BAROQUE

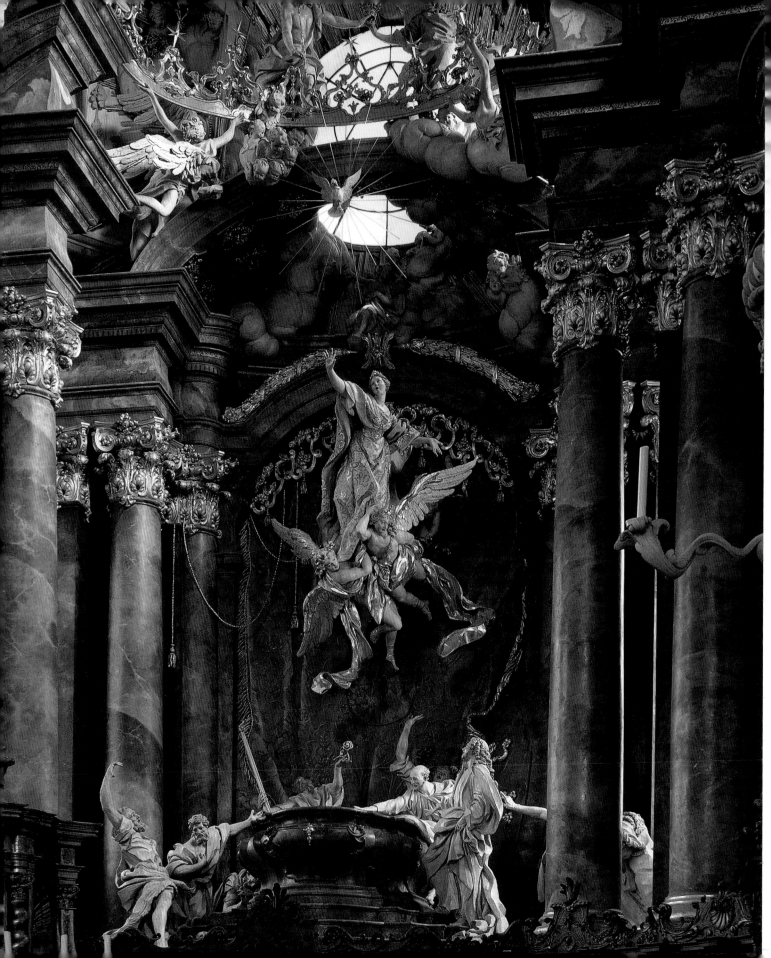

BAROQUE

ARCHITECTURE · SCULPTURE · PAINTING

Edited by Rolf Toman
Photos by Achim Bednorz

ULLMANN & KÖNEMANN

FRONT COVER:
Bom Jesus do Monte, Braga, 1784-1811
Stations of the cross and church facade
Photo: Achim Bednorz

BACK COVER:
Benedictine church of Ottobeuren abbey
Angel of south crossing altar
Ca.1760
Photo: Achim Bednorz

FRONTISPIECE:
Egid Quirin Asam:
Assumption of the Virgin, 1723
Abbey church of Augustinian canons, Rohr (Bavaria)

© 2004 Tandem Verlag GmbH
KÖNEMANN is a trademark and an imprint of Tandem Verlag GmbH
Original title: Barock
ISBN-10: 3-8331-1041-4
ISBN-13: 978-3-8331-1041-2

Editing and production: Rolf Toman, Espéraza, Birgit Beyer, Cologne, Barbara Borngässer, Potzwenden
Photography: Achim Bednorz, Cologne
Picture research: Barbara Linz, Cologne
Cover design: Werkstatt München

Translation from German: Paul Auston, Phil Greenhead, Christine Shuttleworth
Editior of the English-language edition: Catherine Bindman
Typesetting: Goodfellow & Egan, Cambridge

© 2007 for this edition: Tandem Verlag GmbH
ULLMANN & KÖNEMANN is an imprint of Tandem Verlag GmbH
Special edition
ISBN 978-3-8331-3334-3

Printed in China

10 9 8 7 6 5 4 3 2 1
X IX VIII VII VI V IV III II I

Contents

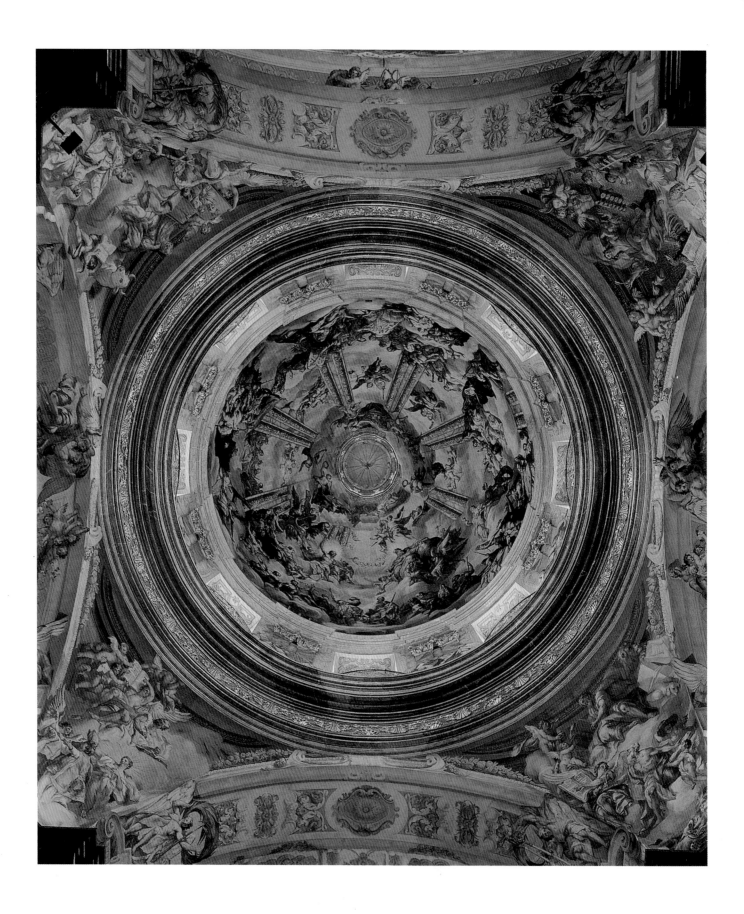

Barbara Borngässer/Rolf Toman

Introduction

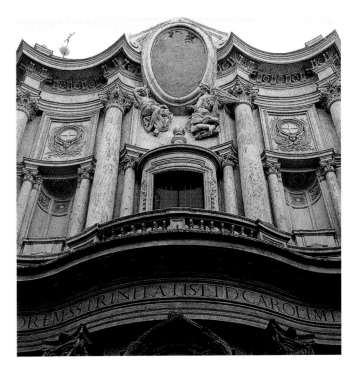

Theatrum Mundi: Life as a Synthesis of the Arts

Rarely has the spirit of the baroque been more powerfully evoked than it is in the work of the Spanish poet Calderón de la Barca. In his allegorical play *El Gran Theatro del Mundo* [The Great Theater of the World], first performed in 1645, he transposes the classical idea of "life as a play" to his own times. The concept suggests individuals conducting themselves as actors before God and his heavenly hosts; the play they are performing is an enactment of their own lives and their stage is the world.

The metaphor of "the world as a stage" was prevalent throughout the baroque period, from the end of the sixteenth to the late eighteenth century. The idea incorporated notable contradictions that could be identified both on stage and "behind the scenes." Reality and appearance, grandeur and asceticism, power and weakness stood as the constant yet oppositional characteristics of the era. In a world convulsed by social upheaval, war, and religious conflict, the image of the vast play seemed to provide a certain stability. At the same time, the flamboyance of baroque rulers, whether popes or kings, seems to have served an additional political purpose: their grand ceremonies might be seen as representing the stage directions for this "world theater" and the mirror of a higher, presumably God-given, order.

The fine arts as much as the performing arts seem to have served two clear functions during the period: they were designed to impress, even to dazzle, the citizens while communicating a specific ideology. The arts provided the setting for the unfolding drama and helpd to create the ideal of a perfectly ordered world. Consider in this context, for example, the artistic perspectives deployed in the ceiling paintings of baroque churches and palaces which open up a realm above the architectural space that appears to give access to the heavenly spheres themselves.

It was not always possible, however, to ignore the contradictions of contemporary life, and these conflicts are to some extent represented in baroque art. The ostentatious displays of material wealth contrasted with a deeply held faith, and the uninhibited sensual pleasure of life was imbued with an awareness of the inevitability of death. The motto *memento mori* [remembrance of death] might be seen as the leitmotif of a disturbed society oppressed by existential anxieties. It is no coincidence then that the richly detailed still-life paintings of the time provide a glimpse of mortality through such distressing images as worms, rotten berries, or half-eaten pieces of bread.

Baroque art tends in the first instance to make a sensual appeal to the viewer: with theatrical pathos, illusionistic devices, and the inter-play of different forms the artist seeks to impress, to convince, and to arouse an internal response. This may explain why the style is often experienced as extravagant, showy, or even pretentious. Towards the end of the eighteenth century, the Italian writer Francesco Milizia was already describing the baroque forms of Borromini's architecture as "an exaggerated expression of the bizarre, or the ridiculous taken to extremes." The baroque has frequently been derided in the twentieth century. The Italian philosopher Benedetto Croce, for example, complained in the 1920s about the insubstantiality of the style. Baroque was "a game… a search for ways to astonish. Inherently, in spite of all its superficial vibrancy and warmth, the baroque… is ultimately frigid. For all the wealth and potency of its images combined, it leaves the viewer with a feeling of emptiness." Such prejudices are still prevalent to some degree. Perhaps our present era, apparently much attracted to surface charm, will achieve a new attitude to this fascinating period in art history.

A more profound appreciation of baroque culture that goes beyond the initial visual, sensual approach can be reached through the examination of individual artists. The historical, intellectual, and social background to baroque art is increasingly the subject of serious art historical study. New research on such subjects as the influence of rhetoric on the structure of the image, the concept of a

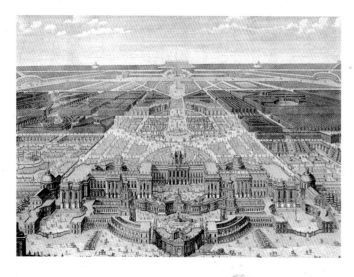

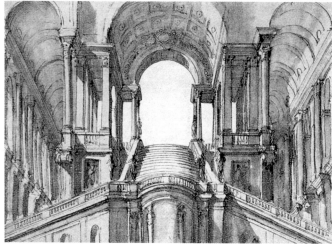

"synthesis of the arts," and the significance of court festivals in the creation of ephemeral works of art are frequently mentioned in the literature.

Baroque as a Concept of Style and as a Historical Era

Contempt for baroque of the kind described above was in fact evident even as it was beginning to emerge as a clearly defined style. In the late nineteenth century, before it had been designated as a specific style, the word "baroque" had been in general use as a pejorative term to indicate anything considered ludicrous, bizarre, florid, ill-defined and confused, artificial and affected. Even in the second edition of Meyer's *Konversationslexikon* [Lexicon of Spoken Language] (1904), the relevant entry reads: "Baroque... originally, rough (used of pearls), hence irregular, strange, peculiar..." It was not until 1956 that Hans Tintelnot effectively questioned some of the views shared by Croce and his colleagues in his historical treatise on "the conquest of our concept of the baroque."

The negative image of baroque as a florid, even ridiculous style was pushed dogmatically by academics schooled in concepts of aesthetic value that were firmly rooted in a reverence for classical antiquity. Scholars like the great German art historian Johann Joachim Winckelmann, for example, saw the baroque period as representing merely "feverish frenzy." Although, Jacob Burckhardt, like Winckelmann, favored the classical idiom, he was the first to examine the architecture of the seventeenth and eighteenth centuries as more than an isolated and anomalous phenomenon, stressing its links to the forms of the Renaissance. While he described the transition from the Renaissance to baroque as the "degeneration of a dialect," his work allowed a more discriminating appraisal of the art of this period and represents the earliest serious study of its compo-

nents. In 1875 he confessed that: "My respect for the baroque is increasing by the hour, and I am ready to recognize it as the true conclusion and ultimate end of living architecture." It was a remarkable change of attitude.

An acceptance of baroque as a subject worthy of academic research finally emerged during the 1880s in the writings of the architect and art historian Cornelius Gurlitt. This was during a time, it should be stressed, when neo-baroque was coming in and a more open attitude to the style was therefore beginning to appear. The designation of baroque as an individual and specific style came about as academically imposed aesthetic standards (based on classical prototypes) were being discarded. Heinrich Wölfflin established a reputation in the field of baroque research over the next decades, most notably in his *Renaissance und Barock* [Renaissance and Baroque] (1888) and his *Kunstgeschichtliche Grundbegriffen* [Basic Concepts in the History of Art] (1915). He attempted to define characteristics specific to the baroque by using pairs of contrasting adjectives such as "linear–picturesque," "vibrant–static," "open–closed." For the first time, psychological factors, the experience of the viewer, and the nature of illusionistic effects were taken into account and decoded for the reader.

Such issues were also investigated by Erwin Panofsky in his famous paper on Bernini's Scala Regia (1919) and by Hans Sedlmayr in his *Österreichische Barockarchitektur* [Austrian Baroque Architecture] (1930). At about the same time, the historical and intellectual context of baroque art was being examined in relation to the Counter-Reformation and to the iconographic sources, a subject which had already been addressed in the revised edition (1593) of Cesare Ripa's *Iconologia*. Over the past decades, our understanding of baroque has been further transformed by the

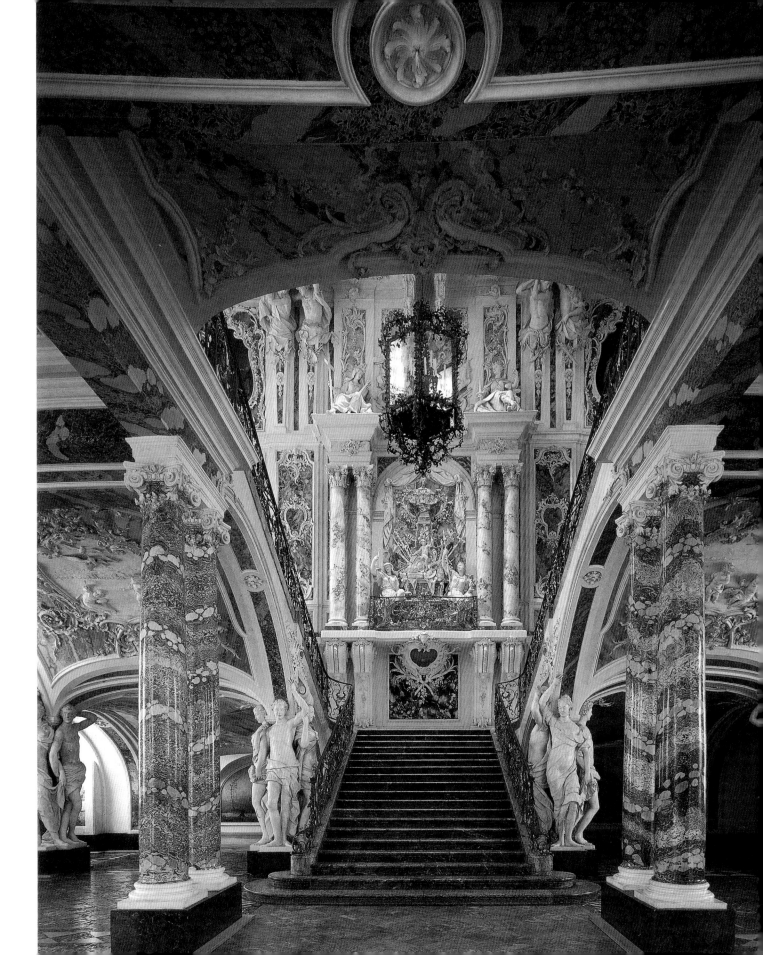

expansion of an interdisciplinary approach to research: an interest in "a synthesis of the arts" is now in vogue, incorporating the combined effects and interaction of types of written and visual culture—the ideas surrounding rhetoric are considered in conjunction with the decorative and fine arts. The concept of the "world theater" currently embodies an essentially much more complex picture of a period no longer viewed as a bizarre incongruity but rather as a setting for intelligent expression.

Pathos and Drama

The Dutch historian Johan Huizinga provided a clear summary of the essential elements of baroque culture in his *Dutch Culture in the Seventeenth Century*: "Splendour and dignity, the theatrical gesture, strictly applied regulations, and a closed educational system were the rule; obedient reverence to church and state was the ideal. The rule of monarchy was worshipped: each individual state advocated autonomy and ruthlessly self-interested nationalistic policies. Public life in general was conducted in an elevated language that was taken entirely seriously. Pageantry and display predominated in spectacular ceremonial events. The restoration of faith took graphic form in the highly resonant, triumphal imagery of Rubens, the Spanish painters, and Bernini." Huizinga used this analysis as a context for exploring the very different nature of Dutch culture: "A rigid style, expansive gestures, and majestic dignity could hardly characterize this country"; it was completely lacking in the theatricality essential to baroque and its artistic imagery.

In order to demonstrate the close links between the theatrical flamboyance of baroque rulers, the need for imposing display, the culture of festivities, and the architectural structures that emerged from them, we will consider here only the most important baroque castles and palaces, especially staircases, which set the best stage for social entrances and exits. Their function is well described by the German literary historian Richard Alewyn: "There is no doubt that what captured the imagination of the age in this particular space was the orientation and, specifically, the possibility of crossing it on the diagonal, a device so elemental to the spirit of the baroque that the space really only came into its own when there was movement. The staircase provided the classic example of the viewer in motion, an essential principle of all spatial art in baroque. As the arrival and reception of guests was of such importance, both the staircase and the hall became significant features and have to be seen in terms of their role as a setting for rows of servants and the display of ritualized greeting."

In addition to this display of ceremonial greeting, the flourishing court culture during the baroque period incorporated a series of other social displays of highly symbolic significance. The most famous are the ceremonial *lever* and *coucher*, the rising and retiring of Louis XIV of France, a spectacle which took hours and which occupied the entire royal household (see pp. 138–39). Today the meaning of these rituals has to a large extent been lost—which does not mean that we have less social playacting. But we no longer know the rules of the old school of drama and, we misrepresent the significance of scenes, gestures, and comportment, since we are unaware of the specific symbolism involved. The same applies to certain poses in portraits of the time.

While life at the baroque court was regulated by rigid ceremony, festivities, although based on definite ground rules, offered an outlet for jollity and high spirits. No era witnessed more sumptuous festivities. Versailles dictated the style, which was imitated by every court in Europe: festivities lasting whole days and nights combined all the arts in a vast synthesis as opera, ballet, and fireworks set new standards of entertainment. Halls decorated with mythological images, gardens, and expanses of water were ideal settings, constantly being transformed into new vistas by illusionistic and mechanical tricks. For a few days the whole royal household slipped into a world of deities and heroes. The effect of these spectacles, as well as the whole culture of the court on state finances, will be discussed later.

Celebration extended into the street. By public decree, the otherwise oppressed cities were decorated with temporary wooden structures and sumptuous decorations for saints' days, processions, and fairs. Theater also featured in street festivities: comedians told crude jokes, reflecting the realities of a world that stood in distinct contrast to the refinements of court society.

Rhetoric and *Concettismo*

The overly flamboyant reputation of baroque art should not obscure the fact that it was subject to strict rules. Just as ceremony influenced the behavior of individuals towards one another, the rules of rhetoric determined the structure of discourse, and of works of art. Rhetoric as inherited from the classical tradition described "the art of measured speech," a style of discourse which formed part of education from classical antiquity until the end of the eighteenth century. It offered a guide to communication between speaker and listener and provided rules for interpreting what was said. It established that the audience must be addressed in the appropriate manner and on a specific subject which had to be clearly explained in order to persuade the listeners after they had weighed up the various issues. This process might include the use of such manipulative contrivances as emotionalism, provocation, and alienation. It was precisely these three elements which proved to be of exceptional usefulness in the reading of baroque art. These rhetorical devices applied just as much to the structure of the image and the construction of the scenes in a cycle of historical frescos as in sculpture, whether in the ecstasy of Bernini's *St. Teresa of Avila* or the horror of a martyrdom in an exaggerated style, each of which was designed to provide the viewer with a sense of immediate experience. "Delectare et movere," "to delight and move," was the aim of both a successful speech and of a well-constructed work of art.

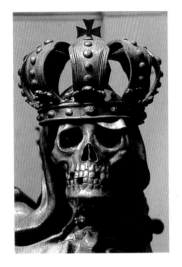

Pieter Boel
Still Life of the Vanities, 1663
Oil on canvas, 207 x 260 cm
Lille, Musée des Beaux Arts

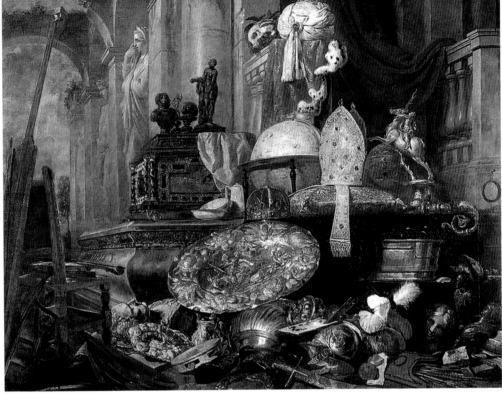

Detail from the sarcophagus
of Emperor Charles VI
Vienna, Capuchin church, vault

Even architecture was subject to the rules of rhetoric which laid down precisely which classical order was suited for each specific purpose and which architecturally significant structures should be included in a church interior, a castle facade, or in the layout of a square. Thus the heavy compact Doric order was assigned to churches dedicated to male saints as well as to the palaces of war heroes. The houses of scholars, on the other hand, were allocated Ionic capitals. The giant orders, where a single group of columns extends across several storeys, had been considered the most noble architectural element of all since Michelangelo. Perspective played an essential role in the layout of baroque castles. Like the ceremonial staircases, these buildings appear to open up as they are approached and crossed: here too—as can be seen in the succession of rooms and courtyards at Versailles—architecture provides the stage directions. As in a good speech, the subject is guided from one experience to the next. While the layout of the inner rooms serves the hierarchical structure of court life, the external structure addresses public life, by serving either to impress or intimidate. Paul Decker's *Fürstlicher Baumeister* [Royal Architecture] is a volume of architectural designs for the court dating from 1711. Decker's imaginative projects were, however, never realized (see p. 8, left). The ascetically strict layout of El Escorial, the Louvre's expansive range of columns, or the positioning of the palace of Versailles which controls the whole landscape, nonetheless provide insight into the means available to architects to persuade the observer or visitor of their patron's intentions.

This calculated use of art presupposes a structured theoretical approach that could have been suggested only by scholars. The spiritual and temporal princes and sometimes even the artists themselves attracted poets, courtiers, and, often, religious figures who provided them with insight into a particular subject. These intellectual contributions were seen as an essential part of the work of art. The artist himself was rarely in a position to work on *concetti* or ideas, yet this was a way to rise above the rank of mere craftsman. Hermann Bauer defined *concetti* as "the transformation of a thought through several stages," "the route from the object to its significance (as a metaphor)"; this was a "constituent" element of the baroque work of art.

The "Last Things"

Let us return to Calderón's "World Theater." During the play, the world provides each actor with whatever he needs for his station in life, whether he is a beggar or a king. The actor comes on stage through a door marked "Cradle" and leaves it through a second door marked "Grave," at which point the actors relinquish their insignia and examine whether or not they have fulfilled their respective roles. The abandoned symbols of authority in Pieter Boel's painting (above) provide a telling illustration of this dramatic scene, which comments on illusion and disillusion. In Calderón's play, only the beggars and the wise remain unblemished by pride and vanity. They alone have understood the moral lesson of the play and in doing so have escaped damnation.

When the curtain comes down, only "the four last things" remain—death, judgment, heaven, and hell. The allegorical representation of these concepts occupied the whole baroque age and supplied the *concetto* for its most moving works of art.

Wolfgang Jung

Architecture and City in Italy from the Early Baroque to the Early Neo-Classical Period

Building the "Thin City"

In his book *Invisible Cities*, Italo Calvino describes a place called Zenobia under the title "Thin Cities, 2." He describes it as an extraordinary city, complex and often contradictory. However, he observes, it was now almost impossible to discern the specific requirements that the city's founders had addressed in establishing the layout of Zenobia as these were obscured by the innumerable architectural layers introduced by subsequent generations. Nonetheless, if you asked an inhabitant to describe his ideal of happiness, the answer invariably indicated a city like Zenobia, not necessarily in its current stage of development, but essentially comprising elements of the initial plan. This said, continues Calvino, it would be pointless to describe Zenobia as a happy or an unhappy city. There is no sense in placing cities in these particular categories; others must be found. Cities should be divided between those where the structures, over many years and after countless alterations, had shaped the desires of their inhabitants, and those which, by contrast, had been sacrificed to the demands of the citizens and where desires and demands were no longer expressed.

The Zenobia which influenced the desires of its inhabitants more than any other European city of the seventeenth century was Rome. One of its most famous inhabitants, Gian Lorenzo Bernini, invited to Paris to tender for the Louvre facade, leaves us in no doubt about this. Comparing Paris, the major European political metropolis of his day, to Rome, Bernini stresses how different Paris is in appearance to his native Rome, with its monuments dating from antiquity and from the Renaissance (he cites in particular the works of Michelangelo), complemented by modern structures, all of which, he observes, are "grandiosi e di un aspetto magnifico e superbo" [full of grandeur and of a magnificent, splendid appearance]. It was primarily these architectural features which molded the demands and desires of Roman artists and patrons, especially the pope and his household. The best example of this is suggested by the fact that Pope Alexander VII, a patron of architecture who had also worked with Bernini on the design of St. Peter's Square, ordered the construction of a detailed wooden model of the center of Rome to be built in his private apartments so that he could immediately test his ideas for architectural schemes.

The apparently unbounded optimism of these years dissolved abruptly after the death of Alexander VII. It quickly became clear that the role of the Vatican in the contemporary European political scene was essentially insignificant. Nonetheless, during this period of decline Rome remained the prime attraction for numerous artists from every Italian and European state. Architects such as Tessin, Fischer von Erlach, Schlaum, Guarini, and Juvarra came to the city, mainly to study the modern architecture of Bernini, Borromini, and Pietro da Cortona at first hand and to gain experience in the great architectural studios which they could put to use on their return home.

Even after the turn of the century, the city of Rome still represented Italian architecture of the late baroque in all its extraordinary guises. This was also a feature of the brief building boom of the 1740s. Other important developments were the growth of visitors' interest in the ruins (these artists and grand tourists might be seen as forerunners of the early romantics) and the emergence of a more systematic, archeological approach to the study of antiquity that was to characterize the neo-classical movement.

The manner in which the Rome of the seventeenth and eighteenth centuries shaped the ideals of its architects and popes and how they themselves were inspired to create the baroque city plan is therefore the principal theme of this study. A variety of issues will be considered in this context, in particular, the role of law and the legal system which allowed the plans to be realized, and the use in architecture of specific formal models, mainly derived from the theater. The interplay of baroque invention and classical tradition—which in many respects defines the era—is emphasized in the discussion of individual architectural designs.

The most important Italian centers of baroque architecture after Rome were Turin and Naples, which assumed great importance in the late seventeenth century as French and Spanish influence declined in the south. Venice will be discussed separately. While it conformed to late renaissance models until well into the seventeenth century, and Roman baroque was never fully established, the principles of neo-classicism were being formulated there by the early eighteenth century, considerably earlier than in Rome, Turin, or Naples.

Methodologically, the focus here is on urban architecture. While the city may mold the ideas of its rulers and their architects, it seems that individuals and their ideas are not automatically incorporated into it. Even during the high baroque period, planning dragged on over years, even decades. New rulers frequently ordered alterations to projects which had been initiated by their predecessors. Similarly, architects were constantly being replaced throughout both the planning stage and construction. This resulted in modifications and new plans, changes to schemes for existing structures, and the partial or complete destruction of sections of buildings. Apparently duplicated planning and artistic expressions of "genius" seem in general to receive more attention than the gradual and thoroughly inconsistent development of city and architecture. This is why a mainly chronological account has been given here.

Late Mannerism and Early Baroque in Rome

Papal policy on construction always had a clear purpose. Impressive architectural structures intended to rival or even outshine the monuments of antiquity were an expression of *auctoritas ecclesiae* [authority of the Church]. At the same time, grand spectacles, *spettacoli grandiosi*, would bolster the weak of faith and lead them back to God. This concept had a long history: as early as 1450, Nicholas

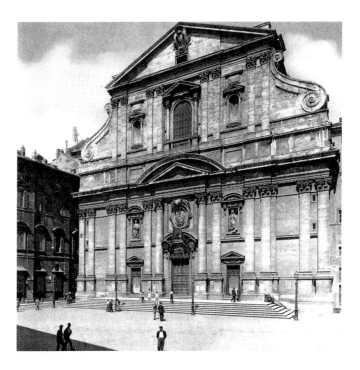

V had introduced building projects of this kind in the name of the Church. These plans remained in operation until well into the baroque era. The designs for St. Peter's Square were initiated on a very similar basis two hundred years later. According to Bernini, St. Peter's, the first architectural undertaking of Alexander VII, was intended to bring all Catholics into the fold and to strengthen their faith, to reunite heretics with their Church, and to shed the light of the true faith on unbelievers.

The further, and often equally important, purpose of papal construction policy was to guarantee the eternal personal glory of the pontiff. This was certainly the case with Sixtus IV towards the end of the fifteenth century. Pope Alexander VII is another noteworthy example of this tendency. In his apartments, his coffin was placed near the wooden model of the city mentioned earlier. The model symbolized Alexander's dream that his building schemes for the city would serve not only to glorify the Catholic church, but also to ensure his own immortality.

The building schemes of the most important popes of the sixteenth century were modeled on Nicholas V's urban plans, schemes which are worth considering in more detail here. Not only did his work provide the basis for all similar ventures during the seventeenth and eighteenth centuries, but the most important architectural features of his city transformations were established at an early stage and used frequently in subsequent plans.

13

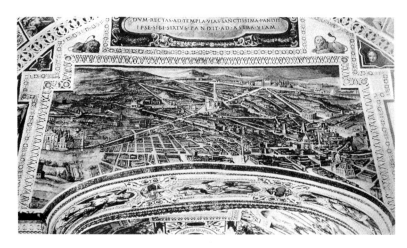

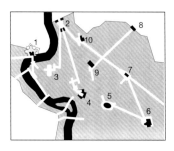

Fresco of Pope Sixtus
V's city plan
Rome, Vatican Museums

BELOW:
Giovanni Battista Nolli
Plan of Rome, 1748

Rome, city planning in the 16th and
17th centuries

1	Castel S. Angelo	7	S. Maria
2	Piazza del		Maggiore
	Popolo	8	Porta Pia
3	Piazza Navona	9	Quirinale
4	Capitol	10	S. Trinità dei
5	Coliseum		Monti
6	S. Giovanni		
	Laterano		

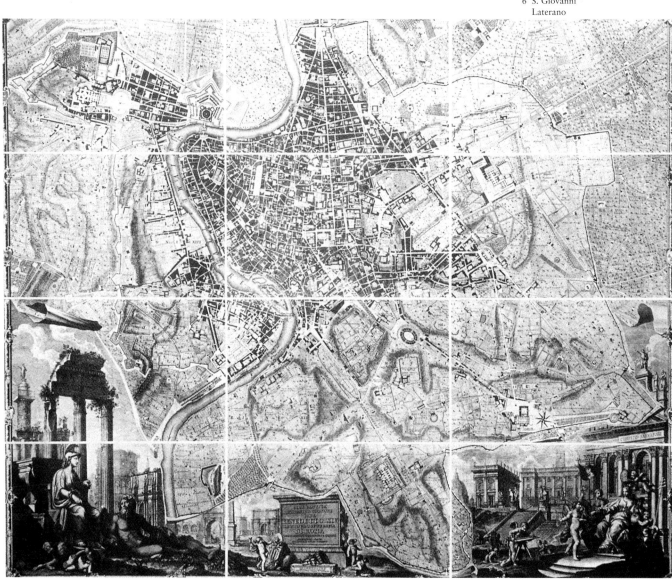

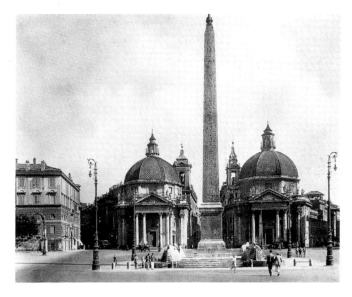

Rome, Piazza del Popolo
View towards Via Babuino, Via del
Corso, and Via Ripetta with the twin
churches of S. Maria in Montesanto and
S. Maria dei Miracoli

From Julius II to Sixtus V

The *renovatio Romae* [renewal of Rome] devised by Julius II and Leo X was driven by desire for power and ostentation; it was a series of plans that mainly concerned St. Peter's, the construction of which had effectively provoked the Protestant Reformation. However, both popes also continued the reorganization of the medieval city which had begun under Sixtus IV. The introduction of straight roads played an important part in this modernization. Via dei Coronari, Via Giulia, and Via della Lungara were built under Julius, and Via Ripetta was constructed under the rule of Leo. The street was no longer seen as a spatial remnant left over from the houses bordering it: it now became an entirely separate entity that defined its environment. The same would have applied to the piazza in front of the Palace of Justice, never completed.

The *trivium* [three roads], extraordinarily influential in the visual culture of the baroque period, also dates back to the first decades of the sixteenth century. Three straight roads which converge on the same corners in a square, or radiate from it, had already been built at Ponte degli Angeli in the *banchi* area. Under Paul III, Piazza del Popolo was also extended to the east, towards the Pincio and along Via Babuino.

The element of theater—and power politics—in the planning of streets and squares was vigorously emphasized by Paul III when he drove the Via Papalis from the Gesù to the Capitol during the Counter-Reformation and commissioned Michelangelo to design the Capitoline Square. The Capitol—like St. Peter's—was not just a focus for papal processions, but a point of orientation throughout the city. The urban plan measured and drawn up by Bufalini under Paul III in 1551 and reissued in 1748 by Nolli provides closer insight into some of these undertakings (see left).

The following designs are taken from a fresco which was produced under Sixtus V (see left). The first is a highly influential design by Michelangelo for the Via Pia, commissioned by Pius IV. This scheme reflected his interest in extending the city over the Campo Marzio area. While the popes had previously restricted their plans to the densely populated late medieval and early renaissance areas of the city, the construction of the Via Pia represented the beginning of the urbanization of the open space surrounding the city center as far as the Aurelian walls, mainly occupied by ancient monuments, early Christian churches, villas, and gardens. Like the Capitol, the Via Pia was laid out along the lines of a contemporary theater. It was a showpiece linking monuments from the ancient Dioscuri to the Palazzo Quirinale and Porta Pia, planned by Michelangelo. Gregory XIII used the Via Pia as a model when he linked the early Christian basilicas of S. Giovanni in Laterano and S. Maria Maggiore. His main contribution to the design of the city, however, was embodied in his edict "Quae publice utilia" (1574), a concept of public utility which established the legal basis for the creation of baroque Rome over the next two centuries. This policy allowed the opening up of new streets and the straightening and extension of existing ones. At the same time, development of the largely empty open areas and the medieval city center was pushed forward. The owners of land along country roads were required to build high garden walls. Meanwhile the concept of the detached building disappeared in the city center: the space between fire walls could now be enclosed and adjacent buildings could under certain circumstances be bought up. As a result, the prevalent two- or maximum three-storey house created the *insulae* system of independent squares.

Sixtus V developed the schemes of Pius IV and Gregory XIII to urbanize the open spaces, but adapted them to a larger scale. Instead of the rather haphazard arrangement of road junctions, he introduced a street system radiating from the seven early Christian basilicas, which stood some considerable distance apart from each other. Essentially, Sixtus' scheme emphasized religious symbolism: the basilicas were to be connected by processional routes. Six roads were constructed and countless others planned, as the fresco illustrates. As the work progressed however, self-interest became very much the focus of the grand design, which ultimately came to center on the papal Villa Montalto.

Nevertheless, the plans of Sixtus and his architect, Domenico Fontana, provided Rome with a structure that was genuinely progressive. Sixtus' schemes provided a comprehensive solution that accommodated the large-scale monuments dating back to the construction of the imperial city to the densely crowded medieval quarter. New roads made the expansion of the city possible while leaving the center intact. Soon palaces and businesses sprang up along the roads connecting the basilicas.

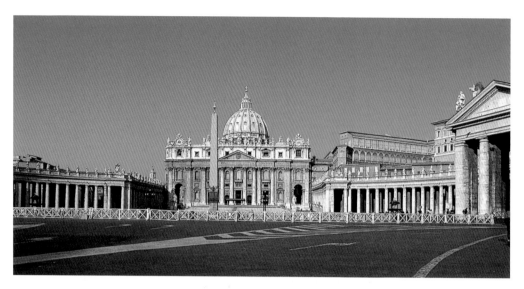

Another significant aspect of baroque urban planning was developed under Sixtus, the introduction of long vistas towards obelisks. Under the rule of Julius II, Bramante had already wanted to align St. Peter's with the obelisks that had been incorrectly attributed to Julius Caesar, and under Leo X, Raphael and Antonio da Sangallo had planned to erect the supposedly Augustan obelisks on Piazza del Popolo (see p. 15). While the question of political representation had dominated such earlier schemes, the stress was now on architectural perspectives. The obelisk became the central point between the line of the buildings behind it and the line of the street. While during the Renaissance architects had focused on the static contrast between palace or church facade and the rectangular planes of perspective and movement, the obelisk allowed space for geometric flexibility and a dynamic viewpoint.

The Via Felice, which starts at the apse of the basilica of S. Maria Maggiore, is a good example of this new concept creating visual links and alignments. If it had been a question of a straightforward connection, a simpler street layout around the hill could have been used. But the real purpose of the enterprise was a symbolic association with the city. There were even plans to extend the Via Felice across the square in front of S. Trinità dei Monti—where the Spanish Steps were later built—diagonally to the Pincio and, irrespective of the building along Via del Babuino, as far as Piazza del Popolo.

It should be noted that Sixtus also extended the legal provisions introduced by Gregory XIII that had been so instrumental in the development of the city. Boundary disputes between landowners could now be resolved more quickly while construction was stimulated by tax relief and the removal of building restrictions.

Thus Sixtus V provided the structural and legal basis for the growth of the baroque city. None of the later popes, not even Alexander VII, was to undertake such extensive urban projects. Nonetheless, Sixtus' successors filled out the structure with magnificent individual set pieces at central points in the city's network of streets.

Paul V Borghese (1605–21)

Papal policy on urban planning at the beginning of the seventeenth century was characterized by major ventures that were to have a huge impact on the future development of the city. At this time, however, there were still some architectural plans being produced in the late mannerist style. This combination defines the transitional period of early baroque.

The completion of St. Peter's after almost one hundred years was of great significance (see above and below). First there had been years of discussion about whether or not the church should be a central structure—as designed by Bramante and planned by Michelangelo. Finally, Pope Paul V decided on a nave. The commission was won by Carlo Maderno. Maderno first produced the design for the facade of S. Susanna (see right). The point of departure for these plans was the unusual position of the facade, parallel to the Via Pia as laid out by Michelangelo, and diagonally across from what is now Via Torino. Maderno's response to the longitudinal and diagonal views was the construction of what was an extraordinarily plastic scheme for its time. His design contrasted strongly with the academic classicism of the single plane as pro-

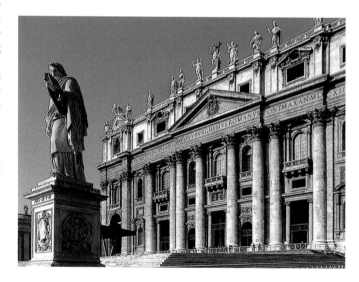

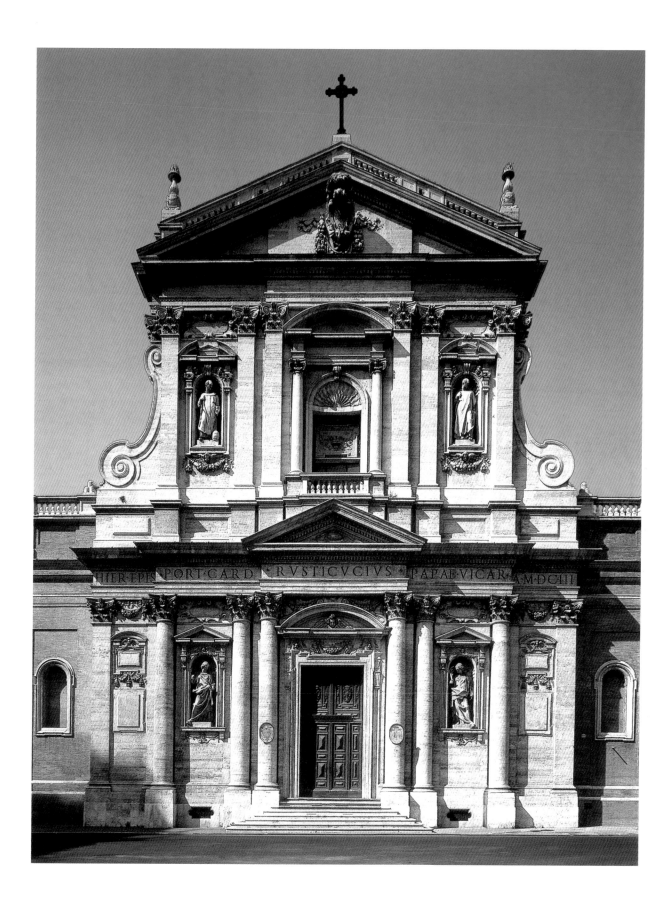

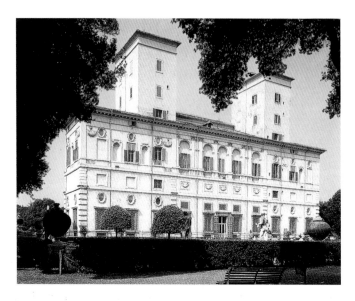

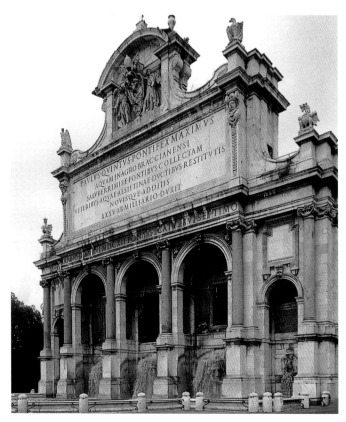

cultural zone between city center and Aurelian wall for villas and parks. Cardinal Scipione appears to have succeeded in incorporating the frequently conflicting aspects of this transitional age in his own personality. He was an enthusiastic collector of Raphael and Titian as well as of d'Arpino and Cigoli. He admired Caravaggio and discovered Bernini, but he commissioned Ponzio and then Vasanzio with the construction of Villa Borghese, which was built between 1613–15 (left). The countless niches, projections and recesses, sculptures, and reliefs scattered across the building by the architects express more than anything else the formalism of the late mannerists.

High Baroque in Rome

This was the context for the development of the high baroque style. The religious and intellectual background to the stylistic changes should be briefly considered here. Under Sixtus V and Paul V there had been some initial political success against the Spanish and French, who dominated the whole Italian peninsula. At the same time, the Protestantism which had been encroaching in the northern regions since 1580–90 was very much on the defensive: the Catholic

duced, for example, by Ponzio and his student, Vasanzio. Maderno reflected the internal structure of the main and side aisles in the facade, providing a concentrated movement towards the center with the bays and columns, and enhancing it with a sense of space and depth. The three compartments interact dynamically with their monumental setting of columns and piers and contrast with the ornamentation of the niches.

Maderno was not able to create the same sort of effect for St. Peter's. The papal insistence on a nave meant that the dome designed by Michelangelo might be completely obscured. Maderno made every effort to respect Michelangelo's design by restricting the height of the facade. At the same time, he designed lateral towers to frame and emphasize the dome. In 1612, at the order of Paul V, work began on the bell towers. However, only the foundations were completed. The problem of the dome, facade, and towers was left for Bernini.

As far as the city plans were concerned, Paul V's interventions were minimal. He ordered the extension of the Roman water supply to Trastevere and commissioned the court architect Ponzio to design a fountainhead (see right). The idea of a fountain within a building which opens onto the street like a stage set is particularly interesting. It expressed Paul's preference for decorating streets and squares with fountains on a large scale. Yet the plans give not the slightest hint that Maderno's design for S. Susanna had been completed more than ten years earlier.

The plans of Paul V's nephew Cardinal Scipione Borghese for a new villa were particularly significant during this period of flux. Under Paul there was an increasing tendency to use the former agri-

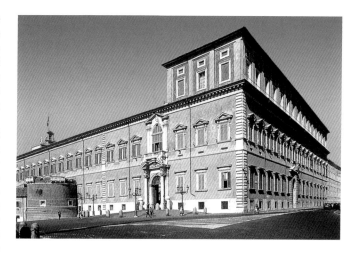

faith had stabilized and was consolidating itself. Under Paul, the covenants for the Filippo Neri Oratory and the Society of Jesus were officially confirmed and on May 22, 1622 Gregory XV declared the canonization of Ignatius Loyola, Teresa of Avila, Filippo Neri, and Francisco Xavier, a particularly significant date which can be seen as marking the end of the transitional period. The revitalization of the church was complete, heralding the beginning of the extravagant fifty-year reign of baroque.

In art, this meant that the formalized mannerist style which had stressed the contrast between the exception and the rule, or between abstract thought and arbitrary fantasy, was replaced by the revolutionary impetus of the baroque in support of the Catholic church. Protestants contended that Christians could do nothing to earn God's mercy; man labored because original sin condemned him to do so, but his work could not actually save him. By contrast, the Catholic church disseminated the creed that God allowed Christians the possibility to actively work towards their salvation. It was the role of the Church to lead men to redemption.

The faith preached by the Catholic church was the property of all believers: it was also essential that they accept it. The poetic theory of the baroque thus emphasized the role of the imagination. Art was representation, but its aim was not merely to permit recognition of an object, but also to impress, to move, and to persuade. Art could not, of course, demonstrate the truth of faith, but it could move the imagination, without which divine salvation became impossible. The boundaries of reality had to be overcome; what was experienced became what was possible.

Urban VIII Barberini (1623–44)

The new era began under the rule of Urban VIII. He confirmed the edicts of the Council of Trent and made the Jesuits his most important allies in the propagation of the Catholic faith. Yet at the same time he permitted an increasing secularization of the papal court, which now entered into competition with the royal courts of Europe. After the anti-aesthetic attitudes confronting the art of the Counter-Reformation, a new appreciation of artistic achievement now began to emerge. Art was no longer merely required to instruct and disseminate the faith, but was also intended to be a repository of aesthetic pleasure.

The first building scheme undertaken by Urban was to affect the entire city of Rome. His idea was to build new walls around the city. Two sections were constructed on the Gianicolo, encircling Trastevere. The plan was to erect walls which were closer in to the city than the Aurelian walls and thus more suited to a defensive role. Urban also ordered the restoration of a series of semi-derelict early Christian churches. Some of these churches were linked by new roads and were included in major plans for the city. The construction of the road from S. Eusebio to S. Bibiana formed part of this work. Urban commissioned Pietro da Cortona to paint the frescos for this church and asked Bernini to design the facade. He also had a road built between Via del

Pellegrino, the pilgrims' route to the Vatican, and the Chiesa Nuova monastery, designed by Borromini. Similarly, he extended Piazza Quirinale in front of the papal palace on the top of a hill to make more space for pilgrims gathering in the hope of receiving a papal blessing. The loggia to the piazza was designed by Bernini, as was the watchtower which cut the square off from the city below. Finally, Urban commissioned a decorative facade to the Trevi Fountain which stood immediately next to Palazzo Quirinale. It was not actually executed until a hundred years later. Meanwhile Borromini was planning Palazzo Carpegna for Piazza Fontana di Trevi.

Above all else, however, Urban VIII favored architecture on a grand scale. Later, the architects he championed, Bernini, Borromini, and Pietro da Cortona made their reputations in quite different ways. Gian Lorenzo Bernini, for example, quickly attracted the attention of Cardinal Scipione Borghese. During his early career, he produced statues of Aeneas and Anchises, and of David. He quickly became the favorite of Urban, who commented that it was fortunate for Bernini that Maffeo Barberini was pope, but that it was even more fortunate for the pope that Bernini was living during his incumbency. Bernini worked continuously for the Church, under Urban's successor Innocent, but mainly, of course, for Alexander.

Soon after assuming office, the pope commissioned Bernini to take on the "shell" of St. Peter's recently completed by Maderno. This work, for which no overall program was ever established, was to occupy Bernini for over forty years, from the design for the baldacchino to the plans for St. Peter's Square. This, more than any other undertaking, became a symbol of the Catholic restoration as well as a seminal structure of high baroque.

The design for the baldacchino over St. Peter's tomb represented an extraordinary synthesis of sculpture and architecture (see p. 282). Bernini based his design on the type of baldacchino normally carried

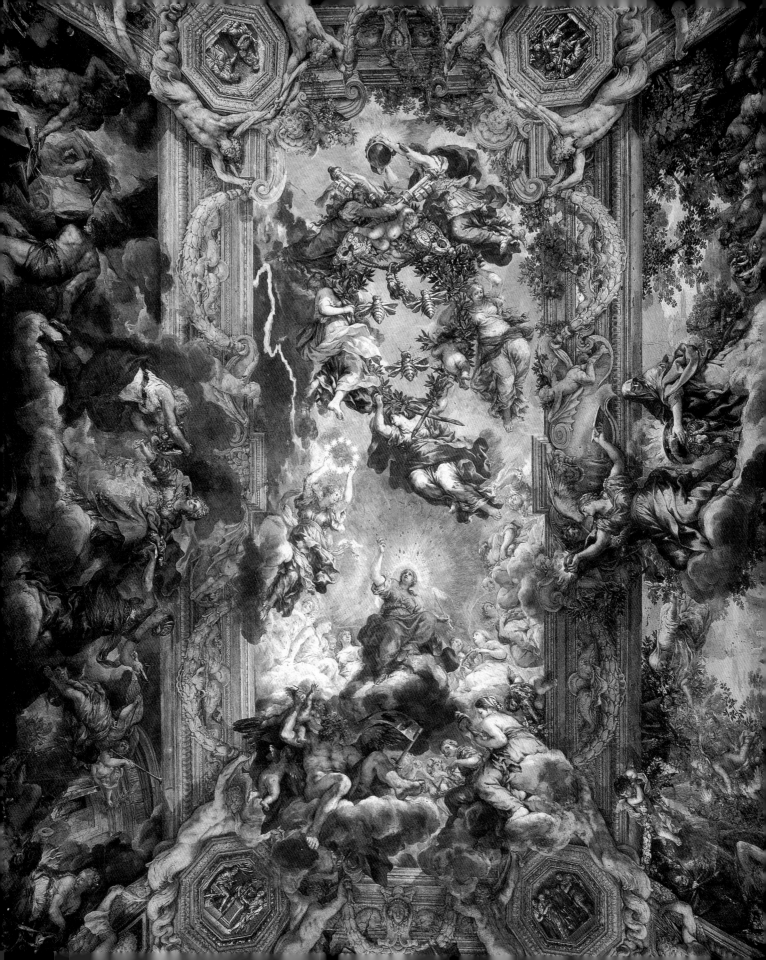

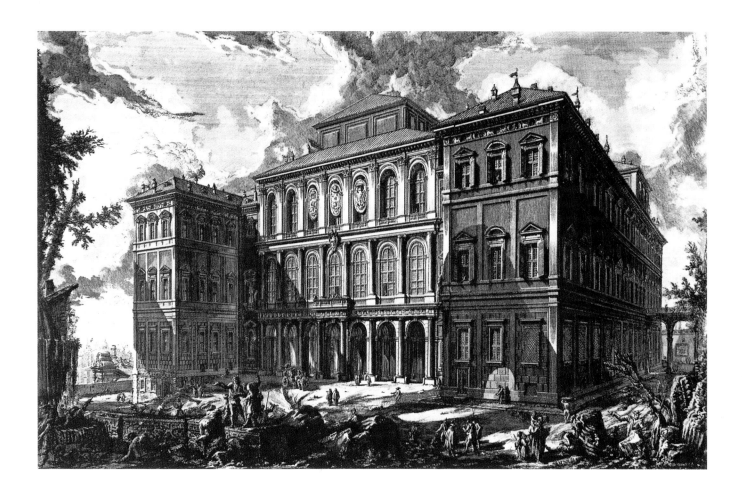

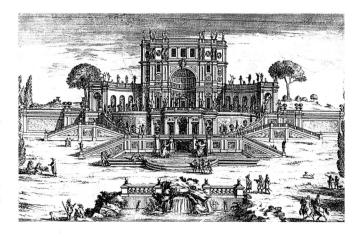

In his plan for Villa Sacchetti, Pietro da Cortona included staircases and terraces, porticos and niches, water features and grottos, in extraordinarily theatrical combinations. The entrance of courtly society could not be better staged. The entrance and garden elevations of Palazzo Barberini are similar in that they encircle the garden and loggia, providing a perfect setting for ceremonials and festivities.

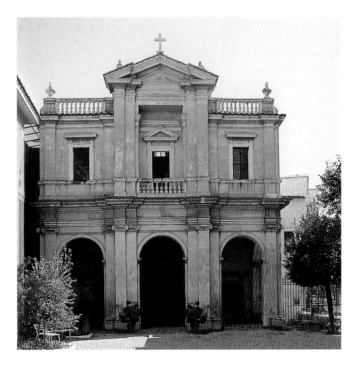

in processions, but enlarged it enormously. The distancing effect is unexpected and surprising: the baldacchino becomes a feature on the aisle to the altar, challenging both the eye and the imagination. Similarly, Bernini referred to the sinuous Salomonic columns round the apse and altar in Old St. Peter's, which again he enlarged considerably. Using these *colonne tortili* [twisted columns], he created a sense of movement at the crossing. At the same time, for the decoration of the piers at the crossing he used the design of the original altar columns for the second storey, echoing the baldacchino and thus communicating a highly complex iconographic message. The use of contrast enabled the artist to suggest the continuity of religious tradition and the transformation from the simplicity of early Christianity to the splendor of the Counter-Reformation.

Borromini, who collaborated with Bernini between 1630 and 1633, produced a series of perspectives intended to situate this scheme convincingly within the nave. They simulate a viewpoint from the level of the first bay before the crossing. According to the account books, Borromini also planned enormous volutes which enhanced the movement of the columns and which were held in place, apparently effortlessly, by four vast angels. The figures in niches around the walls, with their theatrical gestures, provide a fitting reaction to this truly unconventional scheme.

In 1624 Bernini also began his first purely architectural design. He had been hired to create a splendid new facade for the church of S. Bibiana (see left). It is clear, particularly from the windows on the upper floor, that his plans for the church were based on palace architecture, although his version was adapted to a more plastic format. He emphasized the central section of the facade by superimposing one order on top of another and finishing it with an imposing pediment. The upward extension of the columns and the combination of major and minor orders reflect late mannerist motifs, while the inconsistent handling of the design is comparable with Bernini's work on the facade of S. Susanna, completed when he was younger and less experienced.

Pietro da Cortona also developed an early reputation as an architect. Contemporaries praised his first academic studies as comparing favorably with the work of the ancients and of the masters of the high Renaissance. His copy of Raphael's *Galatea* so impressed Sacchetti that he hired him when he was just twenty-seven. Soon afterwards, Pietro met Cardinal Francesco Barberini, the pope's nephew, who became his lifelong patron. Pietro began his career as a fresco painter at S. Bibiana. Between 1634 and 1638, at the height of his fame, he became the president of the Accademia di San Luca.

Between 1625 and 1630, he developed his first architectural work for the Sacchetti family, the Villa Sacchetti al Pignetto, now in ruins (see p. 21, below left). The axial layout of the ground plan here appears to derive from Palladio, while the extensive use of niches points to Bramante and the Cortile del Belvedere; the use of different levels refers to the ancient Roman shrine in Preneste, for which he later completed a reconstruction. Further possible influences on the Villa del Pignetto seem to be drawn from the Villa Aldobrandini, for the layout of the terraces, grottos, and nymphaeae, and from the work of the Florentine mannerist Buontalenti, for the design of the flamboyant curved staircase. A further mannerist element, evident in the contrast between the almost completely austere main facade and the ornate garden facade appears to be based on Giovanni Vasanzio's Villa Borghese. For Pietro da Cortona, history was essentially the interpretation of the visible world; the more sources he deployed in his work therefore, the more decisive was their combined influence on the development of the baroque villa.

The commission for Palazzo Barberini represents a collaboration between Bernini, Borromini, and Pietro da Cortona (see p. 21, above). The old master Carlo Maderno had initially been commissioned to design the palace in 1626, and construction had started after two years of planning. Initially Maderno had chosen a traditional palace layout on a square ground plan. But this design was not particularly appropriate, since the building was to be constructed on the remains of an existing palace on the hill, well away from Piazza Barberini and the Via Pia. He then developed a new design based on Peruzzi's *villa suburbana*, the Villa Farnesina. Two elevations with fifteen axes now faced Piazza Barberini and the Via Pia, while the other sides, with loggias, opened onto the gardens. Maderno emphasized the structural details of the orders and the sur-

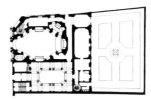

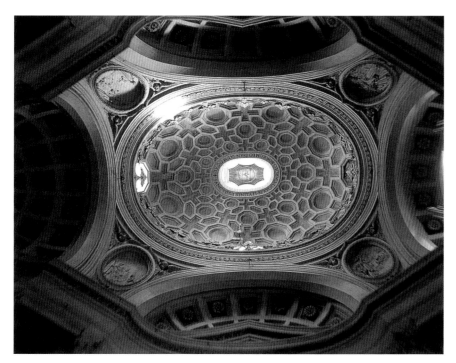

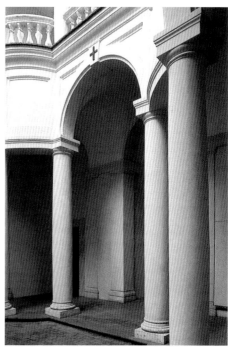

rounding space, especially on the loggia elevations. The window walls are notable for their plasticity of perspective and construction. This link between garden and loggia transforms the facade into the perfect showcase for spectacle and festivities.

In 1629, after Maderno's death, Bernini became chief architect for Palazzo Barberini and Borromini his assistant. Bernini allowed the latter a great deal of freedom in design; this is perhaps best indicated by the side windows of the loggias on the Via Felice facade, on the floor above the piano nobile. Borromini's models here are the windows designed by Maderno for the attic storey of St. Peter's facade, but the dynamic interpretation of detail, including the addition of garland motifs and the forty-five-degree angle of the upper moldings, are already an indication of the tension between architectural elements so characteristic of the master's later work.

Pietro da Cortona participated in the construction of Palazzo Barberini for a short time, but his plans were not ultimately adopted. Only the theater was built, and this has now been altered. Pietro's design for the ceiling fresco of the *Triumph of Divine Providence* in the great hall was considerably more successful, however, and was executed between 1633 and 1639 (see p. 20). It was soon admired as one of the masterpieces of rhetorical art. As his design for Villa Sacchetti demonstrates, art for Pietro was not an ideal, but more a means of defining the visible and the immediately comprehensible.

It was not until 1634 that Borromini was also given the opportunity to complete an independent design. The piece of land on which the monastery and church of S. Carlo alle Quattro Fontane lay occupied a prominent position at the crossroads of the Via Pia and the Via Felice, as planned by Sixtus V. The distinctive feature of this intersection was the fountain which gave its name to the church. Borromini was to complete an extensive building scheme on this small but strategically positioned plot. Work began first on the courtyard, dormitory, and refectory.

Borromini began the courtyard in 1634 (see above right). Considering the restricted space, he decided on very few and very simple component parts. The central motif was provided by the surrounding arcades. He established a coherent rhythm in the design by alternating narrow rectangular openings bearing horizontal cornices with broader semicircular ones. Borromini broke with tradition by placing these two styles of opening on opposing axes. At the same time, he curved the corners of the courtyard inward towards the center. The foundation stone for the church was laid in 1638; it was completed in 1641 and dedicated in 1646 to St. Charles Borromeo. With SS. Luca e Martina, it became the prototype of the Roman baroque. Now all that remained was the design of the interior. Borromini determined the basic structure by introducing an ellipse vertical to the Via Pia and superimposing two triangles. This was

23

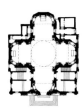
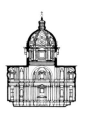

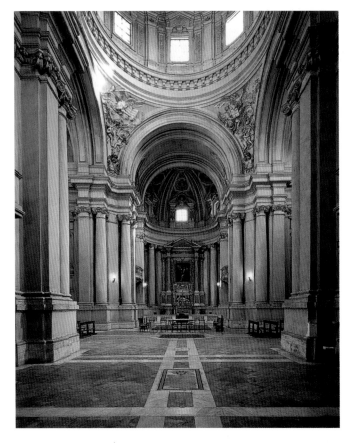

There are clear references here to other buildings. The sweeping movement of the interior can be found in the Piazza d'Oro in Hadrian's Villa and in some of Peruzzi's designs for St. Peter's. The Greek cross form outlined by the diagonally truncated archways is also related to Bramante's design for St. Peter's. An early version of the oval dome, and, in particular the use of lighting from below, can already be found in Serlio's work. Borromini was able to combine these trends into a powerful and inventive whole whose significance was immediately recognized. The builders proudly submitted their work for scrutiny as architectural enthusiasts came from all over Europe to study and copy the new building.

In 1635, only a year after construction started on S. Carlo, the second model of high baroque religious architecture, SS. Luca e Martina, was completed from plans by Pietro da Cortona (see left, right, and p. 26). The site is at least as prominent as that of S. Carlo, and it lies on the papal processional route, beneath the Capitol and with views over the Roman Forum. The architect had received permission to extend the crypt of the church of SS. Luca e Martina at his own expense in 1634. During the excavations, however, the body of St. Martina had been discovered. In 1635, therefore, Cardinal Francesco Barberini ordered the rebuilding of the church from Pietro's plans. In 1644 the building was completed and the interior was finished in 1650.

Pietro's design was based on a Greek cross, with an apse at each of the four ends. He restructured the traditional walls, creating an extraordinarily plastic effect through the alternating use of architectural orders. Three variations on the different conjunctions of walls and columns can be distinguished. In each apse, the columns are set in wall niches; in the adjacent bays, the columns are set in front of the wall (the wall behind is recessed), and beneath the dome piers, columns are set in further piers. In this scheme, the columns have regained the autonomy they had in antiquity and have become more plastic as well as load-bearing. The surrounding row of columns serves both to define a central space and to solve the problem of axial alignment.

The system of decoration here is particularly interesting. The pendentives, spandrels, and vaults are richly ornamented. In the vaults, Pietro superimposed two ultimately contradictory styles of ornament: the panels of the kind used in the Pantheon, a monolithic structure, and ribs of the type used in St. Peter's. Borromini was to create graphic abstractions and variations on this system, while Bernini was to simplify it and to some extent bring it back to its original form. Equally novel was the manner in which Pietro contrasted this decoration with the gables above the windows. This motif is repeated externally on the elevation, except that here the defining features are the highly abstracted window apertures in the tambour and the numerous curves that decorate the lower part of the dome.

No less extraordinary is the treatment of the main facade (see p. 26). While the other sides look like the cut edges of a prism and

developed in the vertical plane by the over-sized columns which seem to define the walls and which, as in the cloister, provide a unifying rhythm. The longitudinal and transverse axes are open, and the four piers are grouped together. In the vertical plane, pendentives rise above the alternately receding and protruding line of the cornice along the entire external perimeter, and the barrel vaults provide a greater sense of depth. Thus Borromini's design leads the eye from the fluid forms of the interior space to the oval of the dome above (see p. 23). Like the vaults over the incipient transept, the dome is foreshortened. The plastic effect of the internal structure of the dome is achieved with lozenge and cross motifs between octagonals to make the dome and lanterns appear higher. The dome is lit by windows immediately above the main entablature. By lighting it from below and from the lantern, Borromini created uniform illumination in the dome, while distinguishing it clearly from the rest of the church interior. The structure appears to be floating above the rest of the church.

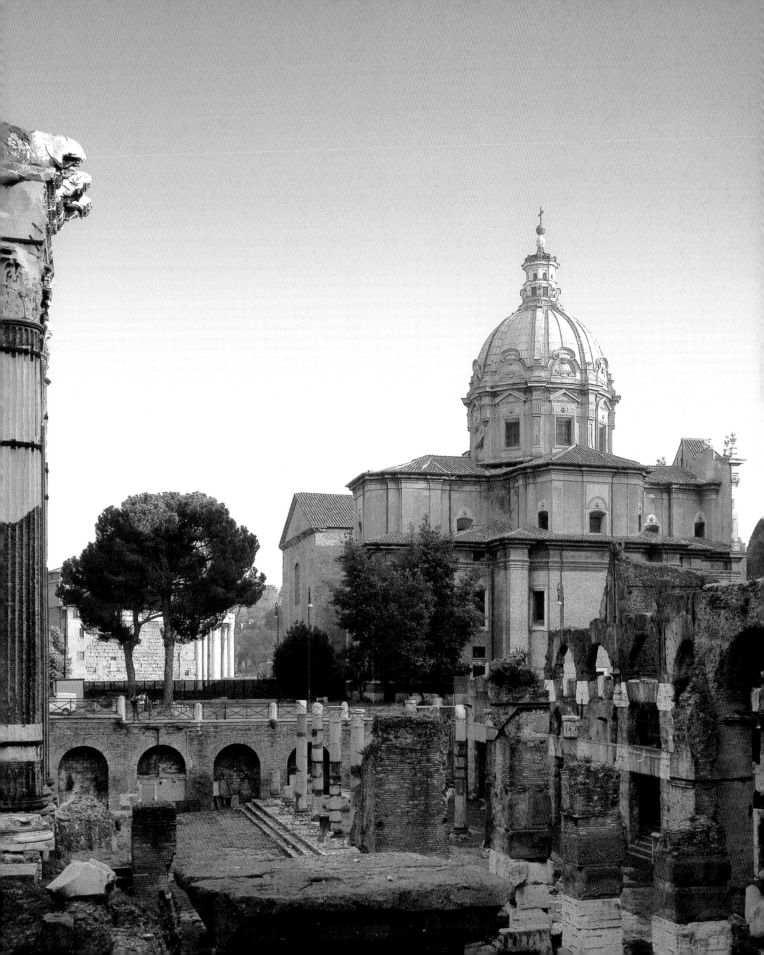

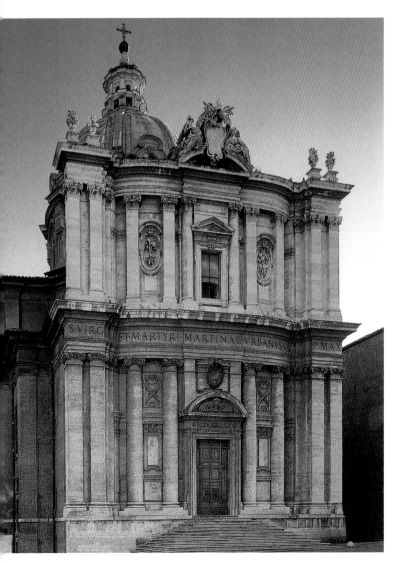

Pietro da Cortona
Rome, SS. Luca e Martina, 1635–50
Facade

Bernini immediately fell out of favor. Nevertheless—or perhaps for this very reason—he produced new proposals the following year. However, they were not taken up and in 1646 the only completed parts of his structure were finally dismantled.

In a late drawing, Bernini used one of Maderno's proposed designs in order to demonstrate the relative superiority of his own proposal (see below). He lowered the towers to lighten the load on the foundations and further reduced their weight by opening them up extensively. A comparison with Maderno's drawing shows how Bernini altered the appearance of the facade, shortening the foreground perspective but not that of the dome on its high tambour. It might also have been appropriate to foreshorten the background. This drawing was presumably Bernini's attempt to persuade the pope of the merit of his proposal.

In 1637 Borromini began the plans and building for the Oratory of St. Filippo Neri, one of the major Catholic congregations after the Jesuits. Like the Jesuits, the community here had opted for a mother house on the Via Papalis at an early stage, although work was less advanced along this route than further south towards Via del Pellegrino. Urban reinforced the link by opening a road from Via del Pellegrino to the square in front of the oratory and the Chiesa Nuova. Borromini's response to the existing facades was the addition of two facades to the oratory. The community's building program included the construction of a sacristy by the church of S. Maria in Vallicella, cells for its members, a refectory, an oratory, and a library. The plans and layout were based on the original designs made by the architect Marucelli, not selected in the 1637 competition. The work proceeded at a brisk pace and the oratory was in use by 1640. The south facade followed and by 1650 the facade on the Via Papalis had been completed.

give only a rough indication of the internal space, the entrance facade seems to be shaped exactly like the interior, curving parallel to the apse behind it. This facade is contained by two abutment-like piers which give the curve a heightened tension. The recess between curve and abutment establishes a visual link with the line of the Via Papalis. The corner piers are doubly reinforced, while the facade curves towards this point, drawing the lines of perspective of the wall towards the street.

At St. Peter's, after work on the baldacchino was completed in 1633, and work on the transverse piers was well enough advanced in the following years, Urban decided to begin a renovation of the facade. Maderno's towers had been completed up to ground-floor level before work was stopped. After reviewing a series of proposals, Urban decided in 1636 to adopt Bernini's scheme to construct bell towers. A start was made on the south tower, but technical problems quickly surfaced. The subsoil gave way and the foundations proved inadequate. There was open criticism of the plan, which became fraught with gossip and intrigue. Building work was suspended and

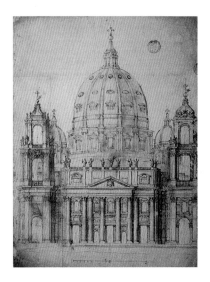

Gian Lorenzo Bernini
Design for St. Peter's facade
with side towers, 1636–41
Biblioteca Apostolica Vaticana
MS. Vat. Lat. 13442, f. 4

Francesco Borromini
Rome, Oratory and mother house of
St. Filippo Neri, 1637–50
Main facade on Via del Pellegrino

Francesco Borromini
Rome, Oratory and mother house of
S. Filippo Neri, 1637–50
Lateral frontage on the Via Papalis

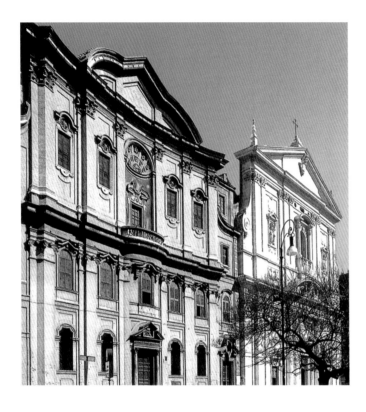

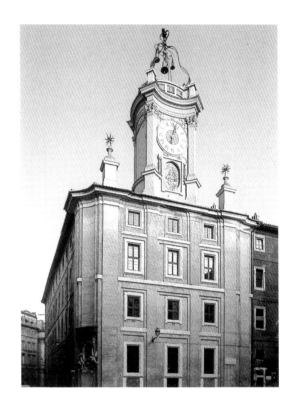

Borromini placed the greatest emphasis here on the south facade which gives onto the square and Via del Pellegrino. The oratory is a real hybrid: it is certainly not a standard church facade but reflects aspects of this tradition while including features of palace architecture. The facade was planned completely independently of the internal layout. The central axis does lead into the oratory, but from the side, below the choir. The main entrance, on the other hand, is hemmed in between the church and the oratory. The new facade was not supposed to compete with the lateral facade of the church and was therefore faced with brick. The facade is composed of a double convex/concave shell and each set of columns is positioned to provide the best perspective for the viewer and to take advantage of the light. The intended interplay of contrasts is suggested by the way the main axis on the ground floor curves in a convex form, while on the first floor the concave niche has the appearance of added depth due to the foreshortening of the arch over it. Similarly, there is an inherent contradiction in the fact that the upper cornice order is corbelled and this "strong" order carries only a double-pitched curved gable. The lower cornice, on the other hand, is interrupted by the window pediments, which negates the visual stability of the whole.

Borromini handled the facade on the Via Papalis very differently.

The whole system of architectural orders is reduced here to a few graphic lines. Only the round bell tower rising powerfully above the facade has any kind of sculptural impact. In this way, the order of Filippo Neri is contained between Via del Pellegrino and the pope's processional route. The life of the spirit is thereby nurtured in this essentially urban space.

Piazza di Trevi lies immediately below Palazzo Quirinale and Piazza Quirinale, both of which were founded in 1635 by Urban with the help of Bernini. Plans for an early Trevi fountain and for the neighboring Palazzo Carpegna to the east had already been started under Urban, but were never carried out. In the years between 1640 and 1649, Borromini drew up innumerable plans for the palace, few ever realized. These are bold schemes which anticipate future developments in palace construction. Borromini initially used Palazzo Barberini as his point of departure, aligning the various parts of the building along a single axis. His approach to the configuration of the great hallway, open staircase, and oval courtyard was revolutionary. The final ground plan selected from a series of proposals shows two staircases rising around the sides of the oval courtyard. It was not until Guarini's plans for Palazzo Carignano that some of these ideas were to be partially implemented.

Francesco Borromini
Plan for Palazzo Carpegna
1640–49

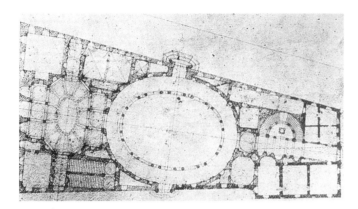

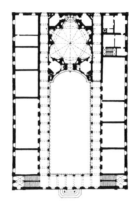

Francesco Borromini
Rome, S. Ivo alla Sapienza
1642–44 (1646–65)
Ground plan and view of the principal
facade

The university church of S. Ivo alla Sapienza (see right) is hardly the product of a single artistic genius. Work on this structure took almost two decades and involved the decisions and revisions of three successive popes. Conflicting political interests and changing tastes inevitably had an impact on the various stages of construction, forcing the architect to change his plans, make alterations, and reinforce parts of the building.

By 1632 Bernini had proposed Borromini, his assistant at the time, as the architect for the university. Borromini immediately began to complete plans for the southern wing of the building that had been started by Giacomo della Porta. In 1642 he then received the commission for the related church. During the next two years building work on the much altered plans reached the level of the lantern. The ground plan for this building was based on two superimposed equilateral triangles, with the apex of each cut off by trapezoid and semicircular apses. The corners are cut by arcs which curve towards the central space.

The essential principle of this plan was similar to the one used in S. Carlo, where one architectural order dominated throughout, as seen here on the pillars. The wide, open entrance from the courtyard lies between these pillars while the altar niche is deeply recessed. Here, Borromini has structured the cupola differently from the one seen in his initial design. While in S. Carlo it was based on a simple oval shape, the form of the cupola now follows the concave and convex curves of the wall. However, the convex sections become increasingly concave as the curve rises, and finally merge with the adjacent sections. It is mainly the ribs between these segments which provide a highly dynamic extension to the upward movement of the corners of the pillars. In this way, the complexity of the basic design is reworked to provide a comprehensive simplicity.

The cupola was completed after the accession of Innocent X, although from a commission dating from the time of his predecessor, Urban. Subsequently, however, work came to a halt, mainly because

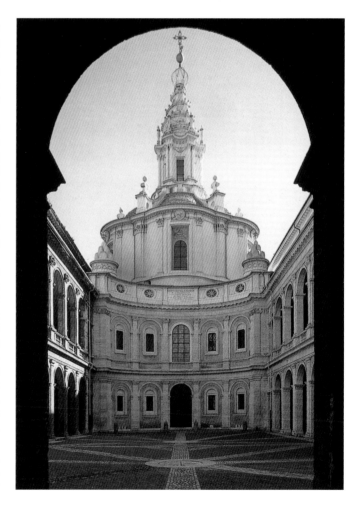

Francesco Borromini
Rome, S. Ivo alla Sapienza
View into the cupola (left)
Lantern (middle)
Plan of the lantern (right)
Interior (below left)

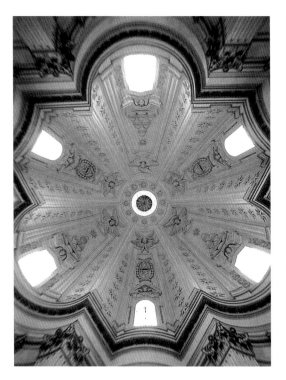

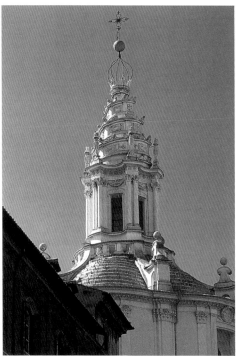

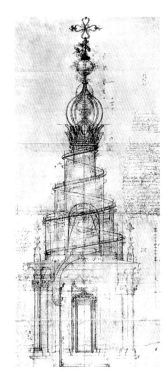

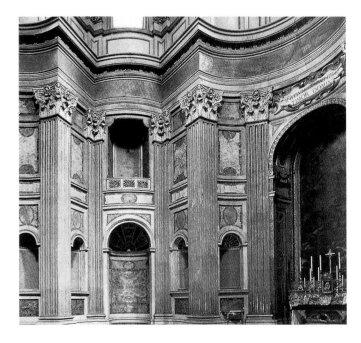

of conflict between the papal families of the Pamphili and the Barberini. Only endless petitions from the builders and the legal faculty of the university forced continuation of the work, finally authorized in 1652. The lantern and the spiral tower were added later. It quickly became apparent that Borromini was not having these elements constructed according to the initial plans, now more than a decade old. This was because the lantern, cramped by the closely packed double column abutments and constrained by the inward curve of the cornice between each pair of columns, threatened the whole cupola structure with collapse. Urgently needed reinforcement resulted in a somewhat improvised appearance due to the insertion of an iron ring at the base of the cupola and the addition of supporting ribs which curve over it.

At this point, the building work as such was finished, but the next pope, Alexander VII, decided on a further series of alterations. This meant that access to the building was rearranged and windows were blocked; externally, the contour of the tambour was altered. While for Bernini, architecture provided a stage for dramatic events, in the case of S. Ivo, the drama of the architecture is an inherent element, a component of its design. However, Borromini probably did not anticipate that this drama would dictate the structure itself.

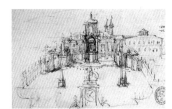

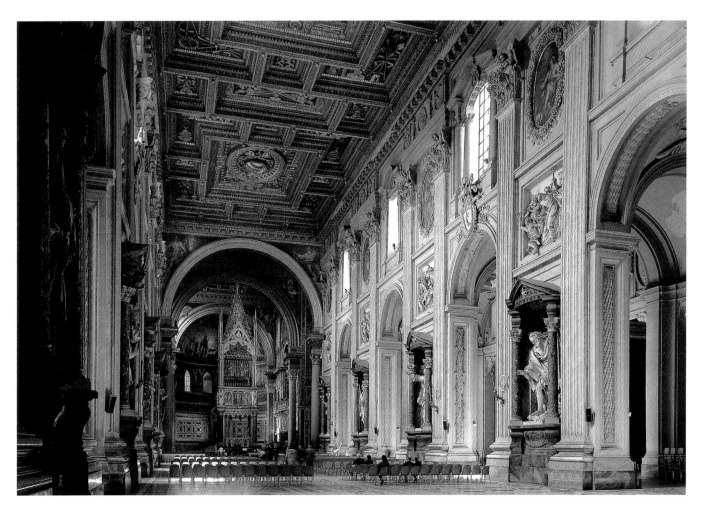

Innocent X Pamphili (1644–55)

By contrast to Urban's many schemes, the building policies of his papal successors concentrated on only a few locations within the city. Initially Innocent's attention had been very much focused on the Via Papalis. First, he commissioned the completion of the Capitol: the third palace there, planned almost a century previously by Michelangelo, was to be sited next to the church of S. Maria in Aracoeli; next, the church of SS. Luca e Martina was to be completed. However, two other plans seem to have aroused more interest, notably the renovation of S. Giovanni in Laterano basilica and the refurbishment of Piazza Navona. While the first would be *ad majorem gloriam Dei* [to the greater glory of God], the second was clearly designed to enhance Innocent's own personal glory.

The renovation of S. Giovanni, which had been hastily initiated in 1646 due to the rapidly approaching jubilee celebrations, and which was completed in the record time of only four years, also included a design for a large square *a forma di teatro* [in the form of a theatre], which was not actually executed. A later sketch by Juvarra (see above) gives some idea of the nature of these plans. Evidently in connection with this scheme, a uniform series of buildings was introduced along Via Merulana, connecting S. Giovanni and S. Maria Maggiore. These twenty-four houses represent the first integrated street plan of the baroque age.

Since the pope's wish was to construct a palace for his family on Piazza Navona, open space had to be found—which meant, in effect, that a serious assault would have to be made on city struc-

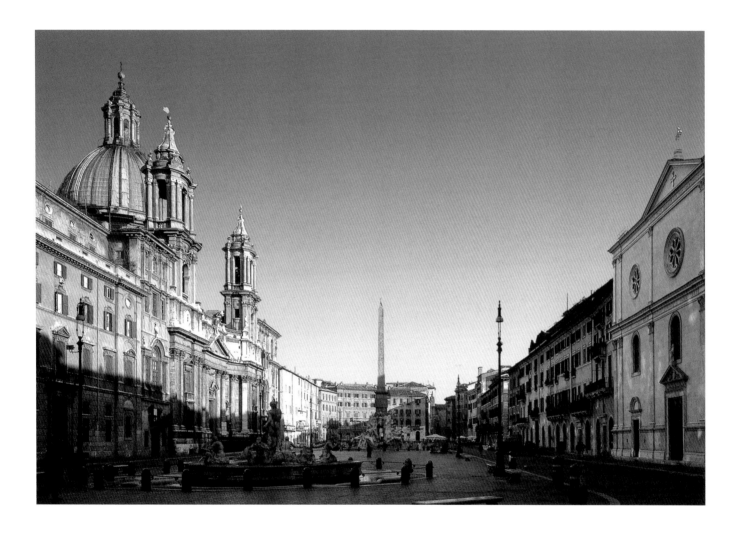

tures, in some cases many centuries old. Moreover, Piazza Navona was an important center of mercantile life. The pope pushed his scheme ahead enthusiastically—and instantly transgressed laws laid down by Gregory XIII almost a hundred years previously. Neighbors were dispossessed and buildings adjacent to the project torn down. To offset the cost of all this, the pope imposed a tax payable by all owners of adjoining properties and property owners in that quarter in order, ultimately, to make the whole square into the forecourt of his private palace.

One and a half centuries before Innocent's 1646 commission for Borromini to renovate the most important church in Rome after St. Peter's, the dilapidated early Christian church of S. Giovanni in Laterano, Bramante had received a similar commission for the reno-

vation of St. Peter's. However, he had been able to persuade Julius II to rebuild. There was no question of such a move with Innocent: his motto was decidedly "retain and improve." This meant that Borromini had to start with an existing structure and the possibilities were necessarily somewhat restricted.

Borromini's chief attention in his renovation was devoted to the central nave of the five in the church (see left). He replaced the forest of columns bearing high walls with giant orders that occupy the full height of the nave. Wide openings to the four adjacent naves and narrow tabernacles create a dynamic rhythm in the new perimeter walls. Early designs show that Borromini first tried to base his design on a diagonal scheme which incorporated the columns, the sepulcher entrances, and the structural features in general. However,

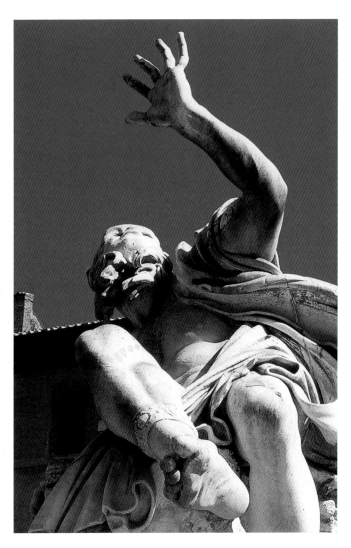

palace, his project was to include the refurbishment or installation of fountains in the square and the building of the church of S. Agnese. Innocent commissioned Giralomo Rainaldi to plan Palazzo Pamphili in 1646 (see p. 385). Rainaldi's plans are diagrammatic and not particularly convincing, presumably the reason why Borromini came to Rainaldi's aid at a late stage. The design for the gallery can be attributed to him, as can the magnificent doorjambs and the central window onto the square, surmounted by an upward sweeping entablature. Frescos were later added to the interior by Pietro da Cortona (see p. 385).

In 1648 Bernini received the commission to plan the Fontana dei Quattro Fiumi, a fountain with four jets, and in 1653 he was asked to redesign the fountains by Giacomo della Porta at each end of the square. The iconography of the urban and natural environments are closely combined in the quadruple fountain (see left and p. 289), which features four giant marble personifications of the rivers Danube, Ganges, Nile, and Plate. The base, pierced on all sides, supports an ancient granite obelisk taken from the Circus of Maxentius, seen by contemporaries as symbolizing the rays of the sun and the triumph of Christianity. The rocky formations are naturalistic, the palms appear to bend in the wind, and the water flows noisily into the basin. The reaction of the river gods to the obelisk reinforces its mystical power as well as that of the pope and the Catholic church.

The commission to build the church of S. Agnese in Agone (see right) close to the family palace was first given to Girolamo Rainaldi and his son Carlo in 1652. They based their design on a Greek cross with a short transom and diagonally curtailed piers with columns. Unfortunately these plans, and especially the main portico and the steps in front of it which extended well into the square, soon became the subject of vigorous criticism. In 1653 Innocent replaced the Rainaldis with Borromini, who was to continue building on the structure that had already been completed to ground-floor level. Borromini was nonetheless able to make several decisive changes. His main achievement is the interior was to project the crossing piers into the internal space, towards the transept. This resulted in an essential change in the architectural rhythm of the interior, since there was now a sequence of almost equal openings. The crossing became an almost perfect octagon. This new vibrancy is further emphasized by the striking contrast between the white church and the red marble columns. The cornice, which projects fully over the columns, is representative of the dynamic tension between the architectonic elements and lends a powerful vertical emphasis in the interior. Borromini's name is also stamped on the tambour, much higher than originally planned, and complemented by the high arching curves of the dome.

Borromini dispensed with the Rainaldi's plan for a vestibule, thus setting back the church facade from the square. At the same time, and in spite of the restrictions imposed by the site, he isolated the central dome and raised it by setting it between the two west towers.

to establish coherence in the central space, he completed a second design where the massive orders project out across the corners of the area and on the front wall, as in the S. Carlo monastery cloister. In this arrangement the convex curves from the tabernacles to the nave serve as a counterpoint. *Verde antico* columns further dignify the tabernacles and provide a strong touch of color. In order to unify the diverse elements of the internal space, Borromini had also planned to instal a barrel vault under the heavy wooden ceiling. However, after the Holy Year this ceased to be an option.

Innocent pushed forward the plans for Piazza Navona as ruthlessly as he had done for S. Giovanni. In addition to his family

With this design Borromini reinforced the role of the central section of the building, an issue much debated in the Renaissance especially after the failure of this idea in the construction of St. Peter's with the building of a nave and the subsequent demolition of the tower. Borromini even achieves here the unity of structure of towers and dome that Michelangelo and Bramante had intended, in spite of the fact that the commission was withdrawn before completion after disagreements with the pope and (after his death) with Cardinal

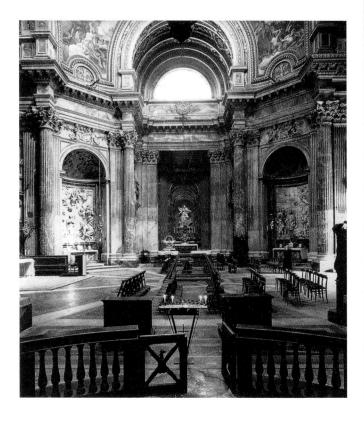

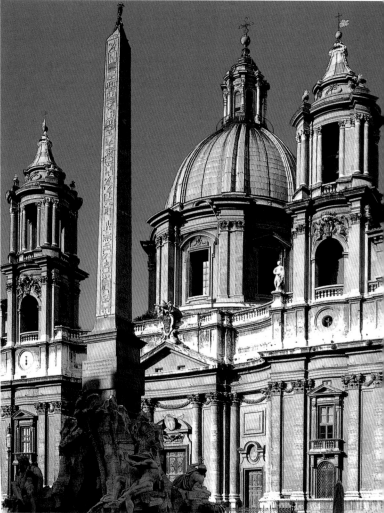

Pamphili. The alterations made by Carlo Rainaldi to the exterior were minimal—an attic storey and simplifying the lanterns and towers.

In addition to S. Giovanni and Piazza Navona, a further series of important building schemes were developed during the incumbency of Innocent: although these were not initiated by him, he followed their progress with considerable attention.

Between 1646 and 1650, Martino Longhi the Younger built the church of SS. Vincenzo ed Anastasio for Cardinal Mazarin on Piazza di Trevi, immediately opposite the site which Borromini had intended for Palazzo Carpegna. The site for the church opened diag-

onally onto the square. This enabled Longhi to create a unique and successful solution for the facade: three free-standing columns set close together on each side of the central axis, with a further set of columns arranged in the same manner on the upper floor (see p. 34). This stepped effect was emphasized by a repetition of these essential architectural elements. Two pairs of columns mark the full width of the facade. The addition of three pediments to the ground-floor level and three differently shaped pediments to the upper storey is strangely effective. The design of the pediments and columns is not particularly coherent and manneristic contrasts can still be perceived. However, Longhi achieved an unusual sense of the size and

Martino Longhi the Younger
Rome, SS. Vincenzo ed Anastasio
Facade, 1646–50

Martino Longhi the Younger
Rome, SS. Vincenzo ed Anastasio
Detail of facade

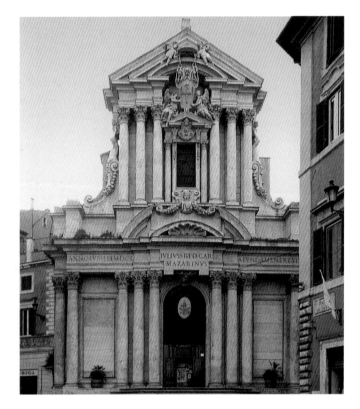

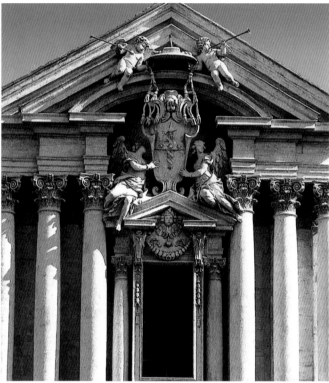

mass of the structures of Roman antiquity with these architectural elements.

The extraordinary patience required by architects involved in any kind of building work during this period is clearly demonstrated by the project for S. Andrea delle Fratte. Borromini received the commission to complete the construction of this church from the Marchese Bufalo in 1653. The protracted building work was stopped in 1655, long before the structure was completed. The sections finished by Borromini to this point are therefore particularly fascinating (see right).

The dome takes the form of a massive brick cylinder incorporating curved abutments. Concave surfaces appear to cut into the dome cylinder, forming convex sections that are emphasized at the junctions by massive columns. There is no lantern but the tower projects onto the street. The first of the storeys, each of which is quite differently structured, is completely enclosed and laid out on a square plan. Columns on the diagonals are pushed outward. Next, above a deeply projecting cornice, can be seen a clerestory which looks like a round temple. It is surmounted by a cornice and an extraordinarily imposing balustrade. Yet another level supersedes this one, with a

receding and protruding design reminiscent of the lantern in S. Ivo, except that here the double columns are decorated with cherubim. Curved volutes rise above this storey, supporting a rather unstable looking scrolled structure surmounted by a crown of thorns. The massive closed tambour and dome structure provides a perfect setting for the tower. The basic sources for this apparently rather curious design are in fact found in antique architecture, and the drum is very similar to that of La Conocchia (first half of the second century AD), a Roman mausoleum at Santa Maria Capua Vetere. It has never been clearly determined whether Borromini saw these motifs or copies of them himself or whether he arrived at this design independently.

Work on the Collegio di Propaganda Fide, a group of buildings which formed the headquarters of the missionary congregation directly adjacent to the church of S. Andrea delle Fratte went on for a fairly extended period (see p. 36). In 1646 Borromini was commissioned to produce new structures for and alterations to the College. The architect very quickly submitted his initial proposals for the compound which was situated at the end of Via del Babuino, one of the roads extending from Piazza del Popolo. The plans included the

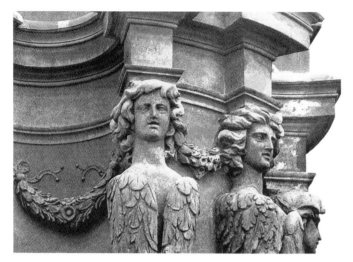

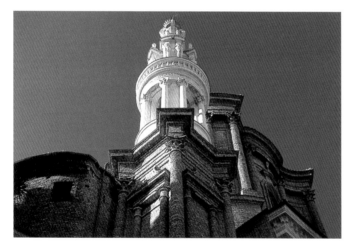

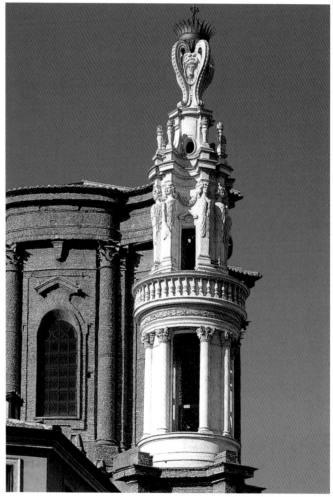

facade to Piazza di Spagna, which had been reworked at Bernini's suggestion, as well as a church that had also been built by Bernini. However, the much altered scheme was not implemented until 1662–64.

Borromini had initially intended to retain Bernini's church, which was similar in some respects to his own first sketches for S. Carlo. However, he finally replaced it with a sort of great hall. Again, he based the design here on Michelangelo's masterly formulation for the setting of major and minor orders. At the same time, the connecting wall behind is made up of many layers comprising independent sections. The external treatment of this extensive complex is similar to that of the Oratory for the congregation of St. Filippo Neri. Borromini planned relatively undetailed orders for the less

important external facades, but for the main entrance facade he used a completely unorthodox design borrowed from the architecture of palaces. In the narrow streets, this facade can only be viewed in a severely foreshortened guise and at an angle. As a result Borromini placed greater emphasis on the seven giant orders marking the bays and the fine details than he had done with the Oratory. He was able to direct light and shade across the complicated window frames and the concave and convex elements, constantly deploying oppositional features in the details. He further rejected the traditional palace facade, lending a completely new interpretation to the orders by abstracting them: he reduced the capitals to a few vertical lines and left the cornice undecorated. The central area is concave in shape, presenting a remarkable contrast to the planes which characterize

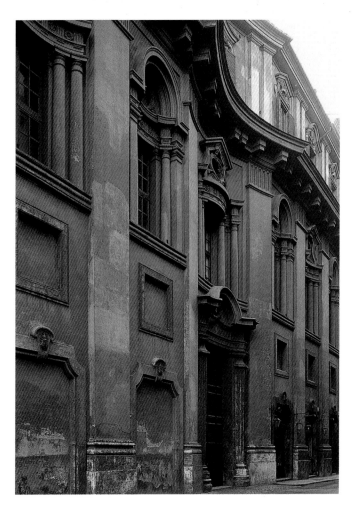

Popolo, St. Peter's Square, and the squares in front of the Pantheon and S. Maria della Pace, as well as renovations to many less well-known squares like those in front of the Collegio Romano, S. Carlo ai Catinari, and S. Maria in Trastevere.

There was certainly a close link between several sites along the Via del Corso, the most important access route from the north into the city and to Piazza Venezia. In 1655, the year Alexander became pope, he commissioned Bernini with the task of reworking the Porta del Popolo, the gateway to the city, and renovating the church of S. Maria del Popolo on Piazza del Popolo. Between 1652 and 1655, Bernini restored the chapel there of the papal family of the Chigi, designed by Raphael. Subsequently, Alexander ordered the straightening of Via del Corso and had it made wider to accommodate two lanes. The ancient Arco di Portogallo proved to be an obstacle to the new building work, but only for a very brief period; experts soon confidently identified it as a mere replica so that it could be torn down without ceremony. Finally, Alexander drove the Via del Plebiscito from Piazza Venezia, providing a direct link with Via del Corso and the Via Papalis.

The real purpose of all this work was to facilitate the construction of a magnificent palace for Alexander's family on Piazza della Colonna, halfway along Via del Corso. Bernini's biographer Manetti gives us detailed information about this scheme. The original idea was to provide a new layout for the square, based on Innocent X's Piazza Navona. Bernini planned to enlarge the square, to relocate the Arch of Trajan from its historic place in front of Trajan's Market, to move the Antonine Column to one side, and to build two fountains. Pietro da Cortona suggested that the nearby water conduit of the Acqua Vergine for the Trevi Fountain should also be extended to the square as the main feature of his design for Palazzo Chigi.

Soon after taking office, Alexander occupied himself with the layout of St. Peter's Square, which he commissioned Bernini to design in 1656 (see right). This square, extending into the surrounding area and linking up with the city itself, became the counterpart to the dome of St. Peter's. The essential feature of this square is a series of constantly changing perspectives and open spaces. An extraordinary interplay between memory and imagination is performed here. But above all the square becomes an allegory of the Church triumphant.

Alexander and Bernini planned and executed this project in the face of internal resistance and intrigue from the Curia. The layout of the square was defined primarily in response to the various rites and processions which were to take place within it. Particularly important in this context was the Easter *urbi et orbi* [to the city and to the world], when the pope blesses Rome and the world. The shape of the square had in some way to express this comprehensive gesture, while still providing a suitable point of departure for papal processions relating to the Via Papalis. In addition, the existing buildings,

the rest of the facade. The richly sculpted openings in the upper storey present a further oppositional dynamic to the stark abstraction of this ground floor, curving inward as though under horizontal pressure from the flat planes of the wall but outward from the concave section. The facade becomes a plain setting for the richly detailed window frames.

Alexander VII Chigi (1655–57)

Compared to Innocent X, Pope Alexander VII seems to have been dominated by an unbounded passion for construction which found expression in a series of major architectural enterprises. The numerous surviving notes and even drawings in his hand concerning his plans for the city demonstrate his untiring devotion to his vision for Rome. The model of the city installed in his apartments, discussed earlier, allowed him to test the feasibility of sudden inspirations at once. While Alexander's schemes mainly involved aesthetic improvements and effects, they hardly represented an understanding of the needs of the citizens.

Examples of schemes designed by Alexander can be found throughout the city, but it is clear that he made only a limited attempt to introduce a truly comprehensive plan of any kind. His works included alterations to such famous squares as Piazza del

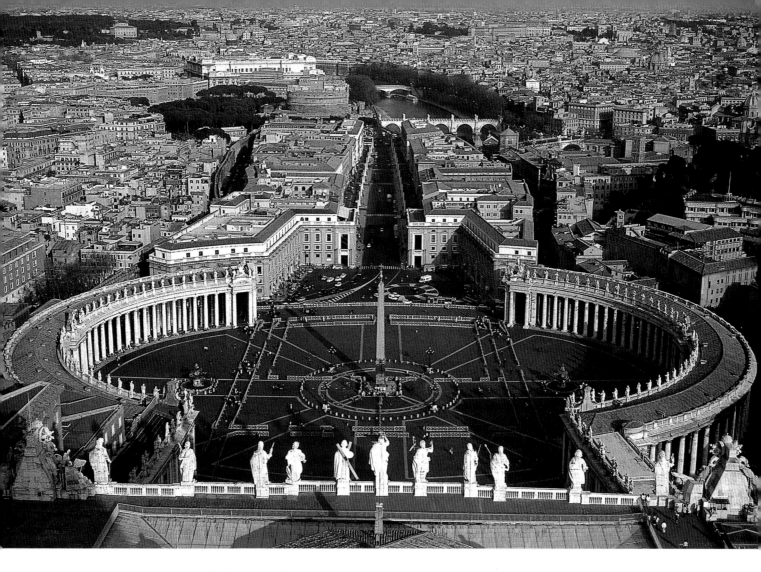

ABOVE AND BELOW RIGHT:
Gian Lorenzo Bernini
Rome, St. Peter's Square, 1656–57
Detail of arcade

Gian Lorenzo Bernini
Rome, St. Peter's Square.
Drawing for the *terzo braccio* [third arcade]
Engraving by Giovanni Battista Falda, 1667

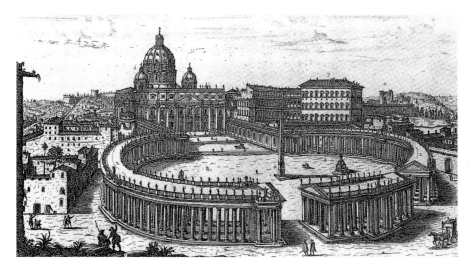

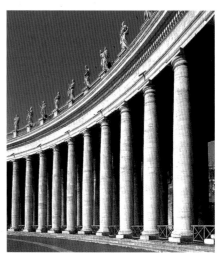

37

Pietro da Cortona
Rome, S. Maria della Pace
Facade, 1656–57

Pietro da Cortona
Rome, S. Maria in Via Lata and
Palazzo Doria (Gabriele Valvassori)
1658–62 (left)

especially the entrance to the papal palace on the northwestern side, had to be taken into account.

Bernini's earliest design for the square took the form of a trapezium with a two-storey facade derived from traditional palaces. But the scheme required the creation of a certain monumentality in the square with the absolute minimum investment, and this restriction inevitably affected the height of new structures. In the spring of 1657, the architect proposed an oval shape, initially with a free-standing arcade of columns; this was superseded over the summer by a portico with horizontal entablature. The design, now free of temporal associations, had finally taken on the ceremonial status for which it was intended. The commission had resulted in the simplest and most expressive form possible. At the same time, the limitation on height which restricted the whole scheme to only one floor provided a wider perspective view; it was also more economical and enhanced the visual correlation between the square and the church

facade in spite of the fact that the geometry of the square was determined by the existing buildings, the Ferrabosco corridor between the Vatican Palace and Castel S. Angelo, the Vatican Palace, and the alignment with the Via Papalis.

Bernini had originally envisaged a third, free-standing section of the colonnade to close off the arms of the square and screen the visitor's view as they approached from the streets of the Borgo. Upon entering the square they would receive a comprehensive perspective on the massive expanse framed by columns curving towards St. Peter's. However, there was never any question of opening up the Borgo for access to Castel S. Angelo.

During this period, 1656–57, Pietro da Cortona was commissioned to renovate the facade of the quattrocento church of S. Maria della Pace (see below left) and to construct a square in front of it. Alexander wanted to make reference to his relationship to his ancestor Sixtus IV. Today the coats of arms of the two popes occupy a

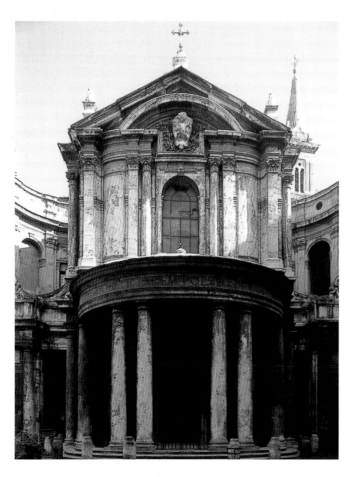

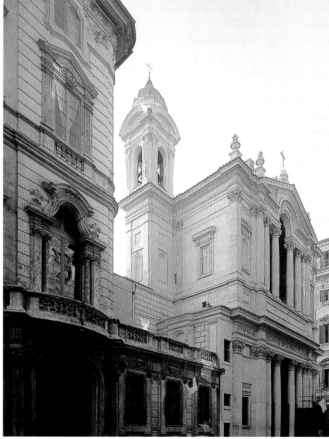

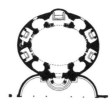
prominent position on the wings of the church. The broad sweep of this facade contrasts with the convex curve of the porch with piers which occupies the entire breadth of the original church facade: here Bramante's *tempietto* is combined with Palladio's stage from the Teatro Olimpico in Vicenza.

The separation of the facade from the church structure is impressive, and the design in this format was new for its time. The facade was no longer a boundary; it now became an independent plastic entity designed specifically for its context. The lateral perspectives open onto the neighboring streets, with the city providing the immediate background. Bernini also applied this system of incorporating the design into the city context directly with S. Andrea. Pietro da Cortona continued to emphasize corners, already an essential feature of the SS. Luca e Martina facade where columns lend space to the facade and lead up to the concave surfaces which project from the upper storey. These walls form the background and are enclosed in pairs of Doric columns, projecting well out into the square. The transition to neighboring buildings is interesting, since it also provides a gradual shift in emphasis from wall to loggia.

It was also Pietro da Cortona's task to provide a facade for an existing building with his design for the church of S. Maria in Via Lata, a project that had been only slightly delayed. However, this was not in the crowded context of the medieval quarter, but on the main access road to the city, Via Lata, now Via del Corso (see left).

In response to this situation, the architect continued to develop ways in which to achieve a simpler monumental effect. The complexity of the designs for SS. Luca e Martina was replaced by a few large motifs, while the classical idiom of S. Maria della Pace, for example, was retained. Again, the architect planned two complete storeys, but this time the central area remained open. Nonetheless, he again used massive structures to flank the portico on the ground floor and the loggia above it. This structure is surmounted by an oversized tympanum. The Palladian influence seems evident to some degree in the classical language of this structure. In relation to the street, Pietro also created a definite sense of depth in the facade, where the columns on the portico and loggia stand out clearly against the shadowy background. Again, the massively formed lateral abutments provide a background and a contrast. Above all, the choice of a facade based on a rectangular ground plan gives it a plasticity of form and monumentality when viewed from the mainly diagonal perspective in the street. Bernini also used this approach in S. Andrea.

Over the same period, Bernini was commissioned to plan three churches in rapid succession, and seems to have worked on all of them simultaneously. These are S. Tommaso da Villanova in Castel Gandolfo (1658–61), S. Maria della Assunzione in Ariccia (1662–64), and, most importantly, S. Andrea al Quirinale in Rome (see above), which was constructed between 1658 and 1661.

Cardinal Camillo Pamphili had commissioned Bernini to plan the

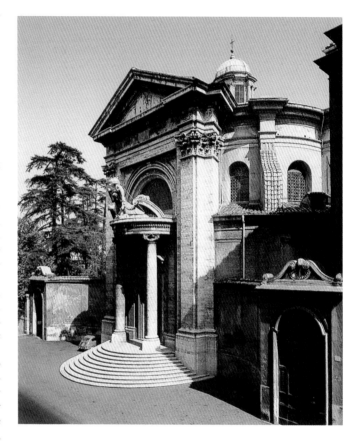

Jesuit novitiate church of S. Andrea on the Via Pia, opposite Palazzo Quirinale and not far from Borromini's S. Carlo. Here Bernini rejected both the circular plan of the Pantheon, which he was renovating at this time, and the Greek cross form that he was later to use in Ariccia, selecting instead the oval shape that he had already used in the plan for St. Peter's Square. However, he was to develop the motif further in a most innovative manner.

The Via Pia constituted a dynamic line extending between Piazza Quirinale and Porta Pia. Bernini captured this dynamic to create a square within the street itself. To distinguish the church as far as possible from the existing novitiate and to pull it back from the street, the oval form was designed to lie lengthwise along the Via Pia. In front of the oval, projecting walls embrace the perimeter of the square. Bernini differentiated the church from neighboring villas and gardens by expanding it to monumental proportions. Each element was both simplified and exaggerated, starting with the monumental orders and the tympanum over them, which dominate the facade. Unlike its predecessors before S. Maria della Pace, the

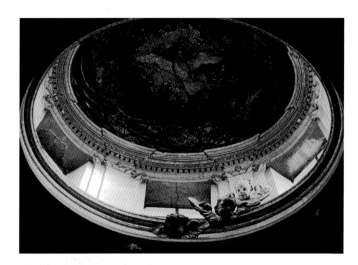

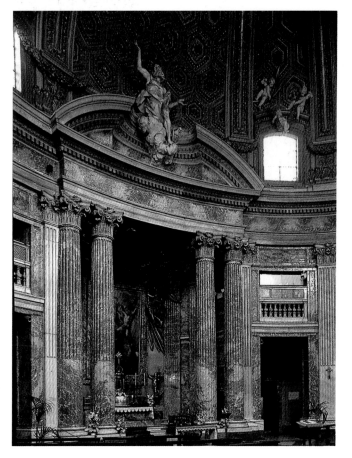

entrance canopy rests on only two columns. Originally only three steps—very wide and spacious—led up to the church. The thermae window over the canopy is vast, the coat of arms seems as though it is about to topple into the street, and the helical abutments to the oval, hardly necessary from a structural point of view, are highly effective and refer to S. Maria in Via Lata. The facade becomes a stage set which exaggerates the structure to monumental proportions. The rhythm and the dramatic use of shadow take on a more significant role in the overall impact of the building than in the basic structure itself.

This very clear emphasis on the vertical axis to the Via Pia is continued in the interior. The thermae window over the entrance is the only feature which disturbs the geometric uniformity of the tambour and dome. Opposite the doorway, Bernini sets the second, internal facade, centering on the altar and an image of martyrdom (see left). This image is emphasized by the plasticity of representation, the use only here of the double column motif, and the oversized tympanum. At the same time, the internal layout stresses the length of the nave with a series of pilasters while the dynamic momentum is underlined by the rhythm of the openings. Two arches lead into equally dark chapels lit only by back light from narrow windows above the altar tables. Two small dark rectangular openings follow. The observer's eye is drawn along the walls inside the oval and then concentrates its full attention on the chancel.

Here we see the representation of martyrdom which, supported by stucco angels, is set out for the observer just like a theatrical scene. This stage is brightly lit from above and appears to open into eternity (see above). To achieve this illusion, Bernini uses glass mosaic which, in varying tones of blue, grows paler towards the central axis. This apparent opening also interrupts the clear outlines of the orders. The altar is the culminating point from every point of view.

The intentional darkness at the lower levels, the white plaster of heaven, the figures arising towards the source of light, and the dove are clearly allegorical. Art is imagination brought to fruition with St. Andrew's ascension into heaven. Besides color, light is used to set the scene for this journey to heaven. In the heavenly spheres far from the earth, and evenly illuminated by windows over the cornice, the colours are white and gold. The chapels are much darker and have only *contre-jour* lighting. There are subtle differences in the lighting from one chapel to another. Both the chapels near the nave are bathed in diffuse light, while the others are very dark. This supports the dramatic tension centering on the chancel.

Each setting for these effects—the square, the entrance, the oval interior, the chancel, and the dome—serves as a backdrop for the perfect performance. They transform the miracle of St. Andrew's salvation to something visible, a miracle the congregation can participate in directly. There has rarely been a more eloquent interpretation of the literal possibility of heavenly salvation through

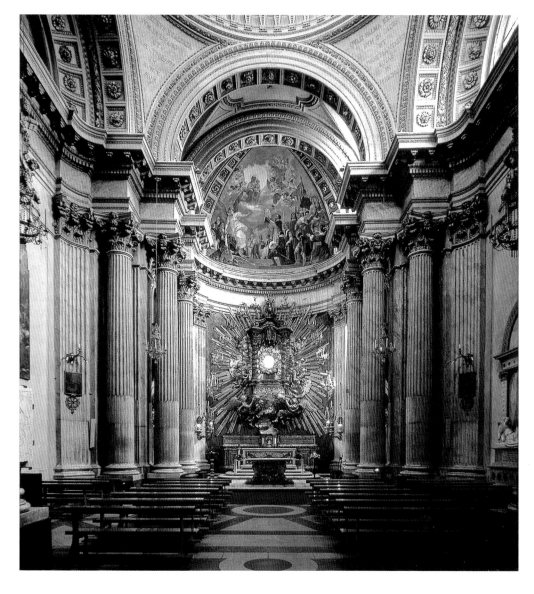

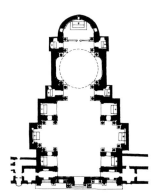

Carlo Rainaldi
Rome, S. Maria in Campitelli
Interior and ground plan, 1660/62–67

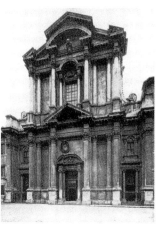

Carlo Rainaldi
Rome, S. Maria in Campitelli
Facade, 1660/62–67

mortal suffering as preached by the Catholic church and expressed here through sculpture, and, above all, through the architecture.

In 1660 Alexander decided to rebuild the church of S. Maria in Campitelli in the ghetto (see above). The commission was given to Carlo Rainaldi. For many years he had worked with his father, who still followed the mannerist tradition of his teacher, Domenico Fontana. After their plans for Palazzo Pamphili and S. Agnese, three important commissions were given to Carlo at about the same time. These were S. Maria in Campitelli (1660-67), the facade for S. Andrea della Valle (1661-65), and the twin churches on Piazza del Popolo.

Over the next two years, Rainaldi developed a series of designs for S. Maria in Campitelli; these demonstrated the various sources he was drawing on to reach an independent and, for Rome, exceptional solution. Initially he reworked the first plans for S. Agnese, the facade of which was based on SS. Luca e Martina. The

next step was to complement the prominent, convex curve of the facade with the features already seen in S. Maria in Via Lata, a double-storey portico and loggia. The ground plan was based on an oval shape to be used for the congregation, and a second, circular space reserved for the miraculous image of the Virgin to whom the church was dedicated. The design derived both from Bernini's S. Andrea and Francesco da Volterra's S. Giacomo degli Incurabili in its treatment of the transept. In this way, Rainaldi combined Mannerist tendencies and the achievements of the high Baroque. In the end, he replaced the oval with a nave, giving special emphasis to the transept. Building commenced in 1663.

There is an extraordinarily scenic quality to which every detail contributes by leading the observer's eye from the body of the church to the rear section of the building. The dynamic of the first section, with floor plan in the shape of a Greek cross, is driven towards the altar by the use of a barrel vault. The emphasis on the

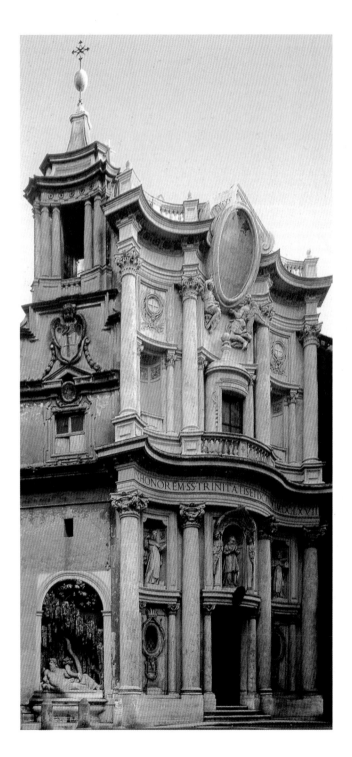

transept, theoretically in opposition to this dynamic, underlines the movement of the nave, particularly through the use of free-standing columns. Carlo used this feature first in the lateral niches, then repeated them in the transition from the body of the church to the chancel, in the chancel itself, and in the transition to the apse, which closes the sequence of internal spaces. Emphasis is lent to these perspectives in that in the completely white internal space gold is used for the arches above the lateral chapels, over the transition to the chancel and to the apse. The cornice over the free-standing columns is asymmetrically corbelled for the same reason. In this way, the cornice points into the side chapels parallel to the nave, emphasizing the existing dynamic. The eye moves from column to column and from one internal space to the next. The way the light is used also aids in this. The first area is only minimally lit by four apertures over the cornice, but it is mainly the two apertures in the transept, facing the observer, which provide the impetus towards the brightly gleaming light of the chancel with their almost dazzling *contre-jour* lighting. Thus, the unresolved mannerist contrast of several lines of sight is replaced in the unification and disposition of mass and lighting typical of the Roman high baroque. This controlled sequence of perspectives is of particular interest to the late baroque.

The main purpose of the twin churches of S. Maria in Montesanto and S. Maria dei Miracoli was to mark the northern approach to Rome, to the then trapezium-shaped Piazza del Popolo and the *trivium* leading from it (see right). This unique position meant that any usual solution such as building on the perimeter of the square would not apply. It was Carlo Rainaldi's specific proposal to make the churches into monuments standing in the square and at the same time use them as anchors for the streets radiating from this point. In this way, the architects succeeded in providing the perfect setting for the *trivium* of Via del Corso, Via della Ripetta, and Via del Babuino begun in the high Renaissance under Leo X and Paul III.

This history of urban planning gives an impressive example of how several architects worked in baroque Rome, either together, at the same time, or one after the other. Rainaldi initially planned two churches with high domes on the same cruciform ground plan. However, as the plots were different in shape, the churches very quickly developed differently, probably under Bernini's influence. The left-hand ground plan became oval in shape. This was an attempt to achieve a complete visual identity by means of differentiation. Up till 1673, Rainaldi also directed the work on S. Maria in Montesanto, which, after being interrupted, was then continued by Carlo Fontana under Bernini's supervision and was completed in 1675. Finally, Rainaldi began the twin church of S. Maria dei Miracoli, which was then completed by Fontana between 1677 and 1681.

The model for these churches was the Pantheon; however, in the very different scale of this interior it was necessary to emphasize the

Carlo Rainaldi, Gian Lorenzo Bernini,
and Carlo Fontana
Rome, Piazza del Popolo
S. Maria in Monsanto (left)
and S. Maria dei Miracoli (right)
1662–67

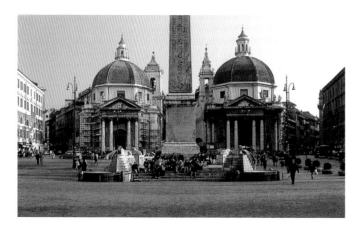

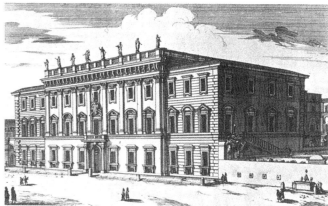

effects of the architectural features, particularly the dome. For this reason, Rainaldi gave both a very deep tambour and dome, with ribs which also use the light that falls on them to added effect. The porch, with classical overtones, is treated in the same way, although the architect reduces this to four pairs of columns surmounted by a pediment. The point of departure for this appears to be the study by Bernini, collaborating with Fontana, for this type of portico in front of St. Peter's, which remained a paper exercise. The monumental model for this, the Pantheon, now became the setting, except that the stage was now Piazza del Popolo.

In the same years, 1664–67, two facade designs emerged which interpreted the urban context in very different ways. Bernini's project for the Chigi palace became a formula for the aristocratic Baroque palace, while on the other hand Borromini's facade for S. Carlo alle Quattro Fontane became a synonym for the baroque "aberrations" so vehemently criticized by classicists. It was the task of both architects to graft a new facade onto an existing building.

Seven highly decorated bays give definition to the central section of Palazzo Chigi, while the three bays at either side are insignificant (see above). The ground floor forms the basis for a row of giant orders two storeys high. The layered effect of decorative architectonic features is impressive, as is the gradual increase in fine detail towards the top. Later, Nicola Salvi and Luigi Vanvitelli doubled the facade, to sixteen window axes.

Parallel to Bernini's design for Palazzo Chigi, Borromini designed a highly discontinuous and fragmented facade, ultimately non-monumental, for S. Carlo alle Quattro Fontane (see left). It was conceived as an object. It projects deep into the Via Pia but makes no attempt to mediate with the street environment.

Bernini had already repeatedly referred to the giant orders developed by Michaelangelo. Borromini's choice of a gigantic order of columns with minor orders inserted and complemented by a horizontal cornice and openings or niches also goes back to Michaelangelo's design for the Capitoline palace. However,

Borromini contradicted this system, which was intended to hold together the full height of a facade, by repeating it over two storeys. He was at the same time contradicting the concept of a unified facade by giving it triple curves. The orders curving in and out in this way form a framework for a large number of contrasts. Niches are opposed to windows, the entrance on the ground floor to an aedicula on the next floor. This niche, in which St. Charles Borromeo stands surrounded by cherubim, contrasts with the medallion held aloft by angels, inward-curving segments of cornice with outward curves, and the continuous cornice on the ground floor with the cornice split by the medallion on the upper storey.

The predominant concept of difference and contrast is typical of Borromini's intellect. The facade reduces sections of wall to a minimum. The eye has little chance to find repose, so densely packed are the columns and sculptures. Architecture had become sculpture for Borromini, quite the opposite to Bernini, who kept them separate because for him sculpture was basically a narrative art, while architecture created a setting for it. But the difference went deeper. With the S. Carlo facade, Borromini made a direct criticism of Bernini's thought on urban planning. For Borromini, the representation of a universal three-dimensional order was not of major concern, but the highly intensive detail was; in the same way, he understood the city not as a reflection of the mightiest powers, for example religious power, but as an intertwining of religious experience and everyday life. Bernini, who was committed simultaneously to the French court and to Borromini's architecture, responded that this brought the anthropomorphic approach of the Renaissance into question, since its architecture—based as much on extravagance as on fantasy—did not follow the rules of composition which were, after all, centered on human points of reference.

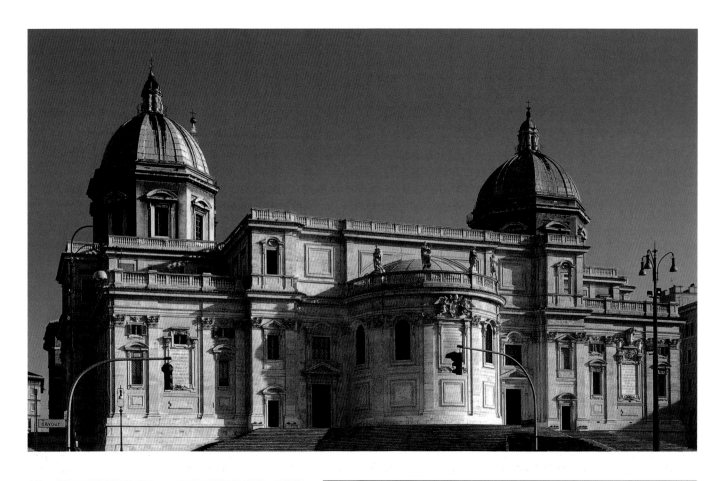

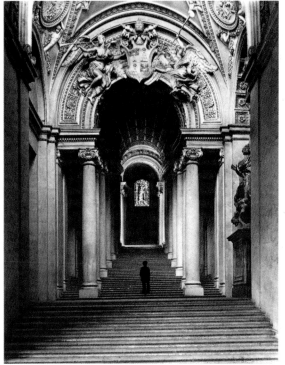

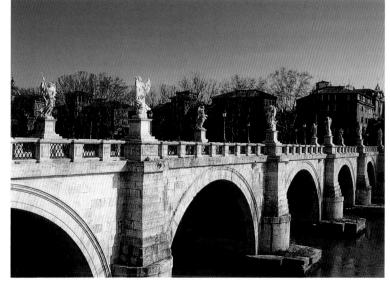

Gian Lorenzo Bernini
Rome, Ponte degli Angeli
1667–68

Gian Lorenzo Bernini
Rome, Vatican Palace
Scala Regia, 1663–66

Local site conditions such as converging walls or immovable foundations made it very difficult to provide a homogeneous design for the Scala Regia. It is all the more impressive that Bernini managed to transform these obstacles and to provide a perspective for the visitor.

Late Baroque and Early Neo-Classicism in Rome

The flamboyant era of high baroque suddenly came to an end with the death of Alexander VII. The Catholic church became painfully aware of its considerably reduced political power. In 1648, the negotiation of the Peace of Westphalia without involvement of the Church had made this loss of influence very evident. At the same time, France's role as the leading European power progressed unchallenged. In architecture, this meant that Rome lost its cultural predominance and the Paris of Louis XIV became the new and dynamic center of artistic production.

Moreover, during the first decades after Alexander's death, not only did the Catholic church become aware of a significant loss of political influence, but its financial situation continued to deteriorate. As a result, building work stagnated. A short-lived recovery and a more active period of construction did not occur until the 1730s and 1740s under Clement XI, Benedict XIII, and Clement XII, whose new schemes gave vibrant expression to the baroque in Rome.

Although little was built in Rome around the turn of the century, the city remained a center of attraction for innumerable artists. In addition, a great number of foreigners came to the city, probably less in the hope of receiving commissions than of making a pilgrimage to the former capital of ancient and modern architecture. The French Academy played a particularly significant role in this development: its scholars studied, copied, and immersed themselves in the ideas of the classical world.

Antiquity was reinterpreted in the following period, its history becoming a theoretical ideal and the products of its art the objects of a new science—archeology. The popes themselves took a particular interest in antiquity. Conservation and restoration became central features of the work at the Vatican Museums even under Clement XI at the turn of the century, and in the Capitoline Museum under Clement XII and Benedict XIII. Finally, Clement XIII appointed the archeologist Winckelmann as director of the Roman collections of antiquities.

Clement IX Rospigliosi (1667–69) and Clement X Altieri (1669–76)

Under Clement IX and his successor Clement X, the rate of construction slowed down considerably. However, work which had not been completed under Alexander VII continued, particularly in St. Peter's Square and the churches on Piazza del Popolo.

Clement IX concentrated on extending the Sistine Via Felice and on the design for the apse of S. Maria Maggiore (see left). The aging Bernini's proposal for the project was rejected in favor of Carlo Rainaldi's less commanding but more economical solution. At the same time, however, Clement IX commissioned Bernini to decorate Ponte degli Angeli, the crucial point on the Via Papalis. The architect planned a group of highly expressive sculptures which appear to float over the waters of the Tiber on the light balustrade that he also designed in impressive opposition to the massive structure of Castel S. Angelo (see left, below). His design also included a square destroyed during the previous century due to works to control the level of the Tiber, the point of departure for the *trivium* in the early sixteenth century. Thus the bridge became a real link between the Vatican and the center of Rome.

Innocent XI Odescalchi (1676–89)

This pope seems to have distinguished himself mainly by his independence from the fashions and trends of the day, by his exemplary piousness, and, in the present context, by his absolute reserve when it came to any building activity. The latter characteristic can be attributed predominantly to the fact that the Vatican was crushed under a heavy burden of debt and was naturally wary in the face of a precarious political situation.

Innocent XI rejected Bernini's proposal for the completion of St. Peter's Square, which incorporated a third colonnade at the base of the square. During his early years in office, he would not even appoint a leading master builder for St. Peter's, in order to save on costs. Only later was Carlo Fontana appointed as the first master builder, but only because the stability of the dome seemed to be under threat. The commission he received to undertake a comprehensive examination of the structure was used by Fontana as the basis for a study in which he traced the construction of St. Peter's back to the time of Bramante. Fontana's *Templum Vaticanum* was published in 1694; in it Fontana proposed two alternative schemes for the completion of St. Peter's Square.

Carlo Fontana soon established himself as the most influential architect of this period. He had worked on drawings in the studios of Pietro da Cortona and Rainaldi and, for almost ten years, in that of Bernini. He begun to work independently in about 1665. His first important work in this capacity, S. Marcello al Corso, which dates from 1682–83, is a key structure in the development of the late baroque and early neo-classical style (see p. 46). The composition of the church facade differs considerably from those of the high baroque period. Here, the treatment of each element is logical and unambiguous: the rules pertaining to the orders are followed and the architectural language is in general easily deciphered. Once again the facade becomes a projection of the interior space, rather like Maderno's design made seventy years previously. The facade is split by three bays, each framed by an order. However, unlike Maderno's design, here each element of the order has an identical counterpart. The drawings indicate symmetrical columns of exactly the same width. The logical design of the ground-floor facade is repeated in the upper facade. Only the central entrance frame with its free floating *aedicula* is clearly set apart.

After this project, Fontana received a great many commissions, including several from abroad, like the one for the Jesuit church and monastery. In Rome, the commissions were very varied in type.

Carlo Fontana
Proposal to extend
St. Peter's Square to the east
Published 1694

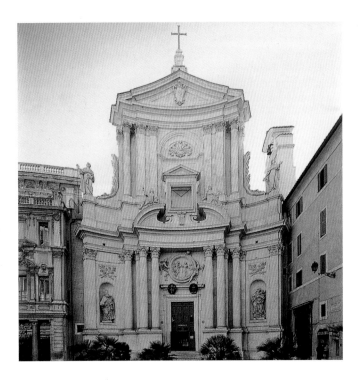

Innocent XII Pignatelli (1691–1700)

Shortly before the turn of the century, the Vatican's financial crisis seemed to have been at least partly resolved, and construction work therefore assumed a more rapid pace. This pope's main interest lay in public buildings and services. In addition to the prison in Via Giulia, the monumental hospice of S. Michele a Ripa Grande (see right) should also be mentioned in this context: as an institution it was responsible for taking in invalids, women, orphans, and three hundred children—and for providing the latter with a trade. The Lateran palace was converted into a hospice for up to five thousand people to the same end. The pope was also concerned with the administration of justice. He not only abolished the sale of public offices to the highest bidder, a practice since Sixtus V, but also demanded a court building large enough to serve the entire city. For this purpose, he commissioned Fontana to complete Palazzo Ludovisi (later called Palazzo di Montecitorio), begun by Bernini under Innocent X.

Fontana's plan to lay out a semicircular piazza in front of the palace was dropped because of the cost of the compulsory purchase, demolition, and reconstruction of the buildings in this square. A more ambitious plan—another paper exercise as it turned out—involved opening this square in front of Palazzo del Montecitorio onto Piazza Colonna, moving the Arch of Trajan, and, between the two squares centering on this feature, building a huge fountain. Another plan extended the Acqua Vergine to this point. However, it seemed that the showpieces that had so much typified high baroque were no longer in much demand; pragmatism was the order of the day. Ultimately, a customs office was therefore erected in the immediate vicinity of Fontana's project in the Temple of Neptune; it was intended for all visitors coming to the city from the north (see center right). A second customs office was set up at the harbor, close to S. Michele a Ripa Grande.

After almost three-quarters of a century of monumental incursions into the city during the high baroque period, a series of what might be seen as specifically middle-class transformations began to be introduced. Notable among these was an appreciable increase in the construction of houses for rent.

Bernini had planned and begun Palazzo Ludovisi between 1650 and 1655, but little of it had been completed by the time of Innocent

Among them were designs for palaces, chapels, memorials, altars, fountains, and festival decorations. Fontana's pre-eminence in the field was recognized when he was appointed director of the Accademia di San Luca, a position which, contrary to accepted tradition, he occupied for eight years, from 1692 to 1700.

In his seminal work *Templum Vaticanum*, as mentioned, Fontana considered two solutions for the completion of St. Peter's Square. The first included the destruction of the central buildings in the Borgo in order to build a road from Castel S. Angelo to the square. Fontana based a second project directly on Bernini's last plan to erect a clocktower outside the oval perimeter of the square, but brought it into the immediate vicinity. He altered the perspective and proposed a second trapezium, reflecting the one in front of St. Peter's which was to cut deeply into the neighboring Piazza Rustiucci and the Borgo (see right). The clocktower was to be placed at the far end of this trapezium. The idea of allowing the whole group of buildings to be experienced as a coherent whole was dropped. An observer stepping into the new square would see the square itself rather than the ground plan. Bernini's arcades would have seemed like the wings in a stage set in this square. Whereas high baroque had played with the concept of a dynamic internal space, here we can see a stage-managed series of interiors that is absolutely characteristic of the influence of the neo-classical idiom on late baroque architecture.

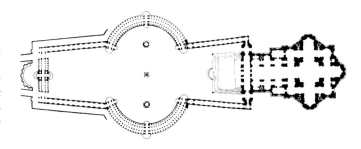

ABOVE:
Rome, S. Michele a Ripa Grande
Tiber facade, c. 1700

MIDDLE:
Carlo Fontana
Rome, Dogana di Terra (Customs
Office; now the Stock Exchange) in
Hadrian's Temple, c. 1700

BELOW:
Carlo Fontana
Plan for the square in front of
Palazzo del Montecitorio, 1694

X's death. Fontana, who resumed the work in 1694, kept mainly to his master's design, although he executed the detail in the academically classical language of his time. The facade of the palace has three sections with a window axis sequence of 3–6–7–6–3. The ground plan is structured on a convex curve. In the center, the different levels of the facade are not superimposed to any great degree. These features are based on both antique sources and elements from Palazzo Farnese.

Fontana's proposal for a semicircular square in front of Palazzo del Montecitorio was formulated, as was the plan for the extension to St. Peter's Square, using specific perspectives. Again, the idea was to direct the observer's eye to specific viewpoints. Instead of the dynamic visual experience established by the architecture of high baroque, we now have a static definition of perspective. Fontana's proposal for a church in the Coliseum can be seen in the same light. The central church was to be sited towards one of the two widths of the structure and set off from behind with oval walls. Again the design refers to Pietro da Cortona's S. Maria della Pace. The scheme was intended to provide an unambiguous demonstration of the predominance of the Catholic church over the entire pagan world.

Innumerable young architects came to Fontana as students. Juvarra, who subsequently traveled to Turin, was perhaps the most famous of these. Other important students were Pöppelmann, von Hildebrandt, and James Gibbs, who spread Fontana's architectural ideas throughout Europe.

Clement XI Albani (1700–21)

Deep-seated political problems and a series of emergency situations again forced the Vatican to restrict building work to essential projects. Only long-standing and urgent restoration work on a series of early Christian churches such as S. Clemente, S. Maria in Trastevere, and S. Cecilia was authorized. Nevertheless, two projects that were vital to the whole city were started at the same time. The first, Alessandro Specchi's Porto di Ripetta, was completed quickly between 1702 and 1705. The second project, Specchi's and Francesco de Sanctis' Spanish Steps, had long been planned, but was not realized until 1723–26.

The ancient ruins and the mythical landscape of Rome attracted an apparently endless stream of visitors. The first place visited after the Piazza del Popolo was the Porto di Ripetta, while Piazza di Spagna became the center of the city. The Porto di Ripetta was an exedra into the river bank, the stepped ramps of which pick up and follow the natural incline (see p. 48). Alessandro Specchi, a student of Fontana who had become well-known as an engraver, created this design. This project, in front of the church of S. Girolamo degli Schiavoni and destroyed by works at the end of the nineteenth century designed to control the river and extend the road beside the river, led Specchi and Fontana towards an increasing use of dynamic perspectives. The interplay between opposing curves in

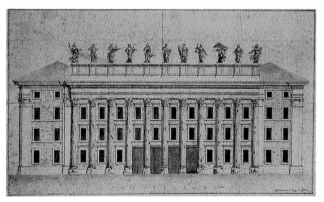

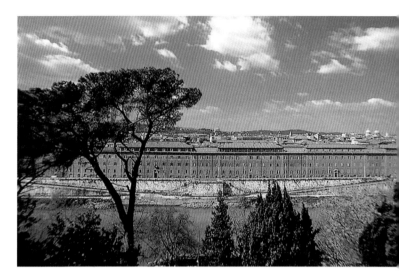

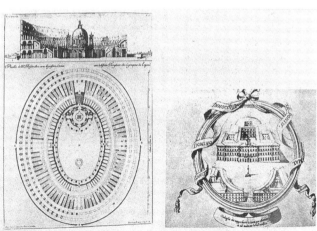

Filippo Raguzzini
Rome, Piazza S. Ignazio
1727–28

OPPOSITE:
**Alessandro Specchi
and Francesco de Sanctis**
Rome, Spanish Steps
and the Fontana della Barcaccia by
Gian Lorenzo Bernini

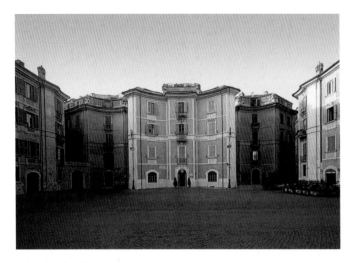

the scheme clearly indicates that the pendulum had swung back towards a high baroque language, more like that of Borromini.

The Spanish Steps were designed in a very similar manner. Years before, Bernini, secretly commissioned by Cardinal Mazarin, had completed an equestrian statue for the steps (see below). The cardinal wanted a mounted statue of the French king to be centered on the flights of steps—an unparalleled affront which Alexander VII could not of course accept. After Bernini's design was discarded due to the political conflict between Mazarin and Alexander VII, the hillside remained bare for some time. At the beginning of the eighteenth century attitudes appear to have changed. In Specchi's design, naturalism and practicality are of particular importance. As in the harbor plan, this scheme rests on numerous flights of steps which expressly follow the natural line of the incline (see right). Above all,

this adds an extraordinary elegance to the comings and goings of visitors. Both designs were on a large scale and aristocratic in character based on the great festivities of the high baroque period. The layout recalls the large scale and far-reaching perspectives achieved by Sixtus V. This sense is particularly well expressed by the engraver Giovanni Battista Nolli, who illustrated the harbor and the steps as though they were on one level.

Benedict XIII Orsini (1724–30)
Surrounded and dominated by decidedly mediocre political advisors, this pope was not only unable to halt the Vatican's rapid loss of prestige but contributed to it. During his incumbency, the Ospedale di S. Gallicano (1724–26) and Piazza S. Ignazio (1727–28) were both planned by Filippo Raguzzini. In both designs the architect took up subjects which had last been used by Borromini almost a century before, but he seemed unable to imbue them with any new energy. The design for the square in particular can be viewed as a counterpart to the Spanish Steps. Its proportions are modest in comparison with the church of S. Ignazio. It is surrounded by simple middle-class houses. No step-by-step stage management here; this particular courtyard plan holds few surprises (see above).

Clement XII Corsini (1730–40)
Under Clement, it seemed for a brief period that building activity in Rome might develop something of the intensity of the high baroque. Clement not only went ahead with the restoration of important churches but also commissioned new buildings like Palazzo della Consulta, for example, directly opposite Palazzo Quirinale and destined to serve one of the many commissions of cardinals. After this, he held two enormously influential architectural competitions in quick succession, one for the Trevi Fountain, the other for the facade of S. Giovanni in Laterano. He also commissioned Ferdinando Fuga to lay out the square in front of Palazzo del Montecitorio; in his

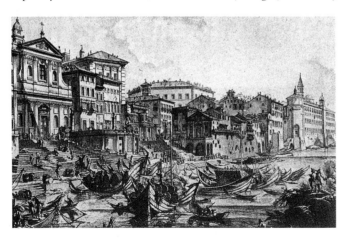

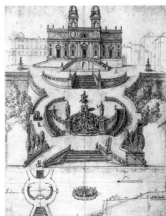

FAR LEFT:
Alessandro Specchi
Rome, Porto di Ripetta
Engraving by Giovanni Battista Piranesi

LEFT:
Studio of Gian Lorenzo Bernini
Design for the Spanish Steps
Rome, 1660
Rome, Biblioteca Apostolica Vaticana

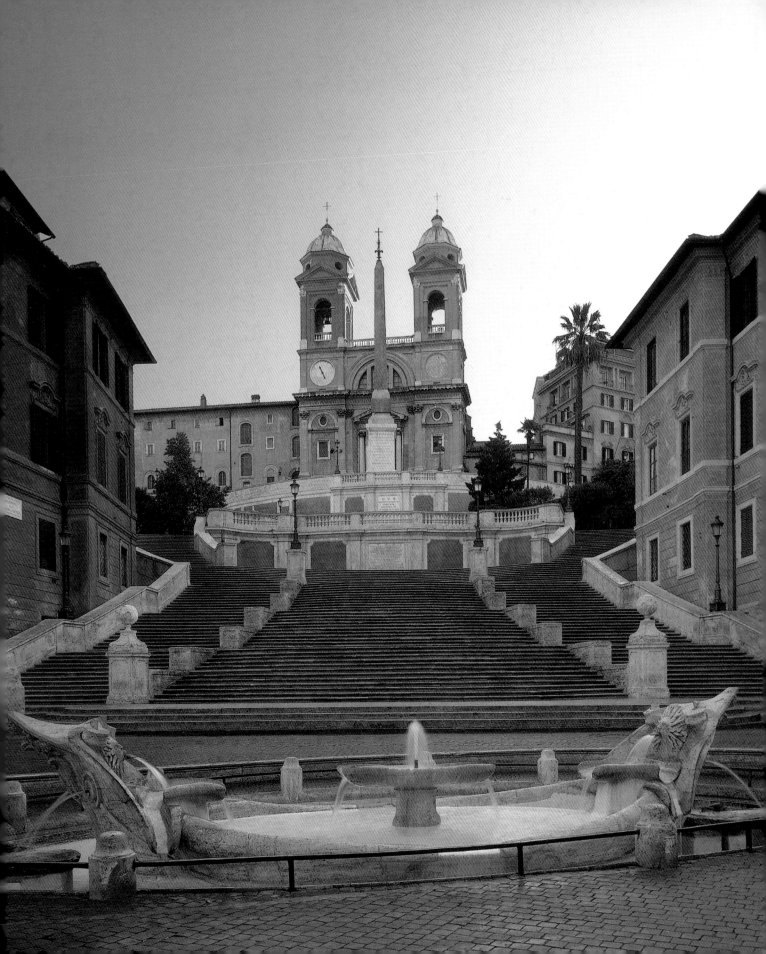

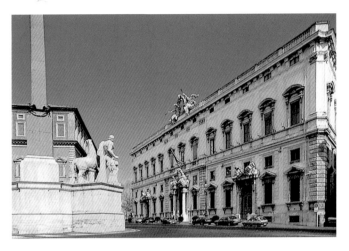

Ferdinando Fuga
Rome, Palazzo della Consulta
1732–35

Giuseppe Sardi
Rome, S. Maria della Maddalena
Facade, 1735

Capitoline palace. Galilei adapted this tradition in the style of S. Marcello al Corso by creating a facade for S. Giovanni with a structure that could be reworked. The relationship between closed and open facade sections was new and produced strongly contrasting light and dark planes which emphasized the orders. A sense of classical discipline pervades the whole design and the large-scale features are directly in the Roman tradition.

Nicola Salvi's design for the Trevi Fountain (1732–62) also illustrates an essentially classical approach (see right and p. 301). The primary source of reference was Pietro da Cortona's design for Palazzo Colonna, which had incorporated a spectacular fountain at the facade. The central triumphal arch motif that developed out of this became the framework for a wealth of allegorical and mythological scenes. The facade also included rococo ornament, a feature in particular of the central niche with Neptune. Thus Salvi combined a variety of different traditions to create a style that was positioned somewhere between Galilei's classicist approach and the late baroque manner of Giuseppe Sardi.

design Fuga rejected Fontana's exedra solution and replaced it with an irregular shape.

In his design for Palazzo Doria Pamphili (1731–34), Gabriele Valvassori reinterpreted the traditional palace facade, providing a picturesque solution with flat surfaces animated only by the window apertures and the alternating pediments over them. He gave added emphasis to the window frames and used more exaggerated curves. The balconies and balustrade reflect the same confident lines. The style is light and elegant (see p. 38, right, to the left of the church of S. Maria in Via Lata).

Only a year later, Fuga was to rework this type of palace facade. His design for the Palazzo della Consulta facade (1732–35) is distinguished by a series of pale frames set against a dark ground (see above). These become a visual framework supporting a number of different motifs, many of which can traced back to Michelangelo. The intellectual abstraction which marks the organization of the structural and ornamental features demonstrates a rare virtuosity. Conceptually, this work anticipates the neoclassical style, although Fuga also incorporates some essentially baroque elements.

Clement XII and Alessandro Galilei were responsible for finally putting paid to the so-called *barocchetto romano* as represented by Raguzzini. In 1632 the pope decreed that a competition should be held for the facade of S. Giovanni in Laterano. Twenty-three architects from Rome and elsewhere took part. The president of the commission was the president of the Accademia di San Luca, and the selectors were all members of the Academy; the result was fairly predictable. Inevitably, the competition became infamous, not least for the intrigue surrounding it. Apart from all this, the ultimate selection of Galilei's design proved to be of historic significance since it served to promote classical architecture during a time that did not generally favor the style (see right).

Galilei had closely followed the discussions in Lord Burlington's circle in London during the 1720s which advocated a return to the classicism of Andrea Palladio. Even though he left London in 1719, when hardly a single building had been executed in the neo-Palladian style, Galilei's experience there certainly had considerable impact on his subsequent work. But the Roman tradition seems to have been an even more important influence, particularly Maderno's design for the facade of St. Peter's and Michelangelo's design for the

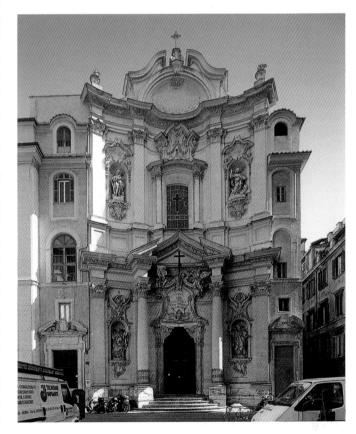

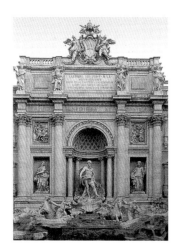

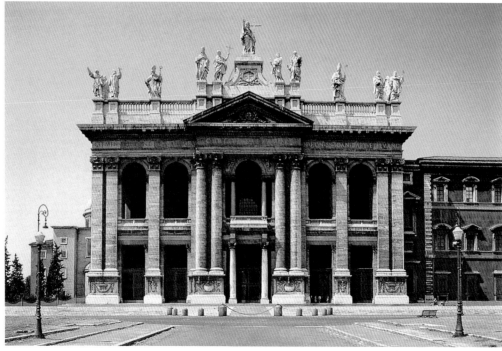

In his design for the facade of S. Maria della Maddalena (see left), Sardi makes direct reference to the work of Borromini, whose plans for S. Ivo and the St. Filippo Neri Oratory had recently been published as engravings. This link is indicated by the layout of the central niches, which clearly dominate the rather conventional structure. Unlike Salvi, Sardi made much more extensive use of exuberant rocaille decoration.

Benedict XIV Lambertini (1740–58)

Benedict XIV also encouraged architectural and urban development to a considerable extent. He continued the restoration of ancient churches such as the Panthenon and S. Croce in Gerusalemme as well as the church of S. Maria degli Angeli that had already been altered by Michelangelo. He took action to ensure the structural stability of St. Peter's dome, had a new facade built for S. Maria Maggiore, completed the Trevi Fountain, and extended the Capitoline Museum. He also took a great interest in the new science of archeology, commissioning Giovanni Battista Piranesi to make a new study of the relationship between the remaining marble fragments of the *forma urbis*, an ancient city plan. At the same time, he had an engraving made of the city layout by Nolli.

Ferdinando Fuga's facade for S. Maria Maggiore (see p. 52, above) dates from 1741–43. It shows the influence of the recently completed facade of the Lateran basilica, particularly in the loggia and the portico. The new facade was set apart from the original one to allow a view of the mosaics. But the details of Fuga's design have an essentially different rhythm and proportions. He not only used a unifying motif for his facade, but also divided the surfaces into individual compartments, varied the openings, and employed split pediment motifs, which stood in contrast to the massive structures.

Finally, and less convincingly, Pietro Passalacqua and Domenico Gregorini attempted in their plans for S. Croce in Gerusalemme (1741–44) to combine the lightness of the so-called *barocchetto romano*, recently demonstrated in S. Maria Maddalena, with the monumental language of S. Giovanni in Laterano. Nonetheless, the vestibule of the building is particularly impressive, reflecting as it does the tradition set by Borromini (see p. 52, below).

In defiance of such repeated attempts to vary the long-standing architectural traditions of the city, Carlo Marchionni decided on an essentially classical approach to his new work. It was his task to construct a villa for Cardinal Albani close to Porta Salaria (see p. 53, below) which was to house his extraordinary collection of ancient statues, amassed with the help of his friend Winckelmann. The garden facade shows a structural framework of great intellectual clarity. Every feature seems to be reduced to its basic elements. Functionalism is the dominant, although not exclusive, basis of this design. This might be seen as the essential tenet of classicism in this context; Pater Lodoli had formulated the theoretical precepts surrounding the style in Venice only a few years previously.

This synopsis of the papal role in the construction of Rome is also intended to demonstrate the essential characteristics of baroque urban planning. What seems to stand out is the close relationship between autocratic rulers and the planning and realization of large-scale projects. Many plans became feasible only because of the interest of the popes and their entourages, although it also seems that arbitrary interventions were equally typical of the system. No less interesting is the manner in which papal incursions and interventions were justified. Their personal schemes were realized in the name of God for the glory of the Church and the person of the pope himself. It was only during the late baroque period that things changed. The influence of the merchant class was growing and insti-

Ferdinando Fuga
Rome, S. Maria Maggiore
Facade, 1741–43

Pietro Passalacqua and Domenico
Gregorini
Rome, S. Croce in Gerusalemme
1741–44

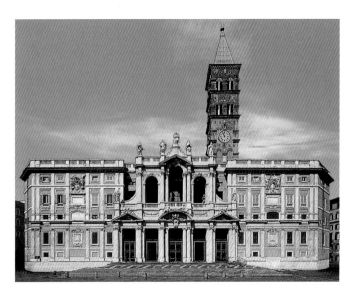

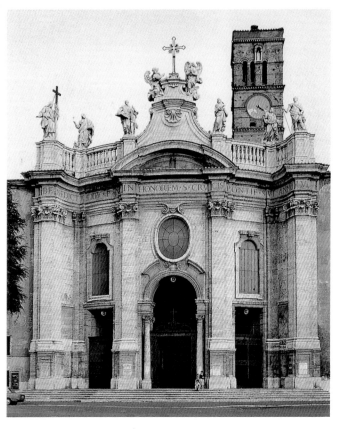

tutions such as courts and hospices as well as ordinary dwelling houses were introduced. A number of baroque cities throughout Europe developed in the same way, although for the most part slightly later (see pp. 76–77).

In Rome the infrastructure necessary for baroque urban and architectural development was established by the new straight roads and the autonomous positioning of the squares, which provided them with an independent environment; the concept of the *trivium* was an important feature of these developments, as was the use of obelisks to unify and to divert multiple lines of perspective and movement.

Finally, the Roman tradition provided an equally definitive influence on the development of seventeenth- and eighteenth-century architecture which, as we have seen, continually juxtaposed the baroque and classical idioms. The impact of a wide variety of stylistic traditions became apparent. Standard references were made to antiquity, the Renaissance, and, ultimately, to the early and high baroque periods. The architectural language was traditional; the range of possible combinations was, however, unlimited.

A new way of looking at architecture first emerged in France. Two theories proved particularly significant. The first advocated a system of standard proportions based solely on classical prototypes. The second was propagated by Louis de Cordemoy in his *Nouveau traité* [New Treatise] of 1706: truth and simplicity should direct the architect, so that the concept for any building could be expressed clearly and comprehensibly. Ultimately these ideas led to a call for "functional architecture." A key factor in this development lay in the sense that baroque had become a purely decorative style which, although technically of high quality, had lost its religious content. As we have seen, architects like Lodoli restricted architecture to its purely structural and functional elements. During the eighteenth century, criticism extended to include not only the apparent insubstantiality of the style but also the methods and aims of baroque art. The liberal, critical position of Lodoli was adopted in Italy by Francesco Milizia (described by Borromini's successors as "the delirious fanatic") and Mengs, who, with Winckelman, belonged to the inner circle around Cardinal Albani.

The following sections address the development of the baroque city and architecture in the most important Italian towns after Rome: Turin, Naples, and Venice.

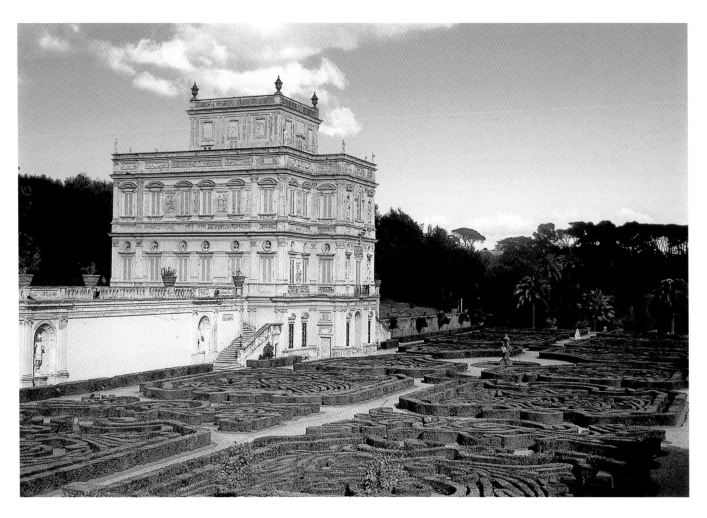

Alessandro Algardi
Rome, Villa Doria Pamphili
c. 1650

Camillo Pamphili rejected Borromini's
first design for the Villa Doria Pamphili.
Borromini had allegorically translated
his client's desire for the greatest
possible peace into a fortress-like villa
aligned toward the thirty-two winds.
The sculptor Algardi, who received the
commission instead of Borromini,
preferred an academic example of a
"museum facade" comparable to the late
mannerist Villa Borghese, in which
countless fragments of sculpture from
Antiquity were displayed.

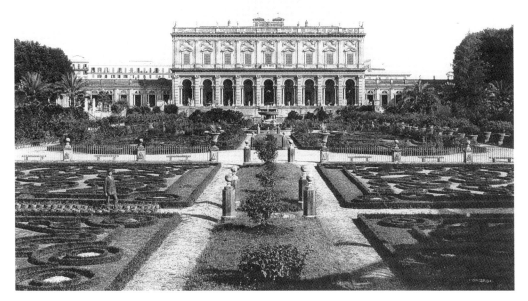

Carlo Marchionni
Rome, Villa Albani
Garden Facade, begun 1743

Developments in Turin

During the seventeenth and eighteenth centuries, Piedmont was the only state in Italy with an established political and economic structure. After Emanuele Filiberto of the house of Savoy had proclaimed Turin as his capital in 1563, architects came to the city until the beginning of the eighteenth century to plan renovations.

Turin had been a Roman castrum. The standard military camp plan used for Roman provincial towns, in chessboard format, had survived in the city for over one thousand years. The city was extended by its rulers south of the city walls in the early seventeenth century, to the east towards the river Po in 1673, and finally to the west, towards Porta Susina, in the early eighteenth century by the architects Ascanio Vittozzi, Carlo and Amedeo Castellamonte, and Filippo Juvarra. Strict laws controlled the work. After Carlo di Castellamonte had completed planning guidelines for the southern Città Nuova, a committee was set up to oversee the execution of the work. Laws were passed on street layout and the height and dimensions of palaces. Aesthetic considerations were very much the dominating factor in the outline of these regulations. In 1620, the first uniform street fronts were built along what is now Via Roma and Piazza San Carlo (from 1638), while in central Italy the autonomous, free-standing palace frontage was still the norm. To achieve a coherent appearance, the regent, Maria Cristina, presented plots of land to the court aristocracy, among other groups, on the condition that any building scheme would follow Castellamonte's plans. The future appearance of Turin was therefore planned with careful foresight and decisiveness; architecture played an essential role in these preparations. When Guarino Guarini came to Turin in 1666, Turin became the most modern and important architectural center in Italy, at almost the very moment when the creative energy of Roman architecture was seen to be fading—particularly after the death of Alexander VII in 1667.

Guarino Guarini (1624–83)

Guarino entered the Theatine order in Modena at the age of just fifteen. He subsequently traveled to Rome to study theology, philosophy, mathematics, and architecture. The newly completed interior of S. Carlo and south facade of the Oratory had a considerable impact on him. By 1647 he had returned to Modena and was working on S. Vincenzo. In 1655 he moved to Messina, where he designed the facade of the Santissima Annunziata (since destroyed). Guarini then went to Paris where he encountered ideas that were new to him. During this period, attempts were being made to reconcile Carthesian principles with religious faith. Debate centered on the apparent conflict between logic and a rational understanding of the world and the leap of faith required to accept as literal truth images of the Resurrection and the Ascension. Guarini's response reflected his role as both mathematician and architect. He understood the imagination as a hypothesis which had to be translated into reality. To do this, it was essential to have a certain skill.

The sort of skill he referred to was apparent in the increasingly dynamic structure of the domes he designed, for example. He was able to set them in a dramatic balance, at the very point where mathematical calculation and divine inspiration seemed to merge. Thus, his most daring and apparently bizarre schemes combined reason with imagination in a carefully judged equilibrium.

The Capella della Santissima Sindone (see right) was designed to house Christ's shroud. After long discussion, it was finally decided that the chapel would be built at the eastern end of the cathedral, directly adjacent to the royal palace (1667–90). Guarini faced a similar situation to the one that Borromini had encountered at S. Agnese. Amedeo di Castellamonte had begun the work on the chapel, reaching the level of the first orders. When Guarini took over the building work in 1667, he had to start with a scheme on a spherical plan with eight monumental piers and nine Palladian structures. He made radical changes to this balanced plan, which had been designed to support a standard tambour and dome construction. Every alternate pair of the nine sections was now given an arch, but pendentives were placed over the other three sections. He enormously exaggerated the ornamental structures laid out in Castellamonte's plan. Each widely curving arch passes over a pier which is not apparently load-bearing, but the main surprise is that he opened broad window apertures in the pendentives, generally the area where the weight is concentrated.

While in many respects Guarini followed in the tradition of Borromini, in the use of triangular forms and ornamental structures for example, it is clear that he had an essentially different approach to design. While Borromini used a great variety of different motifs and forms, he ultimately aimed to achieve a visually coherent scheme. By contrast, Guarini deliberately introduced oppositional elements, creating at times an astonishing dissonance. Thus, one internal space indicated nothing about the one that followed it. These contradictions were reinforced by Guarini through his ornamental, almost fragmented treatment of the surfaces.

In the chapel, a tambour area derived from Borromini can be seen directly above the pendentives. The design is almost traditional, but it appears to have been included simply to set off the structure above it more clearly. Thirty-six arches are inserted along the axis of the tambour apertures and between them to support the dome structure. A large number of window apertures are set under these arches which creates the impression that the structure is floating. The dome is not actually very high, but the foreshortened perspective of the arches gives a sense of height. This complex triangular scheme refers to the Holy Trinity.

The church of the Theatine order, S. Lorenzo (1668–87) (see p. 56), lies directly adjacent to the cathedral and the royal palace. The exterior is minimalist in style: only the dome stands out. The ground plan is based on an octagon with its eight sides convex to the central space. Palladian structures frame these segments. Beyond these out-

Guarino Guarini
Turin, Cappella della Santissima Sindone
View into dome, 1667–90

Cappella della Santissima Sindone
External view of the dome and
elevation

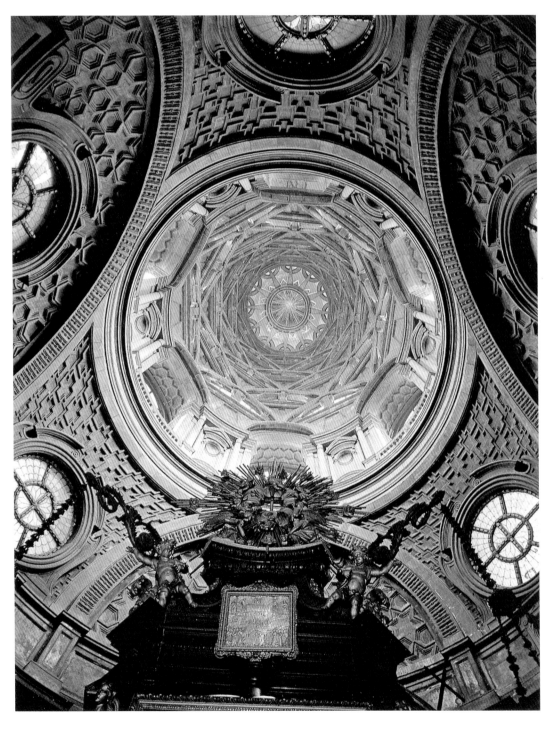

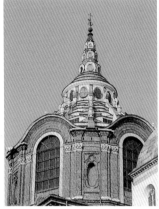

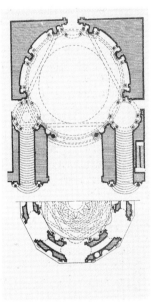

wardly curving areas half hidden by their sixteen marble piers, the eye travels to the outer wall of the building. The continuous repetition of similar features makes it difficult to take in the complete layout: only the cornice brings the whole structure together. But even this respite for the eye is short-lived, for in the area above this the Palladian structures are repeated in a cruciform style. A second cornice follows, interrupted by oval windows which present another structural contradiction. Arches rise from between these ovals, each with three windows, intersecting with the others to form a large octagon. This is surmounted by a second tambour and a second dome. The diaphanous design of the dome is heightened by the lighting. At this point the ground plan continues into a second area of the church which is based on an oval containing a circle, and which contains multiple variations of the features used in the main body of the church.

The principles on which Guarini's design was based are clear: the dome received most of his attention and it was in fact particularly stressed in the introduction to his architectural treatise. Until Borromini, St. Peter's dome had served as a universal prototype. Although Borromini broke with this model, he still adhered to the basic outline. For Guarini's dome, there were no direct formal models but his understanding of the form can be traced back to medieval sources.

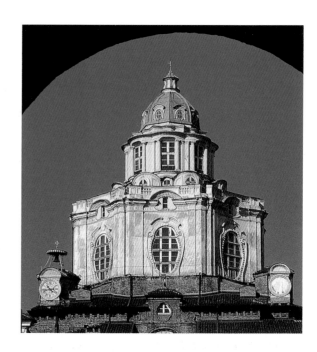

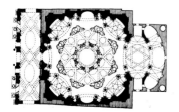

Guarino Guarini
Turin, S. Lorenzo
Ground plan, and interior and exterior of the dome, 1668–87

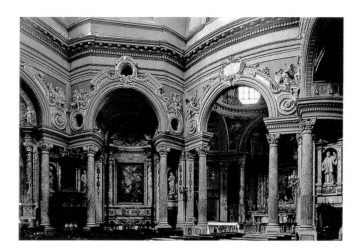

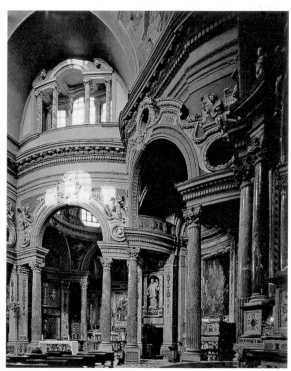

Filippo Juvarra
Turin, Palazzo Madama
Facade, 1718–21

Guarino Guarini
Turin, Palazzo Carignano
1679–81

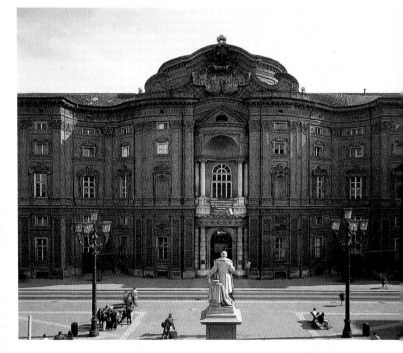

In his treatise he emphasized that gothic master builders had refined the load-bearing structures to such an extent that they seemed miraculously suspended. He developed this concept by replacing the solid hemisphere of the traditional dome with structures that appeared to float, suggesting, like the gothic buildings he admired so much, the mysteries of eternity.

In the rectangular and uniform layout of the city of Turin, the domes of both churches provided a new and extraordinary momentum. This also applied to the facades of Guarini's palaces. With Palazzo Carignano (1679–81), Guarini's combination of mathematical and metaphorical architecture became the official architecture of the absolute monarchy (see right). From Turin, this style was to spread to the whole country.

In Guarini's work we see the end of the classical formats which were predominantly intended for spatial arrangements. At the same time Guarini was the precursor of a form of modern architecture which no longer gave pre-eminence to a representation of space, but stressed the skills of creating internal space and of construction.

Filippo Juvarra (1678–1736)

Guarini died in 1683. After this there was a break in the architectural continuity of the city, since Filippo Juvarra only arrived in Turin three decades later, in 1714. Moreover, Juvarra's approach to architecture was fundamentally different. He had begun his training in

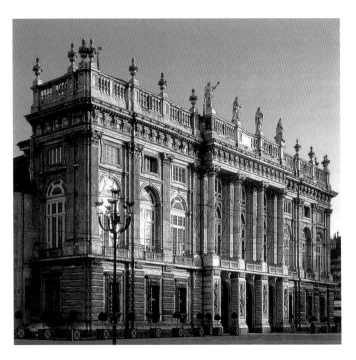

Messina with his father who was a goldsmith. He spent the next ten years in Rome where his master Fontana advised him to forget everything from the past and to study his own style of late baroque academic classicism. But his early, imaginative renovation of the Capitol had already demonstrated a distinctive and highly scenographic approach. Working for Ottobuoni, Juvarra designed many highly inventive stage sets from 1708 on. He earned extraordinary prestige by winning the Concorso Clementino, the architectural competition held by the Accademia di San Luca.

When Juvarra came to Turin in 1714, he was already well-known throughout Europe, especially as a set designer for the theater. His experience in the theater had mainly taught him how to use every possible trick with perspective and lighting effects. Nor did he have any objection to combining different styles and forms of expression, as long as he achieved the desired result. In his official role as "first architect to the king," he subsequently designed churches, royal palaces, and whole city areas, such as the ones between Via del Carmine and Corso Valdoco (1716–28) and between Via Milano and Piazza Emanuele Filiberto (1729–33).

He showed an impressive ability to employ the appropriate idiom for every commission. He took inspiration from Versailles for Palazzo Madama, for example, while for the church of the Superga, he used Roman sources. His fame as an architect quickly became

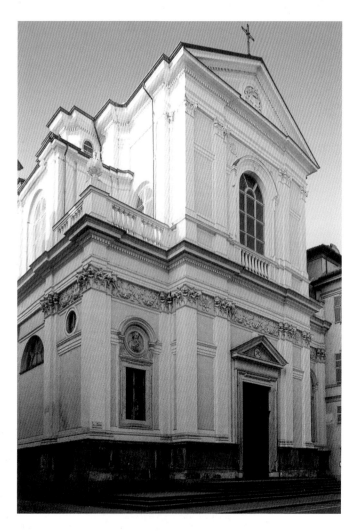

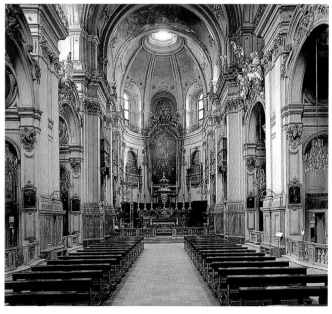

Filippo Juvarra
Turin, Chiesa del Carmine
Facade and view of interior, 1732–35

OPPOSITE:
Filippo Juvarra
Turin, La Superga
1717–31

legendary and he worked alternately in Portugal, London, and Paris, and finally in Madrid, where he died in 1736.

Situated on a chain of hills opposite the foothills of the Alps, the Superga (1717–31) dominates the city (see right). It was both a votive church erected after the victory over the French and a mausoleum for the Savoy family. Juvarra selected a central structure with a pillared portico. It was modeled on the Pantheon—after Bernini's work to open it up. Juvarra worked in the same way. In response to the position above, and remote from, the city center, he exaggerated the individual elements of the design. The tambour is very high and the pillared portico is deep. The large-scale format is reminiscent of the layout of Bernini's S. Andrea. The decision to provide the structure with a background also recalls Pietro da Cortona's S. Maria della Pace. The two wings of the building support the towers, in the tradition of Borromini, and give them added height.

The French court provided a political model for that of Savoy. The fact that Juvarra based his architectural plans for Palazzo Madama (1718–21) on Versailles makes perfect sense in this context. Situated in front of the medieval citadel, directly opposite the royal palace, Palazzo Madama (see p. 57 below) appears to be intended mainly for the purpose of conducting long files of state guests towards the ballroom in the evening: only the staircase lies behind the oversized windows onto the square, under an exaggerated barrel vault. In this space, the stairs become the stage, as in a theater. Compared with the garden frontage of Versailles, the piano nobile facade of Palazzo Madama is more convincing in the clarity of its emphasis.

The Stupinigi hunting lodge (1729–33) lies on flat ground and has an extensive, varied ground plan (see pp. 60–61). The major part of the complex was formed by low buildings of great simplicity which functioned as service and stable blocks. They served as framework and foreground. The stepped structure of the elliptical banqueting hall rises in the center. Galleries ring the interior. From this central space, four further ballrooms extend to form the arms of a cross. The sole purpose of this ground plan seems to be to create a series of theatrical settings. The contrast between the rural landscape and the mirrors and gold leaf of the interior enhanced the dramatic effect. In this way, the landscape became the backdrop, and the interior became the stage itself. This is where court society enacted its various rituals.

The Chiesa del Carmine (1732–35), the high main nave of which is separated from equally high chapels by "bridge arches," gives the impression of a gothic church refurbished in the rococo style (see left). The design of the wall closing the main nave is extraordinary. High galleries run above the three chapels on each side. The "bridge arches" into each of these chapels seem to be hanging in mid-air. The wall closing the main nave has been replaced by a framework of high piers. Only Borromini had treated the wall in such a manner with his design for the chapel in the Palazzo della Propaganda Fide.

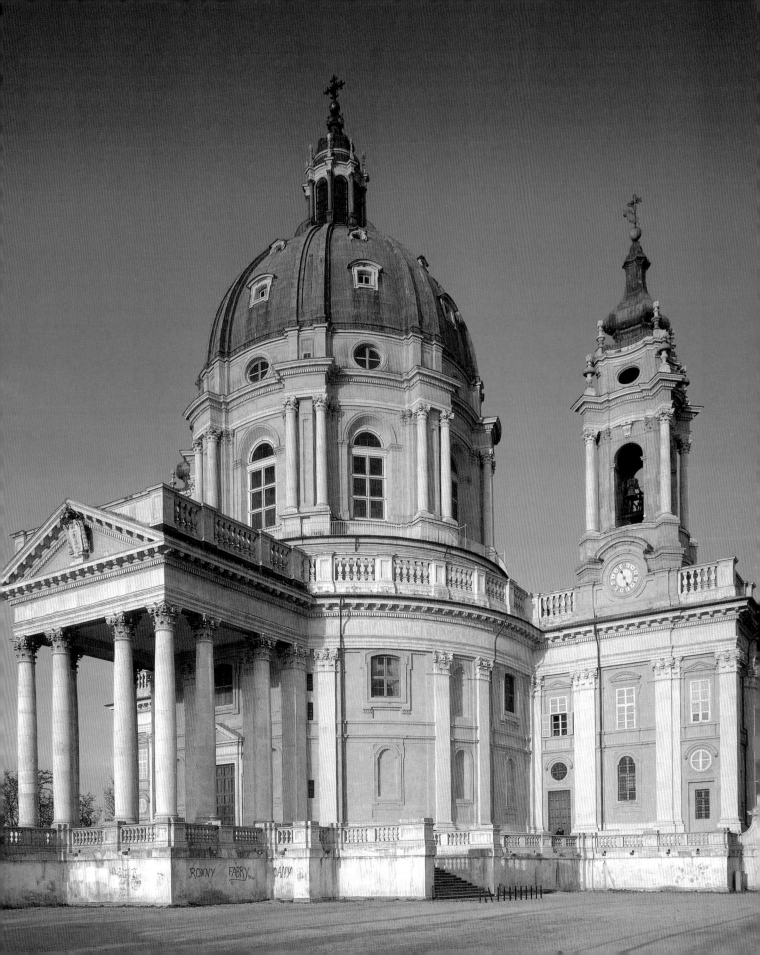

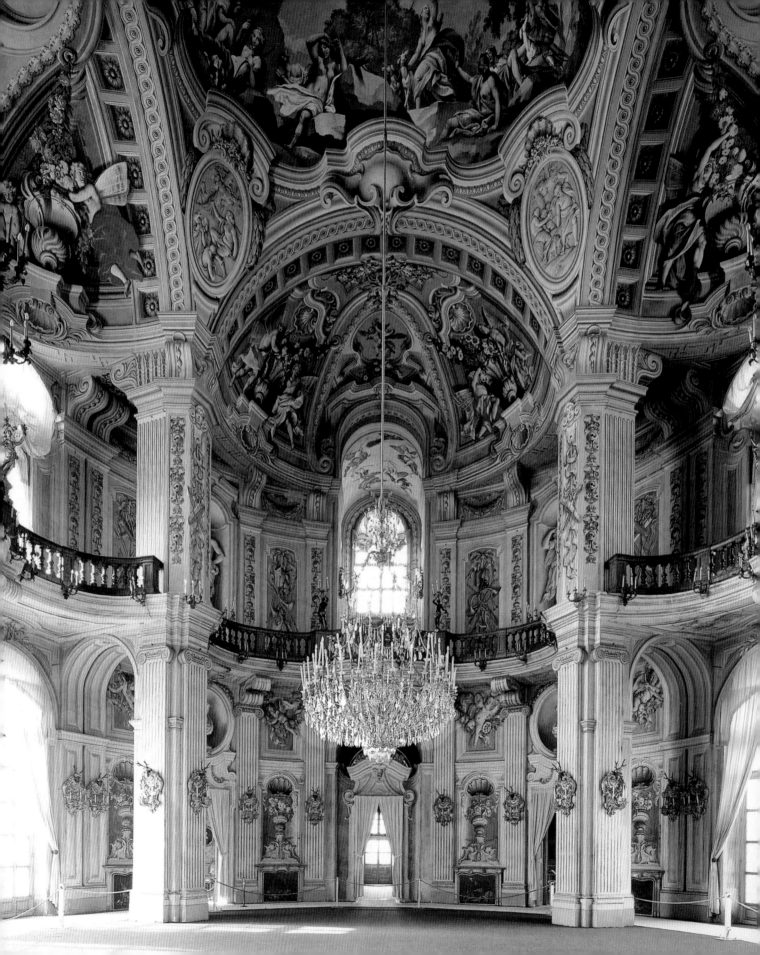

OPPOSITE:
Filippo Juvarra
Stupinigi hunting lodge
Great hall, 1729–33

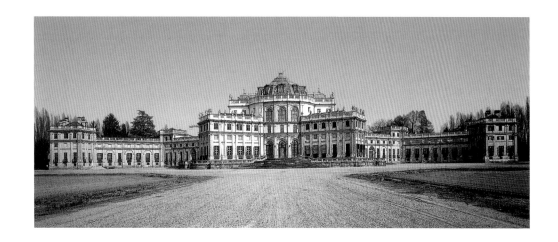

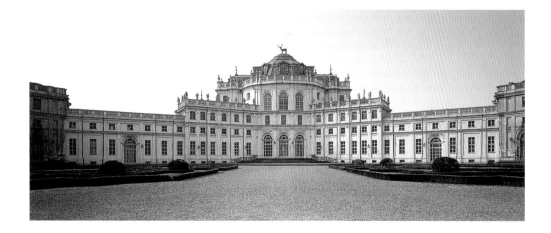

Filippo Juvarra
Stupinigi hunting lodge
External views and ground plan,
1729–33

The Stupinigi hunting lodge was
constructed on flat land with an extensive
and varied ground plan. The major part
of the complex, including service
buildings and stable block, consists of
low structures with very simple lines.
These served as a framework and a
foreground. Central to these rises the
elliptical, stepped banqueting hall.

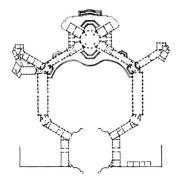

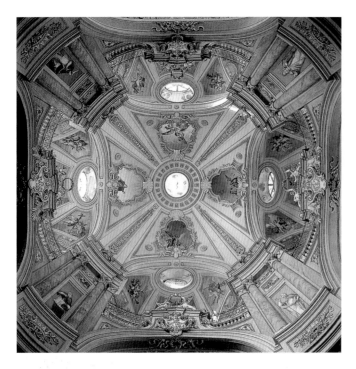

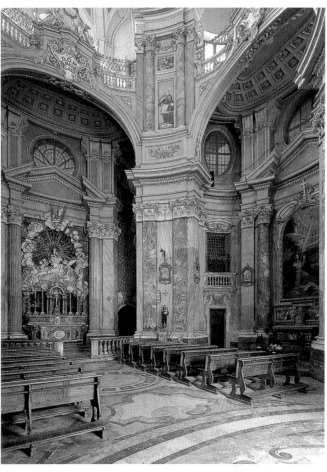

Ignoring Renaissance tradition, Juvarra returned here to a well-used, medieval definition of the wall, of the kind found in S. Ambrogio in Milan. The idea of indirectly lighting the chapel interiors with hidden sources of light, but illuminating the main nave through the broad open aperture above the chapels, was also extraordinary. By 1729, Juvarra had made similar plans for Turin cathedral, but these were never realized. They show how he had applied the revolutionary new definition of the interior wall in the main structure.

Bernardo Vittone (1705–70)

Bernardo Vittone's work combined the achievements of Guarini and Juvarra. He also studied in Rome, where he won first prize in the competition at the Accademia di San Luca. In the following year he returned to Turin, at a time when building work on Juvarra's unusual designs for the Superga and Stupinigi was being completed. After his return, the Theatine order commissioned him to publish the work of Guarini. This project allowed him an intimate knowledge of Guarini's work which he later developed in a series of churches with centralized ground plans. At the same time, he attempted to bring Juvarra's extraordinarily imaginative methods into everyday use.

His design for S. Chiara (1742) was a centralized space bound by four identical chapels laid out as segments of a circle (see left). The shell of the dome is borne by four very narrow piers, and the view from the chapels into the central space is framed by the vertical intersection of two superimposed arches, the upper part of which cuts deeply into the shell of the dome. The structure is decorated in four colors in the lower section and only the calotte is white. In addition, four large apertures in the shell of the dome open up the view to a second shell painted with a heavenly image with angels. The external silhouette of this second space receives direct light from adjacent windows. The area appears to encompass a man-made shell over which the saints and angels of higher spheres appear to be watching: the mortal spheres of this earth stand in contrast with the eternity of heaven as represented by the increasingly complex construction. That this was intended can be understood from Vittone's treatise on architecture.

Vittone remained loyal to the late baroque, even when the classical style began to prevail in the rest of Europe. He himself made a distinction between the classical approach and an architecture "di scherzo e bizzarria" [playful and incongruous], for which he held Borromini and Guarini responsible.

Developments in Naples

With the Peace of Utrecht in 1713, the Spanish crown lost control of southern Italy, which it had dominated for almost two hundred years. Nevertheless, in 1734, the son of Charles III was crowned king of Naples and Sicily, and ruled until 1759. He reigned as an enlightened despot. This new approach, which stands in contrast to

Spanish rule during the seventeenth century, had a direct impact on architectural developments. Over this period, significant large schemes were built, most notably the Museo di Capodimonte, government buildings in Caserta, the Albergo dei Poveri, and the Granary.

Cosimo Fanzago was the most important architect of Naples during the seventeenth century. Like Bernini, he was mainly a master builder and sculptor. His capacity for imaginative juxtaposition and development of architectural features was quite extraordinary. He understood how to combine late mannerist and high baroque elements as well as strictly classical and picturesque effects. In his work, he took advantage of every contemporary style. Nevertheless, his later work demonstrated an impressive simplicity: ornamentation became complementary rather than an inherent element. After Fanzago's death, architecture took two directions: Domenico Antonio Vaccaro and Ferdinando Sanfelice adopted an inventive, unorthodox but elegantly decorative style similar to that of Valvassari and Raguzzini. After their death in 1750, the king summoned Fuga and Vanvitelli to Naples from Rome. Their architectural style reflected the rationalism of late baroque classicism. At the same time, a richly ornamental tradition based more on the arts and crafts expressed bold ideals for social reform. Meanwhile, the excavations in Herculaneum and later in Pompeii made Naples the focal point for travelers from the whole of Europe.

In about 1750, the first concern of the enlightened regime in Naples was to endow the city with an infrastructure. Two enterprises are of particular interest: the Albergo dei Poveri and the Granary. Fuga was initially given the commission for the Albergo dei Poveri, a building which, like S. Michele a Ripa Grande in Rome, was to act as hospice, sanctuary, and educational institution. He planned a building of enormous proportions (see right, below). The longest facade was about 350 meters in length. Transverse structures of the simplest design, intended as sleeping quarters, were aligned with a central church. In 1779 Fuga also designed the Granary. In its extraordinary simplicity the complex, housing a public granary, an armory, and a rope factory, can be seen as a precursor of the industrial buildings of the nineteenth century. The great clarity with which Fuga analyzed and resolved the functional problems heralded the social attitudes which provided some of the basic principles of the neo-classical movement.

Luigi Vanvitelli (1700–73)

The Palazzo Reale in Caserta, near Naples, is a very functional monument. The architect was Luigi Vanvitelli, the son of a painter from Utrecht. He also began life as a painter, participated in the competitions for S. Giovanni in Laterano and the Fontana di Trevi, and subsequently erected a series of utilitarian buildings for the pope including the hospital in Ancona. In Rome, he completed Bernini's Palazzo Chigi.

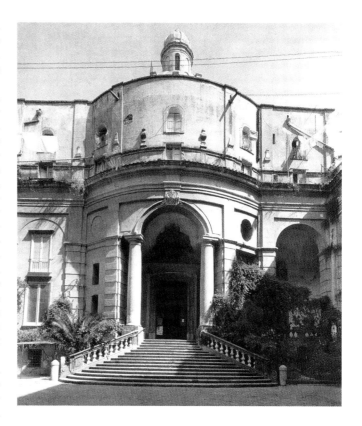

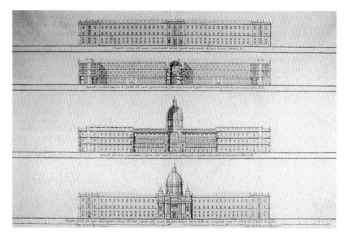

Ferdinando Fuga
Naples, Albergo dei Poveri
Original drawings, 1748

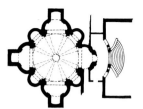

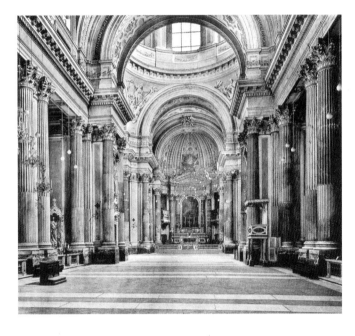

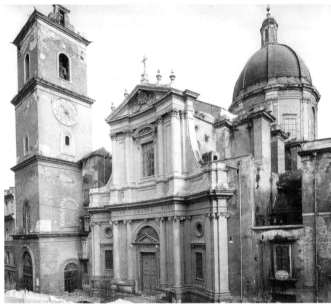

In 1751 he was commissioned by the Spanish king to construct the government palace in Caserta and the neighboring areas of the city. Vanvitelli, who was accustomed to formulating his designs on the basis of clearly defined requirements, first made an analysis of the functions required of the royal palace, which, like Versailles, was to accommodate the whole administration. He proposed a building of enormous proportions (see right). Twelve hundred rooms are grouped around four courtyards laid out as squares. The centerpiece includes a *gran portico* from which four galleries radiate. The facades indicate two main storeys on a high, double-ground-floor structure. Three pavilions, situated at either end and in the center, give definition to the facade. By projecting it onto the exterior in this way, the architect distinguishes the internal structure and organization of the building from the facade. At the same time, the architectonic elements follow the structural requirements very directly. This provided a framework for the layout of the contrived sequences of internal space and perspective which were intended for ceremonial purposes. The model for this was the diagonal stage which became a dominant feature of eighteenth-century theater after its "invention" by the Bibiena family of artists. Thus, Vanvitelli did not open the four courtyards centrally, but on the diagonal. Above all, however, he leads the view along endless prospects, through the whole building, deep into the gardens which appear like a stage set. The essential feature of this theatrical space is, however, the pure classicism of the columns.

A few years later, in 1762, Vanvitelli received the commission for the Chiesa dell'Annunziata in Naples (see above). The remarkable discoveries made during the excavations at Herculaneum and Pompeii provide a context for this scheme. The remains allowed a better understanding of the formal elements of classical antiquity that was evident in the plans for the Chiesa dell'Annunziata. The ground plan followed the pattern developed in the sixteenth century for the Roman church of the Gesù. The nave, side chapels, and a short transept were laid out in a rectangle. The crossing and dome are almost at the center. The way the light is used shows barely a trace of baroque either: the concealed sources of light used to theatrical effect in baroque structures are abandoned here as is the back lighting used to project rays of light in high baroque churches. The light from the dome falls onto fluted columns which reflect it into the surrounding chapels as in the central hall of the Reggia in Caserta. The church was not designed to impress and persuade the faithful, but rather to be a suitable space for church services. The mood of the Enlightenment was clearly demonstrated in Vanvitelli's religious architecture.

Developments in Venice

Throughout the seventeenth century, Venice had been linked with the architecture of Palladio and his successors. Thus, the city became associated with the neo-classicism of the eighteenth century much earlier than Rome, Turin, or Naples.

The specific topographical characteristics of Venice which had developed from fortifications in the lagoon and the integration of

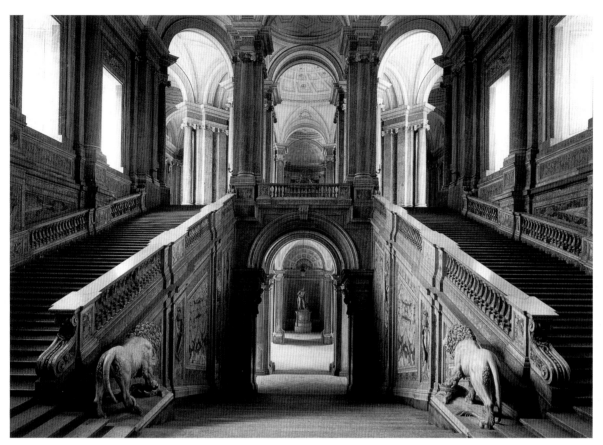

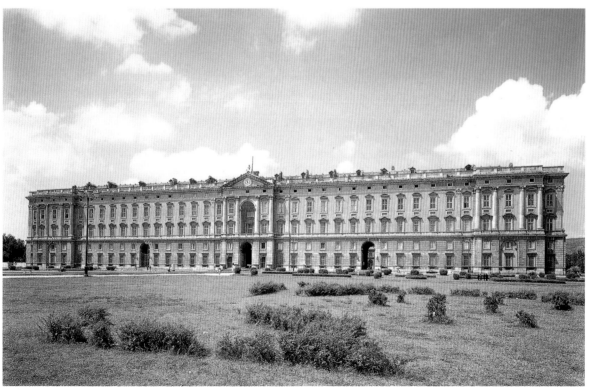

Baldassare Longhena
Venice, S. Maria della Salute
Begun 1630/31
Interior, ground plan, and section

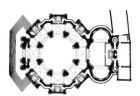

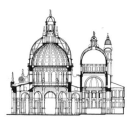

OPPOSITE:
Baldassare Longhena
Venice, S. Maria della Salute
Begun 1630/31

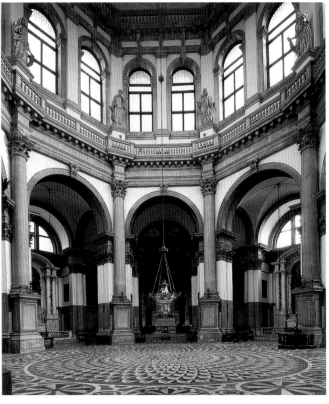

However, Palladio's work was to be of great significance in another respect. During the seventeenth century, his theoretical work was repeatedly reprinted and analyzed. His claim, based on Vitruvius, that architecture should be planned to suit the specific context of Venice, found a sympathetic interpreter in Pater Lodoli. Lodoli rejected all formal solutions which were not suited to structural, functional, and contextual requirements. The absolute principle of rational construction became the point of departure for the neoclassical style in Venice as elsewhere.

Baldassare Longhena (1598–1683)

The most important exception to these trends was Baldassare Longhena's design for S. Maria della Salute (see left and right). Longhena was a student of Scamozzi. His reference point was also the work of Palladio. As a result, his plans were not dominated by a preconceived concept of spatial design, but by an analysis of the specific local context and the functional issues involved. The commission was to build a votive church in thanks for the end of an outbreak of the plague. Longhena accordingly planned two spaces. The first was an octagon with an ambulatory and chapels for the congregation, while the second was rectangular with two apses and intended to be used for services of thanksgiving. The highly prominent site is at the entrance to the Grand Canal, opposite the Giudecca. Longhena proposed a central structure with an elevation which responded to the context, particularly the domes of S. Marco, S. Giorgio Maggiore, and the Redentore. Like these churches it was given a double dome shell with wooden frame to reduce mass and, above all, no ribs. The external walls of the radial chapels give visual support to the powerful volutes, which in turn act as abutments for the tambour and dome.

The design of the interior also followed Venetian tradition in many respects. The gray and white of the architectural elements was derived directly from Palladio. But the purpose of this was not to underline the load-bearing structure; it was intended rather to guide the eye around the building. Thus the white sections of pier lead the eye to the space beyond, while on the other hand the gray color around each opening emphasizes the central structure. The decorative features on the columns were new. They do not continue up to the level of the tambour but are transformed, above the corbelling, into pedestals for imposing statues of prophets. The columns thus become free-standing features reinforcing the circular space. While the octagon is so clearly present, the connection with the chancel is less obvious. It is indicated only by free-standing columns at the entrance to the choir and at the altar itself. The entrance to the church is the focus for the whole design. Longhena created a series of clearly defined perspectives centering on this viewpoint. This sequencing of impressions is particularly Palladian in style. At the same time, however, the Roman baroque was developing an internal coherence of the kind seen in the interiors of the churches of S. Carlo and SS. Luca e Martina.

several independent communities meant that the extensive, large-scale plans which typified baroque architectural schemes were simply not feasible. Palladio had been forced to accommodate these special elements when he planned a bridge to integrate the first of the communities, the Rialto. Even the tradition of building over water and the formation of the Venetian skyline provided few possibilities for baroque architects. Palladio had found an answer to this problem in his church plans. The elemental presence of S. Giorgio and the Redentore, the facades designed in the spirit of the classical late Renaissance, and the high, steep domes still echoing the architecture of Byzantium were designed to be seen across the waters of the lagoon. They became the prototypes for ecclesiastical architecture during the seventeenth century. Venetian palace architecture also followed established traditions. For centuries ground plans and elevations remained unchanged. During the sixteenth century, only the facades were redesigned. The facades of Sanmicheli and Sansevino represented a response to the special play of light from the water in Venice. Subsequently, this became an almost compulsory model. Further, the subsoil of the lagoon necessitated light brick construction and wooden domes.

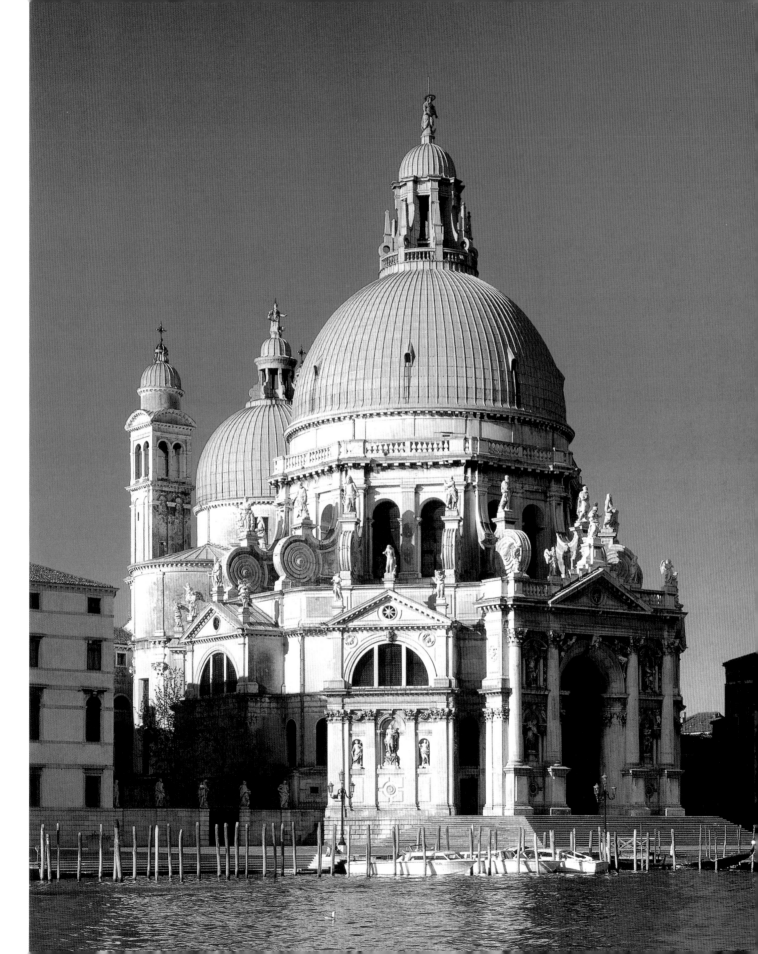

Baldassare Longhena
Venice, S. Giorgio Maggiore
Staircase, 1643–45

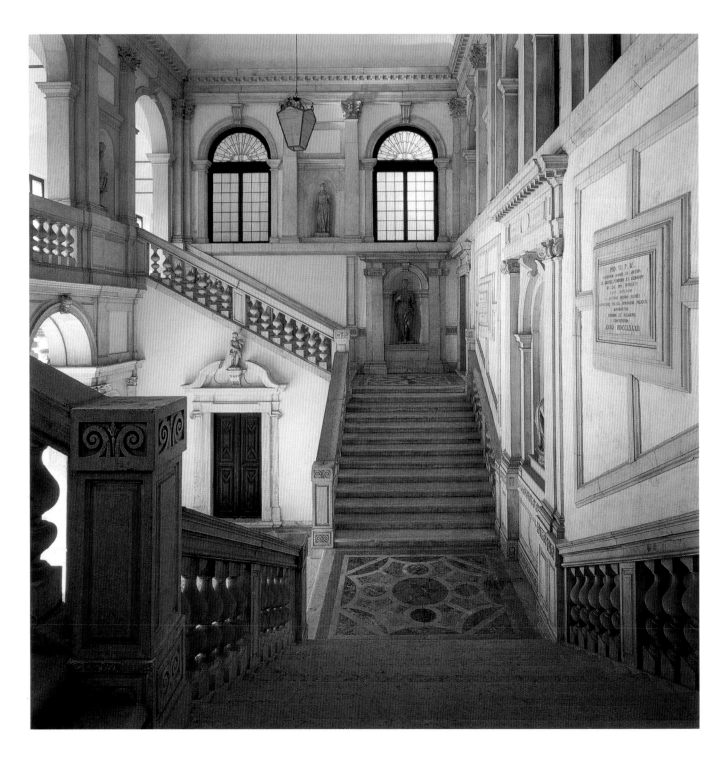

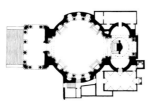

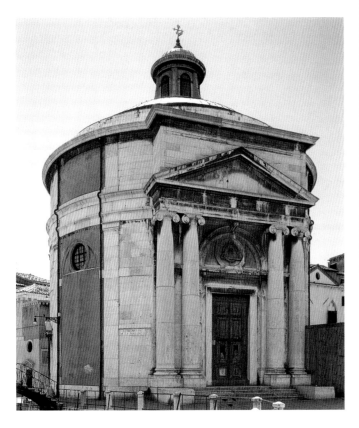

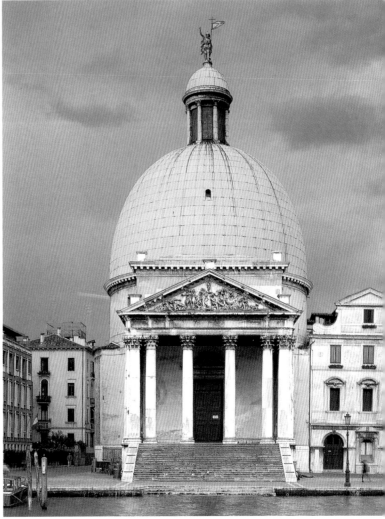

Longhena's design for the staircase in the monastery of S. Giorgio Maggiore is similarly contrived (1643–45). Two parallel flights of stairs rise along the external walls of the hallway to a landing overlooking both the hallway and the adjacent loggia (see left).

In 1652 Longhena began work on Ca' Pesaro (see p. 70). Over the rusticated ground floor rise two further richly decorated storeys punctuated by columns. The plasticity of decoration increases with the height. It seems as though Longhena wanted to increase the number of surfaces which catch the light, contrasting with the shade in the deeply recessed window apertures.

The Palladian tradition came fully into its own quite early in the eighteenth century. A first example is Andrea Tirali's facade for S. Nicolò da Tolentino (1706–14). The design here, particularly for the portico, was strongly influenced by Vitruvius.

An important early milestone in the development of neo-classicism can also be seen in Giovanni Scalfarotto's church, SS. Simeone e Giuda (1718–38) (see above). Again, it was modelled on the Pantheon. The portico and the steps leading up to it were, of course, derived from classical temples, but the structure itself is

nonetheless narrow and high. The wooden double dome still derives from the Byzantine-Venetian tradition. The Pantheon was also the model for the interior, but here the floor plan has an added chancel, as in S. Maria della Salute. The approach was Palladian, although not yet truly neo-classical. Palladian lines also dominated the work of Giorgio Massari, a fine example of which is Palazzo Grassi (see p. 71). The architect left the facade unornamented in order to eliminate any contrast between light and shade. Instead, he alternated the window axes and retained the traditional elements of a Venetian facade.

While Palazzo Grassi was being built, Tommaso Temanza was building S. Maria Maddalena (1748–63; see above right). Temanza had published the theoretical work by Pater Lodoli and was a friend of Milizia, a vehement opponent of the baroque. His work was based on Scalfarotto's plans for SS. Simeone e Giuda which, however, he criticized and amended. He reduced the portico, but the main change here was the elimination of the dome, a decisive and uncompromising return to the classical standards of antiquity.

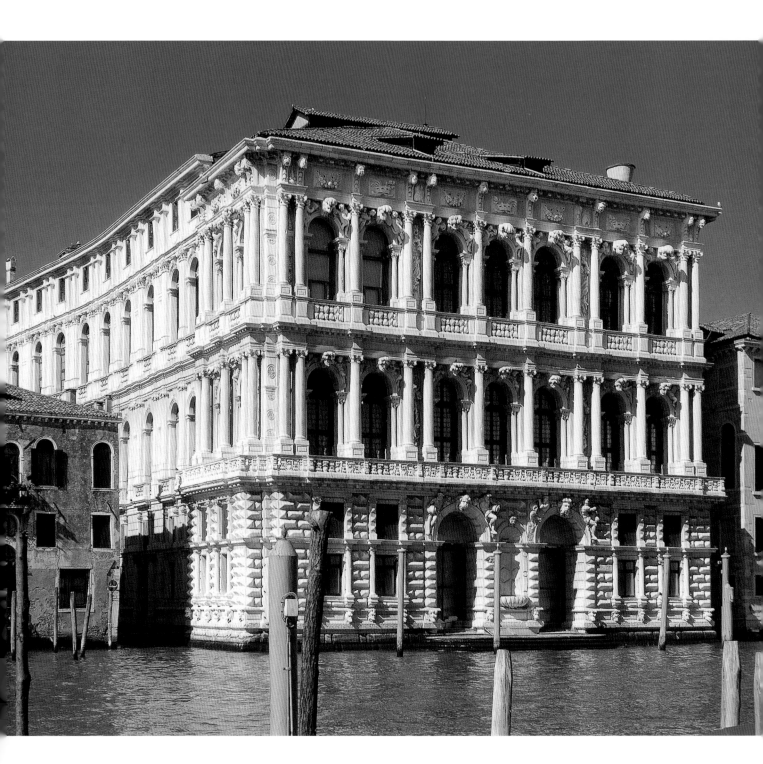

Giorgio Massari
Venice, Palazzo Grassi, begun 1749
Facade

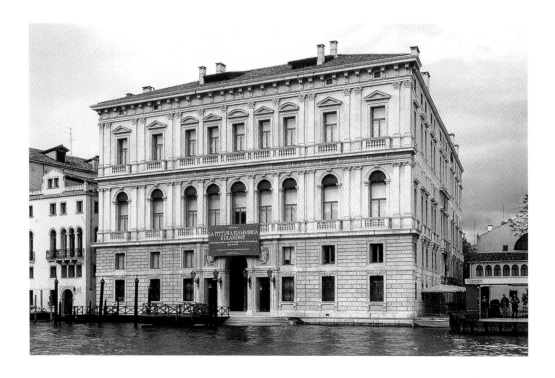

Francesco Maria Preti
Stra, Villa Pisani, 1735–56
Garden facade

In his design for Villa Pisani in Stra, Francesco Maria Preti was looking straight back to the Palladian villa *all'antica*, for instance, in his use of a central temple facade. However, compared with Palladio's villas, the sheer size of Villa Pisani was radically different. This difference in dimensions was due to the influence of palace architecture. This also applied to the addition, on the garden side, of a complete storey on the attic floor.

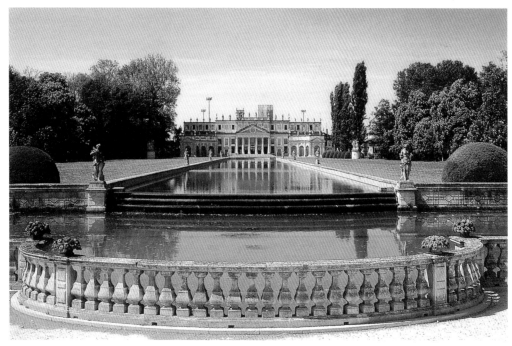

71

View of St. Peter's dome through the
pergola in the garden behind S. Maria
del Priorato

OPPOSITE:
Giovanni Battista Piranesi
Rome, Maria del Priorato
Facade, 1764–68

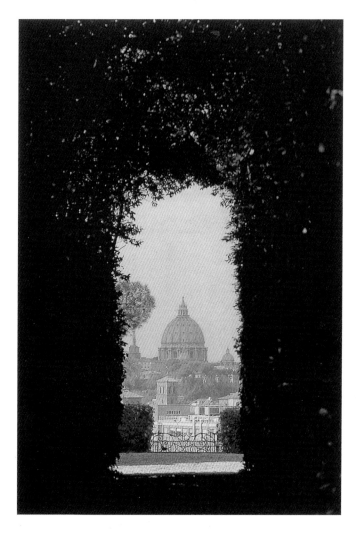

The Thin City as seen by Giambattista Piranesi (1720–78)

On this basis, we should now return to Rome. The initial question was about how baroque Rome influenced the ideas of its inhabitants and how, in return, they structured the architecture of the city. It has been shown that the construction of the city of Rome—that is, Zenobia—was the result of a series of individual enterprises rather than of comprehensive planning. These individual enterprises were often contradictory in nature. They were both baroque and classical in concept and language, and in the manner in which they were committed both to theatricality and to an archeologically accurate reconstruction of antiquity. It was precisely this contradictory multi-

plicity which gave the baroque its extraordinary coherence. It was the work of Piranesi, the most dazzling artist of his age, which demonstrated how architecture and city were viewed during the transition from the late baroque to the early neo-classical style.

Even his training incorporated this combination of apparently contradictory elements. Born in the Veneto, he was trained by his family in the primarily functional skills of stonemasonry and hydraulic engineering. His extraordinary gift for precise detailed analysis and documentation were acquired in Rome with Giovanni Battista Nolli and Giuseppe Vasi: the first was the originator of the 1748 plan of Rome and the second the most important painter of *veduti* [views] of his day. After this, Piranesi studied for a short time in Venice with Canaletto, and became familiar with the theories of Pater Lodoli. Subsequently, Piranesi's chief concern was to enhance both the theatricality of the city and the scientific study of antiquity.

The baroque city made clever use of the dramatic possibilities inherent in it. It often borrowed from the theater for both religious and state processions and festivals. As in the theater, the sets were made cheaply of wood, which also kept them within building regulations. On the other hand, the aim of the baroque master builders was to structure their architecture on the visual experience of processions and festivals, and therefore to transform it into a performance in its own right. It was no coincidence that a series of views of the city engraved in 1665 for Pope Alexander VII were entitled *Il nuovo teatro... di Roma moderna* [The New Theatre of Modern Rome] and a collection of city plans commissioned in 1682 by Carlo Emanuele of Savoy *Theatrum statuum Sabaudiae* [Theatre of the States of Savoy].

Piranesi's representations of city and architecture were no less theatrical. Drama and poetry were the main themes of his engravings, the main subjects of which were his famous picturesque ruins. The approach and technique were essentially those of a late baroque artist. This was demonstrated in the exaggerated proportions and the predominance of the diagonals reflecting the influence of the diagonal stage. Piranesi's *Carceri* seemed to be stage sets from this same baroque theater (though they have also been seen as proto-romantic for the same reasons).

His work as an architect was similar, particularly his plans for S. Maria del Priorato (1763–68). The square and the garden maze designed for the richly decorated church facade (see right), the interior, and, above all, the altar (see p. 75) provide a series of bizarre compositions drawn from archeological finds and following almost incidentally on from each other. Their settings are, however, highly effective.

At the same time, Piranesi was a meticulous archeologist. He documented the finds in Herculaneum with the greatest precision and established a plan of Hadrian's Villa which for over one hundred and fifty years was unmatched in its comprehensive accuracy. Pira-

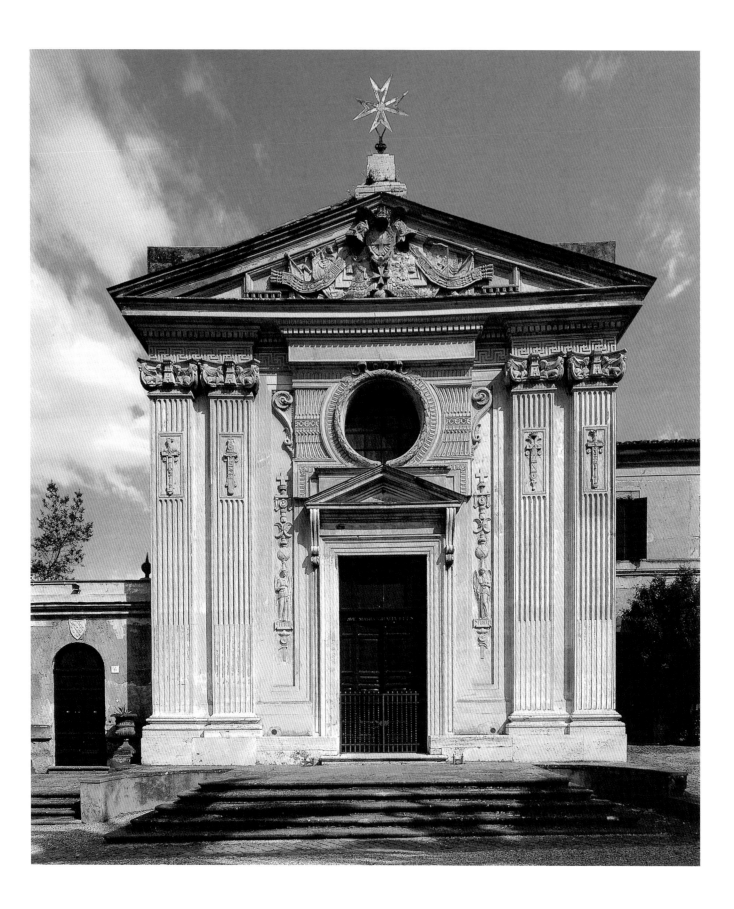

Giovanni Battista Piranesi
Reconstruction of the *Forma Urbis*
From *Le Antichità Romane*, vol. I
Rome, 1756, plate II

Giovanni Battista Piranesi
Campo Marzio
From *Campus Martius Antiquae Urbis Romae*, Rome, 1762, plate V

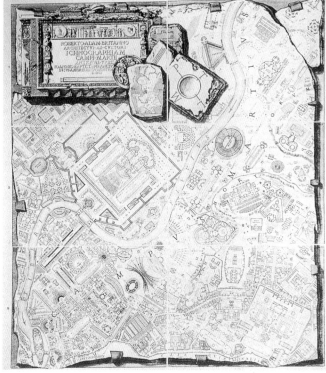

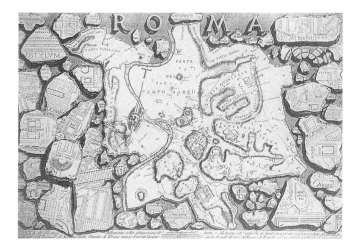

nesi played a major role in the ongoing debates over antiquity. His participation in the Greco-Roman dispute of the day became increasingly polemical. He stressed the prevalence of ancient Roman art and architecture, asserting its primacy over that of Greece. Above all, he argued, the ancients—especially the Romans—should provide the prototypes for a modern style. It would be pointless, nonsense even, to research into the functionality of ancient buildings. A totally logical temple structure did not exist. This would be hypothesis: the ancient way of life had come to an end. Antiquity was to be found in ruins and fragments, and the theoretical basis could not be recovered. Finally, history could be relived only in drawings, engravings, and in the imagination, as suggested by Piranesi's own *Capricci*. This background explains why Piranesi used a diametrically opposed technique in S. Maria del Priorato for the purposes of architectural theatricality. The altar, with an overabundance of references to antiquity on the front, is reduced to its basic formula on the rear elevation.

Theatrical settings and studies of antiquity were combined in Piranesi's most important study of Rome, the *Magnificenza ed Architettura de' Romani* [Magnificence and Architecture of the Romans]. An architectural setting is immediately established as the

essential principle by the way he added fantastical set pieces to the scheme. However, this also provided irrevocable proof that Piranesi had studied the form of the ancient city in the greatest detail and had used it as the basis for his plan. The few remaining fragments of the only surviving ancient map of Rome, the marble *Forma Urbis*, provided an indication of this. Can the plan of Rome be seen simply as a combination of analytical and nostalgic retrospection? Rome has been defined, in the first instance, as the city which, like no other in the seventeenth and eighteenth centuries, molded the desires of its inhabitants. There is no question that Rome comprehensively influenced the world of Piranesi's imagination. On the other hand, could this plan of Piranesi's represent a new, thin Rome, created by his imagination and enthusiasm, undoubtedly exaggerated to a disproportionate degree—and for that very reason so much more clearly defined?

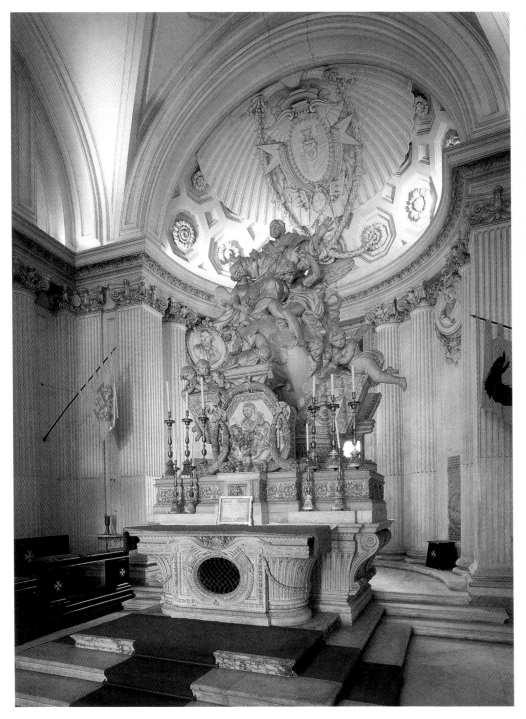

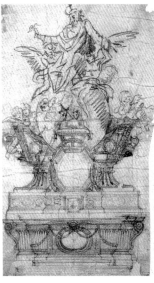

Giovanni Battista Piranesi
Rome, S. Maria del Priorato
Altar, 1764–66

Giovanni Battista Piranesi
Drawing of the design for the altar in
S. Maria del Priorato

Baroque City Planning

Ehrenfried Kluckert

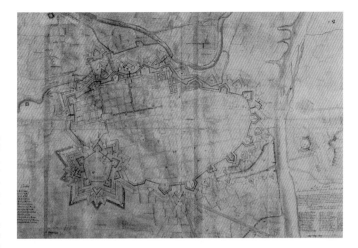

The previous chapter considered the extent to which the development of baroque Rome was influenced by papal construction policy. We will now examine the most important features of urban development in Rome and Turin within the wider context of European city architecture of this period.

The basis for baroque city architecture lay in the renaissance concept of the city, where the city had to respond to the principles of cosmic order and harmony. The relationship between street, square, and building was dramatized in the baroque period, so that the regular rectangular street plan was not always applicable.

Urban architecture as defined by this approach differentiated between refurbishment and expansion of the city on the one hand and new construction on the other. One of the most influential city-planning exercises was undertaken by Pope Sixtus V, who commissioned Domenico Fontana to replan Rome in 1595. In order to open up areas of the city dating from antiquity for large-scale building projects, streets were laid out from the edge of the city into the center and, where possible, connected to each other. Each street ended at a building or a group of buildings with a large square; at the same time, these elements became focal points of the city. The districts of the city opened out from them and were intended gradually to expand into one homogeneous whole. Obelisks were also used as a feature in the development of the concept of visual connections and layout (see p. 16).

The problem of large-scale expansion of the city for the purposes of the state was also apparent in the old Roman and Lombard metropolis of Turin. Here it was Filippo Juvarra who, in 1714, was commissioned by King Vittorio Amedeo to develop the city on the basis of the older grid system (see above). The expansion of the city went according to plan, from the medieval center outwards, forming a sort of almond shape due to the star-shaped fortifications.

While Rome and Turin expanded, mainly for state reasons, elsewhere war was frequently the incentive for new building schemes. The fortress of Neu Breisach (Neuf-Brisach) on the Rhine demonstrates one way in which urban architecture and civil engineering were interwoven. It was founded in 1697 to take the place of the old Breisach, a bridgehead lost in the Treaty of Ryswick (see right, center). The French military architect Sébastien Le Prestre, marquis de

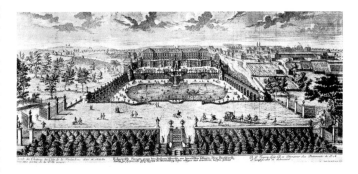

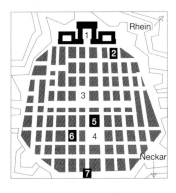

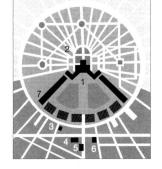

Mannheim
city plan c. 1750
1 Palace
2 Jesuit church
 and college
3 Parade ground
4 Market place
5 Town hall and
 parish church
6 Reformed church
7 Neckar gate

Karlsruhe, city
plan 1780
1 Palace
2 Palace grounds
3 Catholic church
4 Town hall
5 Lutheran church
 (now the Pyramid)
6 Reformed
 church (now the
 "Kleine Kirche")
7 Linkesheim gate
8 Mühlberg gate

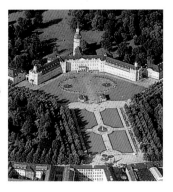

Vauban (1633–1707), the most famous fortress engineer of all times, produced the plans for this installation, designed in accordance with the most advanced military thinking of the time: a star-shaped system of fortifications consisting of a triple ring of walls and bastions surrounded the grid plan of the town with its square central open space. Vauban's strictly pragmatic approach underlies the whole layout of the city, from the public buildings to the decoration on the facades.

In southwestern Germany the Palatinate War of Succession (1688–97), the Turkish Wars (1663–1739) and the War of the Spanish Succession (1701–14) reduced villages, cities, castles, monasteries, and towns to ashes. Like the Neues Schloss in Baden-Baden, the Carlsburg in Durlach was largely destroyed in 1689 by the French. To Karl Wilhelm, who became margrave in 1709 at the age of thirty, there seemed little sense in investing financial resources in the reconstruction of his town. He longed for the plains along the Rhine. He planned a magnificent palace in Hardtwald and, on June 17, 1715, one year after the end of the War of the Spanish Succession, he laid the foundation stone for an octagonal tower from which the town would develop in a fan-shape, like the rays of the sun around the aristocratic palace (see left). As he said, he wanted to have the town built as the "future repose and delight of the soul." "Carlos-Ruhe" [Charles' Repose] was elevated to the role of state capital only two years later. In 1722 and 1724 the town was granted further privileges. Settlers from all parts of Germany moved to Karlsruhe.

The construction of a royal palace was often linked to urban planning. In Ludwigsburg, when the royal residence was built, work also began on developing the town (see above center). The first plans were drawn up in 1709 by Johann Friedrich Nette. The duke was looking for settlers, in order to "settle all types of trade, manufacture and arts there, in addition to the crafts," and he promised to grant building sites and building materials free of charge as well as tax relief, for fifteen years. The town plan, which Frisoni established in 1715, provided for a broad, square market place surrounded by arcades. He differentiated carefully between main streets and side streets and made sure the building plots were spacious.

Versailles was regarded as the ultimate palace prototype by absolute rulers throughout Europe (see right). The unity

Versailles, plan of the whole complex
with view of the city
Engraving after Israel Silvestre
End of 17th century

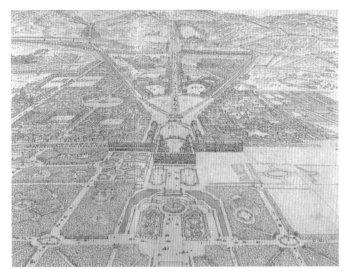

of palace, town, and park and the scale of the links with the extensive landscaped grounds around it were taken as an example of a type of order that could appropriately be imitated by any ambitious ruler. The position of the palace, with its widely extending wings, provided a single central focus which both separated and enclosed the garden side from the town side. The town elevation was set on the road, street, and alley system which radiated like a star from the palace.

Finally, another sort of town should be mentioned here, this time closely associated with the humanist spirit of urban planning: the ideal town. During the Renaissance in Italy, what might be called ideal housing schemes were set up like the one at Palmanova near Udine, the papal town of Pienza, and Sabbioneta. Pamphlets on such ideal theories reached the new world, where all sorts of experiments began to occur. These plans opened new avenues even for new towns in northern Germany: in 1621 Duke Frederick III of Gottorf wanted to give a new home to dissidents from the Netherlands and at the same time to found a center for trade. Thus the town of Friedrichsstadt, named after him, was founded in Schleswig Holstein, between the Trenne and Eider rivers. Traversed by tree-lined canals, the town consisted of rectangular plots. This was the so-called rationalist plan, typical of towns which were built especially for religious refugees.

As the plan of Rome demonstrated, the layout of the squares was of decisive significance in urban planning. While during the late Renaissance and the early baroque periods, a radial layout or squares enclosed on all sides were preferred, as in Piazza del Popolo, for example, and the Place Royale in Paris, baroque urban layout favored a series of squares. Different types of space were combined. Between 1752 and 1755 in Nancy, the architect Héré de Corny created a sequence of three squares to connect the old town with the new.

In the eighteenth century the southern English city of Bath became increasingly important after Charles II's stay at the spa. After improvements to the old town, the neighboring urban areas were also scheduled to be "regulated" and given a new layout. Three main complexes emerged, around three thoroughfares: Gay Street, the Circus, and Royal Crescent. Later Queen Square (see p. 178, below) was added to the south. The architects John Wood the Elder and John

Wood the Younger worked for almost half a century (1725–74) on this design and obtained outstanding results. To the west of the city they established a circular housing development, the Circus (1754), and connected this with the later Royal Crescent (1767–75), a semicircle based on the three-cornered arch with thirty terraced houses forming a single facade opening to the south onto extensive parkland and lawns (see p. 178, above).

These geometrical plans were imbued with a sense of the connecting landscape. Royal Crescent was situated on higher ground overlooking the Avon valley. The park below the complex crossed the terrace leading to the lower town. A "miniaturized" experience of gardening was also intended, since the architects provided each individual section of the building with generous gardens at the rear.

These links between nature and planning within the urban context were unique and reflected a conscious attempt to accommodate middle-class requirements to some extent. The lack of dominant structures and the addition of middle-class houses within the context of an asymmetrical urban complex responded to more universal human needs than merely those of a baroque monarch.

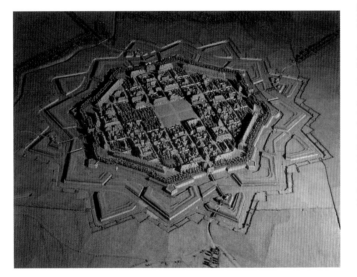

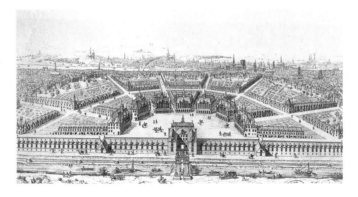

Paris, project for the Place de France
after C. Chastillon
Beginning of 17th century

Barbara Borngässer

Baroque Architecture in Spain and Portugal

The Historical Framework

In the Iberian peninsula—as elsewhere—the baroque period occurred during the seventeenth and first half of the eighteenth centuries. At the same time there can hardly be a clear distinction between the peninsular baroque and both the previous eras of the Renaissance and Mannerism and the subsequent decades of the Enlightenment. This is due to the pervasive influence of powerful factors such as Habsburg patronage or, later, the activities of the academies which discouraged innovation in art. Renaissance and the subsequent decades of the Enlightenment, due to the existence of cultural factors that are not specifically Spanish or Portuguese We will therefore examine more closely the specific historical factors which led to the dominance of baroque in the Iberian peninsula.

In 1492 the conquest of Granada completed the Reconquista, the return of Christian rule to the whole Iberian peninsula. In the same year, Columbus discovered America for the Spanish crown. Portugal had colonized the coasts of Africa long before and had just landed—also in search of a sea route to India—in what is now Brazil. The division of the regions then known as the New World by the Treaty of Tordesillas (1494) marked out once and for all the fields of Spanish and Portuguese influence. With one stroke, the two kingdoms of the Iberian peninsula were masters of territories which until this point had been literally unimaginable.

During the sixteenth century considerable ideological and material capital was made of this situation. The Catholic church, in whose name the Spanish crown acted both at home and in the colonies, supplied contextual justification and practical aid in defense of the claim to power. The religious orders, Franciscans, Dominicans, and, above all, the Jesuits, carried the Catholic faith in the Spanish-Habsburg mold to the farthest-flung corners of the world. Between 1563 and 1584, Philip II built the monastery and palace of El Escorial as a symbol and mark of this sacred kingdom.

In 1561, he designated a hitherto little known spot in the heart of the peninsula—Madrid—as his residence and future capital. Between 1560 and 1640, after annexing Portugal, Spain ruled over the entire Iberian peninsula, all the known areas of Central and South America, and several areas of Asia and Africa. However, the mother countries were confronted with almost insurmountable organizational and ideological difficulties in the establishment of an efficient administration, in the exploitation of minerals discovered in the colonies, in sending missionaries to the "heathens," and, not least, in their foreign relationships. Internal political conflicts were also very much prevalent and had the effect of making the "Golden Age" an era full of contradictions.

Nevertheless, the successors of Philip II, Philip III, and, especially, Philip IV, were patrons of the arts: they drew artists like Velásquez and Rubens to the court, built palaces, and generally promoted the fine arts and science. Their reigns were, however, shaken by great economic and social instability. In spite of the immense wealth pouring in from the colonies to the motherland, it proved impossible to use this for the benefit of the country as a whole. The money flowed out in the wars against the rebellious marches of Portugal and Catalonia, against France in the Pyrenees, and against the Dutch in Brazil. The administration of this worldwide empire was hopelessly inefficient, the economy stagnated—in the seventeenth century the State was declared bankrupt four times—and the population decreased. The Inquisition, fighting for the purity of the faith, and the aristocracy, fighting for the purity of the line, made sure that the country itself dispensed of its productive resources on a large scale. The expulsion of the Moriscos and the resulting decline in skilled work of all kinds was only one example of this self-mutilation.

It was not until the eighteenth century, when the position in southwestern Europe was consolidated with peace in the Pyrenees and with Philip V, a Bourbon, ascended to the Spanish throne, that the position in Spain was stabilized. Aristocracy and clerics lost influence so that, as the intermediate classes increased, trade and commerce experienced an upturn. Improved infrastructures and the exploitation of mineral wealth meant that new economic poles and early centers of industrial production were created. At the same time, cultural centers with pronounced regional characteristics emerged. The court, on the other hand, modeled itself along French lines. Where art was concerned, a radical shift took place in about 1760 with the foundation of the Academy and the rise of a new, neo-classical idiom. The end of the baroque era seemed imminent.

Spanish Baroque Architecture Through the Eyes of the Critics

The late sixteenth and seventeenth centuries were known as the *Siglo de Oro*, the "Golden Age" of Spain. The paintings of Velázquez and Zurbarán and the plays of Lope da Vega and Calderón are renowned as some of the highest achievements of the European baroque period. The architecture of the time, by contrast, is generally experienced through the clichés of travel brochure fantasy. Even quite serious publications give the impression that, between the construction of the monastery and palace of El Escorial and the appearance of an architectural "genius" in the person of Antonio Gaudí at the turn of the last century, there was a vacuum in which Spain—and even more Portugal—produced no high-quality architecture of its own.

Iberian baroque architecture proved itself to be an extraordinarily good export: it was adopted throughout Ibero-America and the most distant regions of Africa and Asia where it flourished as an adaptable and extremely vibrant style of building. Architecture had a greater impact on Latin American culture than any other import—apart from language. As the bearer of a specific ideology, whether of a sociological and political nature as represented in public and administrative buildings, or religious as suggested by the layout of mission stations, monasteries, and churches, it played an important intermediary role between the motherland and the colonies. The transfer of architecture, decorative features, and stylistic elements was so effective that buildings in different corners of the world might on occasion have more in common than those in neighboring regions of Spain and Portugal. Yet the baroque architecture of both these countries is frequently consigned to the categories of regional peculiarities or folk art, or is viewed as a dubious interpretation of foreign models. Spanish baroque architecture in particular has been rigorously attacked over the years. It was, observed the art critic Eugenio Llaguna y Amírola in 1829, like a crumpled piece of paper. He was referring to structures like the facade of the cathedral of Santiago de Compostela, or El Transparente in Toledo, both of which are now highly regarded. The contemporary metaphor was as eloquent as it was damning: paper has no structure, a crumpled heap has no artistic form. Thus, two of the elements of architecture considered essential since the time of Vitruvius were summarily dismissed. The criticism was aimed at the flamboyant decoration and non-tectonic decoration; besides those buildings named above, the objects of this criticism were mainly the works of the Churriguera family, Pedro de Ribera, and Francisco de Hurtado Izquierdo. This view, based firmly on a classical idea of aesthetic value, has not quite disappeared even today.

The fact that the architecture of the Iberian peninsula and its colonies appears to defy the standard stylistic categories of early baroque, late baroque, and rococo may account for these lingering prejudices. This factor was already evident in the art of the fifteenth and early sixteenth centuries, for which the use of phrases such as "late gothic," "Isabelline," and "plateresque" is confusing for the layman. The terms "renaissance," "mannerist," "Herrera style," and "unornamented style" are often used in connection with the architecture of Charles V and Philip II. In the seventeenth century we speak of the "Herrera succession," "early baroque," and "panel style"; in the eighteenth century of "Churriguerism," "Spanish rococo," and—for court architecture—the "Bourbon style." Each of these terms is to some extent a description representing a particular aspect of each style: the character, the econo-political or aesthetic criteria of the era.

Paradoxically, the attachment of a stylistic description to an artist's work did not necessarily involve any particular association with the individual concerned; in fact the case was rather the opposite. As in the case of Herrera and Churriguera, the more their names served to indicate the architecture of a whole period, the less the contribution of the individual was recognized. This is in itself may have been a factor in the lack of interest in Spanish baroque architecture: since the individual architects were not particularly well known, their life and work was never seen as a basis for thorough investigation or even for the emergence of legends of the kind that surrounded the work of Michelangelo and Bernini. Unlike Italy, Spain lacked locally written accounts which might have encouraged the growth of personality cults and the appreciation of individual achievement.

Juan Bautista de Toledo and Juan de
Herrera
Monastery and palace of San Lorenzo de
El Escorial, 1563–84
Entrance building

The Era of Philip III and Philip IV (1598–1665)

In Spain, almost half a century passed between the retreat from mannerist forms and the creation of a national baroque architecture, a timespan which coincided with the reigns of Philip III (1598–1621) and Philip IV (1621–65). In fact, while the first elements of early baroque trends were evident in Valladolid in about 1600, a sustained body of work in this style was not produced until the appearance of Juan Gómez de Moras, whose more freely handled facade designs supplanted the strict classical style of Juan de Herrera's followers. Nevertheless, the influence of El Escorial remained far into the seventeenth century.

El Escorial as a Model for Spanish Habsburg Architecture

The construction of the monastery and palace of San Lorenzo de El Escorial ushered in a new architectural era (see below and right). The choice of a Roman style based on the Vitruvian orders represented a clear rejection of the late gothic and the so-called "plateresque style" that had prevailed in Spain until well into the sixteenth century. The "Renaissance" of classical structures and formulae, already established in Italy by the second quarter of the fifteenth century, did not influence Spain until much later. Even the classical palace of Charles V at the Alhambra in Granada was not widely imitated. This was certainly not true of El Escorial: the rational groundplan, the classically structured facade which avoided the smallest superfluous detail, the ceremonial rigor and monumental proportions of the interior, and, finally, the use of the characteristic gray granite from the local area were to have an impact on court architecture in Spain until the early nineteenth century; the building was still used as a model under the dictatorship of Franco.

The construction of the monastery and palace marked the beginning of absolutism, the rule of one man administering by divine

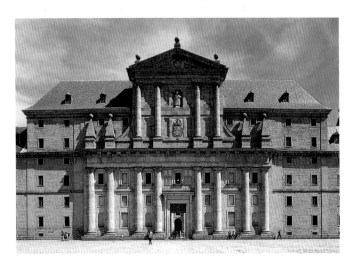

right. With the decision to combine the royal palace and the Habsburg mausoleum with the monastery and college of the Hieronymite order, Philip II sought to combine spiritual and temporal power. The complex, measuring 208 by 162 meters was a synthesis of the Spanish alcázar and a hospital. Scientific and administrative buildings were included, creating a self-supporting environment, a state within a state, a microcosm, the image of a higher order. Symbolically, the complex is laid out axially to the church and the king's private apartments behind it, a concept which was to find its fullest expression in Versailles. It is no coincidence that construction on El Escorial began in 1563, the year in which the Council of Trent, before which the king had presented himself as the defender and unifier of the Catholic church, had ended its business. The extraordinary location of the structure and the possible symbols enshrined in its layout led to a rash of overly constructed interpretations: for some, El Escorial was an image of the Temple of Solomon as described in the Old Testament and was therefore approved by God. For others the grid layout was a mark of the martyrdom on a grill of its patron saint, St. Lawrence.

The various metaphorical interpretations of the structure also reflected a general acceptance of the design, something which had been very much intended. Philip II was conscious of the fact that architecture *a lo romano* would signal the arrival of a new political era. He himself had dabbled in architecture and had tried to find a new idiom capable of representing Spain's position as a world power while freeing it from outmoded medieval traditions. The revival of the "Golden Age" of Augustus seemed particularly appropriate in this context. To realize his ambitions, the king brought Italian or Italian-trained architects to his court and acquired the most important theoretical writings for his library, which were translated for him. Now available in Spanish, the work of Vitruvius, especially volumes III and IV of his *Ten Books on Architecture*, dedicated to the orders of architecture, and Sebastiano Serlio's books of lectures and examples explaining Vitruvius' unillustrated work established the basis for the development of a Spanish understanding of Roman architecture.

Juan de Herrera (1530–97), scholar and confidant of the king, controlled the planning process for all important building projects in the country; he represented a new type of architect, one very different from the medieval master builder and the traditional craft-based technology of the profession. From this point on, throughout the baroque period, the *trazador* or *traçista* dominated the scene, a skilled worker who was responsible for the design of a building and who discussed the plans with the patron. In contrast to the *aparejadores*, who had the responsibility for the realization of any given project, and the *obrero mayor*, the supervisor, the operational architect occupied a superior position: he acted as a kind of artistic manager and as the specialist who worked closely with the patron. The degree of respect accorded to this role is indicated in religious texts describing God the Father as the "highest architect."

Juan Bautista de Toledo and Juan de
Herrera
Monastery and palace of San Lorenzo de
El Escorial, 1563–84
Overall view

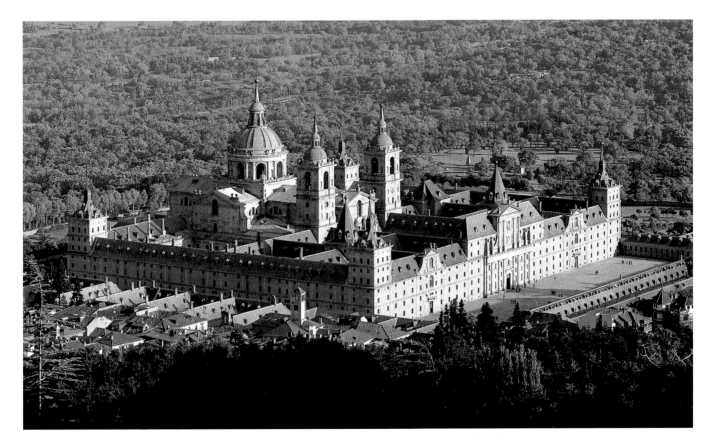

Court architects had an established position and annual salary (comparable with that of a doctor or professor), in addition to generous fees for individual projects. The new professional confidence of architects at this time was rooted in the theoretical precepts of Vitruvius and Alberti and was really the result of a thorough training which complemented the manual skills acquired in apprenticeships to older masters. Usually only members of the aristocracy or clerics could claim this sort of further formal education. The inventories of books held in the libraries of Spanish architects are particularly revealing: Juan de Herrera owned 750 specialist books and Juan Battista de Monego had 610 volumes, among which were the most important Spanish and foreign treatises and practical handbooks.

El Escorial represented a complex prototype that affected the architecture of the Spanish empire at various levels. The close connection between the aristocracy and the court and the spiritual requirements of the Counter-Reformation, combined with the centralizing measures taken by the Spanish crown, made the austere classicism of El Escorial the ultimate model of style. The design and internal organization of court art, reflected in commissions from the aristocracy, had even more impact, in particular the ostentatious efforts at securing personal redemption. Their entire wealth flowed into religious endowments, churches, chapels, cloisters, and monasteries. Civil construction work, which had brought renewed vigour to architecture in Italy and France, seems to have been of little significance in Spain. Apart from ephemera—triumphal arches, catafalques, structures for Holy Week—urban architecture produced only the Plaza Mayor as an indigenous civil structure. Early baroque architecture in Spain was confined almost exclusively to religious structures, in stark contrast to Italy and France. Besides the court, the most important commissions came from cathedral chapters, religious orders, and the numerous religious confraternities.

Herrera's Successors and the Search for a New Language of Form

A rich and important Castilian town even in the middle ages, Valladolid played a key role in the emergence of baroque architecture in the Spanish empire. A devastating fire which destroyed most of its center on September 21, 1561 provided the incentive for a new build-

Juan de Herrera
Model of Valladolíd cathedral, 1585
Reconstruction by Otto Schubert

Ground plan

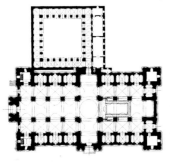

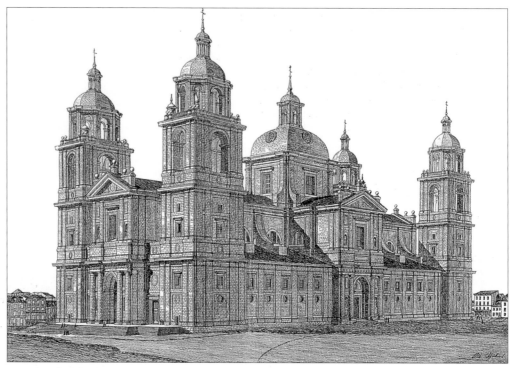

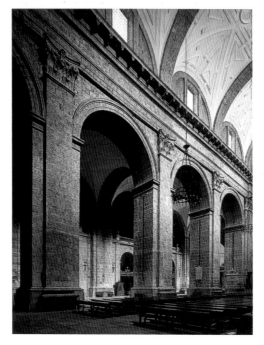

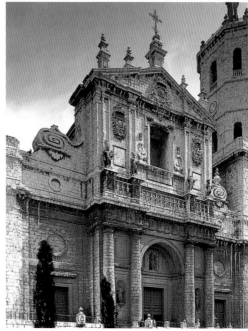

Juan de Herrera
Valladolíd cathedral
Interior, after 1585

FAR RIGHT:
Juan de Herrera
Valladolíd cathedral
Facade, after 1595

Juan de Nates
Medina de Rioseco, Santa Cruz
Facade, begun after 1573

Juan de Nates
Valladolid, Nuestra Señora de las
Angustias facade, 1598–1604

ing scheme. Philip II, born in Valladolid, had promised generous support for the reconstruction of the town, but insisted on his own close involvement in the planning. Concerned as he was for a radical renewal of Spanish court architecture and a link with classicism, he envisaged a clearly structured, systematically built town. Suitable examples were represented in the Italian treatises based on the writings of Vitruvius. Madrid had recently been elevated to the permanent seat of government, and it was therefore in Valladolid that open space suitable for experiments in urban planning was available. The concept of the town as a unit consisting of individual elements, and of the integration of various sections into one coherent whole characterized this project which was unique in Spain. The centerpiece of the whole complex was the rectangular, portico-lined Plaza Mayor with its town hall, which later became the model for many similar squares.

The reconstruction of Valladolid cathedral (see left) also established an important prototype for similar structures. Juan de Herrera, the court architect, received the commission in 1580. Over the late gothic foundations of a complex begun under Charles V, Herrera erected a structure which was significant not only because of its classicism, but also because of the way in which the internal space was organized. In accordance with the insistence of the Council of Trent that the celebration of the eucharist should be "close to the people," he transposed the choir—an area enclosed by massive screens blocking the congregation's view of the high altar—to the eastern end of the church so that a large pulpit area became available between the portal and the crossing. The domed crossing, to the east of which stood the fully exposed altar, became the center of a structure of consistent proportions in both length and breadth. Coherent proportions were also featured in the ground plan, which was now based on a rectangular scheme with four corner towers. Although Herrera respected the original design of Rodrigo Gil de Hontañón, he nevertheless altered the organic medieval approach to the structure in favor of separate areas reflecting the liturgy. It was mainly in the colonies that this pattern was to become compulsory. The impact of Herrera's architecture was even more far-reaching: his style, based on antique forms, gave the decisive signal for the final rejection of late gothic forms and the adoption of a new classical idiom. The vertical elevation of the interior was thus dominated by mighty granite piers with Corinthian pilasters which supported the massive architrave of the central nave. Thermae and barrel vaults emphasized the ceremonial solemnity of the interior. The exterior of the cathedral also reflected these classicizing tendencies. Between the massive corner towers (only a single altered one remains) rose the two-storey gateway pavilion, a triumphal arch with Doric orders on the lower section, and a temple front with triangular pediment above. Although (or perhaps because) the construction of Valladolid cathedral continued until late in the seventeenth century, the style, derived from El Escorial, became the standard for many other religious buildings throughout the Spanish empire.

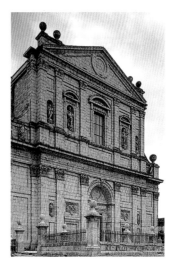
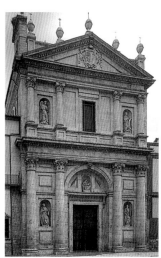

Other significant buildings were constructed in Medina de Rioseco near Valladolid, and in Villagarcía de Campos (in the province of Valladolid). The Jesuit church of San Luís in Villagarcía became, in its classical simplicity (single nave with side chapels, barrel vaults, two-storey facade with intermediary volutes but otherwise without decorative embellishment), the model for innumerable Jesuit churches in Spain; it was designed in 1575 by Pedro de Tolosa, a close collaborator of Herrera. Another model was described by Juan de Nates (details unknown), who first saw a Roman scheme in the facade of the church of Santa Cruz in Medina de Rioseco (see above), the unrealized design by Giacomo Barozzi Vignola for the mother church of the Jesuit order, which he had probably seen in an engraving. Herrera relaxed his customarily austere approach to architectural composition here. The individual architectural elements were treated as subsidiary to a central motif—with the emphasis on the central axis. The complexity of mannerist architecture was superseded by greater elegance and lightness of handling. The church of Nuestra Señora de las Angustias (1598–1604) in Valladolid was also designed by Juan de Nates (see above right). Although the facade was clearly borrowed from Herrera's design for the cathedral, the new baroque principles of style are also apparent here: classical balance has been relinquished in favor of stronger definition and the introduction of a clear hierarchy among the individual elements. Thus, the lower storey is exceptionally high and the massive pilasters dominate the facade.

After Valladolid, which, at the instigation of the Duke of Lerma had again been elevated to the role of court capital by Philip III, the new principles of architectural form and structure established there were adopted in most towns in central Spain. While only a few years earlier it would have been possible to build a cathedral in the late

Sebastián de la Plaza
Alcalá de Henares, church of the mona-
stery of the Bernardine order, begun
1617
Ground plan (right)
Interior (below)

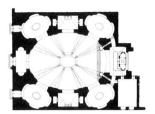

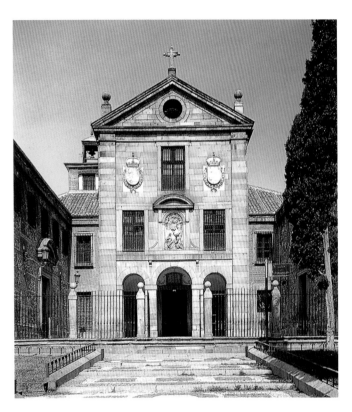

were richly decorated. Significantly, the first monumental structure created for the Habsburgs after the annexation of Portugal also bore the hallmark of the El Escorial school. San Vicente de Fora in Lisbon had an imposing structure with a dominant double-tower facade which made it one of the most impressive buildings of its day in the Iberian peninsula; it was built between 1582 and 1629 by Filippo Terzi or Baltasar Álvares but, in either case, in the manner of Herrera.

An initial indication of a somewhat freer approach to the forms prescribed by El Escorial can be seen in two church facades by Francisco de Moras (died 1610): San José in Ávila (1608) and the Convento de San Blas in Lerma (1604). The proportions were altered to emphasize the height, the lower storey with wide, round-arched portals opened out into a sort of narthex. The wall above was ornamented. Between the classical structural elements cartouches, aediculae, and window openings alternating with wall surfaces appear. The front of the church of St. Teresa of Ávila (Fray Alonso de San José, begun 1515) aroused vehement opposition with what seemed to be overwhelmingly plastic decoration. The most harmonious building of this group of churches is perhaps the Encarnación in Madrid (see left) endowed by Margaret of Austria and Philip III and built from 1611 by Fray Alberto de la Madre de Dios (active during the first thirty years of the seventeenth century). The overbearing heaviness of many of the buildings by the Herrera school was superseded by a greater elegance in architecture which was partly achieved by the upwards extension of facades. A key feature in these later buildings was the use of pilasters which traversed every storey, framing the facade on each side.

gothic style, all buildings were now designed "in the Roman style," *a lo romano*, although frequently more closely based on Juan de Herrera and the El Escorial school than actual classical or Italianate prototypes. Among the outstanding examples of these classical works are the Medina del Campo hospital (Juan de Tolosa, completed 1597), the San Fruto portal in Segovia cathedral (Pedro de Brizuela, 1607), the facade of the Santiago de Uclés monastery (Francisco de Mora?), the chapel of the Afuera hospital in Toledo (Nicolás de Vergara the Younger, begun 1582), and the Capilla Cerralbo in Ciudad Rodrigo (begun 1585). Galicia, in the far northwest of the Iberian peninsula, also boasted a whole series of excellent buildings by the Herrera school of architects, the best of which was the Jesuit college of Monforte de Lemos, built from plans by Andrés Ruiz, Juan de Tolosa, Simón del Monasterio, and others between 1592 and 1619. In Andalusia, a building by Juan de Herrera also set the tone for seventeenth-century architecture: the "Lonja," the stock exchange for the expanding harbor town of Seville provided the ground plan for the so-called *iglesias de cajón* [box churches]. An example of this is the Iglesia del Sagrario (begun 1617, Miguel de Zumárraga); in spite of its modest form its walls

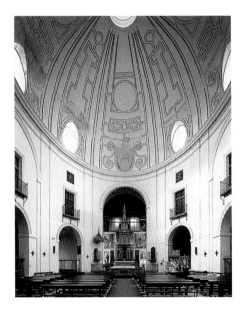

Francisco de Mora and Juan Gómez de
Mora
Lerma, palace of Prince Francisco San-
doval y Rojas, 1601–17

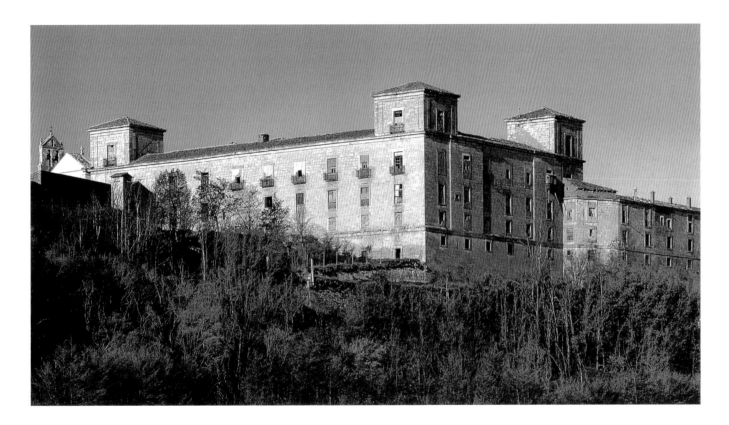

It becomes clear from these examples that architectural innovation was restricted for the most part to religious building and that civil structures played no significant role at the beginning of the baroque era. One of the few exceptions to this was the residence and town at Lerma planned for Francisco Sandoval y Rojas, Philip III's favorite, built by Francisco de Mora and Juan Gómez de Mora between 1601 and 1617. The ambitious prince had his palace built in the form of a four-wing structure with corner towers (see above), modeled, on a reduced scale, on the royal Alcázar in Madrid. This became the prototype for palace architecture in seventeenth-century Spain. Its facades were minimally decorated, only in the arched lintel over the entrance portal. The building was also important for landscape and urban planning: the palace was on high ground with an unhindered view across the fertile plain of the Río Arlanza. The main facade faced the feudal assembly ground, the Plaza de Armas, the former Plaza Mayor of the town, which now had the status of a ducal residence. In tribute to the ostentatious piety of the Duke of Lerma, the palace and medieval town were surrounded by a ring of monasteries which were connected to it and each other by means of covered pergolas. The garden complexes with hermitages were the

inspiration for the later construction of the Buen Retiro in Madrid. In Alcalá de Henares, the church of the Bernardine convent was built as an endowment of Cardinal Archbishop Bernardo Sandoval y Rojas (Sebastián de la Plaza, begun 1617), a building which departed completely from the strict classicism of the Herrera school (see left below). The oval structure with dome (the only surviving one of the period) must have been based on Roman archetypes reported in Spain in the treatises of the day (Serlio's book V) or illustrated in engravings of Roman buildings of oval form (S. Andrea, S. Anna dei Palafrenieri).

Juan Gómez de Mora and the Emergence of Madrid as a Capital
From 1610 there is a discernable trend in the buildings of Francisco de Mora and the church of the Encarnación which may be interpreted as a search for baroque freedom or a relaxation of the formal classical canon. It was apparent particularly in the surfaces of the buildings rather than the ground plans or the structure of the interiors and this was to become a characteristic feature of Spanish baroque architecture. The decisive element in the adoption of the new style resulted from the appointment of Juan Gómez de Mora

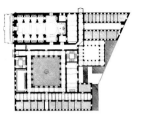

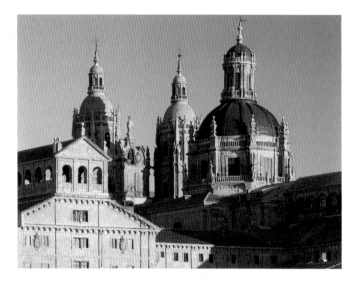

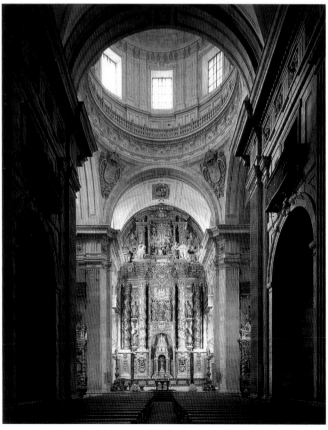

(1586–1648), Francisco's nephew, as "trazador del Rey y arquitecto de la Villa de Madrid," a position which he occupied from 1611. His impact was to be felt on the architecture of the Iberian peninsula for over four decades.

The first major structure built under the direction of Juan Gómez de Mora was the Clerecía Jesuit college in Salamanca endowed by Philip III and Joanna of Austria (see left and right). This building, which dominated the town, an immediate and intimidating neighbor to the cathedral, university, and Dominican monastery, was built in defiance of popular disapproval. This is again typically Spanish: the domination of religious architecture under royal patronage hampered the development of more expansive urban architectural schemes. Begun in 1617 with plans drawn up by Gómez de Mora, the complex of church, college, and monastery was not completed until the middle of the eighteenth century. Today it is laid out roughly in a U-shape with different sections: to the northeast sits the church with the sacristy and monastery on a diagonal, and to the south of this are the college lecture rooms. In between lies the great college courtyard, cut off from the street to the south by the great hall, and to the rear by the chapter hall. The enclosed cloister lies in the space between the college and the monastery. The interior of the church is defined by the ceremonial Tuscan order. The design is similar to that of the Gesù, a four-bay pilaster church with interconnecting chapels, a broad though not sweeping transept, a massive dome over the crossing, and (here) a straight choir termination. There is, however, no evidence of a direct Roman influence on Spanish building of this kind; there were enough existing models in Spain such as the older Jesuit church at Monforte de Lemos (Galicia, begun 1598), Alcalá de Henares (begun 1602), and the more or less contemporary structure of San Ildefonso in Toledo (begun in 1619, now San Juan Bautista), as well as the Colegio Imperial in Madrid (begun 1622, later San Isidro). While the facades of the college reflect the early baroque style of Herrera, the church front is freely embellished with plastic decorative elements. In fact, even here—because of the long construction time—changes to the plans and alterations are apparent, although the two lower storeys with their three axes and the rhythmic traversal of the six powerful three-quarter columns form a setting for the heightened plastic detail decorating the wall surfaces.

The main task of Juan Gómez de Mora was to develop Madrid as the residence of the Spanish Habsburgs. Although it was established as the permanent residence of the king in 1561, it lacked any of the amenities of a capital until well into the seventeenth century: this place with no heritage did not even have its own local legislation. Of course, Philip II had converted the medieval Alcázar to suit the ceremonial needs of Burgundian court ritual, and had built the royal residence and monastery around San Jerónimo el Real in the Buen Retiro district, but his real interest lay in El Escorial. It was only in 1606, when Philip III finally decided that the court should return to

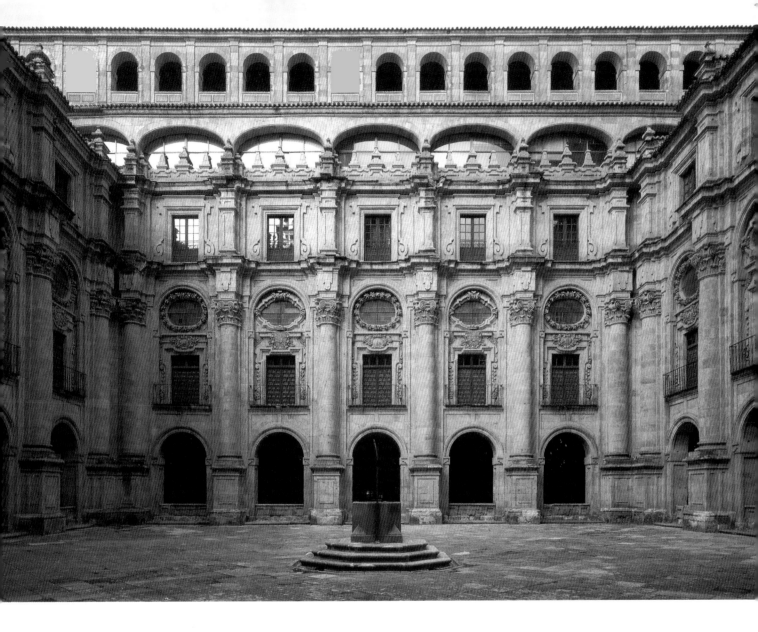

Madrid after a five-year interlude in Valladolid, that a period of intense building activity began which created a suitably impressive setting for the palace.

Juan Gómez de Mora was the major architect for these schemes: in the year he planned the Clerecía he also delivered the first drafts for the Plaza Mayor, the assembly area in the town center which was to serve court and city (see p. 88). In structure, this rectangular complex, surrounded by multi-storey buildings of uniform height and arcades and for the most part closed off from traffic, suggests French (for example the Place des Vosges) or Dutch models (the Grande Place in Brussels). In Madrid, in addition to the official royal offices which served as public administration buildings, it contained the Casa de la Panadería, the city bakery, and therefore served both a community and a commercial function. Gómez de Mora's Plaza Mayor was completed in 1619, after only three years. Subsequently, it became the setting for a wide variety of events: the canonization of the city patron St. Isidro (1620), the proclamation of the future king,

Philip IV (1621), theatrical performances, bullfights, executions, and the notorious *auto-da-fés*, including those of the Inquisition. The history of the construction of the Plaza Mayor is as varied as the events that took place there: it was destroyed several times by fire and rebuilt for the last time towards the end of the eighteenth century, when it acquired its present neo-classical guise.

Between 1619 and 1627, Gómez received the commission to convert the old Alcázar, which through successive building work had developed into a highly complex structure that looked rather like a contemporary residence. Since the building was destroyed by one of the many fires (its reconstruction took place in 1734 under Filippo Juvarra and Giovanni Battista Sacchetti), evidence of its original appearance can only be obtained from historical views, plans, and a surviving wooden model which was probably used as the presentation piece for the planned reconstruction. This indicates that Gómez de Mora had created a new external coherence by using a continuous three-storey facade, emphasizing the corners with towers and

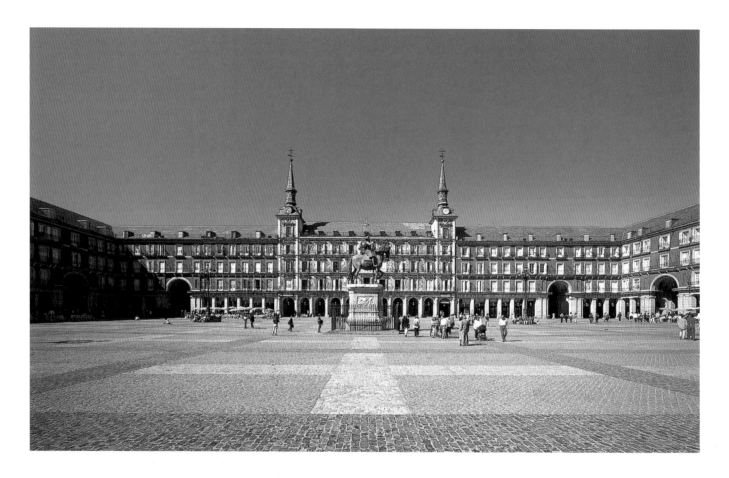

the center with gateway pavilions. The wall surfaces were mainly broken up by horizontal series of windows with triangular pediments; pilasters were used only in the two upper storeys to accentuate the vertical lines. Thus, unlike residences in other countries, the defensive character of the Spanish Alcázar was preserved. The interior housed Philip IV's extraordinary collection of paintings.

The Cárcel de Corte was another building based on a four-wing design; this was the court prison which is now the Ministry of Foreign Relations (see right). In 1629, Gómez de Mora received the commission for the prison and delivered the plans which showed two internal courtyards—a concept derived from the college building. However, the classical structure of three axes in the gateway pavilion surmounted by a pediment seems to follow the traditional scheme. One of his last works in Madrid was the Ayuntamiento, the town hall, begun in 1640, which was similar to the Cárcel de Corte but with an essentially richer and more plastic facade structure. (The portals were added by Teodoro Ardemans during the eighteenth

century.) One of the most ambitious projects, directed by the Spanish king, his wife Isabelle de Bourbon, and Count Duke de Olivares, was never carried out: the construction in Madrid of a cathedral to rival St. Peter's. A drawing by Gómez de Mora in the Biblioteca Nacional testifies that he had begun to work on the designs for a Roman church, with special reference to Sangallo's project. For economic reasons, construction advanced no further than the foundation walls; the work was not continued until 1883, when Madrid finally became a bishopric.

Of the commissions executed by Juan Gómez de Mora outside Madrid, only the most important will be mentioned here, notably the Pantheon in El Escorial (1617–54), an oval structure which was ultimately completed by Crescenzi. His retable for the church in the Guadeloupe monastery (1614) was of great significance for the architectural structure of altar paintings—a commission of extraordinary importance in Spain. The monumental four-storey retable with seven axes is dominated by Corinthian orders assigned to the

Virgin Mary; this forms the framework for statues and panel paintings. Of the few buildings commissioned by the aristocracy, the palace of the Duke of Medinaceli, begun in 1623, should be noted.

Gómez de Mora's buildings combined the strict classical canon of the school of Herrera with an elegant, decorative treatment of wall surfaces. The accentuation of individual structures, the palace gateways, the church facade, the plasticity of the relief ornament, and the use of different, contrasting materials (such as stone and brick) indicate how far Spanish architecture had moved away from the style of El Escorial by the second quarter of the seventeenth century. Gómez de Mora's greatest artistic achievement nevertheless had a much broader context: he formulated a majestic but varied court architecture, as well as a vision of a capital city appropriate to the requirements of baroque court ceremony. Unlike El Escorial, a forbidding monument which represented Philip II's ideology as a statesman, Philip IV's palace was a stage on or before which baroque monarchs and people enacted their various social roles. The Alcázar and the prison, Plaza Mayor, and religious buildings each repre-

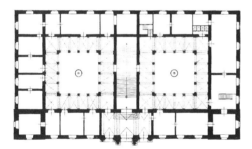

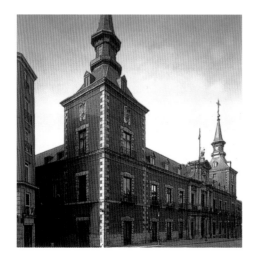

sented a fundamental element of the ideal Vitruvian city, but they now functioned under the control of the absolute monarch. Madrid, "villa y corte," provided the architectural framework for the glorification of the king, and for secular as well as for spiritual life, in which the executions of the Inquisition formed at least a part. As the inventor of such a complex program of urban development, the architect assumed a political and ideological responsibility far beyond the practical requirements of the task, to which he could respond only on the basis of a serious humanist understanding.

One commission which was not given to Gómez de Mora was for the development of the Buen Retiro, a site outside the city intended as a summer palace and retreat for the Spanish king. In 1632 the Count Duke Olivares, minister of Philip IV, had the complex, consisting of a monastery, modest palace, and monastery buildings, converted into a palace to satisfy even the most modern Italian-oriented tastes. This included gardens laid out by Italian specialists, as well as hermitages, grottos, waterfalls, and fountains, all of which were required at the baroque *villa suburbana* of the period for leisure and relaxation. The construction of this scheme underlined the considerable contrast in atmosphere between the official formalities of court life and the needs of the aristocracy who were particularly dedicated to the pursuit of less regulated distractions. The decision in 1633 to refurbish the outdated palace complex resulted in a new design by Giovanni Battista Crescenzi (1577–1660), an architect working for the Duke of Lerma; the scheme marked a departure from the strict, ascetic approach to life of Philip II and even of Philip III. The structure built by Crescenzi and Alonso Carbonell contained only a few imposing salons, and was notable for its introduction of long corridor-like series of rooms which represented a new departure for Spanish palace architecture. Today only the Casón del Buen Retiro, the ballroom, and part of the north wing survive. Its architectural simplicity and use of low-cost materials meant that the Buen Retiro was popularly regarded as rather shabby; the interior, however, certainly defied such criticism. By contrast to the traditional approach of the Alcázar, which was designed to be externally impressive, the most significant references to the prevailing tendencies of court life were assembled here: paintings allegorically representing a return to the countryside and bucolic life—intimate pleasures rather than the centuries-old practice of the virtues and duties of the monarchy. Velázquez, Zurbarán, and Poussin were among the creators of this new ideological program. During a visit to Montserrat, Philip IV had found that he enjoyed the country life, or at least the refined version of it accessible to the baroque court. Thus rustic elements were incorporated into festivities and court spectacles which are represented in Spanish literature of the seventeenth century, such as the plays of Lope de Vega and Calderón. Such features were designed not merely to impress, but for personal enjoyment.

Fray Pedro Sánchez and
Fray Francisco Bautista
Madrid, cathedral of San Isidro el Real,
1626–64
Ground plan and section through the
nave (after Schubert)

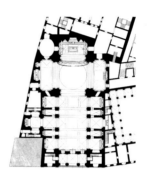
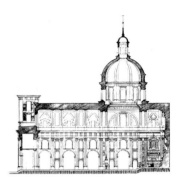

Monastic Master Builders and Architectural Theorists

Ecclesiastical building outside the court was dominated by the religious orders. Fray Lorenzo de San Nicolás (1595–1679), an Augustinian, master builder, and author of the treatise *De arte y uso de arquitectura* [The Art and Use of Architecture] (first published 1633), noted quite accurately that in the seventeenth century a disproportionate number of architects belonged to religious orders. The reason was presumably the fact that many of these individuals had the time and the opportunity for the necessary study of the relevant scientific literature.

While in most European countries the trade of master builder was classified as an engineering trade or as a military skill, in Spain the prevailing image of the architect was of a member of a religious order "spiritually" trained at his mother house. There are a number of reasons for this. The intensive building programs of the orders, mainly the Jesuits and the Carmelites, in the seventeenth century involved a concept of appropriate construction which, while not standardized in any way, certainly reflected the specific spiritual requirements of their congregations. They therefore called on experts from among their own ranks. These architects and builders passed on their knowledge within the order. They were regarded as so highly qualified—not least because of the comprehensive training received by the master builders—that they were frequently given commissions outside the monastery walls. A further reason for the disproportionate number of architects in religious orders lay in the extraordinarily important role played by the orders, and especially the Franciscans and Dominicans, in the colonization of the New World. Church building was an important export and the most impressive manifestation of both Spanish and Portuguese civilization. It served both to legitimize and to provide visible proof of the occupation of "heathen" lands. The religious architect was thus, after the conqueror, the most important tool in the missionary enterprise.

In the mother country, the major architects first emerged from among the ranks of the Jesuits. As Alfonso Rodríguez G. de Ceballos has demonstrated in numerous studies, their work served to spread classical architecture after Herrera. This period also saw the development of the characteristic structure of the Jesuit evangelical church with its single nave hall structure with side chapels and galleries, transept, and crossing dome, a scheme based on the Clerecía in Salamanca described earlier. The trend towards the simplification of the space followed the proclamation of St. Charles Borromeo who, during the Counter-Reformation, had stressed that the high point of the mass lay in the sermon and the open display of the sacrament. This reform, intended to increase the involvement of the laity, required different spatial structures from those that had been required earlier for services where it was mainly the clergy who needed to have sight of the eucharist. Taking the Gesù as its model, the new type of church was introduced into Spain with the Colegiata

in Villagarcía de Campos, and then into Latin America. The construction of a Jesuit church or college was subject to strict controls from the mother house: all plans had to be approved by Rome and the observance of certain regulations and inclusion of specific elements were supervised by *provedores*, who traveled around the provincial orders at regular intervals. Among the best known and most influential of these officials was Giuseppe Valeriani, who crossed half of Europe to make sure that the rules were being followed. However, it seems that ultimately flexible adaptation to local tradition was expected, rather than slavish adherence to every regulation laid down by the mother house.

Among the major architects of the Jesuit order were Andrés Ruiz (details unknown) and Juan de Tolosa (1548–1600), who constructed the College of Monforte de Lemos in Galicia strictly in the style of Herrera. The building became a model for numerous other classical buildings in northwestern Spain. Pedro Sánchez (1569–1633), who was initially active in Andalusia and later in Madrid, experimented with oval structures like those of the churches of San Hermengildo in Seville and San Antonio de los Portugueses; he also designed the church of the Jesuits in Madrid and the Colegio Imperial, now the cathedral of San Isidro (see above). This sober structure, completed by yet another Jesuit, Fray Francisco Bautista, in 1664, incorporated in its internal alternation of wide and narrow bays elements from a fifteenth-century building, Alberti's seminal church of S. Andrea in Mantua. The giant orders of the facade were intended as a conscious reference to St. Peter's in Rome. While not particularly innovative in style, however, one technical detail of the construction was quite new: this was the structure of the dome, recorded as a *cupola encamonada* in the history of architecture, first described in the treatise of Fray Lorenzo de San Nicolás, and soon widely copied because of its practicality. It was structured around an internal wooden frame with an external brick lining which gave the impression of a massive dome. The advantage of this construction lay in the fact it allowed an effective way to build domes for large interiors. Besides the Jesuits, the Carmelites

90

also trained a series of important architects. Among them was Fray Alberto de la Madre de Dios, who like Francisco de Mora worked for the Duke of Lerma and as official *traçista* was responsible for all new foundations by the order. The facade of the Encarnación in Madrid has reently been attributed to him. This structure is, as already mentioned, regarded as representing the transition between mannerism and baroque. The same applies to the church of St. Teresa of Ávila designed by another Carmelite, Alonso de San José.

Most of the important architectural theorists in Spain were also in religious orders: El Greco, whose notes on Vitruvius were not found until the 1970s, was the exception here. The writings and discussion of the reconstruction of the Temple in Jerusalem of the Jesuits Jerónimo del Prado and Juan Bautista Villalpando were in fact more interpretative than pragmatic in nature. The treatise *De arte y uso de arquitectura* by Fray Lorenzo de San Nicolás (1595–1679) is quite different and is specifically addressed to young students in the profession. Here, the Augustinian author provided a highly didactic overview of the major theoretical writings from antiquity to his own day, combining it with practical recommendations for all stages of an architect's training. The Benedictine monk Fray Juan Ricci (1600–81) wrote a large number of papers on the theory of art, among which *Pintura sabia* (not published until 1930) and *Breve tratado de arquitectura acerca del orden salomónico* were the most important. In these works, he developed a theory of the orders of architecture by which—in agreement with Serlio— a specific variation was assigned to each saint. The classical orders—Doric, Tuscan, Ionic, Corinthian, and Composite— were complemented by the "Salomonic" order associated with the twisted columns supposed to have been used in Solomon's temple. Ricci developed these into a complete order including base and capital in a manner which went well beyond Bernini's baldacchino in St. Peter's (see p. 282). As will be seen, the "discovery" of the Salomonic order aroused a great deal of interest, especially in Andalusia.

In Vigevano in 1668, the Cistercian monk Fray Juan Caramuel de Lobkowitz (1606–82) published his *Architectura civil recta y obliqua*, a treatise which also took the description of the Temple of Jerusalem as a starting point. However, unlike earlier authors, he derived from it a criticism of Vitruvius and the classical interpretations of his work. For Caramuel, architecture was not a set of prescribed, established doctrines, but an open discipline subject to change through time. On this basis, his arguments were very similar to those at the same time prevailing between the *anciens et modernes* in the French Academy. Significantly, he developed completely new orders, supposedly at the request of his patron. Among them were the anthropomorphic "Atlantic" and "Paranymph" and even the "gothic," regarded with contempt as obsolete since the end of the middle ages, but essential to a re-evaluation of the aesthetic pre-eminence of classiciam. Even more original than his free interpretation of historical tradition was Caramel's teaching of *arquitectura oblícua*, a complicated theory of perspective which, he asserted, was evident in Bernini's colonnade in St. Peter's Square. Thus he suggested an optical correction of each component of a building, depending on the line of sight. While Caramuel's writings were long considered as purely theoretical, new research indicates that some of his proposals were actually realized.

From the Late Seventeenth Century to the Beginning of the Enlightenment—Social and Regional Differences

While the seventeenth century was a period of crisis and decline of power for the Spanish empire, surprisingly this seems to have had little impact on the patronage of either Philip III or Philip IV. The development of Madrid as a capital, the employment of outstanding artists, and the collections assembled at court give little indication of the advancing economic decline which the country was experiencing. It is true that initially construction work for the court was affected and, at least after the middle of the century, was somewhat slowed. Religious institutions, frequently dependent on endowments from the aristocracy, were sometimes barely in a position to continue with building projects which had already been set in motion, let alone take on new ones. Madrid cathedral, planned by Juan Gómez de Mora and intended by the king to rival St. Peter's, but then barely constructed above the foundation level, was further symptomatic of the declining position of a once prosperous world power. Nevertheless—or perhaps because of this—after the middle of the century, a few centers which had remained in the shadow of the crown for a fairly long period now saw the building of major structures which signaled the replacement of the remaining traces of Herrera's style and a completely new beginning for baroque architecture in Spain.

Galicia

Galicia was among these centers. This region in the northwest of the Iberian peninsula had, by the second quarter of the seventeenth century, already developed specific socio-economic conditions which spared it from the general economic decline. This happy state of affairs was mainly due to the existence of a well-to-do clergy whose estates guaranteed a fair income and made possible the construction of a large number of monasteries and churches. This area had traditionally produced exceptional stonemasons who worked the local hard gray granite with considerable skill. In addition to the monastery of Monforte de Lemos, this material was characteristic of San Martín Pinario in Santiago de Compostela (begun 1596, continued from 1526 by Fernando Lechuga), the monastery church of Monfero (1620–24, Simón del Monasterio), and the strictly classical treatment of Orense cathedral (Simón del Monasterio, 1620–24). The structure of the facades reflects the defining features of Galician architecture particularly clearly: monumental proportions and rigidly classical forms contrast with the rustication of the surface, which appears to be roughened with small pieces of ashlar and rhomboid stonework. The facade of the Benedictine church of Sobrado de los Monjes, with its juxtaposition of classical and completely unconventional elements (Pedro de Montagudo, 1666), is representative of the special creativity emerging in Galician architecture at this time. The nave structure behind it has very different proportions: narrow side aisles flank the broad, barrel-vaulted central nave, possibly suggesting a reference to the original medieval structure.

A particularly productive phase began in 1649, when Canon José de Vega y Verdugo, count of Alba Real, was called to the cathedral of Santiago de la Compostela. His humanist education, which he had enhanced by much foreign travel, strengthened his intention to provide the very traditional church of St. James with a new and more dignified appearance. According to an extremely useful inventory of sources in the *Memoria sobre las obras en la catedral de Santiago* (1657–66), he initiated an ambitious building program which, however, was only completed in stages. The most spectacular measure was the construction of a tabernacle baldacchino over the altar of St. James: this vast structure combining architectural, sculptural, and decorative features was intended to compete with Bernini's baldacchino in St. Peter's; the only major difference was the fact that the canopy was borne by four angels instead of sinuous columns (the dome that had been originally planned was not executed). In addition, alterations were made to the exterior of the building: between 1658 and 1670 José Peña del Toro (died 1676) rebuilt the Quintana Portal (Pórtico Real de la Quintana), the dome over the crossing, and the bell tower, commissioned by Vega y Verdugos. Peña's relatively free approach to the traditional drawings, his feeling for decorative permutations, and the enrichment of classical features testify to a new understanding of form which was beginning to emerge, particularly in Santiago. His successor, Domingo de Andrade (1639–1711), completed Peña's work and built the clock tower himself (completed 1680) over a late gothic core. The downward-facing volutes, represented on each of the towers, accentuate the square upper storey; they seem to have been taken from the mannerist building treatises of Wendel Dietterlin and Vredeman de Vries and suggest that these works had spread as far as the Atlantic coastline by this point. In spite of the impact he had clearly had on the culture of the town, José de Vega y Verdugo had a difficult position in this center of pilgrimage. He left Santiago in 1672; the artistic stimulus which he left behind culminated half a century later in the construction of the cathedral's new facade.

Fernando de Casas y Novoa (about 1680–1749) was entrusted with this task. This architect, who had already created the sumptuous decoration for the cloister in Lugo cathedral, was appointed *maestro de obras* at Santiago cathedral. He first worked on the construction of the still missing north tower, which he matched with the south tower built by Peña de Toro. The construction of a new facade (see right) did not start until 1738. The design required extraordinarily careful planning since it had to accommodate a variety of more or less incompatible requirements: it had to mask and protect the romanesque Pórtico de la Gloria behind and so allow as much light as possible to reach it; it also had to respond to the urban structure of the city of pilgrimage and, in particular, integrate with a baroque flight of steps, the construction of which had already been started. Fernando Casas y Novoa resolved these aesthetic and technical problems in a remarkable way. The romanesque portal was hidden behind the baroque facade with its flanking towers. The facade has three sets of giant two-storey windows which are not apparent as glass surfaces but are concealed by the pronounced projections and recesses of the structures surrounding them and by an almost gothic-looking sweep upwards. A multi-storey pediment crowns the central section, and false gables decorate the lower storeys of the towers and lead the eye to the vertical structures of the surrounding buildings. This *obradorio* facade, so-called because in its filigree lightness it was seen as comparable to goldsmith's work, forms an imposing backdrop which comes into its own only in the context of the urban environment, principally through the interplay of light and shade. On several levels, it could be argued then, that Casas y Novoa created a masterpiece in Santiago, combining classical and apparently medieval structures in a manner that was incomprehensible to the eighteenth century and thus the subject of vehement criticism. He resolved the difficult problem of retaining the dignity of a romanesque building while providing it with a context within the baroque city. The synthesis of old and new idioms seen here anticipates to some extent the architectural eclecticism of later centuries, and the inclusion of such large window apertures was a stroke of technical genius.

Andalusia

Andalusia was a second center that discovered its own architectural language independently of the court. The historical background to these developments were naturally quite different here from that in Galicia. Through the patronage of Charles V, Granada had become the ideal sixteenth-century city: the complex with the Christian palace on the Alhambra, the newly built cathedral, the construction of the university and the Chancellería, the highest court of law, all testify to this. The politics of Philip II, promoting centralization, while driving out the Moriscos and depriving the city of its vital energy, also brought stagnation—even provincialization—to the city. Nevertheless, artistic impetus remained. The creative influence of Alonso Cano (1601–67) was outdone only by Velázquez. Cano, who, like Velázquez, had received his training in Seville with Francisco Pacheco, was the only major all-round artist Spain has produced. His most significant works were undoubtedly the paintings he produced as court artist to Philip IV and drawing master to

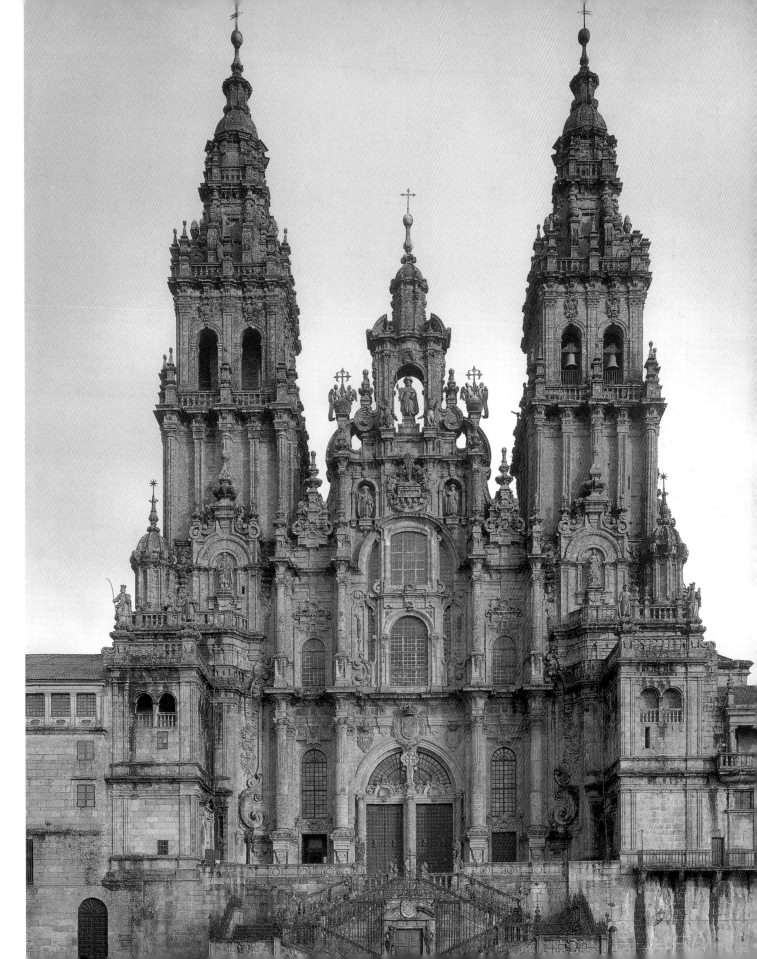

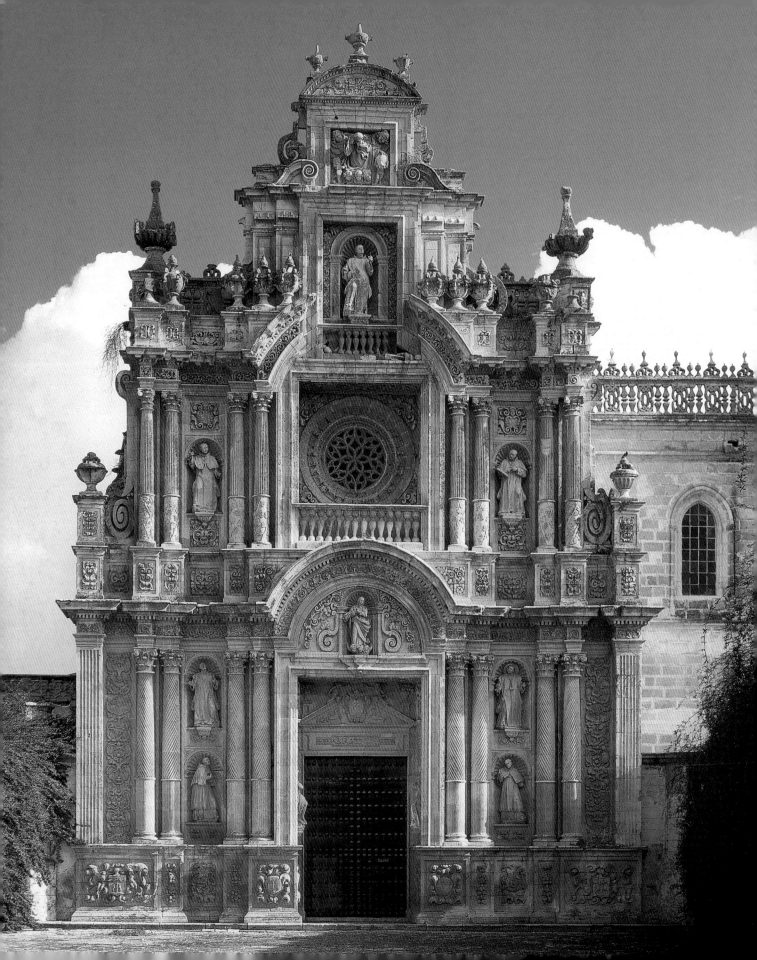

OPPOSITE:
Jerez de la Frontera
Facade of the Carthusian monastery of
Santa María de la Defensión, 1667

Alonso Cano
Granada, cathedral facade
Begun 1667

Prince Baltasar Carlos. However, the plan for the facade of Granada cathedral (see right), which he submitted in 1644, shortly before his death, showed at least as much inventive genius. Although Cano had to respect the nave structure erected by Siloé, he produced a most individual design which went far beyond the other contemporary solutions to this type of problem. Cano selected a framework structure resembling a triumphal arch, behind which he deeply recessed the portals and wall surfaces. Although commonly known since the middle ages throughout Spain and Portugal as the "funnel portal," this structure provided a thoroughly innovative rhythm and dynamism to this facade. The front was dominated by a round arch at the top of the central section, a late reference to Alberti's facade for S. Andrea in Mantua. However, Cano found unconventional solutions even for the detail, as indicated by his use of wall structures instead of capitals and "hanging" relief medallions on the pilasters. Cano's design, which was realized between 1667 and 1684, was imitated throughout Andalusia and the east.

The city of Jaén also made a considerable contribution to baroque architecture in Andalusia. In 1667 work began on the construction of a facade which Eufrasio López de Rojas (died 1684) had designed for the city's cathedral (see right). The massive frontal, with five axes, using giant Corinthian orders and an attic storey, refers to Maderno's St. Peter's. By contrast, the church of the Carthusian monastery of Nuestra Señora de la Defensión, built at the same time near Jerez, looks like a baroque interpretation of a gothic shrine (see left). This is due less to the late gothic nave structure, which somewhat restricted the architectural options here, but to a concept of architecture which saw its objective as a breakdown of structural elements through decoration and the graphic development of the wall.

Seville, the gateway to the New World, had been the richest city of the Spanish empire during the sixteenth century; in 1649 it lost one-third of its population because of an outbreak of the plague and the general decline of the empire. Nevertheless, the Seville baroque, mainly in painting (Zurbarán, Murillo, and Valdés Leal) and sculpture (Martínez, Montañés, and Mena) was one of the major expressions of Spanish art. In architecture, the sixteenth-century concept of space was initially maintained by the continued use of the so-called *iglesias de cajón*, box churches, but at a very early stage plain structures with luxuriant decoration began to take over. An early example of this was El Sagrario, the city's parish church, which was integrated into the cathedral complex between 1617 and 1662 from plans by Miguel de Zumárraga (died c. 1651). Inside the block-shaped structure, the wall and vault surfaces are covered with ornament which pushes the classical forms of the interior into the background. In Santa María la Blanca, a former thirteenth-century synagogue, exuberant stucco decoration, a web of architectural vegetal and figurative set pieces, even decorates the vaulting which was installed in 1659 by the brothers Pedro and Miguel de Borja.

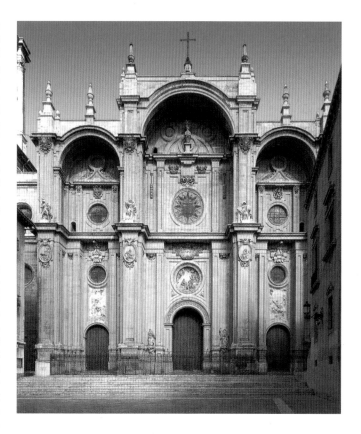

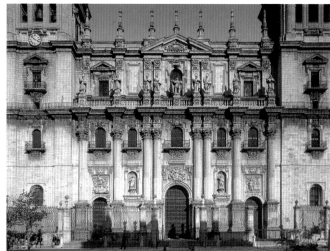

Eufrasio López de Rojas
Jaén Cathedral, facade, 1667–88

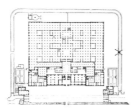

Leonardo de Figueroa
Seville, Colegio di San Telmo
Facade, 1724–34
Ground plan

Sebastian van der Borcht
Seville, tobacco factory, 1728–71

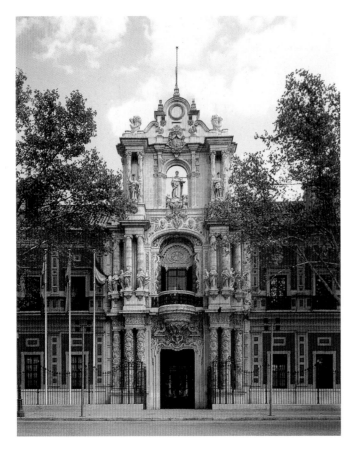

During the final years of the seventeenth century, Leonardo de Figueroa (?1650–1730), an architect from the Cuenca region, introduced some important changes in the architecture of Seville. In the course of his long and extremely fruitful career, he was instrumental in propagating a graphic and decorative approach to all surfaces. Characteristic of his aesthetic ideas, and also of his pragmatic approach, was his use of red brickwork to animate light wall surfaces, creating a color contrast typical of the whole of Andalusia but at the same time reducing building costs enormously in a region poor in suitable stone. While his early work like the Hospital de los Venerables Sacerdotes (1687–97) demonstrates a restraint in his experiments with the "new" (in fact very old) materials and their possibilities, and he worked more traditionally in several buildings which had already been started (San Salvador and San Pablo in Seville, the Colegiata in Jerez de la Frontera), he combined Italian influences with the Andalusian love for ornament in the Jesuit church of San Luis (built between 1699 and 1731), which has been correctly attributed to him. Thus the brick facade contained ele-

ments of Borromini's S. Agnese while the interior ground plan was similarly modeled on Rainaldi's plan for the same building on the Piazza Navona. The defining features of this central structure are the eight giant Salomonic columns, with fluting up to one-third of their height, flanking and adding emphasis and plasticity to the center of the domed building. However, whether this format was a new idea from Figueroa or whether it had been tried out in another context in the Seville area is unknown. At almost the same time it was being used in the upper storey of several bell towers.

Figueroa's late masterpiece was the elegant facade of the Colegio de San Telmo (see left), a foundling hospital established in 1671, where the new generation was trained for the roles of captains of the Atlantic fleet. From 1722 he and his son Matías began work on completing the structure with pronounced corner towers, organizing it around a large internal courtyard. Work went on until 1735 and resulted in one of the most important buildings of the Andalusian baroque. The three-storey central stone pavilion stands out majestically from the restrained brick-built facade. A dramatic effect was achieved by the animated plastic structure with richly ornamented double columns flanking the central axis with its projecting balcony and the aedicula, open to the heavens and containing the figure of St. Telmo. The contrived decorative effect is further heightened through the use of allegorical figures which illustrate nautical science and the importance of Seville, populating the architectural elements of the portal and providing a charming contrast to the impressive architecture. At about the same time, quite close to the Colegio de San Telmo, another major structure was being put up by the military architect Sebastian van der Borcht. This was the tobacco factory which became famous as the setting for the Carmen story. Built between 1728 and 1771, this complex is one of the earliest surviving examples of factory architecture and is based on the type of structure used for hospitals and colleges.

In Granada around 1700, classical forms were overlaid with decoration and completely reinterpreted. The distinctive material here, however, was not brick but stucco, which allows a finer and subtler range of applications and which was most successfully used in the Alhambra. The main person responsible for this innovation—and perhaps the most individual and inventive master builder in Spain—was Francisco de Hurtado Izquierdo (1669–1725), an Andalusian architect, sculptor, and decorator. His decorative forms, deriving from classical elements, but with prismatic angles and multiple ornamental details, influenced Andalusian baroque architecture for decades and have justly been classed as an independent Spanish architectural achievement. In addition, Hurtado, who worked almost exclusively for the clergy, sought to reflect in his work the baroque concept of the total work of art which the faithful considered to be the artistic embodiment of devotion expressed through art.

Hurtado's first important work was the renovation of the Sagrario, the sanctuary of the Carthusian monastery of Granada

Francisco de Hurtado Izquierdo
Granada, Sagrario, Carthusian monastery
1702–20

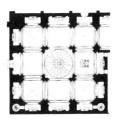

Francisco de Hurtado Izquierdo and
José de Bada
Granada, cathedral sanctuary, 1704–59
Ground plan and interior

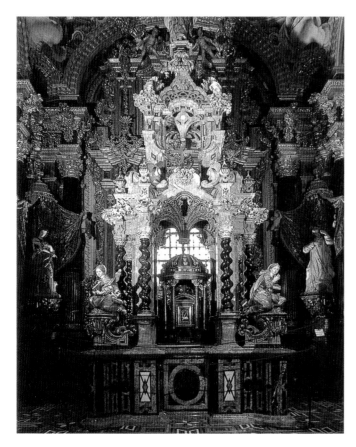

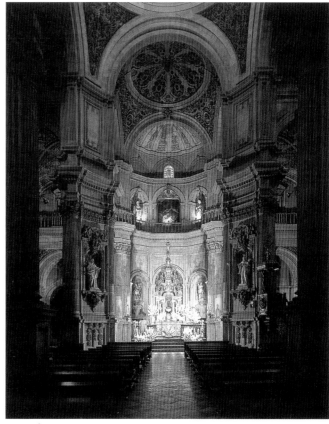

(see above left), which he directed from 1702 on. He designed the tabernacle as an over-sized shrine, the shell of which is a square space with a dome vault. Sculptures decorate the base and black Salomonic columns support the richly ornate baldacchino. From the side chapels, circular windows allow a view of the sacrament. The exaggerated proportions contribute to the effect of the whole, as does the unusual coloring of the marble: gilded capitals and cornice edgings contrast with pink, green, black, white, and gray stone, the tones of which were reflected in Palomino's ceiling frescoes.

In 1706, Hurtado as *maestro mayor*, assumed the responsibility for designing the cathedral Sagrario (see above right); however, this project was to take many years and was only completed by his colleague José de Dada. The classical proportions and orchestration of this central structure represented a notable contrast to his earlier work: the powerful multiple rib piers at the crossing imitate the Composite order used in the cathedral by Diego de Siloé, a design based on the need to set the sanctuary appropriately within the old church. It also documents the versatility of Hurtado's approach to architecture.

In 1718 he designed another Sagrario, modeled on the Granada structure (see p. 98), for the Carthusian monastery of El Paular. Here the sanctuary (realized by Teodosio Sánchez de Rueda), was divided into two areas. The marble and jasper tabernacle was set at the center of the first area, an architectural caprice several storeys high, with four external piers and an internal ring of supports. The space behind this was lit by two circular windows over the upper cornice. The beams of light and the gilding of the retable provide a dramatic contrast with the darker sanctuary. The building, in the mountains behind Segovia, is a rare example of Andalusian art in Castille. In fact, parts of the tabernacle were made in Priego, Andalusia, where Hurtado was employed as a royal tax inspector from 1712.

The most aesthetically remarkable, although least documented, work of the Andalusian baroque was the Sagrario of the Carthusian monastery in Granada (see p. 99). It is known only that the building was planned in 1713 but not begun until 1732. There is no documentation about the architect or architects. As we have mentioned,

**Francisco de Hurtado Izquierdo and
Teodosio Sánchez de Rueda**
El Paular, Sagrario of the Carthusian
monastery Nuestra Señora del Paular,
Begun 1718
Ground plan, interior, and sculpture by
Pedro Duque Cornejo

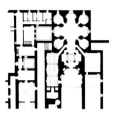

OPPOSITE:
Francisco de Hurtado Izquierdo (?)
Granada, Sagrario of the Carthusi-
an monastery, begun 1732

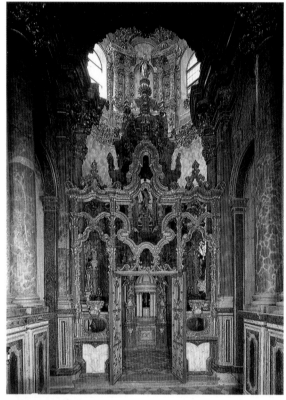

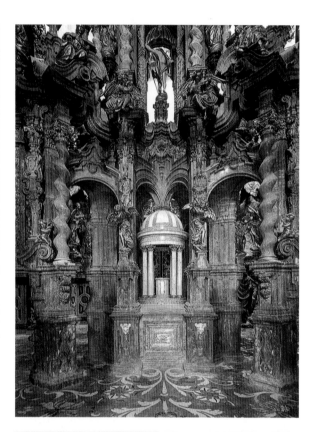

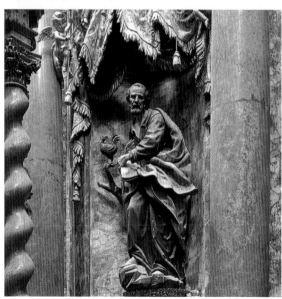

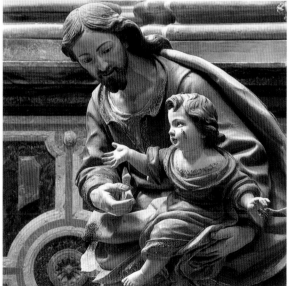

98

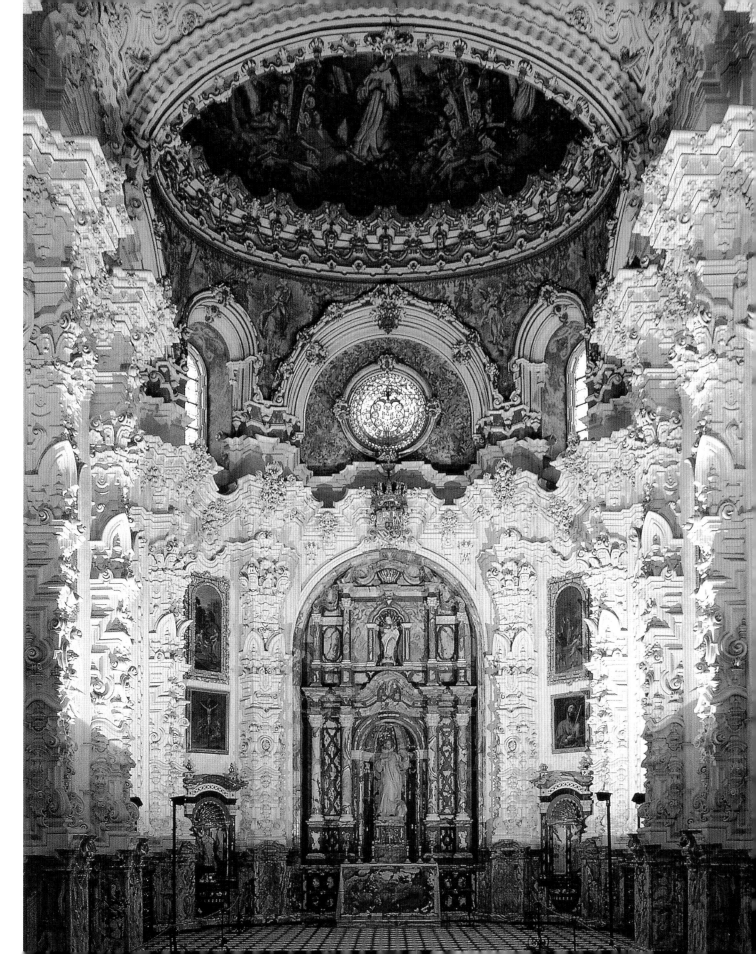

this building was held by later generations to be the ultimate embodiment of the decline of Spanish art; it is only in the past few decades that a more objective evaluation of its design has been made. The compact single nave structure is animated by the exuberant plasticity of the decoration of its structural elements, the pilasters, which remain clearly visible in spite of the luxuriant stucco ornamentation. No fewer than forty-five standard classical motifs—parts of capitals, cornices, volutes, candelabrae, and the so-called "pig's ear" (a segment of a circle superimposed on an angle)—cover the wall surfaces. The corbelled upper cornice follows the wall contours in and out, its course repeated by numerous raised profiles, each one flatter than the last. In spite of the wealth of detail, a uniquely sumptuous space was created, giving the impression of a filigree shrine. Although the realization of this structure was mainly placed in the care of colleagues (Luís de Arévalo, Luís Cabello, and José de Bada), Hurtado's responsibility for the design seems undisputed.

Hurtado, who also enjoyed a certain degree of financial independence due to his position as royal tax inspector, maintained an important school of decorators and craftsmen. They took their art to every corner of Andalusia; traces of their style are even to be found in the colonies, especially in Mexico. As in Andalusia, which incorporated the decorative style of Moorish tradition, Spanish style was combined there with Indian motifs.

The Churriguera Family; Castile, León, and the East

A family of artists from Catalonia gave fresh impetus to the architecture of central Spain: the sculptor José Ratés y Dalmau, from Barcelona, had taken into his workshop the five sons of his late relative Joseph de Xuriguera. After his death in 1684 all of them—José Benito, Manuel, Joaquín, Alberto, and Miguel—emerged as independent architects and retable builders. In 1693, the eldest of the five, José Benito de Churriguera (1665–1725), created the retable in the monastery church of San Esteban in Salamanca (see p. 102), which because of the bold use of Salomonic columns, its spatial arrangements, and its flamboyant decoration established an important prototype. The composition is closely related to theories presented in the treatise by Caramuel de Lobkowitz and also to the writings of Andrea del Pozzo. A fundamentally more severe idiom is apparent in his buildings in Nuevo Baztán, a seat of local government and palace commissioned by the banker Juan de Goyeneche between 1709 and 1713. The church facade flanked by massive towers has an almost ponderous effect, the center being emphasized by Palladian-style pediments set one on top of the other and decreasing in size. Joaquín de Churriguera (1674–1724) also created his most important buildings in Salamanca: the two college buildings, the Hospedería del Colegio de Anaya (begun 1715) and the Colegio de Calatrava (begun 1717), combined classical forms with luxuriant structural decoration originating in the plateresque style, similar to

the dome he designed for the Catedral Nueva. This reference to sixteenth-century style, which was also evident elsewhere, is frequently interpreted as a conscious link with the glories of the Spanish past as well as standing in opposition to the international standardization of architecture under the Bourbons. The youngest of the Churrigueras, Alberto (1676–1750), was overshadowed by his brothers for a long time. It was only after their death that he was free to develop his own style which was already influenced by rococo. His main work was the Plaza Mayor in Salamanca, which he designed in 1728. This rectangular square at the heart of the university town rivaled the older Plaza Mayor complexes in Madrid and Valladolid. It was remarkable for its elegance and the festive and light-hearted decoration of the facades, rising to three storeys over the arcades (see right). Each window had a balcony with iron railings; even today these are the perfect place from which to follow the activity of the square. Two buildings rose above the uniform structures around the Plaza Mayor: the royal pavilion and its great arched gateway, with a medallion of Philip V and the gable over it, and, opposite, the town hall, completed only in 1755 by Andrés García de Quiñones. Alberto de Churriguera received countless other commissions for churches and colleges in Salamanca, but left in 1738 after a dispute about the construction of the tower for the city's new cathedral.

Salamanca acquired a worthy successor to Alberto in Andrés García de Quiñones (active in the mid-eighteenth century). In the years between 1750 and 1755 he completed not only the Plaza Mayor but also the Clerecía; the long-drawn-out construction of this building had been stagnating. The towers and college courtyard (see p. 87) express a quite different and more powerful idiom from that of the Plaza Mayor. Powerful giant half-columns on high pedestals, and a deeply overhanging entablature with its own corbelling lend a dynamic to the facade, which is deeply recessed behind this system of projections. The monumentality of Roman architecture is combined with Iberian surface decoration. The Clerecía courtyard is therefore completely independent of the French and Italian court architecture of the Bourbon regime. Its closest reference point is rather the ceremonial courtyard in the college of San Martín Pinario in Santiago de Compostela.

Narciso de Tomé (working 1715–42) and his brother Diego came from a family of sculptors and ornamental carvers like the Churrigueras; they were the originators of the most spectacular structure of the Spanish baroque, an unimaginably successful total work of art, the *transparente* in Toledo cathedral (see pp. 103 and 369). This structure, built between 1721 and 1732, is a type of *camarín*, that is, a separate, mostly raised but open, space used as a repository. In Toledo this became an architecturally plastic construction behind the high altar, with a sanctuary which was also visible to the faithful from the choir ambulatory, very much in keeping with the edicts of the Council of Trent, which had demanded that the

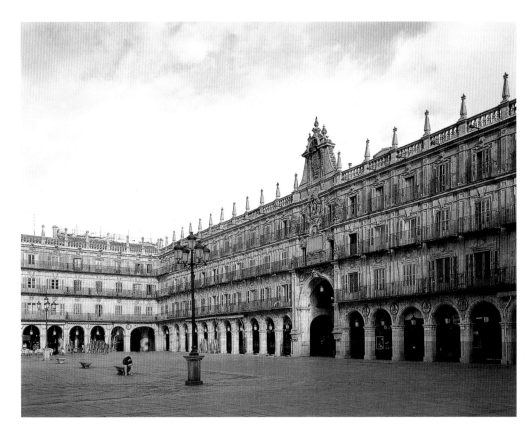

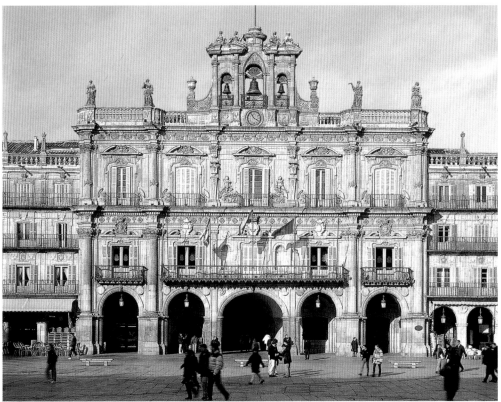

ILLUSTRATION P. 102:
José Benito de Churriguera
Salamanca, San Esteban, altar retable
1692–94

ILLUSTRATION P. 103:
Narciso de Tomé
Toledo cathedral
"El transparente," 1721–32

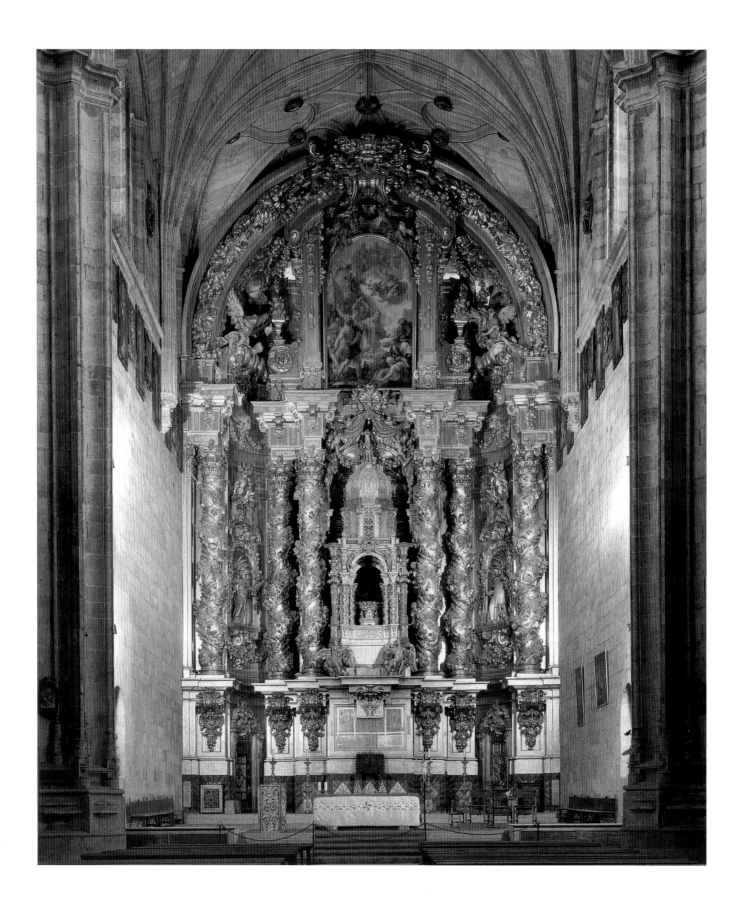

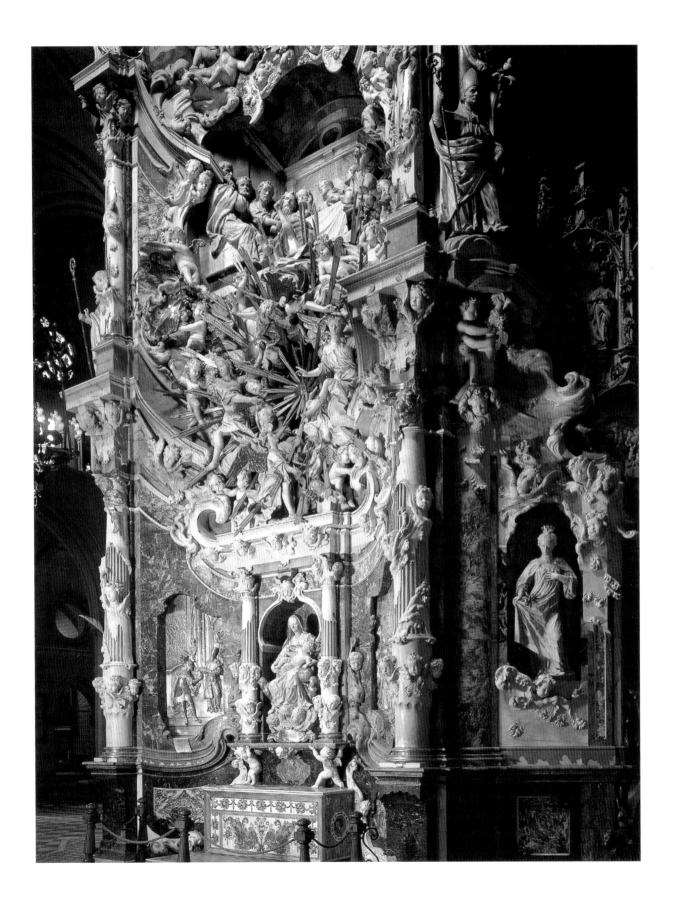

Hipólito Rovira
Valencia, palace of the Marquis of Dos
Aguas, portal, 1740-44

OPPOSITE:
Jaime Bort
Murcia cathedral, 1742-54

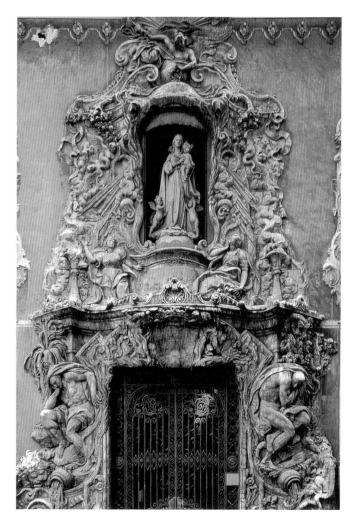

and regarded quite simply as a madman by critics in subsequent centuries. As the *maestro mayor* for Madrid, he occupied an influential position and designed a large number of utilitarian buildings and churches with clear and elegant lines. It was only in the private palaces he built in Madrid and in the Hospicio de San Fernando (1722–29) that he displayed an unparalleled decorative creativity which, however, was confined solely to the main portals and the windows above these. As with a retable, these were enclosed in a framework rising several storeys and with the most exuberant and luxuriant decor—*estípetes*, rocailles, oculi, and so on. The deeply recessed niches contain figures. In Spain, a private palace with a similar facade structure is now found only in Valencia, where the Marquis of Dos Aguas had a city palace built from plans by the painter Hipólito Rovira between 1740 and 1744. Here the theatricality of the setting is pushed to extremes in the allegorical figures (the Valencian rivers, Turia and Júcar) flanking the portal in imitation of Michelangelo (see left). In addition to this structure, Valencia has another monument which represents the quite individual interpretation of the baroque in Spain; this is the alternating convex and concave facade of the cathedral, the work of Conrad Rudolf, a German sculptor trained in Rome. The west front, begun in 1703, shows the influence of Guarino Guarini or of Roman architecture of the late seventeenth century. Traces of this facade structure, unusual throughout the entire Iberian empire, can be seen in the cathedrals of Murcia (see right; Jaime Bort, 1742–54), Guadix, and Cádiz. Their three-dimensional, "broken" facades produce a filigree effect in spite of the monumental proportions, but are far more static than the contemporary structures of Balthasar Neumann or Dietzenhofer. The plasticity of the wall is combined here with the continuing use of the "carpet" surface treatment, a style of ornament which had been prevalent in Spain for centuries.

These regional differences introduced in the development of an individual late baroque architecture must be regarded as one of the essential Spanish contributions to European architecture. Branded since the Enlightenment with the term *Churriguerismo*, a synonym for bad taste, some of these structures have been the subject of more benign re-evaluation in recent years. The extent to which the ornamental style was rooted in Spanish tradition and the influence of the concept of the total work of art on the exuberant decoration and luxuriantly plastic architectural structures was more closely examined. Churriguera, Hurtado, and Ribera are no longer considered uneducated fools, but independent interpreters of the contemporary discourse on the role of the arts. They developed a national idiom which, consciously or otherwise, set itself apart from the style of the Bourbon court.

Bourbon Court Architecture

From 1720 onwards, the varied architecture of the Spanish regions declined somewhat in comparison to the court art of the Bourbons,

laity be included in religious services. A concave, two-storey retable holds a sculptural group of the Virgin and Child in the center of the lower section; above it are scenes of the Last Supper and the eucharist. An opening in the vault allows a ray of light in, suggesting a view into the open heavens, represented as hosts of angels and saints flooded in heavenly light before a background of architectural set pieces. Architecture, sculpture, and painting were so perfectly combined here that contemporaries regarded it as the "eighth wonder of the world." Nonetheless, Ponz, a traveler and art connoisseur in the eighteenth century, saw it as the epitome of the decadence of Spanish art.

Another Madrid architect was Pedro de Ribera (c. 1683–1742), valued by his contemporaries for his astonishing creative powers—

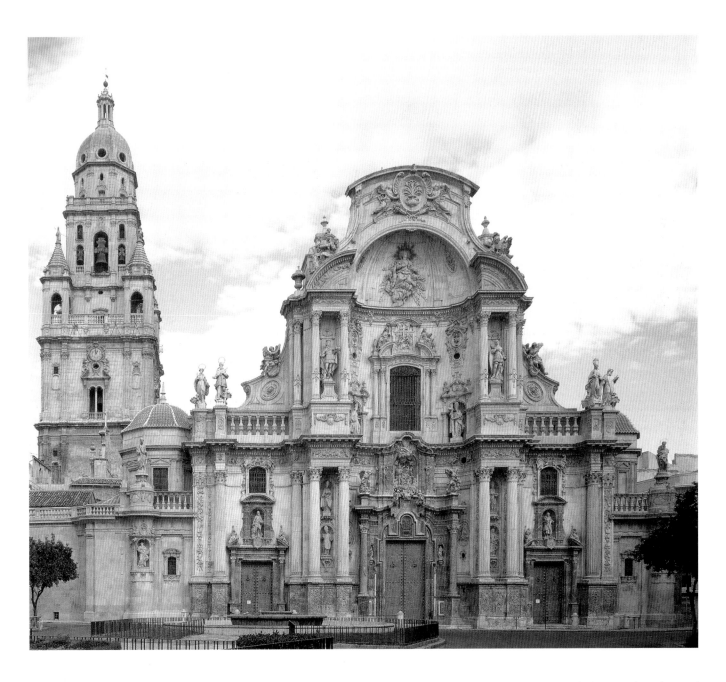

which was predominantly based on the classical baroque of Italy and France. Up to the middle of the century, when the academies were founded, both tendencies continued in tandem, apart from the fact that the imported classical style more or less provoked the development of home-grown Spanish trends. Nevertheless, the underlying themes were also different: the most important commission for the architect was the royal residence, an enterprise that had been badly handled under the Habsburgs since it was almost entirely the province of foreign architects. The Spaniards were either dismissed or relegated to auxiliary tasks. Religious architecture retained its native traditions while the completely outmoded Spanish palaces were seen as inadequate for the needs of the new dynasty.

From 1720 on, therefore, palaces suddenly became the subject of intense activity which lasted until the 1780s. In Madrid, Filippo Juvarra (1678–1736) and Giovanni Battista Sacchetti (1704–64) rebuilt the city palace, which had burned down in 1737, although the compromise with the original alcázar design still remained. For the conversion of the summer palaces at La Granja and Aranjuez, Italian and French principles took over completely.

La Granja was the first major project undertaken by the Bourbon kings (see pp. 106–7). The hunting lodge of the Castilian kings, situated in the mountains, served as summer residence for the Hieronymite order from the fifteenth to the early eighteenth centuries. Philip V acquired the land in 1720 and commissioned his court

Filippo Juvarra and Giovanni Battista Sacchetti
Garden facade of La Granja de San Ildefonso hunting lodge, 1734–36

René Frémin and Jean Thierry
Fountains at La Granja (below)

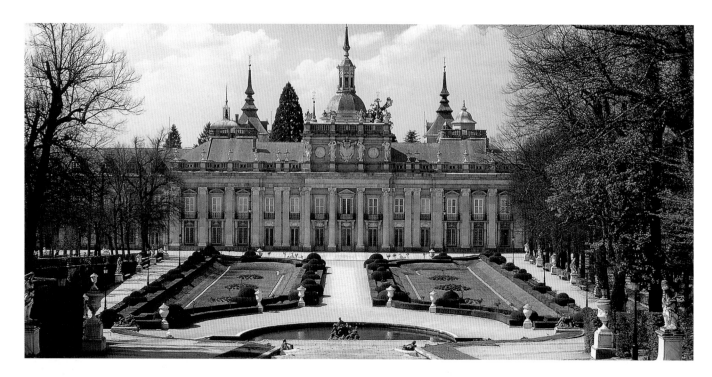

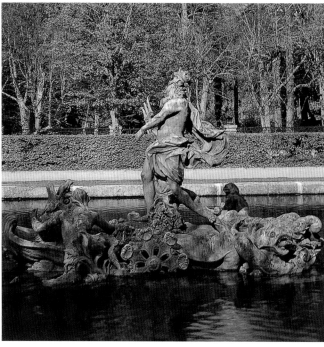

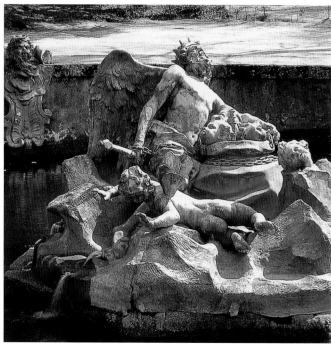

**Filippo Juvarra and Giovanni Battista
Sacchetti**
Detail from the garden facade of La
Granja hunting lodge, 1734–36

architect Teodoro Ardemans (1664–1726) with the design. Initially, Ardemans submitted a traditional Spanish ground plan on the lines of the alcázar, a rectangular complex with corner towers opened to the northwest by a cruciform chapel with dome. Its position made it the focal point of the complex, although the treatment of the facade, with giant orders and an attic storey, is clearly a product of the eighteenth century. The second phase of building was influenced by Italian and French styles, since the work was directed by the Roman architects Andrea Procaccini (1671–1734) and Sempronio Subisati (c. 1680–1758). In about 1730 they extended the main complex with two three-wing edifices, the Patio de la Herradura to the southwest and the Patio de los Coches to the northeast. In this way, the old-fashioned alcázar was served by two *cours d'honneur* at the same time; of these, the Patio de la Herradura was the more elegant and lavish of the two. The concave curve of the central section (hence the name Horseshoe Court) was built over two storeys, with dormer windows alternating with aediculae framed by columns, a motif which is repeated with more restraint on the lateral facades. During the conversion, the old towers of the alcázar were partially removed. The serious evidence of the encroachment of international standardization is manifested in the garden facade at La Granja, which is completely overtaken by the Roman baroque. It was completed in 1736 and built by Sacchetti from Juvarra's plans. Four giant columns in the central pavilion and a subtly graduated row of giant pilasters adjacent to them give the facade a ceremonial power that had not been seen before in Spanish palace architecture. Only later, in the 1780s, was the Colegiata completed, with its outwardly curving facade, designed by Sabatini. It appears to have been inspired by the Salzburg Kollegienkirche which Fischer von Erlach had publicized in his *Entwurf einer historischen Architektur* in 1721. The park layout was placed in the hands of French garden designers and sculptors.

After the Madrid Alcázar and most of its interior had been destroyed by fire in 1734, the construction of a new palace became a major objective. In 1735, Philip V commissioned the Piedmontese architect Filippo Juvarra to prepare plans for the new building. He produced a scheme for a monumental complex larger than Versailles in size (474 meters in length and with twenty-three courtyards), to be situated outside the city. The project was never realized, partly because of the king's disinclination to move the site of his residence, and partly because of Juvarra's death. His successor, Giovanni Battista Sacchetti, altered Juvarra's plans and built the present palace (see pp. 108, 109), a closed four-wing edifice with internal courtyard and corner pavilions, which remained true to the tradition of the Spanish *alcázar*. The structure of the facades combined elements of French and Italian court architecture: from a high square base which forms the ground floor and mezzanine, the three storeys of state apartments rise behind the giant columns and pilasters. An overhanging entablature concealing two further storeys completed the massive structure, designed to be viewed from a distance.

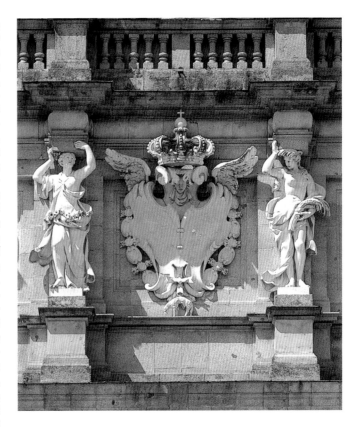

Originally the plan was to place statues on the balustrade; these would have softened the strict cubic lines of the building. The internal layout followed the model of the *appartement double* of contemporary French design. During the course of the planning process, two elements were altered several times: the position and design of the monumental staircase and the treatment of the palace chapel, an oval structure prominently placed opposite the main doorway. In spite of these efforts to give the Palacio Real a contemporary exterior, its origins as a fortress were still very much evident. Up to the present day it still dominates the Manzanares valley, and has little direct connection with the city.

The Palacio Real in Aranjuez (see p. 109, above) was another edifice founded by the Habsburgs which had been converted by Philip V and Isabella Farnese. This former monastery in a well-watered hunting region had been chosen as a summer residence by Philip II although the plans by Juan Bautista Toledo and Juan de Herrera had only been partially realized by Juan Gómez de Mora. Fires caused further damage to the complex in the seventeenth century. In 1731, Santiago Bonavía (died 1759) began to direct the conversion work,

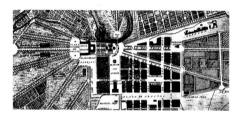

which was set back in 1748 by yet another fire. Rebuilding under Ferdinand VI was mainly based on Herrera's design for a two-storey four-wing building with the emphasis on the west facade and corner towers. Nevertheless, the central pavilion was refurbished and given a double main staircase. The side wings were added in 1771 by Francisco Sabatini (1722–97). Bonavía's sixteenth-century references here surely represent part of a renewed strategy to achieve legitimacy for the second Bourbon on the Spanish throne by embracing the Hispanic tradition of his dynasty more strongly than his predecessor. Around the middle of the century, the palace complex was extended by the creation of today's royal town; a geometric network of streets was added, as well as a performance area for court festivals. The extensive gardens incorporated a unique embarkation point for water-borne spectacles. In addition, the whole complex included the church of San Antonio, a round structure crowned with a dome and with a curved entrance arcade in front, and the Casa del Labrador, a peasant house expanded to become a small three-wing classical structure, which was built under Charles IV.

Further palaces built under the Bourbons during the eighteenth century included Riofrío, a smaller version of the Madrid palace, and El Pardo, the sixteenth-century core of which had been doubled in size by Francisco Sabatini in 1772. These made no innovative contributions to Spanish architecture.

From the Baroque to the Enlightenment

About the middle of the eighteenth century, criticism of the supposed excesses of the baroque and a call for a return to the architecture of Greece and Rome became increasingly strong. The discussions, which had been initiated about three-quarters of the way through the seventeenth century in the *querelle des anciens et des modernes*, was now dying away in Spain too. The effect of the debate had been much more explosive here, since there was a very clear split between Bourbon court architecture, which was predominantly molded by French and Italian baroque classicism, and the lively style of decoration in the traditional centers of the Empire.

During the first half of the century, Spanish artists had already become aware, and appreciative of, the role of the academies in Rome and in Paris and had made representations for the foundation of their own academy of arts in Madrid, particularly since academies of literature and history had existed since 1714 and 1738. In 1742 this project received royal approval and by 1750, two years before Ferdinand VI signed the official deeds for the foundation, the first scholars were sent to Rome. The role of the Academia de San Fernando, which was naturally closely allied with the interests of the court, included scientific research into architecture, an inventory of artistic monuments, and the training of artists. Its control of artistic production went so far that—as an edict corroborates—no public buildings could be started without permission from the Academy, and no master builder could use the title *arquitecto* or *maestro de obras* without first being examined by them. Under these circumstances it was easy to establish the sole predominance of the classical

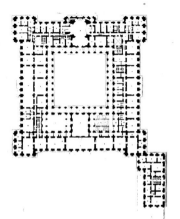

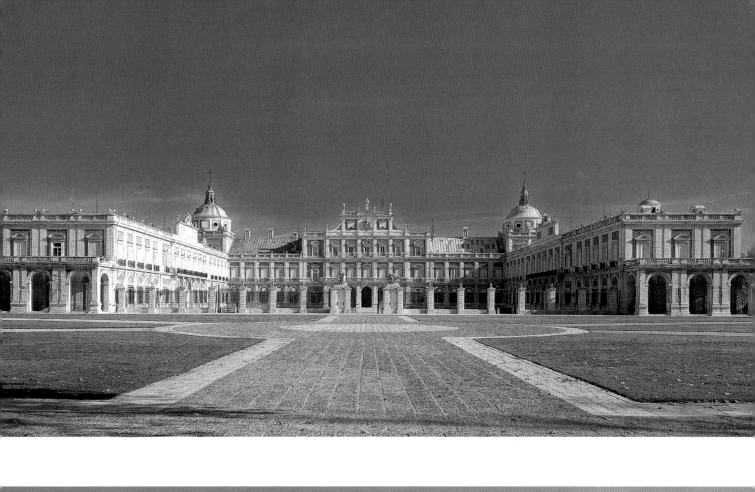

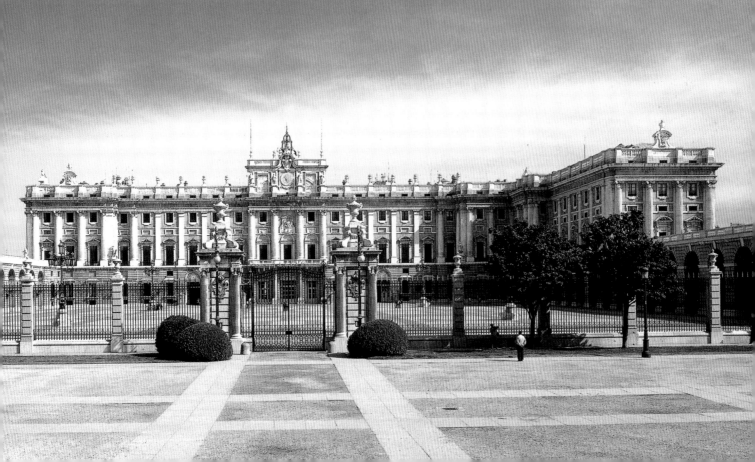

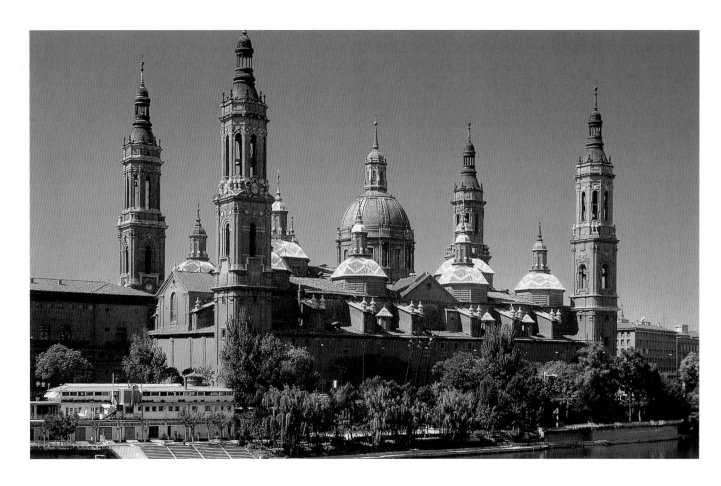

manner in all royal and public art. In Spain, the attachment to a stricter interpretation of antiquity as represented by Vitruvius through Alberti and Vignola, combined with the acknowledgement of Herrera's architectural achievements, further assisted the dominance of a new national style. The return to the forms of the Habsburg palaces from the time of Philip II, as demonstrated in Aranjuez and El Pardo under the Bourbon king Ferdinand VI was therefore doubly legitimized: he was uniting the Spanish heritage with modern international architectural trends.

The work of two architects was seen as embodying the architectural idiom as it was handed down by the Academia de San Fernando. Ventura Rodríguez (1717–85) and Juan de Villanueva (1739–1811) stood at the turning point between two eras, the absolutism of the baroque and the beginning of the Enlightenment. The work of Ventura de Rodríguez, who was trained by Juvarra and Sacchetti, among others, followed the transition from baroque architecture in the academic mold to the classical building styles of the later eighteenth century. Until the death of Ferdinand VI he enjoyed great respect as court architect and later worked as professor of the Academy. Of the innumerable designs he created for the court, the Academy, and for private commissions, about fifty were actually realized. While his early work was still completely under the influence of the Italian baroque of Bernini to Guarino Guarini, by the end of the 1750s the influence of François Blondel's *Architecture française* was evident in his academically classical style.

The discovery of the Greco-Roman remains, however, caused Rodríguez to look again at the work of Juan de Herrera and thus brought about his break with his own architectural heritage.

His first major work, still entirely in the baroque idiom, was the parish church of San Marcos in Madrid (1749–53). From the exterior, with its concave curve, this building is reminiscent of the design of S. Andrea al Quirinale; it thus skillfully exploits an unfavorable location. The interior layout with five intersecting ellipses ultimately refers to Guarini's Divina Providência in Lisbon. In this way, Rodríguez demonstrated that he was one of the few Spanish architects who could deviate from the rigid structure of the rectangular ground plan. In 1750 he undertook the difficult task of converting the pilgrimage church of El Pilar in Zaragoza (see above). The sacred pillar on which the Virgin appeared to the apostle James could not be modified and a solution also had to be found which would accommodate the requirements of the many pilgrims to the site. Rodríguez altered the space immediately surrounding the place of worship to the west of the central nave and designed a domed ellipsis with, in each of the four axes, an apse opened by Corinthian orders on three sides, and closing off the fourth western wall to serve as the altar wall. The saint's image was not centrally positioned but lay to one side of the main axis, in the right-hand exedra. In contrast to this still very baroque treatment of space, his design for the church of the monastery of the Augustinian missionaries to the Philippine Islands in Valladolid (1760) was based on a clear and functional concept, classically structured and directly in the tradition of Herrera's unornamented architecture. Although applied in an academically purified form, the influence of St. Peter's was apparent in the structure of San Francisco el Grande in Madrid (see right), completed only after several setbacks. The facade of Pamplona cathedral had a more striking effect, executed as it was in 1783 in a style which anticipated the nineteenth-century romantic movements in its monumentality and pathos.

The key figure in the spread of neo-classical trends in Spanish architecture was, however, Juan de Villanueva. As court architect to Charles III and Charles IV, he was responsible for redesigning the *sitios reales* of El Escorial, El Pardo, and Buen Retiro and for royal endowments for the Prado Museum and the Observatory.

As *architecto mayor* for Madrid, he controlled the projects for numerous public buildings in the Spanish capital. Several years of experience in Rome, as well as his influence over the teachings of the Academia de San Fernando made of him the mediator of the artistic theories of the age of the Enlightenment in Spain. Villanueva's first major commission was to build two casinos, country houses set in gardens, in the classical style, for Don Carlos, heir to the throne, and his brother, Don Gabriel. His twenty-five-year career as architect in the Spanish capital began when he was appointed *arquitecto maestro mayor de Madrid* in 1786: in these years the city was given a new face. Commissioned by the palace, he first built the colonnade for the Casas de Ayuntamiento and reconstructed the Plaza Mayor, which had been destroyed by fire. However, the construction of the Museo del Prado and the Observatory were to be of greater significance for the history of art: both were royal endowments and anticipated Enlightenment values, as well as being major achievements of neo-classicism in Spain.

The Prado (see p. 112) was not originally designed as an art gallery. In 1785, after the plans of Ventura Rodríguez had been rejected, Villanueva completed several designs for a science museum and the academy of science, which were to be set in parkland close to the Buen Retiro. One of the first sketches envisaged a central rotunda connected with two exedras by porticos and *paseos*; parallel to this a spacious auditorium lay along a second axis, communicating with the rotunda via a narthex and leading through suites of rooms to two corner pavilions. Constructed later, and not finally completed until 1819, after being damaged during the French invasion, the building retained the basic layout but was built on the diagonal. This meant that the *paseos* were converted into Ionic colonnades masking the upper storey, while the lower storey was built with arcades and rectangular niches. The corner pavilions were enlarged and given rotundas. The deeply projecting Doric portico provides access to a semicircular space parallel to the central facade. The exhibition halls are in the Roman style with coffered and dome vaulting. Although there are close ties with the model of the Museo Pio Clementino in the Vatican and various projects for the Academy,

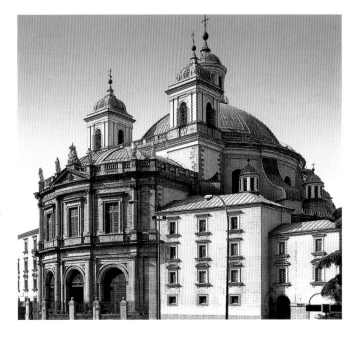

El Prado as a museum open to the public set the standard for later ages.

The nearby Observatorio Astronómico was Villanueva's last great creation (see p. 112). Begun in 1790 and almost complete in 1808, this building on a cruciform ground plan is, in spite of many changes, an important example of how non-classical design penetrated Spanish architecture. Functionality and geometric rigor were the criteria for the design: in contrast with the Corinthian portico with a central reception room dictated by the rotunda, variety was introduced into the scheme and a setting was made for decorative features, a treatment which anticipated the romantic expression of the nineteenth century. Nevertheless, the building is practical to the highest degree. The *tholos* housed the astronomical observatory and its equipment.

Villanueva's influence and his many brilliant buildings and designs demonstrate the final move away from the baroque principles of structure in Spanish architecture. The requirement for a rational approach and the conscious adoption of classical traditions led to the final breakthrough for neo-classicism which merged with a re-evaluation of the national heritage. Villanueva proved to be both a forerunner of the Enlightenment and also an early practitioner of revival styles.

PORTUGAL

In Portugal, the term "baroque" is generally associated with the Restoration and the monarchy of João [John] V, a period extending

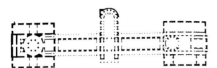

Juan de Villanueva
Madrid, Museo del Prado
1785–1819
Ground plan and main facade

Juan de Villanueva
Madrid, Observatory
1790–1808

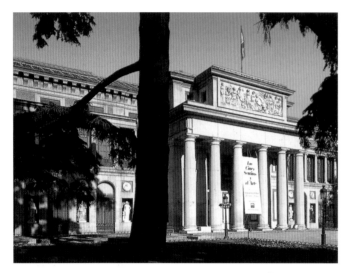

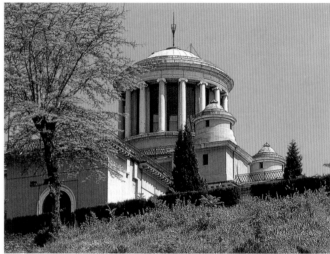

from 1640 to 1750. However, no building activity worthy of mention took place until the last quarter of the seventeenth century. With the discovery of the gold and diamond mines in the Brazilian region of Minas Gerais, the country experienced a quite unbelievable economic improvement. It became, almost overnight, the wealthiest power in the world. The Portuguese court emulated the example of Louis XIV, with the sole difference that it sought to compensate for the lack of tradition with material splendor and the sale of privilege. Thus João V (1706–50) missed the opportunity to develop the country's infrastructure, squandering money and gold in countless building projects, most of which were never completed. He was obsessed by the vain hope of creating a second Vatican at Tejo—an exciting chapter in the history of art. On his death in 1750, however, at least so the story goes, there was not even enough money left in the state coffers for a suitable funeral. Fate dealt his country another blow in 1755 when a major earthquake razed wide swathes of Lisbon and its historic city center. However, this provided the opportunity for a radical new beginning: under the direction of the prime minister Pombal and his modern theories of state. Portugal became an early convert to the message of the Enlightenment.

Any history of baroque architecture must of course start before the eighteenth century. Portugal had already experienced a flowering of the arts under Manuel the Fortunate, when close ties had been maintained with Italy. Classicism had been introduced earlier than in Spain and had laid the foundations for later developments. From 1530 a change was noticeable. Architecture was increasingly characterized by a clear structuring of interior space, block-shaped exteriors, and an extremely spare classical structure. Since the time of George Kubler this style, which has to be seen as a radical negation

of the richly decorative art of Manuel's times, has generally been described as *arquitectura chã* [plain architecture]. Compared with the Spanish *estilo desornamentado*, it was closer in spirit to the characteristically Portuguese traditional preferences for hall churches, and was restricted to smaller, non-monumental structures. The aesthetics of reductionism were rooted in the military architecture which had long become a status symbol for this colonial power, but were given added significance through the ascetic attitudes of João III (1500–57). The radical nature of the switch to the classical style was demonstrated during the construction of the choir chapel in the Hieronymite monastery at Belém. The luxuriantly decorated nave was deliberately contrasted with the purist Capela-Mor (Diego de Torralva and Jerónimo de Ruão, completed 1572).

When Philip II inherited the Portuguese crown in 1580, the western regions of the Iberian peninsula had already developed a high-quality architectural tradition which had made its own individual contribution to mannerist architecture. The construction of a new tower in characteristic style inside Manuel's palace complex on the Tejo was therefore more than just modernization: it was meant to demonstrate in no uncertain terms that Paço da Ribeira had taken possession of the palace which, symbolically, gave access to the city. Filippo Terzi, a student of Herrera, deliberately referred to the military architecture of the country but made the connection with a facade structure like that of El Escorial. A similar compromise in the attitude to Portuguese institutions and a symbolic act of occupation was intended by the construction of S. Vicente de Fora, which—according to the earlier opinion of Terzi and more recent studies by Baltasar Álvares—was realized on the basis of plans by Juan de Herrera. The single nave structure with interconnected side chapels is reminiscent of Vignola's Gesù. The facade with its narthex and the twin towers visible from afar also reflect this Portuguese motif which became a model for almost all the religious buildings of Portuguese baroque.

Philip III's visit to Lisbon on his accession to the throne in 1619, the *joyeuse entrée*, was to have important consequences for seventeenth-century architecture. To mark this visit, a large number of temporary triumphal arches were built, modeled on the monuments created to greet the archducal couple Albert and Isabella to Flanders in 1599. Supported by the treatises by Vredeman de Vries and Wendel Dietterlin which were circulating throughout Europe, the visit of the Spanish king initiated a vogue for the Flemish baroque. An example of this is the facade of Nossa Senhora dos Grilos in Porto (see below), started in 1622, which was another creation of Baltasar Álvares. It shows no trace of central European influence.

A new period, which might be seen as initiating the real baroque, began with the restoration of the Portuguese crown in 1640. Initially it was the aristocracy which made an ostentatious show of their recently regained power. The Palácio Fronteira in Benfica outside Lisbon (begun after 1667), was architecturally still indebted to mannerist models. The perfect amalgamation of palace and park (see p. 114), the masterly setting of the staircase, and the varied decoration of the rooms, based on complex cosmological calculations, were quite in line with baroque concepts. The master of the house,

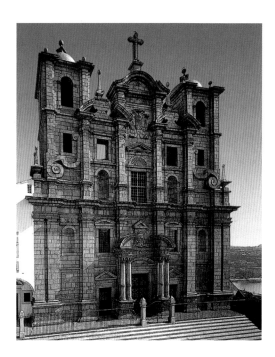

Dom João de Mascarenhas, had himself portrayed life-size on horseback as a stucco bas-relief in the so-called "battle hall." A unique feature here was the series of "tile pictures" using blue and white *azulejos*. Even the walls of the garden pond had portraits of the forebears of the marquis on horseback. Plans by the Italian Theatine architect Guarino Guarini (1624–83) provided the answer to this mysterious scheme. A sketchbook contains the plans and elevation of the church of the Divina Providência in Lisbon, a building which was not constructed to these plans but, with its ground plan based on ellipses, was very unusual for Portuguese architecture of the seventeenth century. Through Guarini's plans, which were published several times, Borromini's influence reached the Iberian peninsula and even extended to Latin America. It is not clear whether the architect himself ever spent any time in Lisbon; there is nevertheless proof of a trip to Spain in around 1657–59, when he examined the construction of Moorish domes, traces of which can be detected in his Turin buildings.

In 1682 the monumental task of reconstructing the church of S. Engracia after it had been destroyed in a hurricane was begun. The central structure with a dome, the work of João Antunes (c. 1645–1712), was influenced by Bramante's 1506 plans for St. Peter's. Although the building had only recently been completed, it represented a new direction for the Portuguese court: Rome had now become the model against which every artistic achievement was measured.

Under João V, imitation of the Eternal City assumed ludicrous proportions. During his reign, from 1707 till 1750, he fantasized that he could build a second Rome, or rather a second Vatican, on the banks of the Tejo. His envoys were to supply him with models and plans of all the Roman monuments as well as the protocols governing papal ceremonial; this alone swallowed unheard-of sums. His building projects, which almost all remained uncompleted, ruined this wealthy country. An outstanding example of his ambitions in this area was the monastery and palace of Mafra, a complex larger than El Escorial and a synthesis of St. Peter's, S. Ignazio, and Bernini's Palazzo di Montecitorio in form. Begun in 1717, the exterior was not completed until the 1840s and it was never inhabited. The director of this project was the southern German architect Johann Friedrich Ludwig (1670–1752), a fairly second-rate designer who worked on the basis of Roman models. At about the same time, the patriarcal palace was being planned; this was a residence and church for the patriarch for which Filippo Juvarra was especially brought to Lisbon. But this project was also realized only in a much reduced and amended guise. Juvarra himself left Portugal after a stay of several months and in breach of all agreements. However, the Royal Library in Coimbra was completed in 1728 by Ludwig, who had taken as his model the court library in Vienna. The votive church of Menino de Deus is of interest from a typological point of view: an irregular octagon with sumptuous internal decoration in which all the arts play a

113

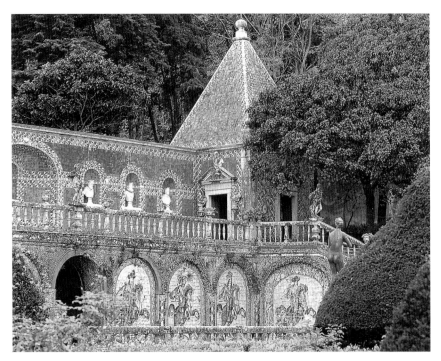

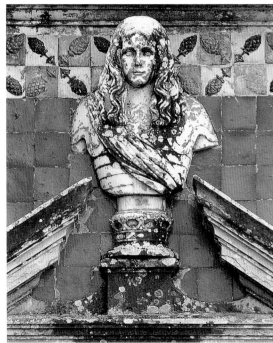

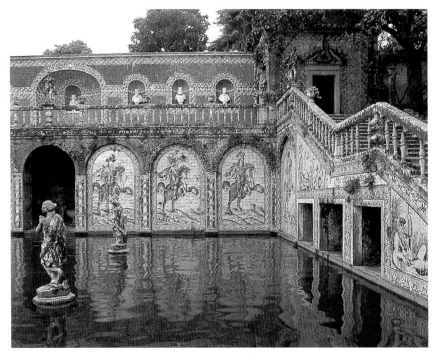

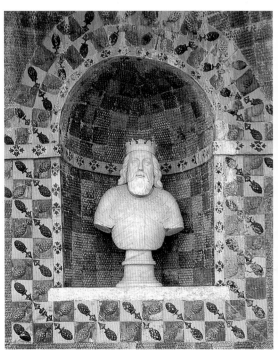

Johann Friedrich Ludwig
Mafra monastery and palace, begun
1717
Ground plan and view of the church
narthex

part. The most spectacular undertaking was the transportation of an entire chapel from Rome to Lisbon for the sole purpose of guaranteeing that João V would receive a building which had been dedicated by the pope. This chapel, designed by Luigi Vanvitelli in 1742 and built by Nicola Salvi, was in effect constructed in Rome, blessed by Benedict XIV, taken apart, and shipped and installed in the church of S. Roque in Lisbon (see p. 118) in 1747. This structure, dedicated to the king's patron saint, St. John the Baptist, was decorated with porphyry, the rarest form of marble, and sumptuous semi-precious stones in the most luxuriant manner; its architectural form already displays the early influences of neo-classicism.

In addition to these monuments, which were designed mainly to glorify the monarch, several institutions which benefited the general population are also attributable to João V. He provided Lisbon with the Aguas Livres acqueduct built in 1729–48, which, with a series of newly built fountains, supplied the city with water. This was one of the great engineering achievements of the age.

In northern Portugal, away from court life, a new individual school of architecture developed after 1725. The founder was Nicola Nasoni (1691–1773), a Sienese painter who only found his true vocation when he came to Porto. His main creation was the Dos Clérigos church (begun 1732), an elliptical structure with a double staircase in front of the western elevation and with the typical single bell tower, attached here to the hospital wing, to the east (see p. 116). Apart from this unusual solution, the facade decoration deviates completely from the grandiose expression of court art under João V. Garlands of flowers, vases, bands, and volutes are all present, with statues, papal insignia, and architectural set pieces decorating the two-storey frontage with window aperture. The result is a picturesque whole which is reminiscent of festival or theater decorations. Nasoni's style, which incorporates elements of Italian rococo, was highly successful, and over the following decades he received a large number of commissions. These included the facade for Bom Jesus von Matosinhos (completed 1748) and the Palácio de Freixo, one of the many late baroque country houses in the north of Portugal and in the Douro valley.

A second center of late baroque architecture established itself in Braga. Archbishop Don Rodrigo de Moura Teles (1704–28) played an important role in this development; he not only extended his palace, installed fountains, and provided new squares in the city center, but also founded a ring of monasteries and convents around the city. The Câmara Municipal (André Soares) was built in 1754, with a facade containing elements of rococo, with curved portal and window coronets. Soares (1720–69) belonged to the confraternity of St. Thomas of Aquinas and built, among other things, the pilgrimage church of Falperra (1753–55), the Tibães Benedictine monastery (1757–60), and the Casa do Raio in Braga (1754–55), where late baroque ornamentation seems to have taken priority over the architectural structure.

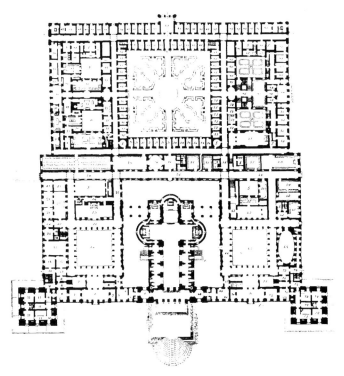

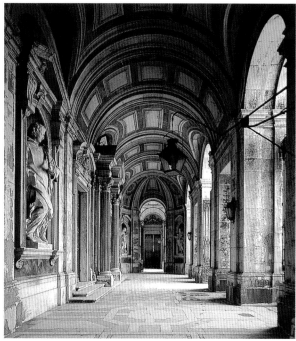

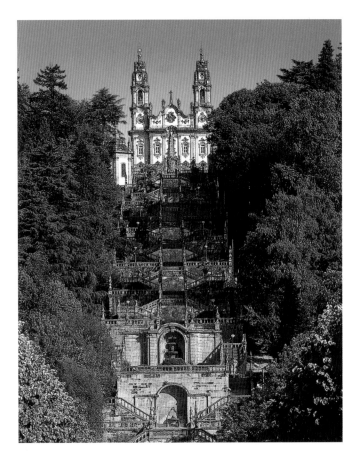

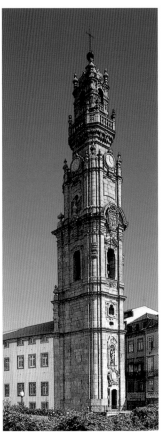

The most breathtaking monument of this era was the Santuário do Bom Jesus do Monte (see p. 117). The shrine, which had stood on a hill outside Braga since 1494, was converted into a *sacro monte* under Dom Rodrigo de Moura Teles. A unique testimony to the combination of Christian and ancient pagan motifs can be found in the stations of the cross which today lead to the church (not completed until the nineteenth century). In the top six levels, connected by stairways, scenes from Christ's passion are represented in square chapels opposite fountain basins with Roman gods; beneath this a second section, furnished again with fountains and statues, combines allegories of the five senses with scenes from the Old Testament. The soul's path to God through the gospel and the senses and the redeeming effect of water are the central themes of this iconographic text, the complete meaning of which has still not been clarified. An outstanding imitation of the Dom Jesus do Monte is to be found in Brazil—although without the spiritual allegory of the staircases—in the Congonhas do Campo Santuário, where the stations of the cross are laid out in a similar manner to indicate the real and the ideal ascension from this earth into the spheres of paradise. Aleijadinho, the legendary black architect and sculptor from Minas Gerais, translated the Portuguese model into a more popular idiom. It is not clear even today how he knew of the original.

While in the northern regions of Portugal relatively constant social and economic conditions applied and provided a basis for continuing architectural development, the seat of government in Lisbon was hit by two severe blows in the year 1755: the death of João V and the earthquake. These led to an abrupt change in building policy. The fact that on December 1 of that year two-thirds of the city lay in ruins and over 10,000 dead were being mourned did not simply signify the end of an era, but a radical change in the history of this colonial power. The consequences can only be sketched out in the present context. They extend right into the age of the Enlightenment and are no longer relevant to this commentary on baroque architecture. Nevertheless, they are too closely linked with the previous era to remain completely unexplored. The empty state coffers, the loathing of the bigoted and profligate dead king, and the almost complete destruction of the old city of Lisbon created the ideal conditions for a new beginning, for the realization of radical, sometimes utopian socio-political ideas.

The rise of the minister Sebastião de Carvalho, later the Marquis de Pombal, brought with it a new era, in urban planning, among other areas. Obsessed by the idea of building the ideal city on the ruins of the devastated Baixa, the lower part of Lisbon, Pombal called on three military architects, Manuel de Maia (1680–1768), Carlos Mardel (died 1763), and Eugenio dos Santos (1711–60). After consideration of various solutions, they proposed an essentially new layout for the flattened city center. This was based on a system of streets intersecting each other at right angles which were to be flanked by two imposing squares, the Terreiro do Paço on the site of the former royal palace, and the Rossio at the upper end of the old city. All building within this grid was to be homogeneous,

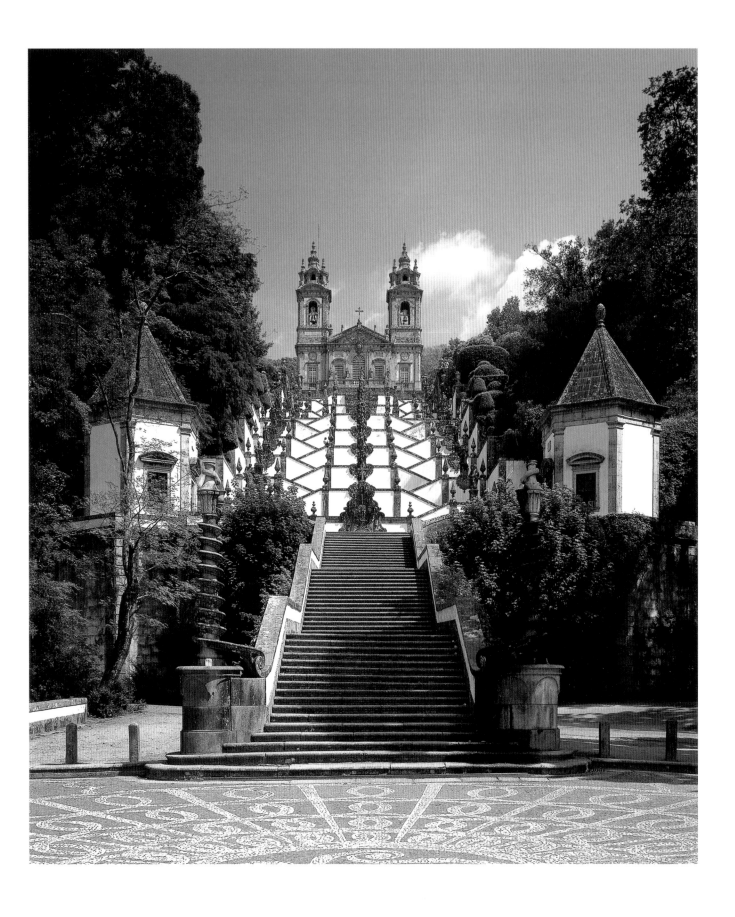

functional, and standardized. These requirements were the most important features of urban development during the nineteenth century.

In addition to these progressive ideas, which were actually to be realized over the next few years, conservative influences inevitably still remained. Thus the summer residence for the Infante, begun while João V was still alive, was completed in Quelez under José I. It is a jewel of rococo architecture in Portugal (see right). Mateus Vicente was the architect of this three-wing complex, constructed around a broad *cour d'honneur*, the interior of which is richly decorated along French lines with rocaille, Gobelins tapestries, and paintings. The grounds also demonstrate the refined taste of the ancien régime, and were laid out from 1758 on by Jean-Baptiste Robillion according to plans by Le Nôtre. The high point, the "jardim pênsil," the hanging gardens built on sloping ground with pavilions and fountains, yet again represented the whole allegorical range of the baroque age. In 1779, building was begun on the Real Basílica e Mosteiro do Santíssimo Coração de Jesus no Casal de Estrela, a votive church built by the Princess Doña María in thanks for the birth of a son; the design very much illustrates the ambivalent mood of the era. The layout on a Roman cross, with a dome and a facade with two towers, is a version of the church at Mafra decorated in the style of the late baroque and absolutely representative of the dignified baroque of the reign of João V.

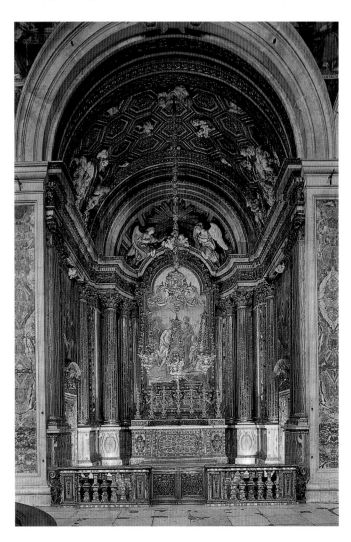

Mateus Vicente and
Jean Baptiste Robillion
Quelez, near Lisbon, Royal Palace
Converted from 1747
So-called "Fachada de Cerimónia"
(above) and views of the Don-Quixote
wing (below)

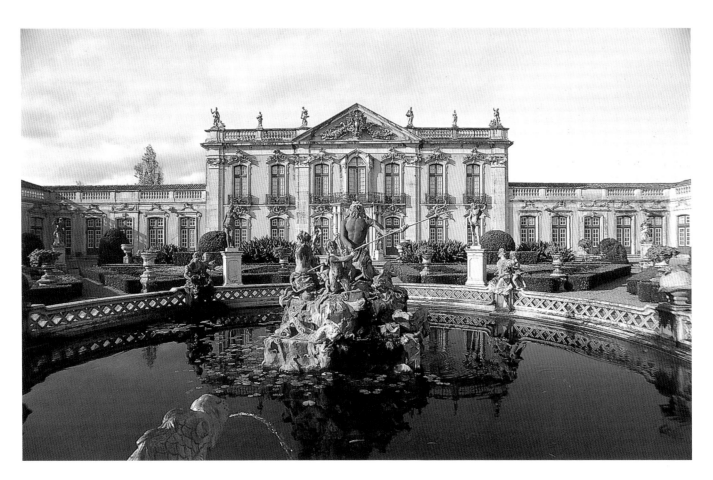

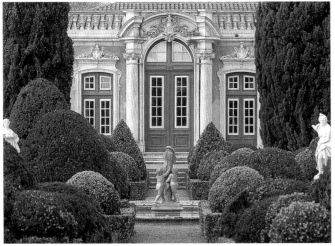

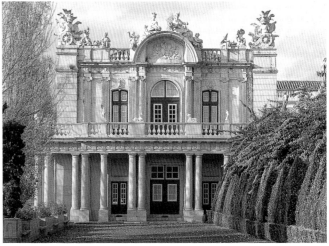

Baroque Architecture in Latin America

Barbara Borngässer

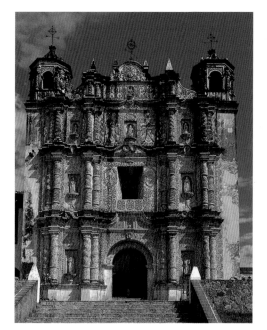

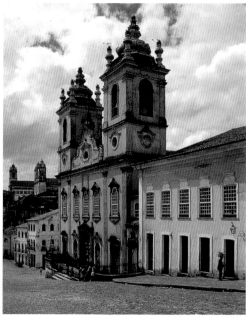

San Cristóbal de las Casas, Mexico
Santo Domingo, facade, c. 1700

San Salvador de Bahia, Brazil, Plourinho with Igreja de Nossa
Senhora do Rosário dos Pretos, second half of 18th century

It is not possible to give anything like a complete overview of the baroque era in Central and South America in the space available here. Nevertheless, this section will address the theme of recent studies which suggest that art historians have begun to develop a less dismissive view of the art of the former Spanish and Portuguese colonies in South America.

In a sub-continent extending over 7,600 kilometers in length and 5,000 kilometers in breadth, whose regions embrace the most widely differing geographic and ethnic features, and with administrations which have been subject to an unusual variety of historical circumstances, it would of course be absurd to search for a consistent style under the nomination "colonial architecture." Undoubtedly common roots in sixteenth-century architecture stemming from the distribution of the treatises by Serlio and Vignola and from the use of traditional architectural orders are more strongly evident in these countries than the remnants of "indigenous" culture. In individual cases, however, the similarities with the architecture of their Spanish or Portuguese origins are often only superficial.

The master builders of the New World were inventive: construction techniques had to be adapted to the geographical conditions. Vaulting was cleverly imitated in wood because of the lack of local stone. Climatic conditions such as extremes of temperature, rain, and drought required new concepts of space; the danger of earthquakes necessitated a new approach to construction. Engineers were often sent to the New World with dozens of sample books in their luggage. They or their indigenous assistants built churches, monasteries, and public buildings on the basis of documents like these. They in turn provided prototypes of a kind for further building work: regional variations developed through this process. This interaction between existing European elements and regional individuality has never been examined in any adequate depth. The cultural context for the settlements and homes of the local population is a new area of research.

The correlation between the foundation of colonial cities and spontaneous settlements, and their relationship to the construction of fortresses and to the *reducciones*, the Jesuit missionary stations, has been the subject of recent

research which explores the role of local contributions to the culture, as opposed to the continuation of Eurocentric investigation of the colonial impact. In general, the New World was ideal ground for experiments in urban planning. Since the city structures had little formal planning, the colonial masters took the opportunity to transform them into urban and social utopias which would have been impractical in the Old World.

The intermingling of different cultures did not, at least in the area under discussion, produce a great deal that was new. The ruling culture was too dominant. Meanwhile, as was the case with the Mexican *atrium* (an area in front of the

church for the instruction of the "heathens"), traditional features, in this case from the time of the early Christians, were revived and adapted to current requirements. The "open chapels," a pragmatic acknowledgement of the Indians' cultural and spiritual link to nature, were as stunning as they were practical. Naturally, new solutions were only found if they were sought. In regions where the conquerors and missionaries came up against primitive tribes or local cultures who fled from colonization, as in the Andes or the sparsely populated regions of what are now Argentina and Paraguay, European principles were applied much more uncompromisingly. The same thing hap-

pened in the Caribbean and Central America. In this area, operating almost as a bridgehead to Europe, Ibero-American architecture retained fairly close ties with the architecture of Andalusia.

Much more than in the mother country, the Catholic church, the real engine of the conquest, was concerned here with impressing and convincing unbelievers. Architecture, with its more or less obvious rhetoric, provided the ideal tool for this purpose. After an initial phase of colonization, occupation, and strategic fortification, accompanied by a wave of missionaries and the establishment of the religious orders, the concern of the seventeenth and eighteenth centuries was to consolidate power.

The monumental new cathedrals, parish and chapter churches, and centers of pilgrimage were obvious signs of a functioning colonial system. Building commissions like these pushed secular architecture almost completely into the background. The bishoprics and the regional capitals like La Antigua (Guatemala), Havana (Cuba), México, Puebla, Oaxaca (Mexico), Quito (Ecuador), Cuzco, Lima (Peru), and La Paz (Bolivia), to name only the most important, bejewelled themselves with extravagant religious buildings as the rate of economic prosperity increased, although such prosperity was frequently threatened by natural disasters.

In the process, the churches in Mexico and in the region of the Andes developed their separate styles, often confusingly treated as similar with the words "typically Latin American," but which ultimately represent a variation on the Spanish originals: the facades, particularly the central section, became a luxu-

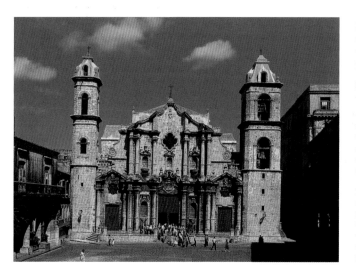

Havana (La Habana), Cuba
cathedral, begun in 1742

riantly decorated showpiece which differentiated itself from the more strongly plastic design of the Central American versions. They were similar in construction to a retable or the temporary triumphal arches often seen in the mother country. Their architectural idiom derived from mannerist treatises. A rich repertoire of figures and ornaments developed on this framework, which also represented Indian motifs, plants, and animals and was quite clearly intended to impress and instruct the native population. To what extent the natives were directly or indirectly affected by the structure of this type of edifice, and the extent to which this could be regarded as an innovative contribution to the art of Spanish America, is an open question. Similarly, the relationship of colonial churches to the interior decoration of Andalusian churches, above all the work of Francisco de Hurtado Izquierdo (see pp. 97–99), who nevertheless preferred purely abstract decorative forms, also remains unclear.

Portuguese colonization was restricted exclusively to the coastal area, where the first settlements had developed around the invaders' fortifications. Up until 1763, the most important city and the seat of government was São Salvador de Bahia, which had "more churches than days in

ABOVE RIGHT:
Aleijadinho
Congonhas do Campo
Santuário do Bom Jesus de Matosinhos
Brazil, 1757–beginning of 19th century

BELOW RIGHT:
Rio de Janeiro, Brazil
Monastery of São Bento
Interior of the church, begun in 1617
Alterations to the plans and decoration
From 1688

the year." Most of these were closely modelled on Portuguese precursors such as the hall churches of Lisbon or Coimbra, the typical double-tower facades, or on the descriptions in Serlio's treatises. Only the church of San Francisco da Ordem Terceira has an aesthetic language comparable to the decorated facades of the countries of the Andes.

In the late eighteenth century by contrast, Brazil developed a unique variation on late baroque style around the region of Minas Gerais, which had grown rich on its gold and diamond mines. The curving ground plans, central interior structures, convex and concave facades with the towers behind them, and the thoroughly plastic interpretation of structure were without comparison in the

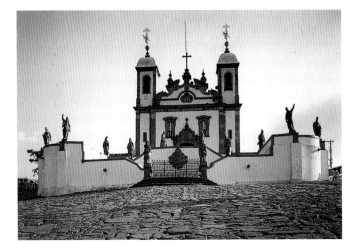

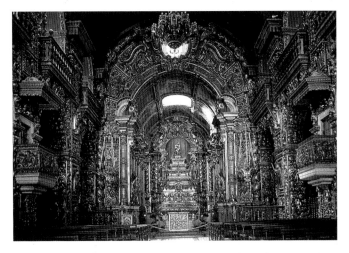

rest of Latin America. The architect, Aleijadinho, is one of the few on the continent whose biography is available. He was of mixed race and disabled (*aleijado* = cripple) and further was mainly self-taught. His work is still proving difficult to research although the gifted master builder soon became a subject of fascination for Brazilian historians. Even today, parallels with the southern German and Bohemian architecture of Dientzenhofer have led to the wildest theories. The influence of the work of Guarino Guarini on this architect is somewhat more likely.

The adherence to tried and tested models, the uninterrupted access to and availability of theoretical literature, and the lack of any formal pressure for innovation meant that late gothic, Mudejar, Plateresque, and mannerist elements

coexisted here until well into the nineteenth century; they were used together quite naturally, even in baroque interiors. This meant that traditional stylistic forms and structures continued almost without interruption right up until the eclecticism of the second half of the century.

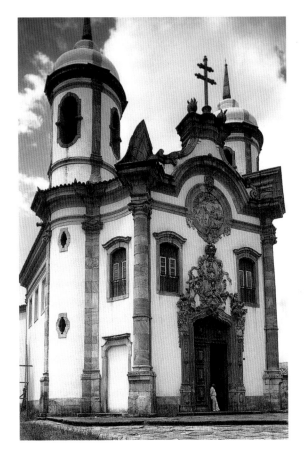

Aleijadinho
Ouro Preto, Brazil
São Francisco de Assis
1765–75

Barbara Borngässer

Baroque Architecture in France

The Historical Context

"The brilliance and splendor surrounding kings establishes part of their power." Montesquieu's observation provides a key to the understanding of French statesmanship and explains its success throughout the baroque age. Urban planning and architecture were put to use as an expression, even a metaphor, of absolute rule that had not been seen in Europe since antiquity. The Place des Vosges and the Place Vendôme, the dome of Les Invalides with the hospital attached to it, the conversion of the Louvre, and the expansion of the palace of Versailles, which ultimately involved relocating the royal residence were only the most spectacular among countless royal building commissions which certainly served practical functions, but were designed mainly to impress.

The resolution with which they were driven forward, the unparalleled financial and organizational investment, and, not least, the quality of the work, meant that France took the lead in architecture within a few years.

The centralization of state power meant that Paris and the court became the nucleus of architectural development; the other regions copied these or subsided into provincialism. Even private palaces modelled themselves on the royal one, so that architecture reflected the hierarchical structure of a society where the highest authority was always invested in the person of the sovereign. Two further constant factors were also essential to French statesmanship: the imitation of classical antiquity and the insistence on classical forms as the most suited to large-scale commissions, regardless of any other contemporary trends. This became the compulsory form of expression for absolute rulers far removed in time and space from France. Although it did develop in France, rococo remained an almost exclusively decorative form.

The period discussed here includes the seventeenth and eighteenth centuries, coinciding with an era of absolutism in France which began under Henri IV and ended with the Revolution in 1789. In these two hundred years, France became the leading power in Europe. After the Bourbon Henri IV (1589–1610) had put an end to the wars of religion with his conversion to the Catholic faith in 1593, and with the acceptance of religious equality as enshrined in the Edict of Nantes in 1598, Henri then embarked on a deliberate expansion of the monarch's powers the restoration of the authority of the state and of economic prosperity. The stabilization experienced in France during his reign was, however, quickly destroyed during Marie de' Medici's regency and the weak rule of Louis XIII (1610–43). In addition to the constantly smoldering conflict with the Huguenots, unrest mainly took the form of uprisings by the aristocracy, who aspired to increase their power. It was only in 1624, when Cardinal Richelieu took over the affairs of state, that peace returned to the internal situation and eventually also to external political relationships. His skillful negotiations meant that the French crown emerged strengthened from the confusion of the Thirty Years War; the power of the house of Austria, on the other hand, had weakened. Richelieu also laid the foundations for the cultural ascendancy of France: the founding of the Académie Française in 1635 was the first of a series of specific measures by which the monarchy sought to promote science and the arts and to make them affairs of state.

Richelieu's policies were continued by Cardinal Mazarin, who directed the administration of Louis XIV (1643–1715) when he was still under age. With the defeat of the Fronde (the uprising of parliament and the upper aristocracy against the absolute monarchy in 1653–54) and the peace treaty with Spain, he put France on the path towards supremacy in Europe. When Louis XIV finally took power himself in 1661, he had secure borders, operational administrative structures, and well-regulated finances which he improved considerably himself through the mercantile policies of his finance minister, Jean-Baptiste Colbert. The expansion of the naval forces now also meant that France was increasing its influence as a colonial power: the marriage of Louis XIV to Maria Teresa, the eldest daughter of the Spanish king Philip IV, brought with it Bourbon claims to the Spanish throne. The extraordinary upturn from the middle of the century also affected the arts and the sciences. Descartes' theory of knowledge, Pascal's critique, Corneille's tragedies, Racine's prose, La Fontaine's fables, and, ultimately, Molière's comedies were all in Colbert's hands; since 1664 he had been the Surintendant des bâtiments and, after the founding of the Academy in 1671, he also had control of a powerful instrument for the formulation of architectural style.

Towards the end of the century, the picture changed: wars on every side drained the state coffers; after the War of the Spanish Succession France's supremacy in Europe collapsed, although Philip V of Anjou, a grandson of Louis XIV, was now on the Spanish throne. Economic, social, and even moral conflict increased and led to the fall of the ancien régime. After the death of Louis XIV in 1715, after seventy-two years on the throne, a period of seemingly endless change began, both in the balance of power and in the economic and social arenas. The regency of the Duke of Orléans followed by Louis XV's own rule (1715–74), from 1723, did little to prevent increases in the national debt, more losses of territory, and finally also the cession of the Canadian colonies to Great Britain. Social reform, above all the equitable taxation of all classes, was blocked by opposition from the court and the aristocracy, whose interests were closely allied. The Parlement demanded wider powers but in vain. When Louis XVI (1774–92) acceded in 1789 to the reinstatement of the Estates General, dissolved in 1614, it was already too late for reform. The Revolution took its course.

French Architecture under Henri IV, Louis XIII, and the Regency of Cardinal Mazarin

The prelude to the almost two-hundred-year pre-eminence of French architecture was the urban development initiated by Henri IV, and

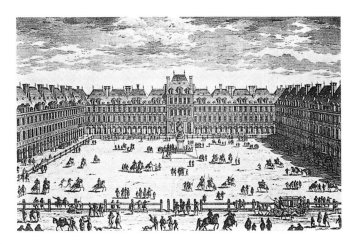

realized with the support of Sully, his minister and architectural planner. Modeled on the measures taken by Pope Sixtus V to improve Rome, Henri's intention was to lay out a "new" city as a reflection of absolutist rule. The responsibility publicly displayed by the monarch towards his people, and, on the other hand, the hierarchical structure of society were constant elements which dominated urban planning and architecture throughout the whole of the baroque age. Even the very first project, the Place Dauphine, which lies between the Pont-Neuf and the Île de la Cité, provides evidence of a great deal of theoretical as well as practical investment. The triangular layout on a prominent urban development site provided a point of departure for a system of axes which was to traverse the entire city. At the same time, it emphasized the Seine as the backbone of the expanding metropolis. A statue of Henri IV, the first modern royal monument, was erected in the center. The second of the king's creations, the Place des Vosges (see above), became the prototype for the Place Royale. This rectangular square in the Marais was surrounded by uniform two-storey brick buildings over arcades. The only emphasis was provided by the two taller pavilions, the Pavillon du Roi and the Pavillon de la Reine, on the widths. The living and business accommodation were originally intended for silkmakers and their businesses, but the square quickly became a meeting place for the aristocracy. Here too, the whole complex is focused on an equestrian statue of the king which, because of late delivery, was adapted as a monument for Louis XIII (erected in 1639). The Place de France (see p. 77) is also worthy of a mention as one of Henri IV's urban planning projects. Its star-shaped, symbolic layout with the roads converging on the city gate bearing the names of eight French provinces was never completed but was nonetheless an important milestone in urban planning.

The emphasis in architectural activity shifted under Louis XIII; previously the main concerns had been the development of the road

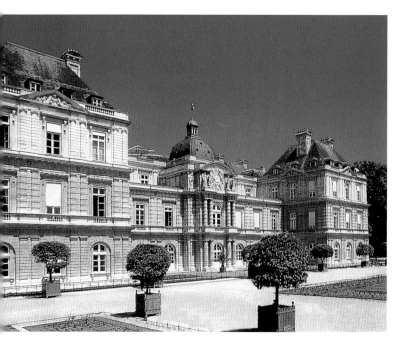

Salomon de Brosse
Paris, Place du Luxembourg
1615–24
Garden facade and ground plan

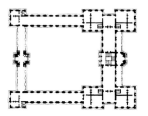

Blérancourt (1614–19), and the Palais du Luxembourg in Paris (1615–24). These were highly regarded and were a major influence on this type of architecture for a long time to come. Blérancourt is the most interesting structure from a typological standpoint, as this was the first break with the standard French U-shaped palace layout; it has no side wings. This reduction to the core structure, the *corps de logis*, and the opening up of the building to the landscape created the conditions for further development in baroque palace architecture throughout Europe.

The original design of the Palais du Luxembourg (see left), built for Marie de' Medici, is shown in an engraving which illustrates the *corps de logis* with corner pavilions, side wings, and a low entrance building, with a domed pavilion adding emphasis to the center. The exterior was severe and clearly structured; the roof held the various cubic structures together. The rusticated facade looks back to Palazzo Pitti, the city palace of the Medici in Florence. The palace, which Gaston d'Orléans used as his residence from 1642 on, also featured innovations in the interior. Thus the corner pavilions were all complete apartments with several distinct rooms, a solution which anticipated future room plans which were designed for greater comfort and functionality. In addition, the gallery of the right wing was decorated with the Medici cycle of Rubens between 1622 and 1625. The left wing was to designed to house paintings on the life of Henri IV, which were never executed. Further works by Salomon de Brosse were the Palais de Justice in Rennes (1618) and the great hall in the Palace of Justice in Paris (1619–22).

network, the provision of a uniform structure for street frontages, and the expansion of the city in general. At the same time, architects like Salomon de Brosse, François Mansart, and Louis Le Vau conducted intensive research into modern methods for resolving traditional building problems. They developed models of palace and church buildings which were to have a lasting influence, not only for French baroque architecture.

De Brosse (1571–1626), court architect and a member of a well-known family of architects, built three major palaces during the second decade of the seventeenth century: Coulommiers (1613),

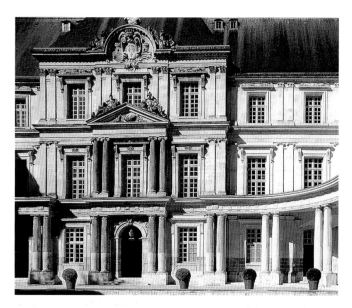

François Mansart, Château de Blois, Gaston apartment, 1635–38

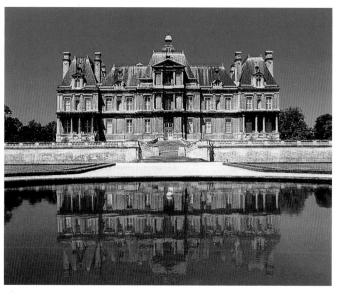

François Mansart, Maisons (Maisons Lafitte) palace, 1642–50

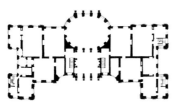

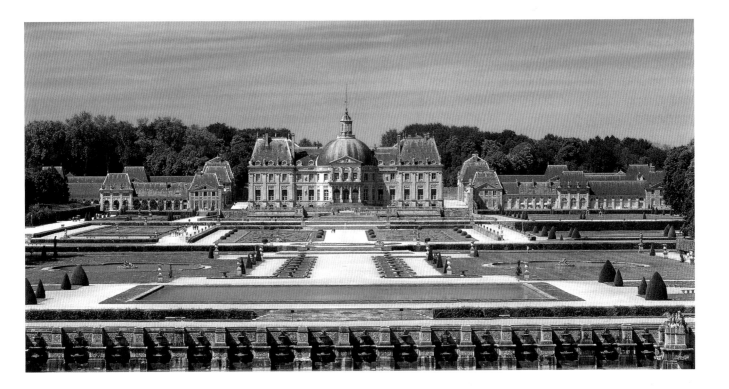

François Mansart (1598–1666), probably a student or younger apprentice with de Brosse, undertook other commissions. He was more interested in the plastic structuring of the facade than the reworking of palace design. His masterpiece was the Gaston apartment at the Château de Blois (see left), which he constructed in 1635–38 for Gaston d'Orléans. The three-wing complex is set around a small *cour d'honneur*, the side wings connected with the *corps de logis* by a curved colonnade. The central pavilion with three axes is extraordinarily elegant, and decorated with three superimposed pairs of pilasters. The large staircase in the central pavilion provides an ingenious link between the different axes of the courtyard and garden facades. The motif used in the dominant central pavilion is repeated in an even more plastic format in the Maisons palace (later Maisons Lafitte, begun 1642), built for the wealthy René de Longueil (see left). Of particular note is the emphasis on the roof through the use of steeply rising surfaces and high chimneys which are reminiscent of sixteenth-century architecture; in addition, typical of the French château, the added wings and pavilions are evidenced by the roof structure. The eighteenth century is heralded by the elegance of the vestibule, which remains classical in format.

The palace of Vaux-le-Vicomte at Melun (see above) was the object of a unique scandal. It was built in 1656 by the court architect Louis Le Vau (1612–70) for the finance minister Nicolas Fouquet in only one year and at considerable cost. This structure, according to contemporaries, outshone everything which had previously been achieved in the field: the château, surrounded by an old-fashioned but functioning moat, opened onto luxuriant grounds laid out by André Le Nôtre (1613–1700) who was at that time an unknown landscape gardener. The complex is approached across a splendid courtyard flanked by service buildings. In the center of the *corps de logis* with its corner pavilions, a rectangular hallway opens onto the courtyard and an oval domed salon faces the garden. The facade consists of a double-storey arcade structure crowned by a triangular pediment, a device which, with its small pilasters, forms a contrast with the giant orders of the wings. The costly interior decoration was the work of Charles Le Brun (1619–90). The major innovation at Vaux-le-Vicomte was its situation *entre cour et jardin*, between courtyard and garden. Its setting within the landscape, the gradual perspective into the palace from the service buildings, across the *cour d'honneur*, and through the hallway to the great salon, and finally the view into the garden landscape, became an essential schematic device for any palace worthy of the name. The interior also featured some major innovations such as the *appartement double* (as opposed to the *enfilade*, or *appartement simple*) which made it

125

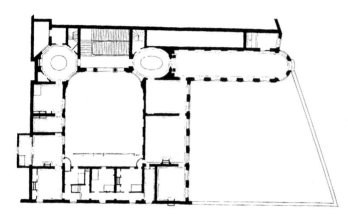

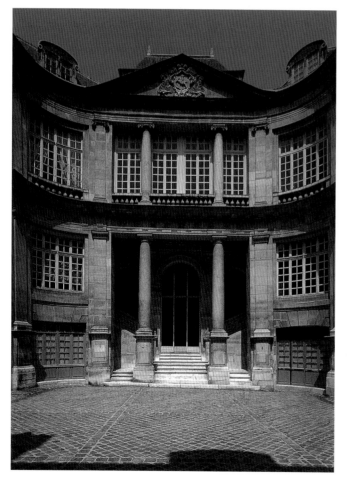

possible to vary the composition of the rooms and allowed a more practical layout which accommodated both ceremonial and domestic requirements. From now on public and private spheres could be more effectively divided. The design of Vaux-le-Vicomte was so influential that it was to become the model for the most important of the French châteaux, Versailles.

Apart from the château, the hôtel, or city palace, led many of the architectural innovations in seventeenth-century France. In Paris, the aristocracy and the *haute bourgeoisie* competed in the construction of splendid residences which, in spite of their ostensibly private function, often became public showplaces. Setting these structures, often on irregular plots, into the urban context and providing practical sequences of rooms was as much of a challenge for the architect as the impressive decoration of the building overall. As mentioned earlier, Salomon de Brosse had broken up the medieval tradition of the four-wing complex with his designs for Blérancourt and the Palais du Luxembourg. He had placed greater emphasis on the *corps de logis* and had given the courtyard a new, more open appearance. These motifs were also taken up in designs for the hôtel, but were naturally adapted to their urban context, which often led to very complex ground plans. Differences in the axes to the courtyard and garden sides were introduced and were frequently affected by the doubling of the size of the *cour d'honneur*. The *appartement double*, a double row of rooms, was also a response to practical requirements. The hallway, staircase, and gallery were designed for ceremonial functions. They were decorated with the most ostentatious architectural elements. Perhaps the most significant of these city palaces is the Hôtel Lambert (see left and right) on the Île St-Louis. Le Vau used a completely new layout here which reflected the narrowness of the site: instead of siting the garden along the portal-courtyard-accommodation axis, he moved it to the right, close to the *cour d'honneur*. The latter, with cut-off corners, opens onto a monumental staircase which, flanked by oval hallways, leads into the gallery which is laid out sideways and is interposed between the garden and open ground. The decoration of the facade combines French elegance and monumental Roman features. Doric orders superimposed on Ionic are used on the courtyard facade and a continuous entablature runs right across the wings. The dominant motif is provided by the stepped entrance with its pediment and free-standing Doric columns at ground-floor level. The garden facades feature Ionic columns with casement doors set between them—one of Le Vau's ideas which was to characterize French palace architecture of the time. In the Galerie d'Hercule the decoration, completed in 1654 (and still preserved), with paintings by Le Brun and reliefs by Van Obstal, sought to evoke antiquity and the heroic deeds of Hercules.

A New Direction in French Religious Architecture

French religious architecture developed with secular architecture, but did not at first demonstrate the same level of creativity. The

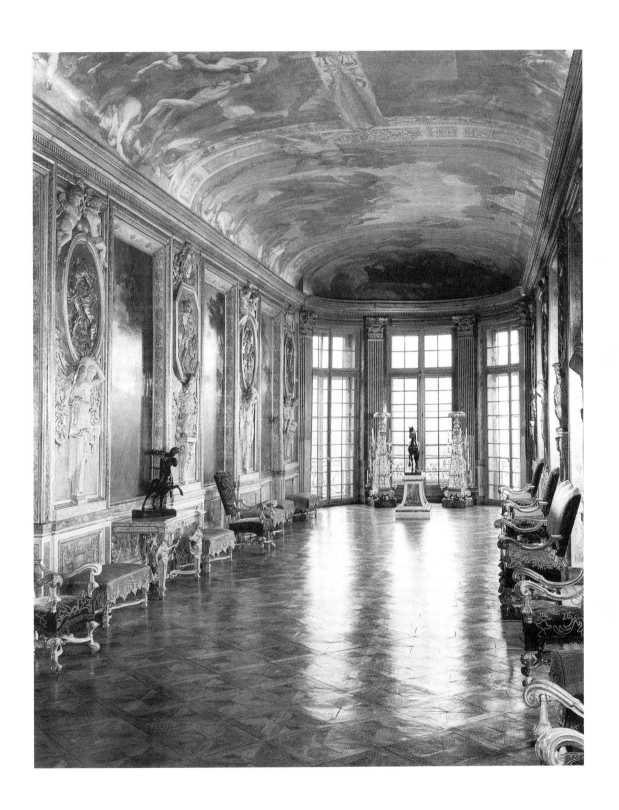

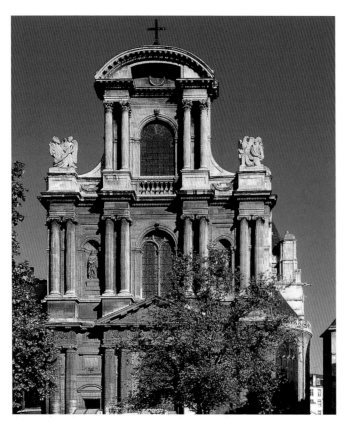

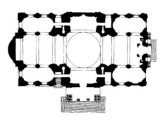

centralized structure dominated by its dome, with a short transept, lengthened transverse arms, and side chapels has a similar ground plan to that of the Roman church of S. Carlo ai Catinari. The west facade reflected the structure of Roman Jesuit churches, incorporating a broad portal *travée* flanked by side niches. The ground floor is dominated by massive Corinthian columns reinforced at the corners, but reduced to pilasters on the upper storey. Powerful entablatures emphasize the horizontal lines. A different design is used for the courtyard facade (see below); the stepped effect of the temple front, triumphal arch, hipped roof, and tambour dome give the picturesque effect of a stage set, a completely idiosyncratic combination of classical and baroque elements.

Another dome structure was built to give thanks for the birth of an heir to the throne, the Val-de-Grâce (see right, below), begun in 1645 by François Mansart and continued by Lemercier, but completed only in 1710 by Pierre Le Muet and Gabriel Le Duc. Here too, Roman architecture provided the basic inspiration, but Mansart, whose plans established the determining features for the ground plan and elevation up to the entablature, was able to provide

search for appropriate forms and an appropriate relationship to the urban context was restricted by the strong links with tradition as represented by a long-standing fascination for gothic as well as the tendency toward imitation of Roman models. France only slowly developed its own baroque style in ecclesiastical architecture which reached its high point predominantly in the use of imposing dome structures.

The first major religious building of the French baroque was the facade of Saint-Gervais in Paris (1616–21), probably built by Salomon de Brosse in the sixteenth-century style (see above). It combined elements of the French palace—after Philibert de l'Orme's mannerist facade at the Château d'Anet—with the grandeur of early Roman baroque. The upward movement of the three-storey front stood in contrast with the weighty plasticity that imitates the Roman prototype. The stepped effect of the various motifs was to become characteristic of French church building.

The Italian influence on religious building increased with the work of Jacques Lemercier. This architect, born in 1585, had worked in Rome between 1607 and 1614, and had studied the work of Giacomo della Porta. Commissioned by Louis XIII, he built the Pavillon de l'Horloge at the Louvre (after 1624). After a large number of hôtels and churches, he designed the palace and setting for the model city of Richelieu, for Cardinal Richelieu (begun 1631) and built the Palais Cardinal in Paris (now the Palais Royal, begun 1633). A milestone in the development of classical baroque in France can be seen as resulting from another commission from Richelieu, that of the church of the Sorbonne (begun 1626). This

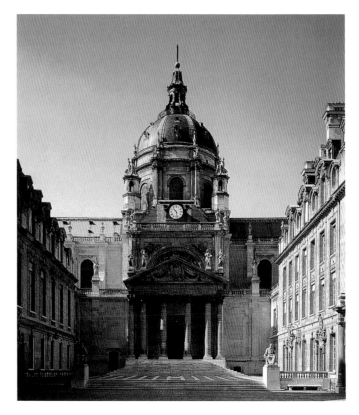

François Mansart and Jacques Lemercier
Paris, Val-de-Grâce, begun 1645
Completed by Pierre Le Muet and
Gabriel Le Duc, 1710

Charles Gamard and Daniel Gittard
Paris, Saint-Sulpice, begun 1646
Interior

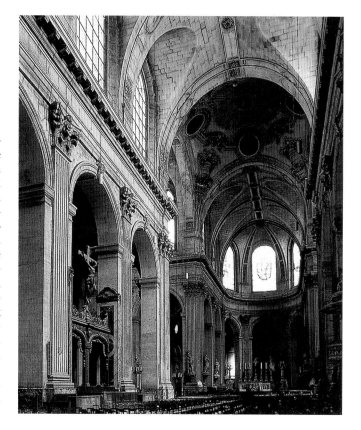

a renewed impetus towards the use of monumental forms. The chapels adjacent to the crossing do not open, as is more usual, onto the nave or transept, but diagonally onto the space beneath the dome in which the high altar is situated, in the manner of Bernini. The tall tambour and dome are supported by massive piers. The Roman design is also considerably modified in the facade; the front, reminiscent of Carlo Maderno's S. Susanna, has a free-standing portico with Corinthian orders. Like the Sorbonne, this gives an impression of depth and provides a base for the stepped organization of the structure. The third dome structure, built in the middle of the century, was the church of the Collège des Quatre-Nations (see p. 130, today the Institut de France), the last of Cardinal Mazarin's foundations, and also his sepulcher. Le Vau designed the main facade facing the Seine within the spirit of the Roman baroque. It displayed curving concave wings framing the central church structure with its oval interior. The edifice is again opened up by a classical portico, and dominated by a high tambour and dome.

Although copied from Roman models, these centrally organized dome churches provided French religious building with its own baroque forms. Nevertheless, other trends coexisted with these

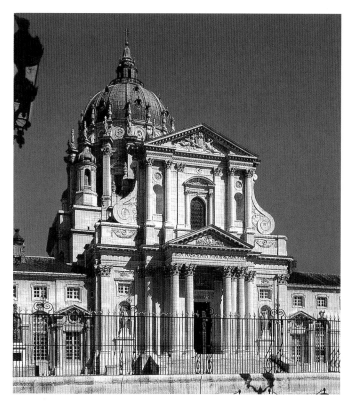

developments. The parish church of Saint-Sulpice (see left and above), built by Daniel Gittard (1625–86) from plans by Charles Gamard from 1646 on, is one example of this. It was a basilica in the medieval tradition with side aisles, transept, and ambulatory, housed in a classical structure.

The Age of Louis XIV

In 1661, after the death of Mazarin, Louis XIV himself took on the affairs of state. Within a few years, the reign of this now twenty-three-year-old monarch had become an example of uninhibited royal power, and the court of the Sun King was transformed into a resplendent metaphor for an absolutist concept of the world. Art and, above all, architecture had an important political role to play in all this. They served to impress the population and at the same time to convey ideological meaning through the use of specific imagery.

Jean-Baptiste Colbert was the driving force behind this statesmanship; already minister of finance and, with Charles Le Brun, president of the Royal Academy for Painting and Sculpture, founded in 1648, he was appointed Surintendant des Bâtiments in 1664, a position which essentially gave him responsibility for all royal building projects. By 1666 the French Academy had already opened its doors in Rome, a clear signal that France, a new world power, intended to emulate the cultural supremacy of the Eternal City and to outdo Rome in developing Paris as a center of the arts. The foundation of the Académie de l'Architecture (1671) was an important stage in this process, an institution which would be the guarantor of standards in training future generations and would take a leading

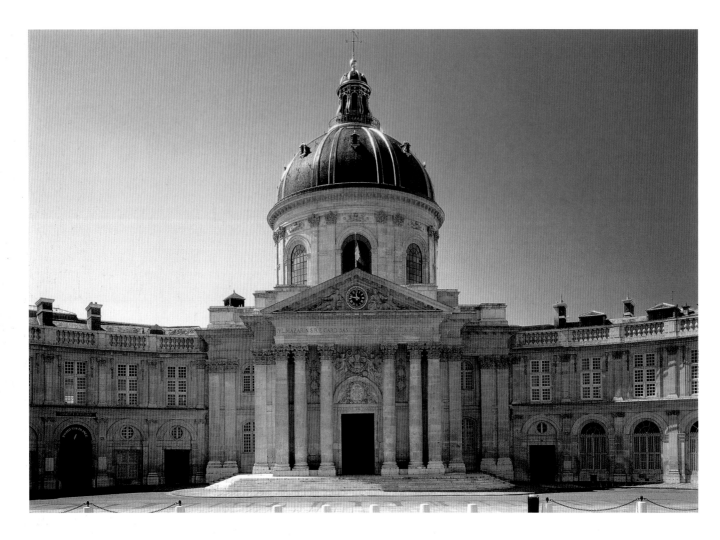

part in theoretical discourse. It became a tool for state control of architectural policy.

Colbert's main concern was the conversion of the Louvre, a fortress-like four-wing structure which had been continually extended and modernized since the sixteenth century, most recently with the clock pavilion by Lemercier and conversion of the eastern half of the Cour Carrée, for which Le Vau claimed responsibility. However, an imposing facade towards the city was still lacking. An initial design by Antoine Léonor Houdin dating from 1661 had already provided the broad frontage of columns, realized six years later by Claude Perrault. Another project by Le Vau consisted of a colonnade, but this time with double columns. The central section was emphasized by a pavilion with pediment, behind which lay a broad oval hallway. Since Colbert would not approve these designs for the east front, he invited the most renowned Italian architects, Gian Lorenzo Bernini, Pietro da Cortona, Carlo Rainaldi, and Francesco Borromini to submit plans for the scheme. Borromini declined and the designs by Pietro da Cortona and Rainaldi aroused no interest, leaving a choice of two proposals by Bernini (see right). The first plan proposed a convex and concave curving front with a transverse oval pavilion crowned by a tambour-like structure. The major order, and the plasticity of the building's contours were reminiscent of St. Peter's Square. This architecturally and effectively open design was rejected by Colbert on the grounds of climate and security. The second, modified version was also criticized. Nevertheless, Bernini was invited to Paris in April 1665 to draw up another plan, the

Claude Perrault
Paris, Louvre
East facade, 1667

Gian Lorenzo Bernini
Initial design for the Louvre, Paris
1664 (center)
Third design for the Louvre, Paris
1665 (below)

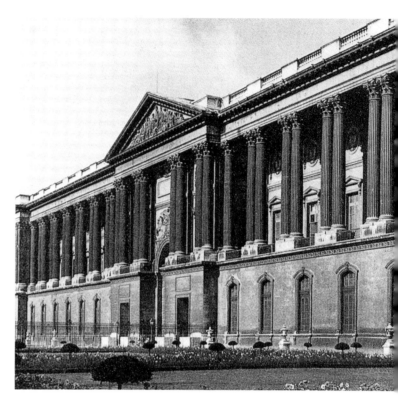

foundation stone for which was laid on October 17 of the same year. Even this project, another version of a straight, block-shaped form, was to have no future: the work barely reached above the level of the foundations.

The reasons for Bernini's failure in Paris are very informative. In the best Italian tradition, Roman architects envisaged a princely residence which communicated with the surrounding city. Thus the open arms of the first design related to an exedra on the opposite side of the palace square. But Colbert demanded a structure that would embody the distant power of absolutism and which would become a monument to the French monarchy. The Petit Conseil, a commission called in April 1667, decided on a compromise which was predictably modified later in the course of further alterations to the Louvre.

The east facade finally built in 1667–68 (see right), for which the doctor and mathematician Claude Perrault claimed responsibility, was indeed an improvement on earlier designs as a monument to the French monarchy. Perrault also used the motif of the colonnade as an appropriate structure for what was essentially a late-medieval palace complex, but his version demonstrated a new classical rigor. Over an escarpment and an unobtrusively structured ground floor lay an elongated columned hall, the corners of which were given added emphasis by pavilions resembling triumphal arches. The central axis is accentuated by a projecting temple frontage. The palace structure is thus enhanced by the religious motif. The extended alignment of double Corinthian columns was the most distinctive and frequently quoted feature here; their impressive weight was further stressed by the ridge line traversing the entire breadth of the building.

The dispute over the Louvre facade and the decision in favor of an academically classical scheme were symptomatic of the understanding of the role of art in absolutist France. Nevertheless, there is no doubt that it was the all-powerful minister, Colbert, rather than the king himself, who set the course in formulating a unified approach to government. The Louvre was to be a paradigm of this. In 1671 he ordered a competition to develop a "French" order of architecture for the internal courtyard; for the apartments he played with the concept of imitating rooms from a variety of different countries, symbolizing a world in miniature, ruled over by the king of France. Pressure from the Fronde and Louis XIV's own plans, however, quickly lead to the end of this idea after the completion of Perrault's facade. The king turned to his favorite project, the conversion of the hunting lodge at Versailles, just outside Paris.

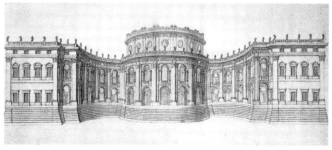

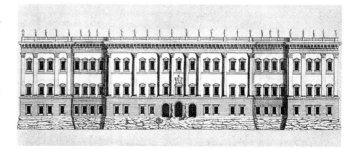

Versailles

Versailles became the ultimate European palace, not only because of its size, splendor, and advanced layout, but also because of the ideal manner in which it expressed absolutist power. Versailles was not the court of a humble mortal like Philip II's monastery and palace at

Louis Le Vau and Jules Hardouin-
Mansart
Palace of Versailles
Views of the garden facade, 1668–78

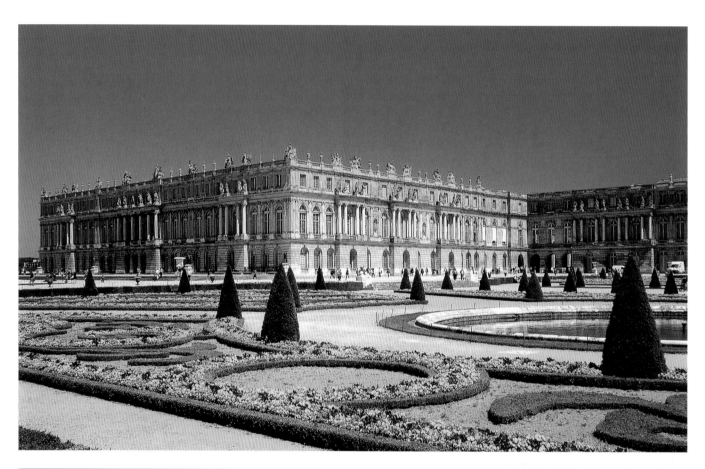

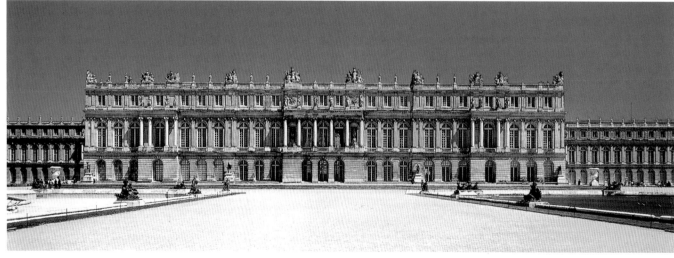

André Le Nôtre and Jules Hardouin-Mansart
Versailles, palace grounds
Latona fountain with view onto the
Grand Canal 1668–86

BELOW:
Versailles, palace and grounds
Engraving after Israel Silvestre
End of 17th century

El Escorial. Versailles was the symbol of timeless domination, the residence of the Sun King, whose life and works were of an exemplary nature and were therefore subject to strict regulation and ritual (see pp. 138–139). Architecture and iconography reinforced these impressions.

Initially extended to make a three-wing complex in 1631, the sumptuous conversion of Louis XIII's small hunting lodge had already been set in motion by 1668. With Le Vau, Le Brun, and Le Nôtre, the king brought in those artists who had already developed significant new concepts at Vaux-le-Vicomte, the palace of his minister Fouquet. Above all, the setting in the natural landscape and the concept of "between courtyard and garden" distinguished this new, but of course much more ambitious, extension. The first measures were to set off the core structure, which now opened on the garden with a broad terrace, to establish the overall scheme, and, finally, to lay out the extensive park itself. In 1677–78, shortly before the Treaty of Nijmegen was signed, thus setting the seal on the supremacy of France in Europe, the king decided to relocate his residence to Versailles, an action which entailed an enormous amount of additional planning, as the entire royal household was also obliged to make the move to the "suburbs." The thirty-one-year-old Jules Hardouin-Mansart was given the responsibility for carrying this through. Over the next thirty years he directed the conversion of Versailles, on which at times up to 30,000 workers were employed.

As a first step, Hardouin-Mansart closed the garden frontage by constructing the Hall of Mirrors to replace the terrace (completed in 1687), endowing the space with a monumental aspect in a style first introduced at Fontainebleau by François I. The old core structure was integrated into Louis XIV's apartments: in the center was the king's bedroom, lying on an east-west axis, since the monarch's day took the same course as the sun. Of the rooms added by Le Vau, those to the south were used as the apartments of the queen, Maria Teresa, and those to the north as reception rooms. These reception rooms, the "grands appartements," ended in the (no longer extant) Ambassadors' Staircase and the Salon d'Hercule; this was where official ceremonies and receptions took place.

The transverse north (1684–89) and south (1678–81) edifices enclosing a second courtyard, the Cour Royale, were added by Mansart to this three-storey core surrounding the original Cour de Marbre. The facade, over 670 meters wide, has an imposing effect. The elevation retains the structure of the old facade; over a banded lower section the main floor rises, with Ionic columns at measured intervals. Ionic pilasters frame the casement doors which provide plenty of light. The final floor is formed by an attic storey crowned with trophies.

The park setting was of great importance for the further development of palace architecture, since, like the palace, it had a ceremonial function, providing an allegorical representation of events. It was used for entertainment—the initial stages of which were none-

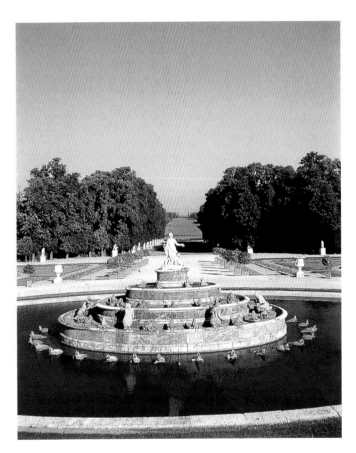

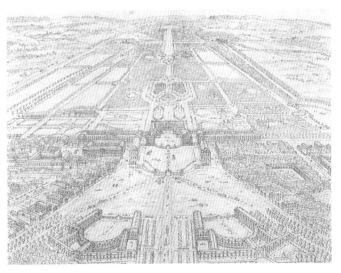

Philibert Le Roy
Versailles, Marble Court, 1631
Facade decoration by Louis Le Vau and Jules
Hardouin-Mansart, 1668

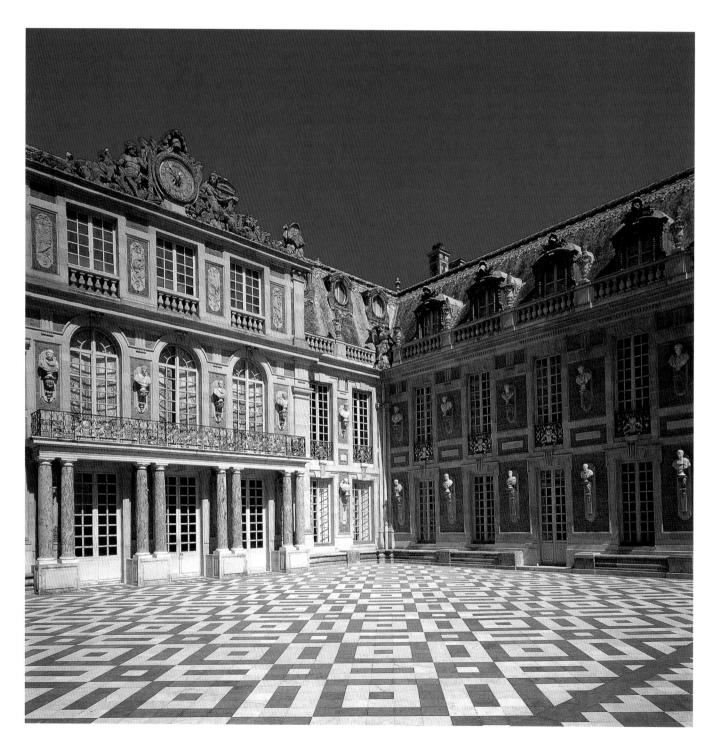

Detail of the palace facade and chapel
from the grounds

Jules Hardouin-Mansart and Robert de Cotte
Versailles, palace chapel, 1689–1710

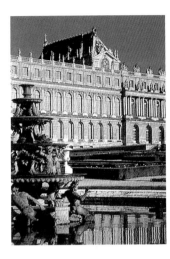

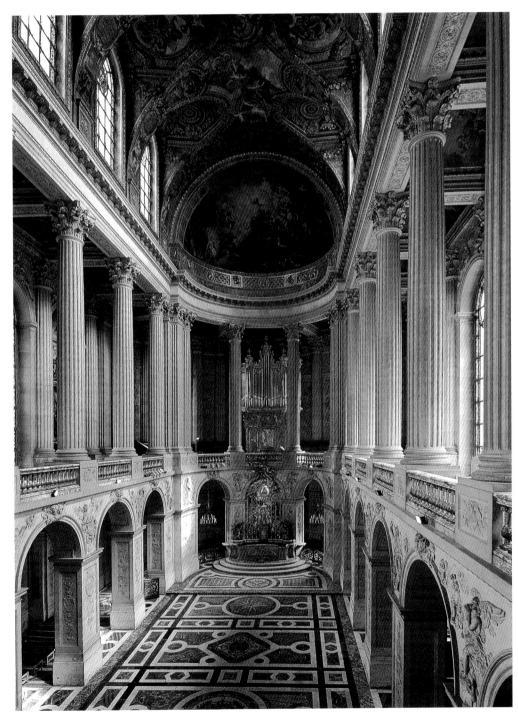

The heart of the Palace of Versailles was the Cour de Marbre, the Marble Court (see left), around which the royal apartments were grouped. It formed and still is the highpoint of three court-yards—the Cour des Ministres and the Cour Royale come first and form the setting for the approach to the palace. The Cour de Marbre, which owes its name to the floor decoration of black and white marble tiles, already formed the heart of the complex which had been built by Philibert Le Roy under Louis XIII. The Cour Royale, five steps higher, was restored in 1980. The facades on the Marble Court were newly structured by Louis Le Vau and Jules Hardouin-Mansart under Louis XIV. They were decorated with balustrades, busts, stat-ues, and vases to provide an impressive setting. The main facade was given a gilded balcony on four pairs of pillars.

The palace chapel (see above and right), which occupies the north wing, is one of the most impressive examples of French late baroque architecture. Begun by Mansart in 1699 and completed in 1710 by Robert de Conte, the galleried church with polygonal ambulatory com-bines classical, medieval, and baroque features and is modeled on St. Louis' Sainte-Chapelle. It consciously serves as a setting for the French monarchy. The rich decoration, the openness to the light and the contrast between the light, stone and the blue background of the frescos (Antoine Coypel) anticipate the aesthetic style of the next few decades.

The Hall of Mirrors, with its con-necting reception rooms, the Salon de la Guerre and the Salon de la Paix, form the

François Mansart and Charles Le Brun
Palace of Versailles, Salon de la Guerre
1678–86

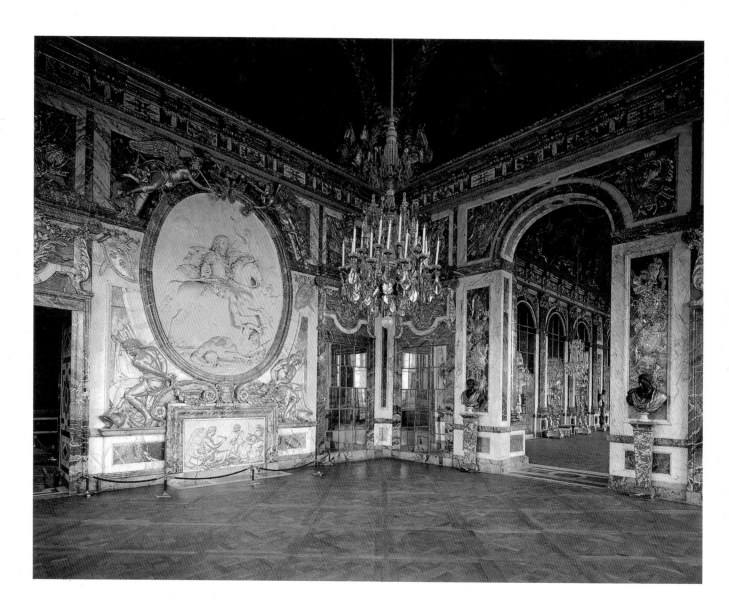

enfilade suite of *grands appartements* linked with the garden. They provided a sumptuous framework for court festivities and the reception of high-ranking guests.

The seventy-five-meter-long Galerie des Glaces, the Hall of Mirrors (see right), was completed in 1687 by François Mansart. The interior decoration was created by Charles Le Brun who, according to Colbert, developed for it a unique "French order of architec-

ture" with which to structure the walls. In the Hall of Mirrors the most refined artistic applications were combined with a complex variety of motifs including allegorical cycles illustrating the history of France up until the Peace of Nijmegen. The outstanding feature here, however, is the reflected light from the countless mirrors. They reflect the sunlight or even the candlelight and effectively realize the metaphor of the "Sun King."

At the ends of the gallery lie the War Salon (see above) and the Peace Salon (Salon de la Guerre and Salon de la Paix), in which the king's military successes are celebrated. In the first, Louis XIV is seen triumphing over his enemies and in the second, the peace achieved during the king's reign is celebrated. The Salon de la Guerre is dominated by a large oval bas-relief by Antoine Coyzevox, showing the king vanquishing his enemies.

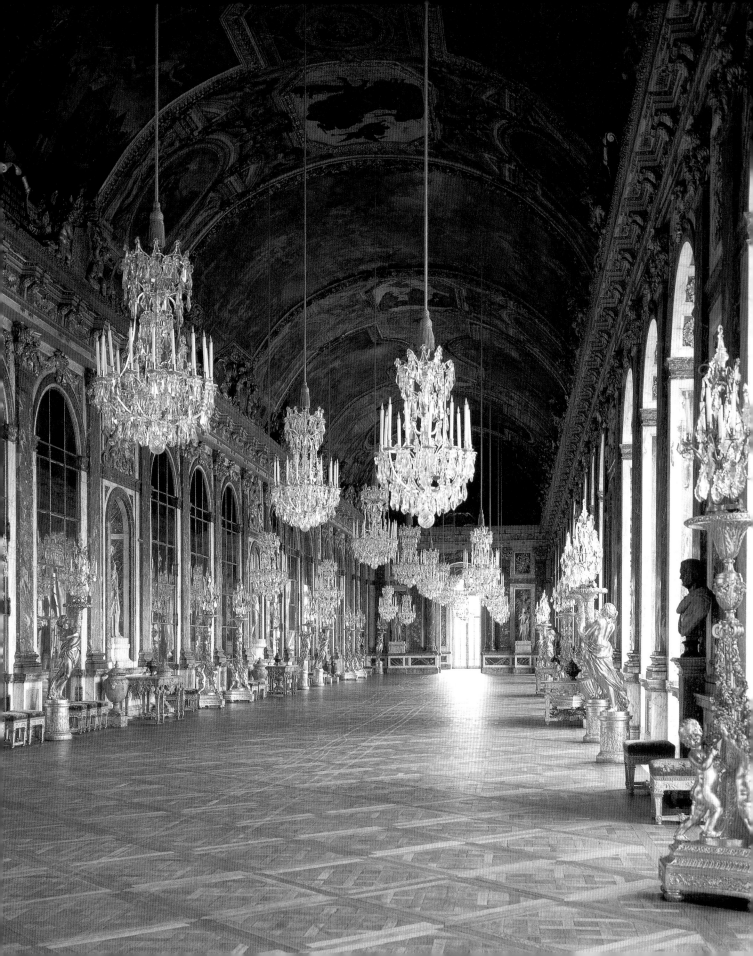

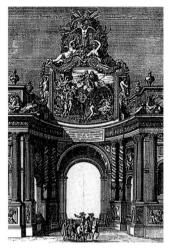

Triumphal arch on the Marché Neuf
Copperplate engraving from the *Entrée
Triomphante*, 1660

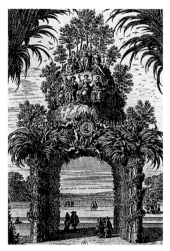

Triumphal arch by the Saint-Gervais
fountain, Copperplate engraving from
the *Entrée Triomphante*, 1660

The baroque age saw itself as a theatrical production: the world was its stage. This concept is reinforced by the fact that innumerable works of the history, culture, and even social history of this period have titles such as *Theatrum ecclesiasticum*, *Theatrum ceremoniale historico-politicum*, *Circus regius*, *Theatrum praecedentiae* and so on. These describe facts and events, but at the same time they provide an interpretation of what might be described as the rules of the game. Thus, life became a story or even a legend; each public action becomes a ceremony and the monarch

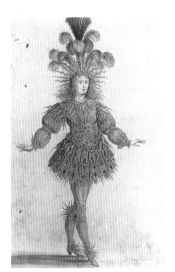

himself the "living image" or *image vivante* of his God-given majesty.

No one embodied this principle better than Louis XIV. At his court, which was viewed as a microcosm of the universe, the king reigned as Jupiter, Apollo, or simply the sun shining over everything. Antiquity and early Christian sources provided the basis for this idea. For instance, in his *Bucolics*, Virgil described the dawning of a new "golden age" ruled by the Sun God. In the time of Constantine, the first Christian emperor, this prophecy was considered to refer to the appearance of the son of God. Early in the modern age, the myth of the sun was equated with the utopian state, as in Tommaso Campanella's *Città del Sole* (1602). Further, the sun god Apollo was represented as the *musagetes*, the leader of the Muses. Encouragement of the arts and of the sciences, encouraging harmony between them and the promotion of peace through their application, became one of the essential iconographical elements of baroque monarchies.

A complex symbolism was deployed here. Images of historical events, portraits, monuments, and medallions were used, and in literature eulogy became an essential tool. The most important symbol, however, was that of the king himself. Louis XIV's daily round was associated with the course of the sun and its effects. Each action, from the ritual *lever* to the *coucher*, the meals, the receptions, even the stroll through the garden, became symbolic actions and a metaphor for his divine presence. Books on court

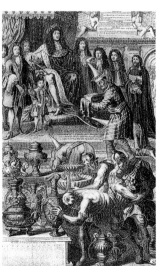

protocol have chronicled the complicated and extended procedures which all took place in open court, sometimes even in view of the general population. The most important activity was the *lever*, when the king arose and dressed at sunrise. Pages of instructions described every step and gesture of the large number of people serving the king. There was a protocol to deal with every eventuality. Thus hours would pass before Louis XIV was out of bed and fully dressed. The royal household was present at every performance; proximity to the king guaranteed them a share in the glory of the very heavens themselves.

It is clear that the palace and its entire program was based on this concept. In Versailles, the residence of the sun god, each separate space reflected this metaphor; there were no private areas. At the heart of the complex, exactly in the middle of Louis XIII's Cour de Marbre,

and aligned precisely on an east-west axis, lay the king's bedroom (see below), where the *lever* took place. It was both a place of worship and the center of power. The sequence of rooms and the degree of accessibility were all part of the ceremony. The more the king favored a courtier, the further he was able to advance through the interior of the palace. The prelude to the real as well as the ideal traversal of the Sun King's palace was the "Escalier des Ambassadeurs," the first and most important ceremonial staircase of the baroque age. In later years it was to become the major feature of palace construction. The ascent of the visitor and the approach of the monarch could be directed here in the most careful fashion.

The "Grands Appartements", for which Le Brun had planned a series of images of the gods of the planets, were used by the king for affairs of state; in

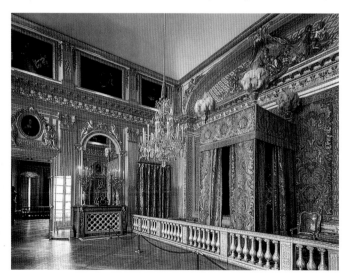

later years they were opened to the public (the upper layers of society) for gaming and dancing three times a week, a gesture of the sovereign's "kinship" with the people. Contrary to early plans, which had shown Hercules as their theme, the Hall of Mirrors, and the adjacent Salons of War and Peace were decorated with "the history of the king, from peace in the Pyrenees to the Peace of Nimwegen." The official ideological interpretation was added by the writer François Charpentier in the form of inscriptions. The sumptuous rooms were, however, only used for important receptions, although the program of events was widely distributed in publications such as the *Mercure Galant*, the monthly reports from court.

The park was at least as important as the palace (see pp. 154 ff, 306 ff). With its summerhouses, fountains, bowers, and groups of sculptures it provided the perfect setting for grandiose festivities. Even by 1664, before the conversion of the old Versailles complex, it was famous for the productions in its park of "Plaisirs de l'île enchantée", a spectacle in honor of the queen (or rather, it is suspected, for Mademoiselle de la Vallière, Louis XIV's mistress), in which the king himself took part as the knight Sir Roger. The highlight of the festivities, on the third day, was the destruction of Alcina's palace, carried out by means of a gigantic fireworks display. On these occasions, temporary structures were erected, included in the drama and then blown up. Louis XIV had already taken part in play-acting during his youth. Between 1651 and 1659 he took part in the "Ballets de Cour" as a dancer, playing the part of Apollo among other roles (see left).

The festivities and the temporary structures they involved played a substantial role in baroque art. Engravings and contemporary accounts tell us how significant these spectacles were, whether their purpose was to amuse the court or to impress the populace on the streets, which saw in them an escape from the oppressions of everyday life. The *entrées solonnelles* of the French king, his processions through the city in continuation of a medieval tradition, were imitated throughout Europe. Extravagant scenarios and expensive accessories, generally wooden triumphal arches, were designed for them (see left above). The triumph was executed like a government program; transcendental government structures, the images of an ideal world, were imparted through the action. The virtues were victorious over vice, faith triumphed over the godless, and order over chaos. At the center of this harmony the king remained a constant, the darling of the gods, and godlike himself, an authority whose acts would always be seen to represent both reality and symbolic gesture. The whole city was the stage for this spectacle: its streets and, more importantly, its squares, were used as assembly ground, theater, and place of execution. These always formed part of a complex

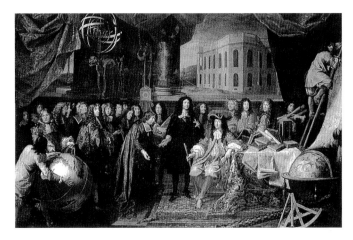

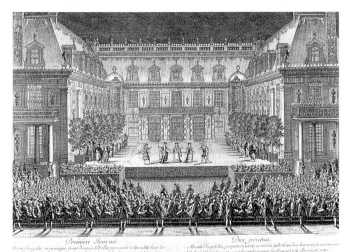

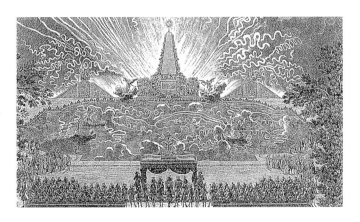

stage set, the backdrop against which the uplifting and serious spectacle of an ideal world unfolded at least in the mind of the sovereign.

These productions, with their propaganda and their jollity, were inspired by both civic and religious festivities. State visits, the accession of princes to the throne, and their weddings, births, and even deaths were celebrated with expensive processions and the relevant architectural structures (*castra doloris*). Church festivals were just as theatrical; the processions during Easter Week or at Corpus Christi for example. The temporary nature of the structures and the restricted time frame of the overall program were interpreted as a sign of the transient nature of existence. The allegories used in sacred and profane imagery were also understood by the uneducated: symbolic scenes, linguistic and pictorial metaphors; rhetorical prototypes, and emblematic structures were much more generally accessible during the baroque period than now (see pp. 428–29).

The content of these productions was elaborated by artists and engineers working together; the design of festive imagery and the theatrical *mise en scène* were regarded as highly creative. In this way, the various art forms eventually combined to establish what became known as the "total work of art."

Jacques Gabriel
Versailles, Petit Trianon, 1762–64
Courtyard facade

Richard Mique
Versailles, grounds of the Petit Trianon
Temple of Love, 1775

OPPOSITE:
Jules Hardouin-Mansart
Versailles, columned hall of the
Grand Trianon, 1687–88.

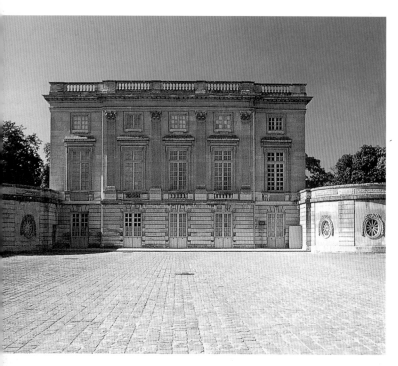

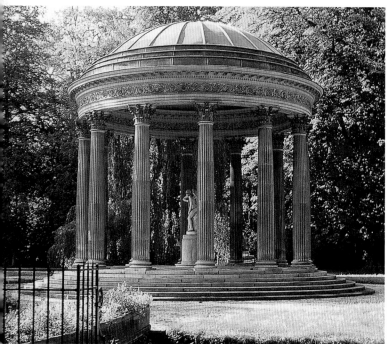

theless ruled by protocol—and formed the natural backdrop for the numerous court festivities. Among the architectural embellishments to the park at Versailles was the Trianon, which stands near the Orangery built by Jules Hardouin-Mansart. In the place of the village of that name, the Trianon de Porcelaine was initially built as an intimate spot for trysts between Louis XIV and Madame de Montespan. Although extravagantly appointed and completely covered in Delft tiles, the unheatable and uncomfortable building was replaced by the Grand Trianon in 1687–88 (see right). In 1687–88, in only six months, Hardouin-Mansart built a permanent structure with an open columned hall and extended single-storey wings. His light-spirited design based on Italian models and the internal appointments based on the notion of *commodité* [comfort] anticipated a more refined approach to architecture based on a less formal, more intimate concept.

Almost eighty years later, Louis XV ordered the building of its companion piece, the Petit Trianon (see left) for his favorite, Madame de Pompadour. Jacques Gabriel, a student of Hardouin-Mansart, gave it a Palladian structure. The same idealization of classical antiquity was evident in the Temple of Love of the Petit Trianon, (see below left), completed in 1775 by Richard Mique, the favorite architect of Marie-Antoinette.

Although the court moved to Versailles, Paris remained the center of architectural development. In the academies, a vehement debate about the theoretical basis for the French view of the state was taking place. In the *Querelle des anciens et des modernes* [Dispute between the Ancients and the Moderns] the relevance of the art of antiquity (more precisely, that of the age of Augustus) was questioned. In the academy of architecture, which, as the educational institution and highest authority in the field, controlled almost all French architecture, an embittered literary dispute had broken out between the president, François Blondel (1617–86) and Claude Perrault (1613–88). This organization was destined to be more than a mere official body; while for Blondel, in spite of a certain freedom of interpretation, the architecture of antiquity represented the basic prototype, Perrault, the natural scientist, pleaded for a more daring reinvention of the classical canon. Imitation of the ancients should not constitute an unwritten law. Charles Perrault, Claude's brother, addressed these issues in the publication *Parallèle des anciens et des modernes* (1668–97). The Paris Observatory (begun 1676) became the manifesto for Perrault's ideas, an unpretentious fortress of a building incorporating classical features, but predominantly a modern purpose-built structure. Blondel's statement is expressed in the Porte Saint-Denis (1671–73), a monumental triumphal arch designed on the basis of a highly refined system of proportions and said to combine the best structures of antiquity.

It was nevertheless Hardouin-Mansart, the architect of Versailles, who was to create the most mature structure of French Baroque. In 1676, Mansart had taken over the direction of the Invalides

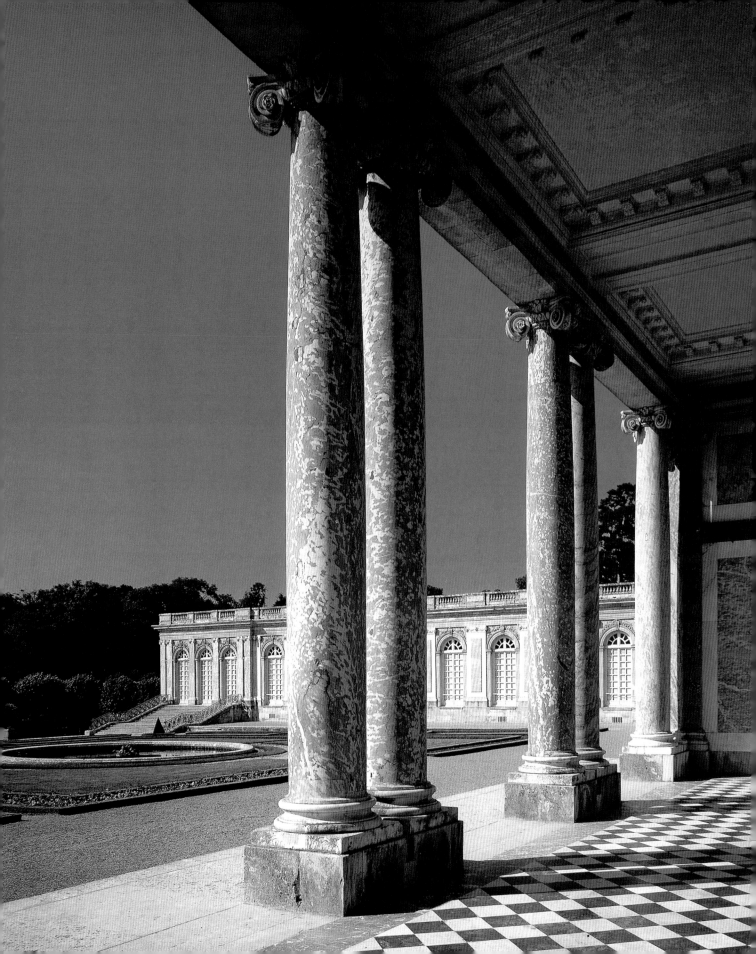

Libéral Bruant and Jules Hardouin-
Mansart
Paris, church of Les Invalides
1677–1706
Interior beneath the dome

François Mansart
Plans for a sepulchral chapel in Saint-
Denis for the Bourbons, 1665

OPPOSITE:
Libéral Bruant and Jules Hardouin-Mansart
Paris, church of Les Invalides
1677–1706

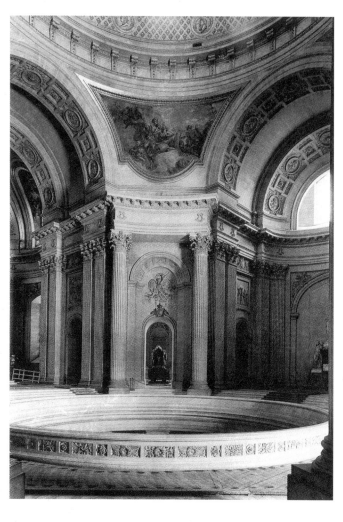

the church of Les Invalides is more closely allied with the Roman baroque. The dome, 105 meters high and opening into an oculus, also dominates the interior. The central space opens onto short transverse arms while over the corners of the square structure are areas with additional domes. As in the Val-de-Grâce, these are diagonally positioned in relation to the crossing. The giant Corinthian order stresses the prevailing vertical lines; here again, the main axes are defined by free-standing columns. The central structure of the complex and the decoration suggest that Louis XIV intended this as his mausoleum. Instead of Louis XIV, however, another monarch found his last resting place here. In 1861, Visconti had a crypt built in the center of the cathedral and Napoleon was buried there. This central structure is closely related to François Mansart's designs for the sepulchral chapels of the Bourbons in Saint-Denis (see below). Although that project was never realized, the ambitious design, with a double-shell dome, was much imitated, not least in Christopher Wren's St. Paul's cathedral in London.

Jules Hardouin-Mansart dominated the architecture of late seventeeth-century France. Master builder at Versailles, in 1691 he became *Inspecteur Général* and *Surintendent des Bâtiments du Roi* in 1699, controlling almost all building projects in the capital as well as in the provinces. In addition to his artistic talents, his success, which earned him a great deal of envy, was undoubtedly due to a well-organized workshop. This inevitably allowed him to undertake large-scale urban schemes. Thus he designed two new focal points for the city: the circular Place des Victoires (1682–87) and the Place Vendôme, at the edge of which a row of royal institutions was originally to be sited. Hardouin-Mansart's influence was transmitted through his students to subsequent generations, so that his style remained influential until well into the eighteenth century.

Regency and Rococo
The political confusion at the beginning of the eighteenth century and the declining power of the French crown had both direct and indirect consequences for architecture. The direct consequence was

hospital, begun six years previously by Libéral Bruant; this was a royal endowment to care for retired soldiers. With the church of Les Invalides, dedicated in 1706 (see above and right), the combination of the nave structure of the simple soldiers' church with a central building produced a magnificent synthesis of two architectural forms, the square substructure with a portal frontage and a dominant tambour and dome. Again, the free-standing double columns animate the structure from base to dome, endowing it with an unusual degree of plasticity. The eye is subtly drawn to the center, where, from the unobtrusive corners of the elevation as far as the portal, the width of the axes changes and the depth of the reliefs on the facade increases. By contrast to the theatrical facades of Lemercier's buildings or the dry classicism of Blondel, for example,

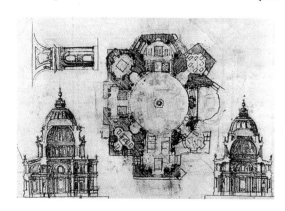

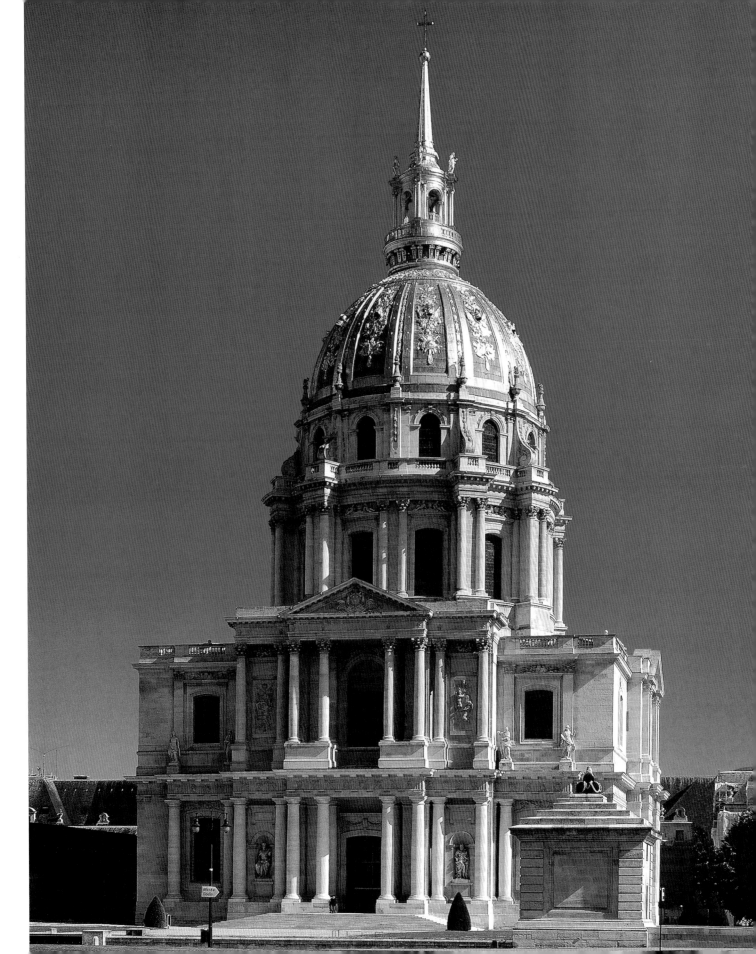

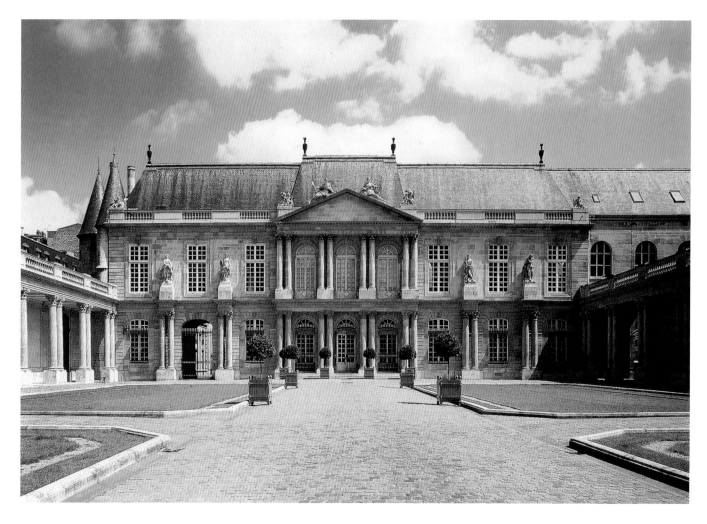

that many royal projects proceeded only slowly or were dropped completely. The indirect, and effectively more lasting, consequence was that the circle of those ready to commission work shifted from the court to the aristocracy and therefore to the provinces; thus the most important commissions were now those for more intimate manor houses rather than monumental palace complexes. During this period there was also a rejection of the bombastic facade structures of earlier years. Instead, the trend was for increasingly expensive, "refined" decoration for the interior, providing greater comfort and convenience in domestic architecture.

The aristocracy, which had been forced to follow the king when he moved to Versailles, now had nothing more pressing to do than to move back to Paris and set themselves up there again, especially now that the Sun King's rays were slowly fading. This meant that city palaces of quality and distinction appeared everywhere: three- or four-wing seventeenth-century structures, but with suites of rooms and decoration much more varied and sophisticated in design than those of their predecessors. Narrow or unsuitable plots of land encouraged the architects to create schemes appropriate to the ground plans. This is found in the Hôtel Amelot (1710), for which Germain Boffrand (1667–1754), a collaborator and student of Hardouin-Mansart, found a novel solution. The complex was laid

Pierre-Alexis Delamair
Hôtel de Soubise
Courtyard facade, begun 1704

OPPOSITE:
Germain Boffrand and Charles-Joseph Natoire
Hôtel de Soubise, Princesses' Hall, 1735

out around a deep oval courtyard, and the rooms surrounding the pointed curve were designed as pentagons.

The radical nature of this shift in focus from grandiose facades to the decoration of the interior was very clearly demonstrated by the Hôtel de Rohan Soubise (see above and right). While the garden frontage (Pierre Alexis Delamair, begun 1704) was still modeled on Versailles, new avenues were being explored in the composition of the living quarters. The son of the patron, the scion of two influential families, had persuaded his parents to fire Delamair and to use Germain Boffrand, who had proved to be a gifted draftsman and interior architect. Boffrand designed several apartments for the palace, interconnected with oval areas. Among the finest rooms of this period were the Princesses' Hall, which was decorated with stucco and paintings by the artist Charles-Joseph Natoire. It displays the new style in its most complete form: the gilded filigree stucco across the walls and ceiling suggests light branches entwined around a pergola, but is nevertheless technically very complete and con-

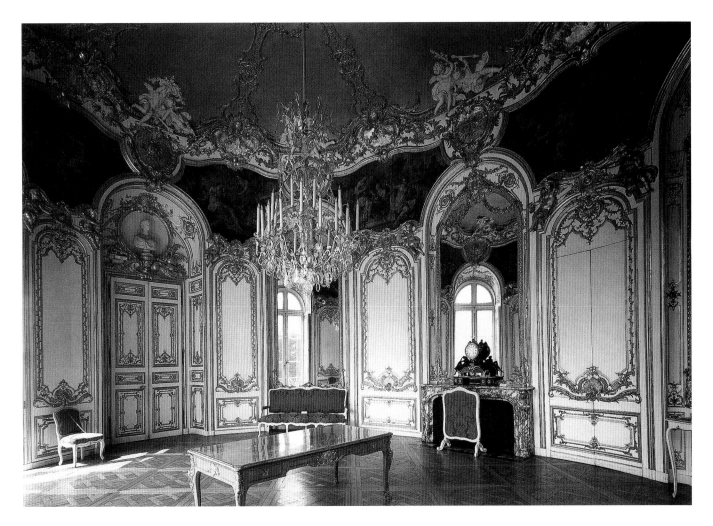

trolled. Round-arched panels alternate with high mirrors which give an impression of space and project multiple reflections of the delicate decoration. A striking feature here is the high division between wall and ceiling; the decoration spills over the main cornice. White, delicate gray-green, and turquoise give the salon its refined and serene atmosphere. On the surfaces between the windows and the ceiling, Natoire's paintings tell the story of Psyche, another indication that the sumptuousness of earlier decorative styles had given way to a more refined style of life and the need for sensitivity.

The new style, which was only later described by the term *rococo* (after *rocaille*, meaning shellwork), became established during the second decade of the eighteenth century. Its essential features, the division of the wall into *panneaux*, mirrors, and overdoors and separating the ceiling into *voute* and *plafond*, encapsulating devices such as the *cartouche* and *lambrequin*, and even the shellwork which was a distinguishing motif of the rococo, were well known throughout the baroque era and even to some extent during the renaissance and mannerist periods. At Versailles itself, early forms of the new style could be seen in some of the suites of rooms and in the decoration in the Grand Trianon. During the regency, when the Duke of Orléans held power, these motifs, still represented within symmetrical structures, began to push the architectural elements into the background,

and later assumed a luxuriant asymmetrical manner. During the 1730s surface decoration in most European centers had adopted to the style, even applying it to the outside of the structure.

In France, the *genre pittoresque*, as rococo had been known from around 1730, was subject to severe criticism. It came mainly from academic circles which still regarded classicism as the only appropriate style for public art. Voltaire's *Temple du Goût* [Temple of Taste] was the literary expression of a faction which saw the new style as the most absolute barbarism after the golden age of culture under Louis XIV. Nevertheless, in practice the two styles coexisted, or were complementary, since even decorative artists had mostly received academic training or had started off as collaborators of Hardouin-Mansart. The delightful results of this combination are demonstrated by the stables at Chantilly, built for the Bourbon dukes (see p. 146) by Jean Aubert (about 1680–1741), Hardouin-Mansart's favorite draftsman. This "palace for horses" which did indeed borrow decisive elements from Versailles, freely interpreted features of French baroque art and added decorative detail.

One of the most influential architects of the first half of the eighteenth century was Robert de Cotte (1656–1735), also a student and collaborator of Hardouin-Mansart. In 1689 he traveled to Italy with Jacques-Gabriel and in the same year he was appointed president of

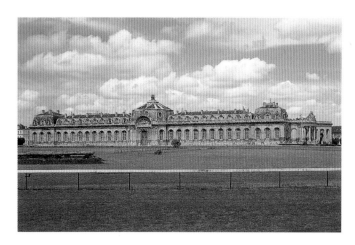

Jean Aubert
Chantilly, stables
1719–35

Robert de Cotte and Massol
Strasbourg, Palais de Rohan
1731–42

Germain Boffrand and Emmanuel Héré
de Corny
Nancy, Palais du Gouvernement, 1715
Detail of facade

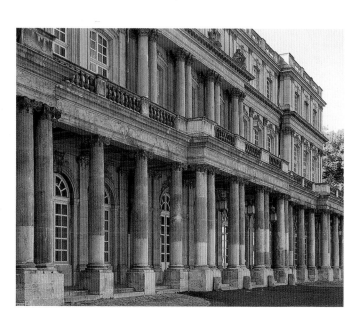

the French Academy of Architecture; after Mansart's death he was appointed *premier architecte du Roi*. Like his predecessor, he used these positions to direct public architectural policy. In Paris he built a large number of hôtels, and adapted François Mansart's Hôtel de la Vrillière to a more contemporary taste. As he ran a well-organized architectural office, he was always working on many building projects simultaneously; among them were the plans for the palaces of Würzburg, Brühl, and Schleissheim and the construction of the Palacio Real in Madrid and the Rivoli Château near Turin. He also supplied plans for public squares such as Place Bellecour in Lyons and Place Royale in Bordeaux, and palace complexes for well-to-do clergy, who exercised considerable influence on French architecture. Nevertheless, de Cotte should be regarded mainly as a planner and designer, since the realization of his proposals was mostly left to other master builders local to the sites. This was how the Strasbourg architect Massol realized his most magnificent project, the Palais de Rohan, seat of the prince-bishop of Strasbourg. The most significant feature of this building, designed as a monumental hôtel (see right), is the facade onto the Ilm, with seventeen window apertures and a dominant central pavilion with giant orders. However, the local architect remained true to the plans of his teacher, who had gone blind, and even added to the effects he had intended. The influence of Robert de Cotte on the attitude to French architecture throughout Europe can by no means be overestimated: his architectural office did more than any theory to disseminate late baroque court style.

The provinces were also increasingly claiming the right to develop independently. The most important example of this was Nancy, the seat of Stanislas Lescinski, the father-in-law of Louis XIV. With the help of his court architect Emmanuel Héré de Corny, a student of Boffrand, he built a most attractive residence which, in its varied forms, integrated with the fortified old town and with the planned new town. It is considered one of the major works of rococo urban planning (see right).

Classicism

In his *Treatise on Architecture* of 1753, the Jesuit abbot Marc-Antoine Laugier demanded a return to the architectural prototypes of antiquity. His rationalist theory was well received by the classical supporters who had never quite been defeated even during the regency and rococo periods. With the founding of a private academy

Emmanuel Héré de Corny
Nancy, Place Royale (now Place
Stanislas), 1752
Fountain and wrought iron railings by
Jean Lamour

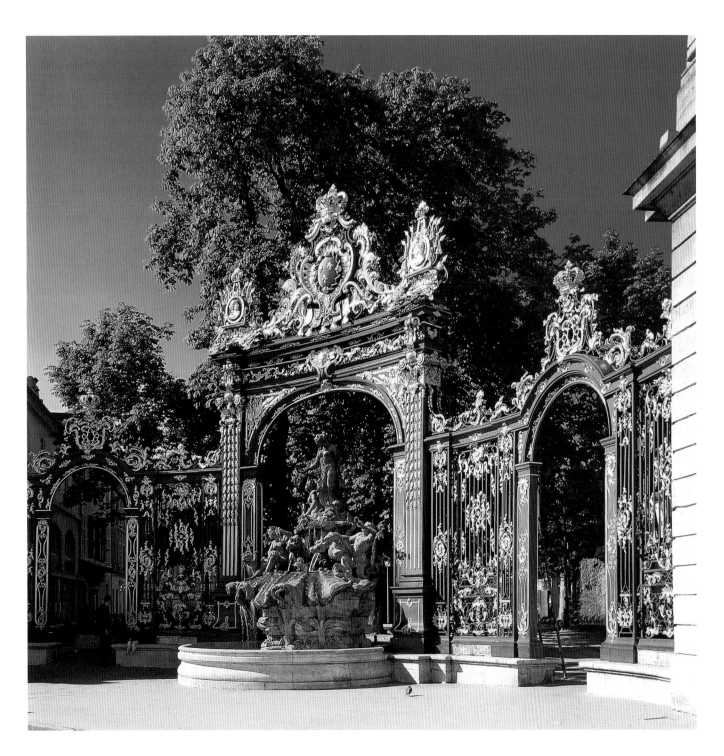

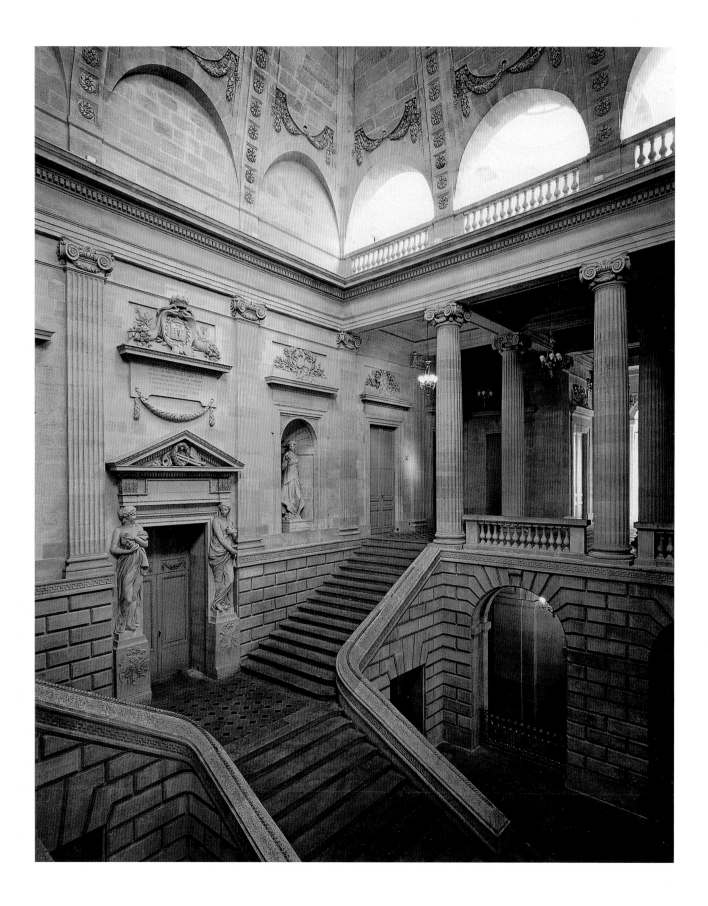

by Jacques-François Blondel (1705–54, not related to François Blondel) ten years earlier, an institution had been created to train the next generation of architects along the lines of the ideals of antiquity. As everywhere else in Europe, the architecture of classical Greece was increasingly influential, although attempts were being made to adapt the style to contemporary and local needs. One architect who was able to accommodate the most diverse requirements was Jacques-Gabriel (1698–1782), whose major achievement was the Petit Trianon mentioned earlier (see p. 140) in the park at Versailles. This square-shaped but decorative building has a Corinthian peristyle in front of the garden facade: the whole concept was closely related to the interpretation of the Palladian villa by the British neo-Palladians. The same sensitivity to nature and the surrounding open space were also characteristic of Place Louis XV, now Place de la Concorde, which was planned by Gabriel in close relation to the Tuileries, the course of the Seine, and the then wooded Champs Élysées.

Jacques Germain Soufflot represented an essentially more rigid perspective on the subject, given the commission to build the church of Sainte-Geneviève (begun in 1756) (see right). Soufflot dreamed of a synthesis of "Greek sublimity and the ethereal Gothic"; he constructed a building on a Greek cross, with portico extension. Its neo-classical interior evoked a sense of lightness in spite of its academic rigor. The crossing piers nevertheless had to be reinforced during construction in order to support the monumental dome. This church, which Laugier celebrated as "the first example of complete architecture," was altered in Republican times and converted for use as the Pantheon. Just as exemplary for the history of art in France after the mid-eighteenth century was the interior of Arras cathedral: here too, an attempt was made to unify ideal gothic structures with classical features. In this case, Pierre Contant d'Ivry (1698–1777) combined a basilica with a nave structure and a Corinthian colonnade, a motif which made the space unusually bright and diaphanous.

There was a more consistent tendency to use neo-classical styles in structures with a less traditional design. This was the case with the independent public theater, liberated from the court context. The building in Bordeaux by Victor Louis (1731–1800), a former Rome scholar from the Paris Academy, was considered by contemporaries to be the loveliest theater in the world. The exterior of this, the Grand Théâtre (see left), built between 1777 and 1780, with the broad sweep of the pillared front of house and its continuous entablature is charming; the magnificent staircase of the interior was the model for the Paris Opéra.

Although constructed under quite different political conditions, the planned workers' city inside the Arc-et-Senans saltworks (see p. 150) provided a foretaste of the architecture of the Revolution. Claude-Nicolas Ledoux (1736–1806), a theoretician with socio-political ambitions, planned an ideal city in an elliptical design combining a patrician scheme—the manager's house was centrally

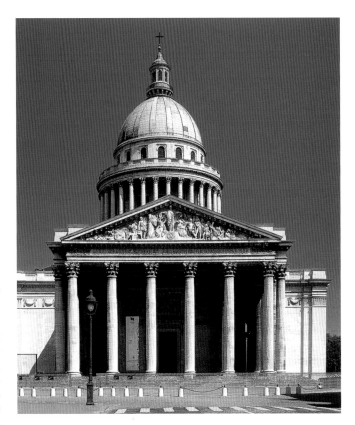

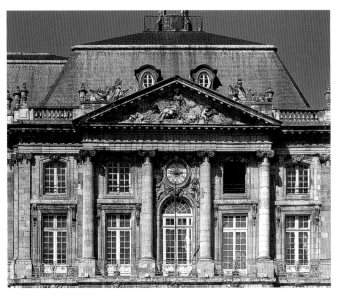

Claude Nicholas Ledoux
Arc-et-Senans, Saline, 1774
Administrative pavilion in the center of
the complex

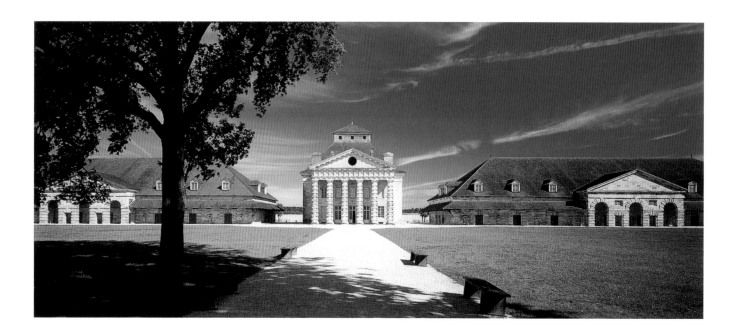

located—with a moralistic utopia. While the overall concept tended towards the traditional, Ledoux provided individual buildings with features that were extremely progressive. Brewing houses decorated with simulated stalactites, the workshop of a tire maker designed in the form of a disk with concentric rings, and undecorated cubic forms embodying abstract concepts were typical of his work here. Ledoux uninhibitedly deployed a full architectural repertoire drawn from history and fantasy, with a freedom which was unusual for its day. His aim, however, was not to revive past idioms but to find a more expressive architecture, an *architecture parlante*, the content

of which was to be revealed not in complex theories and accumulated knowledge, but through the emotions and, ultimately, through nature. Jean-Jacques Rousseau and his book *La Nouvelle Héloise* (1762) had introduced many of these ideas.

Even the court, finally weary of the rigid ceremonies, but at the same time blind to signs of the times, lost its dream of the earthly paradise. A country setting, life in harmony with nature—in a well-ordered formula of course—promised a release from the unpleasant reality of existence. An expression of this attitude can be seen in the buildings of Richard Mique (1728–94) for Marie-Antoinette in the park at Versailles. A peasant farm complete with mill and dairy (see right), complemented of course by a theater, library, and temple of love, makes up this fantasy scheme. Ideas which had been formulated in English landscape gardening were now taken up in French architecture. But the idyll was deceptive: these were the last building projects at Versailles before the Revolution. Only a few years later Mique and his patron ended up on the scaffold.

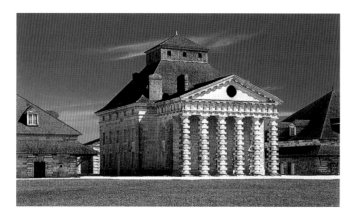

150

Richard Mique
Versailles, Trianon, Hameau de la Reine
Queen's House (above)
and mill (below), 1782–85

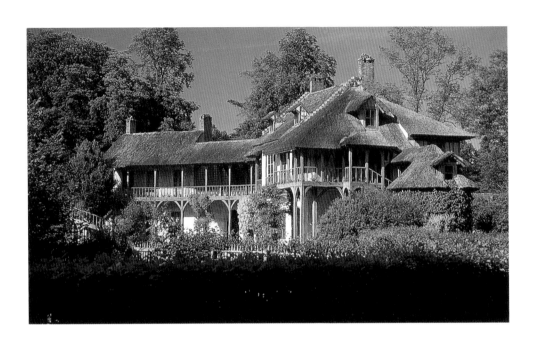

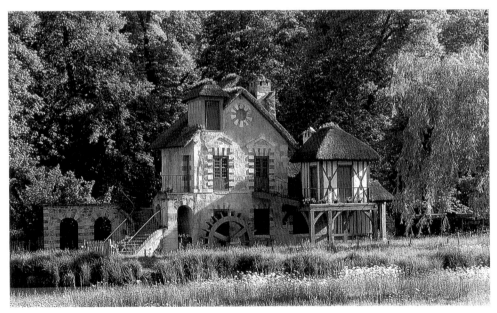

151

Baroque Landscape Architecture

Ehrenfried Kluckert

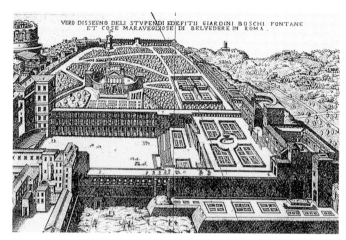

Rome, Vatican Belvedere, engraving by van Scheel, 1579

Two contradictory points of reference meet in the development of the baroque landscape in Europe: geometry and nature. The garden was viewed both as a geometric form and as a demarcated area for organic natural growth. These opposing concepts of landscape resulted in two types of garden, the architectural garden and the country garden. The first developed to its ultimate form in France, the second in England.

The English picturesque garden replaced the strict ornamental formula of the seventeenth-century garden and soon became popular throughout Europe. The charm of luxuriant nature was preferred to the refinement and artificiality of the French garden.

Nevertheless, an important element is being neglected in this analysis: nature, in geometric format or in a regulated system of "free" development, always provided the foundation for landscape architecture. In addition, the standard and popular geometry of French and Italian gardens were not necessarily in accord with the theories on garden arts which had been established there. Thus, for example, in the preface to his *Arcadia*, published in 1504, Jacopo Sannazaro preferred "the proud trees with their abundant foliage which quite naturally cover astonishing mountain peaks without any help from art; these are in general more pleasant to the eye than the scientifically developed, carefully reared ornamental plants in gardens."

Sannazo's *Arcadia* was widely distributed and eagerly read during the sixteenth century, and can be quoted as proof of the preference for country gardens long before the early concept of the English landscape garden. On the other hand, the French baroque garden was not the only representative of the rigidly formal garden. This may well apply to Le Nôtre's artistic plans for Versailles, but certainly not to the gardens of Louis XV dating from around 1750 which were intended as a pastoral revival for Versailles.

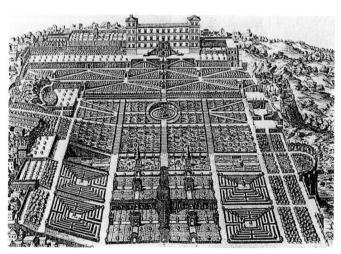

Tivoli, overview of the Villa d'Este, engraving by Étienne Dupérac, 1573

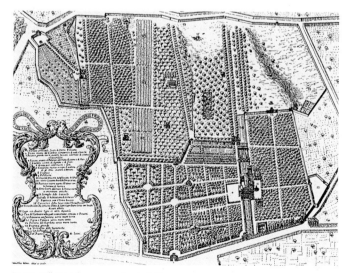

Rome, Villa Borghese, engraving by Selice

Italy

According to Petrarch, nature in the Italian renaissance garden was associated with the search for peace and relaxation. The garden was seen as an arcadian idyll contrasting with the bustle of the city, an artificially constructed refuge. According to Leon Battista Alberti, house and garden had to be an artistic unit based on the same geometric shapes. In his work *Hypnerotomachia Polyphili*, the Dominican friar Francesco Colonna introduced intricate bedding designs and fantastical topiary models which were later taken up in French baroque gardens and adapted in many different ways. The artistic layout of the parterre, symmetrical to the lines of the buildings, with knot gardens and patterns of beds and footpaths, influenced the design of the baroque garden throughout Europe.

The Belvedere garden in the Vatican (see above left) provided a model for garden planning in the seventeenth and eighteenth centuries, as the major architectural motifs were developed here: terraces, flights of steps, ramps, and exedra. Pope Julius II was concerned with harmonious communication between the villa, on a higher level, and the papal palace. Between these two lay more than three hundred meters of ground sloping upwards to the Belvedere.

A good example of the use of architecture in the creation of a garden during this period is seen in the Vatican Belvedere. Pirro Ligorio carried the concept over to another site: the year the Belvedere garden was completed, he was developing a plan for Cardinal Ippolito II d'Este's Tivoli garden (see center left). The cardinal's residence was situated on a hilltop, from which there was a magnificent view of the countryside. The garden complex stretched from a lower level right up to the palace, over five terraces connected with each other by a system of paths, steps and ramps. In *Cicerone*, Jacob Burckhardt enthused about the Villa d'Este as "the richest and eternally unreachable example of a masterpiece with all the advantages of nature."

It was not until the construction of the Villa Borghese in Rome (see below left) that a decisive blow was dealt to the primacy of architecture in the landscape. The master of the house, Cardinal Scipio Borghese, considered that ornamental shrubberies and regular planting of trees were more important than a system of alleyways, ramps, and steps designed in relation to the palace or casino. The extensive grounds were subdivided into several sections which were not laid out with any particular regard for symmetry. Close to the casino, the *giardini segreti* with flowers and useful plants were surrounded by oak, laurel, and cypress groves, and included game enclosures and bird traps.

France

The French were inspired by the new style of the Villa Borghese in Rome. Of course they also took note of the architectural garden scheme in the Vatican. Italian

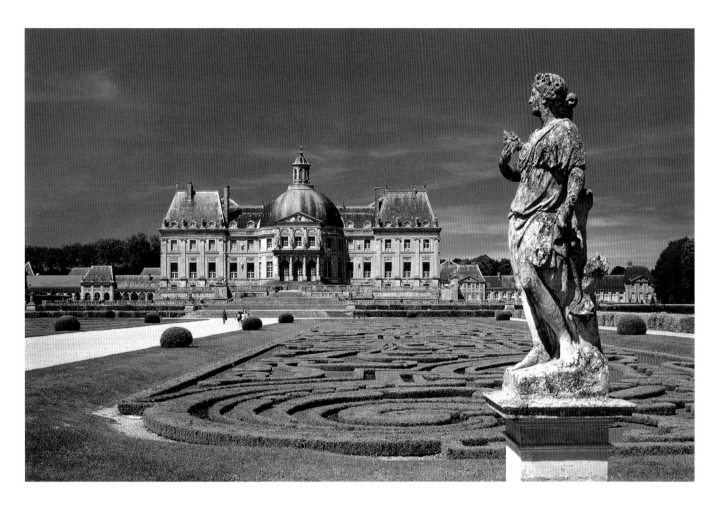

Vaux-le-Vicomte, palace and parterres
Original garden layout by André Le Nôtre

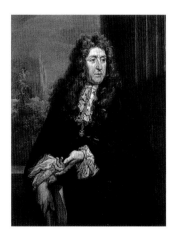

Carlo Maratta
Portrait of André Le Nôtre, 1678
Oil on canvas, 112 x 85 cm
Versailles, Musée du Château

influences on French landscape architecture extend back as far as the reign of Charles VIII who, at the end of the fifteenth century, invited Italian artists to Amboise. Contemporaries reported on "Italian miracles" which were now to flourish in France. However, the influence of Italian landscape architecture was particularly strong in the sixteenth century, during the reign of Henri IV and his wife, Marie de' Medici. The garden at Saint-Germain-en-Laye was extended under Henri IV, and was completed towards the end of the sixteenth century. It was considered to be the eighth wonder of the world. The concept used in the Belvedere, with terraces connected by ramps and steps, as well as the effective siting of summerhouses with exedra-like connecting links, was magnificently implemented here and enriched with many additional decorative features such as galleries, pavilions, grottos, and mechanical curiosities.

From 1612 onwards, after the death of her husband, Marie de' Medici ordered the building of the Jardins du Luxembourg in Paris. They were intended to provide her with a garden in the Italian style as a memento of her homeland and were designed in the form of the Florence Boboli gardens. The arrangement of the shrubberies, for which she had specially grown trees transplanted, the position of the large parterre, and the addition of the transverse pathway were all taken from the Florentine model.

During Louis XIV's reign, however, the French garden developed into an imposing work of art which outshone all other European types of garden. The incomparable gardens at Vaux-le-Vicomte, the Paris Tuileries, and, finally, the undisputed masterpiece at Versailles were—for the most part at least—the creation of the most gifted European landscape architect, André Le Nôtre (see left). It should be added that Versailles itself was the result of the combined talents of the king, his "gardener" Le Nôtre, and, later, the architect Jules Hardouin-Mansart.

André Le Nôtre, born in Paris in 1613, came from a family of gardeners. His father held the position of *jardinier en chef du roi* and worked for a long time in the Tuileries. His son André first won fame in 1656 with the gardens at Vaux-le-Vicomte (see above), which the owner, Nicolas Fouquet, was able to enjoy for only a short time. A few days after the sumptuous inaugural festivities of August 17, 1661, which included a concert, comedy, ballet, and final ostentatious fireworks display in the presence of the royal family, Fouquet was thrown into prison; he did not come out alive. The regent had rapidly reached the conclusion that the enormous expenditure required for the palace and gardens could only have been financed by digging deeply into the state coffers.

Le Nôtre had planned the garden around the central axis of the palace and along this had laid out the individual elements over several terraces built on land sloping down towards the valley. The garden scheme, intended to be seen in perspective from a distance, was accentuated by the double tapestry parterre. In the front sections, Le Nôtre installed two fountains, repeating the theme of the larger fountain at the other end, along the central axis of the terrace. This creative layout directs the view into the distance. The arrangement of the shrubberies on either side also provides a framework, preventing the eye from straying from the central line. Le Nôtre was experimenting at Vaux-le-Vicomte. He adopted devices such as canals, pools, steps, and ramps

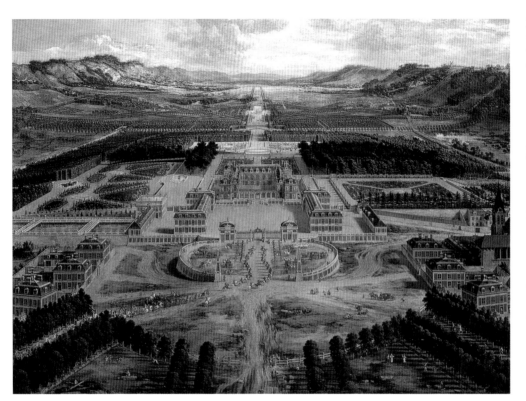

Pierre Patel
Bird's eye view of the palace and
grounds of Versailles, 1668
Oil on canvas, 115 x 161 cm
Versailles, Musée du Château

from various European gardens and found
new combinations of these features.

The young king was undoubtedly
inspired by these extensive and magnificent gardens. For himself, he had only a
modest hunting lodge in the Versailles
forest. In the same year as the festivities
which proved so fateful for Fouquet,
Louis XIV began converting the palace
and grounds at Versailles. Le Nôtre was
recommended as the landscape architect.
Thus the first ideas for the famous gardens of Versailles coincided with the festivities at Vaux-le-Vicomte.

Versailles
A painting by Pierre Patel (see above)
dating from 1668 shows a bird's-eye view
of the garden layout and the palace. In
front of and below the observer, a broad
landscape opens out, framed in the distance to the west in the bluish mist of a
chain of hills, and to the north and south
by softly swelling higher ground. Yet this
panorama does not capture the gardens
completely. It draws the eye over the hilly
landscape and comes to rest beyond the
horizon. The fundamental approach is
therefore based on three areas of the
painting which take the palace as their
point of reference: from this, the pathways radiate outwards like the rays of the
sun, repeatedly branching off to penetrate more sections of the grounds. The
first of the three areas is the present
"Petit Parc," a garden started under the
Sun King's father, Louis XIII, by Jacques
Boyceau. It appears on the so-called
"Plan du Bus" of 1661 (see right), the

oldest known plan of Versailles. The
ninety-three-hectare parterre with its
neighboring shrubberies was bounded by
the transverse path to Apollo's pool. The
second area is ten times larger: the
present "Grand Parc" which, on the painting, reaches the horizon, well beyond
the canal in fact. The third and largest
area, covering 6,500 hectares, is the
old "Grand Parc" and includes the
hunting ground containing villages such

as Saint-Cyr, Rennemoulin, and Marly. A
forty-three-kilometer long wall with
twenty-two gates formed the boundary.

Versailles was not intended solely as
a refuge and place of leisure and entertainment. It was also the incarnation of a
new concept of space, and signified a new
order for the state, and even the world.
The equation of the Sun King Louis XIV
and Apollo was not just playing with
mythology, it was a political ploy.

Apollo, the master of the Muses and the
creator of universal harmony, represented the political aims of Louis, who
saw himself as the new leader of a
Christian world which had to be pacified
and controlled. The grounds at Versailles
reflected the principles of order by which
the authority of state operated and
directed the civilized world.

The layout and iconographic content
of the "Petit Parc" provides a symbolic
representation of great importance for an
understanding of the royal concept of the
world order. Towards the end of his life,
Louis designed a circular walk leading to
the most important points of his park.
Walking through the Hall of Mirrors and
leaving the palace, the visitor will be on
the Parterre de l'Eau, with two pools
designed by Le Nôtre and built by Jules
Hardouin-Mansart between 1683 and
1685. From here the view is directed to
the central axis and sweeps across
Apollo's pool and the canal to the horizon. The world appears to be an ordered
space, a vision of sun and light, since the
water reflects the sky and the mirrors in
the Hall of Mirrors reflect this interplay
as though they were bringing the outside
space into the interior. Passing a bronze
copy of an antique statue of Apollo, and
the Orangery by Jules Hardouin-Mansart
(1684–86), the visitor reaches the maze
with its animal fountains and tortuous
paths, the imaginative creation of Le
Nôtre (1666). According to an old

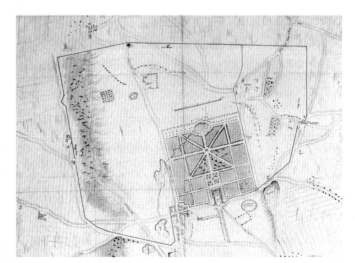

So-called "Plan de Bus," detail, around
1661–62
Paris, Bibliothèque Nationale

Israel Silvestre
Overall plan of Versailles, 1680
Paris, Bibliothèque Nationale

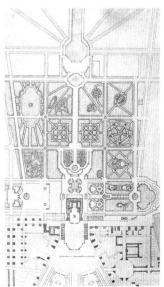

description, getting lost was a special delight. Following this route, the visitor to the park passes twenty-five points and experiences the world of the spirit and of nature through mythological scenes and panoramas and in the actual material surrounding of the vegetation.

The first major building phase here was between 1661 and 1680 (see left). During this time, fifteen shrubberies were planted between the pathways. Each shrubbery was a physical world in itself, architecturally designed and with a variety of stereometric formats. In the Bosquet des Sources, constructed in 1679 by Le Nôtre, the pathways snake between innumerable little brooks, seeming to mock the strict geometric order of the overall layout. For Le Nôtre, order became manifest in disorder. It was probably for this reason that, in 1684, Mansart was commissioned to "regulate" this shrubbery and give it a rotunda (see above right).

This was also the year the king appointed Mansart to the post of artistic director. The format of the gardens now assumed a clearly classical aspect. Architectural installations were much more rigorously separated from the "planted features." Mansart avoided stone retaining walls and used lawned embankments instead. Wherever sophisticated pathways were supposed to lead through woodland, Mansart put down open stretches of lawn.

Water supplies were a major problem. A horse-driven pumping station built in 1664 supplied water from the Clagny pond. Later, there was a connection to the Le Vau reservoir. But supplies soon proved inadequate for the enormous quantities of water required for the palace and its park. Further sources were put on stream and windmills were finally installed to drive the pumps in the 1680s. Water towers were built at the pools themselves, to supply not just the basins but the shrubberies too. Between 1678 and 1685 drainage ditches were laid and a large number of small pools and boggy areas in the Versailles area were drained. The water was channeled to various ponds and then fed to several reservoirs via the canals. Finally, the water reached the palace and the gardens. In Marly, which the king commissioned Hardouin-Mansart to convert into a hermitage between 1676 and 1686, a system known as the Marly machine was installed (see right), with 257 pumps which took water from the Seine and pumped it over the hill to Versailles via an aqueduct.

After the court had established itself in Versailles, the king began to look for retreats. He found them in the Trianon and, as mentioned above, in Marly. After the demolition of the village of Trianon he had the "Trianon de Porcelaine" built for his mistress by Le Vau in 1670; this was the first European summerhouse with Chinese decoration. With the emergence of a new favorite, this pavilion gave way to a new building, the "Trianon de Marbre," built by Mansart and named

Jules Hardouin-Mansart
Versailles, palace grounds
Colonnade, detail, 1684

after the reddish marble used in the pilasters. The parterre was laid out as "Flora's kingdom," a flower garden (see p. 156).

The garden at Marly, laid out between 1676 and 1686 after plans by Mansart, was reputed to be the king's finest garden. Mansart used Le Vau's pavilion at the Trianon as his model and constructed a large two-storey palace flanked by six smaller pavilions and organized around a central axis which was simultaneously used as the center line for the garden layout. Even more than in Versailles, the gardens of which were in a way reflected here in miniature, water played an important role in Marly. The whole complex was laid out on sloping ground so that there was always enough pressure for the fountains and other water devices.

After the death of Louis XIV in 1715, Louis XV took over the grounds, which had changed radically. The trees in the shrubberies had grown to the extent that top cutting was no longer possible. For Louis XV, the Trianon was the ideal place of retreat. Here he set up a menagerie of domesticated animals. The idealization of country life now crystallized into a pastoral vision that can be seen as a precursor to the romantic idealization of nature. The grounds were gradually transformed into a landscape garden. During these years, the king ordered Jacques-Gabriel to build the "Petit Trianon." When the king died in 1774, his successor Louis XVI gave this little palace to his wife Marie-Antoinette, who

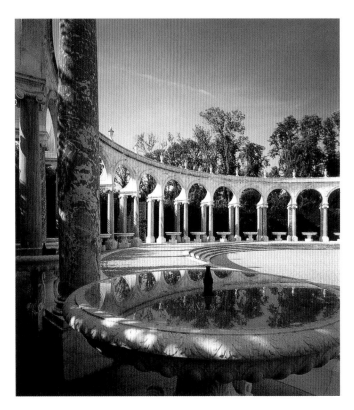

enjoyed the pleasures of country life here until the Revolution.

The English landscape garden was becoming increasingly popular by the end of the eighteenth century, and British gardeners became greatly sought after. In this period, the baroque garden was approaching the end of its dominance. Now elemental nature was in vogue, with contrived set pieces such as cliffs, waterfalls, and wildly overgrown river banks. The rustic view was completed by the construction of an artificial village with eleven thatched houses, the "hameau de Trianon" (see p. 151).

After the Revolution, the garden fell into disrepair. The Trianon complex was not restored until Napoleon's time.

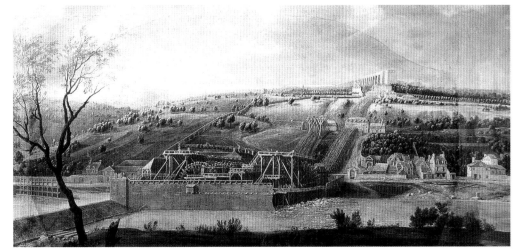

Pierre-Denis Martin, aqueduct and "machine de Marly," 1724, oil on canvas, 115 x 161 cm, Musée Promenade de Marly

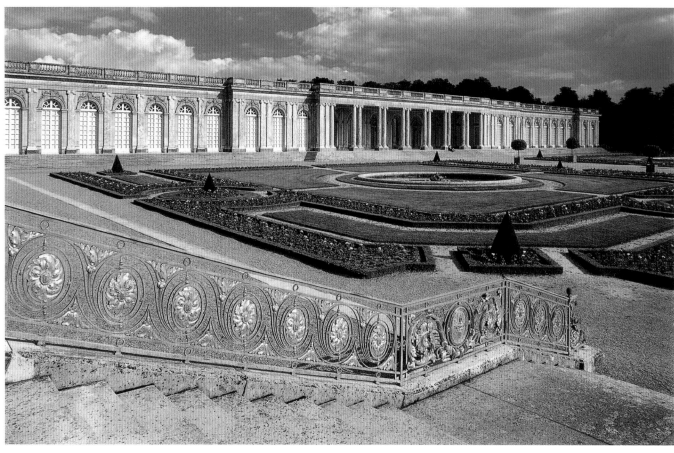

Jules Hardouin-Mansart, Versailles, Trianon de Marbre, with flower beds

Chronology of the Gardens at Versailles

1623 Construction of a hunting lodge
1638 First garden laid out by Boyceau
1661 Park and palace converted
1662 Parterre and shrubberies laid out by Le Nôtre
1666 First festive performance of Molière's *Tartuffe*. Maze constructed
1668 Extension of the palace by Le Vau and demolition of the Trianon village
1670 Construction of the Trianon de Porcelaine (demolished 1687)
1671 Bosquet du Théatre d'Eau laid out by Le Nôtre
1674 Court moves to Versailles
1675 Maze replaced by the Bosquet de la Reine.
1676 Marly Hermitage by Jules Hardouin-Mansart (till 1686). Installation of the Machine de Marly (water conduits and pumping station)
1678 Extensions to the palace under Hardouin-Mansart. 36,000 workers employed in the palace and grounds
1679 Installation of the Pièce d'Eau des Suisses

1680 Completion of the Grand Canal (begun 1667)
1681 Bosquet des Rocailles and amphitheater
1682 Official seat of the French court
1683 Parterre d'eau by Hardouin-Mansart
1684 Construction of the Orangery by Hardouin-Mansart and the second tranche of shrubberies
1685 Construction of the colonnade by Hardouin-Mansart and the aqueducts from Marly to Versailles
1687 Construction of the Trianon de Marbre (later known as the "Grand Trianon")
1699 Construction of the court chapel from plans by Hardouin-Mansart
1700 Death of André Le Nôtre
1708 Death of Hardouin-Mansart
1715 Death of Louis XIV
1722 Louis XV takes over the gardens
1750 Menagerie for domestic animals at Le Trianon
1761 Installation of a show and nursery garden at Le Trianon
1762 Construction of the Petit Trianon by Jacques-Gabriel along the main garden axis, and demolition of the kitchen garden
1774 Clearance of the shrubberies and replanting (till 1776)

1775 Construction of the theater in the Jardin Français
1779 Botanical gardens with pastoral overtones laid out in imitation of an English landscape garden
1783 Construction of the Hameau de Trianon (rustic village complex)
1789 Revolution: all work stops
1793 Execution of Louis XVI; the grounds are divided up and partially devastated
1795 Foundation of the École Centrale; Versailles is opened to the public
1798 Erection of the tree of liberty
1805 Emperor Napoleon I turns the Trianon into his private residence. Restoration of the "Petit Trianon" and the "hamlet"
1860 Clearance of the shrubberies planted under Louis XVI and replanting
1870 Grounds are devastated by Prussian troops
1883 Replanting of the shrubberies
1889 Centenary of the 1789 opening of the Estates General

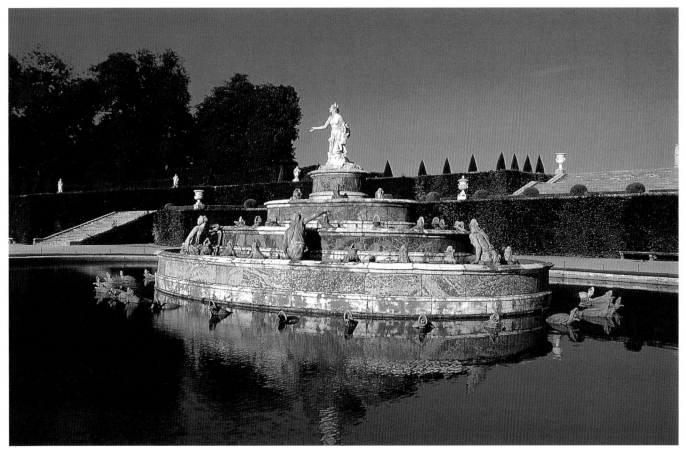

André Le Nôtre and Jules Hardouin-Mansart, Versailles, palace grounds, Latona fountain, 1668–86

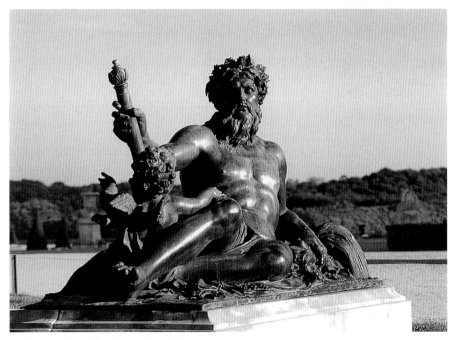

Jean-Baptiste Tuby, "The Rhone," about 1685

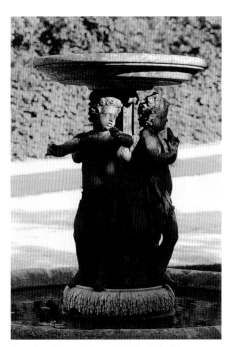

Lerambert (?), small fountain in the Allée d'Eau

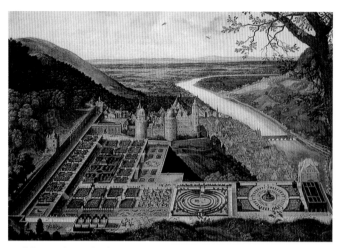

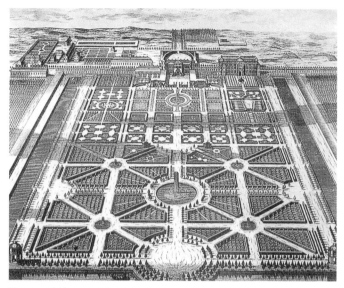

Heidelberg, palace with Salomon de Caus' Hortus Palatinus
Painting by Fouquières, Heidelberg, Kurpfälzisches Museum

Hannover, Schloss Herrenhausen, gardens,
Engraving by Sassen, 1720

Baroque Gardens in Germany

The Hortus Palatinus next to Heidelberg Castle (see above) set the tone for the development of the baroque garden in Germany. The Prince Elector Frederick V of the Palatinate hired the French architect Salomon de Caus for this project. Salomon was personally familiar with the famous gardens of Italy, France, the Low Countries, and England and in 1614 he was able to start on preliminary plans. Hardly anything now remains of the garden itself, but engravings by the architect and the painting by Fouquières give some impression of its size and the layout of the beds. The Italian knot garden with its spiral patterns provided the prototype for the scheme here. Steps, ramps, and exedra were not used because of the problems presented by the sloping grounds. Salomon concentrated his attention on ornamenting the beds in the three parterres. He also planted a shrubbery with shady pergolas next to a water parterre with sophisticated circular paths.

The Heidelberg Hortus Palatinus is regarded as a transitional garden which lies stylistically between those of the Renaissance and the baroque and should be viewed alongside the royal pleasure gardens of Württemberg and Hesse such as the duke's garden in Stuttgart or the royal Brunswick gardens in Hesse.

Towards the end of the seventeenth century, the Grosser Garten of Herrenhausen near Hannover (see right) was created in Lower Saxony. The Princess Elector Sophie of Hannover commissioned her French landscape architect, Martin Charbonnier, with the planning and realization of the scheme. There are obvious

parallels here with French garden design of the period. The central axis of the garden is set on the same line as that of the palace and terminates in a round basin. The layout of the shrubberies and parterres is indebted to the French baroque garden, as are the *giardini segreti* to the side of the palace building. But there are other features which appear to be unrelated to French sources. Shortly before planning was started in 1696, Charbonnier traveled to Holland to explore Niewburg, Honslaerdyck, and Het Loo. His inspiration for the canal sur-

rounding the garden area may possibly have been inspired by Dutch models of this kind. The orchard, with its triangles enclosed by beech hedges, also suggests Dutch sources. However, Charbonnier understood how to mold these features into a unified whole and thus created a style of garden which was to become characteristic of the north German plain.

The garden at Schloss Salzdahlum, residence of Duke Anton Ulrich of Brunswick-Wolfenbüttel, was created at almost the same time as Herrenhausen.

In 1697, the Princess Elector and later Queen Sophie Charlotte, daughter of Sophie of Hannover, had the gardens of Berlin's Schloss Charlottenburg laid out. The plans were drawn up by Siméon Godeau, a student of the famous Le Nôtre.

Half a century later, not far from Charlottenburg, a completely different type of garden was introduced. This was the terraced garden of Sanssouci in Potsdam. The work was completed between 1744 and 1764 (see p. 200).

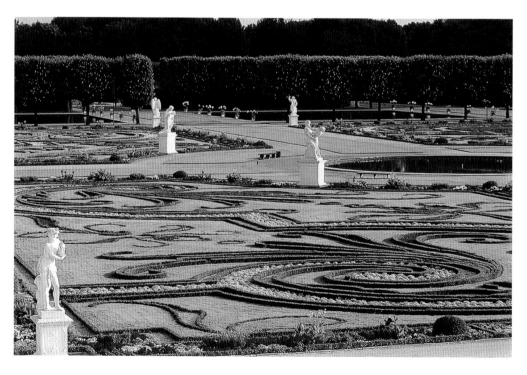

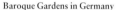

Hannover, Schloss Herrenhausen, gardens

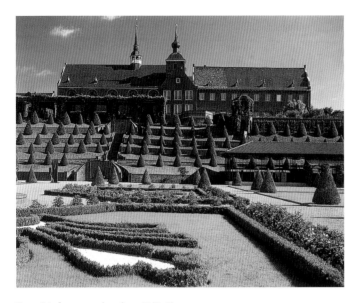

Kamp Lintfort terraced gardens, 1740–50

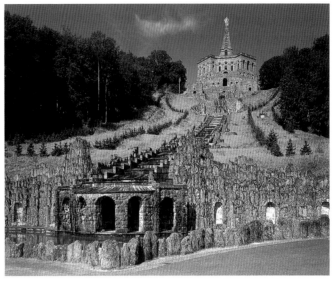

Kassel, Wilhelmshöhe, the setting for the Karlsberg, 1701–11

Frederick the Great provided drawings which he expected his master builder, Georg Wenzeslaus von Knobelsdorf, to follow to the last detail. The palace, the exedra-shaped terraces, the parterre, and the lateral ramps are derived directly from renaissance and baroque models.

Interestingly, at about the same time (1740–50) another terrace garden was built at the former Cistercian monastery in Kamp, on the Lower Rhine (see above). The similarities between these schemes are surprising, although no

direct connection between the two has been established. At least it can be seen that they both drew on similar antique sources in the exedra and theaters of Rome. But pragmatism may also have played a role. Handbooks on landscape architecture describe how concave terraces catch the sun and promote the distribution of heat.

Schloss Augustusburg at Brühl was the favorite residence of the archbishop of Cologne and Prince Elector Clemens August of Bavaria. Dominique Girard

took over the garden layout in 1728 (see below) and based his work on the canal system at Nymphenburg. A magnificent park was created, surrounded by water and dominated by a basin laid on the central axis in imitation of Versailles. Diagonal pathways connected the main parterre with the woodland.

A number of other famous German baroque gardens should be noted here, for example, the Karlsberg grounds near Kassel (see above) (which the English travel writer Sacheverell considered to be

more impressive than Tivoli or even Versailles), the gardens at Weikersheim (1705–25) with their unique figures, the Nymphenburg gardens (1715–20) with grounds rivaling Versailles in scale, and the gardens of Lothar Franz von Schönborn in Gaibach, Seehof, Pommersfelden, and Favorite in Mainz.

In Germany, the era of baroque garden architecture came to an end with Schwetzingen. Between 1753 and 1758, the Prince Elector Carl Theodor, whose plans for a hunting and summer palace were never realized, proceeded with the layout of the gardens instead. The architect Nicholas de Pigage, who worked a great deal in southwestern Germany, and the Palatinate court gardener Johann Ludwig Petri created a garden which was unique in its time. Artificial Roman ruins, a chinoiserie bridge, a mosque and the contrived perspectives that provided a painterly vision of nature transformed the grounds into an idyllic landscape that reflected the prevailing style of the English landscape garden. It was completed by Friedrich Ludwig Sckell, who extended the grounds in the 1770s.

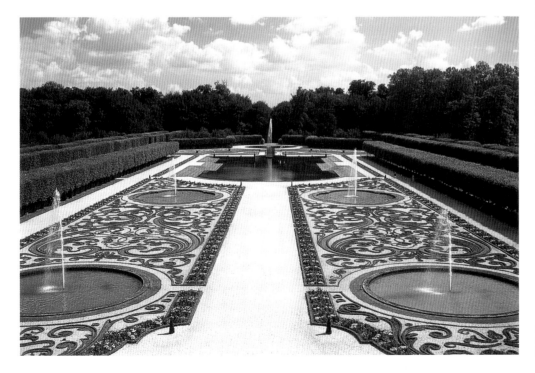

Dominique Girard
Augustusburg, Brühl
Gardens, 1728

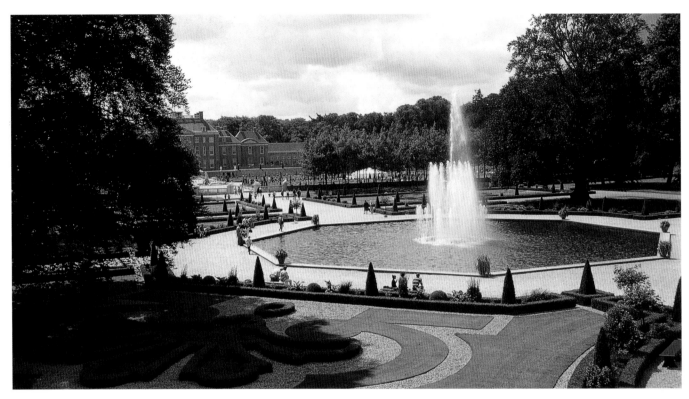

Daniel Marot
Het Loo, garden, 1685, restored 1978

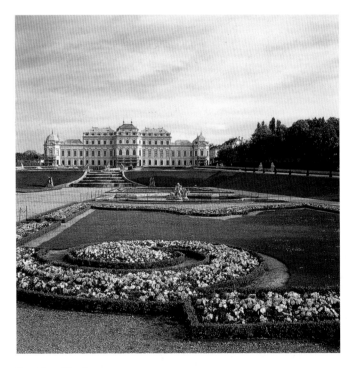

Dominique Girard
Vienna, Belvedere garden, 1717

The Belvedere Garden in Vienna

The layout of the Belvedere garden in Vienna was established in response to the specific contours of the landscape and the position of the two palaces for the victorious Field Marshal Prince Eugene. Between the imposing structure of the Upper Belvedere and the more intimately scaled Lower Belvedere lay a splendid park which can be seen in its original form in an engraving by Salomon Kleiner (see left and p. 254). In 1717, Prince Eugene obtained the services of the royal Bavarian architect Dominique Girard, who had previously worked at Nymphenburg and in Schleissheim.

A slope, deployed here as the transverse axis with steps and a central waterfall, divided the garden into two terraces, thus resolving the problem of the discrepancy in height between the two palaces. A topiary garden was established on the lower terrace. The upper terrace was planted with flower beds and water devices.

The similarities with Versailles are obvious in this garden scheme, but it is certainly not an imitation. The layout of the shrubberies with their diagonal footpaths is described in a garden treatise by Dezallier d'Argenvilles which appeared in 1709 and became the most important source book for garden architecture during the eighteenth century.

Het Loo

The Dutch garden, which reached the heights of creativity from about 1670, also drew extensively on French sources and had a particularly important impact on German gardens. After the north had been freed from Spanish rule, patrician rule came to dominate Dutch cities. It was felt that the court structures should not be relinquished, but they should be symbolically transformed to suit the new political environment.

In 1685, the Dutch governor, later William III of England, used plans by Daniel Marot for a garden at his palace Het Loo (see above). Contemporary etchings and the descriptions of the royal physician Walter Harris provide a very accurate picture of the garden, which was neglected in about 1800 and was not restored until 1978.

The essential concept behind the Het Loo gardens was based on Versailles. This particularly applied to the upper garden, which has a system of paths emanating outwards from the central axis and branching off into the distance. The lower garden, however, dominated by the palace, was more typically Dutch in style. It was divided into individual sections, each contrasting with the next. The tree-lined *allées* and hedges so characteristic of the Dutch landscape could be found throughout the complex.

La Granja in Spain and Caserta in Italy

After the War of the Spanish Succession, Philip V, a grandson of Louis XIV, became king of Spain and Naples. The gardens of La Granja in Spain and Caserta in Italy are therefore closely related in style. At the beginning of the eighteenth century, Philip, who grew up at the court of Versailles, ordered La Granja to be laid out at a height of over one thousand meters in the mountains of San Ildefonso near Segovia. Inevitably, the scheme was based on Versailles. Because of the topography, however, the design could not be as spacious or extensive as its prototype. On the other hand, water was in abundant supply for the countless fountains and water devices (see right and p. 106).

The garden at La Granja is bordered by a mountain range. A similar situation was chosen for the Italian garden at Caserta. Philip's son and successor, the Bourbon king Charles III, bought the village of Caserta in 1734 and had a magnificent palace and park built there to remind him of his home in Spain. The garden rises away from the palace and the view is closed off by a mountain chain.

The essential feature of the view at Versailles lies in its symbolic representation of the world order. In La Granja and Caserta this concept turns in on itself, creating a restricted panorama of a closed space.

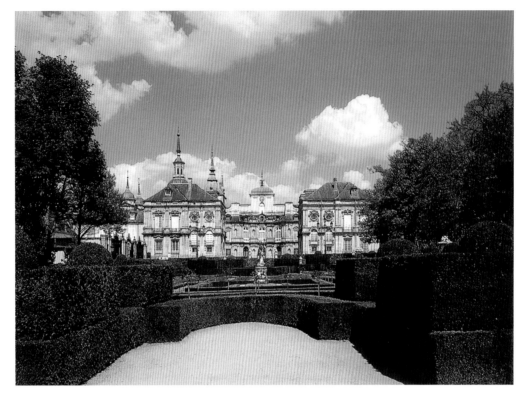

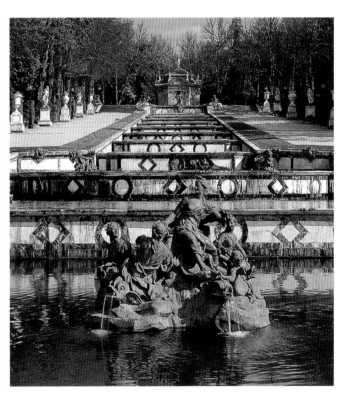

Caserta, near Naples
Overview of palace and garden
Engraving, end of the 18th century

La Granja de San Ildefonso
Gardens (above and below right)

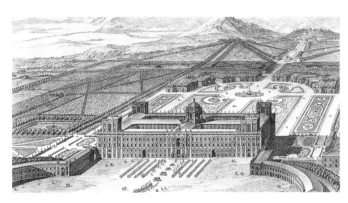

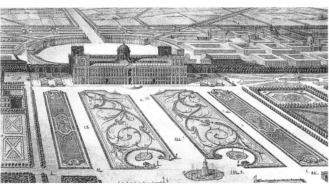

161

Barbara Borngässer

Baroque Architecture in England

Historical Background

In England, the baroque age began with the "discovery" of the Renaissance. Inigo Jones (1573–1652), essentially a maker of images, artist, and set designer, traveled to Venice, Vicenza, and Rome in 1613–14, returning with an enthusiastic admiration for the architecture of Andrea Palladio. Jones was fascinated by the unadorned harmony of the buildings inspired by antiquity; at the same time, the studies of the master builder of Vicenza inspired him to carry out his own research into the ancients. His newly awoken passion for classical architecture, which he shared with the art collector Lord Arundel, not only made its mark on his own work but became the defining style of British architecture until the late eighteenth century.

The era that we will examine here came to an end with the romantic movement and the gothic revival. It can be broadly divided into three phases: the Palladian, which influenced roughly the first two-thirds of the century and was primarily promoted by Inigo Jones, the "true" baroque around the time of Christopher Wren, who came into his own after the Great Fire of London in 1666, and the neo-Palladianism of the early eighteenth century, which was also closely associated with a single individual, in this case the patron of the arts and amateur architect, Lord Burlington. During the second half of the century, a more systematic archeological study of the antique past influenced the emergence of a neo-classical aesthetic that reflected a broader understanding of the architecture of antiquity. The rococo in England can be seen as a frivolous concomitant to the prevailing classical taste and an admiration for the middle ages. Gothic form never quite disappeared. Even before the romantic movement revived the architectural language of the medieval past, Horace Walpole had built a "Gothick" country house at Strawberry Hill.

The English landscape garden provided an ideal setting for experiments with historical styles: the informal environment made it possible to build structures which were unconventional and even exotic for the eighteenth century. This was the context in which the conditions were established for the fashion for the historical and eclectic styles of the nineteenth century.

English architecture during this period emerged independently of contemporary trends on the continent in several essential respects. The era outlined here covers the reign of the house of Stuart, including the Protectorate under Oliver and Richard Cromwell, the installation of the house of Hanover, and Britain's rise to world power. The conflict between Crown and Parliament, which sought to restrict the powers of the monarchy, reached its height with the declaration of the Commonwealth. The victors in the struggle were undoubtedly the gentry and the middle-class merchants who began to control considerable financial assets and who came to wield serious political influence during the eighteenth century. The source of architectural commissions was therefore quite different from that prevailing in the France of Louis XIV, for example, or the papal

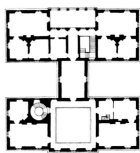

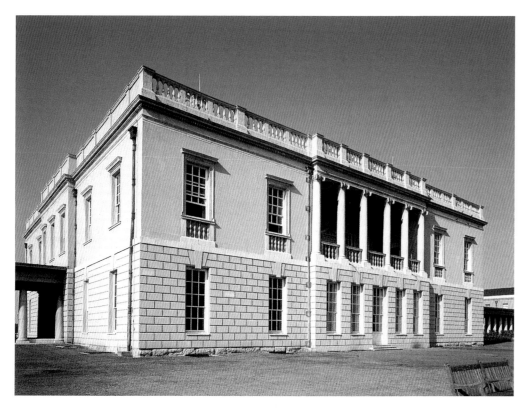

court in Rome, where art became an instrument of government. A second factor that was to be at least as decisive for the singularity of English baroque architecture was the separation from Rome which Henry VIII had effected in 1533–34—less for religious considerations than to enable him to divorce his wife, Catherine of Aragon. This meant that the English church was declared the national church and the monasteries were dissolved in 1536–39 and their lands and treasures handed over to the crown and the aristocracy. Subsequently, many attempts to reverse the break with the Catholic church failed; the Protestant religion remained a characteristic element of English society, although the following centuries were witness to serious conflicts between the absolutist inclinations of the court and its established church on the one hand and the Puritan middle classes on the other. On this basis, it is not surprising that the church was not particularly active as a patron of building: the luxuriant display of splendor which became a feature of the Counter-Reformation on the Continent was out of the question here.

Art therefore was directed to different purposes and other meanings in England from those which molded it in the absolutist Catholic monarchies of the continent. This same architecture was now introduced in the service of a self-confident upper class whose ideals were rather the attainment of a humanist vision than the imitation of courtly style.

Inigo Jones (1573–1652)

The artist who was to lead English architecture away from what might be seen as its impasse came late to his vocation. Jones, a tailor's son, was trained as an artist, costume designer, and set designer and initially worked at the court of Christian IV of Denmark. From 1605, he worked for James I, who appointed him court architect in 1615 in spite of his lack of practical experience. He had already traveled to Paris and Venice, but it was not until his trip of 1613–14 that he developed his characteristic architectural style and created an impetus for change in English architecture.

In the company of the Earl of Arundel, a young aristocrat with whom he was friendly, Jones visited Italy, where they toured Emilia, the Veneto, and, later, Florence, Rome, and Naples. In the Eternal City, Jones and Arundel visited the excavations and acquired sculpture which they sent to England. This was particularly significant since Rome was viewed by English Protestants as a hive of

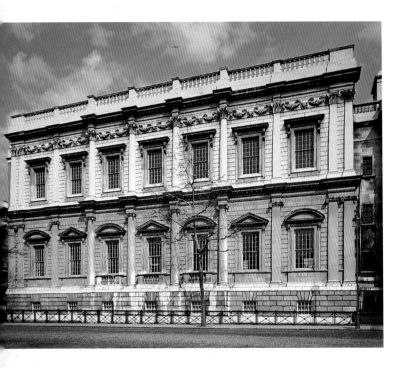

papal intrigues and was therefore officially avoided. Jones spent several more weeks in Vicenza and Venice to further his architectural studies and to copy Palladio's *Quattri libri dell'architectura* (first unabridged publication in 1570).

The immediate response to his experiences abroad was the Queen's House, the queen's palace at Greenwich, for which the foundation stone was laid in 1616 (see p. 163). Although the building was not completed until 1635, after several alterations relating to its setting in the grounds, it suggested an abrupt change of direction in English architecture and a radical negation of the late medieval, mannerist idiom. The Queen's House consists of two rectangular elevations connected by a bridge. Above the rusticated lower storey is a piano nobile which opens into a broad pillared loggia on the garden side. In the northern section, a square hall occupying two floors is concealed behind a modest pavilion. The simplicity of the cubic complex is ennobled by the elegant rows of windows and, above all, by the Ionic orders of the upper floor. It is not hard to find the prototypes for the palace, which is in form a *villa suburbana*, an aristocratic country house: the Medici villa by Giuliano da Sangallo in Poggio a Caiano (1480–85) has a similar block construction opening onto the park via a pillared loggia, and Scamozzi's villas, which Jones visited in Venice, use the same variations for the garden facade. Differences lie mainly in the proportions of the features used. The impression that this house influenced by

the Italian Renaissance made in England should not be underestimated. The Queen's House was described by an observer as "some curious devise," yet its classical architecture structured on primary forms anticipated future developments.

By 1619, Inigo Jones had received his greatest commission, the new Banqueting House in Whitehall, a building for court festivities originally intended as part of a fairly large palace complex (see left). Within only three months, during which Jones experimented with solutions derived from antiquity and the work of Palladio, he created a monumental building comprising a creative mixture of Venetian and Vicenza devices which became characteristic of the English Palladian style. Significantly, the emphasis given to the facade by the use of a pediment in the initial designs was later abandoned in favor of a continuous entablature which accentuated the horizontal lines. The great banqueting room, for which Peter Paul Rubens painted the ceiling frescos, is as wide as an ancient basilica; originally there was even an apse intended as a throne room. The vertical plane is dominated by Ionic half-columns in the lower storey and composite pilasters in the upper storey, a pattern which also appears on the external walls.

The Queen's Chapel (1623–27), the first church designed by Inigo Jones, represents an attempt to find Palladian solutions for religious architecture also. This court chapel, integrated into St. James's Palace, has no side aisles: the box-shaped space has a coffered ceiling and the narrow ends have windows divided into three sections which repeat the Venetian motif combining architrave and arch. A triangular pediment derived from antique models adds emphasis to the entrance wall.

The importance of Inigo Jones's urban development plans should also be considered here. His design for Covent Garden created the first monumental city square with uniform perimeter buildings in the country. Here too Jones relied on classical solutions and their interpretations by the master builders of the Renaissance and the baroque: he must have known the Place des Vosges in Paris, built twenty-five years earlier. The use of this type of layout for a church, as seen in St. Paul's in Covent Garden (completed in 1631, rebuilt after a fire in 1795), was, however, new. Jones constructed the facade strictly according to Vitruvius' instructions for a temple front, with Tuscan orders, a variation of the Doric where the massive columns have no fluting but are provided with a base. Why Jones selected this, the "lowest" order of architecture, more suited to a country environment, for the first church built in England since the Reformation, has never been explained. Did he want to give expression to the Protestant vernacular, or should this be seen as a homage to the Tuscan home of the Medici, with whom Charles I was linked through his wife Henrietta Maria?

A much more monumental project undertaken by Inigo Jones for Charles I fell foul of the confusion caused by the civil war. This was Whitehall Palace, an enormous palace complex which was docu-

Inigo Jones and Isaac de Caus (?)
Wilton House (Wiltshire)
Begun in 1632, renovated in 1647 after a fire
External view and view of the interior of the
"Double Cube"

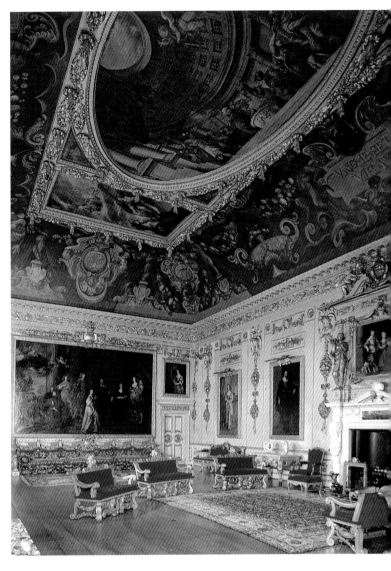

mented through the different stages of planning dating from between 1638 and 1648. The most important drawings, published by Colen Campbell and William Kent in the early eighteenth century, were to have a vital impact on the emerging neo-classical style; they illustrate a rectangle with extended apartments and several internal courtyards. The core of the complex centered on two sequential courtyards, framed with double-storey columns, the first round, the second square. The court chapel and great hall—modeled on the Constantinian basilica—completed the palace, which was designed, like El Escorial, as an architectural allegory of absolutist power. The elevation shows an extended facade featuring giant orders and pavilions, the center of which is emphasized by two tower structures with domes. As in Covent Garden, the boundaries of Inigo Jones' artistic abilities are clearly defined: buildings of harmonious proportions which seemed charming on a small scale became wearisome on a more monumental level as a great variety of elements was added. After the Puritan revolution of 1642, Inigo Jones's career came to an abrupt end, although, in addition to his work as court architect, he also worked sporadically for members of parliament.

There were very few architects, almost exclusively his collaborators and students, who escaped from the shadow of the great innovator. Among these were Isaac de Caus, who, according to recent findings, designed Wilton House (see below; Wiltshire, begun 1632, burned down 1647, renovated). The harmoniously proportioned facade is broad and flanked by high corner pavilions, with a window decorated in Venetian style accentuating the central section (see below). The interior is dominated by a cube and a double cube, two box-shaped reception rooms furnished with the utmost elegance and for which Van Dyck painted portraits of the masters of the house, the family of the Earl of Pembroke. John Webb (1611–72), student

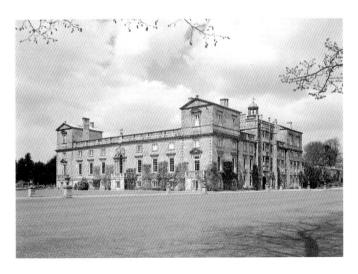

and nephew by marriage of Inigo Jones, designed a large number of country houses in a style very close to that of his master; his most important work was the King Charles Block at Greenwich Hospital (1662–69). Sir Roger Pratt (1620–84), who spent the Civil War years traveling in Italy, France, and the Netherlands, was employed by the gentry after his return in 1649, but built only a few villas. These were, however, significant for the history of architecture. Unfortunately none remains in its original condition. The largest, Clarendon House on Piccadilly (1664–67), was the first classical baroque structure in the French mode in Britain and was much imitated. At the same time, remnants of the late gothic and renaissance styles, particularly those based on Dutch prototypes, were present in England until the middle of the seventeenth century.

Sir Christopher Wren (1632–1723)

It was under Sir Christopher Wren that classicism in the Roman style took hold in England. What is more, this would have been

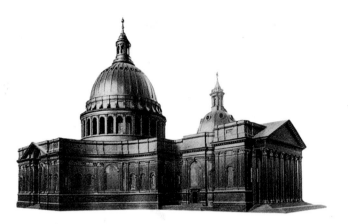

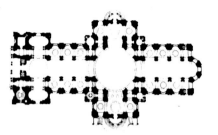

Sir Christopher Wren
London, St. Paul's cathedral
Large-scale model of 1673 and ground
plan, as executed

OPPOSITE:
Sir Christopher Wren
London, St. Paul's cathedral
1675–1711, west facade

almost unthinkable if the political situation had not swung in favor of Catholicism. After the interregnum of the Commonwealth and the Protectorate under the two Cromwells, the restoration of Charles II meant that the crown supported Rome, setting the spiritual climate for several architecturally significant years to come. Fate also played its part: in 1666 the Great Fire destroyed London and devastated 13,000 houses, St. Paul's cathedral, and eighty-seven city churches. Charles II commissioned Christopher Wren and his older colleagues Roger Pratt and Hugh May to submit proposals for the reconstruction and the design of a modern city. The project miscarried, as Wren's proposals proved to be unrealizable. But the new building for St. Paul's and fifty-one further churches were essentially his work. The varied nature of these buildings, their technical accomplishment, and the organizational capabilities behind a reconstruction program on this scale won Wren a great deal of respect and ensured his reputation as one of the greatest English architects.

Sir Christopher Wren was self-taught, like many of his colleagues. The son of a respected learned family, he dedicated himself at an early age to the study of natural sciences; at Oxford he came into contact with a circle of young intellectuals some of whom later founded the Royal Society. In 1651, he became professor of astronomy and in 1661 he was called to Oxford. Immediately after this, his first architectural creations, the Sheldonian Theatre (1662–63) and Pembroke College chapel were built (1663–65), both the work of a gifted "dilettante," but which displayed signs of the creative genius inherent to his later works. In 1665–66 he left for an extended study tour of Holland, Flanders, and France, where he made countless drawings ("I shall bring you almost all France on paper"), and met François Mansart, Louis Le Vau, and Bernini. "I would have given my eye-teeth for Bernini's Louvre design," he admitted later. After his return he became involved in planning the restoration of St. Paul's.

The consequences of the Great Fire and his inclusion in the survey by the reconstruction committee provided Wren with a unique opportunity to realize his own architectural ideas. There was no compulsory model for Protestant religious architecture apart from one or two efforts in the Palladian style and therefore there was every opportunity for stylistic experiments. Wren used a wide range of models and found astonishingly imaginative new solutions; most of his sources were derived from Dutch and French classicism, but many details were also derived from the gothic and Roman baroque.

The official comparison of the scheme with St. Peter's meant that the question of the plans for the new St. Paul's was settled. The so-called "great model" of 1673 (see above) is on the same scale as Michelangelo's domed central structure, although, after countless changes to the plans, a traditional nave structure was built with its famous gigantic, double-shelled dome (111 meters high) over the crossing. The main facade combines double-storey pairs of Corinthian columns with flanking towers (not built until 1706–8). The use of additional heterogeneous features is continued in the interior: the central complex of dome and transept is somewhat arbitrarily attached to the lengthwise nave and choir structures, the vaults of which are an unusual combination of barrel vaulting and round coping. The prevailing style, however, is one of academic classicism. In spite of many conceptual alterations resulting from the long period of construction (1675–1711), St. Paul's, and particularly its dome, became a frequently imitated model for English church building. The application of a ground plan derived from Roman religious architecture was all the more surprising since only a few decades before, new independent structures had been examined and any "catholic" elements had been taboo.

St. Stephen Walbrook (1672–87), a building financed by rich merchants, was one of the most mature of Wren's churches. Here the combination of nave and central structure was resolved in an original manner: inside the nave with its rows of columns and multiple aisles, a square room was set apart, and a wooden dome with pendentives rises over it. In other buildings he experimented with elliptical vaults (St. Mary-le-Bow, 1670–77, restored after being destroyed in 1941) or galleried halls with barrel vaults. While the interior of these churches almost always varied classical motifs, Wren often used gothic features or devices borrowed from Borromini, for example in Tom Tower at Christ Church, Oxford, or in St. Vedast's tower, Foster Lane in London. Trinity College library in Cambridge (see p. 168) is a variation on the Biblioteca Marciana in Venice.

Hampton Court became the Versailles of the British royal house (see p. 169). Between 1689 and 1692, William III and his wife Mary had their summer residence built on the site of a Tudor palace. However, this was only one part of a much larger project which included different wings, "the King's side" and "the Queen's side," galleries,

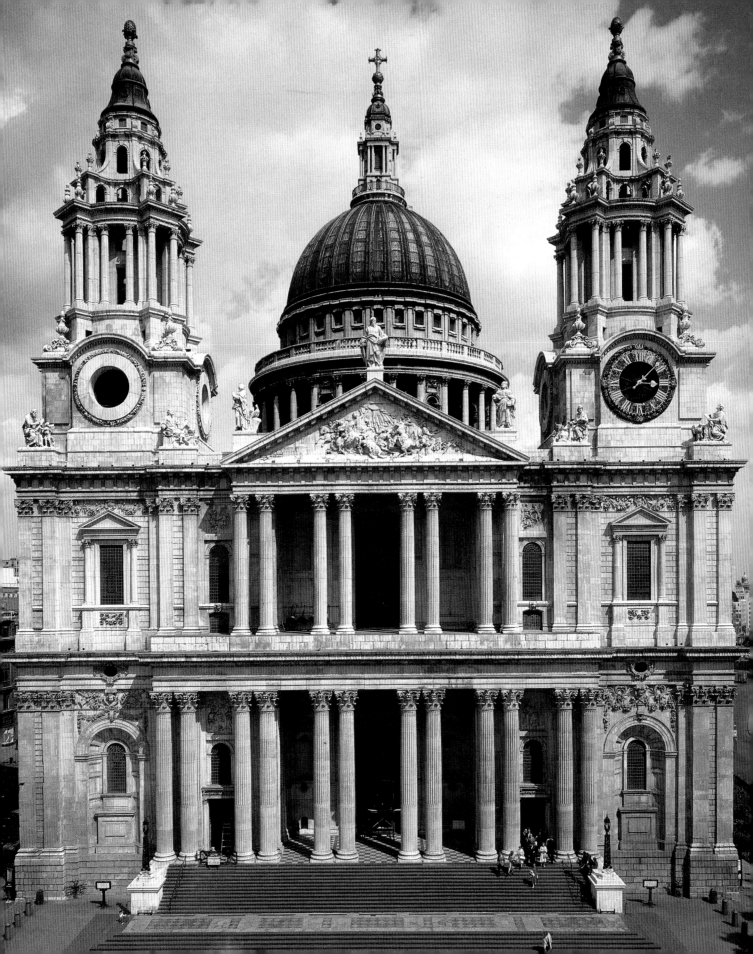

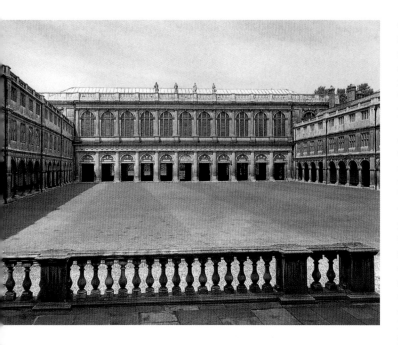

courtyards, and gardens, and was effectively an architectural response to the Louvre. Essential changes were also made to the exterior, so that the building as it now stands should be regarded as a compromise. The lively contrast between the stonework and the red of the brick walls is charming. The French influence is clear in the runs of windows across the facade and the garden facade with its portal and pediment.

Wren's last work was Greenwich Hospital (begun 1695). This complex, a royal endowment, was meant to occupy an extended Charles II building. The accommodation was grouped around several courtyards lying one behind the other on an axis horizontal to the Thames. This sequence copied the pattern of Versailles, which Wren had already reworked in Winchester palace. A unifying motif was provided by the extended colonnade. The extraordinary qualities of the complex within its context are apparent from the river: transverse frontages with double porticos close off the sides of the complex, allowing a view of the Queen's House, Inigo Jones's early masterpiece (see left). At the points of intersection between the courtyards are further transverse buildings, the colonnaded facades of which are dominated by domed towers. These house the chapel and the great hall, with its monumental Corinthian pilasters and highly sophisticated features. The overall complex, one of the high points of English baroque architecture, was completed by Wren's students John Vanbrugh and Nicholas Hawksmoor.

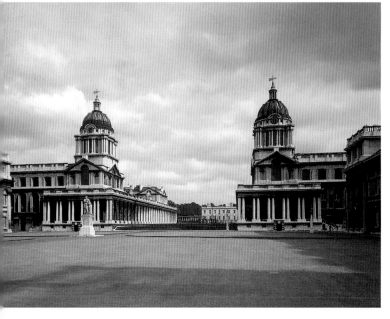

Sir Christopher Wren
Greenwich Hospital, begun 1695

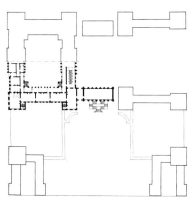

Sir Christopher Wren
Hampton Court
1689 plan

Sir Christopher Wren
Hampton Court, 1690–96
View from the park (above)
Detail of the garden facade (below left)
and the Queen's Drawing Room (below right)

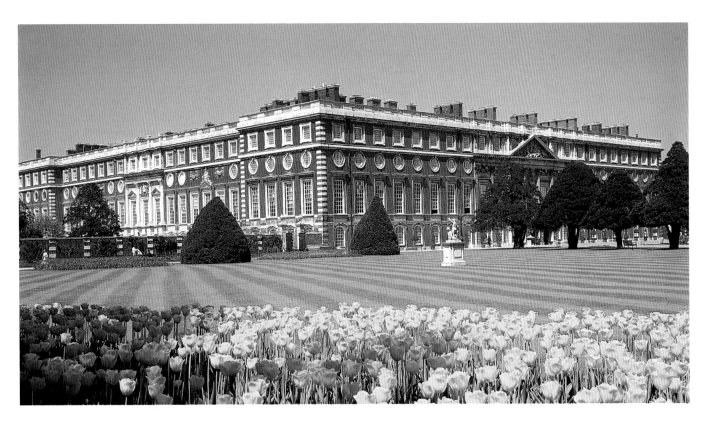

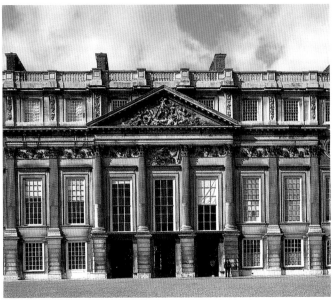

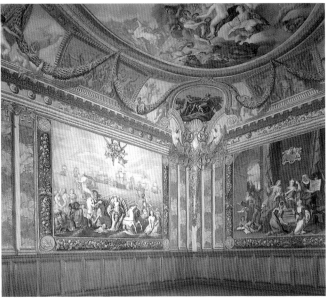

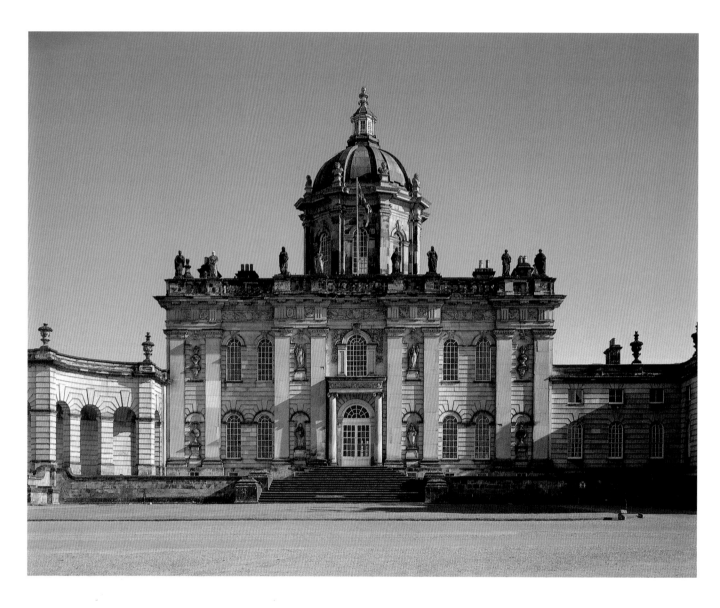

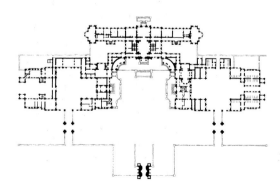

Sir John Vanbrugh and Nicholas Hawksmoor
Castle Howard (North Yorkshire), 1699–1712
Entrance and ground plan

John Vanbrugh and Nicholas Hawksmoor

John Vanbrugh (1664–1726) and Nicholas Hawksmoor (1661–1736) expanded Wren's style to more monumental dimensions, but also into a fundamentally more picturesque idiom. Their creative period coincided more or less with the reigns of Queen Anne and King George I, a time when England was establishing itself as a major power and the aristocracy was extending its influence. Vanbrugh, the son of Flemish refugees brought up in aristocratic circles, came to architecture during an adventurous youth and from the theater. Hawksmoor, a stuccoist, came from an English farming family. Each, quite different in personality and in their approach to architecture, they assisted Wren with the building of Greenwich Hospital. From 1699 they were commissioned to build Castle Howard (completed 1712), a country seat in North Yorkshire, which Vanbrugh had been invited to design by the Earl of Carlisle (see above and right). The complex, as in the French *entre cour et jardin*, between courtyard and garden, consists of corridor-like living quarters. At

Nicholas Hawksmoor
Castle Howard (North Yorkshire)
Mausoleum, begun 1729

Sir John Vanbrugh
Castle Howard (North Yorkshire) 1699–1712,
Entrance hall

their center the salon, opening onto the garden, is balanced on the side of the courtyard by the great square hall. This has the effect of a religious space, with its abbreviated transept and the mighty tambour and dome that had never been seen before in English secular architecture. Concave arcades lead to the lateral facades of the service and stable wings, grouped around further courtyards. The chapel lies at the point of intersection between the palace and stables. The incremental design and the picturesque graduation of individual features clearly point to Greenwich Hospital. While the severe garden facade is reminiscent of Marly, the courtyard facade, with its alternating twin giant Doric pilasters and double window axes is highly original. In the landscape architecture, entrance gates, and side-doors, Vanbrugh experiments with historical elements; the sources here included classical temples, Egyptian obelisks, Turkish pavilions, and medieval towers.

Historicism was very much in vogue at this time. The Viennese architect Johann Bernard Fischer von Erlach was writing his *Design for Historic Architecture*. Nevertheless, the mausoleum built by Hawksmoor in 1729 as the Howard family tomb (see below) was to be a seminal structure for the romantic movement. After discarding the initial designs which were closely modeled on antiquity, he constructed a round temple with Doric capitals based on Bramante's *tempietto* in S. Pietro in Montorio in Rome. The picturesque building sited on higher ground embodies in a unique manner the dramatic creative power of English architecture.

Blenheim Palace (Oxfordshire 1705–25) is yet another remarkable example of baroque palace architecture in England (see pp. 172–73). The palace, a gift from the queen to the Duke of Marlborough after his victory at the battle of Blenheim and the triumph over Louis XIV, was started by Vanbrugh but later, because of

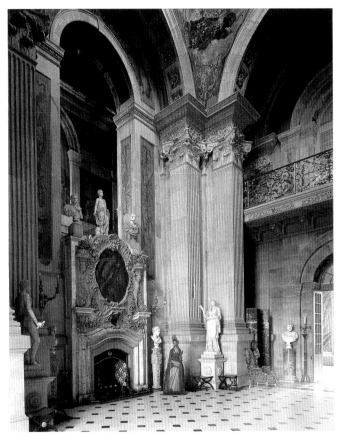

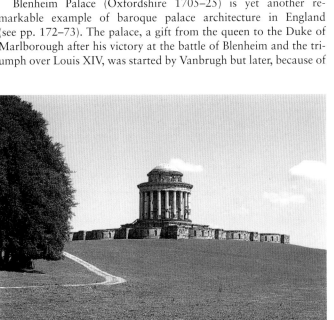

disputes with the queen, was completed by Hawksmoor. The mighty complex measures 275 meters in length and 175 meters in depth, centering on a large *cour d'honneur*. As in Castle Howard, the great hall and salon lie at the center of the longitudinal axis, and the kitchen court and stable court with the relevant appointments are sited on the transverse axis. Here too, heterogeneous architectural elements are used in a sort of collage and colonnades and porticos are again used as links. The building is distinguished from Castle Howard, however, not only in the size of the site. While a large number of European prototypes for the individual buildings can be seen at Castle Howard, here the English heritage is unmistakably predominant. The Corinthian portico had already appeared in the designs for Whitehall and for Greenwich Hospital and the massive corner towers with their chimney-like heads are reminiscent of Elizabethan palace architecture. The decoration designed by Grinling Gibbons is also a clear expression of the national character of this monument.

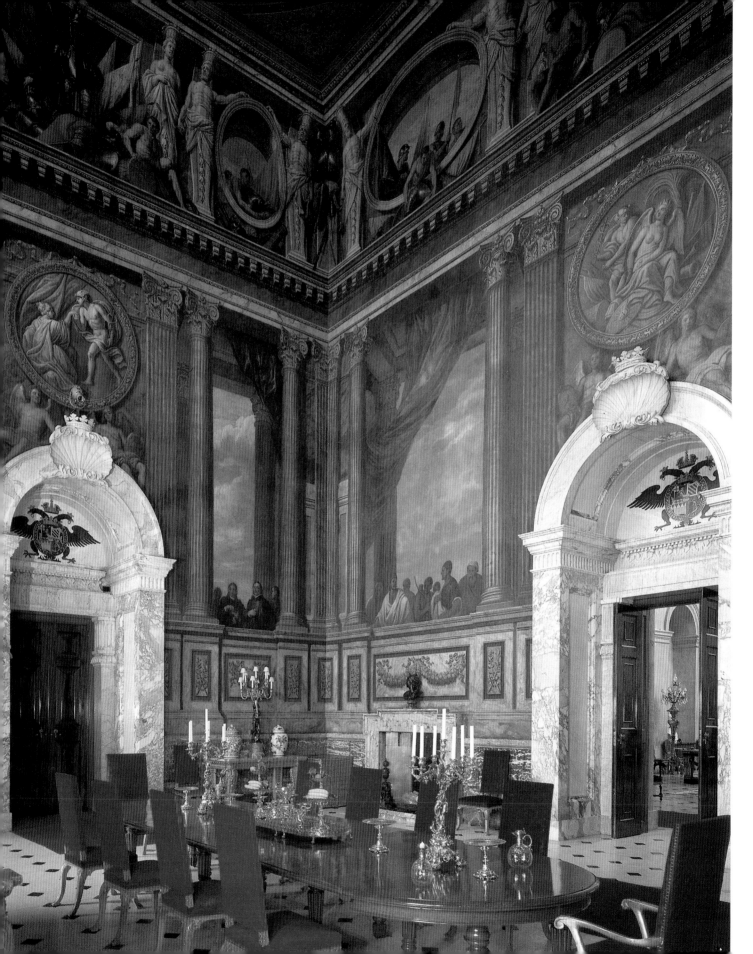

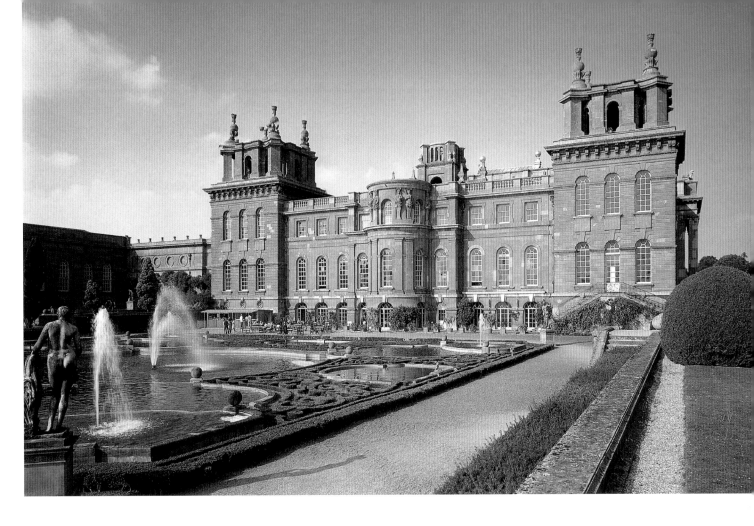

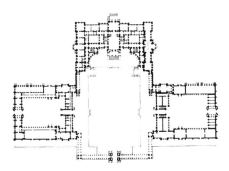

Sir John Vanbrugh and Nicholas Hawksmoor
Blenheim Palace, Oxfordshire, 1705–24
Gallery (above), ground plan, and entrance (below)

OPPOSITE:
Sir John Vanbrugh and Nicholas Hawksmoor
Blenheim Palace, Oxfordshire, 1705–24
Salon

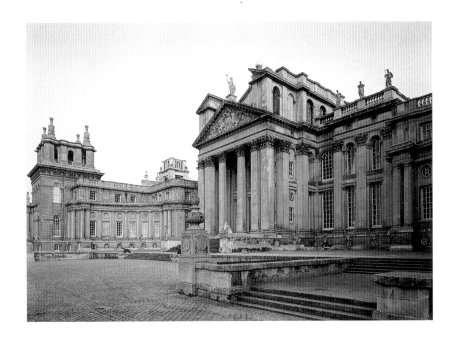

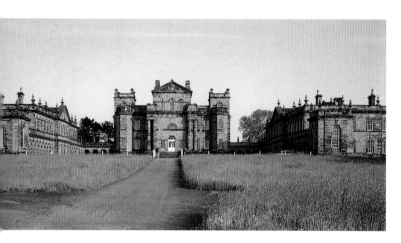

In Seaton Delavel (1718–29), Vanbrugh's later work, the echoes of the middle ages are even stronger. Like a fortress, the house is flanked by polygonal towers and defiant Doric columns frame the rusticated main facade. The Palladian windows provide a unique contrast with the austere architecture.

Church architecture, which Wren had enlivened after the fire of 1666, was left to stagnate for decades around the turn of the eighteenth century. It was only with a bill passed by the conservative Tory government, the 1711 "Act for Building... fifty new churches of stone and other proper materials, with towers or steeples to each of them," that innovation also returned to this architectural field. Vanbrugh's proposals for these churches, mainly intended for construction in the expanding suburbs, reflected a spiritual element that relates them to his palace architecture. Classical, baroque, and even gothic forms stand side by side, on an equal footing. The aim was not so much a consistent architectural idiom, but rather a measured approach to style and materials appropriate to the task. This was very much a renaissance ideal and one which could now be put into practice.

Responsibility for realization of the building program was given to others. Hawksmoor supplied the designs for six churches, among them St. George's, Bloomsbury (1716–27) which consisted of an amalgamation of archeological set pieces, and the church of St. Mary Woolnoth (1716–27), reminiscent of Wren. Significantly, Thomas Archer (1668–1743), who had studied the work of Bernini and Borromini in Rome, created the most baroque formula of the whole program with his design for St. Paul's in Deptford (1712–30), a centralized structure with giant Corinthian orders, in front of which stands a portico consisting of a semi-circular *tempietto*. James Gibbs (1682–1754) also adhered to Italian prototypes, in spite of similarities with Wren's style.

Outside London, it was mainly university towns that built new religious and college buildings. Well-to-do benefactors and intellec-

tual lovers of architecture, the *virtuosi*, competed to endow their colleges with imposing edifices. Thus Henry Aldrich, dean of Christ Church, Oxford, designed the Palladian Peckwater Quadrangle (1704–14), and in 1714 Hawksmoor submitted plans for the conversion of All Souls. The various stages involved in planning indicate the extent to which the gothic style of the historic chapel influenced the designs for the whole quadrangle complex. Several years were to pass before the advent of the gothic revival.

Neo-Palladianism

The generation which followed Vanbrugh and Hawksmoor was vehemently opposed to the architectural ideas of Christopher Wren and his successors. "Thro' several reigns we have patiently seen the noblest publick buildings perish... under the Hand of one single Court-Architect... I question whether our patience is like to hold much longer... Hardly... shou'd we bear to see a Whitehall treated like Hampton Court, or even a new Cathedral like St Paul's." The Earl of Shaftesbury's observations, written in fact in a letter from Italy, reveal more than a dissatisfaction with certain stylistic formulae. During the years following the Glorious Revolution of 1688, the Whigs, who opposed the concept of absolute monarchy, were gaining influence. After the house of Hanover occupied the throne in 1714, the party took over government, administering for several decades. As the balance of power shifted in favor of large landowners and the upper middle class, architectural ideals, especially in relation to grand architectural schemes changed. By contrast with the Roman pathos of many of Wren's buildings, architects and patrons now sought an ideal "founded in truth and nature," an architecture free of frivolous trappings.

The two volumes of *Vitruvius Britannicus* appeared from 1715, the first with one hundred engravings of classical British buildings, the second with a translation of Palladio's *Quattro libri*. Both publications, which were dedicated to George I and described as "Whiggish Products," were published by Colen Campbell; a little later, in 1727, William Kent's versions of Inigo Jones's designs were published. Campbell (1673–1729) and Kent (1685–1748) belonged to the intellectual circle of Richard Boyle, third Earl of Burlington (1694–1753), who was the main propagator of the Palladian movement of this period. Their aim was a return to the "correct and noble rules" as applied in antiquity and which had been interpreted by Palladio and in the work of their countryman Inigo Jones. Classical formulae and national tradition therefore provided the framework for English architecture over the next decades. Mannerist elements, which had been thoroughly effective in Palladio's buildings, were, however, completely eliminated.

The ideas of the artistic circle of *dilettanti* around Lord Burlington mainly influenced secular architecture. Burlington, who had traveled to Italy several times to study Palladio's villas, gave Campbell the task of building Burlington House in 1718–19, passing over

Lord Burlington (Richard Boyle, third
Earl of Burlington)
Chiswick House, Middlesex, 1725–29
Entrance facade (below)
Gallery (right)
Ground plan (below right)

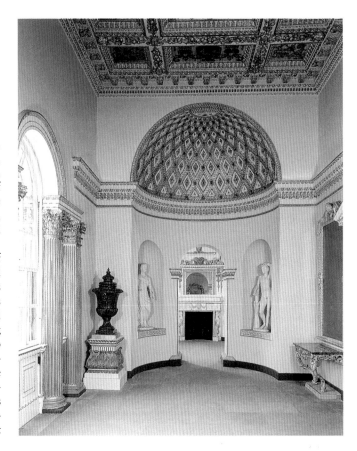

Gibbs, who was more closely associated with the baroque tradition. Campbell's country houses at Mereworth, Kent (1723), Stourhead, Wiltshire (from 1721), and Herbert's House, Whitehall (1724), served as prototypes for English secular architecture for the first half of the eighteenth century. Meanwhile, the sober classical forms were becoming increasingly varied: clear, symmetrical ground plans, temple porticos, colonnades, and domed central areas evoked Palladio's work in ever new combinations.

Lord Burlington himself created the most complete example of Palladian architecture. Chiswick House, Middlesex (see right and below), built between around 1723 and 1729, is closer to the villas of the Veneto than Campbell's country houses simply because of its modest dimensions. The ground plan, a square containing a central octagon, recalls Palladio's Villa Rotunda. A suite of interconnecting geometric spaces surrounds the domed central hall; they extend into apses with statues in the niches. The exterior combines multiple references to antiquity: the six Corinthian columns of the portico are from the temple of Jupiter Stator in Rome. The semi-circular, subdivided windows of the drum are reminiscent of Roman thermal baths and those of the garden facade, with curved arches and inset columns, are a variation on a Venetian prototype. These features do not

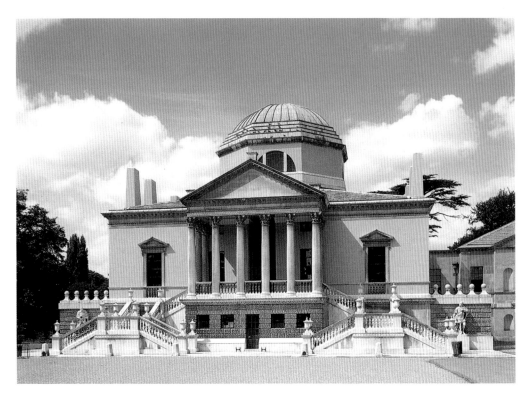

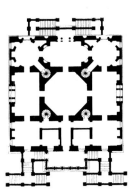

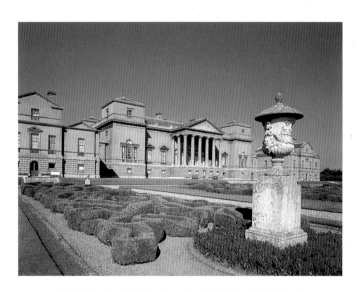

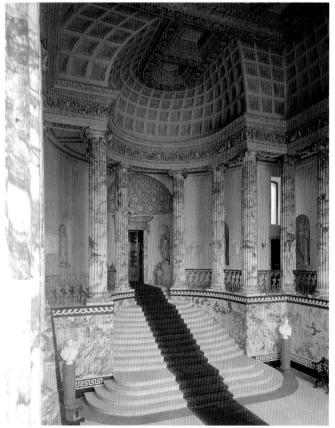

represent a literal quotation from ancient buildings but rather a version of the sixteenth-century interpretations which were accessible to Burlington through Palladio's drawings and buildings. Only the staircases leading up to the dominant portico bring a baroque element into this classical setting. The interior here was dictated mainly by the precepts of Inigo Jones, who, of course, had in his turn interpreted Palladio's schemes. The rooms are all interconnecting and each had clearly defined functions which were reflected in the furnishings and paintings. Reception room, library, galleries, and the "tribunal" in the center of the upper storey point to the mainly ceremonial nature of the villa; nevertheless, the private rooms, among them the bedroom and the red closet, are extremely luxurious, with paintings, chandeliers, velvet, and rare woods.

In contrast to this country house, which was intimate in scale in spite of the vast cost of construction, Holkham Hall (begun 1734) in Norfolk provides us with a monumental transformation of neo-Palladian ideals (see left). Though similarly based on Burlington's neo-Palladian ideas, the palace complex makes Chiswick House look pompous.

The strictly symmetrical ground plan is composed of a central elevation with reception rooms and four service buildings connected to it by corridors. It culminates in the almost religious effect of the entrance hall, where the staircase, surrounded by columns, leads up to the piano nobile. Here too, Roman proportions are evoked through the use of costly materials, classical friezes, and, above all, a formal coffered ceiling. Kent's gift for theatrical settings is also evident on a smaller scale in his design for number 44 Berkeley Square in London; the staircase, with its sinuous curves, enhances what is one of the most impressive interiors of its time.

An exception to the prevailing Palladian manner in early eighteenth-century England may be found in the very individual work of James Gibbs (1682–1754), the master builder whom Lord Burlington had replaced by Campbell for the planning of Burlington House. A Catholic Scot and conservative Tory, Gibbs had sympathized with the exiled Stuart king. In preparation for the priesthood, he had traveled to Rome in 1703, but then went to study under the architect Carlo Fontana. His first building on English soil, St. Mary-le-Strand (1714–17), already reflects Italian antecedents, in this case a variety of mannerist models (see right). His most important work, St. Martin-in-the-Fields (1721–26) demonstrates the freedom with which Gibbs used his historical prototypes. The extended building with a Corinthian portico refers to the Pantheon, here, of course, with nave structure and tower in the manner of Wren instead of the dome space. The original combination of temple facade and a steeply rising tower was to provide a model for many parish churches throughout the country. Previously, however, Gibbs had developed an unusual concept for a city church: a round structure with an internal circle of columns, as proposed by the Italian architect Andrea Pozzo in his treatise on perspective (the text was pub-

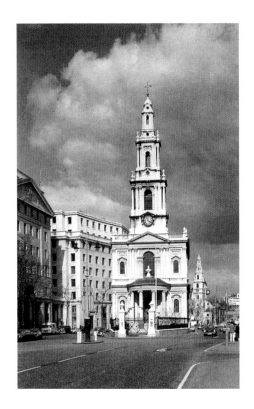

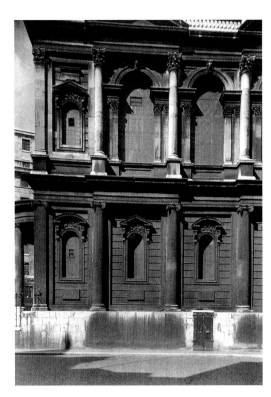

lished in England in 1707). This proposal was not accepted because of the high cost; nevertheless, the central structure in several later plans won approval.

The Radcliffe Camera, the Oxford University library, also stands squarely in the Italian mannerist tradition (see right). The round, domed structure rests on a rusticated base; pairs of Corinthian half–columns animate the facade. Gibbs's individual work, although based on traditional models, was warmly supported in conservative circles. His publications, *A Book of Architecture* (1728) and *Rules for Drawing the Several Parts of Architecture* (1732), were still being used in the nineteenth century.

Bath, renowned as an English spa since Roman times because of its hot springs, became a centerpiece of urban planning which blended with the landscape. Between 1725 and 1782, John Wood the Elder (1704–54) and John Wood the Younger (1728–81/2), father and son, planned the interior of this city on the banks of the Avon in a Palladian style. The backbone of the design was provided by three monumental squares: Queen Square (John Wood the Elder, 1729), the monumental Circus with its star-shaped junctions (John Wood the Elder, 1754), and Royal Crescent (John Wood the Younger, 1767–75), a crescent-shaped complex opening onto broad parkland and flanked by curving access roads (see p. 178). The Woods had encountered the idea of surrounding a square with uniformly structured residential accommodation in the royal squares in Paris, and the circular format in Mansart's Place des Victoires. However, the eighteenth-century architecture of Bath ultimately incorporates much clearer references to Rome than to the French capital. In addition to adopting aspects of the urban schemes found in antiquity, the structure of the facades also uses Roman motifs: thus the sequencing of the orders of architecture used in the Circus, Doric,

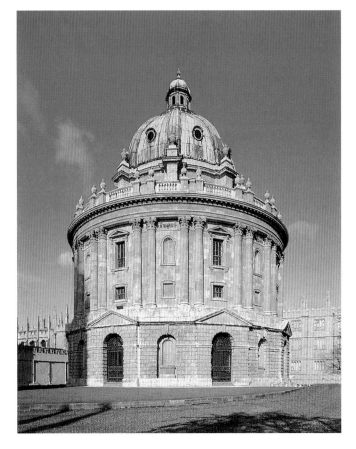

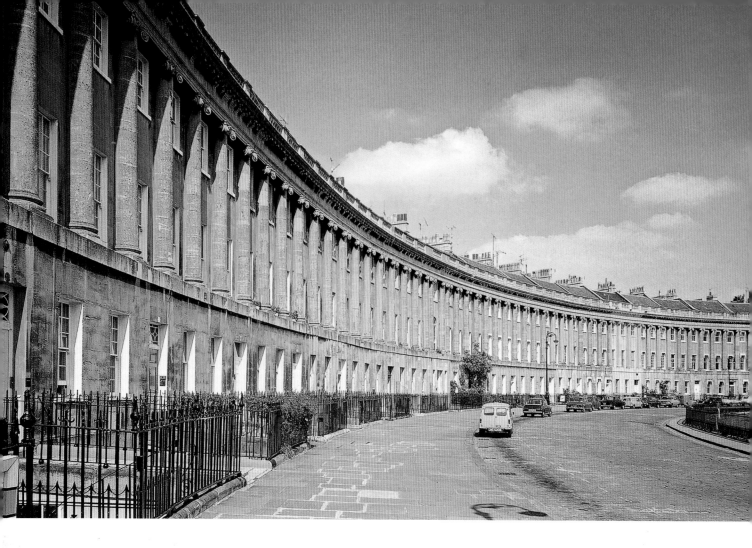

John Wood the Younger
Bath, Royal Crescent (above)
1767–75

John Wood the Elder
Bath, Queen Square (below)
Begun 1729

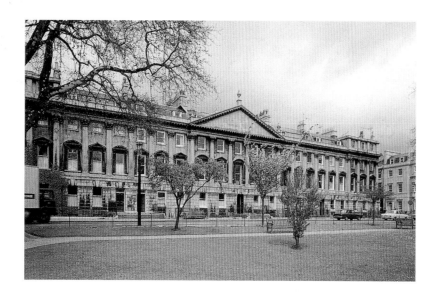

Bath, general layout

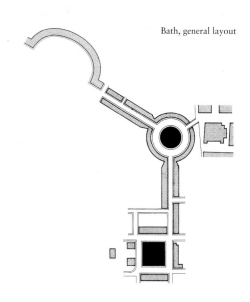

Ionic, and Corinthian, evoke the Coliseum and the giant order used in the Crescent is reminiscent of Michelangelo's Rome. The relationship of Roman buildings to their surrounding landscape also began to influence a new "controlled naturalism" in English gardens of the eighteenth century.

Robert Adam (1728–92) is considered the most important architect of the late eighteenth century. The son of a Scottish architect, he spent a fairly long period in Rome between 1754 and 1758, where he came to know the famous architectural theoretician and engraver Giovanni Battista Piranesi and the French draftsman Clerisseau. He also led an expedition to Dalmatia in order to record the precise measurements of Diocletian's palace at Split. The results of this were published in 1764 under the title *The Ruins of Spalato*. After his return to England, Adam was mainly involved in the decoration of existing interiors. Syon House, Middlesex (1763–64), gives some idea of the way in which he was able to interpret and enhance motifs from a wide variety of classical sources. From 1768 to 1772 Robert Adam and his brother James planned a complex of luxurious urban houses, the Adelphi on the Thames, but this experiment was not successful and brought the family to the brink of ruin.

Although Adam was able to create a vibrant and unique interpretation of decorative elements derived from antiquity, some of his work also reflected the concomitant eighteenth-century interest in "Gothick": Culzean Castle, Strathclyde (1777–96), a castle in medieval style, suggests the emergence of themes that were to be taken up by the romantic movement. The foundations for this process had of course been laid decades before with Horace Walpole's country house at Strawberry Hill (see right): by 1749, the English antiquarian had already acquired the land where William Robinson was to build him a light-hearted neo-gothic structure. Its most important feature was the gallery with fan vaulting (Thomas Pitt), no longer in its original form. It had been modelled on Henry VII's chapel at Westminster Abbey. Walpole's house, regarded by contemporaries as a curiosity partly because of its largely frivolous interpretation of medieval form, was subsequently recognized as an important precursor of the more accurate reproductions of the nineteenth-century gothic revival. This building is a good example of the way in which the vision of an amateur architect influenced architectural history in England.

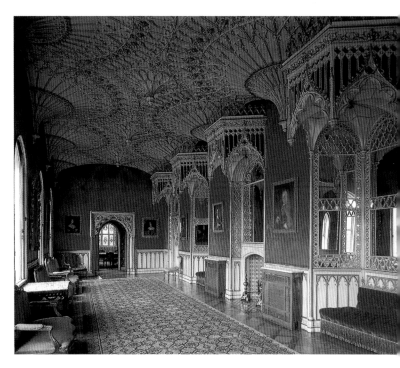

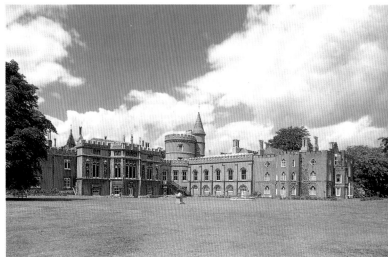

Baroque Architecture in the Netherlands

During the first half of the seventeenth century, the southern Netherlands, later Belgium, experienced a period of economic and cultural expansion. This was reflected more in the fine arts than in architecture however. While Rubens, Van Dyck, and Jordaens explored new dimensions in painting, architecture was still imprisoned in traditional modes. This was due to some extent to the impact of the Counter-Reformation which had provided a bulwark against Protestantism in the southern part of the (still) united Spanish Netherlands. The native gothic inheritance, the persistence of mannerist decorative forms, and the model of France provided prototypes which were utilized by architects in the southern Netherlands but which did not produce any original creativity.

One of the few exceptions was Rubens' house in his Antwerp home which he had designed himself (built 1611–16). The three wings of the complex with courtyard and garden do not reflect a coherent scheme and cannot be classified stylistically. The facade and the fortress-like portico are reminiscent of the mannerist architecture of Italy which Rubens must have studied during the eight years he worked on the other side of the Alps. Nevertheless, the artist's series of engravings, the *Palazzi di Genova* (1622), inspired the design of secular building rather more than his architectural scheme.

There was a change around the middle of the seventeenth century, with the appearance of luxuriantly decorative religious buildings such as St. Loup (begun in 1621 from a plan by Pieter Huyssens), the Jesuit church of St. Michael in Louvain (Willem Hesius,

Brussels
Facades on the Grande Place, about 1700

BELOW:
Willem Hesius
Louvain, St. Michael
1650–66

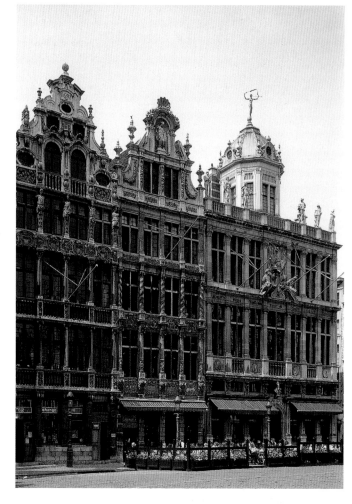

1650–66; see below), St. John the Baptist (1657–77) in Brussels, and St. Peter and St. Paul in Mecheln (1670–1709). The towering facades mostly fronted basilicas with three aisles where gothic structures were combined with classical orders of architecture and mannerist forms of decoration. The embossed columns, pilasters, and arches were characteristic of the architecture of the southern Netherlands and would have been unthinkable in countries strongly influenced by classicism such as France.

The reconstruction of the Brussels market place, destroyed by the French in 1695, demonstrated the persistence of traditional styles. The guild houses that were newly built in 1700 were completely modeled on their historical predecessors: narrow fronts fully taken up by window apertures, richly decorated to stress the vertical lines and with highly ornate decoration, were still reminiscent of late gothic bourgeois architecture. It was not until the eighteenth century that the French style of academic classicism also penetrated to the southern Netherlands.

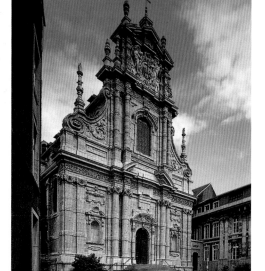

The Northern Netherlands

The architecture of the northern provinces of the Netherlands, which were under Spanish rule until 1648, developed in a completely different direction from that of the south. Their conversion to Calvinism and the decision to found the States General brought with it conflict and separation from the Hapsburg monarchy, and ultimately their release from the Holy Roman Empire. This resulted not only in iconoclasm; religious architecture also developed in a unique way. Economic factors were at least as important: the expansion of trade in the cities of a country that was fast becoming the leading naval power in Europe meant that the bourgeoisie were becoming the most important benefactors and consumers of art.

The expansion of Amsterdam resulted also in a boom in urban planning; the ring of three canals and the radial development plan of 1612 provided an impressive monument to this work (realized from 1615 by Daniel Stalpaert). Straight canals, tree-lined banks, parallel plots, and facades with high brick front-

ages still characterize the city. Like Amsterdam, many Dutch cities enhanced their streets with impressive mercantile houses at the beginning of the seventeenth century. The Rapenburg in Leyden, "the finest canal in Europe," displays some good examples of the individuality of these urban palaces.

Hendrik de Keyser (1565–1621), a leading architect of the day, built a large number of domestic houses and the Stock Exchange (1608), which he modeled on the London building. His churches were innovative, illustrating a new idiom for Protestant church architecture. The Westerkerk, built in 1620, and, to a greater extent, the Noordkerk (de Keyser or Hendrik Staets), begun in the same year, are representative of the Calvinist preaching church and were to become the standard ecclesiastical structure for the entire Protestant world. The central space dominates with its severe and precisely defined geometric features–square, octagonal, circular, or in the form of the Greek cross. The chancel and the font are in the center around which the seats are arranged in an almost theatrical setting.

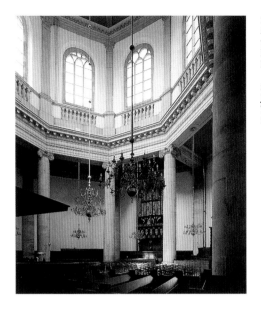

LEFT:
Arent van s'Gra-vensande
Leyden, Marekerk
Begun 1639

RIGHT:
Jacob van Campen
The Hague
Mauritshuis, 1633–44

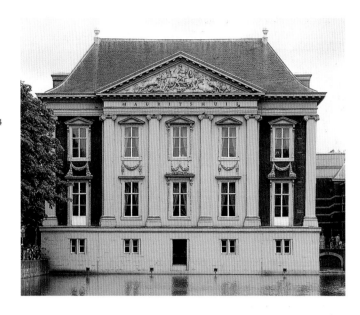

The Marekerk in Leyden, begun in 1639, is one of the finest examples of this type (see above left). The master builder Arent van s'Gravesande used a ground plan de-rived from antiquity, an octagon with ambulatory, which had been interpreted by Leonardo da Vinci. Even later structures such as Jacob van Campen's Nieuwe Kerk in Haarlem (1645), based on a square containing a cross, or the rotunda of the Lutheran church in Amsterdam (Adriaan Dorsman, around 1685) adhered to these structural principles.

Secular architecture underwent considerable change during the seventeenth century. Until shortly after 1600 the renaissance style still dominated architecture in the northern Netherlands. Combining lively mannerist decoration and the traditional brick structures, this style defined the city, as can now be imagined from the meat market at Haarlem (Liven de Keys, 1602–03) or the Kloveniersdoelen (target-shooting range) in Middelburg (1607–10). In court circles, however, a trend towards classicism became apparent after 1620, influenced both by France and by English Palladianism.

Its growing popularity can mainly be attributed to Jacob van Campen (1595–1657), a well-to-do artist and architect who had studied in Italy and now entered the Dutch architectural scene as a great innovator. His very first building, the Coymans house in Amsterdam (1624), indicated his familiarity with the architecture of Palladio and Scamozzi. The Mauritshuis in the Hague, which he built for the great-nephew of the governor Frederick Hendrik Johann Maurits in 1633–44, became the model for a large number of ambitious town and country houses (see above right). The block-shaped structure sitting on a high base features a pedimented giant Ionic order; on the main facade this takes the

form of a pavilion with three axes. In addition to the high hipped roof, the contrast between light ashlar and dark red brick gives the structure a resemblance to Dutch architecture.

Van Campen's undisputed masterpiece was the Amsterdam Town Hall (now the royal palace; see below), started immediately after the Peace of Westphalia was concluded in 1648. The ground plan consists of a rectangle with two interior courtyards centered on an extensive

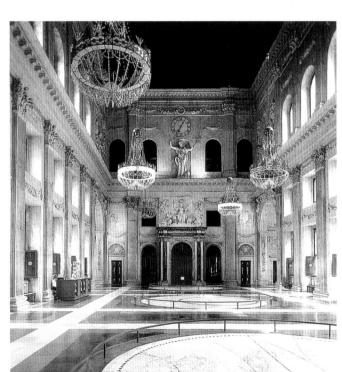

monumental hall, the Burghers' Hall. The barrel vault and the fact that the hall stretches to the full height of the building gives it a distinctly religious feeling; like the exterior, it features two superimposed systems of Corinthian pilasters. The decoration (sculptor Artus Quellinus and his workshop; painting a collaboration between Rembrandt and Jordaens) provides eloquent testimony to the self-confidence of the Amsterdam citizenry. The world lies at the feet of the city's

patron saint, flanked by allegories of power and wisdom. Gods of antiquity, the four elements and the virtues all stand at the service of the young Dutch republic, extolling her glory.

Towards the end of the seventeenth century, French influence again took precedence, as in almost the whole of Europe. This process was given additional impetus by the political circumstances: large numbers of Huguenot architects were leaving their homeland after the Edict of Nantes and were finding employment, due to their artistic skills, in other European courts. The classical baroque was transmitted throughout Europe by these refugees. Prince William III of Orange's hunting lodge, Het Loo near Appeldorn, was an impressive reflection of Huguenot skill. After 1684, Jacob Roman and the Frenchman Daniel Marot (around 1660–1752) constructed the palace and garden, modeling them closely on French academic architecture. As court architect to William III, Marot followed his patron to England, but later returned to the Netherlands and settled in the Hague. There he built several late baroque city palaces, among them the Royal Library (1734).

Jacob van Campen
Amsterdam, Town Hall (now the Royal Palace)
Begun 1648

Baroque Architecture in Scandinavia

Denmark and Sweden made important contributions to seventeenth- and eighteenth-century architecture. Individuality in style was mainly focused on the building materials and the combination of brick walls and sandstone decoration, copper roofing, and so on. The models for Scandinavian architecture, and not just for Protestant religious building, mainly came from the Netherlands; however, during the second half of the seventeenth century, elements of Italian and French architecture can be found in northern Europe. Commissions came from the court and the aristocracy, who had retained their central position in society on their conversion to Protestantism. The middle classes also gave sporadic support to architecture. In Norway, where the crown had been united with that of Denmark, the main source of artistic production could be found in the arts and crafts.

Denmark

As Copenhagen emerged as a modern seat of government, a short flowering of mannerist and early baroque architecture based on Dutch models occurred under Christian IV. The results of this were the summer palace at the palace of Rosenborg (1607–17) and the Stock Exchange (1619–31, 1639–40), built by Hans van Steenwinkel the Younger (see below left). Rosenborg was a broad, stepped building dominated by tall roof dormers and gables for which the king himself is reported to have drawn up the plans. The most ambitious project of the early seventeenth century, an octagonal square in the city center, was never realized because of the Thirty Years War.

The classical baroque style came to Denmark in the guise of the Charlottenborg Palace, begun in 1672. The most important architect of this period was Lambert van Haven (born 1630), who had trained in Italy but whose work nevertheless featured Dutch elements.

Jean de la Vallée
Stockholm, Riddarhus (Ständehaus)
1641–74

The Vor Freslers Kirke (church of the Redeemer) in Christianshavn is a centralized structure combining a Greek cross with rectangles in the corners, thus utilizing a design which had been developed in Protestant church-building in the northern Netherlands. The spiral pinnacle to the tower was added in the eighteenth century (Laurits de Thura). Italian influences are evident in the villa-like complex of the (earlier) Sophie-Amalienborg in Copenhagen.

By the mid eighteenth century, architecture was flourishing again. In 1754 work began on the development of the Amalienborg Square and the Frederikskirke, an urban complex which had been inspired by French planning and which is the most significant work of Danish rococo. The core is an octagon form, the main axes of which are emphasized in junctions with long series of avenues, and the diagonals by four palaces with the stress on the central pavilions of each of the facades.

A second rectangular square has the domed Frederikskirke in its center (not completed till 1849; see below right). The whole plan was designed by Nicolaj Eigtved (1701–1754), a well-traveled gardener and architectural dilettante who had studied with Pöppelmann. The influence of the Dresden architect had marked his first great work, the Christiansborg Palace (1733–45). As court architect to Christian VI and Frederik V, Eigtved was president of the academy of art in Copenhagen.

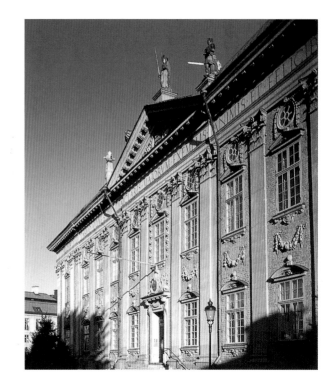

Laurits de Thura (1706–59) also achieved some inter-national reputation, with his "Viennese" hermitage in the Copenhagen deer park as well as the pinnacle on the church of the Redeemer, after Borromini. Between 1746 and 1749 he published the *Danish Vitruvius*.

Sweden

At first the Swedish Academy also based its work on Dutch mannerism, although by 1639, when the French architect Simon de la Vallée (died 1642) was called upon to be court architect, a clear move in favor of baroque classicism had occurred. His son Jean de la Vallée (1620–96) and his student Nikodemus Tessin the Elder (1615–81) gained international respect for Swedish baroque architecture.

The manifesto for the new style was expressed in the Riddarhus in Stockholm (see above), influenced by the Palais du Luxembourg, designed by Simon de la Vallée, and realized, with a few alterations, by Simon de la Vallée and the Dutchman Justus Vingboons during the 1650s. The main facade features a giant

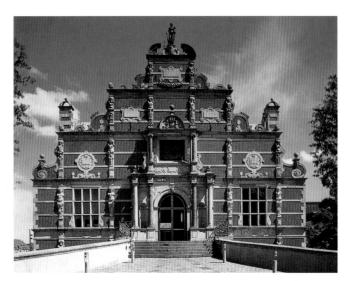

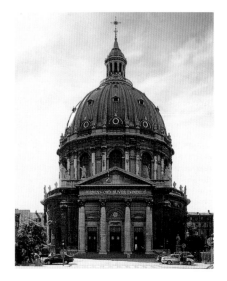

LEFT:
Hans van Steenwinkel the Younger
Copenhagen Stock Exchange, 1619–31 and 1639–74

RIGHT:
Nicolaj Eigtved
Copenhagen, Frederikskirke
1649–1849

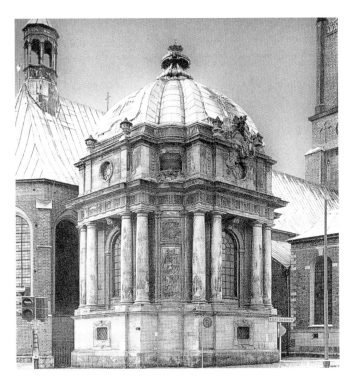

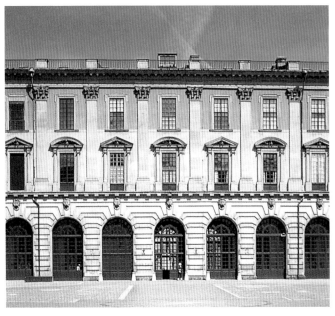

Nikodemas Tessin the Elder
Stockholm, Riddarsholmkirke
Begun 1671

Nikodemus Tessin the Younger
Stockholm, Royal Palace,
Detail of the courtyard facade,
1697–1728

Corinthian order and the slightly projecting pavilion is emphasized by a flat pediment: here too, the contrast between brick and light sandstone was used to good effect. One of the original features here is the two-tier roof with a curved profile to the lower section.

In 1650, Jean de la Vallée began work on the Oxenstierna Palace, which reflected his experience on a recently completed study tour to France and Rome. The Bonde Palace (also 1650) was the first Swedish palace to receive a *cour d'honneur*. The Dutch model continued to dominate in church buildings such as the central structure of St. Catherine's church (1656).

Nicodemus Tessin the Elder was appointed court architect in 1649; shortly after this he undertook a fairly long journey to see the major architectural works of Germany, Italy, France, and the Netherlands. The impressions he brought back with him were to be endlessly represented in his architecture. Thus Kalmar cathedral was reminiscent of the buildings of the Roman Cinquecento whereas the Caroline Museum in Stockholm (1672) was closer to French classicism. In his most important work, Schloss Drottningholm (see right), he initially used the design for Vaux-le-Vicomte, but doubled the *corps de logis* and complemented this with side wings and corner pavilions, producing a complex with two courtyards. The interior of the palace is dominated by a monumental staircase. Construction of the palace and the layout of the extensive grounds was put into the hands of his son, Nikodemus Tessin the Younger.

The younger Tessin (1654–1728) took up his father's position as Swedish court and palace architect in 1681. He too had completed study tours throughout Europe. In Rome, he had close connection with Bernini and Carlo Fontana, whose architecture had a decisive influence on his own creative output. His main work, the reconstruction of the Stockholm Royal Palace (see above), shows that he was acquainted with Bernini's last design for the Louvre and Palazzo Chigi-Odescalchi; however, Tessin transformed these archetypes into a more sober style. The block-shaped four-wing complex with three main storeys resting on a strong base is complemented by curved stable blocks. A mounted statue of Charles XI was to have occupied the great courtyard, just as in the French Place Royale.

Opposite the palace, Tessin built his own town house, an architectural showpiece in which he combined the ground plan of a French hôtel with architectural elements from Roman villas. The garden design resembled a stage set and the architectural structures were set out like monuments.

The classical movement took hold relatively quickly in Scandinavia, at the beginning of the last quarter of the century. The burial chapel for Frederick IV in Roskilde cathedral (C. H. Harsdorff 1774) and the theater at the Gripsholm palace (Jean-Louis Deprez 1743–1804), set the trend for the extraordinarily impressive Greek Revival architecture of the nineteenth century.

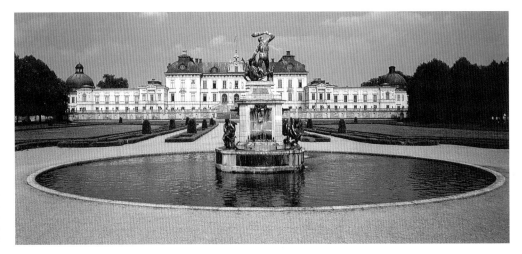

Nikodemus Tessin the Elder, Schloss Drottningholm near Stockholm, 1662–85

Ehrenfried Kluckert

Baroque Architecture in Germany, Switzerland, Austria, and Eastern Europe

Introduction

Homogeneous landscapes of predominantly baroque art in Germany can probably be found only in Swabia, Bavaria, and Franconia. Dresden and Potsdam, to mention two examples, are well known as particularly splendid ensembles of baroque art. Certain types of baroque structure are typical of different regions: the country houses in Schleswig-Holstein, the half-timbered churches in the Vogelsberg area northeast of Frankfurt, the lake mansions of the Münster region in northern Germany. This brief sketch is by no means intended as a comprehensive survey of German baroque culture. It is intended rather to provide a rough outline and an introduction to the subject.

The description of baroque architecture in Germany is arranged here on a geographical basis, in order to explore fringe areas and take account of buildings that have previously been overlooked. This is not to imply, however, that the historical aspects of German baroque have been neglected. Quite the contrary. The historical context demonstrates why the baroque "mesh" is fine in many regions and more loose in others. However, it should be observed that baroque architecture developed conspicuously late in Germany compared to other European countries. This is undoubtedly mainly the result of the Thirty Years War (1618–48) since Germany was its main theater. It was only toward the end of the seventeenth century that secular and ecclesiastical clients had at their disposal the financial means to undertake a more intensive campaign of building in the service of absolutism and the Counter-Reformation.

Country Houses, Mansions, and Churches in Schleswig-Holstein, Mecklenburg, Hamburg, and Lower Saxony

The baroque landscape of Schleswig-Holstein is notable for its seventeenth- and eighteenth-century manor houses and country houses. These display an idiosyncratic baroque rhetoric that takes on a much more varied and dynamic form than the rather spare sober style of Protestant churches. As everywhere in Europe, baroque architecture in Schleswig-Holstein also stood at the political service of duchies, counties, and landed estates. Typical of the territorial claims and counter-claims between the Danish crown and the regional landed estates was the rivalry between the dukes of Gottorf and the kings of Denmark. Between 1698 and 1703 the huge south wing of the Gottorf mansion in Schleswig had been built effectively as a separate palace (see right). In their political dispute, the Gottorfs had gained the backing of Sweden as a protective power against the Danes. It was probably no coincidence then, that the architectural structure and building proportions of the Gottorf mansion resemble those of Stockholm castle, begun by Nikodemus Tessin the Younger in 1697. This suggests more than a mark of favor, however. Danish baroque architecture was indebted to the Dutch ideal, whereas Swedish baroque buildings adopt an imperial, princely style.

In this connection, it should be mentioned that Nikodemus Tessin had submitted designs for the new construction at the Gottorf mansion at the behest of Duke Christian Albrecht. Unfortunately funds were not available for the project and it was left to Christian Albrecht's successor, Duke Frederick IV, to oversee the successful execution of the new building. Unfortunately, he too was unable to move into his new residence. In 1713, even before the interiors were completed, the Danes occupied the "state of Gottorf," including the mansion, during the course of the Great Northern War (1700–21).

Many mansions in Schleswig-Holstein have an Italianate, that is, deliberately anti-Danish, appearance. The best example of this is the hall of the mansion in Damp, where the interior was designed around 1720 by the northern Italian Carlo Enrico Brenno. The lavish stuccoed two-storey hall is surrounded by an ornate gallery at half-height, accessed by a double flight of steps. On the ceiling, richly decorated with rocaille work, angels are seen blowing trumpets and playing flutes. So insubstantial is their physical link to the ceiling that they appear to swoop downwards. The room combines the functions of assembly room, reception room, and private chapel in a most curious fashion.

Two halls in Schleswig-Holstein seem to vie for the crown of baroque achievement. Apart from that in Damp, the other is in a country house in Hasselburg (see p. 186). Here too an Italianate scheme emerges. The painting of the hall in 1710 was probably done for Count Dernath by an Italian assistant of Brenno. Both the stuc-cowork and decoration are restrained in appearance, setting off the gracious sweep of the staircase up to the gallery. Once upstairs, the viewer can look up to another false storey, where sophisticated painted perspectives create an illusion of architecture. This simulated architectural painting with integrated figures of gods is reminiscent of Würzburg and Pommersfelden in the south and Swedish Drottningholm in the north. A vista of the gatehouse built in 1763 opens from the house on a central axis, forming the centerpiece of a courtyard grouping some 650 yards away. Its massive roof sweeps elegantly upwards and culminates in a lantern, giving it the appearance of a pavilion. The articulation with piedroits and undecorated wall areas has a refined and restrained effect, and is appropriate to the sober architecture of the working building—wholly in contrast to the flamboyant hall of the mansion. The utilitarian concerns of agriculture essentially characterize the whole group of buildings here. Decorative additions and pictorial themes are not really relevant. Symbolism always relates to the political obligations of the landed proprietor.

The houses at Emkendorf and Pronstorf (see below right) are comparable in construction to the mansions described above. The facades follow a pattern which can be seen in a number of versions in other manor houses. Typical is a central projection articulated with giant pilasters and surmounted by a segmented or triangular pediment. A double flight of steps leads to a more or less ornate doorway.

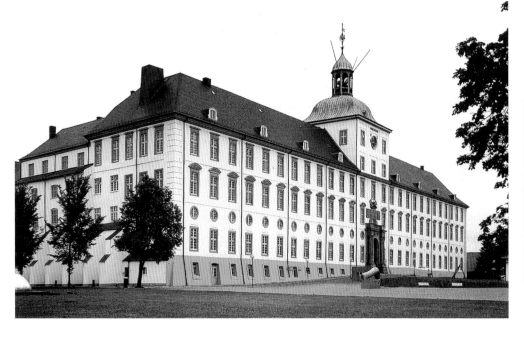

South wing of Schloss Gottorf, Schleswig, 1698–1703

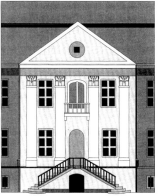

Country house, Pronstdorf

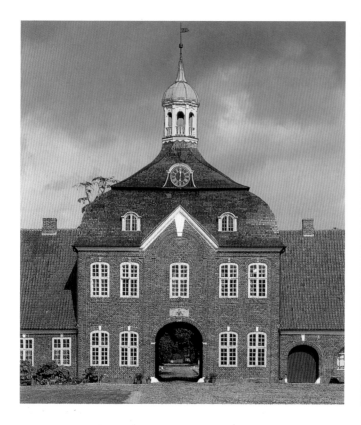

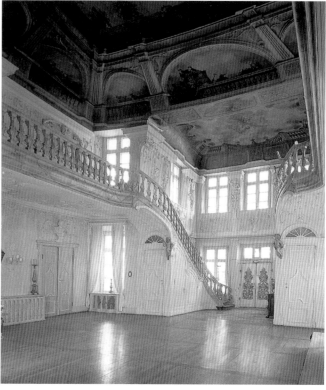

The house at Pronstorf built in 1728 for Detlev von Buchwaldt also shows corner projections that repeat the articulation of the central feature. The mansard roof above lends the building a touch of nobility and grandeur. Whereas in Pronstorf the obligatory brick predominates, towards the end of the eighteenth century an attempt was made to use a wider variety of building materials. The corner pilasters and three-storey pilasters of the central section of the bailiwick in Pinneberg are rusticated with brick, giving the building a sculptured quality. The projection and recession of sections of the facade and the slightly curving edges of the mansard roof lend a dynamic quality to the architecture.

More French and playfully elegant—and already wholly caught up in the rococo manner—is the manor house in Borstel, which was built around the middle of the eighteenth century. A curved double flight of steps sweeps up to the doorway, which is framed by two tall pilasters. The upper window is crowned by an ornate rocaille cartouche, and above it rises a segmented arch that cuts into the roof line. The oval rooms are similarly inspired by the French idiom, particularly unusual in a Schleswig-Holstein house.

The architecture of baroque churches in Schleswig-Holstein is not nearly as striking as that of country houses. One notable excep-

tion is the chancel of the church in Probsteierhagen near Kiel. Originally an early gothic church built of rubble, the building was extended during the eighteenth century. The highlight of the interior is the choir, which dates from 1720. The compact and yet monumental ornamentation corresponds to the Italianate sense of form in the grand hall at Damp. Carlo Enrico Brenno was the stuccoist who carried out the work at both Probsteierhagen and Damp at about the same time.

The churches of Rellingen and Wilster are quite different in appearance. Although they are light inside, their decoration is restrained and sober. Cay Dose, architect of the church at Rellingen (1754–56) (see right), wanted to create a sacred ceremonial hall in the style of those in France and Italy. He announced enthusiastically that he wanted "to accomplish exceptional beauty and magnificence, more immanent than prominent, such as has no parallel in this country, but will probably be found in Italy, France, and England on a far greater scale and different in kind."

For his ground plan, Dose chose a regular octagon, on top of which he placed an elegant mansard roof culminating in a lantern. Piedroits frame tall windows, emphasizing the corner sections. The

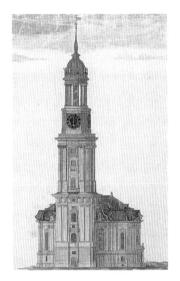

Ernst Georg Sonnin
St. Michael's church, Hamburg
1750–57
Engraving by A. J. Hillers, c. 1780
(below)
View towards choir (right)

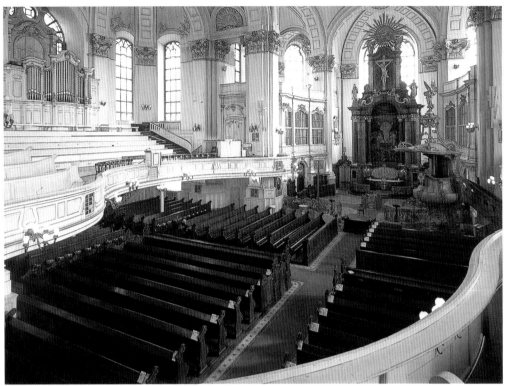

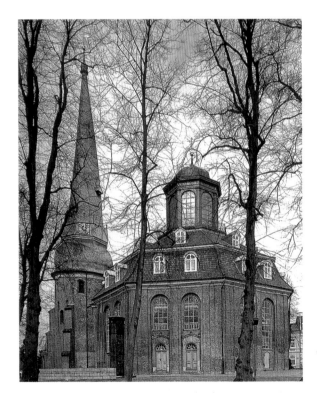

Cay Dose
Protestant church, Rellingen, 1754–56

high interior has a far less expansive and grandiose effect than the exterior would suggest. The reason may lie in the intrusive pillars and galleries, which overlap the window area in an unfortunate manner. They seem to cramp the interior rather than offering the promised "immanent magnificence."

The Brandenburg architect Ernst Georg Sonnin achieved more successful proportional effects with his church buildings, such as the one at Wilster, built between 1775–80. He did more justice to the idea of a grand Protestant preaching hall than his colleague Dose had done, taking as his ground plan an extended octagon with narrow sides which are concave to the western and eastern sections. The simple external articulation is dramatized by a low basement storey and soaring rusticated pilasters. The pulpit projects out from the convex vault of the altar wall and into the interior of the galleried church like the prow of a ship.

Ernst Georg Sonnin designed many buildings in Schleswig-Holstein. He built various noble houses in Wilster, and was also involved in the remodeling of the Kiel Schloss. However, his main work and masterpiece was the reconstruction of St. Michael's church in Hamburg (see above), which had succumbed to fire in 1750. In the same year both he and the Thuringian-born Johann Leonard Prey submitted proposals for the reconstruction of the church. The foundation stone was laid a year later, and the finishing ceremony was carried out in December 1757, although with a tower base barely covered over. It was only twenty years later that funds were made available for the construction of the tower.

This is where Sonnin displayed his genius as a technician and structural engineer—he actually had the tower erected without scaffolding, to the immense astonishment of the public. This structure, which soon became a symbol of Hanseatic Hamburg, was finally opened with great solemnnity in 1786.

The tower and the nave follow different schemes. Whereas the first two levels of the tower grow out of the architectural structure of the nave, the belfry level, clock, and lantern carried on monumental pillars break away from the overall scheme in a design which has no precedent in architecture. Prey had his way with his scheme in the nave, which was still conceived wholly in the late baroque idiom and is marked by a rococo playfulness. When Prey died, shortly before the finishing ceremony, Sonnin took over the project, introducing a more severe architectural language that was strongly influenced by classicism.

Along with the Frauenkirche in Dresden, St. Michael's in Hamburg is considered the most splendid example of a Protestant baroque church. Protestant in conception but Catholic in execution might be a reasonable description of a first impression on entering the building. The spatial proportions and dimensions of the centralized hall are remarkable, especially when viewed from the gallery. The gallery itself runs in elegant curves around the central space and the three transepts up to the choir, with the boxes slotted neatly into the lateral bays. The four piers that mark out the cruciform ground plan support broad coffered transverse arches bearing a lofty trough-shaped vault lined with a broad projecting ledge and an encircling balustrade. From most angles, the eye is led on by the expansive arches into the various spaces and toward the rocaille decoration in the spandrels and the acanthus leaves of the gilt capitals. It is only below the gallery level that the impression of a soberly designed Protestant church interior prevails.

Though the use of the baroque style in churches is often taken as a dominating feature of the urban landscape, and is only rarely considered in the narrow context of the structural environment, baroque mansions cannot be examined in isolation either. House and park usually form an close unit. Moreover, the mansion is often the central point of reference for an urban scheme. Either the mansion was planned and built as the starting point of a new town or it was placed within the context of a town, as at Bückeburg in Lower Saxony, where Prince Ernst von Schaumburg incorporated his castle into the city in the early seventeenth century.

A long wide street led towards the palace which had been a medieval moated fortress with mid-sixteenth-century additions. Four large public buildings—the bursary, built in the same period, the half-timbered town hall (now demolished), the treasury, and the prince's court office—acted as important city landmarks and fulfilled the function of linking town and palace. The market square was left open towards the palace and was otherwise defined by a prestigious group of buildings including a richly adorned palace gateway (see below). Today the palace buildings convey a certain lack of visual coherence, since they incorporate structures of various periods. Bückeburg should be regarded primarily as one of the earliest baroque urban ensembles in Germany rather than as an example of a baroque building.

Whereas in Bückeburg the extended castle structure was incorporated into the urban environment, at Ludwigslust in Mecklenburg a small hunting lodge was expanded into what might almost be

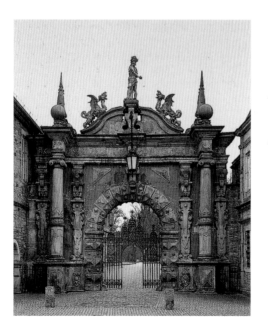

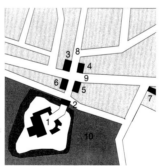

Plan of Schloss Bückeburg: moated palace and adjoining urban area
1   Palace and palace graveyard
2   Palace gateway
3   Site of old town hall
4   Former bursary
5   Prince's court office
6   Treasury
7   Civic church
8   First baroque urban axis (now Bahnhofstrasse)
9   Long street
10 Palace park

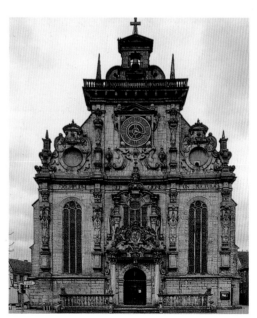

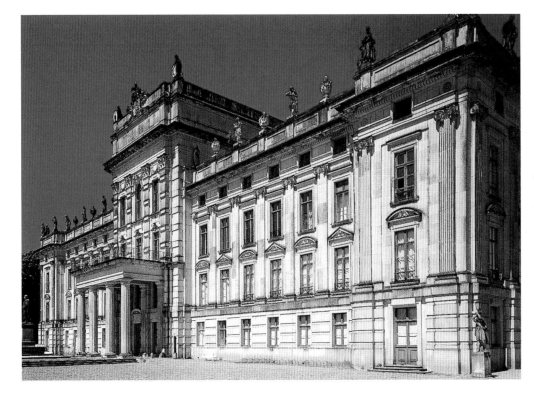

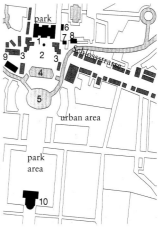

Plan of palace, gardens, and urban area,
Ludwigslust
1 Palace
2 Palace square
3 Service buildings
4 Cascade
5 Pond
6 Fountain house
7 Fire station
8 Courtiers' housing
9 Stables
10 Civic church

described as a baroque urban estate. In 1724 Christian Ludwig II of Mecklenburg-Schwerin commissioned the construction of a cosy princely retreat near the hamlet of Klenow. This lies in the so-called "grizzled district," a region between the Sude and Elde rivers south of Schwerin, notable for its gray sandy soil and forests. He called the lodge Ludwigslust [Ludwig's Pleasure]. His son Frederick was well traveled and had visited Versailles. When he took over the administration, he conceived the idea of creating something like a Mecklenburg version of the magnificent French palace. In 1764 he moved the princely seat from Schwerin to Ludwigslust, entrusting the project to his newly appointed court architect, Johann Joachim Busch. Busch was to remain working on this scheme until he retired in 1796. The houses in the village were demolished and replaced by a planned estate. The palace, royal chapel, and Schlossstrasse are positioned in axial alignment to each other, with the pivotal point formed by the eastern side of the square, where a bridge over the canal marks the beginning of Schlossstrasse and leads into the wide avenue. The ample park to the west forms a counterbalance to the urban area east of the church-palace axis.

The visual impact of the palace (see above) depends on the super-elevated central projection, in front of which is a portico with Tuscan columns. Attached to the central section are two wings terminating in narrow side pavilions, giving the ground plan an overall E-shape. The east wing was designed for the duke, the west wing for the duchess. Inside, the original arrangement of the rooms is still evident. The two stairwells leading up to the two-storey golden hall are entered on either side of the entrance hall. The golden hall gives access to the individual rooms, which retain some of the original furnishings. When Grand-Duke Paul Frederick took over the regency in 1837, the ducal seat was transferred back to Schwerin and Ludwigslust declined into a town of pensioners and garrisons.

Johann Conrad Schlaun
Clemenswerth hunting lodge near Sögel,
1736–45
View towards house and
service buildings

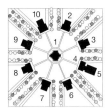

Ground plan
1 House
2 Münster pavilion
3 Hildesheim pavilion
4 Paderborn pavilion
5 Kitchen pavilion
6 Osnabrück pavilion
7 Clement Augustus
   pavilion
8 Cologne pavilion
9 Mergentheim pavilion
10 Chapel with Capuchin
   cloisters

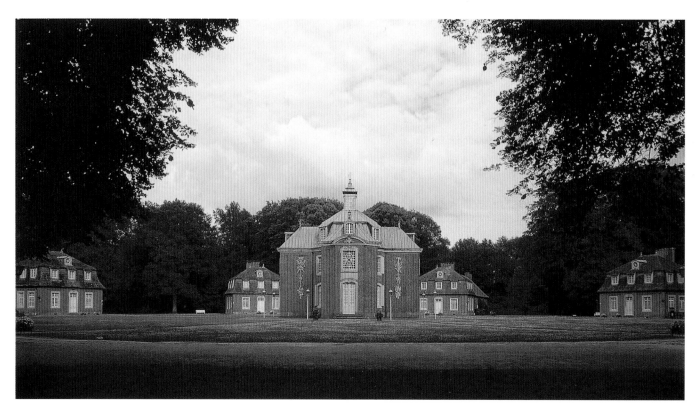

The Architecture of the Electoral Principality of Westphalia—the Architect Johann Conrad Schlaun

The most important baroque architect in Westphalia was Johann Conrad Schlaun (1695–1773), who had already familiarized himself with the major baroque buildings of Europe during his early travels. From 1720–21 he was a pupil of Balthasar Neumann in Würzburg, at a time when the latter had started work on the ducal seat. Directly after this, he traveled to Rome, returning to Münster in 1723.

Soon he was given possibly the most interesting project of his young career by the Elector Clemens August, also archbishop of Cologne, a scion of the house of Wittelsbach. In 1724, already appointed master of works, Schlaun was asked to rebuild Schloss Brühl, near Cologne (see pp. 194–95). It was a difficult commission. On the one hand, the Elector wanted his rank as ruler enshrined in a suitable seat, but on the other, he wanted to save on building costs. He therefore ordered that the ruins of an earlier structure, a moated castle, should be thoroughly explored for materials that could be reused. Schlaun had to take over the ground plan of the medieval edifice, but was at the same time keen to introduce modern Roman ideas borrowed from Borromini and Bernini. His solution obviously

did not entirely satisfy his client. The latter's brother, the Elector Charles Frederick of Bavaria, harshly criticized the architecture, and dispatched his own court architect, François de Cuvilliés, from Munich to Cologne bearing new plans. In 1728 Schlaun was dismissed from the project, but subsequently found employment with the Elector elsewhere.

Cuvilliés transformed Schlaun's traditional castle model with its cramped courtyard and medieval round tower into a modern palace with the character of a summer residence in the French manner. In 1741 Balthasar Neumann came to Brühl and designed the stairwell, built three years later. Thus, after over forty years the palace was finally completed. It contained stylistic features borrowed from prominent baroque buildings in Italy, France, and south Germany.

Between 1736 and 1746, Schlaun was given another large commission by Clemens August, the hunting lodge at Clemenswerth, Hummling near Sögel, north of Osnabrück (see above). No doubt recalling his undignified exit from Brühl, he chose as his basic inspiration the pagoda castle in the park at Nymphenburg palace, near Munich. He also took elements from Marly-le-Roy and the hunting lodge at Bouchefort near Brussels. The result far surpassed all these

Johann Conrad Schlaun
Rüschhaus, Nienberge, 1745–49
View from courtyard

Gerhard Koppers
Hunting lodge, Clemenswerth
Ceiling of stairwell with hunting scenes
1745

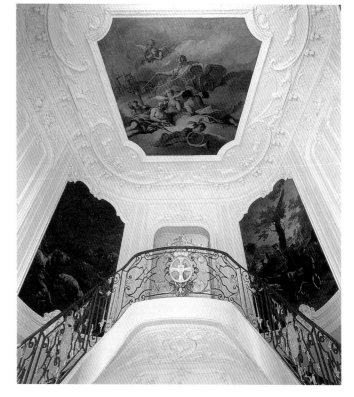

models. The graceful architectural lines of the two-storey lodge are constructed in red brick, articulated with light-colored sandstone on a cruciform ground plan. The tones of the structure contrast with the green of the lawn around. Located at the focal point of eight paths which lead to the cleverly positioned window scheme, the lodge is sparingly ornamented. At the angles of the paths stand eight pavilions, with a small chapel behind and other working buildings. The iconography of the hunting lodge refers to the Elector's hunting exploits, with the Elector himself appearing in four large scenes. Besides the stucco images of hunting expeditions, Diana, the goddess of hunting, features in the great ceiling painting of the stairwell (see right).

At Clemenswerth, Schlaun established his own style comprising straight clean lines and simple, almost unornamented wall divisions. He rejected the decorative flourishes of the newly fashionable rococo, as if intending to move straight from late baroque into the early neo-classicism of southern Germany or France.

While still at work in Sögel, Schlaun received a commission for the construction of St. Clement's Church in Münster. He drew up a central plan, and incorporated it into the building complex of the monastery of the brothers of mercy, later St. Clement's hospital (1745–53). The whole complex was destroyed in the Second World War. The church has been reconstructed, but a parking lot currently occupies the site of the monastery.

Among the papers left by Schlaun is a measured drawing of the Roman church of S. Ivo alla Sapienza (1642–60) by Borromini. Schlaun undoubtedly based his design for St. Clement's on

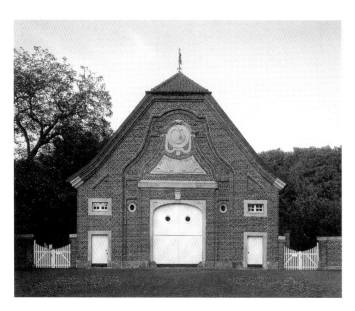

Borromini's sophisticated ground plan, which consists of a triangular shape with an inscribed circle. Piazza del Popolo and the church facades of S. Maria dei Miracoli and S. Maria in Montesanto seem also to have played a decisive role in Schlaun's design.

One of the finest and most daring architectural creations of the Westphalian architect is undoubtedly the Erbdrostenhof in Münster, which he designed immediately after St. Clement's (1749–57; see pp. 192–93). Schlaun was faced with the problem of adapting a corner site in a town. His solution was a barely projecting central block flanked by slightly curving wings running to tapered corners on Salzstrasse and Ringoldsgasse. The elegant and varied facade thus forms a triangular courtyard in front, enclosed by railings. The gate is set at the junction of the streets, and thus also the angle of the courtyard, right on the central axis of the mansion. Coaches could therefore pass in a direct line through the entrance archway of the mansion to the rear elevation, for servicing and to gain access to the stables and outbuildings. Slightly curved staircases lead from each side of the entrance hall up to side rooms, and a further set of steps leads on to the two-storey galleried ceremonial hall over the entrance hall (see p. 192).

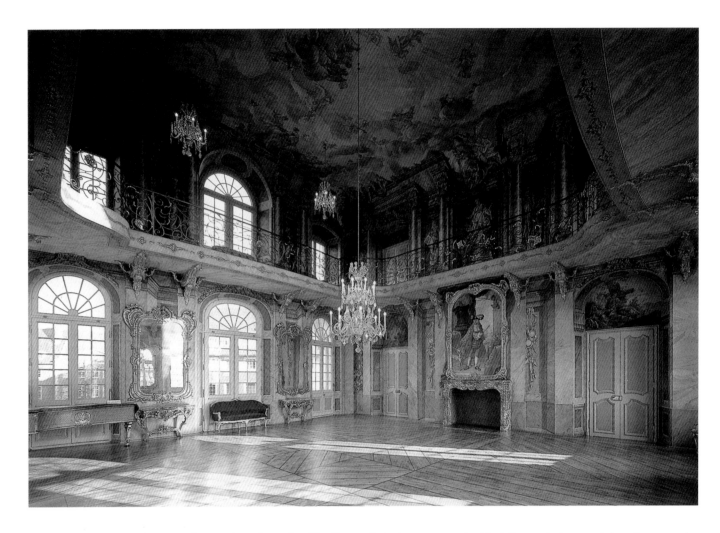

Italian influences are very much in evidence here also. The five-bays of the axial pavilion, a motif which was also used in the town facade of the mansion in Brühl, might have been derived from Borromini's facade of the Oratory of St. Filippo Neri in Rome. There too the middle elevation with its three-centered arch projects out to some degree from the larger curve (see p. 27, left). Bernini's second design for the east facade of the Louvre, made in 1665, was probably of more significance here. In the Louvre facade, a concave central block is flanked by similarly curved wings which are set back, with their narrow sides on the level of the center projection. It seems that Schlaun probably took account of the urban context of his work, since he planned the Erbdrostenhof and the neighboring St. Clement's church, where the facade arches forward, as a coherent grouping.

Not far to the northwest of Münster, Schlaun built himself a country lodge, the delightful Rüschhaus near Nienberge, erected while he was working on the St. Clement's project from 1745–49 (see p. 191, below). In his lodge he succeeded in combining the rustic farmhouse type of the Münster region with the frivolity of the French *maison de plaisance*. A central drive leads to the courtyard facade with its great entrance archway. Working buildings, attached to the main building like wings, flank the courtyard. The garden

front is ornamented with delicate windows and door frames and a flight of steps. In 1825 the Rüschhaus passed to the barony of Droste-Hülshoff, and was from time to time the home of the poet Annette von Droste-Hülshoff.

Schlaun spent the last six years of his life, from 1767 to 1773, on lavish plans and works for the new palace of the prince-bishop in Münster (see right below), intended to be sited at the citadel. The unoccupied ground between the palace and the town was to be transformed into a great park with avenues and squares on the French model. The palace itself was designed around three wings. The narrow sides were given their own facades. The main house therefore gives the effect of very shallow modelling for a baroque building, perhaps anticipating the neo-classical manner just coming into fashion. The prince-bishop's palace can be seen in many of its details as a transitional building. When Schlaun died at the age of seventy-eight in 1773, only the exterior was finished. The interior was executed by Wilhelm Ferdinand Lipper, who completed it in a neo-classical style in 1782.

The Prussian Metropolis: Andreas Schlüter in Berlin
During the Thirty Years War (1618–48) Brandenburg and Berlin were ravaged and destroyed by both Swedish and imperial troops.

OPPOSITE:
Johann Conrad Schlaun
Great hall, 1753–57
Erbdrostenhof, Münster

BELOW:
Johann Conrad Schlaun
Cour d'honneur facade, 1753–57
Erbdrostenhof, Münster

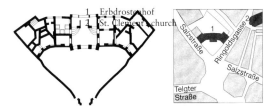

1 Erbdrostenhof
St. Clement's church

BELOW:
Johann Conrad Schlaun
Prince-bishop's palace,
Münster, 1767–73

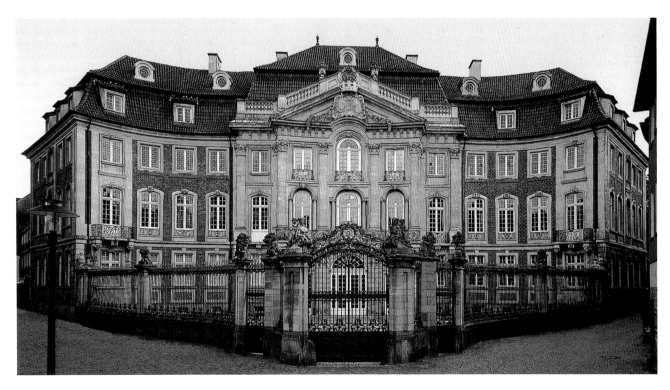

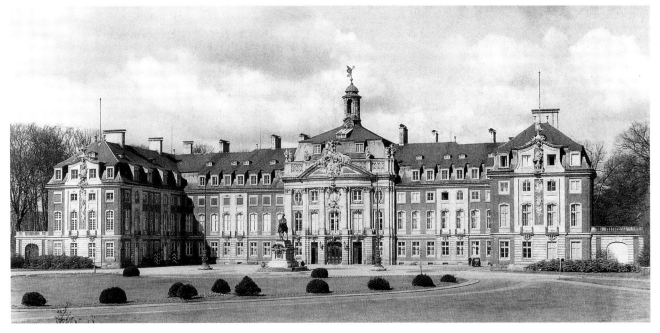

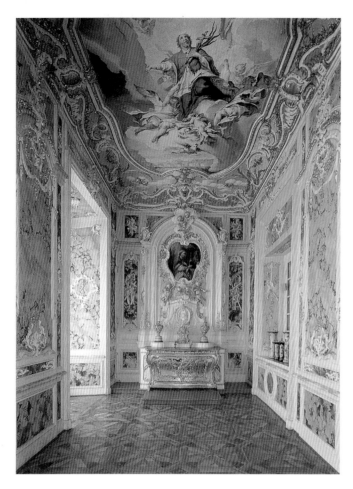

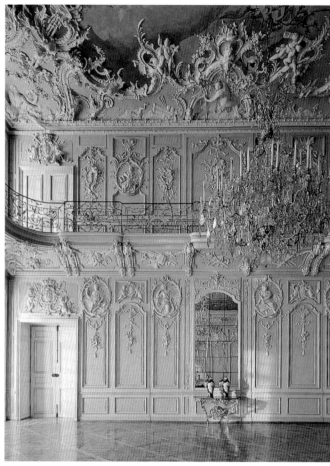

Johann Conrad Schlaun and
François de Cuvilliés
Augustusburg, Brühl
1724 and 1728-40

Nepomuk chapel (above left)
Dining-room (above right)
Facade of palace from the east (below)

OPPOSITE:
Balthasar Neumann
Staircase hall, 1741–44
Augustusburg, Brühl

Brühl was favored by the Elector Clement Augustus (1700–61), the builder of Schloss Augustusburg, because of its glorious surroundings. The Elector spent a lot of time here pursuing his beloved hobby of falconry. Schlaun therefore initially had a hunting lodge in mind. He designed a three-sided layout opening to the east. Following the urgent recommendations of his client, Schlaun incorporated parts of older buildings in order to save money. When the shell was finally complete, Clement Augustus's brother, the Elector Charles Albert of Bavaria, ridiculed the style as old-fashioned.

A change of plan was contemplated. The Munich court architect François de Cuvilliés replaced Schlaun, and transformed his scheme into an official seat with the character of a summer residence. The outer facade was remodeled and the interior was rearranged and refurbished.

The building is remarkable in that it combines Italian, Dutch, and south German ornament. Building was com-

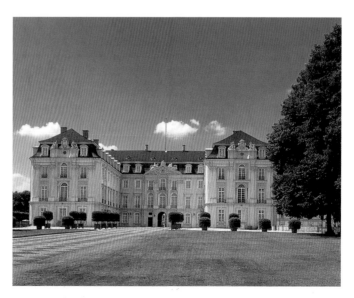

pleted after forty years, and the palace soon achieved a reputation as one of the most splendid rococo palaces anywhere. Clement Augustus did not live long enough to see his magnificent palace completed, though in his last year (1767) he was able to review the sumptuous furnishings of his ceremonial rooms. The paintings in them are particularly distinguished. Clement Augustus was keen on things Italian, and managed to obtain the services of an important artist for the paintings, the Lombard Carlo Carlone, second only to Tiepolo. Carlone designed the paintings for the staircase hall, music room, dining-room and guard-room, as well as the the Nepomuk chapel. He also did canvas paintings, one of which was housed in St. Clement's church. The "painter Carlone" received in all the magnificent sum of 5,325 imperial *thalers* for his work.

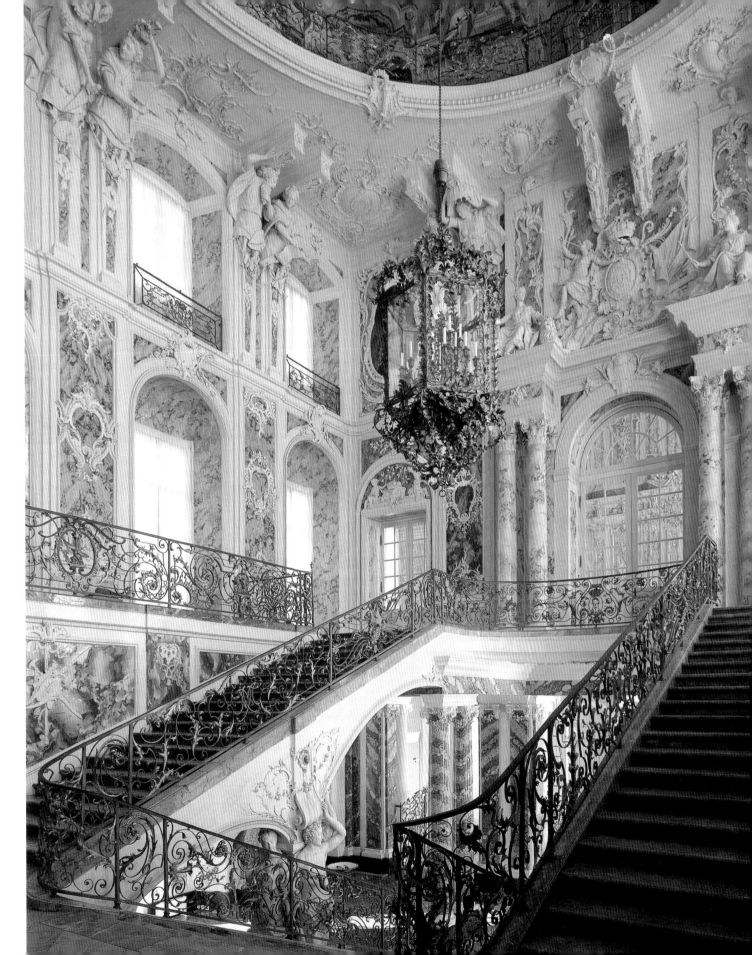

At the end of the war, Elector Frederick William (known as the Great Elector) ordered the fortification of the town. In 1685 he promulgated the Edict of Potsdam, creating a new home for twenty thousand Huguenots driven out of France. Their craft skills and artistic abilities made an important contribution to the economic and cultural flourishing of Berlin. Frederick William's successor, Frederick III, Elector of Brandenburg, had himself crowned king in Königsberg in 1701. A few years later, in 1709, Berlin and Kölln were united with the urban schemes of Friedrichswerder (1669), Dorotheenstadt (1674), and Friedrichsstadt (1688) as the royal capital and seat. During these decades the Elector effectively presided over the transformation of Berlin into a baroque city.

The planning work for these urban developments was assumed by the master of building works, Johann Arnold Nering, who had also transformed the palace of Oranienburg into a three-wing ensemble on the French model between 1688 and 1691. In 1694, a year before Nering died, Andreas Schlüter (?1659–1714) arrived in Berlin. A sculptor and architect, probably born in Danzig (now Gdansk), Schlüter had come from Warsaw, where among other projects he had designed the pediment reliefs of the Krasinski palace. He was commissioned by the Elector to complete the keystones of the windows and doors of the Zeughaus (arsenal) designed by Nering, adding a series of helmets to the exterior and twenty-two heads of dying warriors for the courtyard. After Nering's death, Schlüter took over his other commissions as well. These included redesigning the Stadtschloss in Berlin (see right above). Around 1698 the Elector asked him to supervise work on the palace, and a little later appointed him master of works there. At this time, Schlüter was still busy supervising building work at the arsenal, the foundry, and the parish church as well.

Schlüter was responsible not only for the planning and supervision of the actual building work, but also for the design of the decorative and painted schemes. He knew the plans for the royal palaces in Vienna, Dresden, and Stockholm. He had also become familiar with the plans for Schönbrunn palace when its creator, Johann Bernhard Fischer von Erlach, visited Berlin in 1704. This design was however only of limited relevance to Schlüter, as the specific hill site of the Viennese palace was hardly possible in Berlin. Clearly, however, some of Schlüter's own ideas inspired the Viennese architect, since he borrowed some of the articulation motifs of Schlüter's doorways and window areas for the corner pavilions of the Clam-Gallas mansion in Prague, which he built from 1713.

Schlüter also had contacts with Stockholm. In 1697 the Swedish architect Nicodemus Tessin the Younger, who had discussed the plans for the arsenal with Nering in Berlin in 1688, began work on the royal palace in Stockholm. Tessin was fired by Bernini's designs for the Louvre, and planned a cubic complex with a flat roof and giant orders on the east front. This meant abandoning baroque in favor of a more severe classicism. Obviously news of this novel and unusual style reached Berlin, since in 1699 a request for advice in building matters was sent by the Elector to the Swedish court. The flat-roofed northeastern blocks and the projecting central facade furnished with giant orders on the Berlin palace show the influence of the Stockholm building.

Schlüter's subsequent efforts in Berlin were somewhat less successful. The works on the palace were driven forward with considerable speed. Early in 1705, he also took over the supervision of the building works of the town palace at Potsdam for a short while, as well as working on summer seats and hunting lodges in the area, such as Caputh and Glienicke. Again and again, faults surfaced in the Berlin palace, while in other commissions he undertook, such as the construction of the Münzturm (from 1702), Schlüter made fatal mistakes which caused damage to neighboring buildings. In 1706 the Münzturm had to be demolished for fear of a total collapse. A year later, Johann Friedrich Eosander von Göthe took over the plans for the palace. After the death of the king in 1713, Schlüter left Berlin and traveled to St. Petersburg, to work in the service of Peter the Great. He died there a year later. Berlin's Stadtschloss was destroyed in the Second World War, and in 1950 the ruins were removed. Remains of the architectural sculpture can be found in the Berlin museums.

Potsdam and the Architecture of Georg Wenzeslaus von Knobelsdorff

During a visit by Prince Johann Moritz of Nassau-Siegen to the Great Elector Frederick William in 1664, the prince said of Potsdam, "The whole isle must become a paradise." Frederick Wilhelm had acquired the town of Potsdam with several neighboring villages four years earlier. Now he made Potsdam a second royal seat after Berlin. Potsdam, as Christian, count of Krockow wittily observed, represented the essence of Prussia condensed into pictures and symbols. The "Prussian principle" revealed itself in the utility of form, which displayed at most a restrained flamboyance. It was a concept that can be followed from the sober hunting lodge of Stern on the edge of Babelsberg, commissioned by the "Sergeant King" Frederick William I, right down to the "Frederician" rococo style preferred by his son Frederick II (the Great), who favored a structural elevation with a disciplined application of standard ornamental motifs. Perhaps an appropriate motto for Prussian baroque can be found in the popular saying of the time: "It's an honor to be Prussian, but no fun."

The first building works undertaken by the Great Elector between 1664 and 1670 were for the Potsdam Stadtschloss, which was to replace a medieval castle and its buildings that protected a crossing of the river Havel. Eight years before his death, the palace was completed with the collaboration of Johann Gregor Memhardt, Michael Matthias Smids, and Nering. In the 1690s the Elector Frederick III (son of the Great Elector) who, from 1701 had the right

Andreas Schlüter
Gateway I
Stadtschloss, Berlin
Begun 1698, destroyed 1950

Andreas Schlüter
Great staircase hall of
Stadtschloss, Berlin
Begun 1698, destroyed 1950
(top right)

Georg Wenzeslaus von Knobelsdorff
Stadtschloss, Potsdam
Begun 1664
Extended by Johann Arnold Nering and
others from 1680
Altered by Knobelsdorff 1744–52
Destroyed in the Second World War
(below)

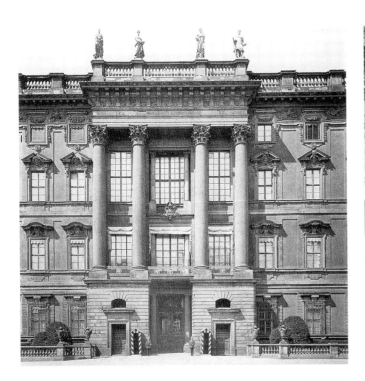

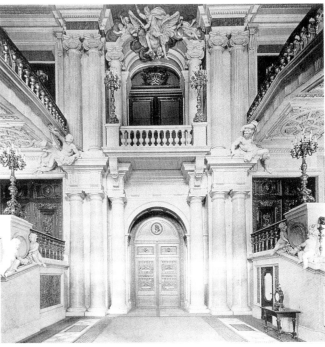

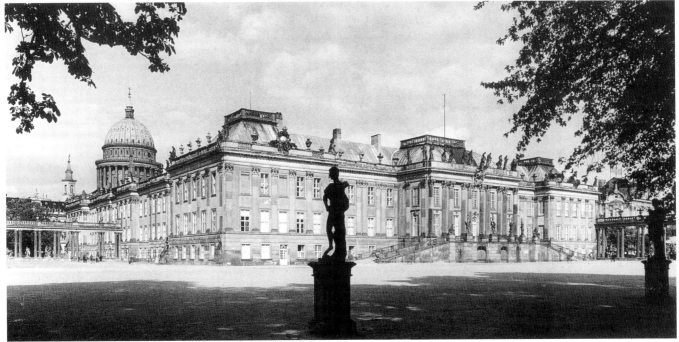

East wing of Golden Gallery, post-1740
Schloss Charlottenburg, Berlin
Reconstructed 1961–73 after destruction
during the Second World War

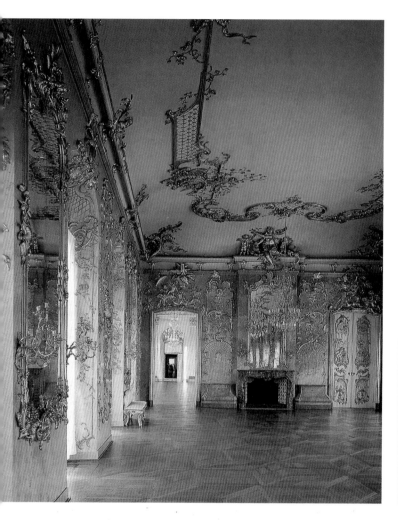

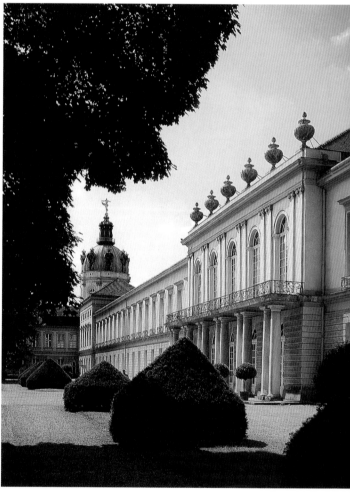

to the title of King Frederick I, had the palace transformed by a scheme incorporating three elevations.

It was not until the accession of King Frederick II, who was interested in both philosophy and music, that the Potsdam Stadtschloss was rebuilt (1744 and 1752). Frederick entrusted this work to Georg Wenzeslaus von Knobelsdorff, whom he had known while he was still crown prince of Rheinsberg. His father, Frederick William I, had bought Schloss Rheinsberg, in idyllic surroundings on Lake Grienerick, for his son who lived here until his accession. In 1737, the crown prince commissioned Knobelsdorff to extend the palace and immediately after his accession in 1740 the new king sent his architect to Dresden and Paris. On his return he appointed him superintendent of royal palaces and gardens, and ordered him to

begin work immediately on extending the little mansion of Monbijou in Berlin. One of the main schemes devised by the king was the development of the Potsdam Stadtschloss (see p. 197, below). Under Knobelsdorff's guidance, the sculptor Johann Michael Hoppenhaupt and the interior designer and decorative sculptor Johann August Nahl from Strasbourg planned the rooms, creating an interior which was later considered to be the masterpiece of Frederician rococo. The palace was destroyed in the Second World War and the ruins removed in 1959.

The first great commission and new building project of Frederick II was awarded to Knobelsdorff immediately after the king's accession in 1740. The architect was instructed to build an opera house in Berlin on Unter den Linden according to the king's specifications.

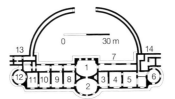

Georg Wenzeslaus von Knobelsdorff
Sanssouci, Potsdam
Begun 1745
Exterior of Marble Hall (below) and
ground plan (left)
1   Entrance hall
2   Marble Hall
3   Reception room/ dining room
4   Drawing-room
5   Bedroom/study
6   Library
7   Little Gallery
8–12   Guest rooms
13–14   Service rooms

The opera house was intended as the monarch's temple, an artistic expression of national status—"Federicus Apollini et Musis" runs one inscription here. To some extent the architectural, or rather the iconographical, structure of the building reflects this concept. Frederick wanted to link court festivities with opera performances in a similar manner to the ceremonies at the Zwinger at Dresden a few years previously. The Apollo Room served as a lobby and dining room. The auditorium and stage adjoined it, with eight Corinthian columns at the sides. The orchestral pit could be raised to the level of the stage, creating a spacious ballroom. The exterior of the opera was left largely free of decoration in the modern French taste. Two flights of steps lead up each side to a monumental pillared portico, through which the Apollo Room is entered. This, an unusually severe form for the period in Germany, had precedents in England, especially in the Palladianism of Inigo Jones, Lord Burlington, and William Kent. These architects and their works were certainly familiar to the king and his master of works and it seems that the English Palladian style gained an early foothold in Germany.

Schloss Charlottenburg in Berlin was the king's residence and official seat. He had commissioned Knobelsdorff to undertake the enlargement of the new wing of the palace as early as 1740, and sent messages to the master of works from the battlefields of the Silesian war, pressing him to complete the work as quickly as possible. A new east wing was to be added (see left) to the main building, partly as a foil to the orangery in the west wing. A graceful stairwell, which reportedly sent the king into rhapsodies of praise, links the lobby with the dining-room. The adjacent Golden Gallery (see left), with its rocaille decoration, volutes, flowers, and dancing putti, displays a stylish but restrained splendor, and is one of the finest rococo banqueting halls in Europe.

It is known that Frederick submitted to his architect not only rough sketches of his ideas but also fully worked out plans. These interventions often led to tension, with Knobelsdorff, of course, always coming off worse from the proceedings, as he was obliged to accommodate the obstinate demands of his royal patron. In the case of the plans for Sanssouci, there were fierce clashes between the two that deteriorated into bitter quarrels. In 1744 the king issued orders for the southern slope of a hillside east of Potsdam center to be terraced, in preparation for the planting of a vineyard. A year later, he decided to build a summer palace (see above and pp. 200–1). His wished to be able to step out through French windows onto the terrace without having to climb steps. Knobelsdorff, on the other hand, conceived of a building that would rise from a low basement storey above the front edge of the terrace. It would then be fully visible in all its glory from the park. The king naturally rejected this scheme, and the royal misjudgment is still apparent today, since the whole thing turned out exactly as Knobelsdorff had feared: the upper terrace overlaps the palace facade to unfortunate effect. A year later, in 1746, Knobelsdorff was dismissed and withdrew from the court. He

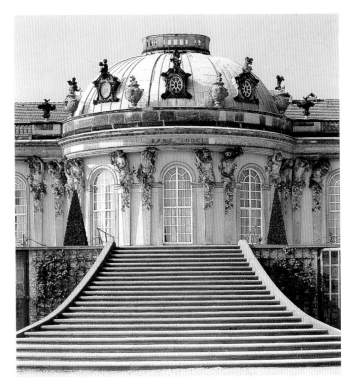

died in 1753. His works were taken over by Johann Boumann of Amsterdam, who had been in residence in Potsdam since 1732, where he had designed the Dutch quarter.

However, the Frederician rococo style at the palace is undoubtedly the work of Knobelsdorff. The French rococo *maison de plaisance*, the garden summerhouse set in natural surroundings, took on a new character under his supervision, although, as we have seen, his ideas were constantly modified by the unwanted interventions of the king. The element of sumptuous display is missing here, as are the endless suites of rooms. The building has an intimate character; it is a retreat with appropriate proportions and exquisite furnishings. Particularly striking are the bacchanalian figures designed by Knobelsdorff, merrily staggering under the effects of wine. Acting as terminal figures with satyrs and nymphs, they are seen supporting the roof timbers and adorning the windows.

Frederick retreated to Sanssouci every summer for forty years. In his will he decreed that he should be buried beside his eleven hounds, "without any pomp and circumstance… quite simply at the top of the terrace, on the right as you go up." The king died in 1786, but the instruction was not to be implemented for a further two hundred years.

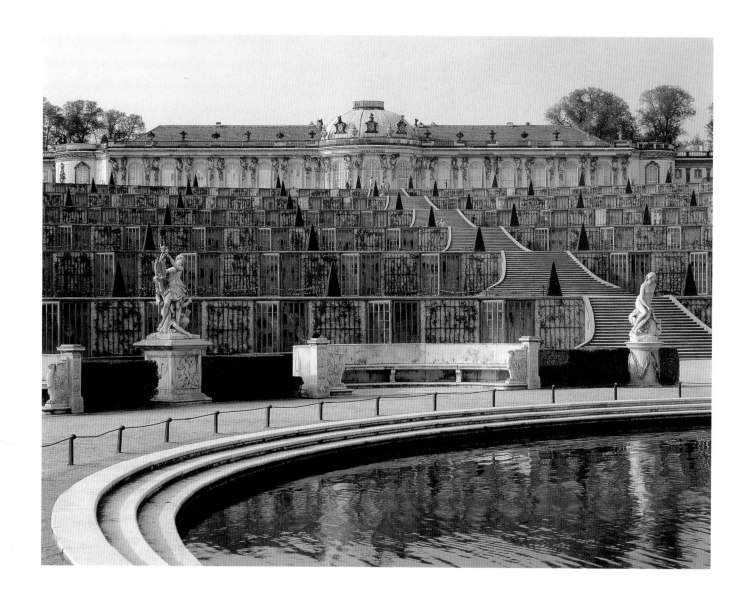

Georg Wenzeslaus von Knobelsdorff
Sanssouci, Potsdam, begun 1745
Garden front with vineyard (above)
Ground plan and elevation, 1744–45
(right)

Sanssouci, Potsdam
In 1744, an artificially terraced vineyard
was laid out with six curved terraces and a
central flight of steps. Frederick II chose this
for his summer residence. The palace of
Sanssouci, together with the extensive gardens, was laid out in accordance with plans
by the architect Knobelsdorff, although
Frederick himself made his own contribution, as surviving sketches indicate.

A mere two years after starting work,
fitting out of the interiors had already
started under Knobelsdorff's direction.
Almost a century later, Ludwig Persius
and Ferdinand von Arnim added the
return wings.

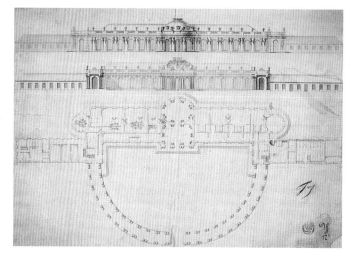

Sanssouci is unmistakable for its oval
central section which also contains the
principal rooms, including the domed
Marble Hall with its colored marble.
Adjacent to it are the king's living rooms,
the music room and bedroom-cum-study.
The circular library with cedar panelling
and bronze ornament is like a precious
gem. The rear courtyard is surrounded by
colonnades.

OPPOSITE:
Georg Wenzeslaus von Knobelsdorff
Entrance hall of Sanssouci, Potsdam
Begun 1745

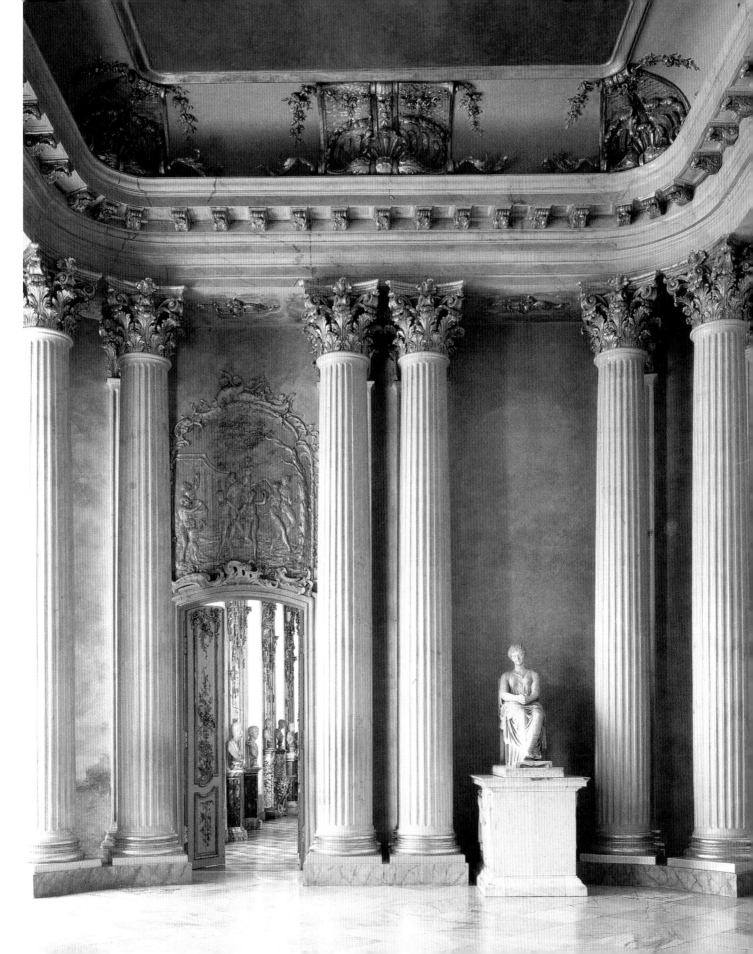

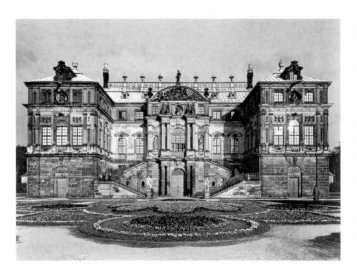

Baroque in Saxony

During his sightseeing tour of Dresden in 1718, the writer Johann Michael von Loen wrote enthusiastically: "The city of Dresden seems like one large pleasure palace, as it were, wherein all the inventions of the building arts pleasantly intermingle, and yet can be viewed separately. A stranger almost needs several months for it, if he wishes to take a close look at everything that is fine and magnificent in this place."

This was the Augustan age, a period when Dresden was considered the finest city in Germany. This was due not only to the palaces and churches, but also to the unusually rich art collections. The archeologist Winckelmann praised the collection of classical antiquities, which was considered the greatest of its kind north of the Alps. For the poet Goethe, the art gallery founded in 1722 with 284 pictures was "a shrine."

Frederick Augustus I (the Strong) (1670–1733) and his son Frederick Augustus II (1696–1763), a passionate art lover who relinquished his official business to his chancellor Heinrich, Count Brühl in order to devote himself to art, together transformed Dresden and Saxony into a grandiose baroque treasure chest. The great literary critic Herder commented that nowhere in Germany were art collections laid out as superbly and liberally as in Saxony. Moreover, Saxony could claim a position at the center of German music during this period. In Leipzig, Johann Sebastian Bach, choirmaster of St. Thomas's church, was developing his new music, and in Freiberg Gottfried Silbermann was ensconced in his organ workshop, famous all over Europe.

The cultural flowering of Saxony came to an end when Prussia annexed Austrian Silesia. Sixteen years later, the Seven Years War broke out (1756–63), laying waste to the country. War damage was estimated at over three hundred million thalers, and it was declared that the rebuilding of the country would take over twenty years.

Saxony's prosperity had begun before Augustus the Strong came to power, shortly after the Thirty Years War, when the Elector John George II appointed the architect Wolf Caspar von Klengel (1630–91) as principal architect for the province. Klengel had made an intensive study of Italian architecture. In 1661 he was commissioned to do some work at the sixteenth-century castle of Moritzburg, nine kilometers northwest of Dresden. Named after Duke Maurice, the lodge was among the finest renaissance buildings of Saxony. Klengel's task was to build a chapel, which he produced with high arched windows to link his new work to the old. The interior contained curved galleries, anticipating the interior of the opera house in Dresden, which Klengel was building at the same time (1664–67). Its appearance is known only from an engraving, as the building was to be permitted only a short existence.

Another important architect of the Augustan period is Johann Georg Starcke (1640–95), who in 1678 was asked by the Elector John George III (known as the subjugator of the Turks) to build a palace in the Grosses Garten at Dresden (see left). The garden had been laid out in the French style two years earlier by Johann Friedrich Karcher at the behest of the Elector John George II. The model was of course Versailles, which influenced the straight avenues intersecting at the palace. Taking an H-shaped ground plan, Starcke erected a palace of two and a half storeys. The double flight of steps fits into the space left in the H, leading up to a splendid doorway flanked with columns on the first upper level and thence to the grand hall. The Elector himself sketched out the architectural scheme for the palace, possibly inspired by an architectural idea of Klengel's. Starcke's execution of the scheme constitutes an interesting combination of the styles of the Italian summer residence and the French town palace. The core of the building and the arrangement of the steps are reminiscent of Italian country villas, but the window frames and architectural decoration follow closely the ornate character of French palaces. The palace became the prototype for baroque architecture in Saxony.

In the 1680s, three important figures arrived in Dresden: Marcus Conrad Dietze from Ulm, Balthasar Permoser, who had just spent a long time in Italy, and Matthias Daniel Pöppelmann from Westphalia. They were not to play a role until the following decades, however, after Frederick Augustus I, Elector of Saxony, succeeded to the throne in 1694; three years later he also acquired the royal crown of Poland and gained the title Augustus II of Poland. The "double king" commissioned the sculptor and architect Dietze to plan a new royal seat. He wanted an orangery built on the fairground and tournament field between the old castle and the outer bailey, and drew up a sketch for it himself. Dietze's design showed a horseshoe-shaped building, which formed the first element in the complex later known as the Zwinger (see pp. 203–05). The central

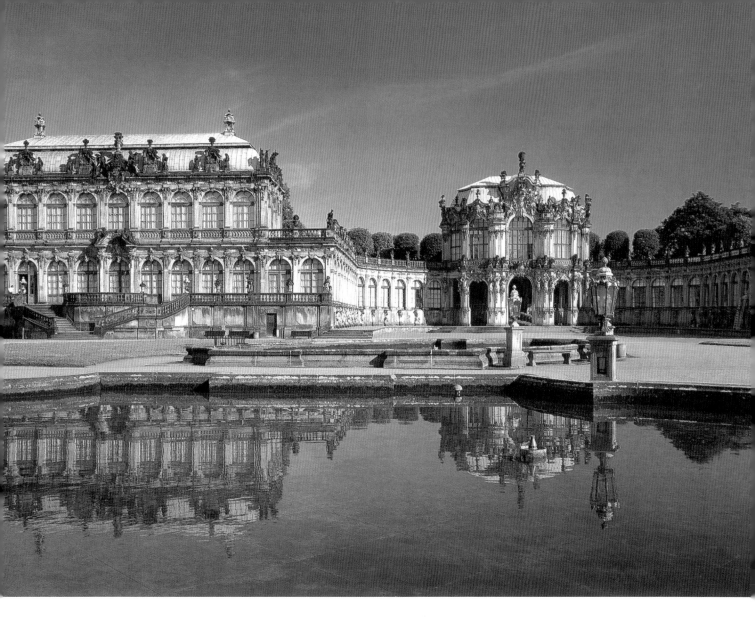

pavilion was supposed to be built on the model of Dietze's "green" gateway to the palace, which he had designed in 1692.

In 1704 Dietze had a fatal accident. The Elector appointed Pöppelmann and Permoser as his successors. In 1709 Pöppelmann began drawing up comprehensive plans. In 1716 the single-storey gallery buildings of the orangery formed an omega-shaped ground plan, with the Wallpavillon added over the stairs midway along the curved galleries. Two years later the royal client came up with his master plan. He probably recalled the visit by the Danish king in 1709, when he had ordered a wooden amphitheater with arcaded corridors to be erected to frame the festival ground for the king's reception. Perhaps he also had in mind the celebrations planned for the occasion of the marriage of the heir Frederick Augustus to the Archduchess Maria Josepha of Habsburg, due in 1719. In any case, he entertained the notion of a spacious and unusual festival ground without any direct link to the architecture of the palace. The court architecture would provide its own ceremonial delimitation of the

area. He therefore issued instructions that "this Zwinger garden structure" should be "built on the approved ground plan as a special structure... not aligned in symmetry with the palace." Pöppelmann evidently took these requirements literally, likewise remembering the amphitheater structure built for the Danish visit. He submitted a simple but inspired plan which included a new group of buildings that was a mirror image of the existing ones. One longitudinal axis now ran through the Wallpavillon, while its counterpart ran through the carillon pavilion. The center axis was marked by the Kronentor, on which work had been proceeding since 1713. Construction of the Zwinger was completed in 1728. The end piece on the River Elbe side was formed by an insubstantial "temporary' wooden gallery, which was in fact not replaced until Gottfried Semper built a permanent gallery between 1847 and 1854.

The Zwinger at Dresden is a good example of the often improvised, stage-set character of baroque palaces. The delay between the design of a building and its realization often seemed to princes and

Matthias Daniel Pöppelmann
Terms on rampart pavilion
Zwinger, Dresden, 1697–1716

Matthias Daniel Pöppelmann
Detail of Crown Tower
Zwinger, Dresden, 1697–1716

OPPOSITE:
Matthias Daniel Pöppelmann
Zwinger, Dresden, 1697–1716

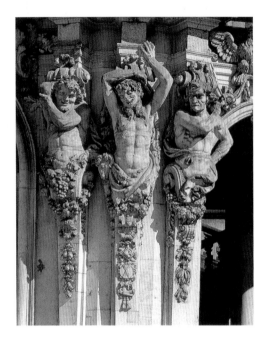

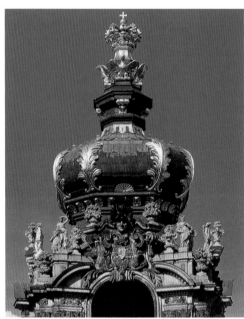

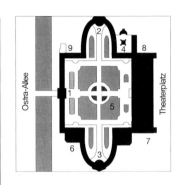

Zwinger, Dresden
Overall plan
1 Crown tower
2 Rampart pavilion
3 Glockenspiel pavilion
4 Nymphaeum with fountains
5 Court festival ground
6 Salon of Mathematics and Physics
7 Art Gallery
8 Historical Museum
9 Porcelain Museum

kings so great that their impatience forced a premature conclusion or allowed them to intervene with spontaneous changes of plan. The baroque period has been appropriately described by the German literary historian Richard Alewyn as reflecting "a culture of impatience."

The Zwinger was conceived as a space for receptions and court festivities. The omega form laid out by Pöppelmann must have been inspired by French palace architecture. The Trianon de Porcelain in Versailles, built 1670–72, possibly provided a model here; it was demolished a few years later in favor of the Grand Trianon. Italian garden architecture may be another source for this scheme. Sculpture and architecture at the Zwinger are closely unified. They are both at the service of pomp and festivity. For the Wallpavillon, Balthasar Permoser designed an allegorical scheme which pays homage to the glory of the Elector.

From 1720 to 1723 Pöppelmann was at work on another project which was similar both in concept and topographical situation, Schloss Pillnitz on the Elbe. The owner of the old mansion, Countess Cosel, had fallen out of favor at court and the Elector commissioned a summer pleasure palace. Pöppelmann designed the "Wasserpalais," an extended elevation along the banks of the Elbe, with curved roofs in the fashionable *chinoiserie* style (see p. 206, above). Four years later he constructed its counterpart, the "Bergpalais." The two elevations thus framed a courtyard area where a pleasure garden was installed. Permoser was not involved in its design, as he

preferred the more severe lines of French architecture and tried to maintain a clear articulation of wall surfaces. The architect was probably influenced by his colleague Zacharias Longuelune, an architect and painter from Paris who had collaborated with Pöppelmann since 1715 and who definitely favored the stricter French style.

In 1723, directly after finishing the work at Pillnitz, Pöppelmann was summoned to Moritzburg with Longuelune to rebuild the renaissance-style mansion there in the baroque style (see p. 206, below). The external walls were torn down, and Klengel's monumental chapel was balanced by a ceremonial hall. To ensure harmonious proportions, the architect enlarged the three round towers. Four palatial halls and more than two hundred rooms were splendidly decked out in the Saxon baroque colors of ocher and white. In 1730 the French park was enhanced by a great lake, which was often used subsequently for the staging of mock sea battles. The Fasanenschlosschen [Little Pheasant House] lies near it, built between 1770 and 1782 in the rococo style by J. D. Schade and Gottlieb Hauptmann.

One of the most important ecclesiastical buildings in Saxony is the Frauenkirche in Dresden (see p. 207), built by Georg Bähr, a carpenter from Fürstenwalde south of Dresden. Or at least this is how he is described by Count Wackerbarth, director of building in Dresden. In 1705 Bähr rose to the position of municipal master car-

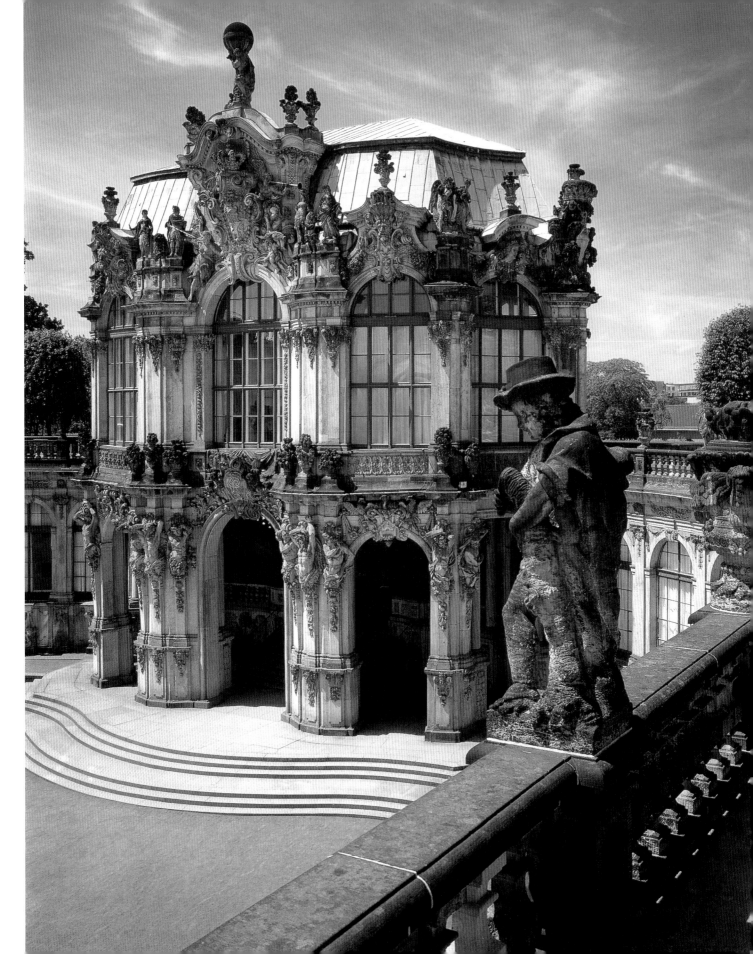

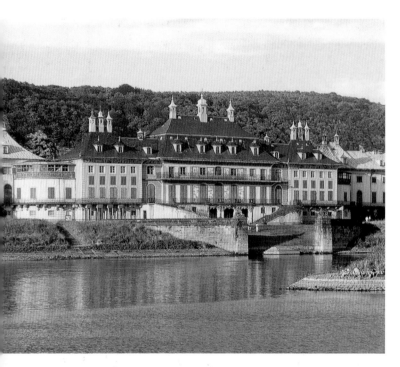

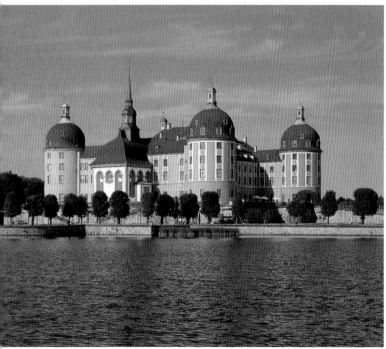

penter and after he obtained the commission for the Protestant structure in 1722, he was allowed to call himself building steward.

Bähr produced a square ground plan with three monumental facades and four diagonally set turrets housing the gallery stairs, the whole structure crowned by a high dome. It was modelled on a design by Giovanni Antonio Viscardi for the Mariahilfe church in Freystadt (Upper Palatinate), begun in 1700. However, the concept of a Protestant central plan was probably derived from a much closer source, namely H. G. Roth's church at Carlsfeld (1684–88) in the Erz mountains, Bähr's homeland. Bähr raised the choir somewhat and placed two curved flights of steps against the front choir piers to overcome the difference in level. A similar solution was found to deal with the discrepancy between central area and choir in the palace chapel at Rastatt, built a few years earlier (1719–21). The eight slender detached pillars present an effect of open space reminiscent of a ceremonial hall (see right). The growing importance of church music under the influence of the work of Bach and Handel must also have had some impact on the design of the plan. The organ—designed by Gottfried Silbermann of Freiberg—towers imposingly above the altar. The choir stalls were set laterally above the level of the altar. Altogether the church had five galleries, raising the overall seating capacity to five thousand.

The huge dome, crowned by a lantern known as the "stone bell" to the people of Dresden, was executed only after Bähr's death in 1738, by Johann Georg Schmid. The site supervisor Johann Christoph Knöffel, who had disagreed with Bähr over many details, delayed the completion of the dome because he claimed that he had no faith in the "carpenter's" ability to solve the complex technical problems involved. Nonetheless, the structure withstood bombardment by the Prussians in the Seven Years War and for a time also survived the blanket bombing of 1945, collapsing only two days after the bombardment onto the burnt-out sandstone building. Until recently, the ruin was treated as an anti-war monument. It has now been decided to rebuild the church by the year 2006, when the city celebrates its eight-hundredth anniversary.

In 1719 Frederick Augustus II, ruler of Protestant Saxony, converted to Catholicism in order to ascend the Polish throne. As a Protestant Elector and Catholic King, he had a Catholic church built in Dresden to provide proof of the dual religious allegiance of the monarchy. This is the Hofkirche, or court church, at the end of the Augustus Bridge. Gaetano Chiaveri, a Roman who had just come from planning parts of St. Petersburg, was given the task of designing a powerful counterpart to the Protestant Frauenkirche. Work began in 1738. Ten years later the painter Canaletto happened to be in the area and painted a unique view of the Elbe embankment with the Hofkirche and its still unfinished tower, the Augustus Bridge, and the imposing dome of the Frauenkirche (see right). This "last baroque structure" of Dresden was completed in 1755. Chiaveri's time in St. Petersburg and Warsaw had familiarized him with north-

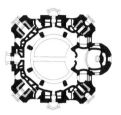

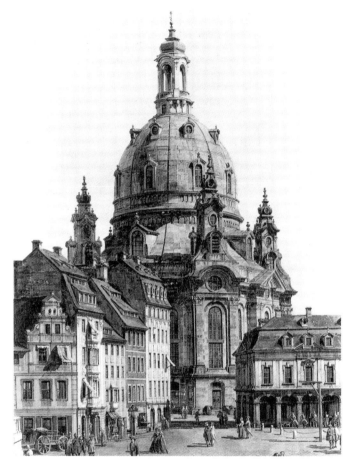

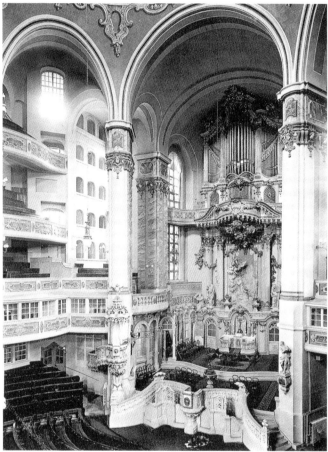

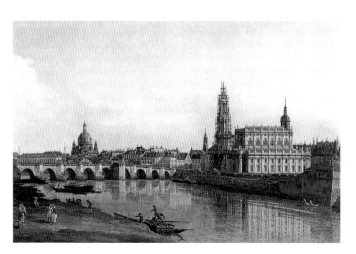

ern church architecture. He therefore made the west tower dominant, giving it a filigree, rather gothic appearance. Seen from the Elbe and the Augustus Bridge, the tower stood at the intersection of the lines between the palace tower and the Zwinger. It thus formed a pivotal point from which the structure of the city unfolded. The nave, pointing into the city, is a basilica with semicircular endings on the eastern and western sections, and ornamented with balustrades and with plinths bearing lively-looking saints by Lorenzo Mattielli.

Baroque half-timbered architecture

Components of timber buildings
1 Sill/ground plate
2 Joist/ floorboard
3 Nogging piece
4 Bracket
5 Panel   8 Upright
6 Brace   9 Lintel/crossbar
7 Brace   10 Window

Doorway, half-timbered church
Büssfeld (Hesse), 1699–1700

Even in Carolingian days, stone-built churches north and northeast of the Alps were something of a rarity. Most buildings were of timber. However, wooden churches were not always half-timbered. Churches of the half-timbered type are found in Europe in a region stretching from Holland across northern and eastern Germany as far as east Prussia (now northeast Poland and the Russian enclave of Kaliningrad). Isolated examples are also found in Normandy and southern England. Half-timbering is, of course, not peculiar to baroque architecture, but it is a building style which reveals a new aspect of baroque culture.

The unique concentration of half-timbered churches in Hesse should be considered in conjunction with the Reformation. The Reformation was introduced here in 1526 at the Synod of Homburg under Count Philip the Magnanimous of Hesse. Many daughter communities that had not previously had their own church building and whose inhabitants had often had to trudge to the mother church now received permission to build a church or chapel of their own. As the village congregations had to raise the costs themselves, simple and unprepossessing little churches and chapels were erected—often influenced by native housebuilding styles such as half-timbering. In Hesse, half-timbering was

further encouraged by the arrival of French religious refugees in the seventeenth and eighteenth centuries. Thus, especially in the Vogelsberg, Hesse developed a cultural landscape of half-timbered churches which flourished particularly during the baroque period. Over one-tenth of Hessian village churches are completely or substantially built with half-timbering.

Half-timbered churches of the pre-baroque or early baroque period (c. 1500–1670) were typically steeply proportioned and had an upper floor which in many cases was used for everyday purposes, like the fruit store in the church at Wagenfurth. East ends were generally straight, becoming polygonal only in the eighteenth century. Then there was often a period of mixed construction types using uprights and nogging. It was only after around 1700 that the really splendid half-timbered churches began to appear which still grace the landscape today. These are grand buildings with tall naves, terminating at the west end in substantial ridge turrets. East ends were henceforth generally polygonal in order to further emphasize the liturgical focus of the buildings. External walls are divided into two or three sections to absorb the lateral thrust of the tall roofs. To give the wall structure the necessary dynamics and strength, it was reinforced at the corner

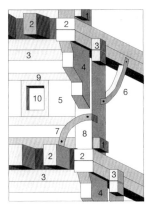

or head posts or studs with braces. The churches of Dirlammen, Sellnrod, Stumpertenrod, and Breungeshain are good examples of this.

The half-timbered church at Stumpertenrod, built between 1696 and 1697 (see below) is the largest of its kind in the Vogelsberg area. The wall structure is complex. Additional crossbars were also used over window lintels as the wall surfaces between the tall windows were too extensive. Corner posts, braces, and vertical studs transform the wall surfaces into a dense network of timbering. The

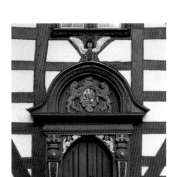

lateral thrust of the roof and vault is strongest above the windows.

For this reason, the area between the upper wall plate, where the vault begins, and the point where the upper part of the roof starts, is subdivided by a cross rail. The brace motif of the "husband" and the angle braces give this upper part of the wall the necessary rigidity.

Other characteristics of baroque half-timbered churches in Hesse are the ornate doorframes and carved pillars of the interiors. The doorways in Stumpertenrod and Büssfeld (see below) are par-

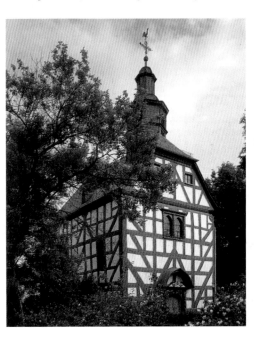

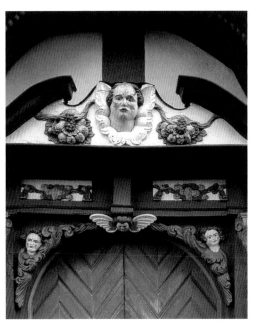

Half-timbered church, Stumpertenrod (Hesse), 1696–97
Diagram of half-timbering

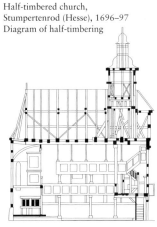

FAR LEFT:
Half-timbered church, Stumpertenrod (Hesse), 1696–97

LEFT:
Detail of doorway, half-timbered church, Stumpertenrod (Hesse)

Doorway of a half-timbered house, Seln-
roth

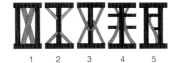

Alemannic half-timbering motifs also
used in baroque buildings
1 St. Andrew's cross
2 "Swabian wife"
3 An early form of the "husband"
4 "Husband"
5 "Half-husband"

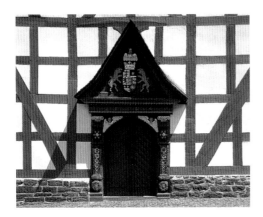

ticularly notable. Artistically finished
chancel and pews join the pillars in
Hohenroth with their rich ornament of
foliage and spirals from the first half of
the eighteenth century.

The persistence of Alemannic timbering into the seventeenth and eighteenth
centuries and its link with Franconian
ornamental motifs are specific to southwest German "half-timbered" baroque.
The picturesque little town of Mosbach
in the Oden forest is a treasure trove of
baroque timber-building motifs. Particularly of note are the sixteenth- to eighteenth-century residential buildings around
the market square above all the Palmisch
house (see right), with half-timber rising
on a stone plinth. Alemannic motifs such
as "husband" and saltires are harmoniously combined with Franconian decorative motifs like curved braces and crosses.
Balcony and windows have carved
frames and consoles, and many timber
structures are filled out with a variety of
rosettes and foliage motifs.

In the old town of Sindelfingen it is
possible to trace the cultural history of
half-timbering virtually from its origins
to the baroque period. Remarkably, the
half-timbered houses with striking decorative forms tend to belong to the
Renaissance rather than the baroque era.
In Württemberg, baroque half-timbering
is conceived structurally, more with an
eye for symmetry, than the ornate stonework of the princely pleasure palaces.
The reason was that half-timbered
houses are bourgeois houses and their
residents regarded the extravagant activities of the capricious circle around the
duke with suspicion and distaste. In a
bourgeois household, a single wax candle
was often considered a luxury; for the
duke, who might have thousands of can-

dles to illuminate a banquet, it was a
trifle. In contrast, the middle classes demonstrated simplicity and piety in the aesthetic style of their homes and public
buildings. Such severity of form was most
obviously evident in the Protestant districts of Württemberg. In Catholic areas,
the timber structures are often lightened
with Franconian decorative motifs, especially on the houses of well-to-do citizens
of the seventeenth and eighteenth centuries like the "Swede's House" in Altingen,
near Herrenberg (see right).

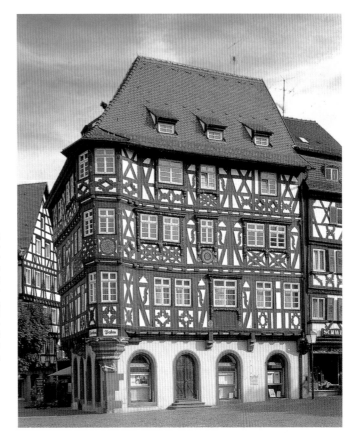

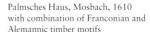

Palmsches Haus, Mosbach, 1610
with combination of Franconian and
Alemannic timber motifs

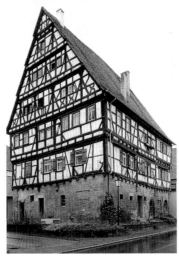

RIGHT:
"Schwedenhaus"
Altingen, near Herrenberg
17th century

Maximilian von Welsch,
Balthasar Neumann, and others
Garden front of Schloss Bruchsal
Begun 1720

Balthasar Neumann
Staircase hall, Schloss Bruchsal

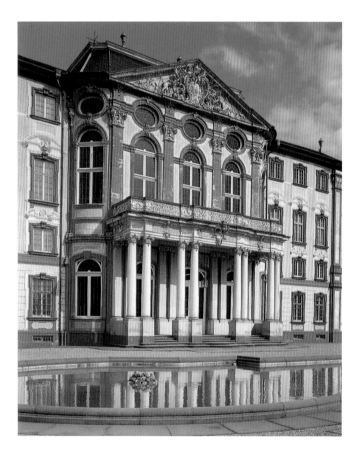

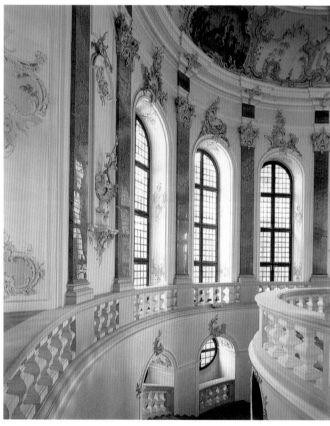

Palaces and Churches in Franconia

Baroque architecture in Franconia is particularly associated with one city and one name, Würzburg and Johann Balthasar Neumann (1687–1753). Though this association does not do justice to the variety of baroque art in this part of southern Germany, it does highlight a specific aspect of German baroque architecture. It was Neumann's good fortune to be born into what was even then known as the "Schönborn age," a period in the eighteenth and nineteenth centuries characterized in Franconia by magnificent building schemes and a brilliant artistic life. The rulers of the house of Schönborn in Franconia and the Rhineland were all patrons of architecture and thought nothing of employing famous architects like Johann Dientzenhofer or Johann Lukas von Hildebrandt.

The head of the family was the Elector Lothar Franz von Schönborn (1655–1729), also archbishop of Mainz, imperial archchancellor and prince-bishop of Bamberg. His nephew Johann Philipp Franz von Schönborn (1673–1724) was prince-bishop of Würzburg and Neumann's client. The latter's nephew, Friedrich Karl (1674–1746), was imperial vice-chancellor in Vienna and from 1729 prince-bishop of Würzburg and Bamberg. They were all, as a contemporary saying had it, "bitten by the building bug." Lothar Franz employed Maximilian von Welsch (1671–1745) as director of works and Johann Dientzenhofer. The Elector also employed Hildebrandt of Vienna as guest architect, who had been specially recommended by the Elector's nephew Karl.

The specific nature of the connections between client and architect is of great importance in explaining Neumann's activities at the court of Würzburg. When he received the commission for the Würzburg Residenz in 1719, Neumann had just returned from the Turkish wars in which he was held the rank of lieutenant. He was thirty-two years old, and was now given the opportunity to work with famous architects such as Maximilian von Welsch, Johann Dientzenhofer, Hildebrandt, and the Frenchmen Gabriel Germain Boffrand and Robert de Cotte.

Work commenced in 1720. In 1722 Neumann became involved with Welsch and Hildebrandt in the planning of the Schönborn

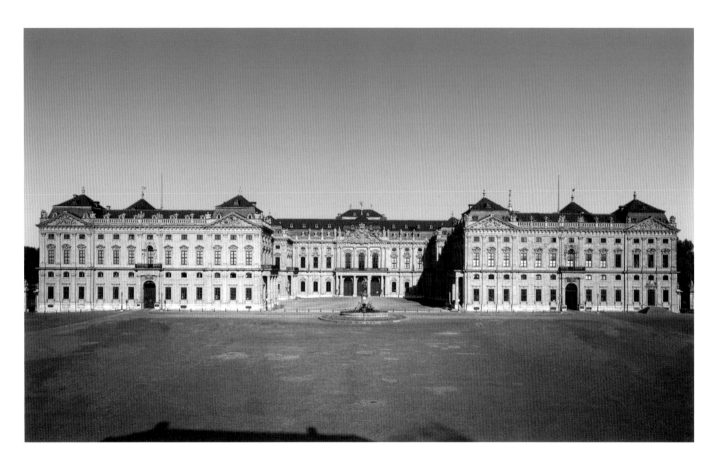

chapel in the cathedral, where he directed building work until 1736. In 1723 he traveled to Paris to discuss the plans for the palace with Boffrand and de Cotte. These discussions are well documented in Neumann's letters to the prince-bishop.

De Cotte's harsh criticism of the spatial disposition of the Würzburg Residenz highlights two fundamentally different approaches to architecture. For Neumann, rectangular interior courtyards were "an instrument of architectural articulation," whereas for de Cotte they represented a waste of building space. Neumann stood firm, arguing that his plan started from the "principal figure," that is from outside in, in order to achieve homogeneous and proportionate elevations. De Cotte, on the hand, planned from the inside out, in order to do justice to the palace's ceremonial functions. He therefore complained about the absence of a central palace chapel, and proposed that one of the staircase halls be replaced by a church which should not be too far from the center of the palace. The quick-witted Neumann immediately countered with the example of Versailles, where the palace chapel is also situated some way from the center of the palace.

A year later, in 1724, the prince-bishop died. When Bishop Christoph Franz von Hutten was elected, work on the Residenz was at first suspended. In the following years Neumann continued work on the Schönborn chapel. Not long afterwards, in 1727, he was summoned to Bruchsal by Cardinal Damian Hugo von Schönborn, prince-bishop of Speyer and brother of the late prince-bishop of Würzburg, to take on the construction of the palace there. Work on Schloss Bruchsal had already begun in 1720, initially following designs by Welsch and under the site direction of Neumann's pupil Johann Daniel Seitz. This task was later taken over by Michael Ludwig Rohrer from Rastatt, who promptly fell out with the prince-bishop. In the following years, quarrels blew up between client and architect, to the point where Neumann's dismissal was considered. He submitted new plans, however, including the famous curving double flights of stairs executed in 1731 by Johann Georg Stahl. The staircase sweeps up to the piano nobile from a rectangular vestibule, rising around a circular space, which is surmounted by a wide dome. It is a remarkable structure, and one that was ultimately to establish the fame of the palace (see p. 210, right).

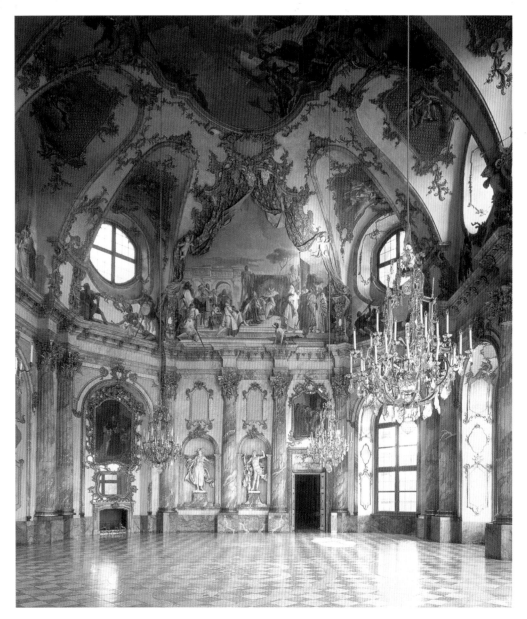

OPPOSITE:
Maximilian von Welsch, Johann Lucas von Hildebrandt, Balthasar Neumann, and others.
Center block, garden front
Würzburg, Residenz, 1720–44

Maximilan von Welsch, Johann Lucas von Hildebrandt, Balthasar Neumann, and others.

Emperor's Hall (left) with frescos by G. B. Tiepolo, completed 1752
Würzburg, Residenz, 1720–44
The pictorial scheme of the Emperor's Hall depicts the history of the city of Würzburg. Scenes include the bridal journey of Beatrice of Burgundy, her betrothal to Frederick Barbarossa (1156), and the confirmation of the bishop's power by the Emperor (1168). The stuccowork was by Antonio Bossi.

The new prince-bishop of Würzburg only lasted until 1729. His successor, Friedrich Karl von Schönborn, gave orders for the immediate resumption of building work on the Residenz. By 1737 work was progressing so well that a start could be made on laying out the staircase hall. By 1742 the vault was in place. In the same year the great vault of the Imperial Hall and the White Room were completed, and the shell of the house was finished—after twenty-five years of construction—in 1744.

When he signed the declaration of war against Prussia in front of the palace on October 2, 1806, Napoleon is supposed to have observed to his generals that he was standing on "Europe's largest vicarage lawn." The monumental space in front of the huge building is 180 yards long and 100 yards deep; with the magnificent palace, it was intended to show Europe's rulers that the house of Schönborn could offer something that was the equal of the famous palaces of Versailles and Schönbrunn, the centers of power of France and the Habsburg. The main elevation of the building is framed by wings, each with a pair of interior courtyards, which serve to emphasize the dominant projecting central elevation. The structural plan can best be seen from a distance. From the lower end of the square, the facades of the wings and the central elevation appear to lie approximately on the same plane, creating the impression of a single long palace facade. But then the facade begins to move: the projecting center section with its pillared portico appears to recede, although still remaining dominant. The wings open up to reveal a depth focusing on the center of the palace. The centralism of the Catholic church and the status of the ruler are effectively represented by this dynamic architectural arrangement.

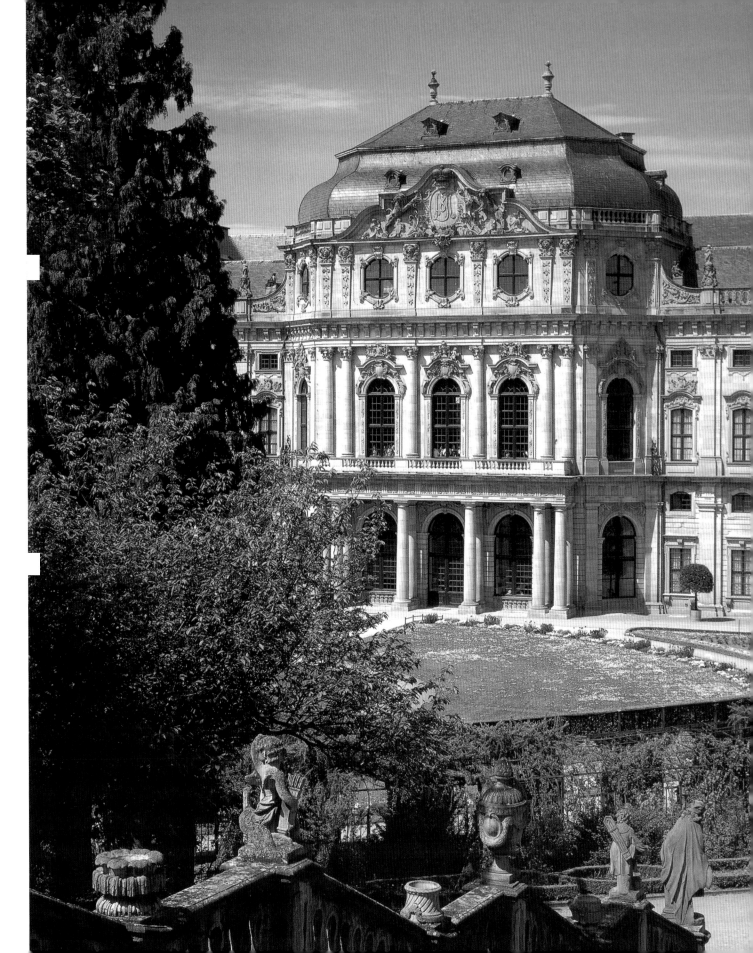

Balthasar Neumann
Interior of Dreifaltigkeitskirche,
Gaibach, 1742–45

Balthasar Neumann
West front of pilgrimage church of
Vierzehnheiligen, 1743–72

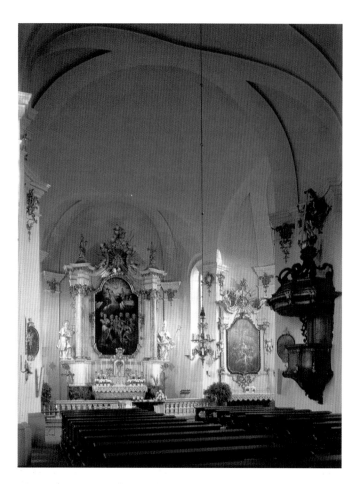

age church at Vierzehnheiligen which was set high above the Main valley (see right). The design that he had successfully introduced into the Trinity church, in particular the fusion of different sections into a dynamic and light interior layout, he brought to perfection in Vierzehnheiligen. Despite the planning problems of the site, which were partly the result of the designs of the Thuringian court architect G. H. Krohne and the interventions of the Schönborn prince-bishop of Bamberg, Neumann was able to achieve his ideas for this project. The nave is formed by three large ovals with circular transepts; it projects into the choir and is set off only by circular side chapels or aisle chapels. However, since a crossing—as indicated by the ground plan—is "outplayed" by the depressed vault of the nave, the nave expands into these side zones, attaining an architectural culmination in the chancel. Here the eye is caught by an intricate theatrical interplay of light, architecture, and plasterwork. Neumann placed the spiritual focus—the pilgrim's altar of grace—at the center of the church, about halfway between the entrance and the altar, a design based on an idea of his colleague J. M. Kuchel, who was also involved in planning this church. Thus the external basilica form is transformed into a centralized plan in the interior.

Barely thirty years separate the construction of Vierzehnheiligen and the monastic church of Banz opposite it, designed by Johann Dienztenhofer between 1710 and 1718. Whereas Neumann sought

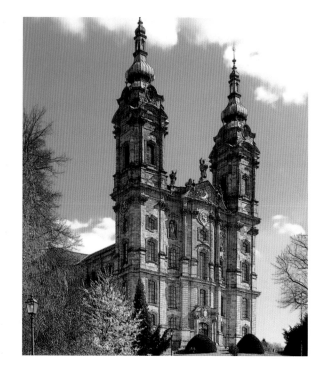

While he was working on the Residenz Neumann was also engaged in various other projects such as the country house and garden of Werneck (1733–45) and building the Dreifaltigkeitskirche (Trinity church) in the Schönborn village of Gaibach, near Volkach am Main (1742–45). The new ground plan and vaulting scheme of the Trinity church are particularly unusual (see above). The interior consists of a nearly spherical oval shape that is set crossways and therefore also functions as a crossing. Three elliptical smaller spaces adjoin it on the east side, forming a choir and transept. The pillars project and support strap-like diagonal arches which are elegantly joined in the vaulting of the choir and transept, then part again to continue down to the pillars opposite. The fusion of the crossing vault with those of the transepts and choir is one of Neumann's characteristic devices. The interior is lighter, with a greater sense of breadth and height.

During the same period that he was working on the Trinity church in Gaibach, Neuman also developed a plan for the pilgrim-

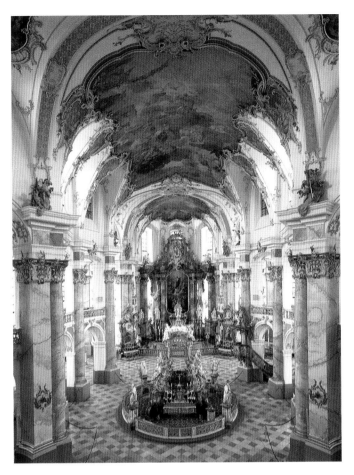

Balthasar Neumann
View of nave (left), ground plan (right),
and altar of grace (below)
Pilgrimage church of Vierzehnheiligen
1743–72

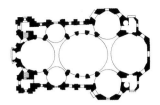

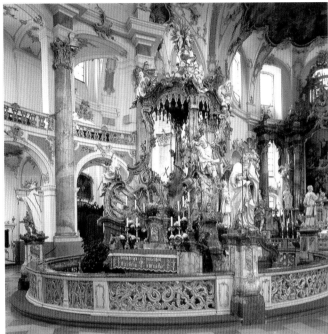

a homogeneous spatial scheme through the interplay of ground plan and vault, Dientzenhofer articulated the church interior by means of cross-placed ovals which become narrower in the extended choir. The bays have their own well-defined window areas and vaulting schemes, so that a spatial rhythm develops that leads dramatically toward the end of the choir.

With Vierzehnheiligen, Neumann went far beyond the architecture of Dientzenhofer, abolishing the traditional iconology of church interiors. The crossing dissolves in an area where the extended ceiling vaulting drops in the direction of the upward sweep of the choir vault and where airy side spaces—once the realm of the transept—are crowned with circular domes. The liturgical focus moves back into the center of the nave where the pierced walls are articulated by half and three-quarters engaged columns, pilasters, and a gallery. Unfortunately the architect did not live long enough to see his miracle finished. When he died in 1753, the shell remained uncompleted. The vaulting was not executed until 1763 and the actual dedication of the church was another nine years later.

In 1745 the Habsburg Emperor Franz Stephan and Empress Maria Teresa visited the Würzburg Residenz. Neumann took over the guided tour, and it is possible that during this the talk turned to building work in Vienna. Hildebrandt died in that year. At any rate, two years later, in 1747, Neumann submitted new plans for the Hofburg in Vienna. The Empress acknowledged receipt by sending

him a gold snuffbox. In the same year he drew up new plans for the palace in Stuttgart. He presumably even spent some days there at the seat of Württemberg. It is certain, however, that he visited the Elector Clement Augustus of Cologne in Bad Mergentheim. Neumann's availability for outside work at this point may be associated with the death of his patron, the prince-bishop of Würzburg; his successor, Count Anselm Franz von Ingelheim, had promptly dismissed Neumann as director of building works. The refurbishing of the Würzburg Residenz faltered and soon ground to a complete halt.

During this period of travel and architectural planning, Neumann also went sightseeing in Neresheim, and subsequently drew up plans for a new abbey church there (see pp. 216–17). Two years later he supplied a more detailed proposal. In Neresheim, Neumann was able to realize his vision of a combined longitudinal and central plan—an architectural concept that spans the transition from late baroque to early classicism. The starting point is a cruciform ground plan: on both east and west sides a pair of crossways-set domed and vaulted oval areas run into a space marked out by four free-standing pairs of columns delineating a round temple that separates two side areas. Longitudinal and circular structures are united. The remaining basilica feature is evident in the narrow apses accompanying nave and choir. Wall-piers and free-standing piers break up the walls and transform the basilica into a hall. The light and airy grandeur of the space is particularly enhanced by the high

Balthasar Neumann
Ground plan (right) and interior of
Neresheim abbey (below), 1745–92

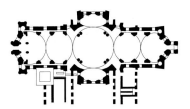

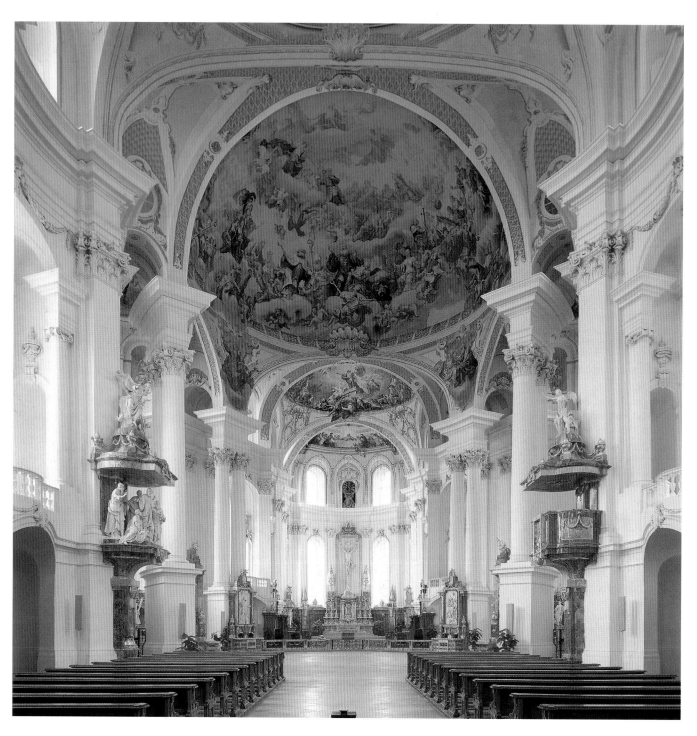

galleries set above plinth level. The upper wall area is thus bright-
ened and lends the sequence of bays a captivating rhythm. The
vaulting accents each bay while appearing to gravitate towards the
central dome which is the main feature here. The flattened transverse arches separate the crossways-placed oval domes. This is a
more controlled and yet more commanding version of the
Vierzehnheiligen arrangement, where the transverse arches inter-
weave.

On December 13, 1750, the court quartermaster of Würzburg
noted: "Yesterday the Venetian painter Tiepolo arrived, bringing
with him his two sons and a servant. He is housed at court in the
corner room in the Rennweg garden and has five rooms at his disposal. Food was laid on for him at table in the courtiers' house, initially
along with the valets because it was more convenient for him, but he
was finally left to eat alone, and he had eight dishes at lunchtime and
seven in the evening. For the rest, he was allowed to want for nothing and was treated splendidly in every respect."

Tiepolo had been commissioned to paint the frescos in the
Imperial Hall, an extended octagonal banqueting room with a high
vaulted ceiling. These occupied him until 1752. During this time, the
painter must have walked through the staircase hall every day, and
must have marveled at the 6,500 square feet of ceiling vault that
remained unfinished. Tiepolo was thus able to study the way in
which the light changed according to the seasons, and was presumably impressed by the boldness of the structure. The staircase hall as
it was finally executed was as Neumann had originally conceived it.
In his initial plan, he had provided for a small double staircase. It
was only in 1735 that he finally decided on his "theater of light"
solution: the free-standing double staircase is set in the staircase hall,
and runs straight up in a shallow rise towards the ceiling; it then
turns in the opposite direction, swinging further up into the space
beneath the surmounting vault (see p. 219). It appears that
Neumann derived some of his ideas for this design from Schloss
Weissenstein in Pommersfelden (see pp. 220–21)—but he deployed
them quite differently. Pommersfelden had been built in a record five
years between 1711 and 1718 by Dientzenhofer and Hildebrandt.
The stairwell on which they collaborated is just one component in a
monumental space vaulted by a huge ceiling. By contrast,
Neumann's stairwell at Würzburg forms a coherent spatial entity
which defines the surrounding area. Whereas in Pommersfelden the
viewer is presented with an aesthetic cornucopia comprising painting, plasterwork, and architecture, in Würzburg the scheme choreo-
graphs the eye as space and ceiling paintings successively unfold
before it.

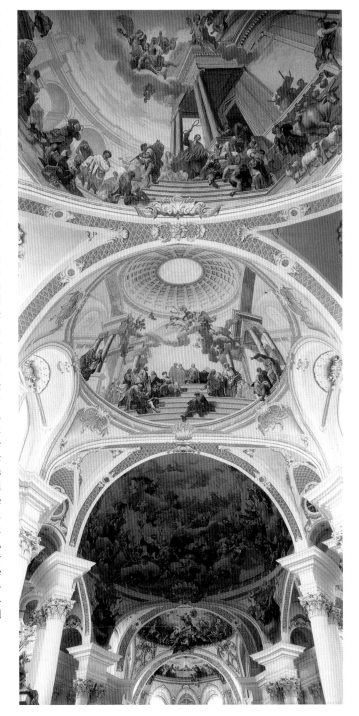

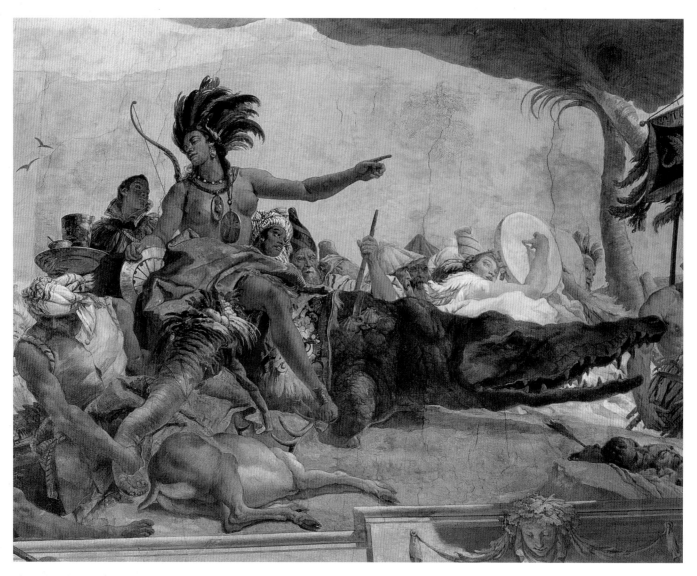

Giovanni Battista Tiepolo
Detail of the allegory of the continent of America
Ceiling fresco of staircase hall, 1751–53, Residenz, Würzburg

The celebrated Venetian fresco-painter Tiepolo took advantage of the dramatic possibilities of the staircase hall and drew up a "narrative plan" for the pictorial program. As the huge ceiling gradually unfolds going up, the observer is supposed to read the scene literally step by step, like a motion picture. Thus, in Tiepolo's design, the overall scheme is not a total composition to be read within a single frame but a map to follow. Going up, the America fresco (above and diagram A) comes into view. Bit by bit the heavens unfold, with Apollo in a burst of light and restless, populated trails of cloud. At this point, Asia and Africa steal into view. In the meantime, the observer reaches the landing, where the stairs turn 180 degrees and divide. Apollo (diagram B) moves suddenly out of the center and,

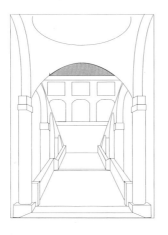

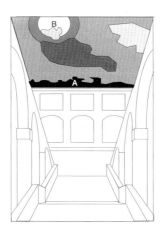

separated by a huge bank of cloud, Mercury sweeps in, pointing southwards towards Europe, the center of civilization. The perspective is laid out at this point so that the architectural elements can most effectively showcase their effects.

OPPOSITE:
Balthasar Neumann
Staircase hall
Residenz, Würzburg, 1735

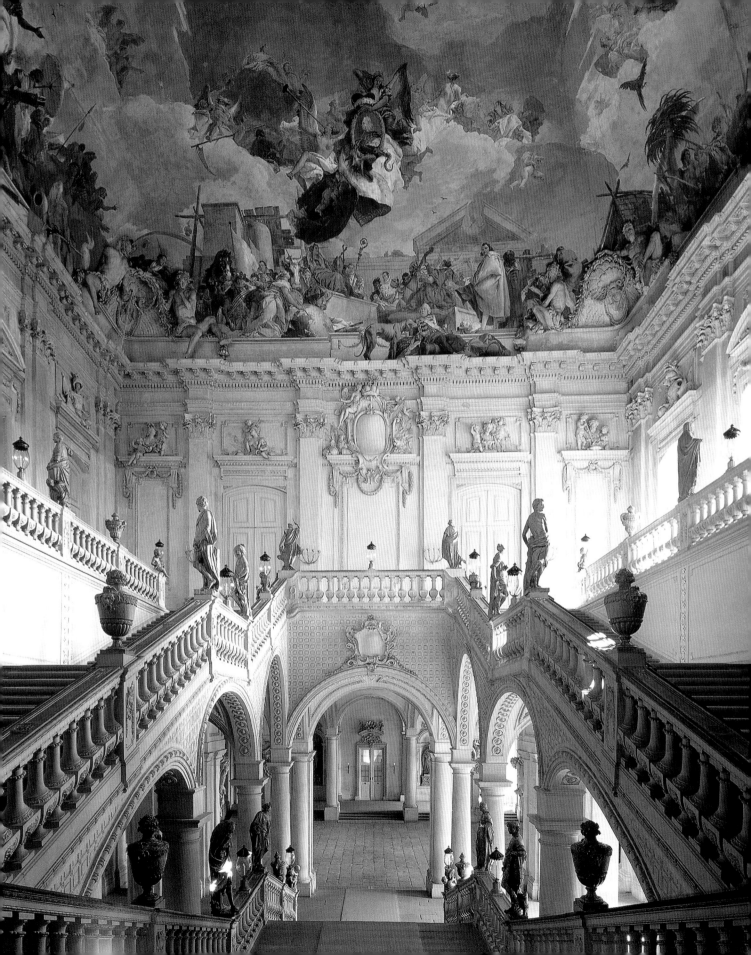

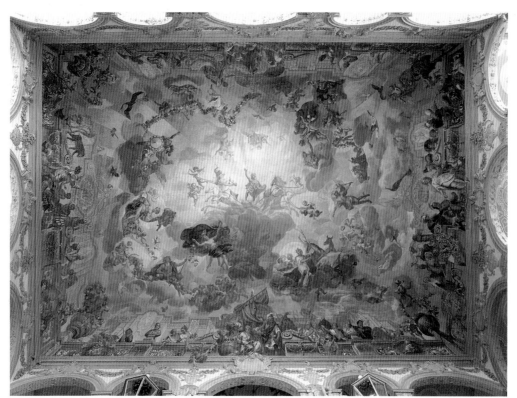

Johann Dientzenhofer and Johann Lucas von Hildebrandt
Staircase hall, Weissenstein palace, Pommersfeldern, 1711–18

Johann Rudolf Byss
Ceiling fresco in stairwell of Weissenstein palace, Pommersfelden, 1713

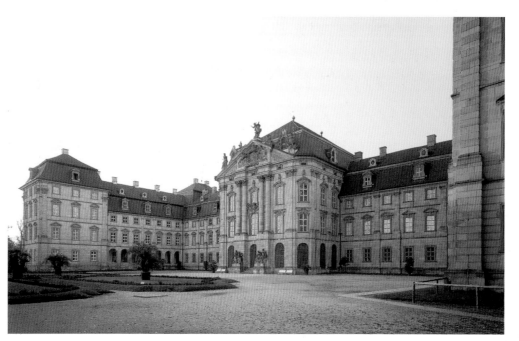

Johann Dientzenhofer and Johann Lucas von Hildebrandt
Courtyard view of Weissenstein palace, 1711–18

The staircase hall at Weissenstein palace, Pommersfelden (see right), was conceptually a grand room for which Johann Dientzenhofer first drew up plans in 1712. His original idea for the ceiling was a vast fresco. The stairs would run round and so open up the scenes optically to the observer. A year later, the plans were handed over to Hildebrandt for reworking. The Viennese architect adopted a different approach to the spatial situation from his colleague Dientzenhofer and suggested including a gallery. With this approach, the openness of the space was retained, but the ceiling was reduced to a size where it could impress in proportional relationship to the height.

Balthasar Neumann later proposed yet another approach for Würzburg. He saw the staircase structure as an independent architectural component in the spatial organisation of the palace, a building within a building.

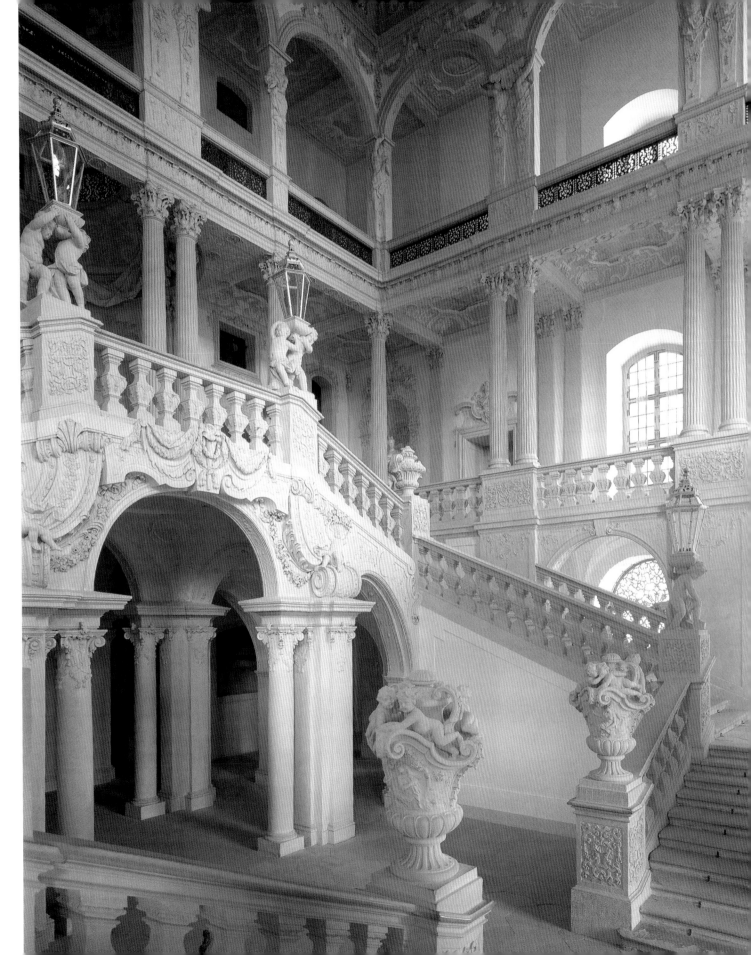

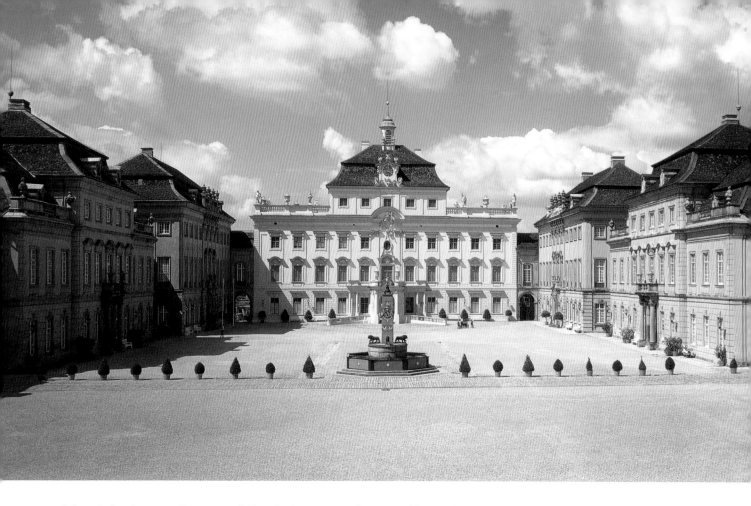

Palaces in Southwestern Germany and Churches in Upper Swabia

The baroque period in southwestern Germany was marked by the military conflicts of the Nine Years War (1688–97), the Turkish wars (1663–1739), and the War of the Spanish Succession (1701–14). Villages, towns, palaces, monasteries, and castles collapsed in rubble and ashes, and new towns and palaces were built. Above all, the Nine Years War, characterized by the cruel military actions of Louis XIV, caused enormous distress among the populations of Baden and the Palatinate and transformed the cultural landscape.

The daughter of the Palatine Elector, Elizabeth Charlotte, nicknamed Liselotte of the Palatinate, was married to the younger brother of the Roi Soleil, Philippe d'Orléans. After the line of electors from the Rhineland Palatinate died out in 1685, the French king sought to enforce his claim to Liselotte's homeland. When this was rejected, he declared war and laid the principality waste. Not only did he destroy the Palatinate cities of Heidelberg and Mannheim among other towns, but Louis also wreaked his revenge on the margravate of Baden, the Carlsburg in Durlach, and the Neues Schloss [New Castle] in Baden-Baden.

These were soon replaced by new palaces, however, as well as new princely seats. The defining architectural characteristics of a baroque prince's principal seat should be considered here. In Ludwigsburg palace (see above), for example, the individual phases of the building work can be clearly distinguished. The starting point for the plans for the town and palace might have been the cramped old princely capital of Stuttgart. An alternative might have been the Erlachhof in the heart of the old hunting reserve of the dukes of Württemberg north of Stuttgart which had been destroyed by Louis XIV's troops. Eberhard Ludwig was only sixteen, but the Emperor declared that he had officially reached his majority. He therefore ordered the project to be started in 1704. Initially, it was only a case of rebuilding the hunting lodge at Erlachhof. Then Ludwig's mistress Wilhelmine von Gravenitz, whom the public saw as the source of national ruin, intervened. Presumably it was she who urged the young duke to transform the hunting lodge into a palace. The new Erlachhof arose from the northern section of the old *corps de logis*. The architects were Philipp Joseph Jenisch and, later, Johann Friedrich Nette, who transformed the building into an Italianate palazzo. The flat-roofed three-storey building was given a pillared portico on the central axis that had side entrance arches for coaches. In 1709 Nette added the right wing (the so-called orders elevation), a largely unadorned three-storey building with a mansard roof. Three years later he added its counterpart on the left side (the so-called giant elevation). Though originally planned as a hunting lodge, the structure had now become a palace.

When Nette died suddenly in 1714, Giovanni Donato Frisoni of Lombardy took over the project. Following Nette's plans, he enlarged the former central elevation with galleries and pavilions, and erected palace and orders chapels at the end angles of the wings. These were all completed by 1720. Over the next ten years courtiers' housing and galleries were set in alignment to the wings, a theater

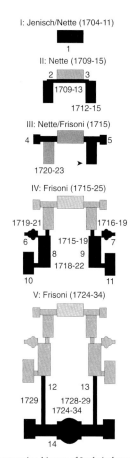

I: Jenisch/Nette (1704-11)

1

II: Nette (1709-15)

2　　3
1709-13
1712-15

III: Nette/Frisoni (1715)

4　　5
1720-23

IV: Frisoni (1715-25)

1719-21　　1716-19
6　1715-19　7
8　9
1718-22
10　　11

V: Frisoni (1724-34)

12　13
1729　1728-29
1724-34
14

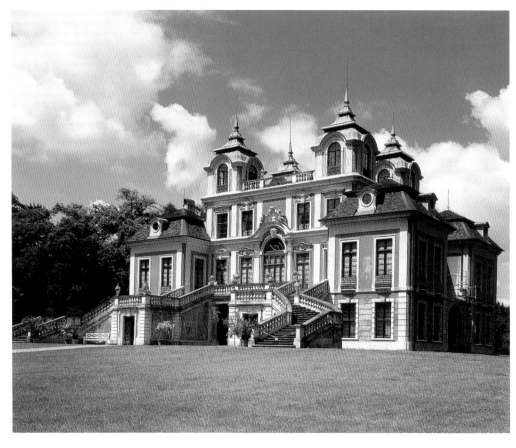

Construction history of Ludwigsburg
1　Old corps de logis (prince's house)
2　Orders building　3　Giant building
4　Hunting chapel　5　Gaming pavilion
6　Orders chapel　7　Palace chapel

8, 9　Courtiers' housing
10　Festin building 11　Theater
12　Picture gallery　13 Portrait gallery
14　New *corps de logis*

PAGE 222:
Jenisch, Nette, and Frisoni
Internal courtyard with the old main
house
Ludwigsburg, 1704–34

ABOVE:
Giovanni Donato Frisoni
Favorite, Ludwigsburg,
1718

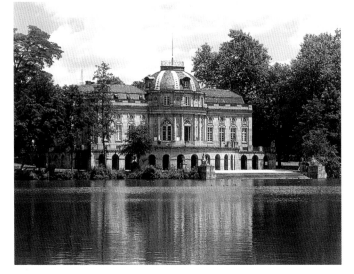

Philippe de la Guêpière
Monrepos, near Ludwigsburg

was constructed, and the Festin house built alongside the courtiers' housing.

In addition to their main palace (the Residenz), baroque princes also maintained small country houses in the immediate vicinity as summer residences or hunting lodges. Eberhard Ludwig had a hunting lodge built called the Favorite on a small hillock about 380 yards north of his palace (see above). The commission for an outline scheme for this building was given to Frisoni in 1718 while he was still occupied with planning and building the eastern courtiers' house at the palace. A cube-shaped, two-storey central block with four corner towers rises above a broad lower floor with rusticated ashlar blocks. The corners are flanked by four pavilions with mansard roofs. The four small belvedere towers recall contemporary Bohemian architecture, while the drive and the wide span of the free-standing steps are reminiscent of Italian baroque villas.

A wonderful avenue of poplars once led through the Favorite park from the Ludwigsburger Schloss to a little lakeside mansion commissioned by Duke Charles Eugene from his architect Philippe de la Guêpière between 1760 and 1765 (see left). The core of the building is an oval central elevation set in a rectangular front with adjoining wings. As it stands on a hill that runs down to the lake, the

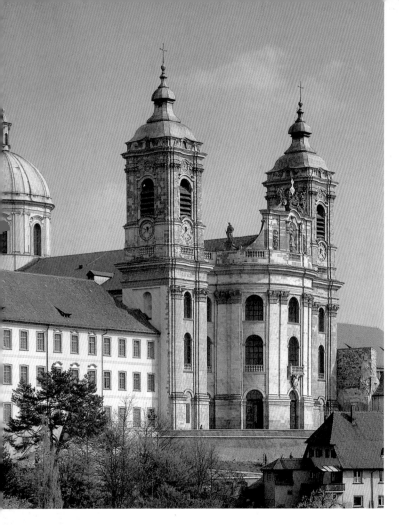

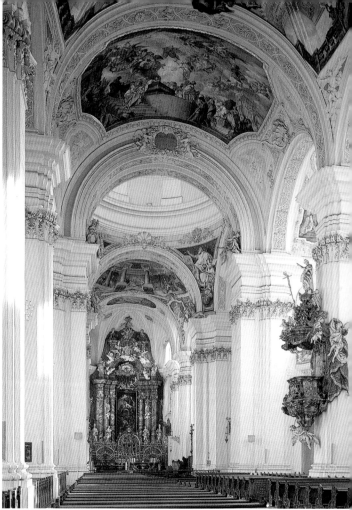

lakeside front had to be set on a plinth. The courtyard front was at ground level. The plinth level, formed of an arcade of semicircular arches and broad piers, rises above a large terrace, on the other side of which steps lead down to the lake. The French architect probably modeled his scheme on the chateau of Vaux-le-Vicomte near Melun. Associating it with his country houses in Finland and Lake Geneva, King Frederick called this little folly Mon Repos.

Court festivities and theater performances allowed baroque princes and dukes to extend their experience into the realm of illusion. Indeed, as the eighteenth century progressed, aesthetic attitudes moved towards illusionistic modes of representation. It was no longer enough to evoke a golden age redolent of pastoral scenes or idyllic but melancholic stage sets. A new approach was required.

Architecture was extended into a divine realm by ceiling paintings. The monastic church of Weingarten near Ravensburg in Upper Swabia, dedicated in 1724 (see above), was painted by Cosmas Damian Asam between 1718 and 1720. Asam had studied in Rome. Like Lanfranco, Guercino, and Pozzo, he was capable of creating an illusion of space through the deployment of various perspective devices. In the vault of the basilica at Weingarten, he painted halls with columns and domes, steps and pillars, creating a fascinating architecture of the imagination which appeared to extend the actual architecture of the church. Heavenly access was opened up in the

vortex of the vaulting, and the heavenly host appeared to descend to the faithful. Twisting banks of cloud wind around the pilasters, enshrouding angels or saints. The tremendous, solidly built columns of the nave extend subtly above the cornice and arches as painted columns.

A favorite architectural illusion is often deployed in stairwells, which move into the curve of the vaulting, arch swinging upwards in a graceful sweep. They act as an intermediary between the two levels of reality, functioning as a theatrical setting. In Weingarten, visitors sit on the steps and gaze upwards in astonishment, following the Assumption of the Virgin in the manner of the faithful below, who in their piety similarly aspire to ascend this "heavenly staircase."

The artist Franz Joseph Spiegler, who was born in Wangen in Allgäu in 1691 and died in 1757, created an unusual result from such a scheme. In Friedolinsmünster in Bad Säckingen (see p. 226, above), he integrated the steps into a sort of "heavenly architecture" in several cases. Spiegler was given the commission for the painting in 1751. In the *Apotheosis of St. Fridolin*, the staircase winds

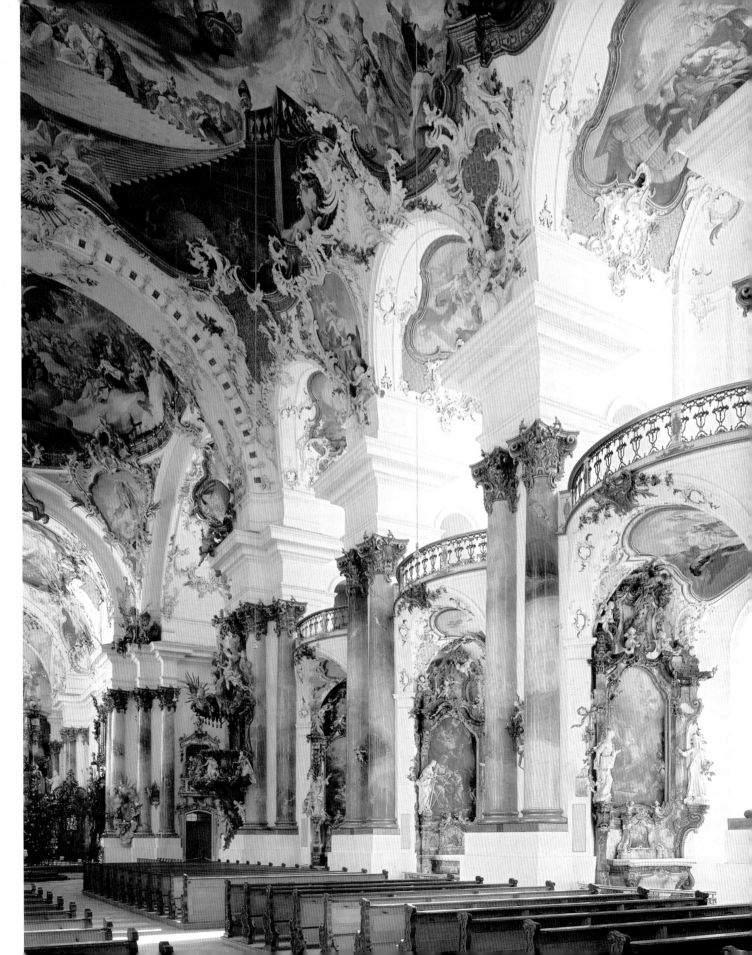

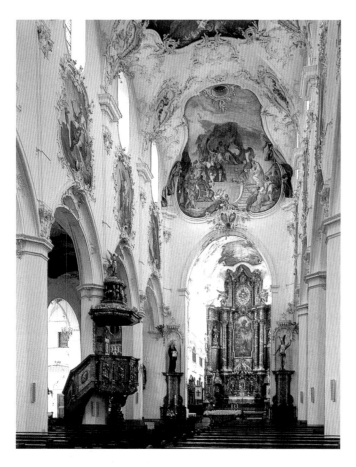

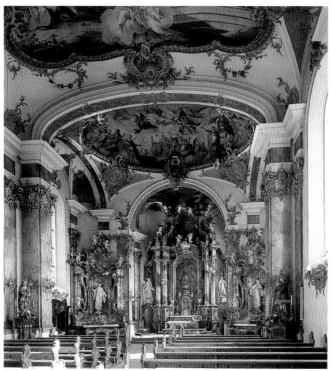

upwards out of the stucco of the vault and is continued by curving paths of cloud, only to reappear on the opposite side where steps again descend toward the stucco and a more earthly realm. The staircase device further structures the composition of a ceiling painting covering over 5,300 square feet in the Benedictine abbey of Zwiefalten (see p. 225). The painting extends across four bays and down over the arches. The painted city architecture rises and falls with the rhythm of the pendentives and arches of the bays, and opens upwards along the longitudinal axis of the vault in steeply rising staircases. Figures stand here and on the breastwork of the parapet, with Clovis the Merovingian king and Benedictine missionaries beneath them awaiting the intercession of the Virgin.

The unity of architecture, plasterwork, and painting in Friedolinsmünster reflects the harmonious collaboration between Spiegler and the sculptor and stuccoist Joseph Anton Feuchtmayer (1696–1770). In Bad Säckingen, Feuchtmayer's use of rocaille is notably restrained. The architecture remains the dominant feature, and also forms the basic structure for the illusionistic painting schemes. Only the ornamental foliage springing from the cartouches projects onto the painted ceiling, where it is echoed by rocaille motifs. In Zwiefalten, by contrast, the architecture appears to dissolve into the dense plasterwork, gracefully overlapping the ornamental areas of painted architecture.

This ornamental exuberance, this sumptuous interplay of soaring pilasters, undulating cartouches, and architectural elements which soar upwards, represents the astonishing ornamental flamboyance of German rococo of the southwest. Rococo ornament of this kind achieves new heights of extravagance in the pilgrimage church of the Virgin at Birnau, on Lake Constance, the "Hall of God" (see p. 228). Feuchtmayer's work as a sculptor and stuccoist effectively defines the characteristic rococo manner of Upper Swabia in Birnau. Using as his canvas the architecture of Peter Thumb of Vorarlberg, he composed an incomparable work of art (1748–50). The relatively wide windows of the church allow plenty of light into the interior, illuminating even the rocaille cartouches that are concealed in various nooks and crannies. The balustrade around the galleries, repeatedly interrupted by small-scale ornamentation that seems almost to overflow from its setting, dissolves into curved interlaced forms. In the midst of this controlled undulation and surging of tumbling paths of cloud and burgeoning plaster branches, putti are seen peeking out, half concealed by the plasterwork, or stepping out unexpectedly beside an altar, among them the famous putto shown licking honey.

Above, the space opens on an imposing ceiling painting by Gottfried Bernhard Goetz, a Bohemian by birth. Relays of pilasters lead the viewer's gaze toward the choir, curving upwards into groin arches that delimit the painting while providing illusionary supports for the painted cornice, from which marbled double columns soar into a sky formed by a swirling vortex of clouds. At the top sits the

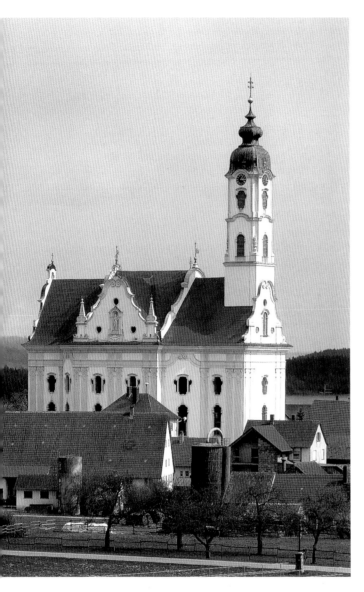

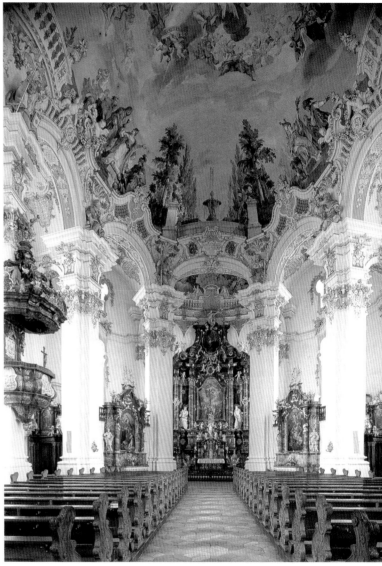

Virgin as the woman of the apocalypse on a crescent moon, casting the vermin of hell into the deep.

The pilgrimage church of St. Anne in Haigerloch (1753–55), although not as magnificent as that at Birnau, provides a similar impression of spatial harmony and of the coherence of the architecture, painting, and sculpture (see left). The plans for the church were probably provided by the celebrated Munich artist Johann Michael Fischer. The stuccoist Feuchtmayer, the sculptor J. G. Weckenmann, and the painter Meinrad von Ow then transformed the little building into a magical work of art. Ideal proportions—the length of the nave equals the width of the transept—unfold in front of the choir. It is like the curtain going up on a stage set. The nave expands into the transept, then contracts as it moves towards the choir. The piers and pilasters of nave and choir stretch in relays into the depths of the apse. The viewer's gaze is led upwards to the volutes of the altar, moving on to an ornamental frenzy with cavorting putti. The orna-

mentation branches off over the dome of the choir and finally ends up in the cartouches of the great ceiling vault, in which the story of St. Anne, the mother of the Virgin, is depicted.

In Birnau and Haigerloch, architectural, stucco, and painted decoration combine to create two masterpieces of spatial illusion. Perhaps we should refer to "rococo space" rather than "baroque space" here, since rococo is more usually associated with the use of illusionistic devices of this kind. Further heights of rococo extravagance can hardly be imagined, unless we consider a building like the church at Steinhausen in Upper Swabia, where art and illusion unfold in space in a new way (see above). The pilgrimage and parish church of St. Peter and St. Paul was built between 1728 and 1733 by Dominikus Zimmermann, to whom we shall return in connection with the Wieskirche. Here Zimmerman successfully combined a hall built of free-standing piers with a central plan. Into the oval ground plan he introduced a further oval form, a "pier oval" which rein-

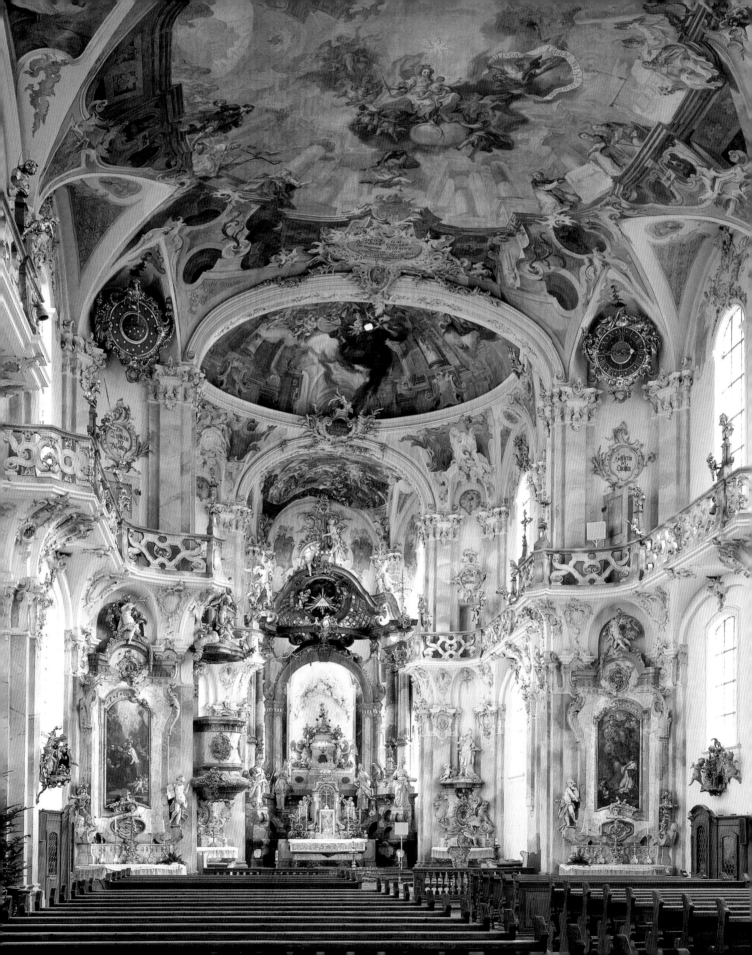

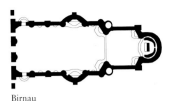

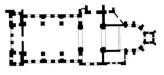

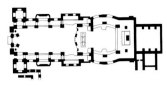

Birnau   Ebersbach   Weissenau

forces the impression of a homogeneous space, terminating in the ceiling vault. Zimmermann deliberately steered clear of dramatic architectural set pieces like those in Birnau and Haigerloch. Instead, he emphasized the sense of height in the oval dome, which his brother, Johann Baptist Zimmermann, filled with an illusionist fresco showing the world, depicted allegorically by the four ends of the earth and symbolically by Paradise, into which the church interior opens but to which human beings have no access. This zone on the ceiling, inaccessible to believers, is made accessible only by realistic details—various animals are visible in the plasterwork, including a woodpecker on the pier, a magpie in its nest, a butterfly, a squirrel, and a hoopoe. The garden of Paradise thus beckons to the believer.

The Courses at Au or the Art of Constructing Galleries: the Vorarlberg School

At Birnau the interplay of decoration and architecture sets the illusionistic tone. We should of course not talk of "illusionistic architecture" in reference to such works, but rather to the wall-pier architecture of Vorarlberg (now part of Austria). The leading architects of the Vorarlberg School include Peter Thumb (the builder of Birnau), Michael Thumb, Johann Michael Fischer, Franz Beer, Johann Georg Kuen, and Kaspar Moosbrugger. Their architectural ideas and theoretical principles are recorded in the manuals *Courses at Au*, named after the village of Au in the Vorarlberg. Both volumes include perspective drawings, patterns of types of architecture, and outlines of major Roman baroque churches, in addition to drawings of the authors' own work in Vorarlberg.

A specialism, although not an actual invention, of the Vorarlberg School was the use of wall-piers and galleries, known as the "wall-pier church" style. Peter Thumb was the first to introduce the idea at the Benedictine church of Ebersmünster in Alsace between 1719 and 1731. Before drawing up his design, he studied Franz Beer's plans for Obermarchtal and Weissenau. These buildings were also models for Thumb's Benedictine abbey of St. Peter in the Black Forest (1724–27), north-east of Freiburg. Using the wall-pier system, he enlarged three pairs of side chapels in which he installed galleries. The fourth bay was expanded into a "supported" transept. At Birnau (1746–50), Thumb developed some unusual designs. He compressed the transepts by turning them into triple arches and placed the wall-piers right against the wall. This produced a projecting space, which he integrated into the structure of the nave by means of an excessively large ceiling. Space was thus left for stucco and frescoes. The subtle transition from nave to choir and from there to the apse is marked by splayed altar niches. The galleries embrace the wall-piers as well as the wall, and seem to function like a curved ornamental ribbon decorating the interior. It was an inspired architectural solution to a problem Thumb had been wrestling with in his buildings in the Black Forest and Alsace.

The wall-pier system is, as we have said, not an invention of the Vorarlberg School. Wall-piers had been used in late gothic and renaissance churches, such as the municipal church in Schwaigen (1514) or the castle church in Haigerloch (1584). However, the Vorarlberg architects around the Thumbs and the Beers came up with their own individual and artistic applications of the feature, thus setting the style for the German-speaking southwest. The decisive years for the establishment of the style were probably 1705–25.

This was the period when Franz Beer (1660–1726), having completed the building of Obermarchtal (1690–92), turned in a new direction in his work. His progress can be most clearly seen in the Premonstratensian imperial foundation of Weissenau (1717–24). Here he extended outwards the middle of the three-nave bays in the manner of chapels and turned the next but one bay into a transept, producing a crossing effect with four columns. Above this he erected a flattened cupola, bearing a high false dome scheme. Above the chapel areas left blank by the wall-piers runs an elegant gallery that is flooded with light. The concept became positively monumental in the designs for the Benedictine monastery church of Weingarten. The plans are certainly by Beer, and he was evidently in charge of building work from 1715–16. After that, the project was supervised by Andreas Schreck and Christian Thumb. The large dimensions meant that there was space for high passageways to be included in the galleries. At the crossing, the wall-piers look like monumental columns; above them rises the drum of the Italianate dome. As Norbert Lieb has observed, this Italianate approach—highly unusual in southwestern Germany—had already featured in Beer's design. It cannot therefore be attributed to the "Swabian" Italian Donato Giuseppe Frisoni, who had been appointed master of works in Württemberg and was involved in the building work from 1718. His sole contribution was the concave structure of the galleries.

The Vorarlberg architects produced curved wall designs "tamed" by a strict articulation system, which can be observed in many churches of Upper Swabia, but is unusual for southwestern Germany in general. It is not clear, however, that this formula should be considered as an early example of neo-classicism and therefore representing a transitional style, since new ideas of this kind would not be introduced until the arrival of French architects from the Académie Française in Paris.

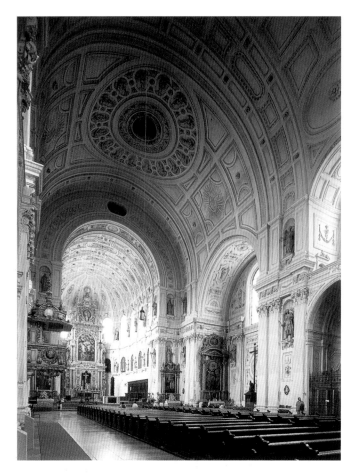

View towards choir of
St. Michael's, Munich,
begun 1583 (left)
Ground plan (right)

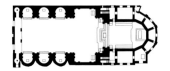

cousin Franz Beer, both also from Vorarlberg. The characteristic wall-piers with galleries and the windowless barrel vault arching above must therefore have been inspired to a considerable extent by St. Michael's in Munich.

The Vorarlberg principle was seen at the time as a kind of counter to the prevailing Italianate grammar of architecture. Although the spatial structure of St. Michael's is certainly influenced by Italian architecture—probably based on S. Andrea in Mantua—the symbol of grandeur in Italian baroque architecture, the dome, was deliberately rejected here, and thus also the model of the Gesù. One of the first baroque church buildings after the Thirty Years War is the former collegiate church (now Catholic municipal parish church) of St. Lawrence in Kempten (see below). This was begun in 1652 following plans by, and under the supervision of, Michael Beer, and conceived in such a way that the obligatory dome above the crossing must have seemed superfluous. Beer erected an octagon over the nave which marks the choir area, effectively creating a separate chapel delimited by the four piers. It is nonetheless a halfhearted solution, since the choir octagon with its low dome and substantial lantern still echoes Italian domes. This spatial concept does not merely accommodate aesthetic considerations, however. Beer was faced with the problem of combining a parish church with a monastic building. The congregation's desire for an untrammeled view of

Bavarian Baroque

The Jesuit church of St. Michael in Munich (see above), built at the end of the sixteenth century, was the model for many later baroque churches. This is true not only of Jesuit foundations or churches in Bavaria, but also applies generally to baroque church buildings in south Germany. The wall-piers, the broad windowless barrel vault with transverse arches, and the chapels with lateral barrel vaults and galleries inspired the designs of numerous later churches. Begun in 1583, the final scheme was effectively a building made to order, as the various designs and proposals were worked over by the duke's director of art, Friedrich Sustris, and the construction was supervised by building foremen, among them Wolfgang Miller.

Barrel vaulting supported on wall-piers and a separation of stories by galleries reappear in Michael Thumb's Premonstratensian abbey church at Obermachtal, built a century later in 1686–1701. It is true that in this case the vaulting does not come down to gallery level, but terminates far above the gallery parapet on protruding capitals. To this end, Thumb continued the wall-piers high up, creating tall arcades that would allow light into the interior. It was a concept that Thumb had put into practice shortly before in the pilgrimage church of Schönenberg near Ellwangen (1681–95). Unfortunately Thumb did not live to see these two churches completed, as he died in 1690. The architect's supervisory role in Obermarchtal was taken over by Thumb's brother Christian and

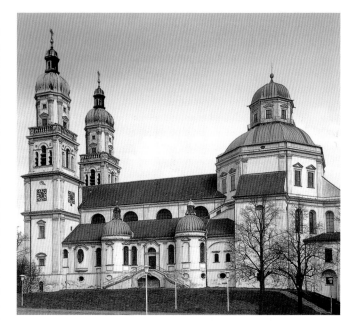

Michael Beer, civic parish church of St. Lawrence, Kempten, begun 1652

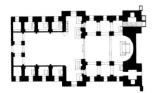

Johann Michael Fischer
View of choir of St. Michael in Berg am
Laim, Munich, begun 1739

LEFT:
Ground plan of former
Premonstratensian church of St. Peter
and St. Paul, Obermarchtal

the choir had to be considered in addition to the monks' wish for a separate area for the purpose of divine office. A short time later, construction work began in Munich on a church that was truly in the Italianate manner. The Theatinerkirche, designed in 1663 by Enrico Zucalli, was modelled on the Theatine church of S. Andrea delle Valle in Rome. It borrowed such features as the compressed transept, broad nave, and semicircular apse. The drum of the crossing supports a high dome, and this, together with the four-storey towers, dominates the townscape. This building was exceptionally unusual by the standards of southern Germany.

Native architects such as Johann Michael Fischer and the Asam brothers in Munich gradually superseded the Italian taste. In 1739, two years after the foundation stone was laid for the parish church of St. Michael in Berg am Laim in Munich, Fischer took over the supervision of the site (see right). He linked the congregation area with the choir, combining these two central areas with each other on the principle of the golden section. He then subdivided the choir into an ante-choir (the central space) and a laterally elliptical chancel, and the congregation area was given two short transept arms. This produced a completely new style of ground plan. There are certainly elements of the traditional spatial features of the rotunda and basilica here, but the visitor also experiences a quite unusual sense of space. The prominent red marbled three-quarter columns dominate the interior; they combine with Johann Baptist Zimmermann's painting and plasterwork to create distinctive theatrical effects.

Fischer delighted in experimenting with auditoria like the one in Berg am Laim. A little earlier, he had been working in Ingolstadt, where between 1736 and 1740 he built the Augustinian pilgrimage church. Stylistically this structure, destroyed in the Second World War, seems to have anticipated his design for St. Michael's.

The former monastic church of Maria Himmelfahrt in Diessen on Lake Ammer (1732–39) also belongs to this group of experimental churches, although in this case the architect followed the traditional scheme of the wall-pier church. The momentum of the five-bay nave moves towards the domed rectangle of the choir and encloses the chancel. Transverse arches vault across the space between the pilastered piers in rhythmic motion, seeming to lead the eye forward into the choir. To enhance the theatricality of the spatial effects and thus the significance of the liturgical symbolism, Fischer designed transverse arches for the last bay before the choir, marking the transition between the auditorium-style main area and the choir.

The building of the new Benedictine abbey of Ottobeuren (see pp. 232–33) was one of the largest construction projects of southern German baroque architecture. The planning history of this scheme is immensely complex, and can therefore be only briefly discussed here. The foundation stone was laid in 1737, but plans by several well-known architects, including Dominikus Zimmermann, were rejected. A less famous Swabian architect called Simpert Kraemer

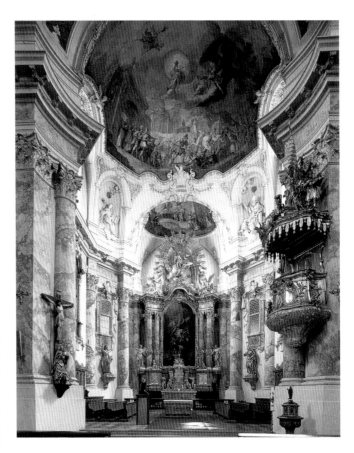

was awarded the contract, but he was forced to hand over his design to Joseph Effner, court architect of Bavaria, for reworking. Effner tightened the lines of the design in the emerging French classical style and proposed a straight choir ending. In 1748 Johann Michael Fischer was called in to work on the designs. He modified the cool severity of Effner's reworking, while maintaining the ground plan.

Fischer concentrated the spatial effects here on the central crossing, which is crowned by a huge domed vault. The central area comes to life—or this is at least the effect on the observer—as they walk in the direction of the choir. The bays before and behind the crossing are vaulted with oval shapes set lengthways; they therefore appear to be compressed, suggesting a gathering effect on the longitudinal axis. Piers and three-quarter columns seem to tower over the cornice and transverse arches into the heavenly realm of the painted architecture. This linking of architecture and vault or dome painting is further enhanced by the vigorous rocaille ornament, executed by Joseph Anton Feuchtmayr between 1757 and 1764. The perspectives of the frescos develop out of the built architecture; they were

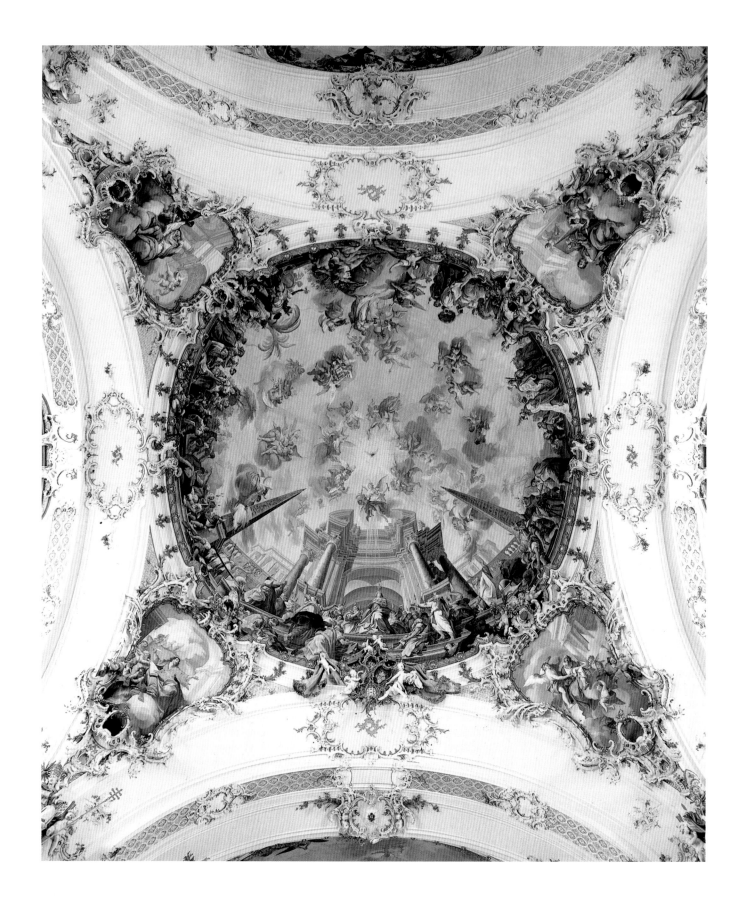

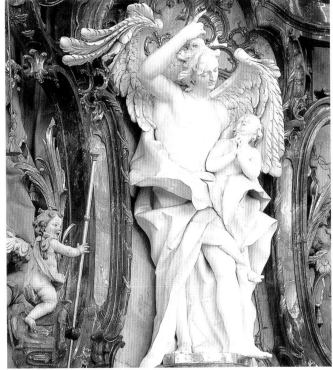

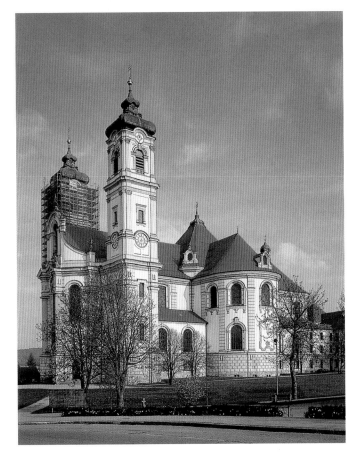

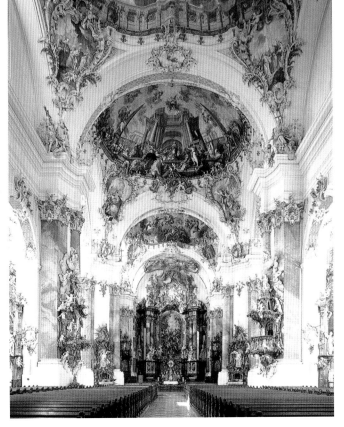

produced at around the same time as the stucco by Johann Jakob
Zeiller.

A typical feature of Bavarian baroque architecture is double-
layering: interiors and exteriors do not correspond. The external
wall with its windows does not necessarily define the interior layout.
In Ottobeuren, for example, the interior orchestrates an emotional
response in the observer that is not indicated in any way by the exterior; it is almost as if the architectural elements were presenting a
dramatic performance of their own. This theatrical effect is not confined to the choir and altar area, as at Diessen and Berg am Laim,
but extends to the entire space.

The Asam brothers were particularly famous for their manipula-
tion of illusionistic tricks of this kind. The Munich church of St.
John Nepomuk, known as the "Asam church" (see p. 234), reflects
the work of both the sculptor Egid Quirin Asam and the painter
Cosmas Damian Asam, both also trained architects. Between 1729
and 1733 Egid bought four houses in Sendlinger Strasse in Munich.

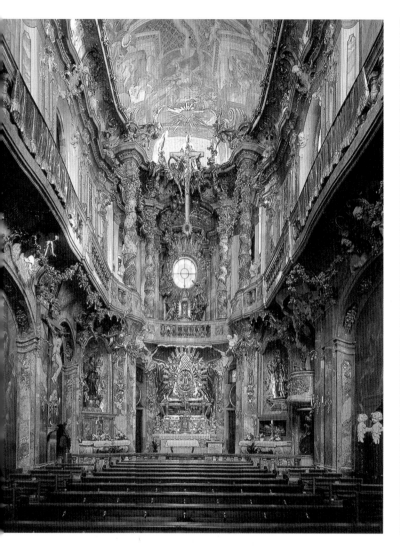

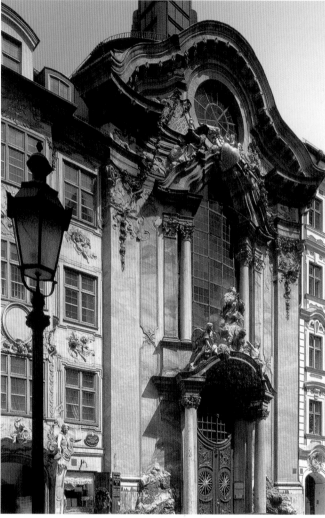

He converted one into a home for himself, and set two aside to be used for the church while the fourth was later bought by the cleric Philipp Franz Lindmayr and furnished as a priest's house.

The two-storey bowed facade of the church opens the row of houses with its pillared doorway, high window, and curving pediments. The upward thrust of the facade is repeated endlessly in the interior by Cosmas' illusionistic paintings of 1735. The upper storey is terminated by a curving gable, above which is a barrel vault lit by windows to the east and west. If you stand beside the altar and let your eye glide up the sinuous columns, the "heavenly architecture" suddenly opens up above you, with its columns, consoles, and cornices framing the scenes from the life of St. John Nepomuk. The diffuse light, steep perspective of the architecture, and sculptural ornament dissolve the boundaries between real and painted architecture so that the believer feels transported to a parallel, sacred world.

Cosmas had been trained in Rome and knew how to construct illusionistic space and combine painted architecture with real architecture with precise perspectives in the Italian manner. In Munich he and his brother Egid succeeded in creating a work of art that opens

Egid Quirin Asam and Cosmas Damian Asam
Interior (left) and west front (right) of St. John Nepomuk church (the "Asam church"), Munich, 1733–34

OPPOSITE:
Cosmas Damian Asam
Dome fresco of Benedictine abbey of Weltenburg, 1716

out a narrow space which grows increasingly restricted as it reaches upwards into an illusion of the "architecture beyond."

Cosmas's picture puzzle of reality and illusion at Weltenburg on the Danube (see right) is even more remarkable than his work in Munich. The Benedictine abbey was constructed in 1716. On top of the main space, which is oval in form, Asam places a double-layered dome, effectively a stretched elliptical space. Above this is a flat roof with painted columns which appear to be severely foreshortened, supporting a painted drum with a ring of cloud and a lantern. This painted architecture contains a fresco showing the Church Triumphant. The illusion is perfect. The painted illusion is hardly detectable as such—just like the flat ceiling, which curves with different illusions of perspective from every viewpoint. Illusionistic devises used in the service of a sacred cause and inspired by Italian

234

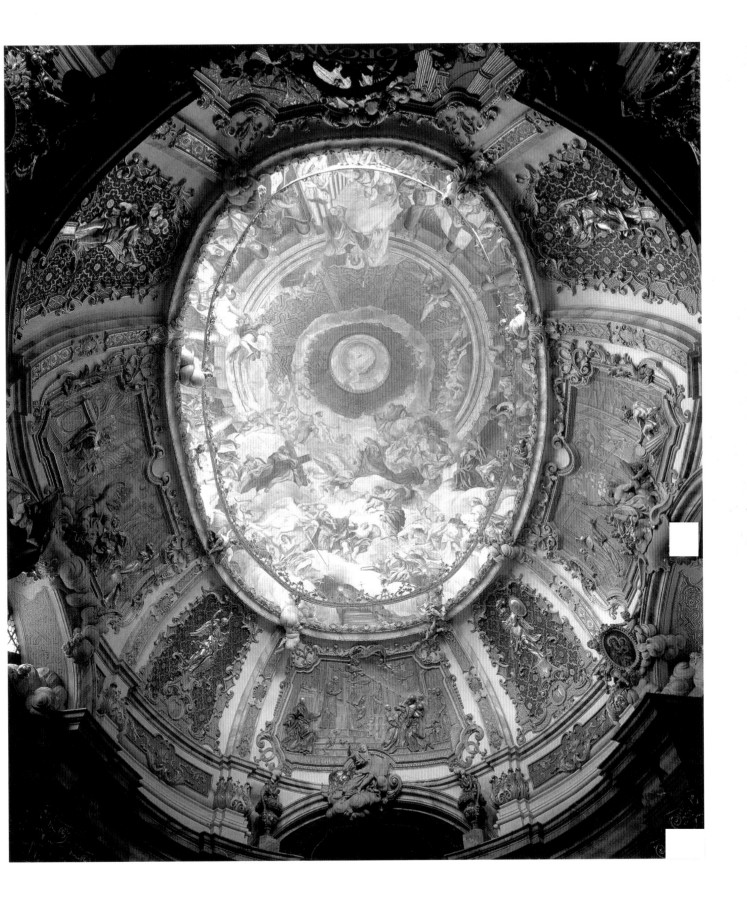

Dominikus Zimmermann
The Wieskirche, begun 1743, seen from
the southwest (below)
Ground plan (right)

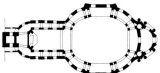

models reach a high point in the work of the Asam family. The effects appear almost excessive, the theatrical effects almost overly contrived.

The spatial effects achieved by Dominikus Zimmermann from Wessobrunn are quite different. In 1743 he was awarded a contract by Abbot Hyazinth Gassner of Steingaden to build the pilgrimage church of the Scourged Savior, known as the Wieskirche (see below and right). For Zimmermann, the Vorarlberg philosophy was definitive. In *Courses at Au*, he found oval ground plans and hall choirs, already used to some extent by Kaspar Moosbrugger. In addition, he had chosen an oval shape as a ground plan years earlier (1728–33) for the pilgrimage church at Steinhausen in Upper Swabia (see p. 227). Steinhausen reappears, extensively transformed and dramatically enhanced, in the Wieskirche.

Zimmermann chose an unusual design incorporating twin piers as supports for the main oval section, with shafts with four ridges. In contrast to Steinhausen, he placed a lengthy choir east of the oval main area in order to intensify the effect of the "ritual perspective" from the entrance. A stuccoist himself, Zimmermann designed the architecture in conjunction with the ornament. The rich flamboyant rocaille stucco appears to dematerialize the architectural forms and this was clearly the intended effect. At critical points in the structure, at the top of an arch for example, or zones of the upper storey where free-standing piers normally support the weight of the ceiling or where piers draw off the lateral thrust of the vault, graceful little rocaille cartouches or filigree ornament suddenly appear. Architecture and ornament are inexorably linked. In Steinhausen, the oval of the dome seems to rest directly on the arches springing

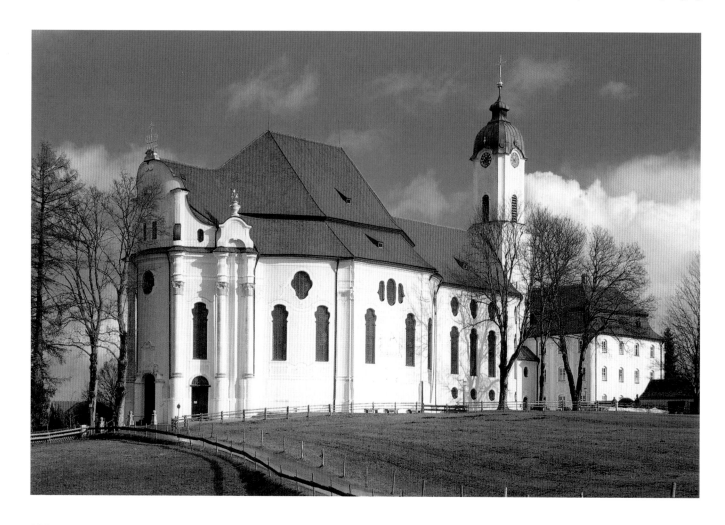

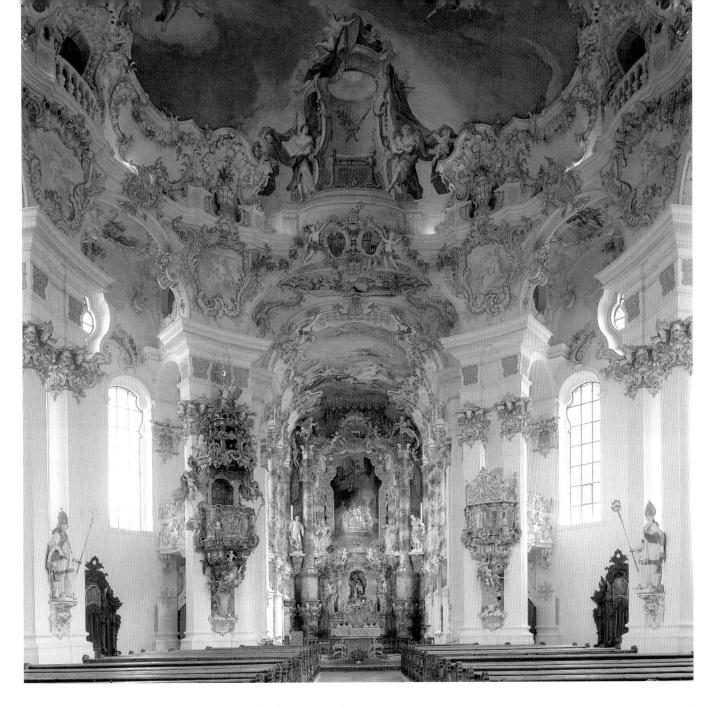

from the capitals of the columns. At the Wieskirche, by contrast, the rocaille decoration frames the picture on the ceiling, allowing the architectural frame to be dispensed with. An architectural vault is represented by an illusionistic one which, with the exception of the painted doorway, is otherwise unpainted. The great ceiling fresco of *Christ Made Man and His Sacrifice* is a collaboration between the architect and his elder brother, Johann Baptist Zimmermann. In this case the concept of the "ornamentalization" of the architecture can be taken literally: plaster actually forms the architecture here, since the flat dome consists of a timber frame suspended beneath the roof truss and plastered solely as a ground for the fresco—an ingenious solution.

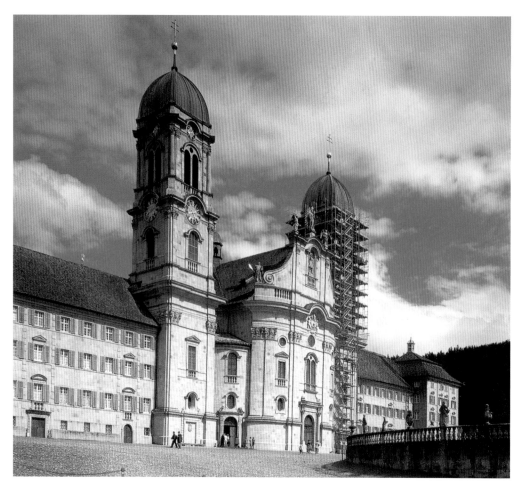

Kaspar Moosbrugger
Benedictine abbey of Einsiedeln,
1691–1735
West front (left) and plans (below)

TOP TO BOTTOM:
Design of 1691–92
Design of 1705
Final design, 1719

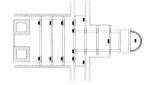

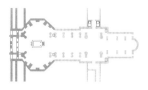

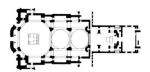

Churches and Monasteries in Switzerland

Baroque church building in Switzerland is marked by the inventiveness of the Vorarlberg school. It can be observed in monastic buildings and ecclesiastical foundations in particular, for which the architects of the Vorarlberg provided numerous designs. Such ecclesiastical structures often featured linked spaces that were distinguished by ritual symbolism.

The ground plan of the Benedictine abbey of Einsiedeln is confusing at first (see above). The history of this abbey in the canton of Schwyz may explain to some degree its apparently unusual structure, as only the origins of Einsiedeln illuminate its functions as a commemorative church and shrine, and thus the baroque planning process that went on for more than thirty years.

In 861, the story goes, a hermit called Meinrad living at Einsiedeln was killed by robbers; he soon became venerated in the area. Several hermits settled here. Barely sixty years later, Eberhard, a canon of Strasbourg, succeeded in transforming the hermits into a Benedictine community. Their church was dedicated to Our Lady of the Hermits. In the mid-fifteenth century, the late gothic Madonna of Einsiedeln was created and pilgrimages were made in her honor. This statue of the Virgin stood in the holy chapel, Meinrad's cell, in the Lower Minster. The abbey church, the Upper Minster, adjoined it on the eastern side.

This was how the buildings were laid out prior to the baroque additions. In 1674 the Vorarlberg architect Johann Georg Kuen built the choir. There was a pair of Romanesque towers at the west end, and initially the plan was to integrate these into the church facade of the new foundation. The longitudinal axis of the building site was thus established in advance. The chapel of grace in the interior of the old building, a sacred place that had to be preserved, was also supposed to be linked to the new building project.

In 1691 Kuen's pupil Kaspar Moosbrugger started planning. He designed a ground plan in which the nave was accommodated to the pier-church system of his teacher. In a further ground plan the architect first defines a scheme where the first space is centralized, an element which was retained in the final plan. Planning went on at this level until 1693, but it was only ten years later that the decision was finally taken to rebuild the church. An architect from Milan who had been called in as a consultant in 1705 suggested an oval area for the chapel of grace, which was supposed to continue into a piered nave and then open up in a central domed area. The notion was brought into various designs by Moosbrugger and developed, over ten years later (1717–19), in his final plans which treat the various ritual functions of the building in an inspired way. The grace area, flanked by towers, forms an irregular octagon with two flat rectangular transepts. A comparable scheme had in fact been proposed by

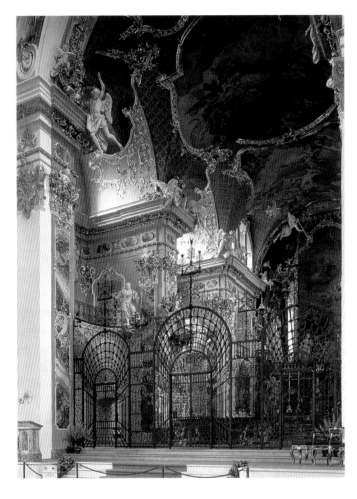

Kaspar Moosbrugger
Benedictine Abbey of Einsiedeln, 1691–1735
(Left) View of choir
(Below) Pilgrimage area, with Chapel of Grace

a specific relationship to the nave and choir reflecting the rituals of pilgrimage. However, only one architect really produced a successful synthesis of these different spatial concepts and this was Neumann at the pilgrimage church of Vierzehnheiligen (see pp. 214–15).

The baroque church of the foundation of St. Gall (see pp. 240–41) was also more than thirty years in the planning, although the end result is less complex than the one at Einsiedeln. The first designs, by Moosbrugger, date to 1721. To link the shrines of St. Gall and St. Othmer, he designed a double crucifix with two domed crossings. After Moosbrugger's death in 1723, another Vorarlberg architect, Johann Michael Beer from Bleichten, took over the work, producing alternative plans that included a large octagon in the middle of the nave. Between 1730 and 1754, six other architects came forward with proposals, among them the architect of the Teutonic Order, Johann Kaspar Bagnato. In each case, an attempt was made to combine the schemes of Moosbrugger and Beer. Finally, Peter Thumb triumphed in 1755 with a version of Beer's scheme linking a longitudinal design with a central plan. Wall-piers and a pier system placed in relation to them run through the whole space to create a coherent whole. The two choirs appear not as separate entities but linked together at the central point. Moreover, the entrances to the church are placed in such a way that the building is powerfully represented not just by the facade of the choir towers but also in the effect of its breadth. Work was com-

Michael Beer around 1652 for St. Lawrence in Kempten (see p. 230, below). The pulpit area leads from it, marked out by four piers and roofed by a suspension dome. Here too it is adjoined by a pair of flat rectangular transepts. Both spaces are linked by galleries that extend into the domed area.

The facade anticipates the broad entrance area and the chapel of grace. Single and double pilasters mirror the inner arrangement of the piers (see above). The spatial effects are concentrated on the preaching area behind the chapel of grace where the vaulting gains height and finally peaks in the domed area where the galleries end. At this point, we are on the threshold of the choir, where the spatial effects become less contrived. Moosbrugger died in 1723. The dedication of the church took place only twelve years later, in 1735.

The choir and domed area are the province of the prince-abbot and his foundation, while the broad grace area is devoted to pilgrimage. In one sense, however, the whole architectural sequence is designed for pilgrims, who are intended to experience the truths of their faith as they proceed through the different sections of the building.

The idea of integrating different types of space for ritual reasons may, as already mentioned, have first been seen by Moosbrugger in Beer's plan for Kempten. In the new minster at Würzburg in 1711, Joseph Greissing similarly tried to set an octagonal western space in

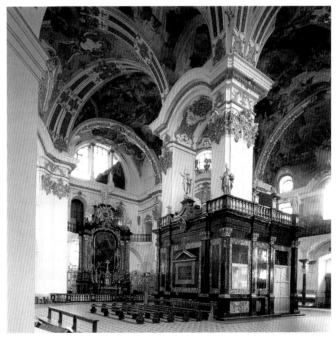

Heinrich Mayer
Jesuit church of Solothurn,
begun 1680

Kaspar Moosbrugger, Michael Beer, and
Peter Thumb
Interior of St. Gall collegiate church,
1721–70

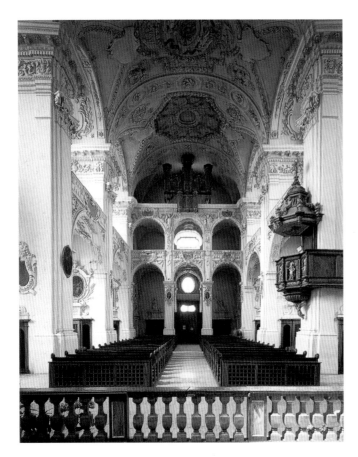

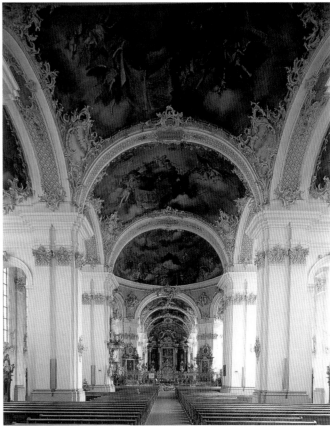

pleted in 1770. Two years later, yet another Vorarlberg architect, Johann Georg Specht, adopted the concept for his ground plan for the Benedictine abbey church of St. Martin in Wiblingen, thereby introducing the first elements of neo-classicism into southwest Germany.

A close relationship can be identified between the Jesuit architecture of Switzerland and the activities of the Vorarlberg architects; in the Jesuit church at Solothurn (see above left) this can be traced back to the southern German baroque architecture of St. Michael's in Munich. It was the Jesuit building supervisor Heinrich Mayer (1636–39) more than anyone else, in fact, who endeavored to assimilate the novel architectural ideas of the Vorarlberg school.

Three architects are recorded as having worked on the Jesuit church in Lucerne, including one "from Bregenz," which probably refers to Michael Kuen of Voralberg. The building, constructed between 1666 and 1669, certainly represents a version of the Vorarlberg pier system. The Jesuit church in Soloturn dates to this

period, and a foundation stone was ceremonially laid in 1680. Mayer may have worked out the definitive plans along Vorarlberg principles. In Solothurn, the wall-pier arrangement is pure Vorarlberg. Michael Thumb must have studied Swiss Jesuit architecture during this period, as he built the Jesuit church on Schönenberg near Ellwangen following the Solothurn scheme. In 1683, a year after the foundation stone was laid, Heinrich Mayer was moved to the Jesuit establishment in Ellwangen and took over as building supervisor at the church there, reinforcing the Voralberg trend.

However, both Jesuit churches are derived from the Jesuit church of St. Michael in Munich (see p. 230) especially the hall church design, the arrangement of the galleries, and the very basic transept.

Kaspar Moosbrugger, Michael Beer, and
Peter Thumb
St. Gall collegiate church, 1721–70

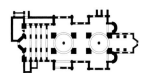

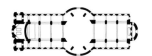

LEFT:
Design by Kaspar Moosbrugger, 1719
(far left) and ground plan of church as
built, 1755–68

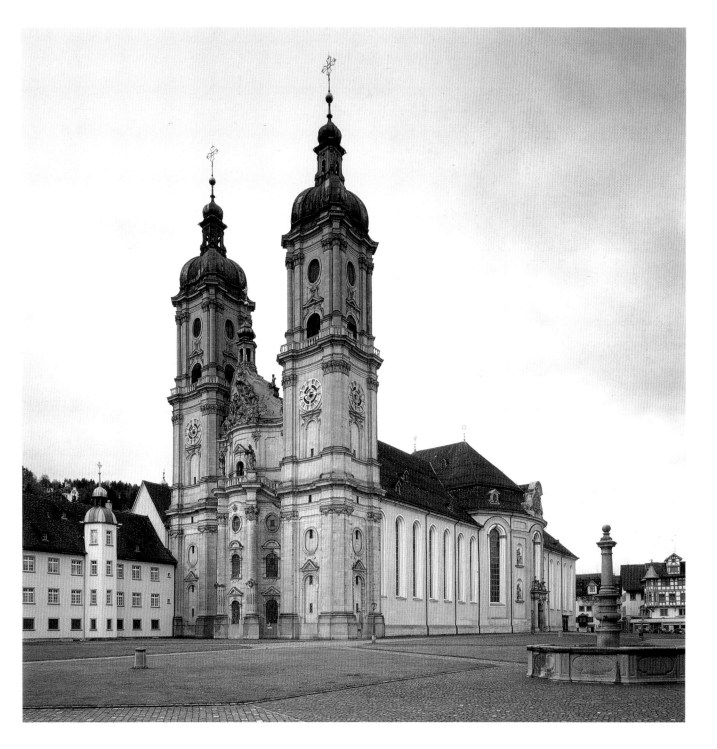

Collections of Art and Curiosities and Libraries

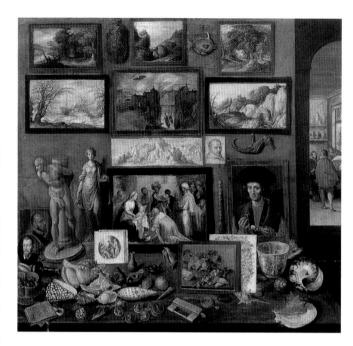

There is a direct line of progression from the early hunter-gatherer days through the *Kunstkammern* [art collections] and *Wunderkammern* [curiosity collections] of princes and kings to our modern museums. A passion for collecting, whether in order to maintain existence or hoard treasures, led to exquisite cabinets of valuables or art rooms. Collecting is linked to curiosity and even in early days there was a fascination with exotic items from remote parts of the world. Curiosity activated the thirst for knowledge so that collections of curiosities ultimately led to encyclopedias. Collections of art and oddities were in many cases established near major libraries, or vice versa.

In 1565, a Dutch doctor, the collector Dr. Samuel von Quicheberg, published an system called the *Methodology of the Theatrum Sapientiae* [Theatre of Knowledge] which became standard for many art collections. He divided his *Theatrum* into five sections, with various subsections called *Inscriptiones*. The first relates to the collector or founder and his family history. Here are found historical family tables and family trees and portraits as well as representations of the local environment. The second section corresponds to the content of the familiar art room of the time, with various art objects, coins, and exotic implements or models. The third section was devoted to nature, and the fourth to technology. For

the fifth section, Quicheberg envisaged a picture gallery. For the Dutch doctor, this *Theatrum Sapientiae* was the ideal image of a collection, which, together with the library attached to it, would form a "walk-in" encyclopedia.

According to an inventory of 1598, the ducal collection in Munich was set up along these lines. The collection dated back to at least the mid-1500s, but towards the end of the century Albrecht V had expanded it within the area of the modern palace and linked it with the library. After the occupation of Munich by the Swedes in 1632, the collection

was plundered. During the eighteenth century, it was reassembled in the Cologne Room of the palace. It formed the basis of the modern Bayerisches Nationalmuseum.

The Dresden collection was begun around 1560 by the Elector Augustus in the recently built new wing of his official palace. He was interested in physics and mathematics, so clocks and geodetic instruments for measuring the land formed a major part of the collection. Supplies of money and secret state papers were also kept here. After a fire in 1701, which fortunately hardly touched the collection, Augustus the Strong had this secret closet transformed into a museum-style complex. His fondness for the fine arts meant that the rooms were full of paintings, sculptures, and craft objects. He set up a room for bronze, ivory, enamel, and silver objects as well as a room for valuables. The high point of the collection was his room full of gems with sets of ceremonial jewelry. Until the palace is rebuilt, the collections are on display in the Green Vault of the Albertinum in the Zwinger.

In addition to the art collections of Prague, Salzburg, Ambrase, and Berlin, the collection of the Count of Hesse-Cassel, established towards the end of the sixteenth century, brought together strange artifacts such as expensively mounted ostrich eggs and nautilus shells with astronomical instruments, and a collection of ethnological costumes and antiquities acquired from France. Between 1776 and 1779, Count Frederick II founded the Museum Fridericianum in Cassel, the first museum in Europe. When this was rebuilt as an assembly chamber, the collections were distributed among other buildings in the

town. The valuable baroque instruments, clock mechanisms, and craft objects can be admired in the Hessisches Landesmuseum in Darmstadt and the Museum für Astronomie und Technikgeschichte in Cassel.

Baroque collections are typically characterized by a juxtaposition of scientific devices and mysterious objects. The confusing wealth of encyclopedic knowledge is combined with inexplicable freaks of nature such as mandrakes and similar objects that had a special curiosity value. There is a certain relationship to the medieval speculations of the alchemist's laboratory here. Even in the seventeenth century, efforts were being made at many courts scientifically to establish marvels of nature or inexplicable phenomena; attempts were still being made to verify the theory expounded in Virgil's *Georgics* that bees originate from animal corpses.

Such curiosities or marvels appear in the *Prodromus*, a volume of copper engravings published by Stampart and Prenner in 1735 that presents a selection of objects contained in the Viennese treasury and documents the baroque love of placing precious things alongside oddities and natural objects alongside artificial ones. Combinations of this sort were often found in libraries of the baroque period, as is shown by an engraving from the Viennese court library in the time of

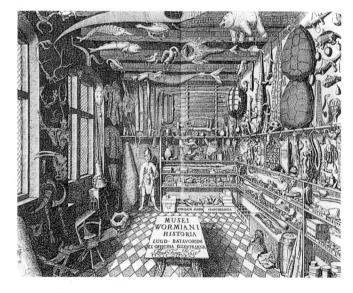

Museum Wormianum, engraving, 1655
Schleswig-Holstein Landesmuseum, Schleswig

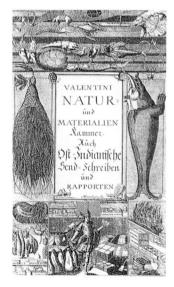

Title engraving from Valentini's
Museum Museorum, 1704

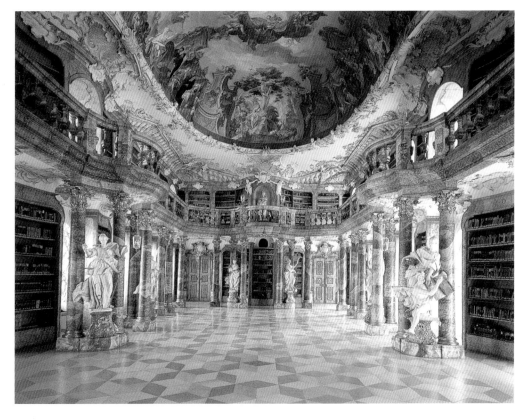

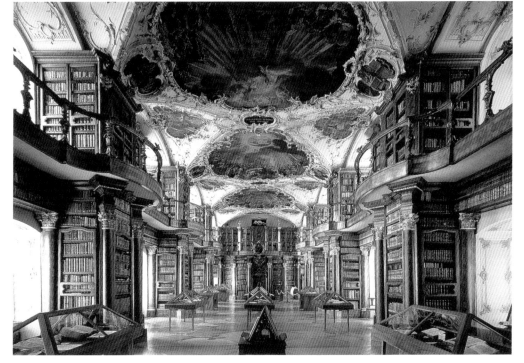

Peter Thumb
Monastery library at St. Gall, completed 1766
Woodwork by Brother Gabriel Loser

Emperor Leopold I (second half of seventeenth century). It is a view through a room many feet high. The walls are stuffed to the ceiling with books and other spacious rooms festooned with stuffed exotic beasts can be seen. Cupboards are placed on the floor and the drawers are being opened by curious onlookers. Clearly this is a place for admiring curiosities and valuables.

This engraving was printed in Nuremberg in 1711, and shows a view of the immensely rich stock of books owned by the Habsburgs, housed in makeshift accommodation in the rooms of the imperial chancellery of the Hofburg. Eleven years later, Emperor Charles VI commissioned Johann Bernhard Fischer von Erlach to extend the Hofburg and to rebuild the library, making use of a riding school building that had been started in 1681. This set the site and shape of the wing as an extended rectangle. In the center of it, Fischer placed an oval with a tall dome, thus creating an individual building (see pp. 244–45). The space soaring above the top of the upper level vaults majestically upwards to where light streams into the hall through large round-arched windows. The iconographical scheme of the dome, painted in 1726 by Daniel Gran, presents an allegory of the patron of the arts and sciences, Charles VI. The bookshelves reach up to where the vault springs. The upper shelves at the lower level are reached by ladders. For the upper level, galleries were provided, similarly furnished with ladders. Many of the volumes refer directly to this confrontation between curiosities and learned knowledge, such as Valentini's *Museum Museorum* from 1704 see p. 242 right).

Forty years later the room had to be reinforced. Fischer's almost seamless transition from the oval dome to the longitudinal axis was provided with a cesura. Transverse arches and pilasters and double columns placed in the room now separate the two side rooms from the central oval.

Besides magnificent and monumental libraries, small, intimate closet libraries had to be produced that continued the tradition of the art room/marvel room type. An example of this is King Frederick II's small library in Sanssouci. The east rotunda is the only room in the palace not directly accessible. This holy of holies of the philosopher king is accessed via a narrow corridor. As the door in the inner room itself takes the form of bookshelves, the impression is given of a humanistic study room. The

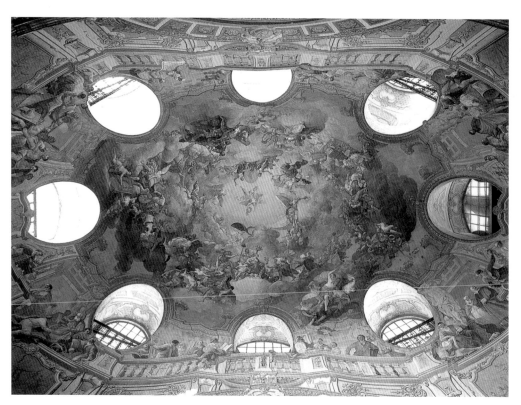

OPPOSITE:
Johann Bernhard Fischer von Erlach
Hofburg library, 1722
Vienna

LEFT:
Daniel Gran
Ceiling fresco, 1726
Hofburg library, Vienna

hundred thousand books. Construction was completed in 1766 under the direction of the Vorarlberg architect Peter Thumb. The space is divided vertically by four wall-piers on each side, which a gallery connects all the way round. The plasterwork was by Johann Georg and Matthias Gigl of Wessobrunn, while the woodwork is by Brother Gabriel Loser. The theme of classical and Christian learning familiar from Wiblingen is adapted in a curious fashion in St. Gall. According to the ceiling paintings by Josef Wannenmacher, it is a matter of defending Christian teaching with the help of theological and scientific arguments.

wainscoting is decorated with graceful bronze reliefs depicting allegories of the arts and sciences. Among these, on consoles, stand four antique busts acquired with the collection of Cardinal Polignac in 1742.

It was not only emperors, kings, and princes who wanted to establish libraries and thereby secure the corpus of knowledge of their time, but traditionally ecclesiastical orders such as the Benedictines or Cistercians as well. In the mid-eighteenth century, a library was built for the Benedictine monastery at Wiblingen near Ulm, probably by Christian Wiedermann (see p. 243 above). It contains an elegant curving gallery supported on thirty-two red and green marbled wooden columns. In balanced color contrast to these are white-painted wooden figures standing on low pedestals, allegories of the virtues and sciences. The ceiling, painted in 1744 by Franz Martin Kuen, unfolds the theme of this unique baroque room in an effective motif-led structure. Earthly and heavenly shapes allegorically glorifying classical and Christian learning circulate between rocaille-adorned architectural elements in the middle of a paradisical garden environment. Above them soar angels trailing clouds and drapery, and proclaiming divine wisdom.

When the new monastery was built at St. Gall around 1760, the collegiate library was built as the same time (see p. 243, below). It contains over two thousand old manuscripts and one

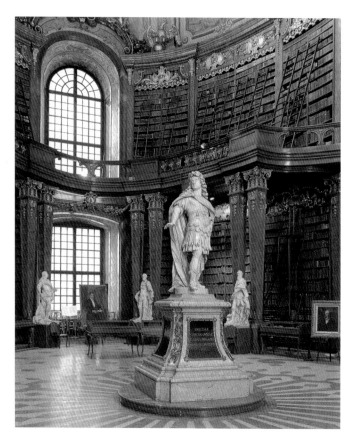

LEFT:
Johann Bernhard Fischer von Erlach
View of oval of Hofburg library, 1722
Vienna

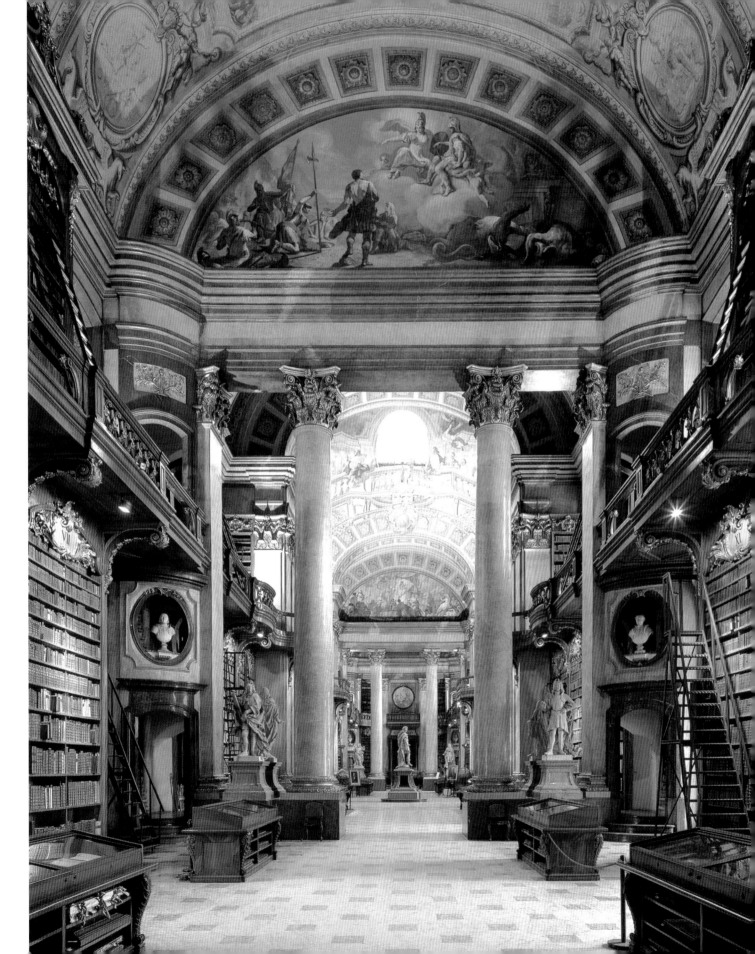

Country Houses, City Palaces, Abbeys, and Churches in Austria

The three major architects who defined the splendor and magnificence of Austrian baroque architecture are Johann Bernard Fischer (1656–1723) from Graz, on whom the noble title "von Erlach" was conferred in 1696, Johann Lukas Hildebrandt (1668–1745) from Genoa, and Jakob Prandtauer (1660–1726) from Stanz in the Tyrol. Fischer and Hildebrandt had spent a great deal of time in Rome. Hildebrandt received his training from the Roman architect Carlo Fontana, and served from 1695–96 as an engineer with the imperial army under the command of the celebrated "Hammer of the Turks," Prince Eugene. After his discharge, he settled in Vienna and devoted himself mainly to the building of palaces.

Fischer was the son of a sculptor from a prosperous workshop. He went to Italy for further training and experience in sculpture. However, during his time in the studio of Johann Paul Schors in Rome (1775–84), which maintained good contacts with the leading artists of the period, especially Bernini, he soon moved over to architecture, which later became his principal profession. The younger

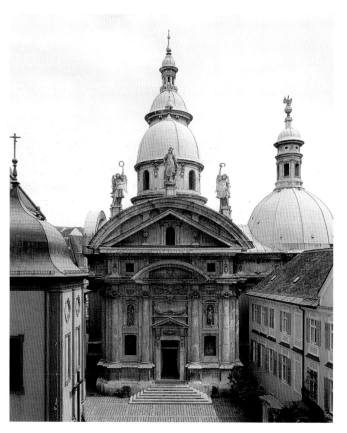

generation of artists were heavily influenced by both classical architecture and the highly imaginative use of the formal language of antiquity in the baroque style of Roman architects.

The overwhelming Italian influence on the baroque architecture of Austria during this time was soon molded into a definable individual style by the three artists mentioned above. Fischer von Erlach and Hildebrandt were virtuoso architects who countered the Italian style with their own, highly sophisticated Habsburg manner. However, Prandtauer, who had a special feeling for monumentality and grandeur, clung to the roots of his native soil and worked soberly with traditional building forms.

The Italian approach in Austrian baroque architecture is most clearly reflected in the mausoleum of Ferdinand II in Graz (see left). Before his accession as archduke of Styria, he was an emphatic advocate of the Counter-Reformation. Ferdinand commissioned plans for the structure from the Italian architect Pietro de Pomis. Construction probably began in 1614. Pietro de Pomis was probably the first architect to make use of an oval ground plan north of the Alps for this mausoleum in St. Catherine's church. He envisaged a two-storey circular structure surmounted by an oval dome, a characteristic Italian motif. The east front is similarly indebted to the Roman baroque tradition. Architectural features such as three-quarter columns, pilasters, window frames, and cornices are treated sculpturally. The alternation of triangular and segmental pediments is strictly maintained. The broad final segmented pediment is set over the triangular pediment of the roof storey—a motif borrowed from the facade of the Gesù in Rome (1577)—and supports three massive statues (two angels and St. Catherine).

After the death of de Pomis in 1633, construction was suspended for half a century until Fischer von Erlach was commissioned to fit out the half-finished shell in 1687. He was probably fascinated by the use of the oval form, which would have been familiar to him from his Italian period. In any case, it was to become a prominent feature in his later designs.

A few years later he was able to put these new ideas into practice. In 1694 he was commissioned by Archbishop Count Thun of Salzburg to build the Trinity church there. The archbishop was as obsessed by building schemes as the Schönborn of Würzburg, and wanted to transform Salzburg into the "Rome of the North." The construction of four major churches was planned, and Fischer seemed the ideal architect for them. In an engraving from 1699, the archiepiscopal client is depicted among his foundations, which are exclusively the work of his architect Fischer (or, after 1696, Fischer von Erlach): the seminary and Trinity church (from 1694), St. John's hospital and church (from 1694–95), the collegiate church (from 1696). and the Ursuline church (from 1699).

Fischer's task was to set each new construction aesthetically and functionally within the context of the townscape, and he therefore faced a fundamental problem of urban planning. He had to consider

Johann Bernhard Fischer von Erlach
West front (below) and ground plan
(right) of Trinity church, Salzburg,
begun 1694

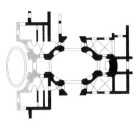

Johann Bernhard Fischer von Erlach
View from west (below) and ground
plan (right) of collegiate church,
Salzburg, begun 1696

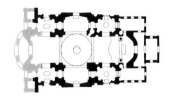

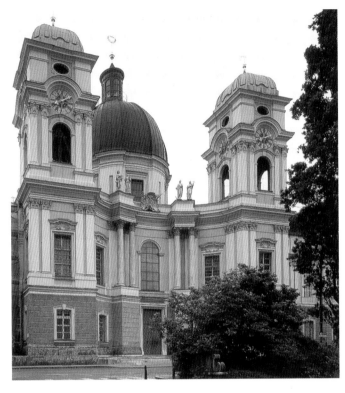

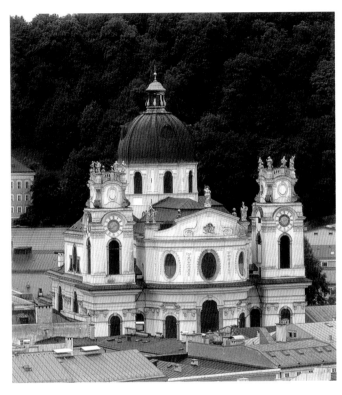

how a church facade could be presented to good effect in the framework of the city environment. In the case of the Trinity church, it was a matter of positioning a facade with the corresponding wings of the seminary in an appropriate relationship to the square in front of it. Fischer took his bearings from the church of S. Agnese in Agone in Piazza Navona in Rome, also a domed church with two towers flanking a concave columnar facade. Fischer was clearly taken with Francesco Borromini's elegant design. The Roman architect had not in fact been able to carry the momentum of the facade through to the ground plan; the interior might have been more effective if it had been designed as a similar oval. However, for reasons of space, the Rainaldi brothers, who had worked on the design before Borromini, had created a building with a circular ground plan. By contrast, Fischer's interior reflects the arch of the concave external wall structure, with an oval nave stretching right up to the high altar. Above this he placed a steeply proportioned rotunda, an architectural feature that would henceforth define the spatial organization of his church interiors.

His design two years later (1696) for the collegiate church in Salzburg (see above right) was even more imaginative; it was also commissioned by Archbishop Thun. Fischer improved on his design

for the Trinity facade in a most original way, here setting it clearly apart from the flanking towers and bringing its convex outline forward in front of the line of the towers. This design resulted in three distinct architectural components which are linked in harmonious motion. The impact of this scheme was felt as far away as southwestern Germany and Switzerland, in Weingarten, Einsiedeln, and Ottobeuren.

The spatial arrangement of the building is familiar from Rosati's church of S. Carlo ai Catinari in Rome (from 1612). Fischer von Erlach must have studied this church in detail during his stay in Rome, because his work improves significantly on the spatial effects of the original. The ratio of height to breadth is around 4:1, creating the sense of a vast ravine-like space.

Fischer von Erlach's two church designs served as an excellent basis for the procurement of further employment in Vienna. In the plague year of 1713 Charles VI, who had had himself crowned emperor in 1711, vowed to build a church dedicated to St. Charles Borromeo if the disaster could be averted. Planning began two years later, and an architect was sought. Fischer von Erlach was up against formidable opposition, including the imperial court architect Hildebrandt and Ferdinando Galli-Bibiena. Fischer drew up a plan

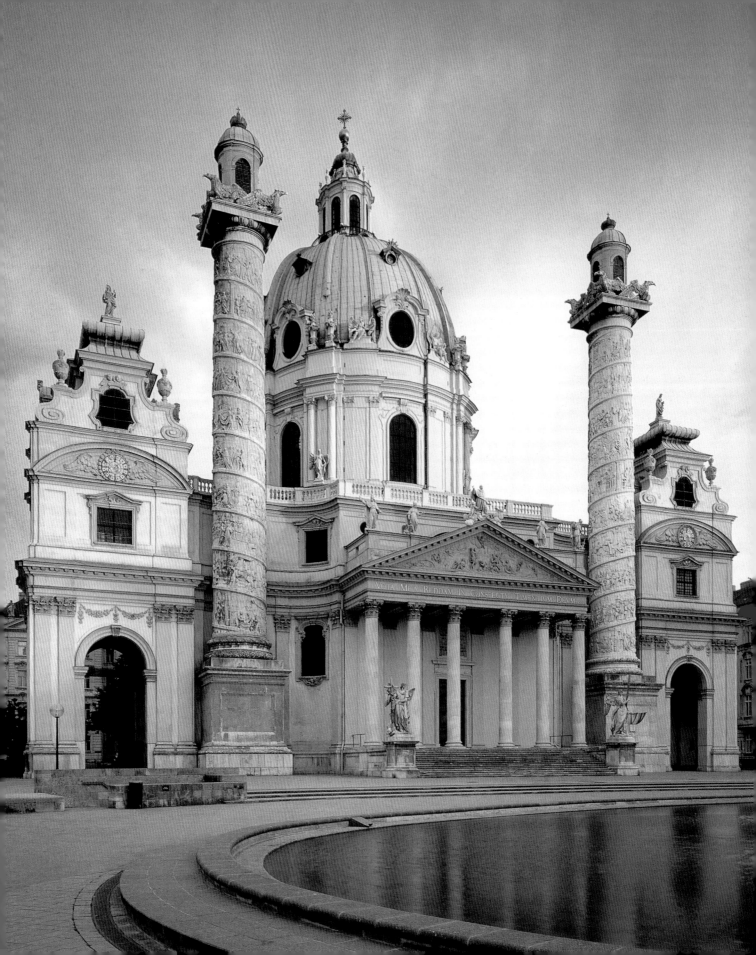

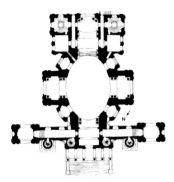

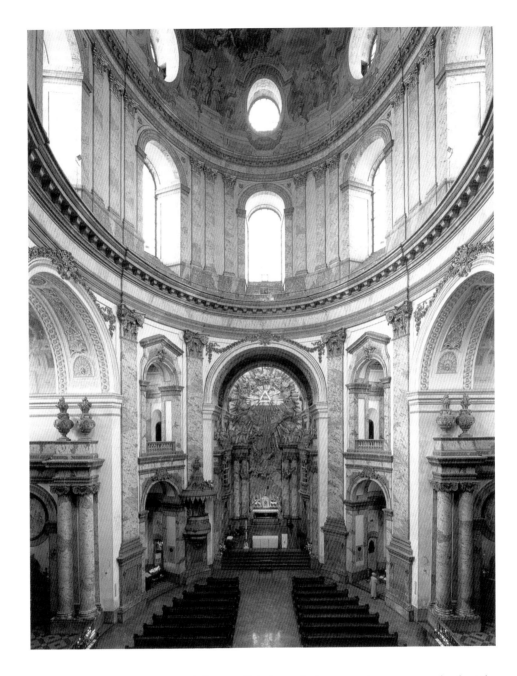

The unusually imposing quality of the Karlskirche depends not just on the triad of pillared portico, dome, and triumphal columns. Fischer von Erlach saw the dome as the focal point of the scheme. The oval is the core of the composition. Above it rises the dome on a high drum. Inside, the nave seems to extend both horizontally and vertically. The choir, chapels, sacristies, and side-rooms are arranged around the choir.

The east-west axis of the nave is crossed by the axis of the west front. The facade's restfulness and linearity is broken up in the interior and transformed into a dynamic design. On entering, the observer is drawn up towards the light, which then unfolds the movement of the architecture before him. Both structurally and empirically, the focal point of the building remains the dome. Its dominance is perceived both internally and externally.

linking the notion of a votive building with that of regal display—a sacred monument of *pietas austriaca* [Austrian piety] (see above and left). This building, with its tall drum and dome rising behind a classical pillared portico and flanked by two classical triumphal columns is a spectacular version of the two Salzburg churches. The church is clearly the product of a native tradition, thereby symbolizing the political ambitions of the Habsburgs—the Roman roots of the Empire, bound up with the Emperor's claim to Spain. The classical temple facade and the triumphal columns, although homogeneous parts of the whole building, appear as heavily symbolic set pieces, almost as if they had been taken from an imaginary architectural pattern book.

Fischer von Erlach was in fact at work on a pattern book at the time, which in due course became the core of *Historic Architecture*, a folio of engravings showing the roots of modern architecture. The book is unconventional in that it fails to address the theoretical matters customarily represented in such works, such as the orders or architectural proportion. For Fischer, examples of exotic architecture like the pyramids of Egypt were just as important as the visual representation and depiction of Deinocrates' works as recorded in Vitruvius. According to Vitruvius, the Macedonian architect drew up a plan to transform Mount Athos into a seated figure of his royal patron Alexander the Great, with the city laid out across his lap and beneath his huge outstretched arm (see p. 250).

Johann Bernhard Fischer von Erlach
Engravings from *Entwurff einer historischen Architektur*, 1721
TOP TO BOTTOM
Two vases and a summer residence (plate 10, vol. V)
Mount Athos, with Alexander, Plate 18, Vol. I
First design for Schönbrunn (plate 2, vol. IV)

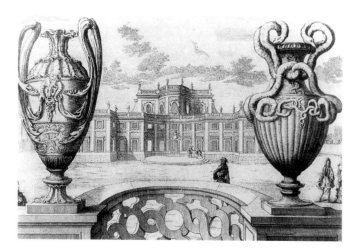

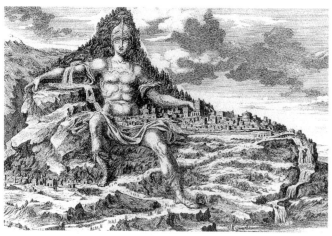

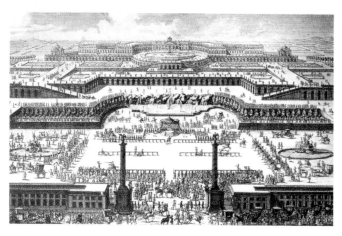

An engraving in volume V of Fischer's book spreads before the reader a view of a garden and summer palace between two antique vases (see left above). The facade is a subtle design with a concave ground floor front, surmounted by a graceful but convex central elevation behind a parapet with statues. This unusual combination of convex and concave facades had already engaged Fischer's attention while he was in Rome, as is evident from numerous sketches of country buildings (see right, above). Certainly Bernini's first project for the facade of the Louvre in Paris had an influence here. While training as a sculptor in the workshop of Johann Ferdinand Schor in Rome. Fischer may have met Bernini shortly before the latter's death in 1680, as his frequent presence in this workshop is well-attested. When it came to planning garden palaces and "pleasure buildings," Fischer turned back to his early sketches and reworked them, sometimes to dazzling effect. This is true of the palace of Klesheim which he worked on from 1694, described by the artist as "the little pleasure palace of the archbishop of Salzburg, Ernestus von Thun" (see p. 252, above left). The ground plan consists of three ovals attached to each other as in a clover leaf, with three rectangular corner buildings set in the spandrels. A facade effect was underplayed in favor of the interior design and outlook.

A similar starting point can be identified for the facade of the collegiate church in Salzburg, built two years later. In his sketchbook, later known as the *Codex Montenuovo* (now in the Albertina in Vienna), Fischer presents plans for garden lodges, thus setting the pattern for the typical Viennese summer residence. There is a certain irony in the fact that his greatest rival in palace architecture, Hildebrandt, made use of Fischer's inventions for his scheme for the garden palace of Starhemberg. This was probably not his own choice but the result of pressure from his client. Fischer's garden palace variations soon became popular with the nobility, and a standard model for this type of building evolved from his designs that became an obligatory formula even for the competition.

Fischer also knew how to monumentalize his cosy garden lodges, as is evident from his first design for the palace of Schönbrunn in 1688. This was an ornate design intended mainly to impress future clients (see left below). The garden was laid out in 1695, and a year later he designed a hunting lodge which, at the prompting of Emperor Leopold I, was to be extended by two courtyards and corresponding wings "so that it should be suitable to hold the whole imperial household." This variant is depicted in volume IV of *Historic Architecture*. With the death of Joseph I in 1711, Schönbrunn declined in importance. It was left to Maria Teresa to organize and transform the palace complex from 1743.

In 1696 Fischer von Erlach was awarded the commission to build a town palace for Prince Eugene of Savoy. He designed a building of seven bays which was to be extended in later years. In comparison to the garden palaces, his design seems astonishingly sober, quite different from the Viennese taste of the time. The facade is made up of a

Johann Bernhard Fischer von Erlach
Sketches for country houses, c. 1680

Johann Bernhard Fischer von Erlach
Staircase hall of Prince Eugene's former city palace,
Vienna, begun 1695

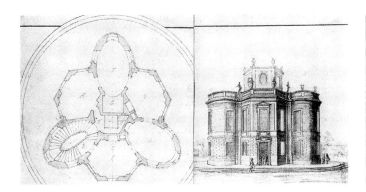

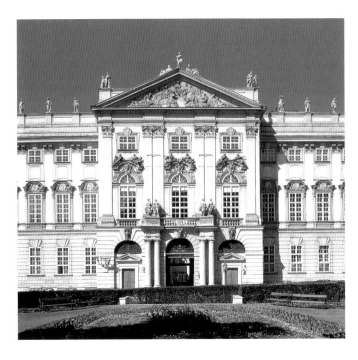

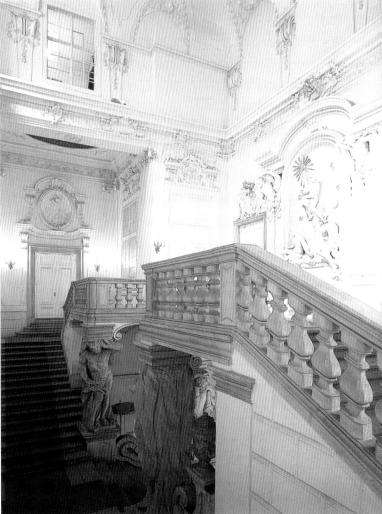

Johann Bernhard Fischer von Erlach
Main front of Gartenpalais Trautson,
begun 1710

Johann Bernhard Fischer von Erlach
Schloss Klesheim, Salzburg
1700–09

Johann Lucas von Hildebrandt
Stadtpalais Daun-Kinsky, Vienna
1713–16

Johann Lucas von Hildebrandt
Central elevation of garden front
of Lower Belvedere, Vienna,
1713–16

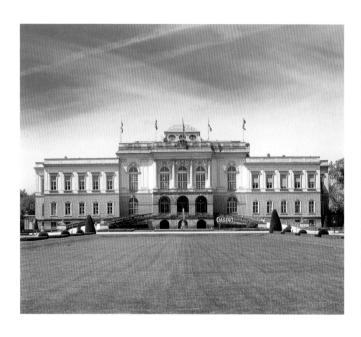

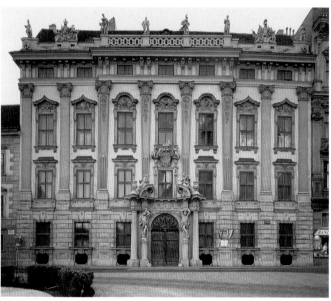

Johann Lucas von Hildebrandt
Garden front of Palais Schwarzenberg
(previously Mansfeld-Fondi), Vienna,
1697

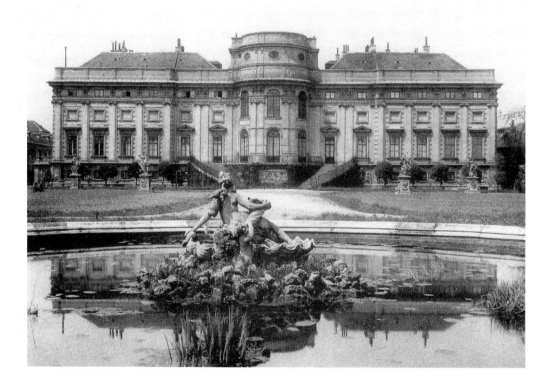

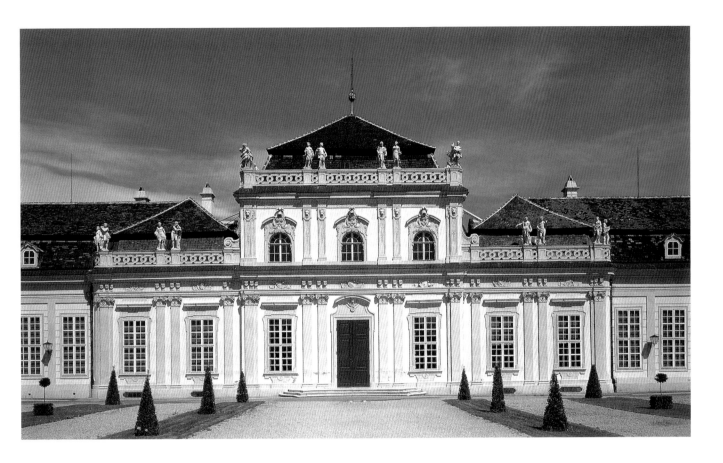

somewhat unvarying conglomeration of pilasters—essentially, the design was old-fashioned. This may have been the reason why Prince Eugene took the commission from Fischer and from 1700 gave it to his great rival Hildebrandt. In any case, things changed for Fischer von Erlach in Vienna. The ornate architectural grammar of Hildebrandt's style suddenly came into greater favor. Nonetheless it is evident that Hildebrandt appreciated Fischer's popular palace design, which he adapted in the garden palace of Mansfeld-Fondi, built in 1697 (see left, below). A central oval block, accessed by two flights of steps on the garden side, is flanked by a pair of wings. Hildebrandt was unable to finish the building. Until 1716, when Prince Schwarzenberg acquired it, it remained a shell. Four years later, Fischer von Erlach was awarded the job of fitting out the now renamed Palais Schwarzenberg. It was a notable event. Fischer thoroughly altered the external appearance, replacing the ornate aedicules with round arches and making the articulatory features such as cornice and pilasters more prominent and three-dimensional. The decorative design typical of Hildebrandt, which included the oval central projection, was not implemented. Fischer moved the central oval forward as an independent and prominent architectural feature.

The different styles of the two architects can be seen most clearly in Hildebrandt's Daun-Kinsky Palais, which he built between 1713 and 1716 (see left above). The town house has a distinguished appearance, with a very busy, richly decorated facade. The pilasters of the slightly projecting central elevation re-emerge in the lower third, where they are coarsely fluted. The window pediments are varied on the upper floor—some are elegant segments and others are ogee arches. Above an upper mezzanine floor a graceful balustrade is crowned with classical figures on lofty pedestals. Hildebrandt's feeling for the awkward detail is best expressed in the interior. The scrollwork of the balustrade in the staircase hall concentrates on foliage and volutes, or unfolds into large-scale triangles.

During these years, Prince Eugene's plans for a residence outside the city were well advanced. In the 1690s, Hildebrandt had started work on laying out the terraces of the garden outside the gates of Vienna. In 1714 he devoted himself to building the Lower Belvedere, a lengthy single-storey building that has an upper floor only in the modest center elevation (see above). Work was completed two years later.

The designs for the Upper Belvedere (1721) were decidedly more majestic (see pp. 254–55). The super-elevated central middle pavilion with the marble hall is preceded by the staircase hall and a vestibule with a curved segmented gable. Each wing terminates in an octagonal pavilion, their circular domes continuing and concluding the rhythm of the various floor levels. It is a novel and unusual scheme. The wings are layered: the first five bays on each side of the central pavilion have a second storey that stretches behind the gable of the vestibule. Behind it the central pavilion rises, its roof crowning the whole structure. The rising and falling outline of the roof, together with the projecting and receding building elevations, are set in dynamic tension through the use of a coherent system of decora-

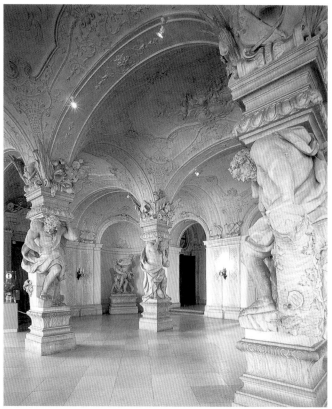

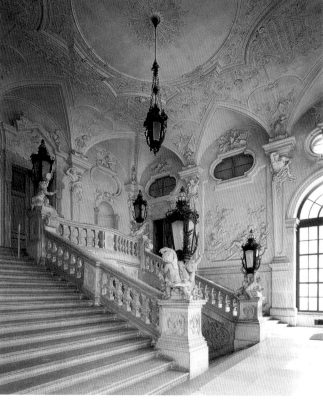

Johann Lucas von Hildebrandt
Sala Terrena (left) and
staircase hall (right)
Upper Belvedere, Vienna, 1721–23

BELOW:
Overall view of Belvedere, Vienna
Engraving by J. A. Corvinius after a
drawing by Salomon Kleiner, 1740

OPPOSITE:
Johann Lucas von Hildebrandt
Exterior elevation of Upper
Belvedere, Vienna, 1721–23

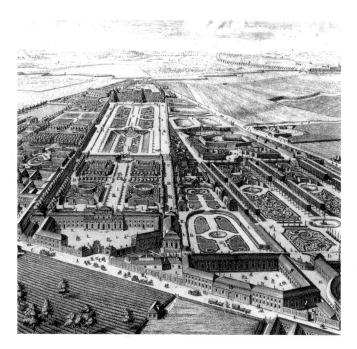

tion. The continuous lower storey, with its entablature carried right
across and round the corner pavilions, provides the unifying principle of the system.

No other work by Hildebrandt reveals his feeling for three-
dimensionality and its effect as definitively as the dynamic facade of
the Upper Belvedere. The same applies to the interiors, especially the
staircase hall. Its construction may be explained by an examination
of Franconian sources. In 1711 Hildebrandt was summoned to
Schloss Pommersfelden to solve the problem of the staircase hall
there (see p. 221). The client, the Elector and Archbishop Lothar
Franz von Schonborn, had allocated too great a space in his design
for the staircases. Hildebrandt solved the problem by introducing a
three-storey gallery, with the stairs linking just the lower floors.

This relationship between the spatial proportion and stairwell
dimensions must have come to mind when Hildebrandt was faced
with the same problem in Vienna. He found an elegant solution,
creating a "sliding" spatial sequence between the Sala Terrena, the
entrance hall, and the marble hall. From the vestibule, the visitor
enters the staircase hall, where two outer flights rise to the Marble
Hall and apartments at the side. The center flight descends to the
Sala Terrena.

Hildebrandt's imaginative and yet formal style also characterizes

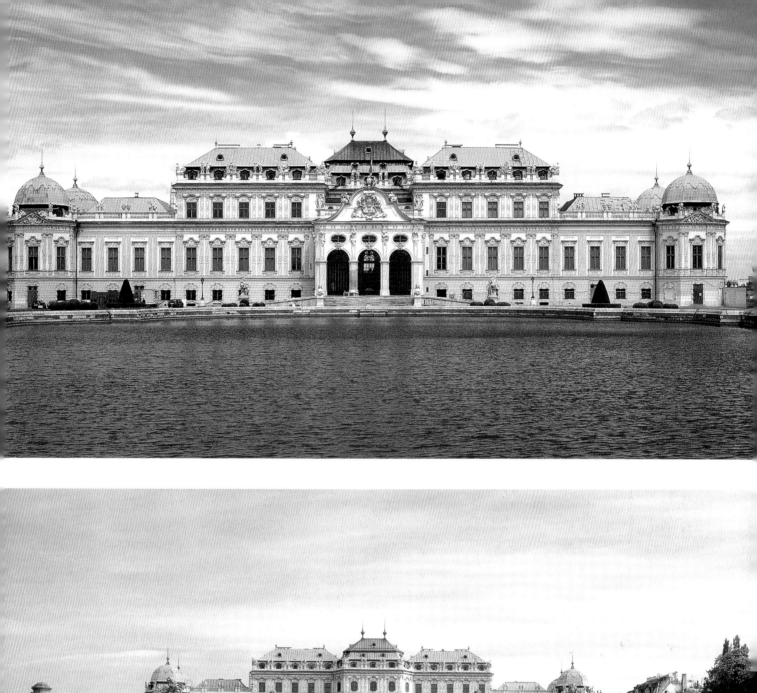

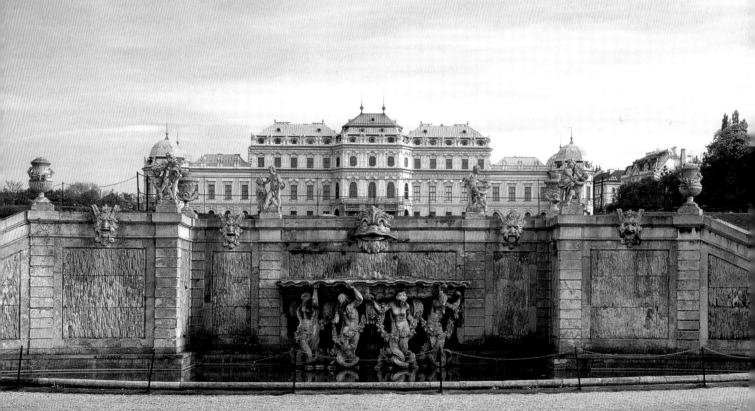

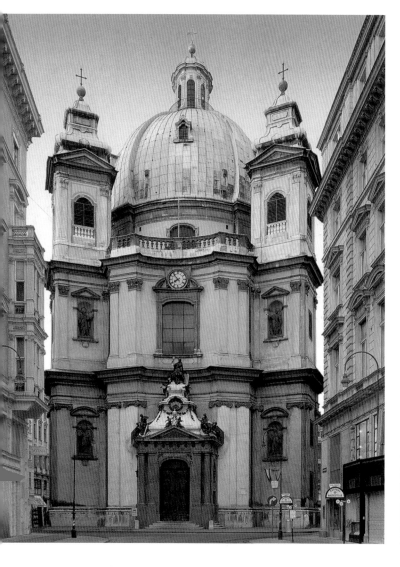

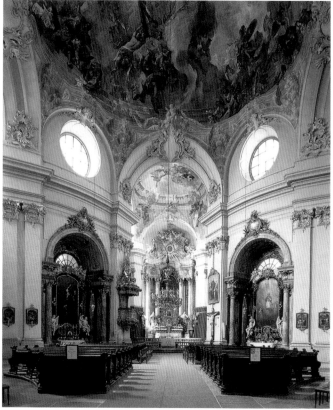

his church buildings. He submitted plans for the Piaristenkirche (see p. 256) in Vienna in 1698, but construction was begun only in 1716. Later, Kilian Ignaz Dientzenhofer became involved in the scheme.

The facade of St. Peter's (see above left) is somewhat squat but nonetheless bears an elegant curve between the two flanking and somewhat recessed bell towers. A huge dome rises above the concave central elevation. The building was constructed between 1702 and 1733. Hildebrandt envisaged a similar bold curve for the facade of the parish church of Göllersdorf, built between 1740 and 1741. Another important work in this context is the seminary church in Linz, formerly the Deutschordenskirche Heiliges Kreuz (1718–25).

Splendid apartments, stairwells, and ceremonial halls belong not only to the fixed repertory of princely palaces and summer houses but featured also in large abbeys. Powerful abbots or prince-abbots had estates and political influence—or at the very least, they maintained excellent contacts with the imperial court in Vienna. The splendor of imperial power emanating from the prevailing ruling house thus shone also on the ecclesiastical sphere, setting the tone

for the layout and implementation of monastic buildings.

One of the grandest and most magnificent abbeys in Austria is undoubtedly the Benedictine Abbey at Melk on the Danube (see right and pp. 258–59). Its history goes back to the year 985, when Margrave Leopold I of Babenberg founded the monastery. Around a century later the Benedictines moved in. The present group of baroque structures set on a rocky salient high above the Danube is the result of collaboration between Abbot Berthold Dietmayr and the architect Jakob Prandtauer (1660–1726).

Prandtauer began his career as a sculptor, as Fischer had done, but then turned to architecture. From 1701 he planned and organized various abbeys from his base in St. Polten. They included Sonntagberg, Garsten, St. Florian, Kremsmunster, and Melk. He did not restrict himself to drawing plans like Hildebrandt, but also took over the supervision of the building work. Prandtauer was a pragmatist—a master mason in the traditional sense.

The ceremony for the laying of the foundation stone was held at Melk in 1702. The shell of the building was completed sixteen years

Johann Lucas von Hildebrandt
Overall view of Gottweig collegiate foundation, according to plan of 1719
Engraving by Salomon Kleiner

Antonio Beduzzi, Lorenzo Mattielli, and Peter Widerin
High altar of Melk collegiate church, 1727–35

later. Work on the interior proceeded briskly; however, Prandtauer died in 1726 and did not live to see his work finished. The entire site was taken over by Josef Munggenast, who implemented everything as his great predecessor had intended.

The main axis of the 1,050 foot long complex runs from the entrance gateway in the east across the forecourt and the prelates, court through the choir and nave of the abbey church and exits through Coloman court, finally terminating at the western balcony above a sheer drop to the Danube.

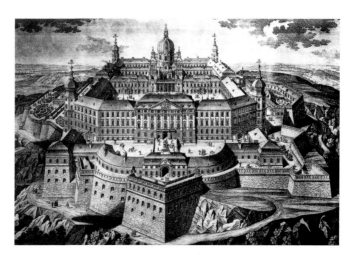

The visitor approaching the abbey along the bank of the Danube from the southwest can appreciate the scale of the ensemble and its principal components from below. The semicircular western gallery and balcony with a semicircular arch at its vortex is flanked by wings comprising a marble hall on the south side and a library on the Danube side. The balcony, with its columns and semi-circular arch, was probably derived from the Venetian villa architecture of Palladio. The bastion-style curves of the gallery on each side of the balcony follow the form and movement of the cliff, and carry the rhythm of the rock up into the soaring architecture. Prandtauer undoubtedly contrived this interplay of movement between the natural rock and the constructed gallery, since the architectural motifs recur in versions in the side wings and church facade.

The facades of the twin buildings adjoining the gallery on each side of Coloman court are articulated by slender pilasters, and continue up to the west front of the church, which is surmounted by two towers with onion domes. The onion domes stand in remarkable contrast to the architecture of the towers. The formal arrangement comprising double pilasters, simple framed windows, and solid arcading bears no relationship to the concave and convex play of turrets, clock towers, and onion domes. In 1738, a long time after Prandtauer's death, fire destroyed parts of the church, and Munggenast designed new tops of the towers—although not quite in the spirit of his predecessor's original conception.

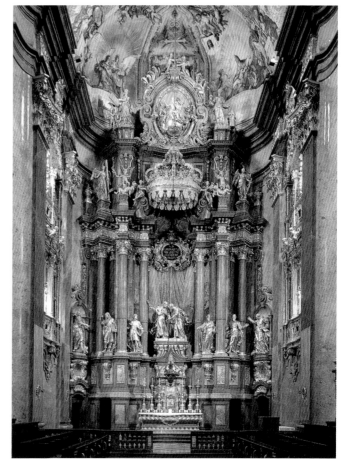

Above the crossing rises a dome on a tall drum, surmounted by a graceful lantern. The abbey fortress seems to sail along like an oversized ship. This movement towards the promontory is dramatically represented by the immensely long south front, which terminates in the western gallery and balcony. The scheme emphasizes Prandtauer's essentially sculptural approach, which is repeatedly expressed in a number of unusual associations. The sophisticated interplay of architecture and scenery reinforces this impression. The monastic complex is enthroned on top of the cliff like a monumental sculpture. The topographical situation presented a challenge to Prandtauer as a sculptor and an architect. His response was to release his architectural creation from the rock and project it into the sky.

The powerful exterior effects are also carried through into the interior of the abbey church. A striking feature here is the expansion of the architectural parts such as piers or fluted pilasters like filigree

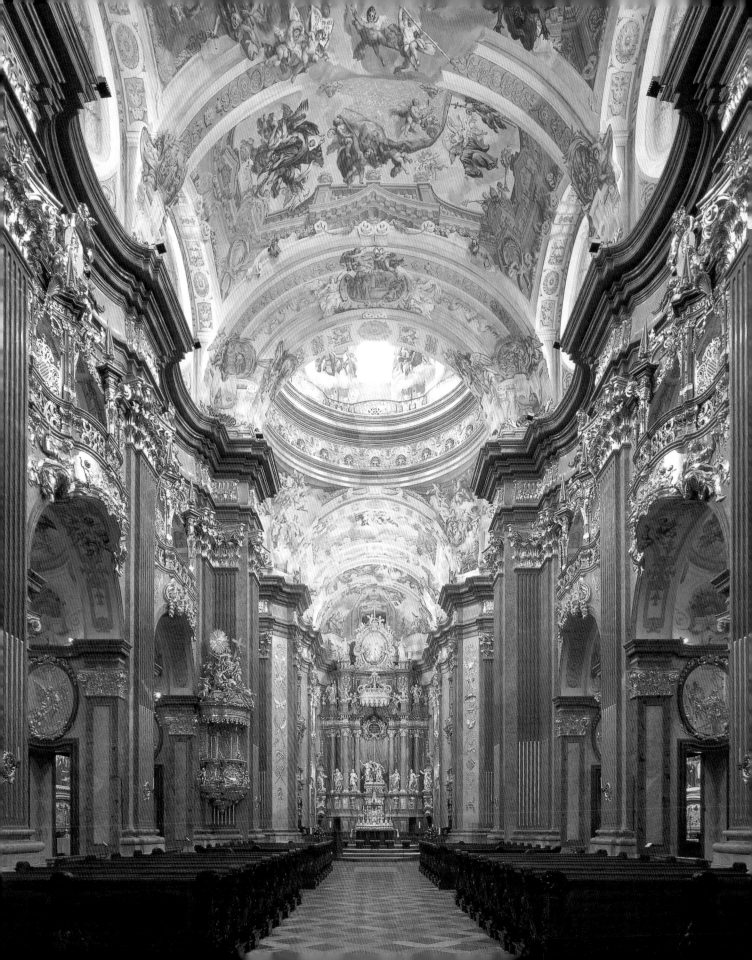

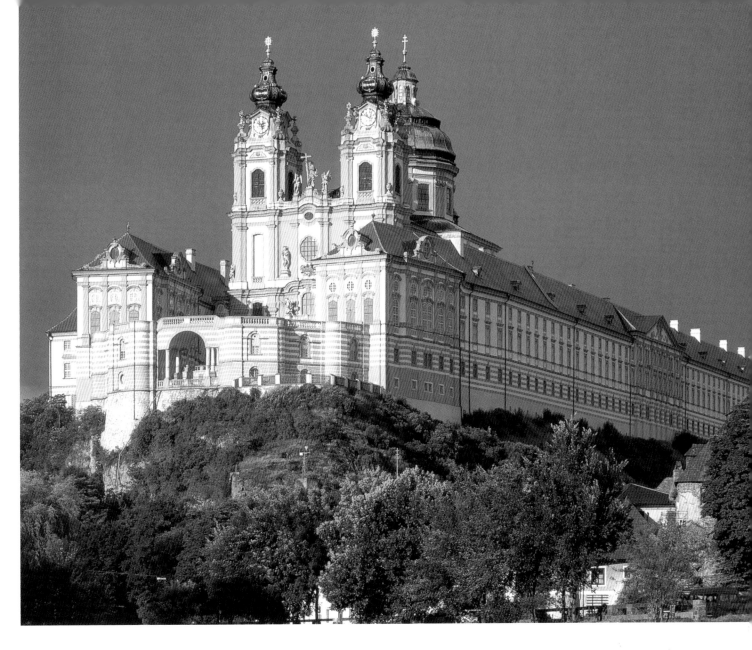

Jakob Prandtauer and Josef Munggenast
View from the Danube of the
Benedictine foundation of Melk,
1702–38

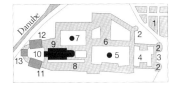

Ground plan of Benedictine foundation
of Melk

1 Gardens
2 Bastions
3 Entrance gateway
4 Forecourt
5 Prelates court
   with fountain
6 School
7 Monastery court
8 Emperor's
   court
9 Collegiate
   church
10 Coloman court
11 Marble hall
12 Library
13 Balcony

OPPOSITE:
Jakob Prandtauer
and Josef Munggenast
Interior of church, Benedictine
foundation of Melk, 1702–38

work into the richly adorned transverse arches and the vault and dome areas. Light falls into the crossing through the large windows of the drum and is diffused into the adjoining areas, where it illuminates the sculptural quality of the plasterwork.

For Prandtauer, Melk was not just an experiment in handling the three-dimensional and dynamic aspects of architecture. It was here that he also acquired experience in planning complex ensembles consisting of numerous different structures that had to be absorbed into a homogeneous whole. The specific topographical situation may have provided a welcome challenge, as the various alternatives were otherwise somewhat restricted.

The construction at Durnstein on the Danube, only a few miles northeast of Melk, was similar in many respects. In 1716 Prandtauer designed a building complex with west towers and a terrace at the front, set in a dramatic relationship to the Danube rather like the buildings at Melk. From 1724 Munggenast took

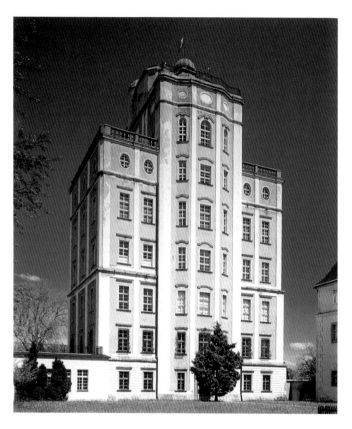

P. Anselm Desing
Observatory at Kremsmünster
Completed 1758

the church: the victory of faith, signified through the Church, is connected with the vanquishing of unbelief. This is the theme of the decoration of the marble hall, where Martino Altomonte's ceiling frescos depict Prince Eugene, representing imperial power, conquering the Turks. His portrait is placed in this room opposite that of the Emperor Charles VI.

The library in the east wing was not built until 1744 to 1751, long after Prandtauer's death. Altomonte's son Bartolommeo painted the ceiling fresco, the *Marriage of Religion and Science*, evidently intended to provide a further allegory on the theme of worldly and spiritual power. The monastic buildings and church are organized according to a heavily symbolic system of order. The doorway, library, marble hall, and choir of the church are set on axes that intersect in the cloister. The active encounter between faith and science in the library finds its basis in the church and its protection in the veneration of the monarchy in the marble hall.

The third member of the triad of great Austrian abbeys is the Benedictine foundation of Kremsmünster, which was rebuilt during the seventeenth and eighteenth centuries. Between 1709 and 1713 the romanesque-gothic church was renovated in the baroque manner. Carlone, the architect of St. Florian, had built an imperial hall around 1692, and a few years later Prandtauer designed the entrance court.

The observatory, built between 1748 and 1760 does not belong to the standard baroque typology (see left). The initiative for the construction of this building lay in the rivalry between Benedictines and Jesuits: the former wanted to counter the educational enthusiasm of the Jesuits with something of equal weight. The Benedictines therefore had the idea of building an observatory as part of their academy for young nobles which would be set in a picturesque location on a hill in Kremsmünster. This impressive building is astonishing simply for its height. Almost a skyscraper, the central convex elevation rises over seven floors. It is articulated by two corner pilasters and two central pilasters, which run up uninterrupted to the terminal wall. Adjoining blocks with two bays have roof balustrades which echo the sixth floor of the projecting central elevation.

Outside Austria there are probably no baroque abbeys where the sacred and imperial spheres are so palpably interwoven. Melk, St Florian, and Kremsmünster could almost be designated imperial palaces. The *unio mystica et terrena*, the fusion of God and the world in the imperium, is, however nowhere as explicitly expresses as it is in Klosterneuburg. Established in the twelfth century high above the Danube near Vienna by the Babenberg Margrave Leopold III, the monastery foundation was noted as due for rebuilding by Charles VI around 1730, when it was planned as a "Habsburg Escorial." Of the four courts planned, only the northeastern one was executed, and work was stopped in 1755. The original building scheme had incorporated a close connection between the imperial wing, church, and

over the supervision of this site also, overseeing the completion of the work.

The situation in St. Florian (Upper Austria), south of Linz (see right) was quite different. The buildings of the Augustinian choral foundation were initially begun by Carlo Antonio Carlone in 1686. He constructed a church based on the proportions and with the structural organization of the Jesuit church of the Gesù in Rome. Apparently the scheme was for an aiseless nave with galleries above the side chapels. After Carlone's death, Prandtauer continued the work from 1706 to 1724. He designed the monastic ensemble as a large-scale rectangle. From the west front of the church he developed an elongated wing with a richly sculptured doorway and an adjacent stairwell, the latter already complete in 1714. The steps lead to the Emperor's apartments and are magnificently adorned with arcades and a substantial arch with columns. Prandtauer planned an elegant marble hall for the center of the south wing. This project occupied him until his death. The hall extends to the full depth of the wing, and on the courtyard side projects beyond the line of the building. This was intended to emphasize a symbolic bridge to

Carlo Antonio Carlone
and Jakob Prandtauer
St. Florian collegiate foundation,
1686–1724
Doorway with sculptures by Leonhard
Sattler (above left)
Library (below left)
Staircases (above right)
Marble Hall (below right)

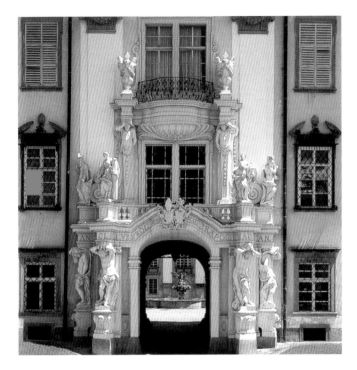

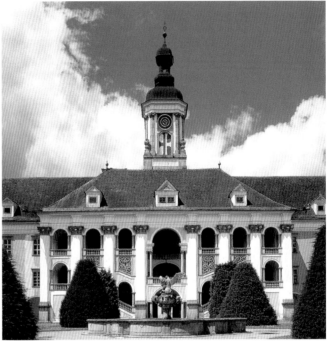

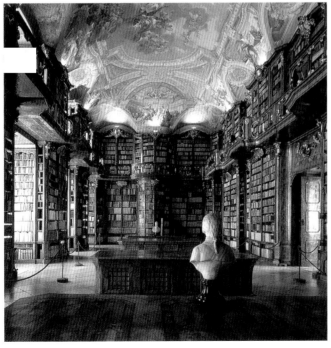

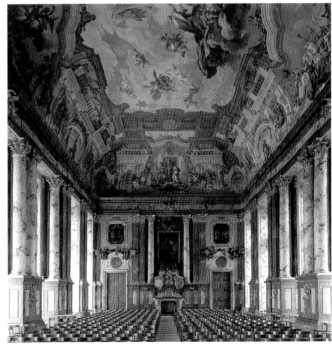

**Johann Bernhard Fischer, Joseph Emmanuel Fischer
von Erlach, and Nicola Pacassi**
Great Gallery of Schönbrunn, Vienna
Begun 1696, altered 1735 and 1744–49
Ceiling frescos by Gregorio Guglielmi, 1760

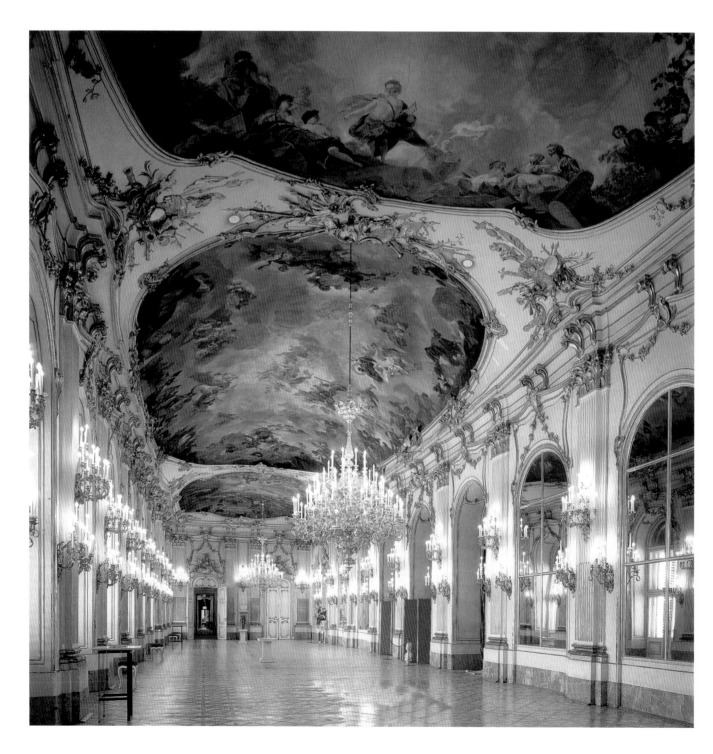

CENTER RIGHT:
Johann Bernhard Fischer, Joseph Emmanuel Fischer von Erlach, and Nicola Pacassi
Garden front of Schönbrunn, Vienna, begun 1696

BELOW RIGHT:
Ferdinand Hetzendorf von Hohenberg
Gloriette, Schönbrunn, Vienna, completed

1775
RIGHT:
Daniel Gran
Dome fresco of Klosterneuburg collegiate foundation, 1749

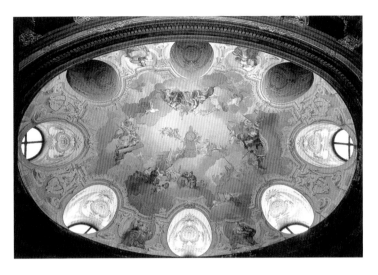

cloister. High on the central pavilion of what is today the residential wing sits a monumental imperial throne, while the mitre of the Austrian archbishop looms over the left-hand pavilion, and the imperial eagle hovers over the stairhall. The unexecuted right-hand pavilion was designed to bear the crown of Spain—a symbol of mourning for the lost Spanish empire. Lost because Joseph Franz, who had become Emperor Charles VI in 1711, had not been able to enforce his claim in the War of the Spanish Succession in the face of his French rival Philip V. At the Peace of Utrecht in 1713, Spain had been promised to the Bourbons by Britain and Holland.

The concept of the cosmocrator, the ruler of heaven and earth, unfolds in the fresco in the central dome of the imperial hall in Klosternneuburg (see above right). The artist Daniel Gran represents Charles VI as the Holy Roman Emperor and lord of war and peace. He sits on his throne surrounded by the virtues, arts, and sciences and has himself glorified in the "world center" of Vienna.

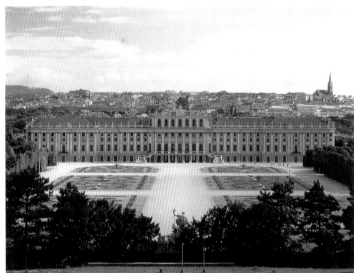

The political dominance of the Habsburgs in Europe, embodied in the Holy Roman Empire, is seen in opposition to the French regime. The architecture of the church of St. Charles in Vienna was intended to embody this imperial notion. Fischer von Erlach's dream project at Schönbrunn (see p. 250, below) must be viewed in the same way. Even if never implemented on this scale, it was supposed to represent a challenge to Versailles, functioning also as a focus for the other, non-French, parts of Europe. At that time Paris and Vienna were the political and cultural centers of the continent. The major impetus for baroque architecture originated in Vienna. Fischer's plans and buildings, like the palaces of Hildebrandt, were models for other European baroque schemes.

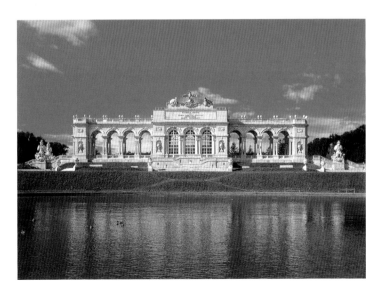

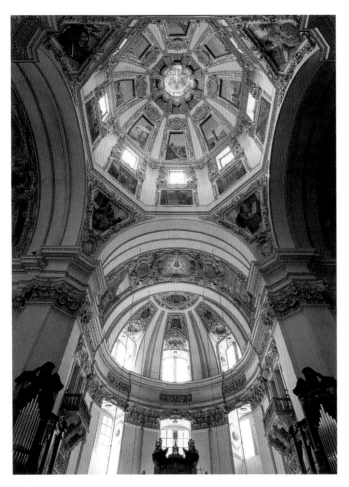

Santino Solari
West front and view into dome
Salzburg cathedral, 1614–28

Solari built Salzburg cathedral from 1614 to 1628, but the eighty-meter west towers were added thirty years later. This church was the first baroque building north of the Alps. The interior structure and west front were modeled on the Jesuit church of Il Gesù in Rome. The four giant statues depicting national patrons Rupert and Virgil (outside) and the Apostles Peter and Paul (inside) relate to the architecture characteristic of baroque.

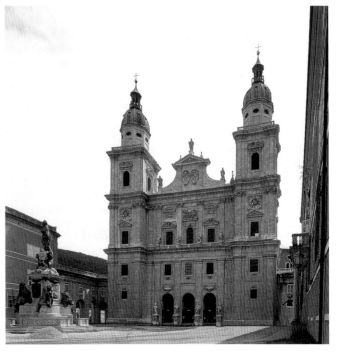

RIGHT:
Hippolytus Guarinoni
St. Charles Borromeo, Volders
1620–54

A doctor and polymath, Hippolytus Guarinoni supervised the building of the church according to his own plans between 1620 and 1654. His intention was to translate the principle of the Holy Trinity into building. Three chapels branching from the circular central space illustrate the Trinity. This ground plan motif is repeated on a small scale in the tower. The decorative forms sometimes appear to have been arbitrarily combined and the overall impression of the building is not entirely homogeneous.

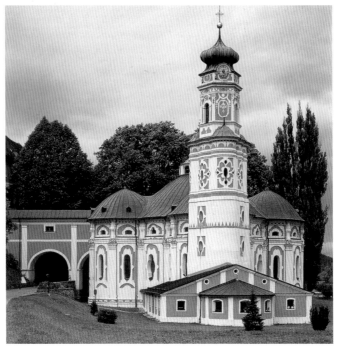

OPPOSITE, BOTTOM RIGHT:
Johann Michael Prunner
Trinity church, Stadl-Paura near Lambach, 1717–24

The foundation of this church goes back to a plague vow by Abbot Maximilian Pagel. The three-cornered, curving ground plan is marked out by three corner towers. The cornice curves elegantly around the whole building, thus incorporating the pilasters of the towers with the main structure.

Andreas Stengg
Pilgrimage church of Our Lady of
Consolation, Graz, begun 1714

A miraculous icon led to the construction
of this pilgrimage church. Strengg
designed a staggered wall-pier church
with galleries. The building was finished
by his son Johann Georg in 1724.

Matthias Steinl
Tower front of collegiate church, Zwettl,
1722–27

The Cistercian foundation of Zwettl
dates from 1138. The church forms the
centerpiece of the ensemble, and is notable for its unusually high tower (nearly
one hundred meters) built by Josef
Munggenast in 1722–27. The figures,
urns, and obelisks are cleverly fitted into
the architectural structure as decorative
forms. The baroque dome is surmounted
by a gilt figure of Christ.

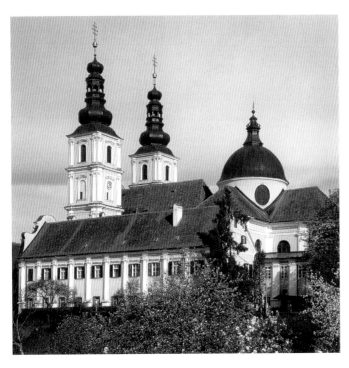

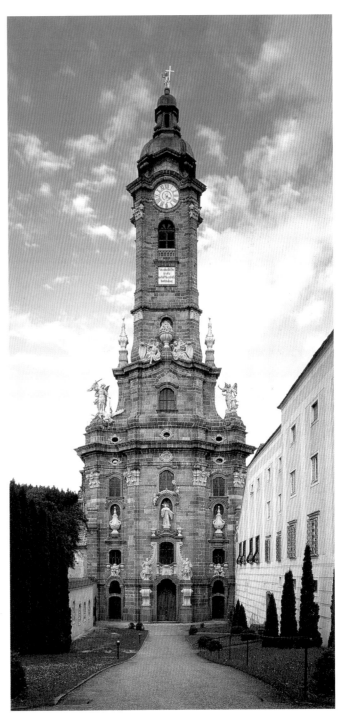

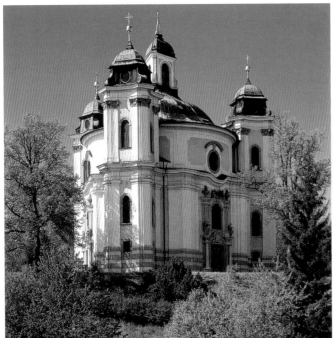

Francesco Caratti
Palais Cernin, Prague, 1668–77

Jean Baptist Mathey
Archeipiscopal palace, Prague, 1675–79

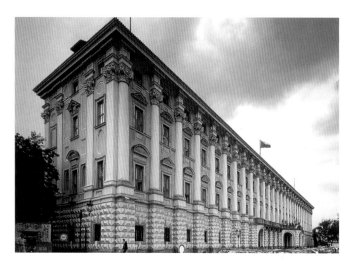

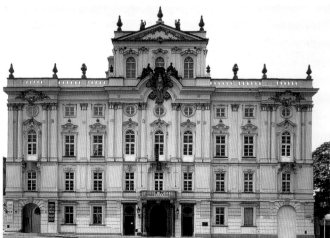

The Baroque City of Prague and Architecture in Bohemia and Moravia

Before the Dientzenhofer family of architects made its appearance, the aristocracy of Bohemia and Moravia had favored buildings on the Italianate model. Count Cernin, who had visited Rome several times, desired a prestigious building "in the Roman style." His palace in Prague (see above left) was constructed between 1668 and 1677 by Francesco Caratti in the Palladian manner. A solid rusticated ground floor terminating in a balustrade supports a two-storey upper building surmounted by a mezzanine floor. The whole front is articulated by giant columns.

By contrast, Count Johann Friedrich von Waldstein, archbishop of Prague, endeavored to introduce a new mood into the architecture of Prague. He commissioned the Frenchman Jean Baptist Mathey of Dijon to build his palace (1675–79, see above right). This, like the other palaces and villas designed by Mathey, was conceived as a three-sectioned ensemble with a raised central elevation and external stairways.

Mathey remained in Prague until 1694. He built among other structures the church for the Augustinian choral canons, which is designed with transepts leading off a domed oval central space—a scheme which was to be an important source of inspiration for Fischer von Erlach's Dreifaltigkeitskirche church in Salzburg and Karlskirche in Vienna. Similarly the church of St. Joseph in Prague's Malá Strana [Lesser Town] seems to have been an important model for Fischer, who recorded it in his sketchbook.

Johann Dientzenhofer (d. 1726) has already been mentioned in connection with Banz and Pommersfelden. For the Dientzenhofer family, which came from Upper Bavaria, the wealth of French and Italian buildings in Prague presented both a stimulus and a challenge. It was Johann's brother Christoph (1655–1722) who first developed an unusual style in Prague and the surrounding areas, and his son Kilian Ignaz (1690–1751) who effectively gave the city its present baroque countenance. Kilian trained under Hildebrandt, and refined his artistic skills on extended study trips to Italy and Paris.

The church of St. Nicholas in the Lesser Town (see right, below) was celebrated as one of the loveliest churches in Europe. It certainly must rate as one of the masterpieces of the architect Christoph Dientzenhofer, who built the nave (1703–11) and west front (1709–17). The model for the west front was Borromini's playfully curving S. Carlo alle Quattro Fontane in Rome. But whereas the Italian architect had restricted himself to a strict subdivision of the two storeys, and repeated the elevation system of the lower front in the upper story, Dientzenhofer monumentalized the facade of the church. He broadened the storeys, thereby allowing space for the movement of the alternating concave and convex bays. Following the principle of modelling the structure more lightly as it goes up, he echoed the massive double columns of the doorway with flat pilasters, which are repeated on a lesser scale in the tall pedimented gable. The niche in the gable is occupied by a statue and surmounted by a shell shape that pierces the cornice, which curves itself into the fluid architectural line of an undulating triangular pediment.

The vigorous facade and the lively effect of the pierced entablature with its layers of pediments is continued in the interior. The corner piers that delimit the nave with double columns and pilasters are set well forward, suggesting an oval ground plan if the viewer follows the course of the adjoining bay with its concave chapel niches and galleries. Above the capitals of the double columns and pilasters is a tall impost area with markedly projecting coping slabs,

Christoph Dientzenhofer
St. Nicholas, Lesser Town, Prague
West front, 1709–17 (below left)
Interior, 1703–11 (below right)

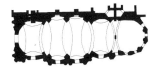

Christoph Dientzenhofer
St. Margaret's, Brevnov, 1708–21
Exterior view (below)
Ground plan (left)

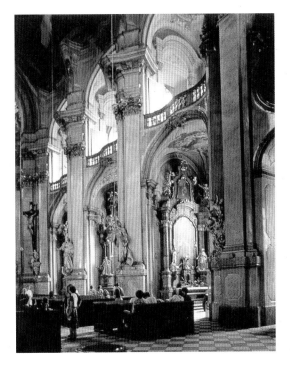

from which the vault emerges steeply, interrupted only by the arches of the bay. The effect of this German-Bohemian architectural language outdoes not only the Roman examples it follows but presents a completely novel, alternative approach to what had been the obligatory Italian mode.

The Margaretenkirche at the Benedictine monastery of Brevnov (1708–21, see right) is another of Dientzenhofer's masterpieces. The southern side of the exterior effectively serves as the facade, as the two central bays are raised like a centerpiece crowned by a gable and flanked by engaged columns, as on a palace. The effect of the choir and west entrance front is consequently somewhat muddling. Seen from the broad (south) side, they look like asymmetrical additions. The protruding and receding motion of the different parts of the exterior is dramatically enhanced in the interior. Piers rise from triangular pedestals, the tops of which point into the nave. They are thus set diagonally to the interior. The transverse arches do not run directly by the shortest route across the nave but in a slight bow. The oval sections of the vault overlap the oval ground plan of each bay. This oppositional motion of vault and ground plan gives the whole space an odd sense of oscillation, which recedes only in the apsidal termination of the choir.

Mention must also be made of Georg Dientzenhofer, Christoph's elder brother, the oldest member of the family and father of Johann

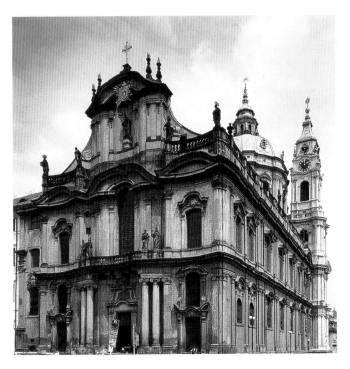

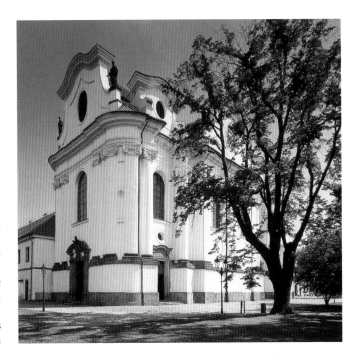

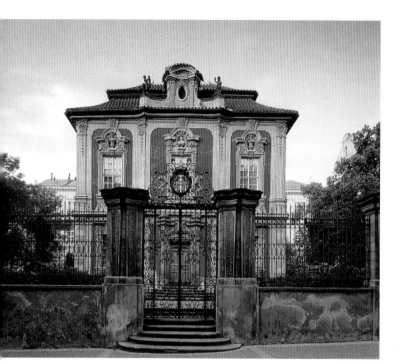

Kilian Ignaz Dientzenhofer
Villa Amerika, Prague
1720

onal ground plan, but extend it and give it with straight sides. This is what he did at the churches in Ruprechtice and Hermanice; in the latter he designed an exterior with concave walls and the interior with convex walls. This was in fact a ground plan first used by the third celebrated architect of Bohemia and Moravia, Johann Santin-Aichel. However, it was Dientzenhofer who used the motif extensively in his churches.

The combination of a circular central plan with removed or overlapping ellipses was given virtuoso treatment by Johann Santin-Aichel in the votive chapel of St. John Nepomuk on the Green Hill (1719–21), a design inspired by Kappel. Five ovals alternate with five triangular niches arranged regularly round a circle. This produces a linear dynamism which is taken up in the cornice of the dome. For Santin-Aichel, this shape was the symbol of a sacred event: when St. John Nepomuk was drowned in the river Vltava, five stars were supposed have circled over his head. Pointed shapes and half oval roundels refer to the martyr's crown with the five stars.

The ground plan of the votive chapel is comparable in shape to that of the gothic cinquefoil. In Lomec near Prachatice in southern Bohemia a quatrefoil ground plan was deliberately chosen for the chapel. Santin-Aichel could not have been the originator of this idea since he was born in 1677 and would therefore have been too young to have been involved in the construction of the Lomec chapel (1692–1702). A name mentioned in this connection is the stonemason Mathias Tischler from Rozenberk; in any case it is possible that this church was the model for Santin-Aichel's votive chapel.

Santin-Aichel's preference for gothic forms might also derive from his work in transforming gothic churches into baroque ones. Such jobs could also be considered a source of the picturesque motifs in which baroque architecture in Bohemia is particularly rich. The sensitive manner in which Santin-Aichel treated the restoration of a gothic church is evident in the Benedictine abbey church of Kladruby (1712). It is true that he was allowed largely to eliminate the medieval decoration, but he nonetheless retained the structure of the late gothic vault with its foils and star motifs. Half-columns with octagonal half-capitals set in front of the piers, together with narrow finely profiled straps, give some sense of the original gothic idiom.

There are many surviving examples of the unusual versions of baroque architecture that are characteristic of Bohemia and Moravia and represent the cultural landscape of baroque idiosyncrasies. The obligatory "Italian mode" and the stylistic features of French taste that rivaled it, together with the proximity of the baroque metropolis of Vienna, were combined with the activities of the highly imaginative Dientzenhofer family to create a fusion of aesthetic forms that was unique in Europe.

Dientzenhofer. He died in 1689 in Waldsassen, East Bavaria. Here, near the Bohemian border, during the last four years of his life he designed and built the pilgrimage church of Kappel, a structure that is more in the spirit of the Bohemian rather than the German cultural tradition (see right, above). This must be the most unusual religious building north of the Alps. The ground plan describes a trefoil with three semicircular chapels arranged around a triangle the intersection and marked by three minaret-like turrets with onion domes. The whole building is surrounded by a gallery, elegantly following the movement of the chapels and curves of the towers. The idea was taken up twenty years later by Santin-Aichel and elaborated in St. John Nepomuk on the Green Hill in Zdar, which will be discussed later.

After the death of Christoph Dientzenhofer, his son Kilian built the choir and crossing vault of the church of St. Nicholas in Prague (1737–51). The choir was laid out as a central circle overlapped by three ellipses, two lateral chapels, and the altar area. This ground plan indicates a rococo playfulness that stands in contrast to the contemporary trend toward classical severity. Another building which demonstrates a strong rococo affinity is the facade of the shrine of Our Lady of Loreto in Prague (see below right). It was built from 1721 according to plans by Christoph Dientzenhofer, but the work was again completed by his son Kilian. The broad facade is dignified and restrained; only the two end bays allow the front to curve slightly. The bell tower dominating the facade provides the most decorative feature. The Villa Amerika must rank as one of Kilian's finest palaces (see above); he built it in 1720 for Duke Johann Wenzel Michma. It is a finely articulated variant on the style of his mentor Hildebrandt.

Kilian Dientzenhofer studied many baroque plans, adapting them to his own purposes. He might, for example, choose an octag-

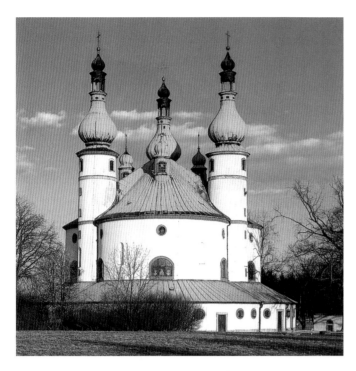

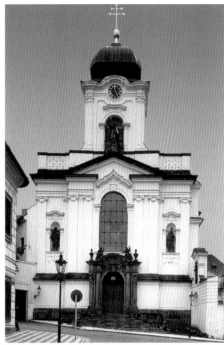

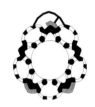

FAR LEFT:
Georg Dientzenhofer
Pilgrimage church, Kappel
1685–89
Ground plan below
(upper diagram)

ABOVE CENTER:
Johann Santin-Aichel
Votive church of St. John
Nepomuk on the Green Hill,
Zdar, 1719–21
Ground plan above
(lower diagram)

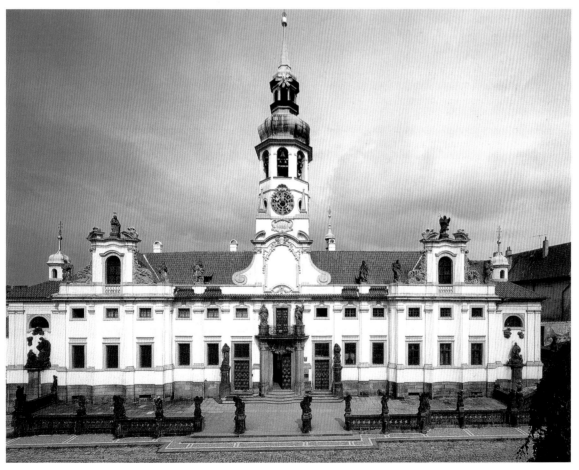

**Christoph and Kilian
Ignaz Dientzenhofer**
Facade of pilgrimage
shrine of Our Lady of
Loreto, Prague, begun
1721

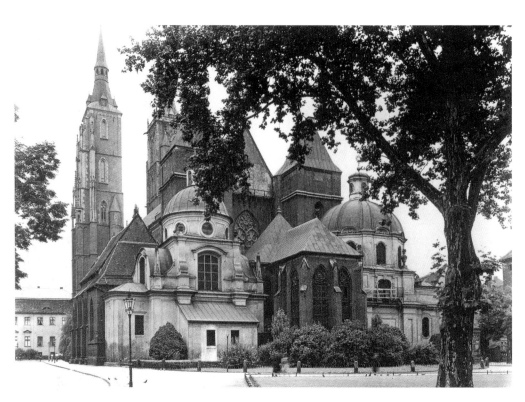

Cathedral of St. John the Baptist,
Wrocław
East end, with baroque additions by Scianzi (Elizabeth chapel, left) and Fischer
von Erlach (Elector's chapel, right)
1716–24

Baroque Variants in Silesia and Poland

Two trends typify the development of baroque architecture in Silesia. Building commissions by the Catholic church and the Catholic nobility were focused on the centers of Vienna and Prague. In the eighteenth century, with the predominance of Prussia, Berlin became another important point of contact. However, traditional architectural styles were retained, and were favored by the religious and political opposition. Artistic models were sought mainly outside the great centers. Alongside splendid flamboyant facades based on Bohemian and Italianate forms can be found native half-timbered facades with small onion towers.

The Elector Franz Ludwig of the Neuburg Palatinate (1683–1732), the bishop of Breslau (now Wrocław, was known as an active and liberal patron of architecture. But ecclesiastical commissions were also forthcoming from the rich Cistercian foundations and the Jesuits, the Premonstratensians, and the Augustinian choral canons.

Rome provided the main model for Silesian art. When the landgrave of Hessen, Cardinal Frederick—a connoisseur of Roman art—was appointed bishop of Breslau, he used his close connections with the Eternal City to arrange for the design of his memorial chapel in Breslau cathedral to be executed in Bernini's workshop. Construction was also entrusted to an Italian, Giacomo Scianzi. The Elector Franz Ludwig was the successor to Bishop Frederick. As the brother-in-law of the Habsburg Emperor Leopold I, he was close to the Viennese court. Between 1716 and 1724 his electoral chapel (the chapel of the holy sacrament)—another addition to the cathedral—was built by Fischer von Erlach. The oval of the dome rises above a rectangular ground plan. Lofty pendentives, set above a strongly

protruding cornice, reinforce the sense of height and thus the impression of power and rank.

A glance at the east end of the cathedral (see above) allows a striking comparison of the two chapels which stood close together, separated only by the straight-ended choir. The typical Fischer elevation with the clearly articulated walls and the high windows of the drum looks more "native" than its more elegant Italian rival, which is more graceful and better balanced in its proportions. The flat-framed tondos in the narrow drum are in harmony with the tall vault of the dome, which is crownd by a slender lantern. Fischer's building is provided with a relatively flat dome the top of which is formed by a lantern that appears somewhat squat compared to the lower part.

In 1705 Hildebrandt also provided the plans for the Breslau house of the Viennese merchant and imperial trade commissioner Gottfried Christian von Schreyvogel. Building work finished in 1711.

Italian and Austrian architects dominated Silesian baroque architecture in the second half of the seventeenth century. Later, in the first decades of the eighteenth century, Swabian, Bavarian, and northern German architects arrived to work for the bishops. The contrasts and conflicts of their different approaches are undoubtedly responsible for the quality and charm of Silesian baroque architecture.

Toward the end of the seventeenth century Poland experienced a brief period of cultural glory under King Jan Sobieski. Years earlier Sobieski had successfully defeated the Turks; after his coronation, he had played a decisive role in repelling them from the gates of Vienna in 1683. Now he was ready to establish an environment for the

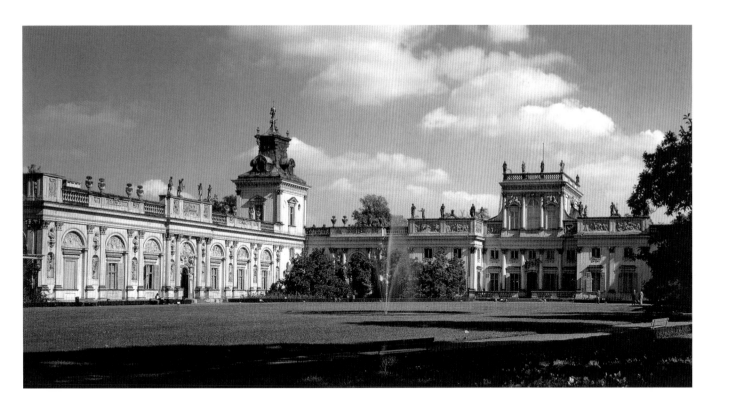

flourishing of culture. The Dutch architect and engineer Tylman van Gameren worked for Queen Maria Kasimira. In Warsaw, he adapted the churches of the Holy Ghost, St. Casimir, and St. Boniface, among others, to the baroque manner. He also completed the Krasinski palace, begun by Giuseppe Bellotti in 1682 (see below) where Andreas Schlüter did the sculptural work.

Along with Tylman van Gameren, the royal architect was Agostino Locci, who turned the former manor house at Wilanów (see above), about eight miles south of Warsaw, into a splendid palatial ensemble with pavilions and flanking galleries framed with two-story towers. On the advice of Schlüter, and following his designs, the central elevation was raised in 1692.

Under the Saxon Elector Frederick Augustus I (Augustus the Strong), who was King Augustus II of Poland from 1697, Dresden-based architects came to the city of Warsaw. The most prominent among them was Johann Friderich Karcher, who was appointed court architect of Poland and Saxony and drew up plans for enlarging the royal palace.

In 1728 the leading Saxon architects Pöppelmann and Longuelune reached the Polish capital. Pöppelmann's son Karl Friedrich drew up numerous plans and designs which he submitted to the king for approval. He was obviously involved in the building of the Blue Palace for Countess Anna Orszelska in Warsaw. In style and architectural concept, this building is comparable with his father's plan of around 1730 for the "Saxon Palace" in Warsaw. The son was also involved in the design of this palace, of which only the central section was completed.

Due to the wars in Poland, and most significantly the bombardments of the Second World War, little remains of the splendor of the Warsaw baroque. Only the wonderful views by Canaletto in the National Museum in Warsaw bear witness to this once splendid baroque metropolis.

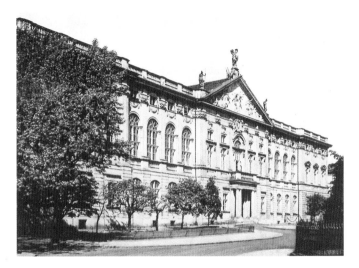

Tylman van Gameren
Palais Krasinski, Warsaw, 1677–82
Pediment reliefs by Andreas Schlüter

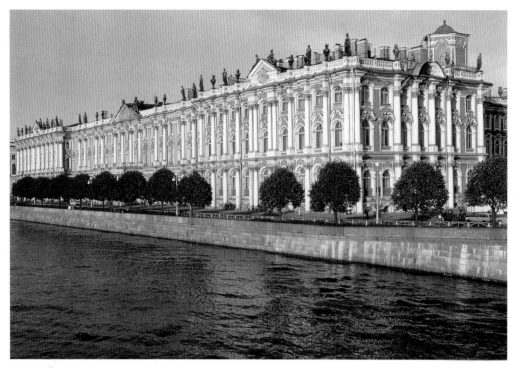

LEFT:
Bartolomeo Francesco Rastrelli
Facade of Winter Palace on the Neva,
St. Petersburg, 1754–62

The most important urban developments of the eighteenth century were the Palace Square, Admiralty Square, and Senate Square. A decisive factor in these schemes was the Winter Palace, which was to be integrated into a comprehensive urban development design. The Building Commission for St. Petersburg and Moscow in 1763 accepted the plan by A. E. Kvassov, who designed grand entrances to the city including existing buildings in the plan. Most important among these was the Winter Palace (see left), built between 1754 and 1762 by Count Rastrelli. The leading architect of his time in St. Petersburg, Rastrelli was of Italian origin. He trained in Paris, and was summoned from there in 1741 by the tsarina Elizabeth and appointed court architect. His father, the sculptor Carlo Bartolomeo Rastrelli, had sculpted the equestrian statue of Peter the Great in 1716.

The Winter Palace was built in a pure French late baroque style. Its facade dominates the Neva embankment, and, with the Admiralty, forms the core section of the city. Rastrelli planned the Smolny monastery opposite, with its powerful dome and four towers (see right), as a foil to the palace. The view of the city center is dominated by Palais Stroganoff, which rises in an exposed position where the Nevsky Prospekt crosses the Moika.

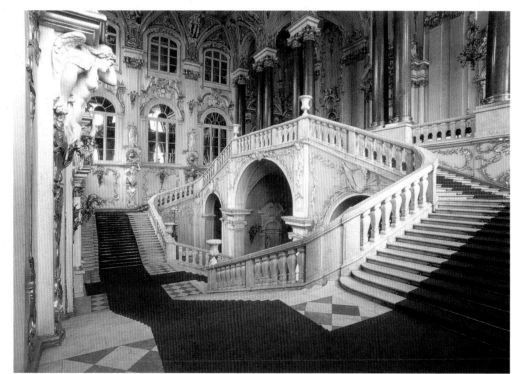

LEFT:
Bartolomeo Francesco Rastrelli
Ambassador Staircase ("Jordan Staircase") in Winter Palace, St. Petersburg, 1754–62

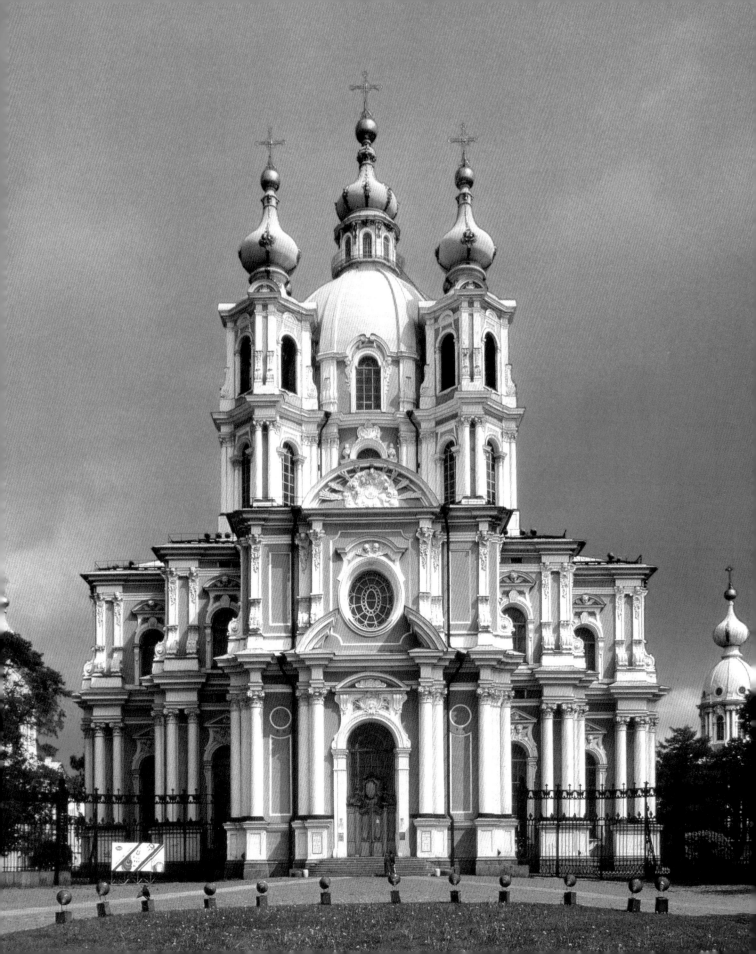

Uwe Geese

Baroque Sculpture in Italy, France, and Central Europe

Sculpture between the Renaissance and the Age of Baroque

During the Renaissance, sculptors had returned to classical antiquity for inspiration, but at the same time had developed concepts of form which asserted the modernity of their work. The ideal of the perfect human body, for instance, was associated more with a prevailing humanist ideology than with the classical canons which defined the architectural orders. Renaissance sculptors believed that antique sculpture had captured nature in such an exemplary manner that the study of such works of art should take precedence over the observation of nature itself. Michelangelo, for example, according to a remark attributed to him, considered that the Belvedere Torso was such an exemplary classical work of art that, the man who made it was wiser than nature. He also noted that it was a great misfortune that the piece had survived only as a torso.

The painter, architect, and art historian Giorgio Vasari was one of the theorists who introduced a new system of aesthetic values during this period, one that was based on a notion of individual genius. A great artist was distinguished by his *maniera*, an individual and unmistakable personal style in his work; it was a concept which changed the classical ideal of the Renaissance. During the course of the Cinquecento, it became the standard ambition of sculptors not merely to produce an accurate imitation of natural forms but to surpass nature in sheer inventiveness. This tendency anticipated in some respect the work of the mannerists, which was much derided until the art historians Max Dvorak and Hermann Voss rehabilitated the style in the twentieth century. Among its essential characteristics are elongated limbs and proportions, artificial poses, and a combination of different materials and surface treatments. Mannerist sculptural compositions might also deploy such oppositional elements as age and youth, beauty and ugliness, or male and female figures. Among the most striking inventions of mannerist sculpture is the *figura serpentinata*, a complex twisting movement of figures and groups that spirals upwards from the base, apparently defying gravity. Michelangelo's *Victory* and *Dying Slave* (see right), dated at various times between 1519 and 1530, established the motif, but retained the central perspective of a principal aspect turned towards the beholder. The depressed position of one figure and elevation of the other in the opposite direction is also inherent to the subject of victor and vanquished. When Giambologna took up the *figura serpentinata* motif and developed it into a new form, he created a group intended to be viewed from all sides; the complexity of the structure can only be appreciated as the viewer circulates around it. New views constantly open up, but they always accentuate the closed upward motion of the whole group. In further contrast to Michelangelo's *Victory* and *Dying Slave* group, the mannerist *figura serpentinata* reflected above all Vasari's notion of a *maniera*, which some argued ultimately degenerated into excessive virtuosity. This interim mannerist period of intense fascination with artistic perfection and elegance can be seen as anticipating the baroque style in art, which emerged after the Council of Trent called for religious renewal. Giambologna nonetheless remained the most influential Italian sculptor of the period, and his art set the tone for European sculpture of the late sixteenth and early seventeenth centuries. His work can be seen as representing an artistic link between Michelangelo and Bernini. Art historians, especially during the first half of the twentieth century, were preoccupied with examining the true nature of the highly complex art of baroque, and their enquiries and discussions revolved mainly around matters of stylistic history. Reference is often made, for example, to the permeation of late decorative mannerism by naturalism and the picturesque, or to the importance of naturalism as a reaction to mannerism. It can be argued that the reduction of analysis to the straightforward history of form in this way allowed the broader cultural and historical context of art to be overlooked.

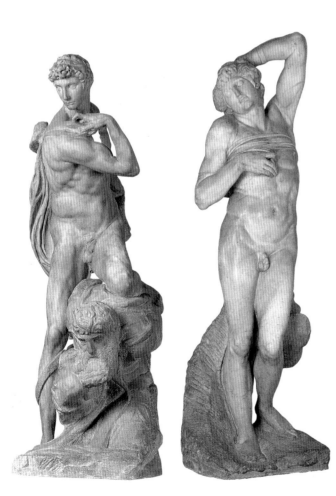

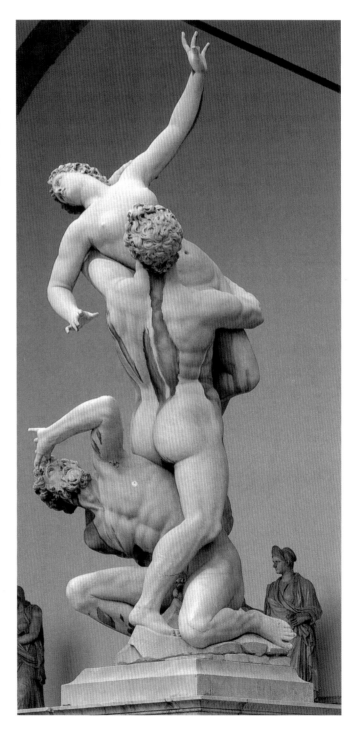

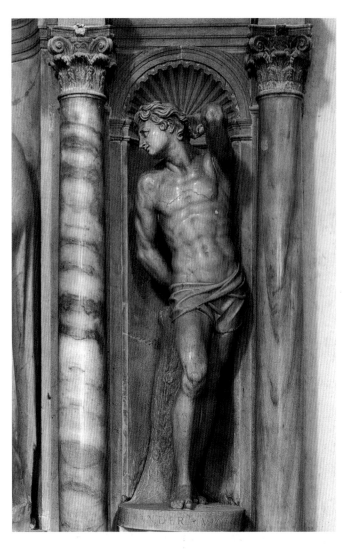

Alessandro Vittoria
St. Sebastian, 1561–63
Marble, height 117 cm
S. Francesco della Vigna, Venice

OPPOSITE:
Alessandro Vittoria
St. Sebastian, c. 1600
Marble, height 170 cm
S. Salvatore, Venice

In the early 1950s the Italian art historian Giulio Carlo Argan introduced the concept of rhetoric into our understanding of the baroque by describing the style as an "art form of rhetoric" in which the main emphasis was on *persuasio*, persuasion. This puts the beholder into a wholly different relationship with the work of art. "Previously, art was supposed to awaken an almost objective admiration of the beauty or perfection of the natural phenomenon being represented; thus the response of the beholder to the art work was the same as, or resembled, his response to the reality it illustrated. In the seventeenth century, a new relationship between the observer and work of art is understood by the artist. The work is no longer an objective fact, it is a means to action," writes the Polish art historian Jan Bialostocki.

From Mannerism to Baroque Rhetoric in the Work of Alessandro Vittoria

Between 1563 and the end of the century, the Italian sculptor Alessandro Vittoria (?1525–1608) produced several sculptures of St. Sebastian in Venice. The earliest major Venetian work by Vittoria is the altar of the Montefeltro family in the church of S. Francesco della Vigna. The altar was commissioned in November 1561 and was due to be completed by September 1562, but work seems to have dragged on until the end of the following year. In the right-hand niche of the altar, which is articulated by columns, can be seen the figure of St. Sebastian leaning against a tree-trunk (see left). A mannerist *serpentinata* is incorporated into this figure, as is evident from a comparison with its main source of inspiration, Michelangelo's *Dying Slave* in the Louvre (see p. 275). Whereas in Michelangelo's sculpture the whole figure is turned towards the onlooker in a classical presentation of form, Vittoria's St. Sebastian seems to be twisting away from the viewer's gaze. The stance of the lower body, turned towards the left and almost a step forwards, is offset by the extreme rightward rotation of the head, which is intensified by the position of the arms. This posture is the most powerful element of the sculpture. The fact that it is intended as a representation of St. Sebastian cannot be ascertained from the figure itself except for the telling detail of the arrow wound on the left chest. In fact, Vittoria later produced a small bronze replica of this figure which he entitled *Marsyas or Sebastian*.

Among Vittoria's major late works is another altar with a statue of St. Sebastian, in the church of S. Salvatore in Venice (see right). There it forms the right-hand flanking figure, the pair to a statue of St. Roch on the left-hand side of an altar of the Scuola dei Luganegheri where both statues are placed in front of the outer, slightly recessed column. The statues are dated between 1594 and 1600 to shortly before 1602. Standing somewhat under five feet, seven inches tall, more or less life-size, the figure of St. Sebastian is balanced on its right leg, which is at a slight angle and rests only on the ball of the foot. At the same time, the body leans against a thick tree

If Luther's Reformation had split Europe into two powerful ideological camps, it was in cinquecento Italy that forces emerged in opposition to it, even to the extent of producing a new unity between faith and the Church. Eventually the celebrated Council of Trent sat between 1545 and 1563; although it resulted in the internal consolidation of the Catholic church, at the same time the intellectual climate turned against the classically inspired arts of the Renaissance, and absolutely against the spirit of humanism. The extent to which the general cultural environment and the religious attitudes of the public and of artists in particular were affected by historical events can be well illustrated by the example of the sculptor Bartolomeo Ammannati.

Ammannati initially devoted himself to studying the sculpture of the Renaissance and antiquity, producing vast fountain figures in Florence in the mannerist spirit of the late Renaissance. Following a crisis in his personal life, however, he turned away from the style and subject matter of his early work. Condemning it wholly in the spirit of the Counter-Reformation and above all for its incorporation of the nude human figure, he bequeathed his inheritance to the Jesuit order.

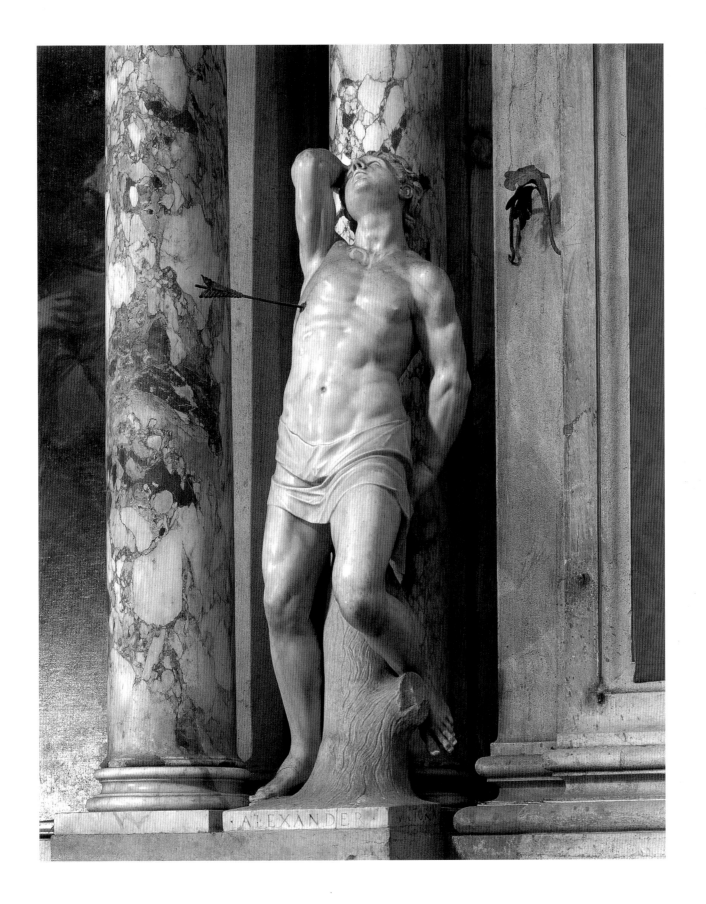
ALEXANDER

Pietro Bernini
Assumption of the Virgin, 1606–10
Marble relief
S. Maria Maggiore, Rome

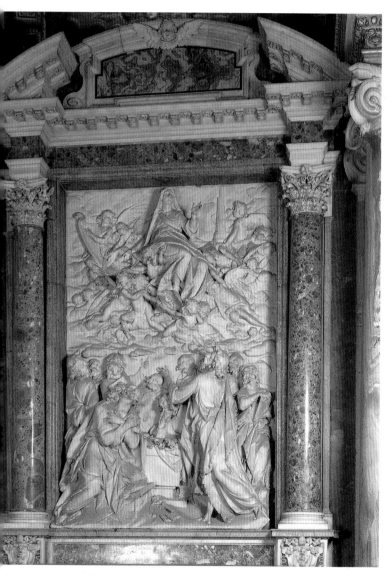

stump, which is visible between the legs only up to thigh height. At calf height, the stump of a bough branches off to the left, and the bent lower left leg rests on it.

In this sculpture Vittoria abandons the classical posture of *contrapposto* in favor of a severe separation of the sides of the body. The elevated right arm follows the pivot of the right leg, while the left arm is dropped towards the lower left leg resting on the stump of the bough. A figure once shaped by the formal concepts of the Renaissance has been transformed into a baroque form in a manner which at once reinforces the element of suffering. The artist is no longer aiming to achieve a perfect natural realism in his sculpture. The artist's work is focused directly on moving the emotions rather than provoking admiration for a precise imitation of nature.

Gian Lorenzo Bernini (1598–1680)

Donatello's predominant influence in the development of quattrocento sculpture and Michelangelo's similarly powerful role during the following century prefigured the career of Bernini in baroque Rome. Like his two predecessors, Gian Lorenzo Bernini was an artistic personality who dominated the artistic world of the seventeenth century in Rome, but it can be argued that his influence on the art of his time far exceeded that of any artist before him.

Born on December 7, 1598 in Naples, he was trained in the workshop of his father, the painter and sculptor Pietro Bernini, who was summoned to Rome in 1605 by Pope Paul V to create a marble relief of the Assumption for the church of S. Maria Maggiore (see left). Inspired by the artistic legacy of Rome and of classical antiquity, the younger Bernini was also deeply impressed by the spirituality of St. Ignatius Loyola. His first artistic endeavors were in painting. Nonetheless, his biographer Filippo Baldinucci, whose life of the artist appeared in Florence in 1682, informs us that Bernini had already begun to make sculptures at the age of eight, and was taking on his own commissions when he was just sixteen. In early works such as *Young Jupiter with the Goat Amalthea and a Satyr* (see right) in the Villa Borghese, his virtuoso handling of the marble demonstrates a precocious genius, which is also suggested by the manner in which the artist integrates the sculpture into the existing space.

The four famous marble sculptures of the Villa Borghese designed by Bernini for his patron Cardinal Scipione Caffarelli Borghese between 1618 and 1625 marked a first sustained creative phase that established his fame as Italy's leading sculptor, the "Michelangelo of his age." Bernini also restored classical forms in his work with an evident enthusiasm, particularly those which were seen as having been degraded by the distortions of mannerism. The *Aeneas and Anchises* (see p. 280, left), in which Bernini translated into marble Virgil's account of Aeneas' flight from burning Troy, was already in place in 1619.

The work is intended to embody the imperial Roman foundation myth, according to which Aeneas' flight from Troy led to the founda-

Gian Lorenzo Bernini
David, 1623–24
Marble, height 170 cm
Galleria Borghese, Rome

Gian Lorenzo Bernini
*Young Jupiter with the Goat Amalthea and
a Satyr*, c. 1611–12
Marble, height 45 cm
Galleria Borghese, Rome

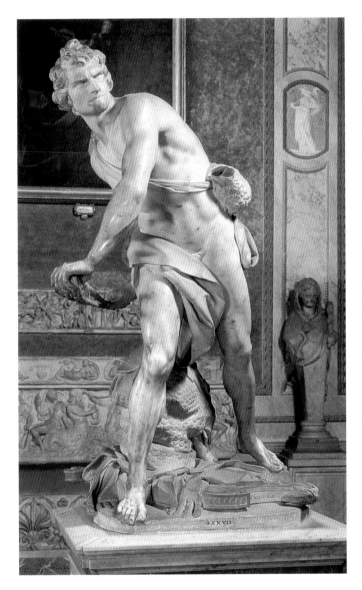

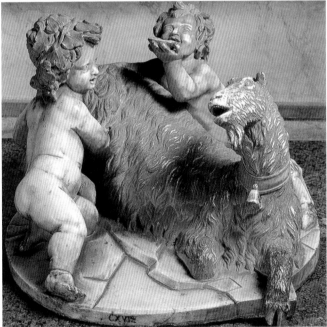

the extent that the front view captures the full energy of the impending impact of the stone, creating a heightened expectation of victory in the profile. David's lyre lies on the ground before him, a reference to his youthful musicality, which he was able to combine with courage and strength. In this sense, David is set in specific opposition to his enemy, the lascivious Goliath, described in contemporary literature as a depraved monster and the son of a whore. *Apollo and Daphne* (1622–24) (see p. 281), the most famous of these Borghese sculptures, narrates the scene from Ovid's *Metamorphoses* where the youthful Apollo, burning with passionate love, thinks he has caught the nymph as she flees in fear of her life, only to find her transformed into a tree in his grasp. Enfolded in the bark and boughs of laurel, she becomes a natural element in the form of a laurel tree which is henceforth sacred to the grieving Apollo.

tion of Rome and Aeneas himself is therefore represented as the ancestor of Church and papacy. Literary models for the *Rape of Proserpine* (see p. 280, right), completed in 1622, include Ovid's account of the seizure of the future goddess of the underworld. In contrast to the mannerist the *Rape of the Sabine Woman* by Giambologna, Bernini reduces the sculptural perspectives to frontal and half-left, greatly intensifying the immediacy of the event. The perspective angles in *David* (1623) (see above) are differentiated even further, to

While work on the baldacchino of St. Peter's was still in progress, Urban VIII commissioned Bernini to provide sculptures for the four piers of the crossing, as an extension of the baldacchino structure. While the statues of St. Andrew (1629–39), St. Veronica (1631–40), and St. Helena (1631–39) were carried out by Duquesnoy, Mocchi, and Bolgi respectively, Bernini himself worked on the figure of St. Longinus (1631–38) (see p. 284), the Roman soldier who pierced the side of the crucified Christ. The result of more

Gian Lorenzo Bernini
Aeneas and Anchises, 1618–19
Marble, height 220 cm
Galleria Borghese, Rome

Gian Lorenzo Bernini
Rape of Proserpine, 1621–22
Marble, height 255 cm
Galleria Borghese, Rome

OPPOSITE:
Gian Lorenzo Bernini
Apollo and Daphne, 1622–25
Marble, height 243 cm
Galleria Borghese, Rome

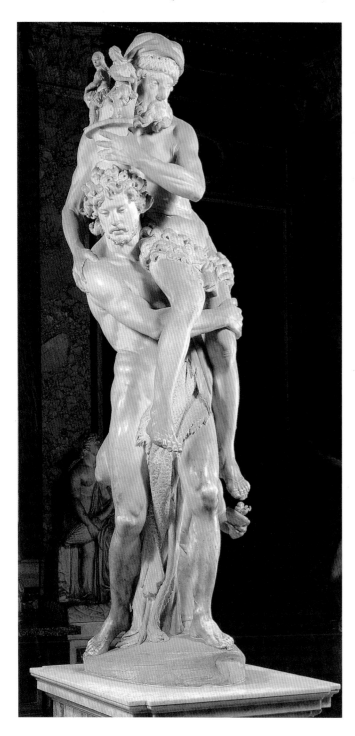

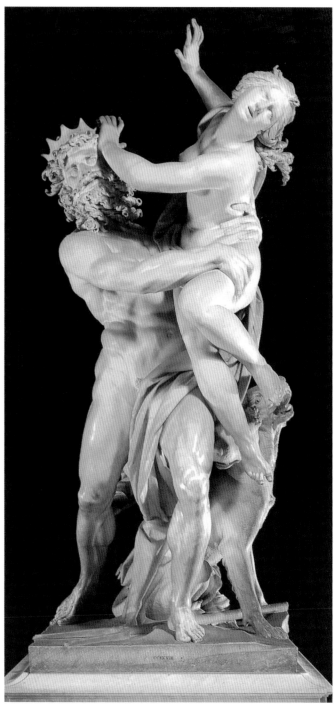

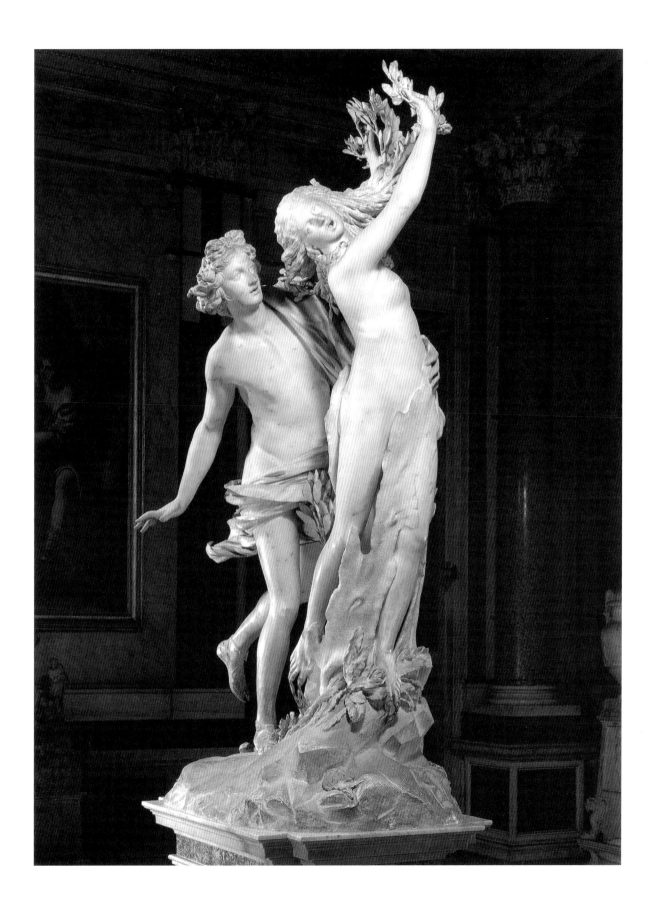

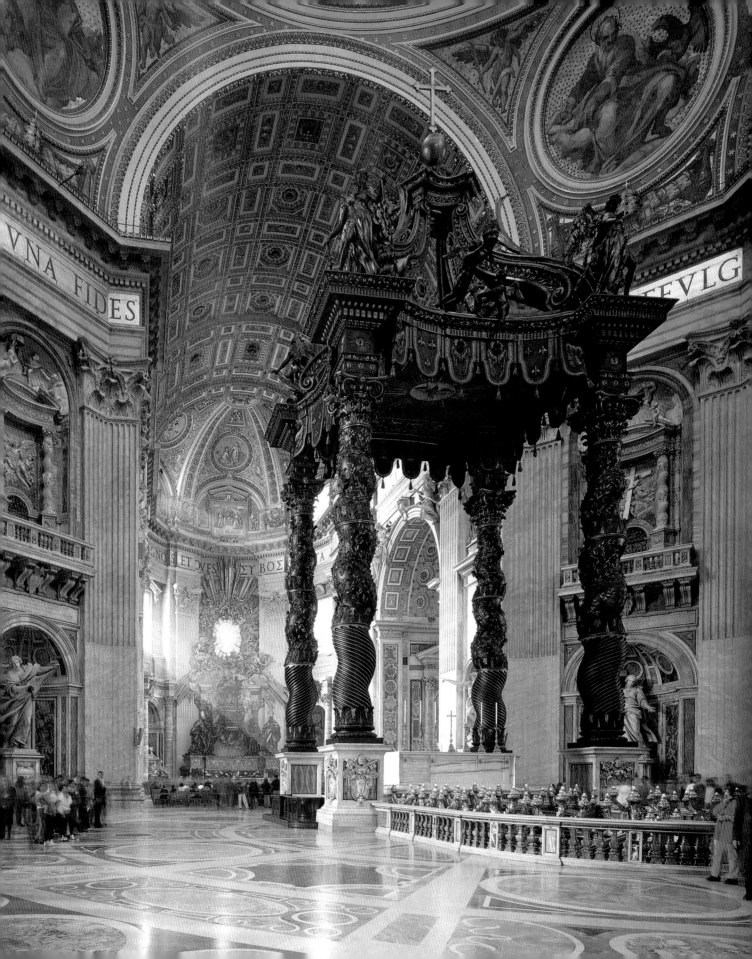

OPPOSITE:
Gian Lorenzo Bernini
Baldacchino, 1624–33
Marble, bronze, and gold, height 28.5 m
St. Peter's, Rome

Gian Lorenzo Bernini
Tomb of Pope Alexander VII
1673–74
Marble and ormolu
St. Peter's, Rome

A major new period of creativity began for Bernini in 1623 when his amiable patron and powerful sponsor Cardinal Maffeo Barberini became Pope Urban VIII and he was entrusted with extensive works on the interior design of St. Peter's. The commission for the immense baldacchino over the tomb of St. Peter and the papal altar was preceded by his appointment as director of the papal casting workshop. Considering the colossal task ahead of him, this appears to have been an almost essential precondition.

The challenge to Bernini was to fill the huge, capacious crossing of St. Peter's with a liturgical structure that would stand out in the existing architecture. His solution was an inventive combination of architecture and sculpture: he raised four twisted bronze Salomonic columns on marble plinths (see left). These support a ciborium surmounted by a baldacchino formed of four volutes ornamented with sculpture. Unfortunately Bernini's first design for this scheme, which placed a bronze figure of the risen Christ on top of the baldacchino, proved impossible to implement due to the excessive weight of the figure. It was replaced by a globe and crucifix, symbolizing the triumph of Christianity over the world.

Bernini again cleverly combined architecture and sculpture to good effect in the tomb of Pope Alexander VII (see right), which he completed a few years before his own death. He designed it for a niche in the aisle of St. Peter's which contains the door to what was then a sacristy. The door is drawn into the sculptural composition, reinterpreted as the entrance to the tomb, or indeed as the door to death itself; from it emerges a skeleton with an hourglass in the manner of a *memento mori*.

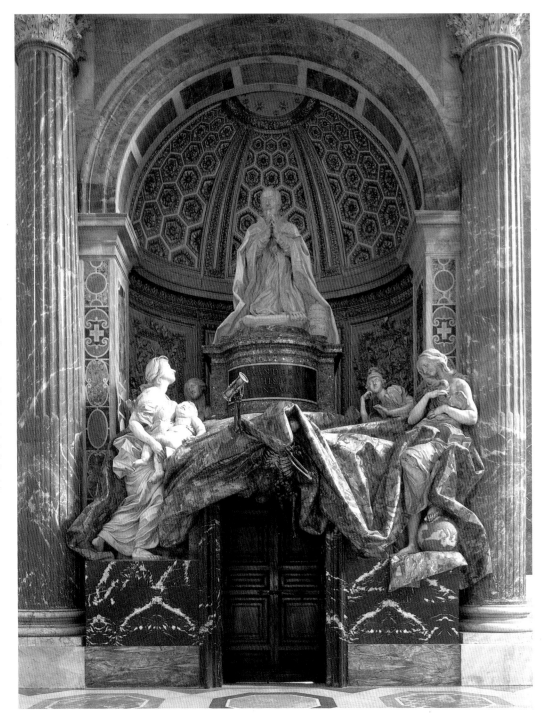

Gian Lorenzo Bernini
St. Longinus, 1629–38
Marble, height 440 cm
St. Peter's, Rome

Gian Lorenzo Bernini
Costanza Bonarelli, c. 1636–37
Marble bust, height 72 cm
Museo Nazionale del Bargello, Florence

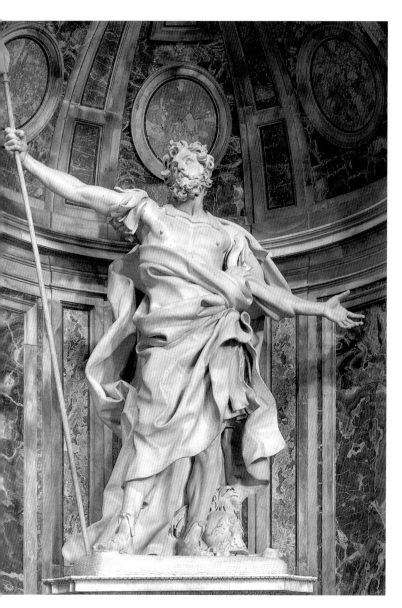

whole personality of the person depicted, displaying particularly expressive and immediate qualities. Here his work moves beyond the formal concepts of the genre, and may have been influenced in this respect by the portrait paintings of Velázquez, Rubens, and Hals. His ability to create such singular likenesses enabled him to become the most sought-after portraitist of his time.

The inspiration for his portrait bust of Costanza Bonarelli, the wife of his colleague Matteo Bonarelli, was evidently a romantic attraction so violent on Bernini's part that in the end the pope himself was forced to intervene. The bust of Costanza (see below) is the only sculptural record of Bernini's private life, and is thus portrayed in an personal rather than a grand manner. With a slight turn of the sitter's head to the left, her parted lips, and watchful, interested gaze, Bernini represents her in a moment of intimate naturalism but also in an attitude of intimate closeness.

Shortly before work was finished on the bust of his patron Scipione Borghese (see right), Bernini discovered a flaw in the marble running across the forehead. He finished the work nonetheless, but immediately ordered a new block of marble in order to prepare a replica as quickly as possible, which he presented to the cardinal at the unveiling of the defective bust. Bernini's bust of Louis XIV (see above right) can be seen as representing the high-point of baroque

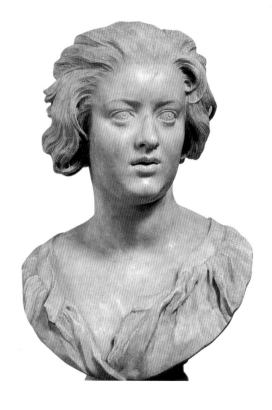

than twenty maquettes, Bernini's sculpture shows the Roman in the moment of his conversion. With arms outstretched in the shape of a crucifix, he looks up at the cross and acknowledges the son of God. In contrast to Michelangelo's stipulation that figures had to be as it were "liberated" from a single block of marble, Bernini used no fewer than four blocks for the figure, which is nearly fifteen feet tall. Nonetheless, the extraordinary monumentality of this piece and the design of the other statues take into consideration the architectural setting designed by Michelangelo who had made the crossing the aesthetic and spiritual center of St. Peter's.

During the Borghese period Bernini embarked on a series of busts, which he released from the architectural niches that were the characteristic mannerist settings, bringing baroque portraits of popes and absolutist rulers to new artistic levels. Although usually only a partial portrait, Bernini's busts are always imbued with the

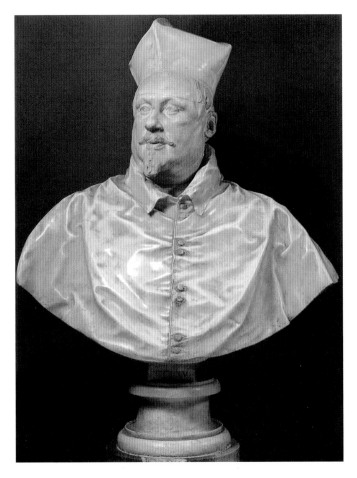

Gian Lorenzo Bernini
Cardinal Scipione Borghese, 1632
Marble bust, height 78 cm
Galleria Borghese, Rome

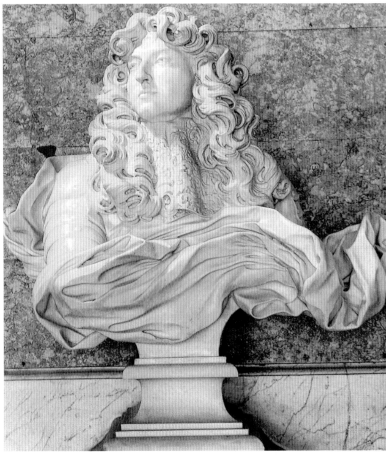

Gian Lorenzo Bernini
King Louis XIV, 1665
Marble bust, height 80 cm
Musée National de Versailles et du
Trianon, Versailles

portrait sculpture. The history of the creation of this piece is documented, more fully than any other work by Bernini, in Chantelou's account of the journey to France. Bernini started work on the sculpture directly after his arrival in Paris in June 1665, finishing it shortly before his departure in October. The sculptor had prepared the design of the bust in numerous sketches and clay models before asking the king to actually sit for the portrait. Here Louis is shown in the imperious pose of the absolute monarch, as if he is about to issue instructions to his court officials. Bernini's later religious enthusiasm finds expression in the portrait of the doctor Gabriele Fonseca (see p. 287, below left), who was one of the first to use quinine as a medicine after its discovery by Jesuit missionaries. Bernini was commissioned to design his memorial chapel in S. Lorenzo in Lucina in Rome; he shows the doctor clasping his left hand to his breast in a moment

of religious fervor as he gazes at the miracle of transubstantiation on the altar.

With the death of Urban VIII in 1644, twenty years in which baroque art dominated by Bernini had flourished in Rome finally came to an end. As the Barberini pope was replaced by the Pamphili Pope Innocent X, Bernini's influence waned and he was removed as chief architect of St. Peter's. The new pope favored the architect Borromini and the sculptor Algardi. In 1647 Bernini began work on his most admired but also most controversial sculpture, the *Ecstasy of St. Teresa of Avila* for the chapel of the Cornaro family in S. Maria della Vittoria. Separated from the nave of the church only by a low balustrade, the chapel resembles a theater set in several respects. The chapel itself forms a kind of stage, while the altar creates a secondary tier behind which the retable forms a third level set in an elliptical niche flanked by double columns where the mysterious angelic

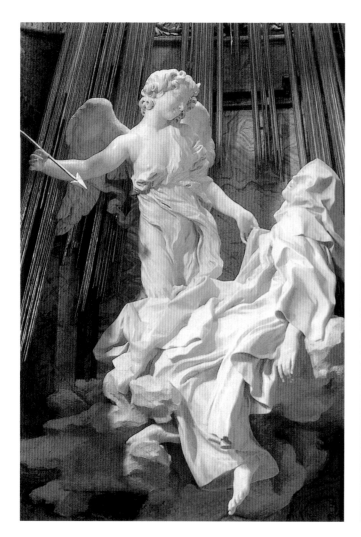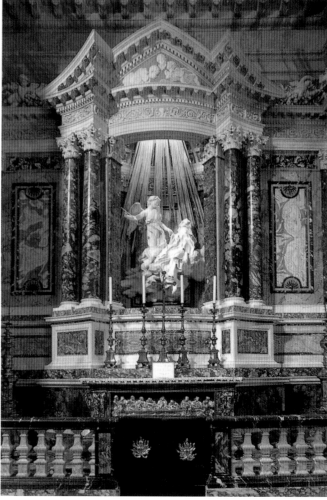

visitation is enacted. The figural group illustrated the moment of religious ecstasy described by St. Teresa of Avila herself: "One day an angel appeared to me who was lovely beyond compare. I saw in his hand a long spear, the end of which looked like a point of fire. I felt it pierce my heart several times, pressing into my innermost being. So real was the pain to me that I moaned out loud several times, and yet it was so indescribably sweet that I could not wish to be released from it. No joy in life can give more satisfaction. When the angel withdrew his spear, I was left with a great love of God." Borne aloft in a cloud, with her whole body except her left hand and foot enveloped in billowing drapery, the saint awaits the angel's dart, which he aims at her with his right hand. The combination of natural light streaming in through an invisible window with the supernatural light of the golden rays transports the saint into an unreal, visionary realm that defies gravity. Set in this divine ambience, St. Teresa communicates the force of religious faith to the beholder, who is drawn under her spell by Bernini's carefully contrived dramatic illusion and aesthetic rhetoric.

However, the observer is not a lone witness to the event; on closer inspection they become aware of other onlookers. The family of the patron is seated in a box in the side walls (see right); the viewer therefore becomes a participant in a mystery already watched by others and to which they can become a witness only by intruding on the intimacy of the family group. At the same time it is also obvious that the spectators in the box are more given to the distractions of a casual theatrical audience than to the higher drama of the mystical event before them; the observer thus finds himself focusing on his religious faith at a more serious level. The full spectacle represented by the chapel is defined by clearly designated formal relationships and symbolic references between the individual elements of the ensemble, as Matthias Kross has conclusively shown.

St. Teresa was greeted by rapt praise from contemporaries and Bernini himself considered it his most successful work. However, the sculpture was the subject of sustained criticism during the following centuries, a response which, it could be argued, is based on a trivialization of the saint's religious ecstasy in terms of a superficial eroticism.

Bernini's allegorical fountains appeared to fuse water and stone in a new way; the many mythological sea and river figures are no longer bound together in any kind of formal structural relationship.

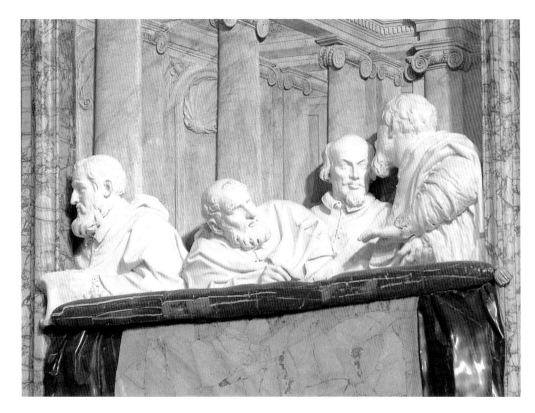

Gian Lorenzo Bernini
Chapel of the Cornaro family, 1647–52
Balcony in side wall with donors

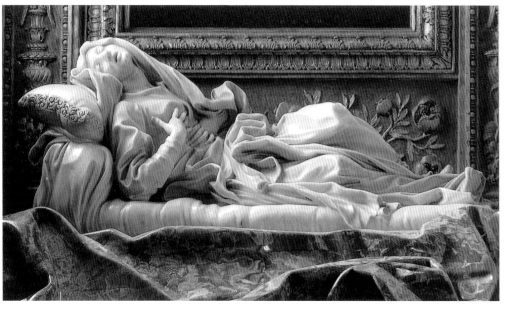

Gian Lorenzo Bernini
Blessed Ludovica Albertoni, 1671–74
Marble and jasper, length 188 cm
S. Francesco a Ripa, Rome

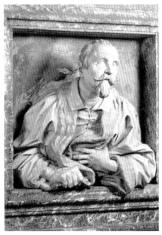

Gian Lorenzo Bernini
Doctor Gabriele Fonseca, c. 1668–75
Marble relief, over-life-size
S. Lorenzo in Lucina, Rome

Gian Lorenzo Bernini
Triton fountain, 1624–43
Travertine, over-life-size
Piazza Barberini, Rome

OPPOSITE:
Gian Lorenzo Bernini
Fountain of the Four Rivers
1648–51
Overall view and details
Marble and travertine
Piazza Navona, Rome

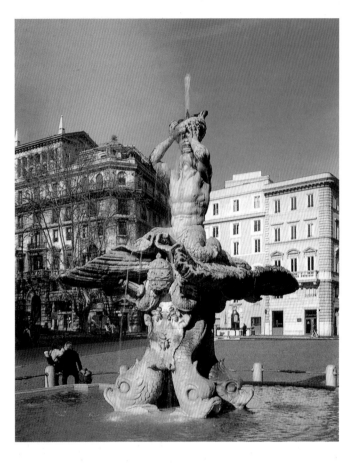

The Triton fountain (see above) was commissioned as an object of self-glorification by Urban VIII, who survived its completion in 1643 by only one year. The fountain is characterized by its essentially sculptural quality which neglects the usual architectural elements. The fountain illustrates the narrative about the end of the Flood in Ovid's *Metamorphoses* (I, 330 ff): "Nor does the rage of the seas continue; the ruler of the seas sets his trident aside, smoothes the billows, and summons the sea-blue Triton who towers up over the depths... and commands him to blow into his sounding shell and by his signal recall the waters and the rivers. He takes the hollow horn that spirals like a snail from the lowest coil into the distance; as soon as this horn has taken air in mid-sea, its voice fills the coasts lying towards sunrise and sunset." The scene is set at the moment when four dolphins rear out of the water supporting an open scallop shell on which the son of the sea god reaches up to blow into the triton's shell, a trumpet, and thus end the Great Flood.

On the axis of front and rear views the papal insignia of tiara and key are combined with the three bees of the Barberini arms, forming a heraldic reference to the donor. In addition to this display of grandeur, the design incorporates further allegorical motifs and relationships: the good-natured dolphins represent social conscience while the open shell from which water pours alludes to the powers of benediction; the three bees of the Barberini are associated with the concept of selfless activity in an orderly state, and the glory of the benign Barberini pontificate is proclaimed to the world by the triton blowing into the shell horn.

The commission for the Fountain of the Four Rivers (see right) was given to Bernini by Pope Innocent X. The widest variety of forms and elements are combined here to create a vast fountain monument that dominates Piazza Navona. In order to lend appropriate visual emphasis to the obelisk, which formed part of the original commission, Bernini was forced to raise it on a plinth. In bold contrast to the urban architecture of the square, he introduced into the heart of the city a grotto mound of the kind found in the gardens of villas, which, like the combination of obelisk and fountain, represented an entirely novel scheme. Bernini's design for the fountain can be associated with the early Christian concept which locates the source of the great rivers watering the four continents in a single mountain (analogous to the four rivers of paradise); the fountain comes to represent the center of the world. At the foot of the four cliffs lie the river gods representing the continents: the Ganges for Asia, the Nile for Africa, and the Plate for America. The fact that here the Danube rather than the Tiber represents Europe in paying homage to the papal insignia may be because the Tiber stands for the center of faith from where the missionary conquest of the continents originates, which for areas far north of the Danube meant above all reconquest during the Counter-Reformation. Imperial Roman symbols of this kind are usually complemented not by towering antique obelisks but by the cross, the symbol of Christ's victory over them, to which they are subordinated. In this case of course the monument is crowned by the personal emblem of the Pamphili pope, the "innocent" dove bearing an olive branch in its beak and proclaiming divine peace. In the sense that the allegorical significance of this fountain extends across both territorial regions and historical periods, the pontificate of the reigning pope and his historic message dominate the scheme. To complete the layout of Piazza Navona, Bernini was commissioned to create the Moro Fountain (see p. 290, left).

After his return from the court of the Sun King in 1665, Bernini received a final commission from Pope Alexander VII. As with the Fountain of the Four Rivers for Innocent X, he was to design a sculptural base for an obelisk recently excavated in the cloisters of S. Maria sopra Minerva. The idea of the saddled elephant (see p. 290, right) derives from an earlier design for a sculpture that had never been executed. The Christian church dedicated to the Virgin stands

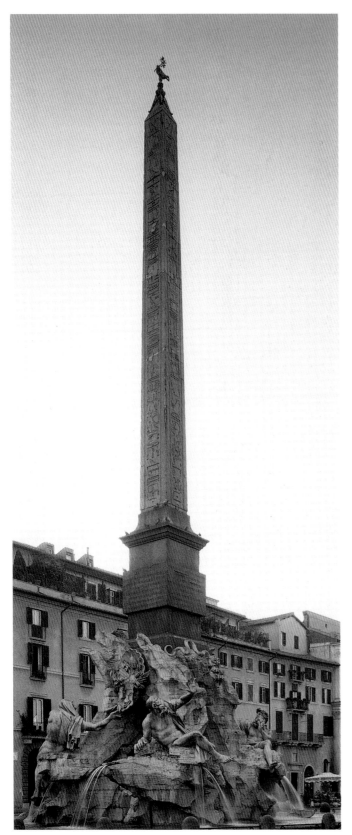

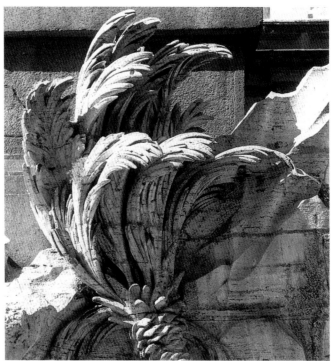

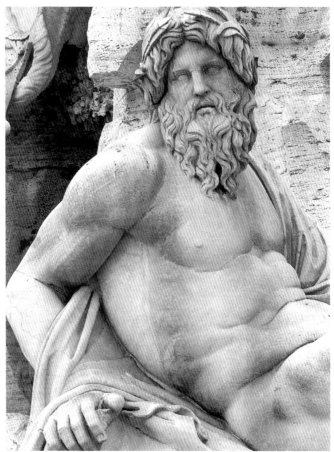

Gian Lorenzo Bernini
Moro Fountain, 1653–54
Marble
Piazza Navona, Rome

Gian Lorenzo Bernini
Elephant and obelisk, 1665–67
Marble
Piazza S. Maria sopra Minerva, Rome

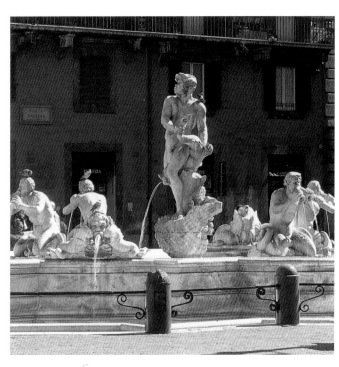

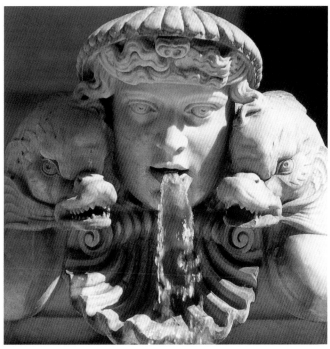

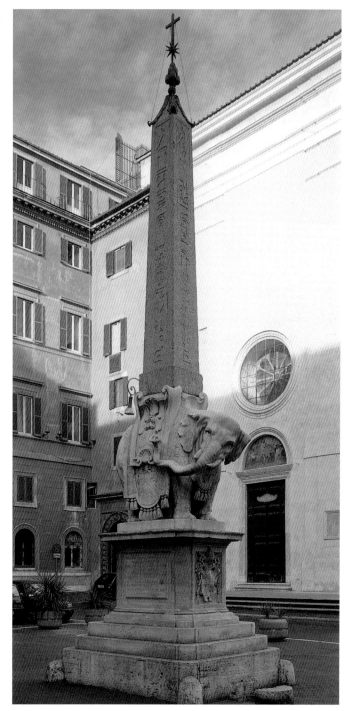

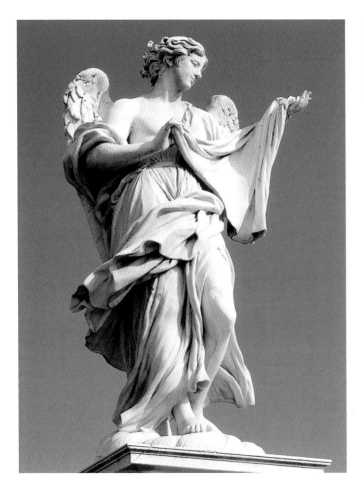

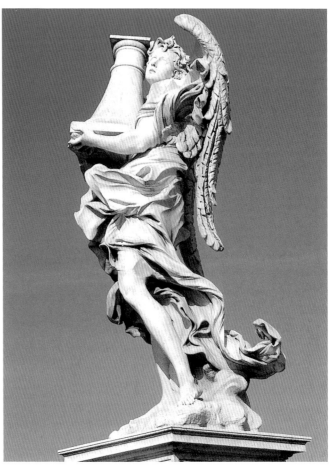

on the site of a Roman temple of Minerva and an earlier Egyptian shrine of Isis, in the tradition of the embodiment of divine wisdom.

Although Bernini had enjoyed the highest reputation as a sculptor among his contemporaries, after his death in 1680 he was derided as a "despoiler of art." "Bernini is the biggest ass among modern sculptors," wrote the German critic Winckelmann from Rome in 1756. It was an assessment that would not be revised until the late nineteenth century.

Camillo Mariani
St. Catherine of Alexandria, 1600
Plaster
S. Bernardo alle Terme, Rome

Francesco Mocchi
Equestrian statue of Alessandro Farnese
1620–25
Bronze
Piazza Cavalli, Piacenza

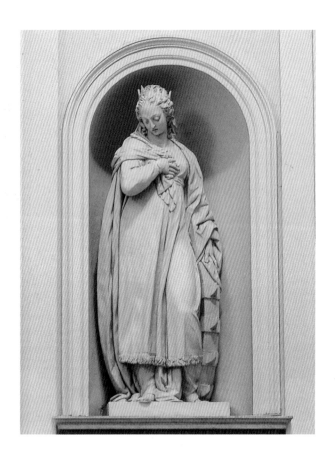

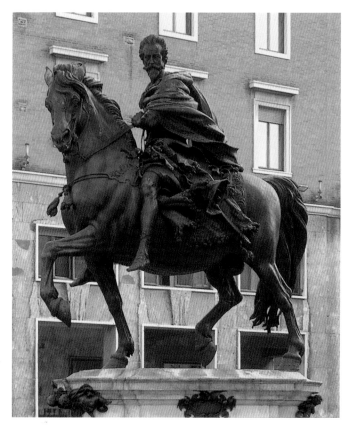

Sculptors in Italy before and after Bernini

During the seventeenth century, Rome retained its position as the pre-eminent artistic capital. Numerous artists were attracted to it from all over Europe, wishing to school themselves in the famous works of antiquity and of the great masters, as well as finding commissions from wealthy patrons. Not one of the leading sculptors of the period was Roman, and to work in Rome as a sculptor meant either challenging the superior might of the famous Bernini, who dominated the field, or actually working for him.

Camillo Mariani (1556–1611) from Vicenza was one of the first to arrive and he soon become a member of the Congregazione dei Virtuosi. Although he was ranked among the most talented of sculptors, the difficulty of obtaining regular commissions meant that he was often reduced to making plasterwork for painters. With Pietro Bernini and others, he was involved in the work on the tomb of Clement VIII, and in 1603 he produced eight large niche figures made of plaster for S. Bernardo alle Terme (see above), presumably assisted by his pupil Mocchi.

Born in Montevarchi near Florence, Francesco Mocchi (1580–1654) began his training with the Florentine painter Santi di Tito (1536–1603) before doing his apprenticeship under Camillo Mariani in Rome. However, his more important early works are found not in Rome but in Piacenza, where he worked from 1612 to 1630 on equestrian statues for Ranuccio and Alessandro Farnese, creating a new baroque style in this sort of sculpture (see above right). His *St. Veronica* in the crossing of St. Peter's (see right) was so large that it had to be made from several blocks of marble; the figure appears to be striding violently out of the niche with her drapery billowing up in such a manner that she almost appears to be floating. Although he should really be seen as an early baroque predecessor of Bernini, Mocchi held his own alongside Bernini for a time before moving away from "the history of sculpture unfolding in Bernini's work," as Norbert Huse puts it, eventually turning the special character of his art into the "capriciousness of an eccentric." This process itself suggests how powerfully Bernini's art determined the prevailing baroque taste in Rome.

Stefano Maderno (1576–1636), who came from Lombardy or Ticino, like Mocchi was active artistically between two distinct stylistic periods. He worked initially as a restorer of antiquities while producing numerous small-scale copies of classical and contemporary sculptures, many of which were cast in bronze. His earliest large-scale sculpture is also his most important work. *St. Cecilia* lies in a red marble niche in the church of S. Cecilia in Trastevere in Rome as if displayed in an open coffin (see right). In this work, Maderno devises an impressive composition. For the first time, a moving moment from the legend of a religious martyr is captured not as a narrative scene of the kind found in a relief, but as sculpture. Here the artist can be seen as having anticipated the powerful expressiveness of Bernini's works in marble.

Alessandro Algardi (1598–1654) was born in Bologna and first trained in the academy there which was run by Lodovico Carracci (1555–1619). He then worked in Milan (for Vincenzo Gonzaga II) and Venice before moving to Rome, probably in 1625. Through his

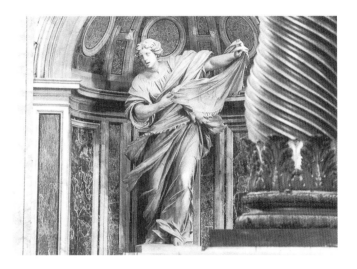

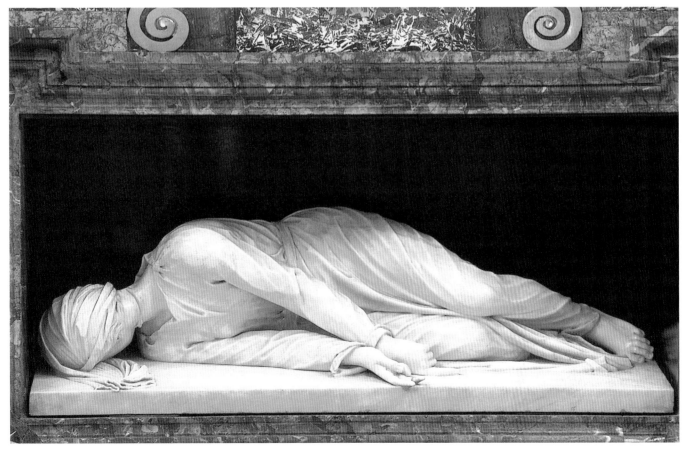

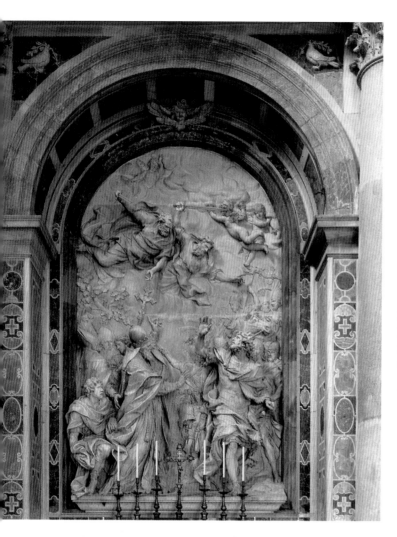

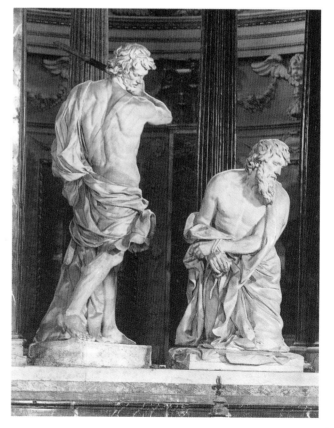

Alessandro Algardi
Pope Leo the Great and Attila
1646–53
Marble relief
St. Peter's, Rome

Alessandro Algardi
Beheading of St. Paul, 1641–47
Marble, height of St. Paul 190 cm, executioner 282 cm
S. Paolo Maggiore, Bologna

tion, which occasionally slips into a monotonous inventory of detail, may explain why Algardi was also one of the most sought-after portraitists of his time.

François Duquesnoy (1597–1643), known in Italy also as Il Fiammingo [the Fleming], came from Brussels, where he trained in the studio of his father Jérôme Duquesnoy. After his arrival in Rome in 1618, he made ivory figure carvings and restored classical antiquities. This close contact with classical sculpture and an appreciation of the paintings of Raphael formed the basis for his own style, which was further developed by his studies with Nicolas Poussin (1594–1665) of Titian's *Bacchanalia* in the Villa Ludovisi. This was possibly the Flemish sculptor's source of inspiration for the characteristic putto type which appears in his subsequent work. In 1626, Duquesnoy was sharing a house with his friend Poussin. A summons from Paris to become court sculptor to Louis XIII remained unfulfilled as Duquesnoy fell ill on the way there and died on July 19 1643. He was probably the most prominent Low Countries sculptor working in Bernini's Rome.

fellow-citizen Domenichino, he obtained commissions for plaster work and smaller sculptures, and spent a considerable period restoring antique statues. After creating a portrait of Cardinal Laudivio Zacchia in 1626, he received his first major commission for the tomb of Leo XI in St. Peter's. By the time the Pamphili pope Innocent X arrived on the papal throne, Algardi was in direct competition with Bernini. Although the pope had no particular interest in art and no special preference for Algardi's style, he evidently preferred his more relaxed character. A stronger motive for the promotion of Algardi at this point was most probably a general enmity for the Barberini and their favorites.

Among Algardi's most famous works is the great marble relief of *Pope Leo the Great and Attila* (see above). It shows Leo turning back Attila and the Huns. Pope Leo had gone to the banks of the Po to counter the invasion of Attila and his army by dissuading him from conquering and destroying Rome. A vision in which the apostles Peter and Paul appear in the sky with swords drawn against the cowed leader of the Huns finally persuades the invader to retreat. In this relief, Algardi's style appears to be cooler and more precisely detailed than Bernini's passionate manner. This clarity of observa-

François Duquesnoy
St. Susanna, 1629–33
Marble
S. Maria di Loreto, Rome

François Duquesnoy
St. Andrew, 1629–33
Marble, height c. 450 cm
St. Peter's, Rome

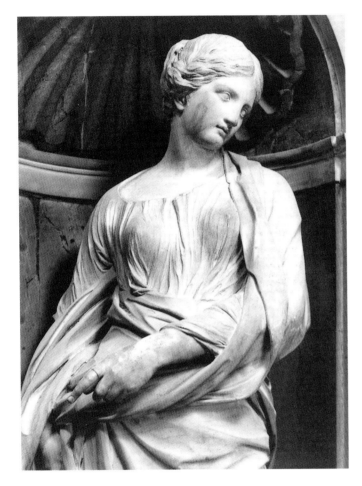

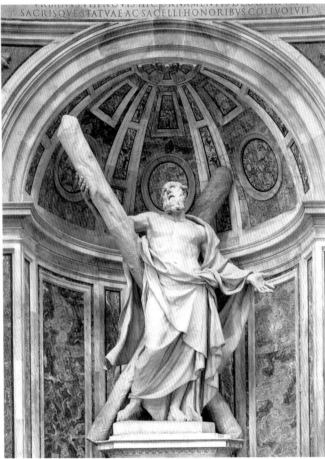

Whereas Algardi's work had reflected the influence of Bernini, Dusquesnoy's *St. Susanna* (see above) suggests an abandonment of Bernini's influence, although to some degree it equals the quality of the master's religious sculptures. The saint does not look upward to heaven like most other Roman figures of the Seicento, but downwards at humanity. In this pose, which is very much based on a classical aesthetic, she contrasts with Bernini's mystification of naturalness and humanity. Further, through his use of an antique style of drapery in which the body is carefully enveloped, Duquesnoy shows the saint as she essentially is: chaste, pure, virginal. As an outstanding masterpiece in Duquesnoy's œuvre, even for contemporary commentators it represented a model of the progressive, classically oriented tendency in baroque sculpture. The other large figure by Duquesnoy, the *St. Andrew* in the crossing of St. Peter's, is therefore a source of some confusion. In complete contrast to

St. Susanna, it is conceived wholly in the spirit of Bernini's baroque pathos. The mystery of how a sculptor of such ability could produce two such different works at the same time is at least partly resolved by current art historical suggestions that Bernini himself was heavily involved in the design of the figure.

Antonio Raggi (1624–86) was born in Vico Morcote near Como, and worked initially in Algardi's studio in Rome before gaining employment with Bernini. At this point he was mainly involved in simply executing Bernini's models, but also appears to have produced independent work which allowed him ultimately to establish his own professional reputation. His sculpture of the death of St. Cecilia on the left-hand side-altar of S. Agnese in Piazza Navona (see p. 296) shows a predilection for painterly relief, a characteristically baroque form of sculpture, which he filled with a scene with many figures. The opposing motions represented in the body and drapery

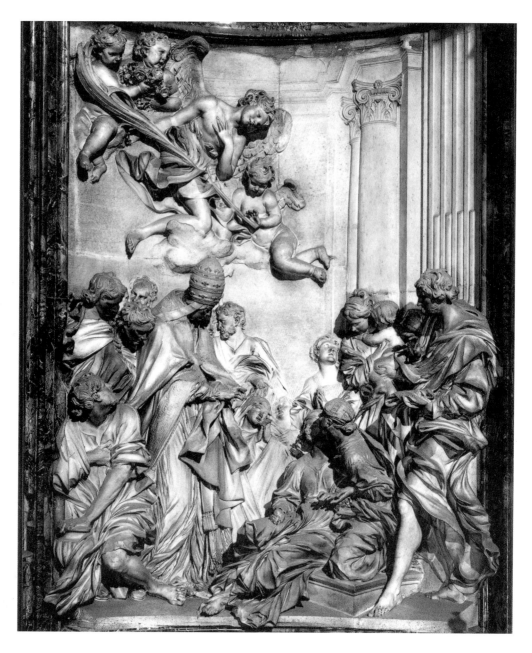

of the figure standing on the right, the extension of the pictorial space by cutting across the frame, and the emotional abandon of the remaining figures have led to Raggi being known as "the second-generation Bernini."

Ercole Ferrata (1610–86) came like Raggi from the Val d'Intelvi near Como, an area with a rich artistic tradition. He studied first in Genoa, but in 1637 was recorded as a member of the sculptors' guild of Naples. In 1646, after a year working in L'Aquila, he finally came to Rome, where he studied first under Bernini and then under Algardi. After the latter's death he set up his own studio, where he nonetheless continued to carry out Bernini's commissions. At the same time he trained numerous young talented sculptors revealing himself as a good teacher of judgment and taste. His reputation as a

teacher and the fact that he was thought to be the best connoisseur of antiquities in his day contrast with the rather modest and simple nature of his compositions.

His marble relief of the *Stoning of St. Emerentiana* (see right) was conceived as a counterpart to Raggi's relief for the right-hand side-altar of S. Agnese. Ferrata captures with profound sympathy the moment of martyrdom, which is mentioned in the *Golden Legend* only in two sentences: "But when friends buried [St. Agnes's] body, they were scarcely able to escape the stones thrown by the heathen. Emerentiana, St. Agnes's foster-sister, who was very holy even though she had not yet been baptized, remained by the tomb; she punished the heathen with harsh words until she herself was stoned by them."

Ercole Ferrata
Stoning of St. Emerentiana, begun 1660
Marble relief
S. Agnese in Piazza Navona, Rome

Ercole Ferrata
Burning of St. Agnes, 1660
Marble
S. Agnese in Piazza Navona, Rome

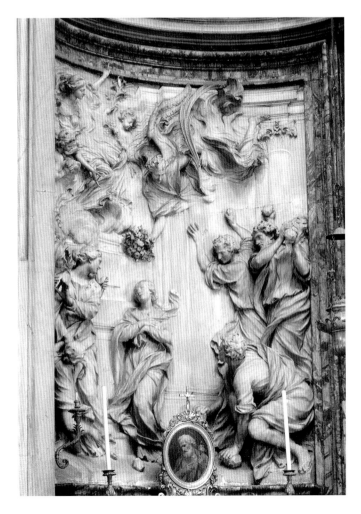

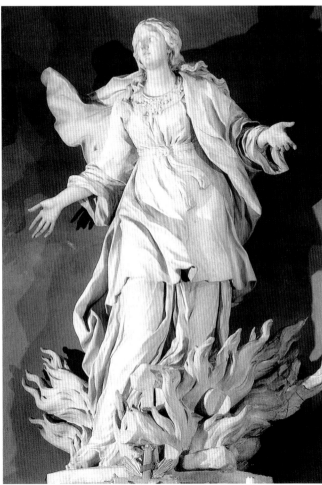

Domenico Guidi (1628–1701) was apprenticed at first to his uncle Giuliano Finelli (1601–57) in Naples before joining Algardi's workshop in Rome in 1649, where he remained until the latter's death. Like Ferrata, he also set up his own workshop, although he seems to have been less interested in teaching than Ferrata and was more interested in establishing a commercial enterprise which supplied patrons throughout Italy as well as Germany, Spain, France, and even Malta. Apart from an exceptional design for the angel with the spear for the Ponte degli Angeli, he never worked for Bernini. As a self-assured artistic entrepreneur who considered himself of equal rank to his great rival, he apparently maintained a professional distance from the master. After the deaths of Bernini, Ferrata, and Raggi, Guidi at last achieved his ambition of becoming the leading sculptor in Rome. In addition, his intervention on behalf of Charles Lebrun reinforced the influence of French sculptors in Rome. His own reliefs, however, can be seen as lacking depth, and are ultimately superficial.

The Genoese sculptor Francesco Queirolo (1704–62) passed through Rome and on to Naples, where he worked on the furnishing of the Cappella Sansevero de' Sangri, the tomb of the Sangrio family. Large-scale representations of the deceased were increasingly being replaced during this period by allegorical figures or groups, with those buried in the tomb appearing only in medallion portraits. The *Liberation from Error* (see p. 299, below) alludes to the worldly life of Prince Antonio Sangrio who became a monk after the death of his wife. The sculptural representation of a net, the allegorical form of

297

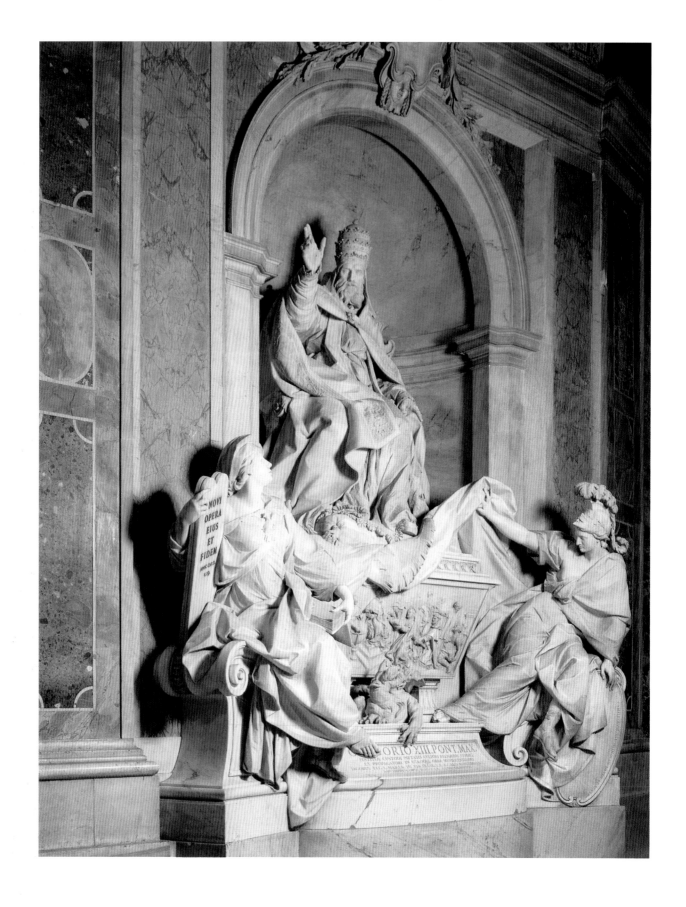

human and worldly error, is translated with impressive naturalism, achieving a three-dimensional illustration of a painterly subject that was characteristic of baroque sculpture.

The Milanese sculptor Camillo Rusconi (1654 or 1658–1728) came to Rome around 1680, where he was numbered among the many collaborators of Ercole Ferrata. Stylistically, his work remained at first within the Roman tradition of Bernini's baroque, distinguished mainly by a restless monumentality and massive weight of drapery. Later Rusconi simplified his style by paring down the movement in the surface of garments, removing excessive folds and formally stressing the monumental appearance of the apostles in S. Giovanni Laterano, for example (see p. 300, right).

One of the few important Roman sculptors was Pietro Bracci (1700–73). A pupil of Rusconi, along with Filippo della Valle, his work is characterized by a softer treatment of light. His aim was to reinforce the painterly qualities of the work, which were further emphasized by the use of colored marble as in the tomb of Pope Benedict XIII in S. Maria sopra Minerva (see right). In later works, his figures throw off the weight of heavy draperies, establishing a classically oriented rococo style.

Filippo della Valle (1697–1770) began his training under his uncle Giovanni Battista Foggini (1652–1737), but after Foggini's death worked for Camillo Rusconi in Rome, where he began to

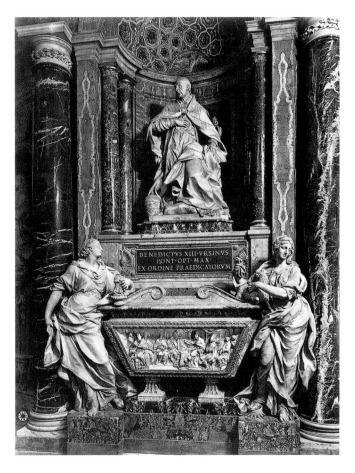

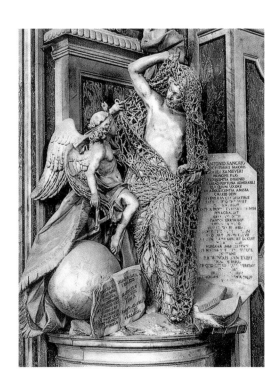

develop his own style. Shortly afterwards he won joint first prize with Pietro Bracci in the Concorso Clementino of the Accademia di San Luca but after Rusconi's death in 1728 he returned to Florence.

The accession of the Florentine-born Lorenzo Corsini as Pope Clement XII and in particular the nepotism of Cardinal Neri Corsini resulted in the award of numerous commissions to Filippo della Valle in Rome after 1730. He was one of ten sculptors to work on furnishing the Capella Orsini in S. Giovanni Laterano; in 1732 he produced *Temperance* (see p. 300, left), an allegory of moderation, in which he represses the overbearing pathos of Roman high and late baroque in favor of a soft mobility. A restrained classicism is evident in the depiction of the female statue figure.

The Trevi Fountain (see p. 301) is the last great collaborative work by Roman sculptors. Its present form is based on plans by Nicola Salvi (1697–1751). The grand ornamental facade in front of Palazzo Poli is in the style of a Roman triumphal arch with a massive

299

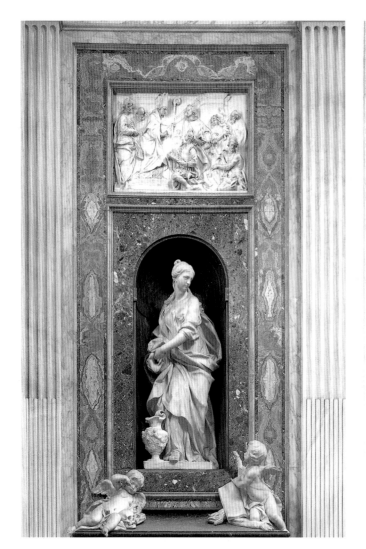

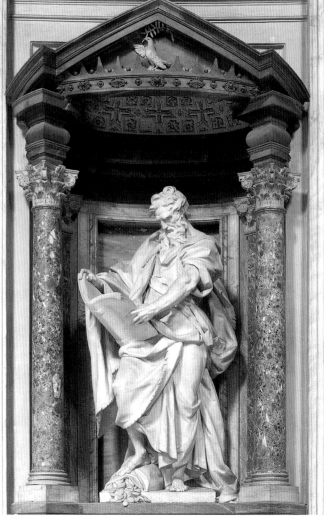

semicircular niche in the center. A rectangular niche on the left side holds a figure intended as an allegory of abundance, while a niche on the right is the setting for a personification of healing; both were made by Filippo della Valle. Above, the relief on the left-hand side by Giovanni Grossi (dates unknown) shows Agrippa examining the design of the aqueduct, while in Andrea Bergondi's relief on the right (second half of eighteenth century) the Virgin points out the spring, the *Acqua Vergine*, to the Roman soldiers, as described in the ancient legend. In the central niche, Oceanus, ruler of the waters and its inhabitants, steps forth on a shell held up by sea creatures, assisted by horses held by tritons. This group is the work of Pietro Bracci, possibly according to designs by Giovanni Battista Maini (1690–1752), the third major pupil of Rusconi. The Trevi Fountain can be seen as representing the end of Roman baroque.

Baroque Sculpture in France

During the first half of the seventeenth century, French baroque sculpture seems to have had little of the aesthetic coherence that would come to characterize it after Louis XIV became king. Before

Filippo della Valle
Temperance, 1732
Marble
S. Giovanni Laterano, Rome

Camillo Rusconi
St. Matthew, 1708–18
Marble, over-life-size
S. Giovanni Laterano, Rome

OPPOSITE:
Nicola Salvi and others
Trevi Fountain, 1732–51
Marble
Palazzo Poli, Rome

this, French sculpture was dominated to a considerable degree by the various styles of other European sculptors or schools of sculpture. It is possible to discern here the influence of Roman baroque as well as Netherlandish sculpture, and sometimes elements of the work of the mannerist sculptor Giambologna. The prevailing tendency was towards monumentality, as developed in the transition to early French baroque in the work of such artists as Germain Pilon (c. 1525–90).

Pilon's influence permeated the training of the Parisian sculptor Simon Guillain (1581–1658) under his father Nicolas before he went to Italy sometime before 1621. In the 1630s, he worked for the

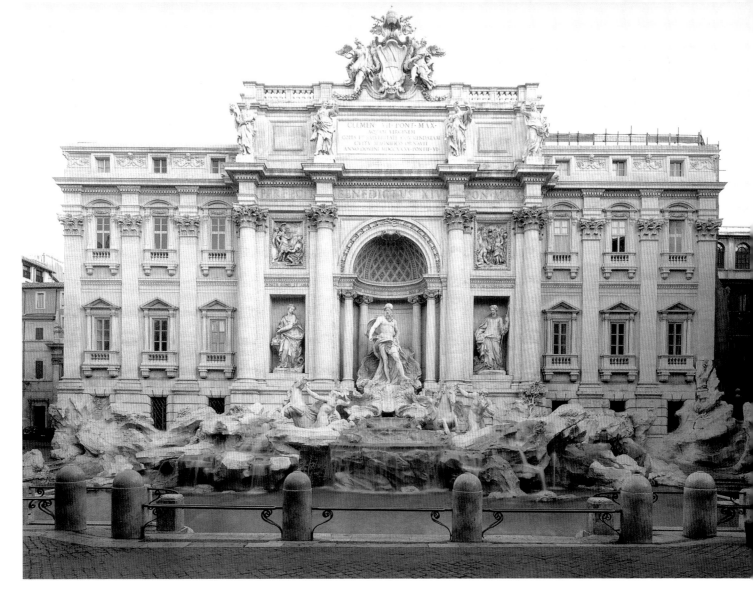

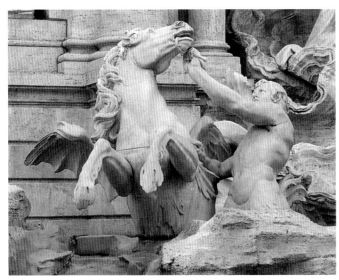

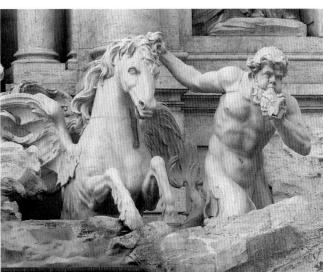

Simon Guillain
Louis XIII, 1647
Bronze, height 200 cm
Louvre, Paris

Jean Warin II
Cardinal Richelieu, c. 1640
Bronze bust, height 70 cm
Bibliothèque Mazarin, Paris

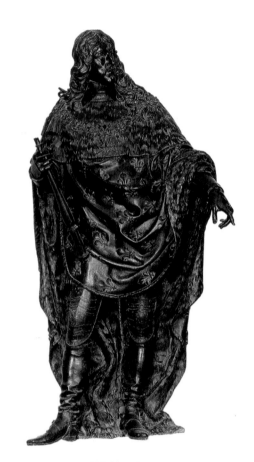

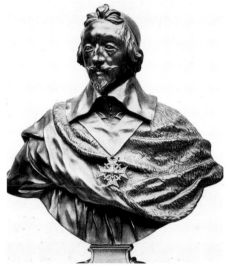

royal château at Blois (among others) and is recorded in 1648 as a founding member of the royal academy of painting and sculpture, becoming its president a year before his death. The bronze figure of Louis XIII (see left) with Anne of Austria and their ten-year-old son Louis XIV in coronation robes is Guillain's masterpiece. Made in 1647 and now preserved in the Louvre, the group was originally set into a triumphal arch on the narrow side of a block of houses opposite the Pont-au-Change. The naturalism and monumentalism of these figures indicate their stylistic dependence on the Pilon school.

Jean Warin II (1604–72) was raised in the traditions of a Liège medal-making family. In 1625, he moved to Paris and became France's leading medal-maker. Almost twenty years before his election to the Academy in 1665, he was appointed Graveur Général des Monnaies de France, and in 1648 Controlleur Général des Effigies. In his role as director of the Mint, he undertook the reorganization of French coinage. While his portrait medals reflect the stylistic tradition of Germain Pilon, his portrait statues are imbued with a notable intimacy beneath formal exteriors. Thus the raised eyebrows of Cardinal Richelieu (see left) and other physiognomical details reveal something of the personality of the sitter. This sculpture was produced during Richelieu's lifetime and six casts were made of it after his death.

Active both as a sculptor and painter, Jacques Sarrazin (1592–1660) was trained by Nicolas Guillain until he left for Italy in 1610. In Rome, where he worked until 1628, he made the acquaintance of Bernini and Duquesnoy. He subsequently produced numerous garden figures as well as several statues for the high altar of S. Andrea della Valle. Sarrazin was an early practitioner of neoclassicism, a style which developed from his study of classical antiquity and the sculpture of Michelangelo. Once back in France, he produced sculpture for a wide range of ecclesiastical and secular buildings such as the Château de Maisons (1642–50) in Maisons-Laffitte and the park at Versailles (1660). He was a founding member of the Paris Academy in 1648 and became its president in 1655. His caryatids on the Pavillon de l'Horloge (see right) on the west wing of the Louvre in Paris were conceived as pilasters because of the cubic entablature (and in the case of the inner pairs, as offset pilasters) which removed problems of arrangement otherwise arising from the rules of the classical orders. Both the *contrapposto* arrangement of the statues and the treatment of the robes indicate the direct influence of classical models.

Whereas Sarrazin had an influence on the classical tendency of French baroque sculpture, the work of another artist, Pierre Puget (1620–94), similarly inspired by Michelangelo and in particular by Bernini, is imbued with baroque pathos and emotion rather than with academic concerns of form. Puget came from Marseilles, and gained his early training in the shipyard carving workshop. In 1638, he went to Italy and worked presumably as a stuccoist and painter under Pietro da Cortona. From 1643 he practised sculpture and

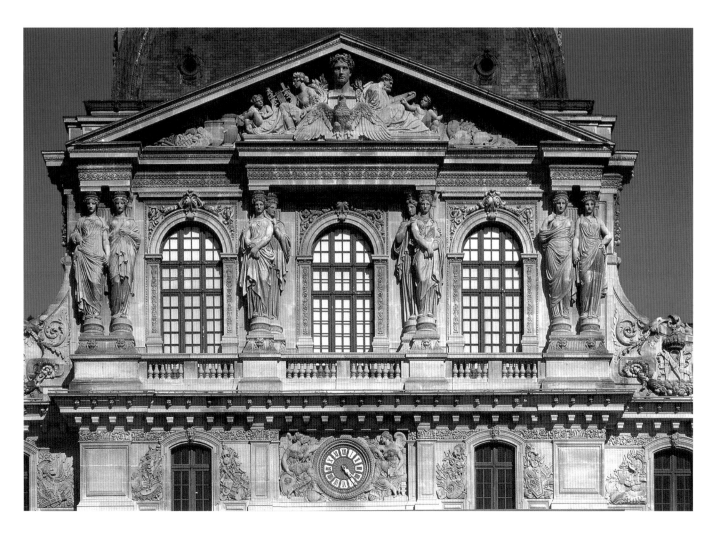

painting at Toulon arsenal, the largest shipyard in France, where he worked mainly in the woodcarving workshop; the decoration of ships constituted his main activity from 1643 to 1679. His paintings were mainly of religious subjects in the manner of the Carracci and Rubens. Among his first significant architectural and sculptural commissions was the entrance to Toulon city hall (1656). A second tour of Italy took him not only to Rome but also to Genoa, where among other works he created two monumental figures, *St. Sebastian* and the *Blessed Alessandro Sauli*, for the dome piers of S. Maria Assunta di Carignano (1664–68). These works, commissioned by the Sauli family, show Puget working wholly in Bernini's Roman high baroque manner. Back in Toulon, he is known to have become director of shipbuilding in the shipyard around 1670, but evidently

still found time to act as *architecte de ville* for Marseilles where he produced ambitious urban development plans including such buildings as the fish markets, and designs for large town houses in Aix-en-Provence.

The beginning of Puget's late period is marked by the marble figure of Milon of Crotone for the park at Versailles (see p. 304, right). One of his principal works, this powerful design illustrating the moment when Milon is attacked by a lion combines naturalistic representation with extreme dramatic tension. A contemporary of Pythagoras, Milon was a famous wrestler from Croton who in Ovid's *Metamorphoses* (XV, 229 ff) complains of the infirmity of age. The face contorted by fear and the violent rotation of the athlete as the beast of prey sinks its paws into his thigh seem to

Pierre Puget
Alexander's Encounter with Diogenes, 1692
Marble relief, height 332 cm, breadth 296 cm
Louvre, Paris

Pierre Puget
Milon of Crotone, 1672–82
Marble, height 270 cm
Louvre, Paris

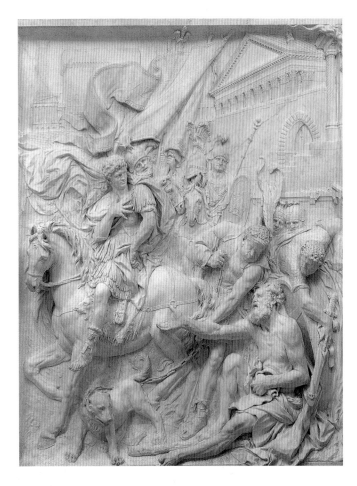

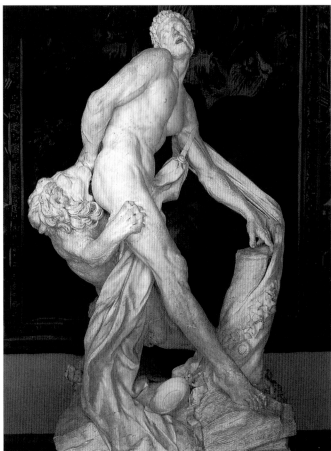

represent a deliberate aesthetic challenge to the elegant court art of the day.

Although the marble reliefs *Alexander's Encounter with Diogenes* (see above left) and *The Liberation of Andromeda by Perseus* were acquired by Louis XIV, Puget failed to obtain further commissions from the court. Nonetheless, the vibrant restlessness and naturalism of his figures give his work an exceptional place in French baroque sculpture.

François Girardon (1628–1715) from Troyes was an explicit adherent of the Paris Academy and its notions of form. After his early studies in his home town he travelled to Rome between 1648 and 1650, where he made the acquaintance of Bernini. His work is ultimately characterized, however, by a rejection of Bernini's baroque manner and a return to the formal models of antiquity. The famous *Apollo Tended by the Nymphs* (see p. 307), an allegory of

the Sun King, is the dominant symbol of the gardens and sculpture at Versailles. The model for Apollo was the classical Apollo Belvedere in the Vatican. Having returned home in the evening after his journey in the sun chariot, Apollo is bathed and anointed by nymphs, while his fiery steeds (see p. 306) are led off to be watered to the left of the grotto. The image embodies a symbolic reference to the Sun King, who, like the sun god, in unflagging service of his people, merits respectful homage. It was a symbol that would have been clear to every contemporary beholder.

The tomb of Cardinal Richelieu, produced between 1675 and 1694, originally stood at the central axis of the church of the Sorbonne in Paris, from where the statesman, accompanied by the allegorical female figures of *religio* and *scientia* (knowledge), could look directly towards the altar. Girardon's sculpture promoted a style of classical tomb art in which the deceased, represented in an active

Francois Girardon
Tomb of Cardinal Richelieu, 1675–94
Marble
Chapel of the Sorbonne, Paris

Francois Girardon
Rape of Proserpine, 1677–99
Marble, height of group 270 cm
Versailles, park

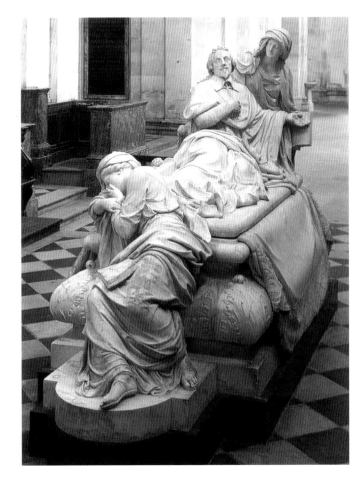

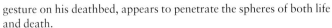

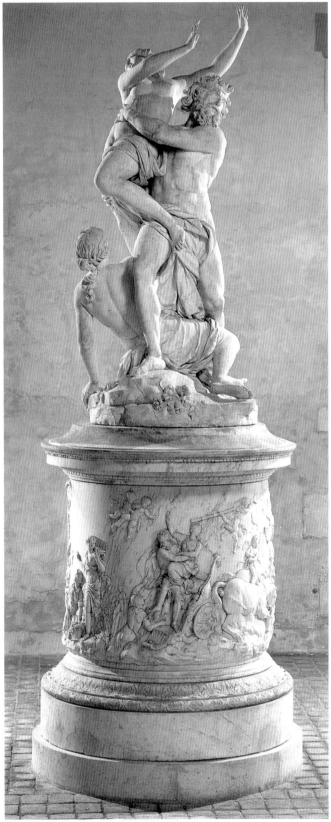

gesture on his deathbed, appears to penetrate the spheres of both life and death.

By contrast to the multi-dimensional quality of Giambologna's *Rape of the Sabine Woman*, Girardon's *Rape of Proserpine* (see right), which is to some extent modelled on Giambologna's design, is so one-dimensional that it seems more like a relief than a sculpture. There are of course baroque elements of motion, but at the same time the inner tensions and emotional force of the piece are restrained by a clearly defined order and a tendency towards symmetry of form.

Antoine Coyzevox (1640–1720) was a rival of Girardon and was also substantially involved in the furnishing of Versailles. The son of a sculptor from Lyons, he came to Paris in 1657 where he was initially employed by Louis Lerambert. By 1666, at the age of twenty-six, he had already achieved the title of Sculpteur du Roi,

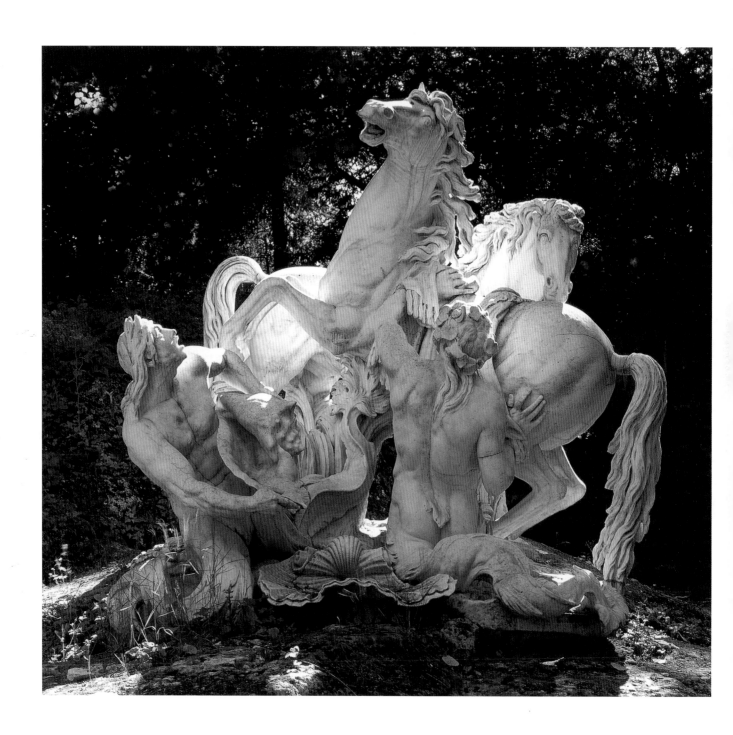

François Girardon
Apollo Tended by the Nymphs, 1666–75
Marble, life-size
Versailles, park

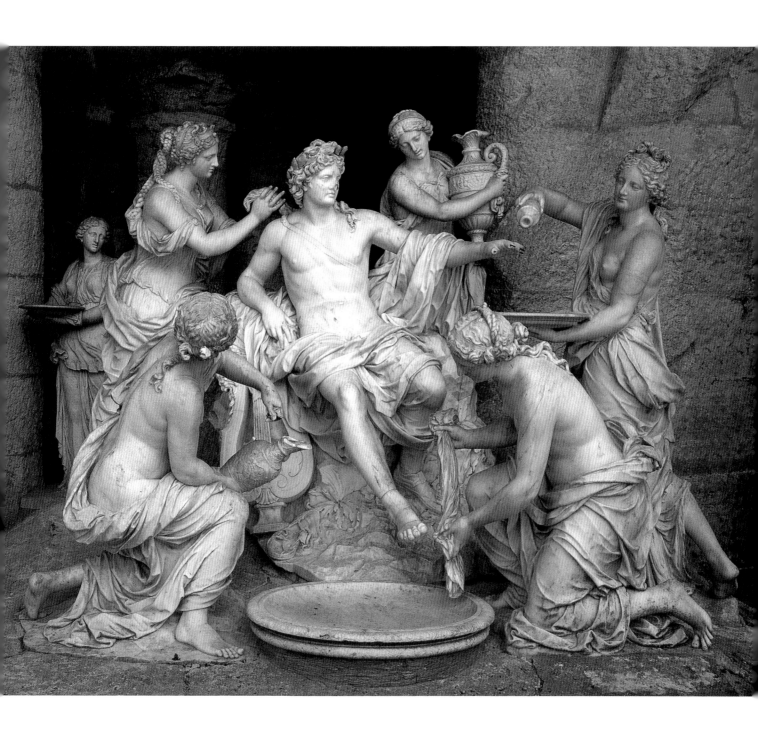

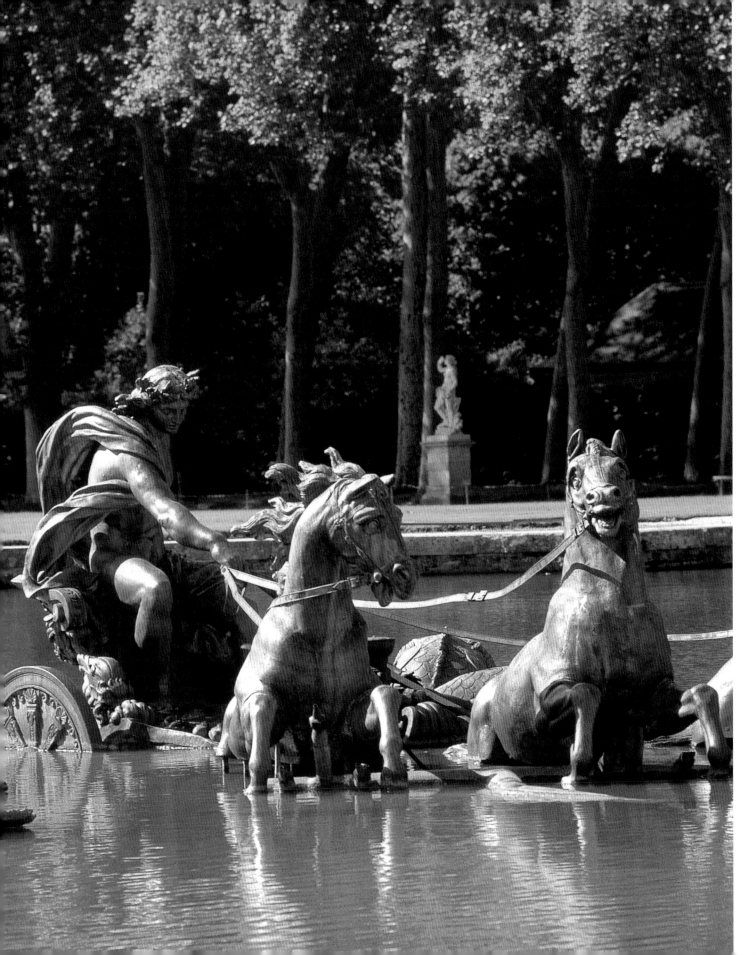

ABOVE LEFT:
Régnaudin(?)
Ceres or *Sun Fountain*, 1672–79
Lead and gilt
Versailles, palace gardens

BELOW LEFT:
Jean-Baptiste Tuby
Flora or *Spring Fountain*, 1672–79
Lead and gilt
Versailles, palace gardens

ABOVE RIGHT:
Gaspard and Balthasar Marsy
Bacchus or *Autumn Fountain*, 1672–75
Lead and gilt
Versailles, palace gardens

BELOW RIGHT:
François Girardon
Saturn or *Winter Fountain*, 1672–77
Lead and gilt
Versailles, palace gardens

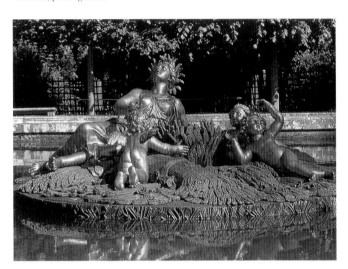 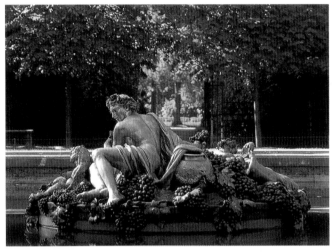

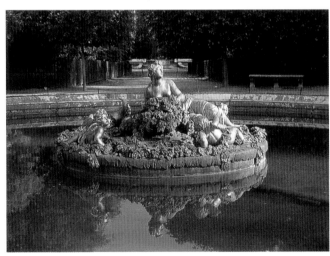 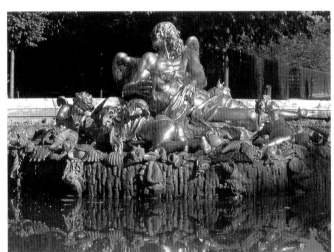

OPPOSITE:
Jean-Baptiste Tuby
Detail of *Apollo* fountain
Apollo on his chariot, 1668–70
Lead, formerly gilded
Versailles, palace gardens

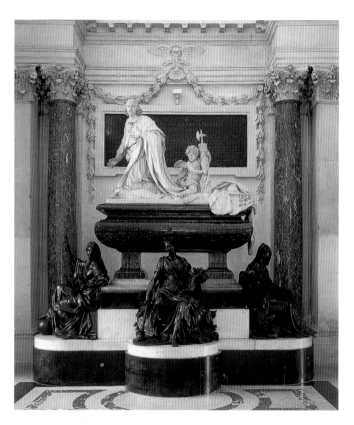

Antoine Coyzevox
Tomb of Cardinal Mazarin, 1689–93
Marble and bronze, height of cardinal 160 cm
Institut de France, Paris

court sculptor, and in 1678 was appointed to the Paris Academy as a teacher. He was to be elected director of the Academy in 1702. Coyzevox was the most successful of Louis XIV's sculptors: he received an annual stipend of four thousand *livres* and taught an entire generation of sculptors, including his nephew Nicolas (1659–1733) and Guillaume Coustou the Elder (1677–1746). He thus wielded a decisive influence on French sculpture of the eighteenth century.

A large number of portrait statues and busts demonstrate that Coyzevox was a close observer of nature; he by no means idealized his portraits but nonetheless was able to convey the required sense of display through showy dress, pathos of gesture, or classicizing elements. He clothes a sculpture of the Duchess of Burgundy, Marie-Adelaide of Savoy, in the late Roman costume of the goddess *Diana*, for example. The monumental plaster relief, *The Triumph of Louis XIV* (see p. 136), is among his most important works, executed as part of the wall decoration of the Salon de Guerre in Versailles. Riding over the battlefield in the manner of a late-Roman apotheosis, the king is here elevated to the role of divine ruler, the heir of the

Jean-Baptiste Tuby
Allegory of Prudence
From the tomb of Cardinal Mazarin, 1693
Bronze, height 140 cm
Institut de France, Paris

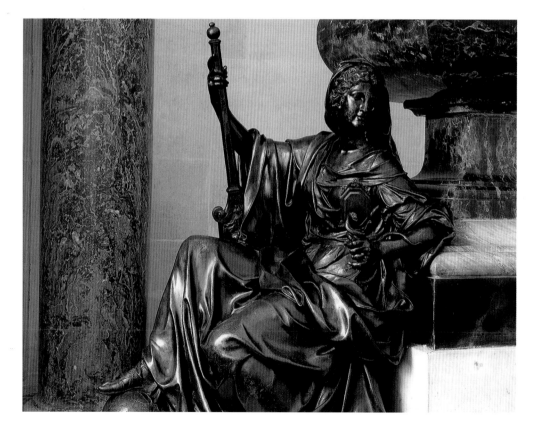

La Perdrix
The Melancholic, 1680
Marble
Versailles, palace gardens

Étienne Le Hongre
Air, 1685
Marble
Versailles, palace gardens

Laviron
Ganymede, 1682
Marble
Versailles, palace gardens

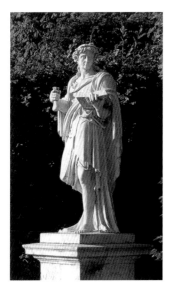

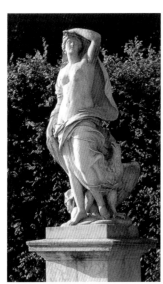

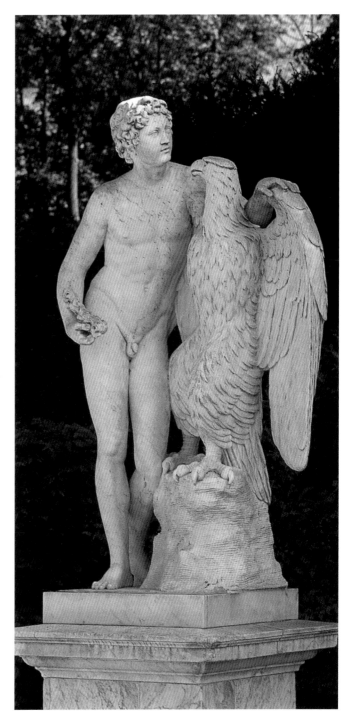

Caesars. With his gaze directed into the distance and the future, this subjugator of his enemies awaits the crown of victory that is proffered by the figure of Victory appearing above him.

Coyzevox's work for the court aristocracy consisted of a series of tombs. Among them those of minister Colbert and Cardinal Mazarin (see left) are notable for their formal references to the artistic traditions of the sixteenth-century royal tombs in Saint-Denis. In splendid garments, the dead cardinal kneels on the raised sarcophagus, while a putto squats holding the lictor's bundle of fasces. Both marble figures and one of the bronze allegories of virtues derive from some of Coyzevox's own earlier works, while the other two virtues were produced by the sculptors Étienne Le Hongre (1628–90) and Jean-Baptiste Tuby (1635–1700).

Although his garden sculptures were often reduced to the level of mere copies of antique works, Coyzevox was nonetheless later able to shake off the lifeless and rigid constraints of the Academy. Beyond its art historical significance, his work (which today includes around two hundred known pieces) offers an informative view of the cult of divine rule surrounding Louis XIV.

Like his brother Nicolas Coustou, who was a nephew and pupil of Antoine Coyzevox, Guillaume Coustou the Elder was also a colleague of Coyzevox at one time. Between 1697 and 1703 he was in Rome on a scholarship and returned there in 1704 to become a member of the academy of fine arts, where eventually, in 1735, he became president. Among his outstanding works is the *Horse-Tamer* (see p. 313), originally commissioned for Château Marly but now at the beginning of the Champs-Élysées. The horse rears up in an elegant riding-school pose and is held on a bridle in an almost playful

René-Michel (Michel-Ange) Slodtz
Tomb of Languet de Gergy, 1753
Marble
St. John the Baptist chapel,
Saint-Sulpice, Paris

OPPOSITE RIGHT:
Edme Bouchardon
Fountain in Rue de Grenelle, Paris,
1739–45
Paris with personifications of the rivers
Seine and Marne
Marble, height of statue c. 210 cm
Rue de Grenelle, Paris

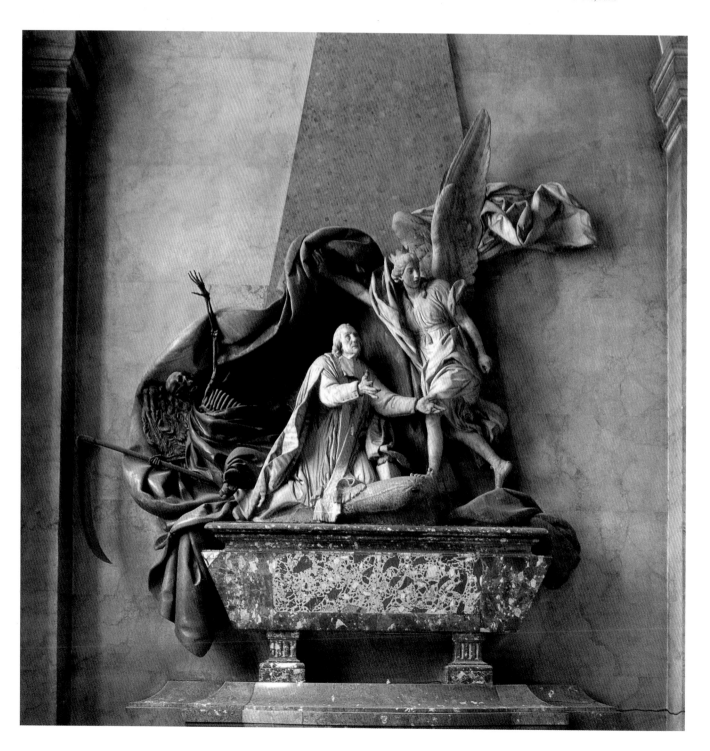

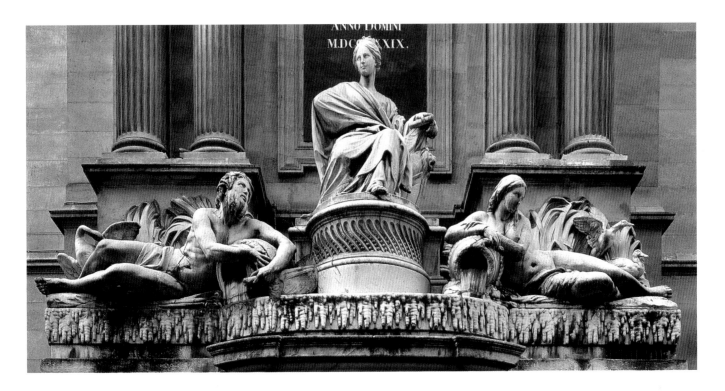

manner. What is supposedly an elemental force is in fact portrayed as nature firmly under human restraint. Mane and hair remain ornaments in the subdued illusion of rococo.

Edmé Bouchardon (1698–1762), a pupil of Coustou, combined late French rococo with formal classical elements in an early version of neo-classicism. His principal work, the Fontaine de Grenelle in the Rue de Grenelle in Paris (see above), is incorporated into a classical columnar facade which relates to the monumentality of the fountain figures. The sculptural structure of the fountain was inspired by the Medici tombs by Michelangelo in Florence.

The work of René-Michel Slodtz (1705–64) is still largely influenced by the formal framework of Roman baroque; his sculpture is comparable in style to the pre-classical manner of Bouchardon. Born to a French artist family of Flemish descent, he was trained by his father Sébastien Slodtz (1655–1726) before obtaining a scholarship from the Academy. He finally established himself as an independent sculptor in Rome between 1736 and 1746. His principal works date from this period. They include the marble *St. Bruno Rejecting the Rank of Bishop* in St. Peter's (1740–44) and the tomb of Alessandro Gregorio Marchese Capponi in S. Giovanni dei Fiorentini (1745–46). In Paris he worked in collaboration with his brothers Sébastien Antoine (1695–1754) and Paul-Ambroise (1702–58), principally on decorative works for the court. The only monumental work of his later life was the tomb of Jean-Baptiste Languet de Gergy (1757) in the church of Saint-Sulpice in Paris (see left).

The work of the Parisian sculptor Jean-Baptiste Pigalle (1714–85) reflects the aesthetic transition from rococo to neo-classicism. His work embodies the contrast between an almost radical naturalism in translating anatomical details on the one hand and the polished, classically derived forms and clear straight lines of the Louis

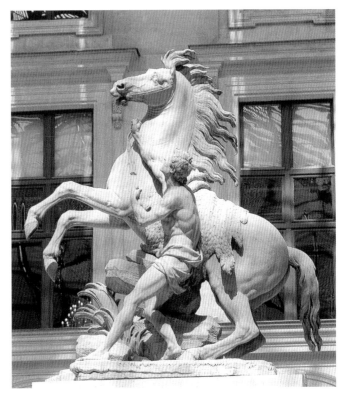

Guillaume Coustou
Horse-Tamer, 1745
Marble, height c. 350 cm
Louvre, Paris

XVI style on the other. Trained under Robert Le Lorrain, in 1735 Pigalle was employed in the studio of Jean-Baptiste Lemoyne II; he left the following year for a prolonged stay in Italy. Three years after his return, in 1744, he became a member of the Academy. He was appointed professor there in 1752 and finally elected president in 1777. In his work Pigalle sought to represent the individual with idealization and in all his intimate humanity. This is particularly evident in his portrait bust of Diderot (1777), and in the seated figure of the unclothed Voltaire produced the year before. This is also how the deceased Henri-Claude d'Harcourt is presented on his tomb in Notre-Dame in Paris (see below). The gaunt corpse endeavors one last time to rise from the coffin, but shrouded Death holds up the hourglass which has run out, and the torch held by the dead man's guardian spirit standing at his feet has gone out. Even the widow who stands beside her husband's discarded military equipment no longer looks at the deceased but laments to herself in prayerful entreaty. Although features of the baroque *memento mori*, the reminder of human mortality, are suggested here, this composition is essentially very untypical for a baroque tomb. The figures stand in a very distant relationship to each other, and this is mirrored by the limited degree to which the beholder is drawn into the scene; the mourning figure takes on a posture that, almost memorial-like, conjures up the relics of the deceased.

Although Jean-Baptiste Lemoyne II (1704–8) was awarded the Grand Prix in 1725 and was later appointed president of the Royal Academy, his reputation as the pre-eminent French rococo sculptor was established only by art historians of the twentieth century. Influenced by Diderot and imbued with classicist fervor, contemporary art critics saw in his busts only a moderate talent for portrait likenesses—which was, in any case, considered inferior to the abilities of his pupil Jean-Antoine Houdon (1741–1828). Lemoyne's bust of the Comte de la Tour d'Auvergne in Frankfurt (see right) is notable for the ambiguity it incorporates between the hardness of the representation of the eyes on the one hand and the almost picturesque, soft aspect of the drapery and fleshy facial features on the other. The way in which the sculpture catches the subject in the attitude of an instant is particularly characteristic of Lemoyne; further, in giving expression to the individual being, this bust is distinguished from the pretentious conventions of court portraiture. The portrait of the Comte de la Tour in the French rococo manner nonetheless appears to be entirely in accord with the highly educated and elegant lifestyle of French aristocratic life in the eighteenth century.

Also in the Liebighaus in Frankfurt is the portrait bust of Mademoiselle Servat (see right) by Lemoyne's most important pupil, Jean-Antoine Houdon. This work is even more ambiguously executed. The piece is in some respects meticulously detailed, as in the fine lace of the décolletage, for example, but elsewhere, such as in the drapery or face, the composition is overly finished and highly stylized. The hairstyle seems oddly enough to create a new expressive element, linking the disparate styles represented in the composition; without excessive elaboration each individual hair becomes visible. However much Houdon's work reflected the naturalistic and human tendencies of portraiture during his early artistic career, it appears that he was equally concerned to conform to the aesthetic canons of classicism. His career took him not only to Italy and Germany but also, in 1785, to North America, where he was involved in the execution of a memorial for George Washington. In the transition to a new age, his work was essentially more forward-looking than historicist, but was very much informed nonetheless by an understanding of the artistic language of the classical past.

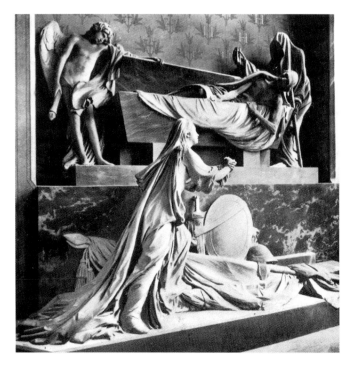

Jean-Baptiste Pigalle
Tomb of Henri-Claude d'Harcourt, 1774
Marble
Notre-Dame, Paris

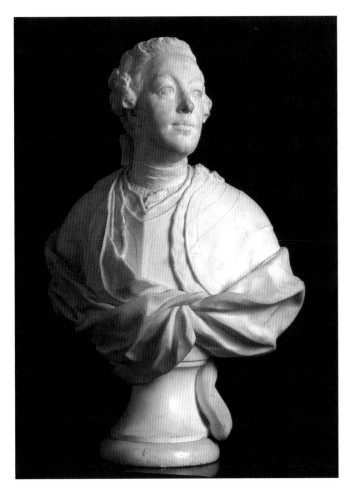

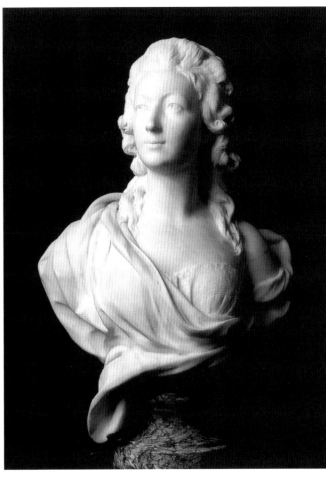

Jean Baptiste Lemoyne II
Comte de la Tour d'Auvergne, 1765
Marble, height 71 cm
Liebighaus, Frankfurt

Jean-Antoine Houdon
Mademoiselle Servat, 1777
Marble, height 76.5 cm
Liebighaus, Frankfurt

Hendrik de Keyser
Tomb of William I, 1614–22
Marble and bronze, height 765 cm
Nieuwe Kerk, Delft

Artus Quellinus the Elder
Anton de Graeff, 1661
Marble
Rijksmuseum, Amsterdam

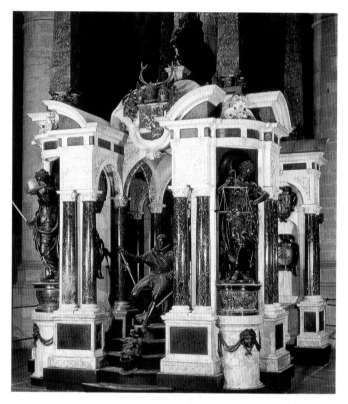

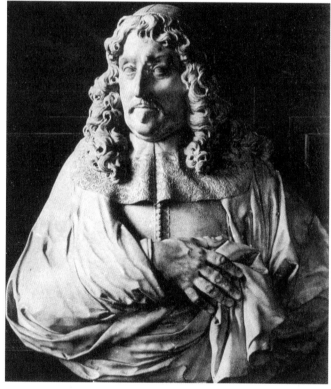

Baroque Sculpture in Holland and Belgium

After the religious partition of the Netherlands during the seventeenth century, only one sculptor from the Protestant north achieved any kind of international artistic status. This was Hendrik de Keyser (1565–1621), the sculptor and architect who later became municipal architect of Amsterdam. His sculptural work, like his architecture, drew on Italian mannerist sources, but his work in this style hardly compares, it can be argued, with the outstanding sculptures of an artist like Adriaen de Vries, for example. It was not until the year of his death that Hendrik de Keyser's masterpiece, the tomb of William I of Orange, commissioned in 1614 for the Nieuwe Kerk in Delft, was completed by his son Peter (see above left). In a light and richly decorated pavilion of black and white marble, the reclining figure of the ruler is flanked by his portrait in bronze while at his feet is an allegory of Fame. In the puritan spirit, not one of the four bronze cardinal virtues in the corner niches is depicted either fully or partly nude. Hendrik de Keyser established no school, and few sculptors were trained by him; after his death artists from the southern part of the country moved to the north to fill the artistic void.

Even though many Netherlandish artists worked mainly abroad, including Jan van Nost and Pieter-Denis Plumier, Aegid Verhelst, Guillelmus de Grof, Gabriel Grupello, and Peter Verschaffelt, the Quellinus workshop under Artus Quellinus the Elder (1609–68), the principal master of Dutch sculpture in the seventeenth century, is representative of an important native school. Born in Antwerp and trained by his father Erasmus Quellinus (1584–1639), Artus went initially to work for François Duquesnoy in Rome, returning to Antwerp in 1639, where he joined a wider circle around Rubens. In 1650, Quellinus went to Amsterdam, where he remained for fifteen years, producing allegorical reliefs and four female caryatids for the decoration of the town hall. His signed marble bust of Anton de Graeff (see above right) from this period shows this member of the ruling family in formal dress and pose. Quellinus' most important artistic contribution was his translation of the aesthetic philosophy of the painter Peter Paul Rubens into sculpture.

Born in Mechelen as the most important member of the artistic Fayd'herbe family, Lukas Fayd'herbe (1617–97) went at the age of nineteen to Rubens' house in Antwerp and worked with him for three years. Like Quellinus, Fayd'herbe also followed Rubens' stylistic

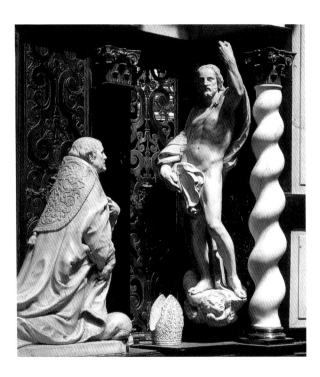

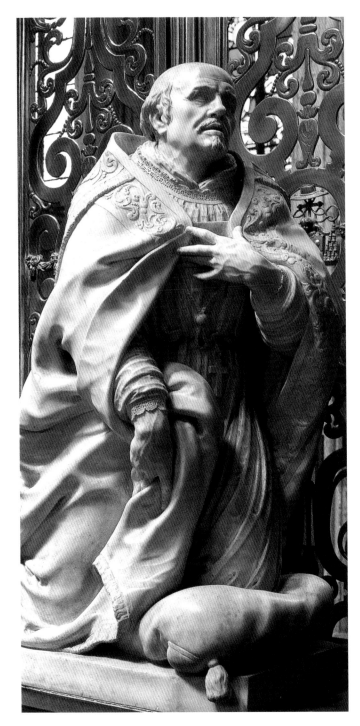

models in his small-scale ivory carvings as well as his other work. His eclectic manner undermines the coherence of handling in the design and arrangement of figures, and this is still more evident in his large-scale figures, where the influence of Bernini can also be seen. The tomb of Archbishop Andreas Cruesen in Mechelen cathedral (see left and above) shows the bishop in full vestments kneeling before the figure of the Risen Christ. His miter is placed before him on the ground, while behind him Chronos, symbolic of transience, is on the point of turning away. Fayd'herbe's principal work in his capacity as an architect is the church of Our Lady of Hanswijk in Mechelen.

Rombout Verhulst (1624–98) was also from Mechelen; in 1648 he collaborated with Artus Quellinus on the work on the town hall in Amsterdam. He soon developed a reputation with Quellinus as one of the leading Dutch portrait artists of the second half of the seventeenth century and was sought after to create tomb sculpture throughout the country. His numerous tomb monuments include the one for Johan Polyander van Kerchoven in Leyden (see p. 318, above) which is considered one of his best funerary works. The deceased is portrayed as if merely resting, with his head propped on his left hand. Verhulst's sensitive handling of the physiognomy and hands as well as the naturalistic treatment of clothing and hair define him as one of the finest Dutch sculptors of his time.

Among the extraordinary sculptural achievements of the south-ern Low Countries are pulpits, objects which have generally been

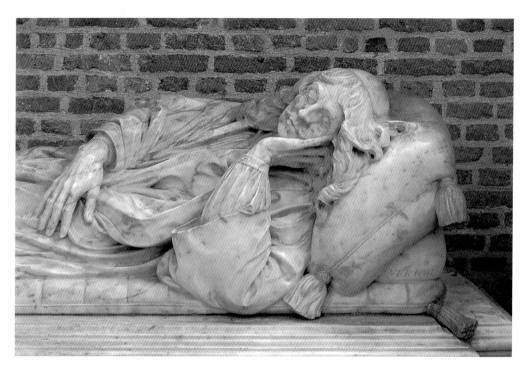

Rombout Verhulst
Tomb of Johan Polyander van
Kerchoven, 1663
Marble
St. Peter's, Leyden

BELOW AND OPPOSITE:
Hendrik Frans Verbruggen
Pulpit and detail (Eve and Death before
the expulsion from paradise), 1695–99
Oak and gilding
Height c. 700 cm, width c. 350 cm,
depth c. 200 cm
Church of St. Michael and St. Gudula,
Brussels

ignored by art historians. The church decoration in the nave of St. Gudula in Brussels is outstanding in both size and design. Before Hendrik Frans Verbruggen (1654–1724) was commissioned by the Jesuits in Louvain to work on this project in 1695, he had worked on numerous decorative schemes for churches in Antwerp, like his father Pieter Verbruggen (1615–86). In his master work at St. Gudula, Verbruggen chose to combine scenes from the Old and New Testaments in a representation of salvation and redemption. The platform is supported on a massive tree trunk, the boughs and branches of which extend beyond the tester. In front of it, Adam and Eve are seen being driven out of paradise by an angel brandishing a sword. In an iconographical deviation from the typological pattern, they are accompanied by the skeletal figure of Death. This scene is paired by that of the Virgin with the Christ Child on the tester, where the mother of God is represented as the new Eve and redeemer of humanity who kills the serpent. Whereas the naturalistic representation of flora and fauna refers to the earthly realm, the tester, borne up by angels, floats in the heavenly sphere. Between them is the platform, its shape hinting at the globe of the earth, suggesting not only a burden on the backs of our progenitors but also, as an attribute of the Virgin, an ideal link to the mother of God. "The platform as the globe becomes a place where the... Church involves its earthly representative in the visual unfolding of the Redemption and proclaims its message from there," writes Susanne Geese. Erected in 1699 in the Jesuit church in Louvain, the pulpit was moved to its present position after the dissolution of the Society of Jesus in 1773.

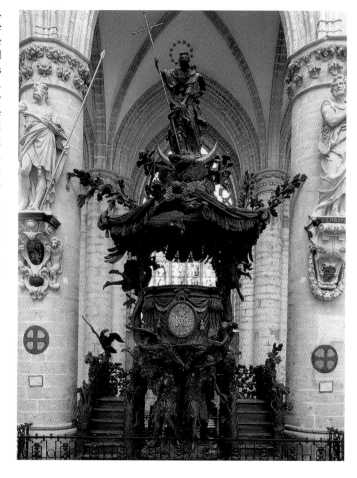

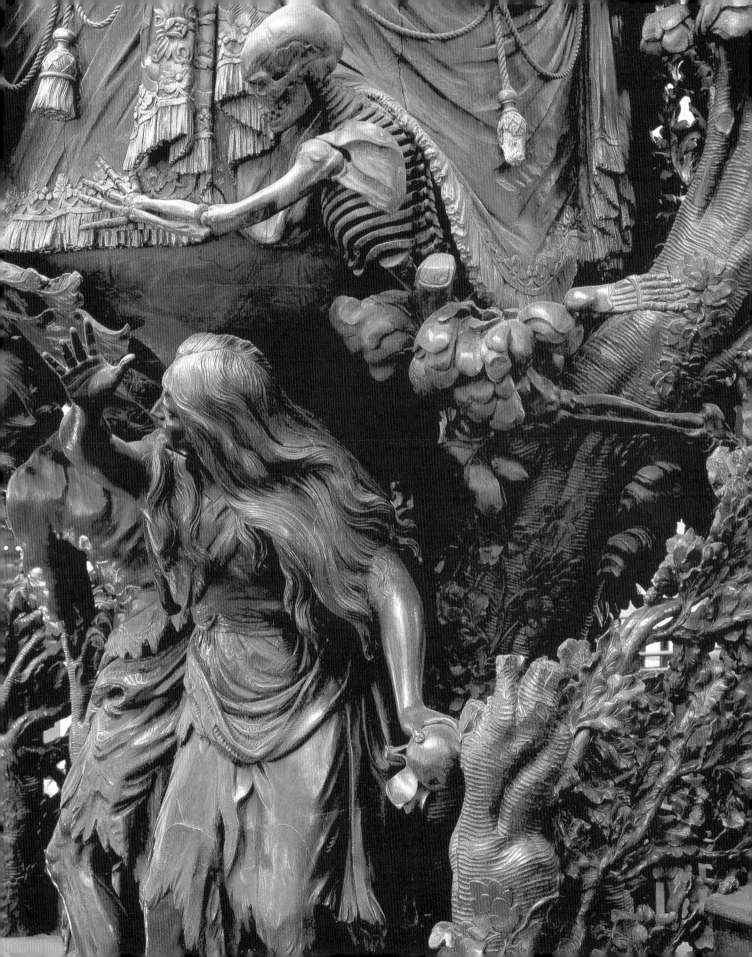

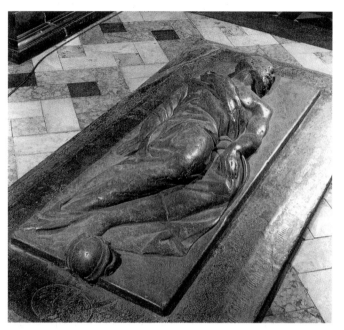

Nicholas Stone the Elder
Tomb of Sir William Curle, 1617
Marble, lifesize
Hatfield House, Hertfordshire

Baroque Sculpture in Britain

While English art of the first half of the seventeenth century was largely dominated by the architectural achievements of the London painter and architect Inigo Jones (1573–1652), sculpture of this period was influenced particularly by trends brought over by refugees of the religious wars on the European continent, in particular Holland. One of the major English sculptors of the period is Nicholas Stone (1586–1647) from Woodbury, near Exeter. He spent the last two years of his apprenticeship in the London workshop of Isaac James, who may have recommended him to Hendrik de Keyser in 1606, during the latter's two-year stay in England. Stone returned to Holland with Hendrik as his associate, where he remained until 1613 and married his teacher's daughter before returning to London.

In the Dutchman's workshop Stone came into contact with sculpture of an artistic quality that he had not encountered in his homeland and which was ultimately to play a considerable role in the revival of contemporary English sculpture, particularly in the important field of tomb monuments. It was Stone who introduced the reclining figure without hands raised in prayer into the canon of English sculpture. The tomb of Lady Elizabeth Carey, created during the subject's lifetime, shows the deceased lying on a raised tomb (see left)

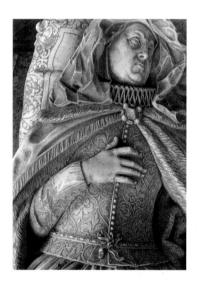

Nicholas Stone the Elder
Tomb of Lady Elizabeth Carey, 1617–18
Marble, lifesize
Stowe Nine Churches, Northamptonshire

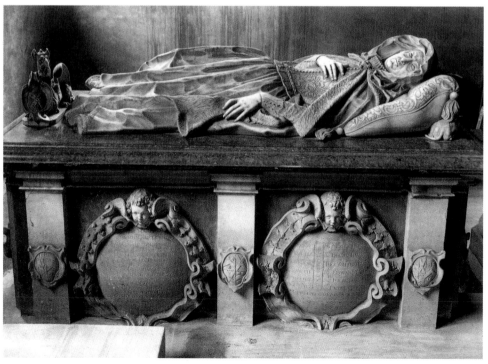

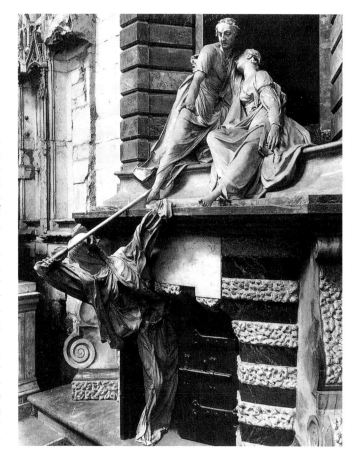

with her right hand on her breast. The black marble slab forms a simple but effective contrast to the carefully detailed figure. The splendid and minutely finished clothing is matched by a naturalism in the depiction of the dead woman's face that is carefully observed and reflects the general trend of the period for the replacement of the prestige tomb by a more intimate portrayal of death. In the tomb of Sir William Curle (see left), the deceased appears to be sleeping, with limbs relaxed on a tombstone that scarcely rises above ground level. The naked corpse is covered only by a thin cloth. Stone's many innovations had a notably enlivening effect on contemporary English sculpture. He was also active as an architect and site supervisor on some of Inigo Jones's projects. His son Nicholas the Younger (1618–47) was both pupil and assistant in his workshop. Two surviving notebooks provide a detailed insight into the life, work, and output of the Stones.

The leading English rococo sculptor was in fact a Frenchman born in Lyons. Louis-François Roubiliac (1702–62) probably trained under Balthasar Permoser in Dresden and then under Nicolas Coustou in Paris. In 1730, as a pupil at the Académie Royale de Peinture et Sculpture he was awarded second prize in the Prix de Rome competition. Around 1730 he went to England and in 1735 married a Huguenot, Catherine Helot. Even his first work, commis-

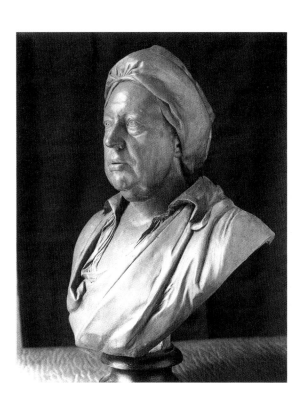

sioned by Jonathan Tyers, the proprietor of Vauxhall Gardens, a seated figure of George Frideric Handel (1738), brought immediate success. Instead of Apollo or Orpheus, the traditional subjects of musical allegory, Roubiliac chose to portray the famous living composer on a pedestal playing his lyre. In composition and expression this piece may be seen as one of the principal works of English rococo; it is also one of the earliest memorials to a living artist.

Among Roubiliac's best known works is the tomb of Joseph and Lady Elizabeth Nightingale, (1758–61) (see above). Lady Elizabeth died in 1731 after a miscarriage brought about by shock caused by lightning. Her son commissioned the tomb after the death of his father in 1752. In this composition, Death steps forth from his black vault and aims his thunderbolt at the young swooning Lady Elizabeth, while her horrified husband attempts in vain to ward off the event. Like many tombs of this period, it illustrates a story, although this is not a conventional tale of Christian redemption but one representing the tragic triumph of death.

Roubiliac was known as a virtuoso portrait sculptor who was more interested in creating realistic likenesses than idealized, pretentious depictions (see left); his sitters are often shown in simple contemporary clothing.

Hans Krumper
Duke Albrecht V of Bavaria, from the
tomb of Emperor Ludwig the Bavarian,
1619–22
Bronze, over-life-size
Frauenkirche, Munich

Baroque Sculpture in Germany and Austria: Late Sixteenth to Mid-Seventeenth Centuries

After Protestant iconoclasm had been pushed back in parts of the Holy Roman Empire in favor of the aesthetic demands of the Counter-Reformation, towards the end of the sixteenth and during the seventeenth century, centers of art emerged in southern Germany. In particular, this led to a strong demand for contemporary large-scale sculptures. Dutch artists were prominent both in architecture and sculpture, which entered into a new relationship with each other during this period, partly on the basis of the artists' extensive training in Italy.

The Amsterdam sculptor Hubert Gerhard (c. 1550–1622/23), for example, had worked in the Florentine workshop of Giambologna until he was summoned to southern Germany by the banker Hans Fugger to produce what was to be the first monumental fountain in the Florentine style north of the Alps for his country house at Kirch-

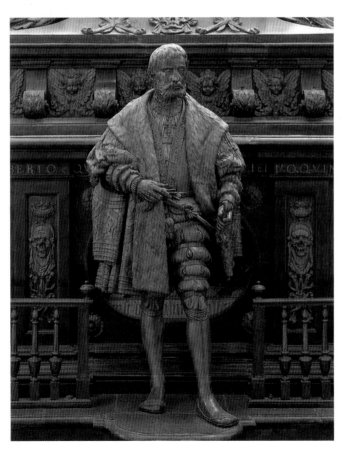

heim. Gerhard was commissioned to produce a fountain to commemorate the Emperor Augustus, the legendary founder of Augsburg (see right); the scheme was commissioned by the city on its 1,600th anniversary in 1589. Four river gods set on the edge of the fountain basin symbolize the four rivers of Augsburg and their individual economic roles, while the figure of Augustus turns with raised arm towards the town hall, the seat of the citizens whose only allegiance is to the emperor. Gerhard's bronze figure of the Archangel Michael (see right) conquering the dragon adorns the facade of the church of St. Michael in Munich, built in 1583–90 by the architect Friedrich Sustris for the Jesuits. The figure is an allegory of the triumph over unbelief in the struggle of the Counter-Reformation against Protestantism.

Hans Krumper from Weilheim (1570–1634) worked in close collaboration with his teachers Gerhard and Sustris. On completing his training in 1590, Krumper went first to Italy, then two years later married Sustris's daughter and by 1594 was taken on as William V's court sculptor. It was probably due to his father-in-law's rank that in 1599 he was also appointed court architect. As architect and sculptor, Krumper combined two key roles in the large-scale rebuilding of the official electoral palace, decorating it with allegories of the cardinal virtues and the "Patrona Bavariae" [patron of Bavaria] in the middle of the facade (see right). The mother of God appears as the queen of heaven with crown and scepter in her left hand. She rests her right foot on the crescent moon, while holding the child with the imperial orb with her right arm. Planned by Krumper from 1611, modeled in 1614, and cast by Bartholomeus Wenglein the following year, the figure provides the palace (and thereby the rule of Maximilian I) with an element of piety and legitimacy against a background of blossoming Counter-Reformation religiosity. Krumper's ducal figures from the tomb of Ludwig of Bavaria (see left) were originally intended for the tomb of William V. They were executed by Dionys Frey and are among the leading examples of bronze-casting in Munich.

Adriaen de Vries (c. 1545–1626) was another Fleming who passed through the Florentine workshop of Giambologna. There he absorbed a formal mannerist repertoire, moving on in 1588 to the duchy of Savoy, where he was appointed court sculptor. Between 1596 and 1602, he executed the two other major fountains in Augsburg, a further expression of imperial ostentation. These were the Merkurbrunnen [Mercury Fountain] and the Herkulebrunne [Hercules Fountain] (see right); the bronze sculptures on these structures were produced in the bronze foundry of Wolfgang Neidhart the Younger.

Among the most impressive works by Adriaen de Vries is the *Man of Sorrows* (see p. 324, below) executed in 1607 at the commission of Prince Carl von Liechtenstein, when the artist was already established as the official sculptor to Rudolf II at the court in Prague. The typology of the man of sorrows sitting alone on the Via

Hubert Gerhard
Archangel Michael, 1588
Bronze, over-life-size
West front of St. Michael, Munich

Hans Krumper
Patrona Bavariae, 1615(?)
Bronze, height c. 300 cm
Facade of ducal seat, Munich

Hubert Gerhard
Augustus Fountain, 1589–1594
Detail of bronze figures
Augsburg

Adriaen de Vries
Hercules Fountain, 1596–1602
Bronze figures
Augsburg

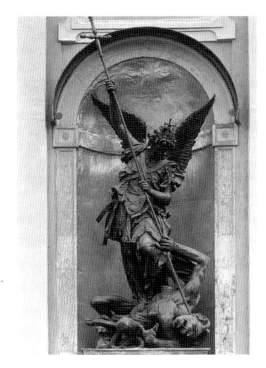

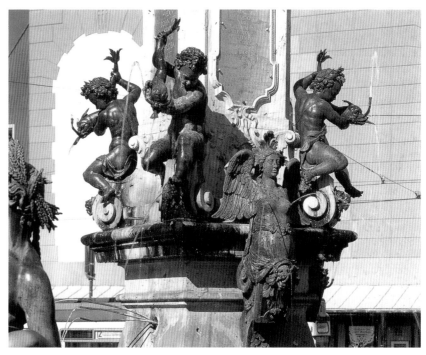

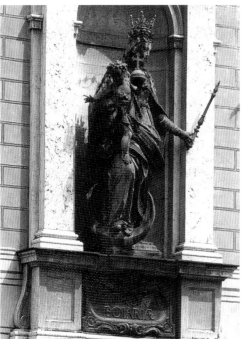

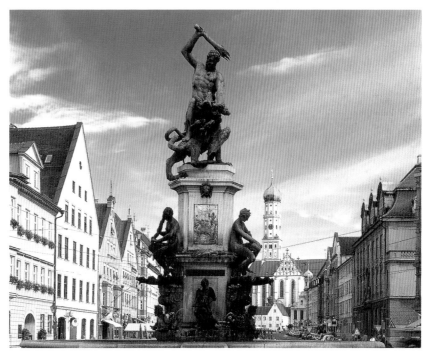

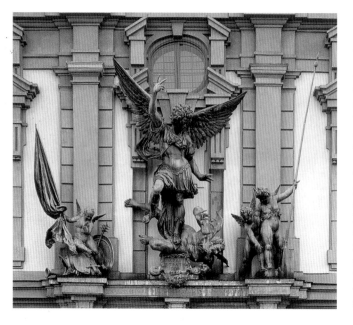

event. Reichle's mastery of the medium is still more evident in the bronze figures of the altar of the crucifix in St. Ulrich and St. Afra (see right and p. 327, top left). With wide gestures, the voluminous figures lay claim to the broad space of the crossing, in which they are clearly defined by sharp lines. The group, which consists of Christ on the cross and the grieving Virgin, with St. Mary Magdalene and St. John standing by, may be considered as the joint work of the sculptor and the Augsburg bronze foundry run by Wolfgang Neidhart the Younger, a member of an old brass-founding family. Neidhart's skills were clearly equal to those demonstrated by the foundry in Nuremberg.

The light late-gothic church interior of St. Ulrich and Afra is distinguished by the three multi-storey monumental carved altars (see right) by the Weilheim sculptor Hans Degler (1564–1634/35); their structure derives from the type of the now lost tabernacle in the Dominican church of Augsburg which was built in 1518 in the renaissance style. On a plinth running the breadth of the altar table rests a distinct tabernacle area. Above this rises a massive main storey in the style of a classical triumphal arch. It takes up the principal theme in its central arch, while saints in the pierced side arcades witness the event. Through the broken pediment of the attic storey rises another system of niches, which again supports the extension.

Dolorosa was introduced in the title page of the *Large Passion* (1511) by Albrecht Dürer (1471–1528). Nonethelesss, this composition does not represent a straightforward adaptation of the image in a woodcut into a three-dimensional bronze sculpture. Whereas Dürer had intended to establish the concept of the passion and generalize it by showing Christ with the crown of thorns and wound marks, Adriaen de Vries shows the momentousness of human suffering on the edge of the Via Dolorosa, matching a Counter-Reformation need for empathetic piety. However the expression of suffering on Christ's face in the sculpture stands in stark contrast to the athletic body modeled on the Belevedere torso, suggesting an art in transition from late mannerism to baroque.

Shortly after Adriaen de Vries, Hans Reichle (c. 1570–1624) from Schongau found himself in Augsburg; his principal works are a series of outstanding monumental bronzes. Reichle, another pupil of Giambologna who is recorded as being employed in his workshop in Florence from 1588, came to Augsburg in 1602 and in the following year began work on the *Archangel Michael* for the Arsenal (see above), completing it by 1606. Over-life-size, the archangel stands with flaming sword (lost) raised triumphantly over the body of the fallen Lucifer, whose horror is expressed in a grisly naturalistic grimace. Clearly owing much to a work illustrating the same subject produced by the Flemish sculptor Hubert Gerhard, Reichle's group is nonetheless more spatially expansive, and as the sculpture is not confined to a niche here, the ensemble is widened to make room for the flanking putti; the entire facade in fact serves as a stage for the

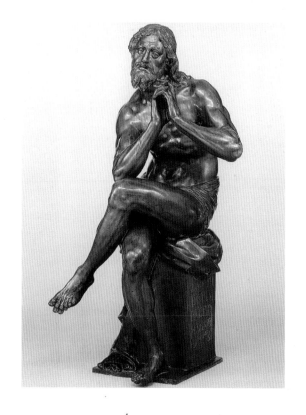

Choir with *Crucifixion* by Hans Reichle, 1605
Altars by Hans Degler, 1604–7
Collegiate church of St. Ulrich and St. Afra, Augsburg

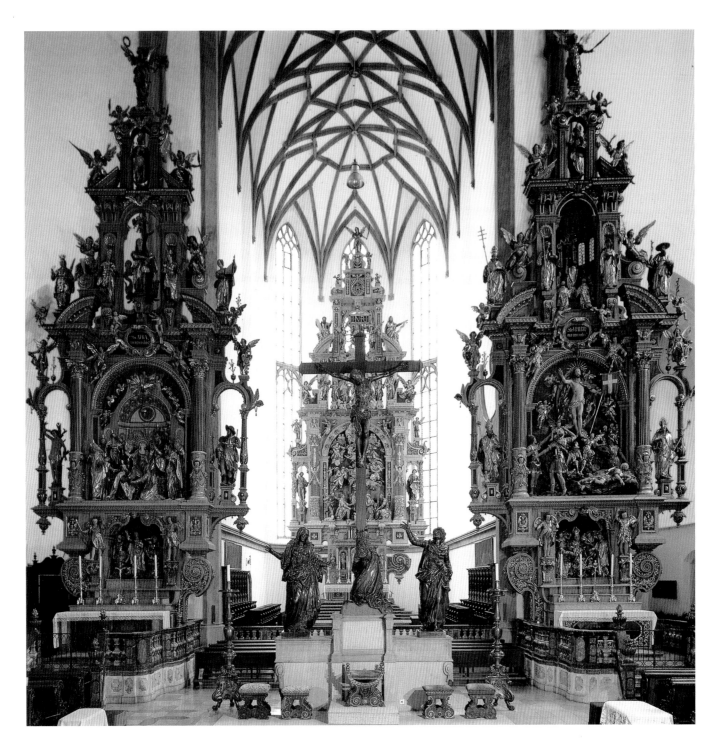

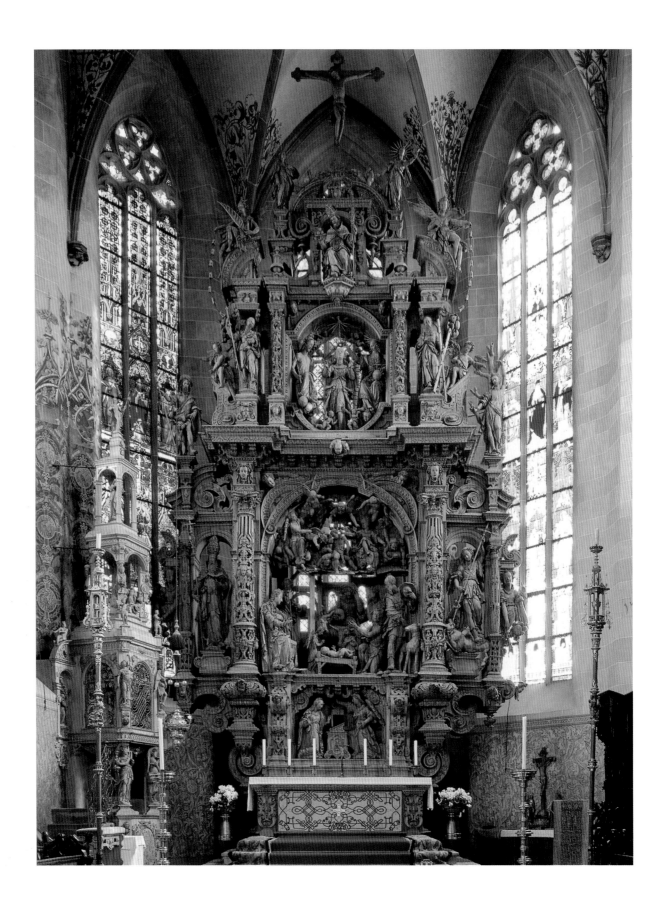

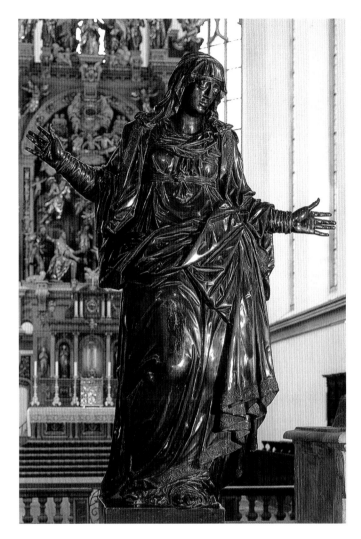

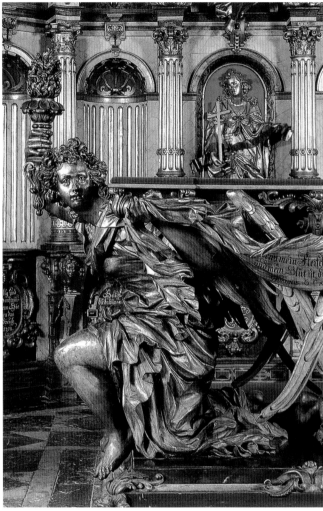

Hans Reichle
Mater Dolorosa (figure from
Crucifixion), 1605
Bronze, height 190 cm
St. Ulrich and St. Afra,
Augsburg

Eckbert Wolff the Younger
Altar table (left)
Detail of angel holding torch,
1601–4 (above)
Wood, gilt
Palace chapel, Bückeburg

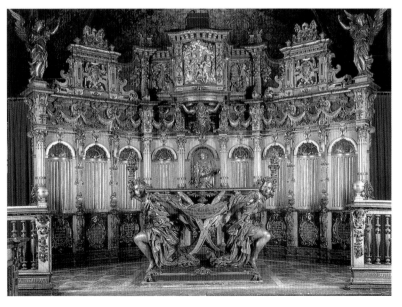

OPPOSITE:
Jörg Zürn
Altar of Our Lady, 1613–16
Limewood, unpainted
Church of St. Nicholas,
Überlingen

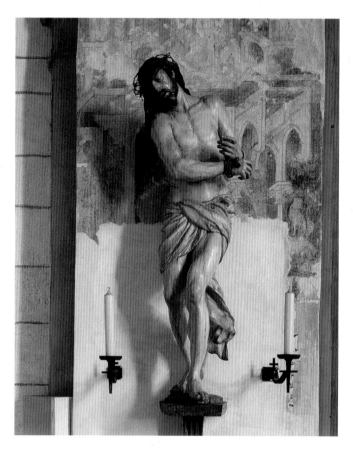

On numerous projections, capitals, and volutes, putti and saints populate the altar structure. As on the stage of the spiritual drama of the Counter-Reformation, the main themes of the altars appear in the central arches of the main storey, specifically the high feasts of the church year, Christmas, Easter, and Pentecost.

In other areas of Germany great altars were produced even before the Thirty Years War; these can be partly considered successors to Hans Degler's altar in Augsburg. The splendid altar of Our Lady in the church of St. Nicholas in Überlingen (see p. 326) was created by a pupil of Degler, the woodcarver Jörg Zürn from Waldsee (c. 1583–1635), between 1609 and 1613. Over the Annunciation in the predella, a central arch opens with the adoration of the shepherds. Above this is a depiction of the coronation of the Virgin and the patron saint is seen in the extension. Even though this enormous assembly of sculpture still bears many of the features of late gothic winged altars, it does contain novel lighting effects and naturalistic, stage-like, three-dimensional set pieces in a complex spatial relationship. Further, the unpainted figures continue the German tradition of woodcarving. This work represents a transition from the German altarpiece of the late gothic period to the high baroque altar. By contrast, the passion altar created around 1610 for the palace chapel at Aschaffenburg by the leading Franconian sculptor of the early seventeenth century, Johannes Juncker (c. 1582-post 1623) suggests a strong adherence to a late renaissance formalism, with a strict structure formed of red and black marble; the many alabaster figures and scenes filling the intervening areas point to an almost mannerist *horror vacui* [horror of emptiness].

During the early seventeenth century countless grand houses and churches were built, and even in the Protestant areas, where the princes took over ecclesiastical possessions almost entirely, new palaces provided sculptors with a numerous opportunities. The court in Bückeburg, for example, developed into a center of independent artistic activity as a result of the cultural renaissance along the Weser. Three members of the Wolff family, Eckbert the Elder and his sons Eckbert the Younger (died c. 1608) and Jonas all worked on the furnishing of the palace at Bückeburg. In the palace chapel, life-size kneeling angels support the altar table (see p. 327), each carrying a burning torch. This composition was produced between 1601 and 1604, like the Venus on the Door of the Gods in the Golden Hall; with this design the younger Eckbert seems to have translated German mannerism into the forms of an early native baroque style.

As in many other places, developments of this sort were impeded by the Thirty Years War. However, Georg Petel of Weilheim (1601/2–34), probably the most outstanding and best-known German sculptor of the early seventeenth century, seems initially to have avoided the decline. Presumably trained by his guardian, the sculptor Bartholoma Steinle, his travels as a journeyman took him from Munich (c. 1620) to the Netherlands and then to Paris before he went to Italy for an extended period. In Rome, he was in close contact with the Flemish sculptor François Duquesnoy and the painter Anthony van Dyck. He produced numerous sculptures in wood and bronze which display a monumentality sustained by the expressive richness of baroque rhetoric but which at the same time can demonstrate restraint in movement in the manner illustrated by the *Ecce Homo* (see above). Petel also produced small-scale works in wood and ivory, creating innovative designs that are in some respects even more interesting than the large-scale works. In 1633 Petel set off on another trip to the Low Countries, where he made a terracotta bust of Rubens, an artist who had shown a paternal interest in him. When Augsburg was besieged the following year by the imperial army, the thirty-three-year-old Petel was among the twelve thousand victims of who died of starvation and plague.

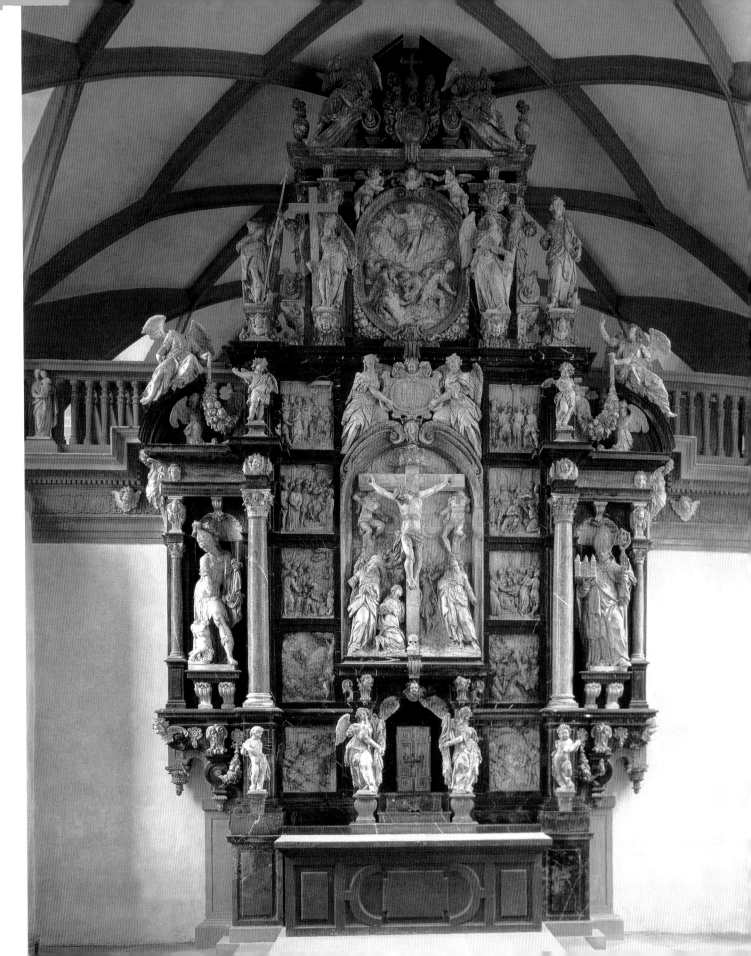

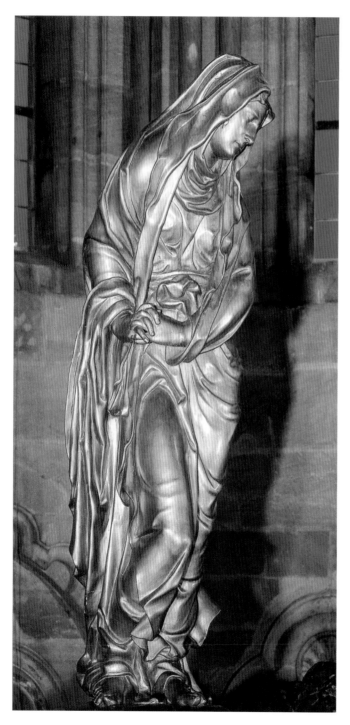

Justus Glesker
Crucifixion (right)
Mater Dolorosa (below) 1648–49
Wood, regilded, height of Christ 220 cm
Bamberg cathedral

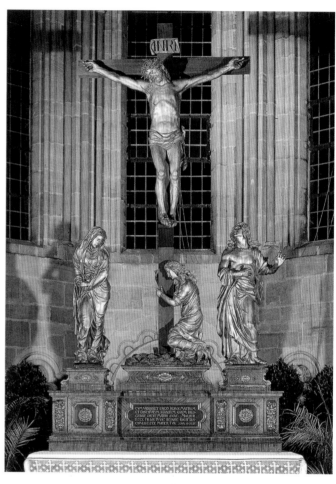

The Second Half of the Seventeenth Century

During the Thirty Years War, the production of large-scale sculptures virtually came to a halt in many areas. The Frankfurt sculptor Justus Glesker (born between 1610 and 1623, died 1678) was fortunate in obtaining the first important large-scale commission in Franconia in 1648, the year of the peace treaty (presumably on the recommendation of the younger Matthias Merian) for the refurbishing of Bamberg cathedral in the baroque style. Glesker was a native of Hamelin but his early life is shrouded in mystery. Even the year of his birth can only be loosely established, and the information that he traveled first to the Netherlands and then Italy is known only from Sandrart. The sudden emergence of this sculptor during a period when continuous artistic activity in the field was almost impossible was considered until recently a source of irritation to art historians more than anything else. This evident annoyance appears to be com-

Martin and Michael Zürn
Holy Knights St. Florian (above) *and St. Sebastian*, 1638–39
Wood, height of St. Florian 286 cm, St. Sebastian 289 cm
Sculpture gallery, Staatliche Museen, Berlin

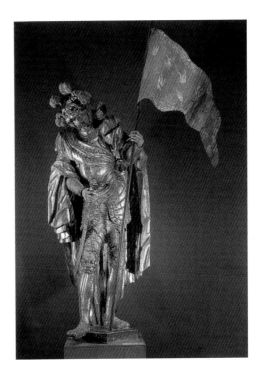

pounded by the fact that little of what is believed to have been an extensive œuvre exists today, but the surviving works are of astonishingly high quality. Taking into account the inevitable gaps in our current knowledge of Glesker's work, his *Crucifixion* (see left) from Bamberg should nonetheless be seen as one of his principal works. Even from an art historical perspective, however, his work is difficult to categorize on the basis of conventional stylistic criteria. His knowledge of Roman art as translated by the mannerism of the 1630s and 1640s is most evident in the *Mater Dolorosa* from the *Crucifixion*. Not only is the shape of the body recognizable beneath the drapery, but the pose of the Virgin herself adopts the *figura serpentinata* motif. The concentrated inner tension in which the grieving figure is frozen suggests a direct derivation of the classical *contrapposto* concept of movement. In such naturalistic anatomically detailed representations of the naked body, as seen in the Florence ivory figure of St. Sebastian (see p. 352, below right), Glesker reveals his exceptional artistic talents as well as his thorough training in the sculptural art of antiquity and the Italian Renaissance. These aspects of his work also made Glesker an isolated phenomenon in the stylistic development of contemporary sculpture.

The monumental *Holy Knights* carved by Martin Zürn (1585/1590–after 1665) for the high altar of the parish church at Wasserburg am Inn are, by contrast, entirely in the mainstream tradition of German gothic. These figures were removed from the church in the nineteenth century and were long believed to be lost until they turned up in the mid-1950s in a Californian hotel, from where they were acquired in 1958 by the Staatliche Museen in Berlin. The figures were produced as a result of an oath by the citizens of Wasserburg in the plague year 1634 to renovate the parish church from top to bottom and install new altars. The job was awarded to the Swabian immigrant brothers Martin and Michael Zürn who were based in nearby Seeon.

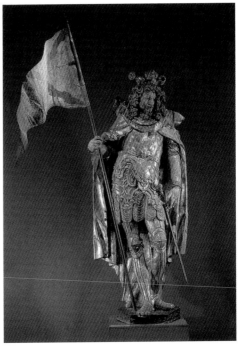

In marked contrast to Glesker's figures, for example, the Zürn brothers' *Holy Knights* owe little to an understanding of the ideal of beauty absorbed from classical sculpture in the depiction of the human body. The translation of facial features and limbs to wood bears little relation to anatomical reality and does not constitute an imitation of nature. In fact, they are representative of a surviving medieval tradition in sculpture where the main focus was on the illustration of the saint and aspects of his life in three dimensions. These works (which are characteristic in this respect of much contemporary sculpture in southern Germany) indicate how closely the sculptural activity of the time was associated with the artistically confining guild system run by the burghers. "That the Zürns and others never had any association with more international artistic trends, and probably never tried to, was based primarily on socioeconomic factors. The basis of their economic existence lay precisely in the fact that they were first-class guild craftsmen who were known and recommended as such in burgher circles," writes Claus

Thomas Schwanthaler
Double altar, 1675–76
Wood, painted and gilt
St. Wolfgang am Abersee,
Salzkammergut

BELOW LEFT:
Meinrad Guggenbichler
St. Sebastian, c. 1682
Painted wood, slightly under life-size
Mondsee Museum

BELOW CENTER:
Meinrad Guggenbichler
St. Roch, c. 1682
Painted wood, slightly under life-size
Mondsee Museum

BELOW RIGHT:
Meinrad Guggenbichler
Christ with Crown of Thorns, c. 1682
Painted wood, slightly under life-size
Former monastery church, Mondsee

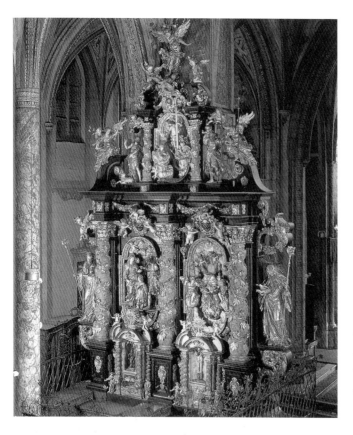

Zoege von Manteuffel. Thus, training in the workshops focused far less on academic canons and more on traditional craft skills. As a result, patrons of major standing (the nobility or wealthy bourgeoisie) would give preference to foreign artists from Italy or the Netherlands. Sculptures of this kind could be of high artistic quality nonetheless, and this is demonstrated by the intelligent manner in which the content is of these figures is related to the context of the altar.

In October 1633 a sculptor is mentioned in the wedding register of the parish of Ried in the district of the river Inn who, as it turned out, was to be the ancestor of a family of sculptors active over five generations or more than two hundred and fifty years. Hans Schwabenthaler (c. 1600–56) worked in the style of the Munich court sculptors, mainly Krumper and Degler; he brought their style to Ried and passed it on to his son Thomas. Although Thomas Schwanthaler (1634–1707; he had changed his name by 1679) was originally intended for the priesthood, at the age of twenty-two he was obliged to take over his father's business. However, it was not until he married the daughter of a member of the bourgeoisie that he gained extensive commissions and established a reputation in the face of his competitors. Commissions in Zell am Pettenfirst, Atzbach, Ungenach, and Haag were followed by work in Salzburg, Kremsmünster, and Lambach, and, finally, Mondsee monastery, St. Wolfgang am Abersee, and the collegiate church of the Augustinian canons in Reichersberg am Inn. His *Madonna of the Misericordia* in Andorf near Schärding displays softly handled heavy drapery, its billowing folds, held up by angels, providing shelter for the faithful. The iconography is derived from the medieval law which permitted aristocractic women to grant refuge under their veils or cloak to vic-

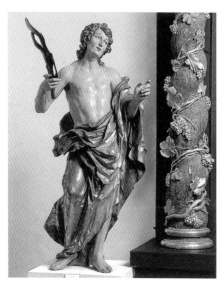

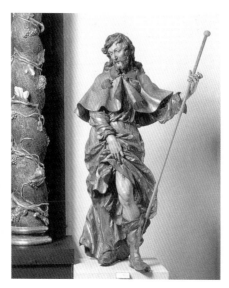

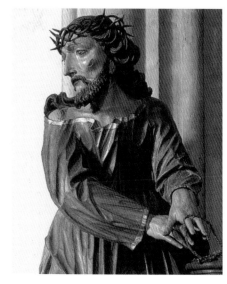

Salzburg Master (Waldburg?)
Coronation of the Virgin altar, 1626
Wood, painted and gilt
Former monastery church, Mondsee

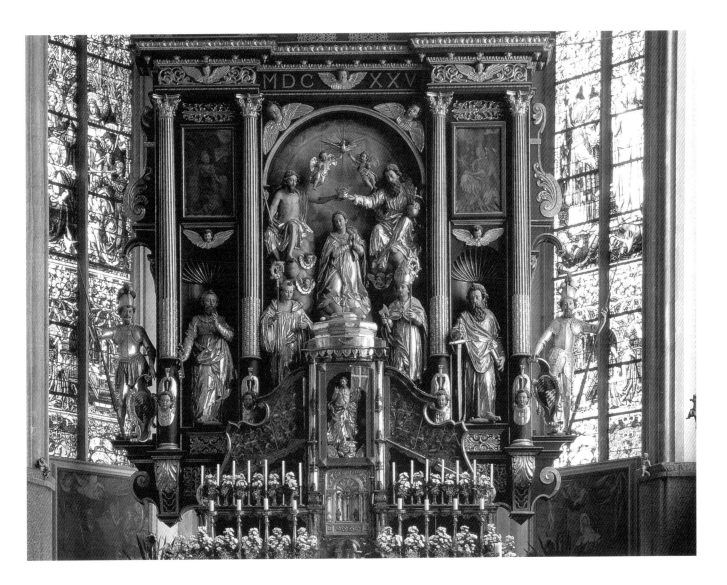

tims of persecution who called on them as advocates, a legal practice that was later frequently symbolically applied to female saints and to the mother of God in particular.

Johann Meinrad Guggenbichler (1649–1723) continued the Alpine carving tradition of Schwantaler and from 1675 was employed in the monastery at Mondsee. From the workshop he established there in 1679, he turned out numerous painted wooden figures in which he developed the heavy representation of drapery and body gestures used by older masters as a means of expressing spiritual introspection. Around 1690, the expressions of his figures,

in the restlessness of drapery and intensfied pathos of gesture, become almost transfigured; the sculptor's empathy for the martyr-dom of the passion is linked by an evident feeling for beauty (see left). At the same time, Guggenbichler uses forms which, with their fleshy physiognomies and their fluttering draperies, serve to rein-force somewhat the widely held prejudice that baroque sculpture is essentially about "plump little angels." Nonetheless, Guggenbichler's work is entirely representative of Alpine baroque sculpture.

Before Matthias Rauchmiller (1645–86) from Radolfzell on Lake Constance went to work in the Rhineland around 1670, he went on

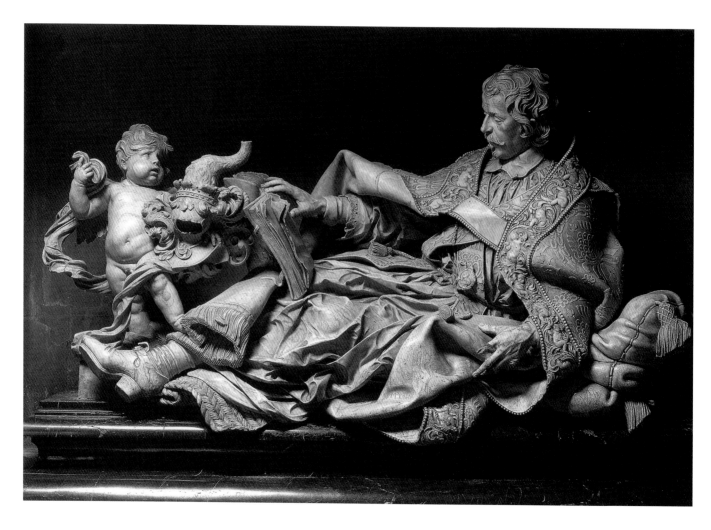

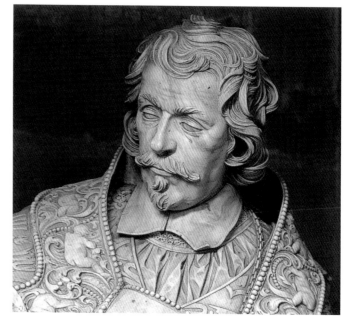

Matthias Rauchmiller
Tomb of Karl von Metternich, and detail (left), c. 1675
Marble, slightly over-life-size
Frauenkirche, Trier

his journeyman travels to Holland and Antwerp where he came into contact with Rubens and his circle. Shortly before he settled in Austria, he designed the tomb of Karl von Metternich (see above and right) in Trier in 1675. This powerfully expressive work suggests a completely new approach to memorial sculpture under the German high baroque. The figure of the deceased reclines with his sightless eyes apparently having just read a book, in a composition which seems to enhance the sense of immediacy in the scene. The forehead is wrinkled in a frown, the hair falls casually about the head. The veins stand out on his hands, and the pages of the book seem to have been flicked over. Even the splendid regalia has slipped and is crumpled. All courtly pretensions are rejected here in favor of a memorial to the man himself. Just a year later, when already in Vienna, Rauchmiller produced the famous signed ivory tankard featuring the *Rape of the Sabine Woman*, now in the Liechtenstein collection in Vaduz. In Prague in 1681 he made a terracotta maquette of the figure of St. John Nepomuk, destined for the end of the

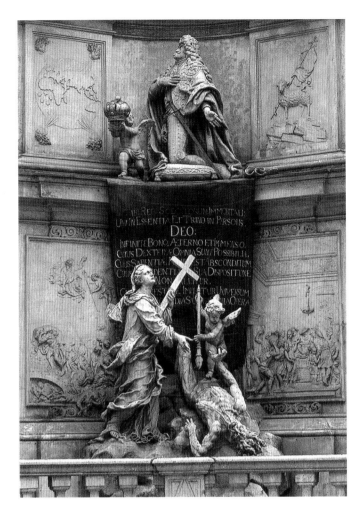

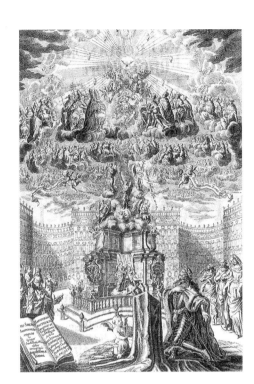

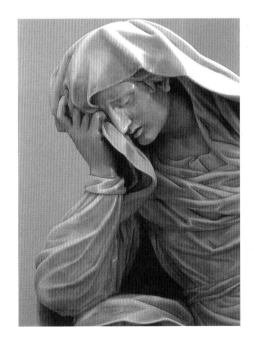

Charles Bridge. This was a devotional image that would serve as a model for countless imitations.

Among his late works was a design for the Trinity Column in Vienna. Like the *Holy Knights* of Wasserburg, the *Trinity Column* or *Plague Column* (see above) is a highly important monument. Situated in the Graben in Vienna, it was built as a result of Emperor Leopold I's vow in 1679 to erect such a memorial in honor of the holy trinity in order to hasten the end of the plague. A design was first sought from Matthias Rauchmiller to replace an early temporary wooden column by Johann Frühwirth (1640–1710) with a marble structure, but the Turkish siege and the death of the sculptor in 1686 meant that this scheme was never carried out. Eventually an amended design by Johann Fischer von Erlach (1656–1723) and Ludovico Burnacini (1636–1707) was erected. The plinth is triangular, symbolizing the Trinity, and each face is devoted to one of the three divine aspects. Six reliefs showing "histories," principally referring to representations of biblical history, were executed by Johann Ignaz Bendl, based on instructions by Fischer.

Burnacini gave the column the shape of an obelisk shrouded in cloud, while Paul Strudel (1648–1708) executed the prominent sculptures on the plinth. On the main face is the *Allegory of Faith* (see above), in which the plague is pushed into the depths by a

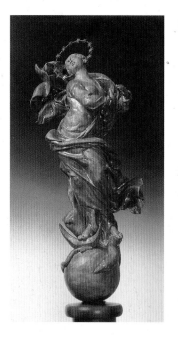

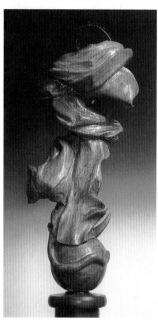

Matthias Steinl
Virgin of the Immaculate Conception (front and rear views), 1688
Wood, once gilded, height 93 cm
Liebighaus, Frankfurt

Ehrgott Bernhard Bendl
St. John the Evangelist, 1697
Painted wood, height 197 cm

Germanisches Nationalmuseum, Nuremberg
OPPOSITE:
Andreas Schlüter
Equestrian statue of the Great Elector, Frederick William I of Brandenburg, 1689–1703
Bronze, height 290 cm, height of stone plinth 270 cm

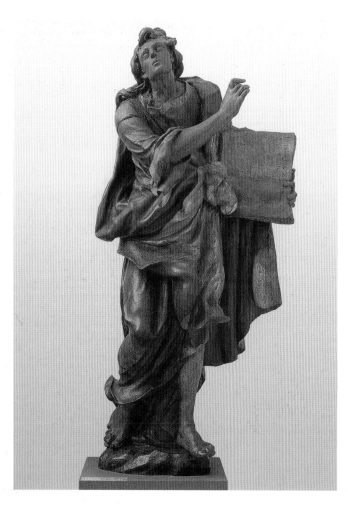

woman, while above, the kneeling emperor calls for divine assistance. Building the column consumed the enormous sum of seventy thousand florins in 1692; the dedication took place in 1693.

A bold design by the Viennese court sculptor Matthias Steinl (1643–1727) for the Madonna of the Immaculate Conception is a fine example of Austrian high baroque (see left, now in Frankfurt); it was executed as a study. Standing with her right foot on the crescent moon, balanced on the globe, the figure is shown defying gravity in a violently contorted pose, as prescribed by the Italian mannerists. Like the apocalyptic woman in Revelations (12, 1), she is ringed by twelve stars. Following the perspective around, the beholder's gaze is led by the spiral line of the drapery in a perpetual transformation of physical substance to the point of complete dematerialization. In the rear view, the figure appears merely as the shape of a cloud floating on the sky. Within the framework of Counter-Reformation iconography, the image of the Immaculate Conception represents the central religious symbol of the Catholic church, which in the imperial house of Habsburg forms part of a further tradition of war-related veneration of the Virgin. A monumental version in bronze, which was not executed, was probably based on the formerly gilt Frankfurt figure, and would have been conceived as part of a spatially expansive ensemble, whose religious protection was intended to encompass the whole of Vienna in the face of the Turkish siege.

Ehrgott Bernhard Bendl (1660–1738) came from Pfarrkirchen in Lower Bavaria and was trained initially by his father. He spent six years on the road as a journeyman before settling in Augsburg where in 1687 he acquired master status in the guild. His work in all the major sculptural media was of such notable quality that even in the eighteenth century he was compared with Georg Petel. His *St. John the Evangelist* (see left) belongs to a group of six massive statues comprising the four evangelists, St. Paul, and a figure of the Savior, which were erected in St. George's in Augsburg in 1697. With his head raised in visionary pose, the evangelist is portrayed at the moment of divine inspiration, which is transmitted to his writing of the gospel. In his left hand he holds the open book with the opening words: "In principo erat verbum" [In the beginning was the Word]; his right hand once held a quill which is now lost. The weighty, scrolled folds of drapery enhance the pathos of the composition, a style which would gradually be toned down as Bendl modified his style in the eighteenth century.

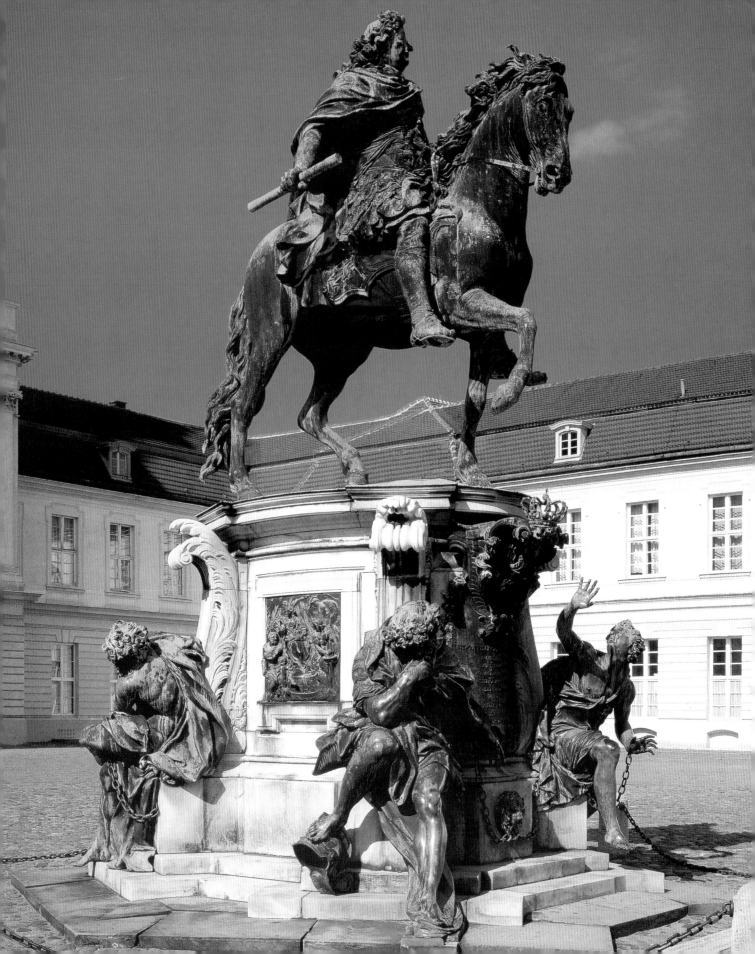

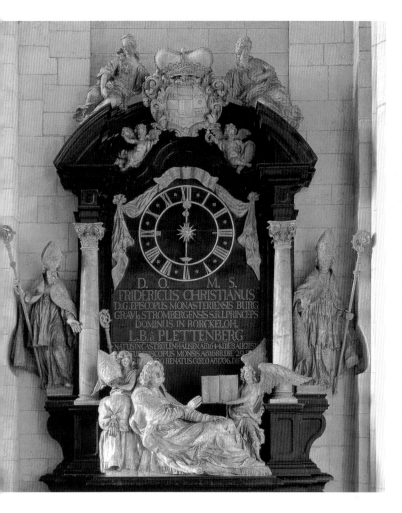

Johann Mauritz Gröninger, Johann Wilhelm Gröninger, and Gottfried Laurenz Pictorius
Tomb of prince-bishop Friedrich Christian von Plettenberg, begun 1707
Marble and alabaster
Münster cathedral

The Eighteenth Century and Rococo Sculpture

Among the outstanding European sculptors and architects of the turn of the century was Andreas Schlüter (c. 1660–1714) who came from Gdansk (Danzig). As a sculptor, he trained under Christoph Sapovius; as an architect, he was self-taught. Between 1681 and 1694 he was involved in numerous projects in Warsaw, but in 1694 came to Berlin as official court sculptor to the Brandenburg Elector. His principal sculptural and architectural works were produced in Berlin. In 1707, he was suspended from office as palace architect and left Berlin for St. Petersburg on the invitation of the Czar. He died there in 1714.

Schlüter's most important sculptural work is the monumental equestrian statue of the Great Elector, Frederick William I, in Berlin (see p. 337). It is not only one of the most important equestrian stat-

ues in the baroque style but also the first monument of its kind in Germany to be displayed outside. The imperial posture of the Elector, whose strength alone is capable of reining in the elemental energy of the horse, gives expression to the fame of the ruler who founded the power and political influence of Brandenburg. Accordingly, the monument was originally set up in a dominant urban position on the Long Bridge on the lines of perspective leading towards the King's Gate of the palace in Berlin. The figures on the plinth are four slaves symbolizing the temperaments and were designed in the tradition of the late Renaissance; they were executed by other sculptors.

Balthasar Permoser (1651–1732) from the Chiemgau region, spent fourteen years (from 1675 to 1689) living and working in Italy before he was summoned to Dresden as court sculptor. He worked during his early career in Venice, Rome, and Florence. Bernini had the greatest impact on his work, but Permoser's many sculptures also demonstrated elements of renaissance restraint. In Dresden, where he had been summoned by the Elector John George III, he produced numerous garden figures in addition to high-quality ivory sculpture. Among his principal duties as a sculptor was the ornamentation of the Zwinger, where he was able to import Italian concepts of form into Germany. His main late work was the *Apotheosis of Prince Eugene* (see right), showing the prince who had put an end to the Turkish threat to Europe in 1697. Clad in dress armor and wearing a full wig, the figure of the military leader rests his right foot on the cowering figure of a defeated Turk. Prince Eugene, bearing a lion's pelt and cudgel, is further idealized as Hercules. A genius holds up the sun of fame before him, while Fama, blowing a trumpet, proclaims his glory. Beneath the grandeur of a baroque apotheosis, Permoser nonetheless succeeds in capturing some of the individual human characteristics of Eugene of Savoy. In this sense, Permoser's baroque gesture can be clearly distinguished from the imperial repose evident in the works of Schlüter for example.

In Münster (Westphalia) there was another family of sculptors which was active over several generations. In the works of both the father Johann Mauritz Gröninger (1650–1707), who was trained by Artus Quellinus in Antwerp and worked as court sculptor in Munich, and the son Johann Wilhelm Gröninger, the flamboyance of Italian baroque is considerably reduced, possibly because of the father's training in Flanders (see left).

The brothers Cosmas Damian Asam (1686–1739) and Egid Quirin Asam (1692–1750) received their early training from their father, the painter Hans Georg Asam, before setting out together for a study trip to Rome (1712–14). Whereas Cosmas worked principally as a ceiling painter, Egid worked mainly as a sculptor and stuccoist, but both were active as architects. In this as in their other skills they complemented each other splendidly and collaborated on many projects. As a sculptor, Egid was strongly influenced by Bernini; in his own works he unites Roman influences with native elements to produce a style of sculpture which was to provide the basis for

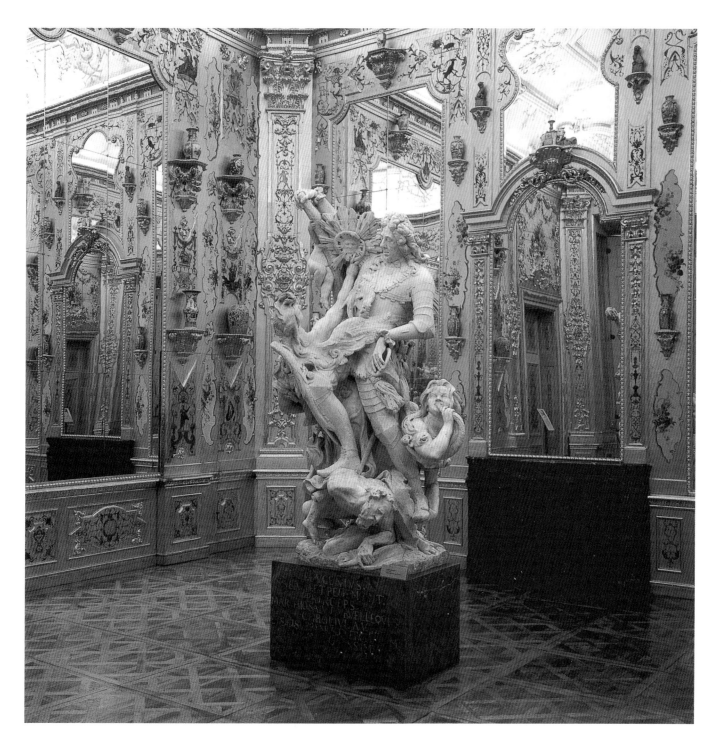

Egid Quirin Asam
St. George Fighting the Dragon, 1721
Plaster, gilded and silvered
Benedictine abbey church, Weltenburg

OPPOSITE:
Egid Quirin Asam
Assumption of the Virgin, 1723
Plaster, decorated with gold
Abbey church of Augustinian canons,
Rohr (Bavaria)

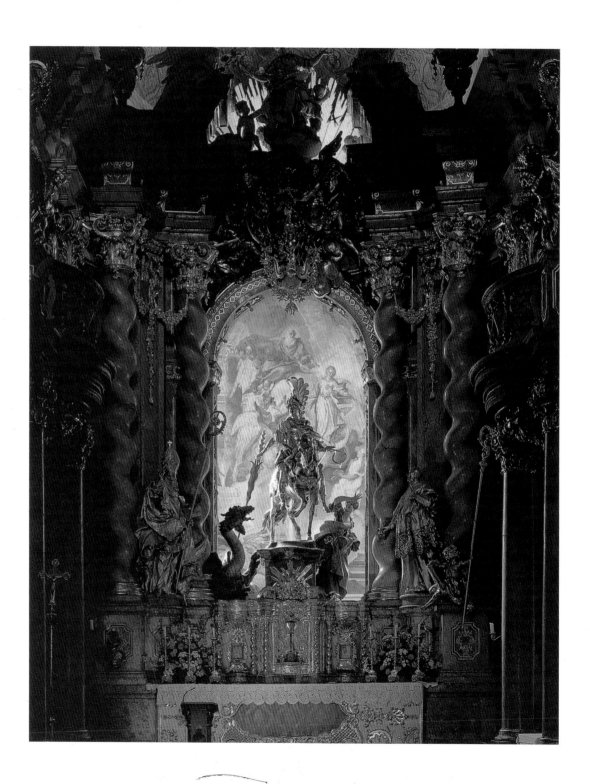

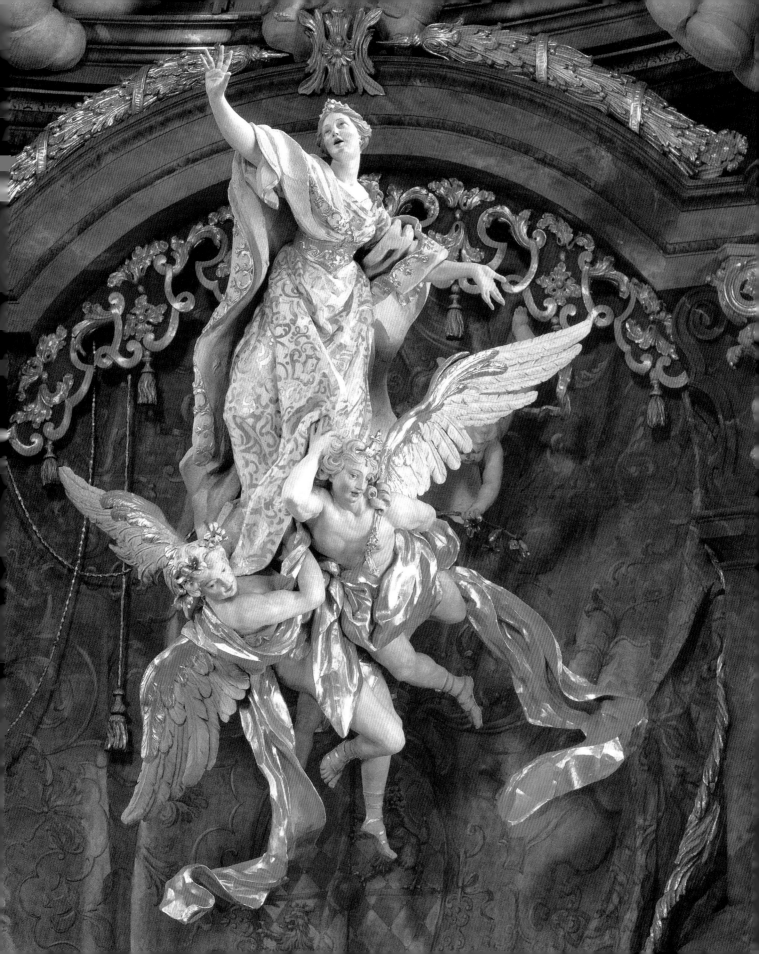

Johann Paul Egell
Deposition, c. 1740–50
Limewood, height 45 cm, width 28 cm
Liebighaus, Frankfurt

BOTTOM:
Johann Franz Schwanthaler
St. Margaret, c. 1750
Wood, painted and gilded
Parish church, Wippenham bei Ried

OPPOSITE:
Georg Raphael Donner
Flour Market Fountain, 1737–39
Lead, height 337 cm
Österreichische Galerie, Vienna

River March Personified as a Young Girl
(opposite, bottom left)

River Enns Personified as an Old Man
(opposite, bottom right)

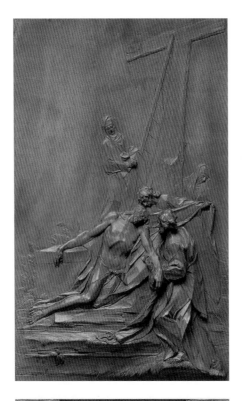

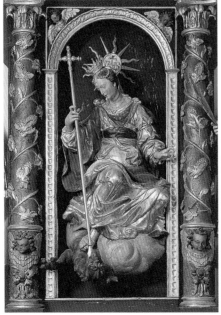

southern German rococo. Their first major commission was the decoration of the Benedictine church of St. George and St. Martin in Weltenburg, for which Egid executed *St. George Fighting the Dragon* in plaster coated with silver and gold (see p. 340). In the *Assumption of the Virgin* over the altar of the monastery church at Rohr (see p. 341), the late baroque altar arrangement becomes a totally theatrical set piece linking architecture and "floating" sculpture; the wildly gesticulating disciples participating in the event below form only one part of the illusion (see frontispiece). The church of St. John Nepomuk in Munich's Sendlinger Strasse, known as the Asam Church, is a unique structure. It was erected at the architects' own cost, which meant that they were not required to consider the views of a client in the architecture or the internal decoration (see p. 234).

Johann Franz Schwanthaler (1683–1762) was the youngest son of Thomas Schwantaler (cf. p. 332); in his work Johann sought to continue his father's artistic legacy. Taking over his father's workshop in 1710, he found himself overwhelmed by debt, which his ensuing marriage did nothing to reduce. Under huge pressure to economize, Schwanthaler slowly worked his way up and eventually earned an outstanding artistic reputation. He left an extensive body of work. He gradually adapted to the style of the time, producing more lyrical, introverted pieces than his father had done (see below).

Johann Paul Egell was trained by Balthasar Permoser (1691–1752) and returned to his native city of Mannheim around 1720 to become official sculptor to the electoral court; in this capacity he was involved in furnishing Schloss Schwetzing and the park. The small *Deposition* relief (see above) reveals his particular skill in sensitively uniting the various aspects of his artistic work as a sculptor, plasterworker, ivory-carver, and graphic artist. This is one of a whole series of small-scale reliefs conceived as devotional images which point to the apparently organic connection in his work between graphic and painterly elements of form and sculptural ones, a feature which prompted Klaus Lankheit to describe them as "paintings in limewood." The artistic charm of these pieces lies in a delicious tension between the flat surfaces, which serve as a plain ground for drawing, and the male heads, sculpted in high relief or even three dimensions, around which the dynamics of the scene revolve both formally and in terms of subject matter.

Georg Raphael Donner (1693–1741) belongs among the leading sculptors of Austrian late baroque. His development as a sculptor involved numerous phases, including travels to Dresden and Italy. His favored material was lead or terne metal. His best-known work was the Mehlmarktbrunnen [Flour Market Fountain] (see right), erected between 1737 and 1739 as a commission by the city of Vienna, a project which established him as a sculptor of European importance. The lead figure of Providentia sits on a plinth surrounded by putti, here represented as an allegory of the human virtues of prudence and shrewdness rather than divine providence. On the original edge of the fountain, four figures in the shape of youth

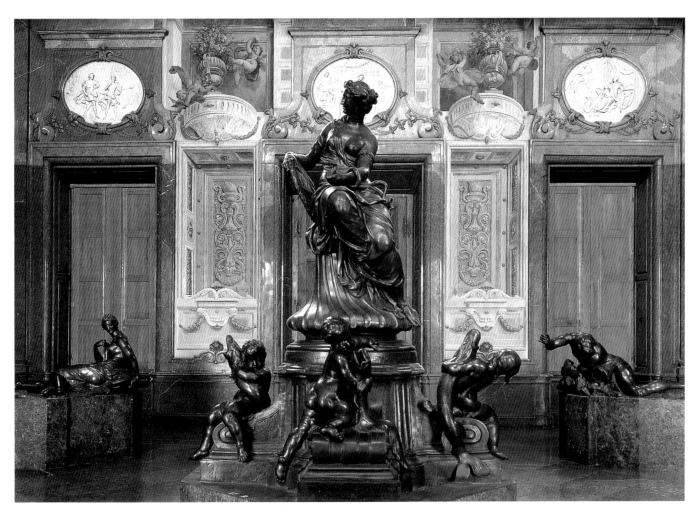

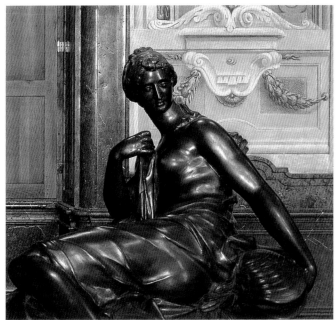

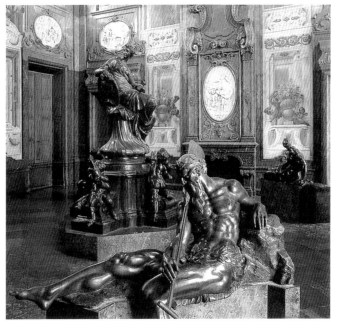

Georg Raphael Donner
Pietà, 1740–1741
Lead, height 220 cm, width 280 cm
Gurk cathedral

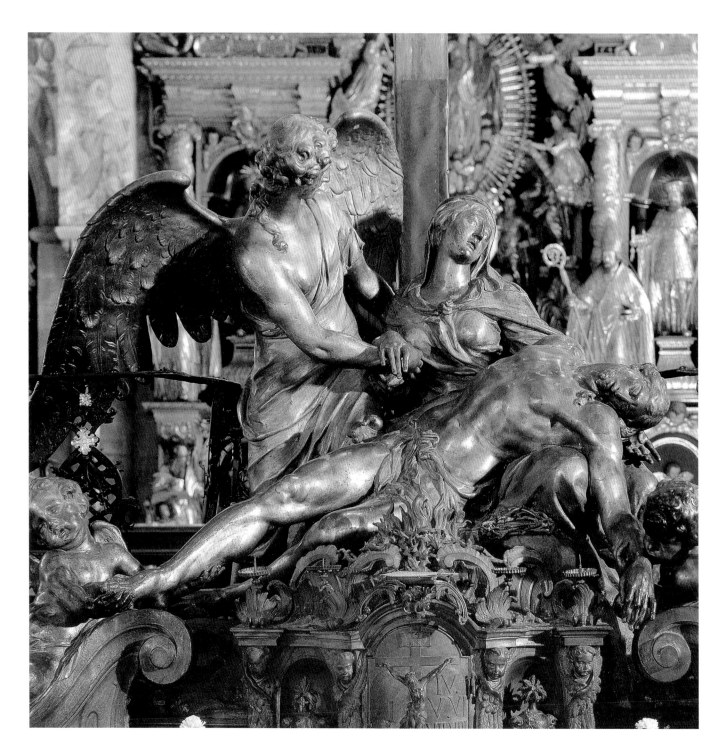

Johann Joseph Christian
The Prophet Ezekiel, 1752–56
Plaster, life-size
Benedictine abbey church, Zwiefalten

Joseph Anton Feuchtmayr
St. Joachim, 1749
Plaster, life-size
Pilgrimage church, Birnau

Johann Baptist Straub
St. Barbara, c. 1762
Wood, painted white with gilded decoration
Monastic church, Ettal

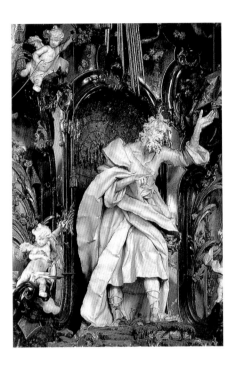
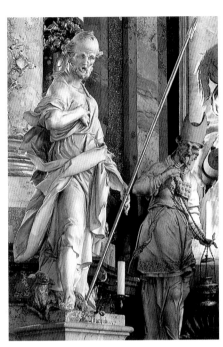
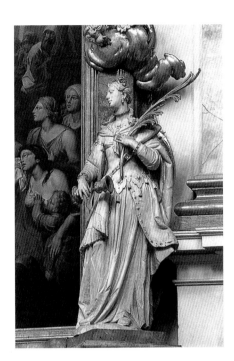

and age, girl and woman symbolize the four most important tributaries of the Danube, the Traun and Enns, March and Ybbs. The Danube is represented not in the sculpture but in the water of the fountain itself. Among Donner's late works is the *Pietà* in the cathedral at Gurk (see left), which shows the inner distress of the mother of God as she sits grieving by the corpse of Christ, supported by an angel. Donner's style is difficult to characterize. His art moves into a rococo realm far from removed from heavy baroque pathos, revealing classical elements that are forward-looking for their time.

Two sculptors who settled in Upper Swabia in the mid-eighteenth century used plaster as their main sculptural medium. One, Joseph Anton Feuchtmayr (1696–1770), came from a family of stuccoists from Wessobrunn, and is considered one of the principal masters of southern German rococo. His life-size figures in the pilgrimage church at Birnau (see above) are notable for their intense physical agitation, which is intended to suggest inner spiritual torment; their symbolic representation was evidently more important to Feuchtmayr than their specific anatomical attributes. The Riedling-based sculptor Johann Joseph Christian (1706–77), who occasionally collaborated with Johann Michael Feuchtmayr, owed his considerable reputation among Upper Swabian rococo artists to his work at the abbey church of Zwiefalten (see above) and Ottobeuren.

Johann Baptist Straub (1705–84) from Wiesensteig in Württemberg had a great influence on the rococo sculpture of southern Germany. He trained initially under Gabriel Luidl in Munich but then spent almost ten years at the academy in Vienna, where the work of Georg Raphael Donner provided a strong influence. Although he was court sculptor in Munich from 1737, Straub often undertook commissions for ecclesiastical and monastic clients. He became the leading sculptor of southern German rococo with Egid Quirin Asam, and his reputation was surpassed only by that of his most important pupil, Ignaz Günther. His figures, which are mainly carved in wood, are notable for their graceful elegance which, like the figure of St. Barbara in Ettal (see above) seem eloquently to express a sort of courtly refinement.

A pupil of Christian, of Straub, and of his own father Wenzeslaus was Christian Jorhan the Elder (1727–1804), who was based in Landshut. Among his works, which are found principally in Lower Bavaria and around Erding, are several series of half-figures of the apostles on rocaille bases.

Libraries in aristocratic houses and in monasteries were among the great variety of interiors that artists were asked to furnish. The principal work of Josef Thaddäus Stammel (1695–1765), born in Graz, was produced in Admont in Austria. After an Italian sojourn from 1718 to 1725, Stammel remained in Admont until his death, working as collegiate sculptor. In addition to such structures as the high altar in St. Martin near Graz, which was constructed between 1738 and 1740, he carried out the sculptural work for the ornate

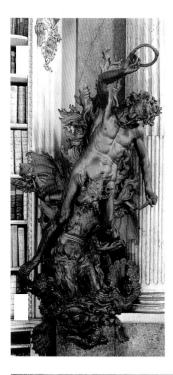

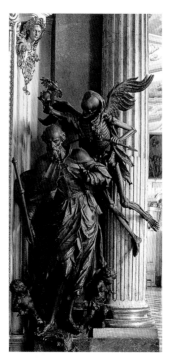

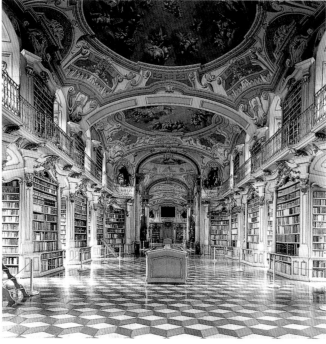

collegiate library (see left below) from the late 1740s to around 1760. His extraordinarily expressive figures, in which local stylistic traditions are combined with formal concepts of the Italian baroque, are based on allegories of transitoriness and motifs of Vanity. The allegorical figures representing the "Four Last Things," including the sculptures *Hell* and *Death* (see left below) seriously admonished the visitor to the library to be mindful of the earthly power of death and to put the books at the service of future spiritual salvation.

With commissions from the Viennese court and well-placed citizens, the German sculptor Franz Xaver Messerschmidt (1736–83) spanned the transition from Austrian rococo to neo-classicism. Trained by his uncles Johann Baptist Straub in Munich and Philipp Jacob Straub (1706–74) in Graz, he enrolled as a student at the Vienna Academy in 1775. He became a teacher there in 1769, hoping eventually to be appointed director. As this promotion was denied him, in 1774 he turned against the Academy and retired to Bratislava, where he devoted the rest of his life to his character heads, works as mysterious as they are spectacular, and which were to establish his modern reputation (see right). In a short but impressive study, Herbert Beck reveals how much this series of what amounted to sixty-nine sculptures owes to an existential tension between the physical nature of the sculpture and its intellectual and historical mastery on the threshold of the Enlightenment. Physical movements stand in proportional relationship to the head; its mimed response depicts what is happening to the body: this might sum up the sculptor's rather simplistic idea here. As the body feels itself plagued by bestial sensuality, however, it tries to protect itself from evil by physically manifesting its unhappy fate in a grimace. The frequent recurrence of portrait features in these character heads, "which due to their intimate nature are curiously styleless," may have had an negative impact on the success of the intended apotropaic effect. Messerschmidt's intention was to get close to the idea of a "true proportion," that of "the ideal, beautiful body purged of sensuality." This however he did not undertake or dare to represent sculpturally. Cut off as it were from the grimacing head, the body was supposed to be realized in the imagination from the facial expression alone. Beneath every character portrait there was always an immaterial body, one which only a classical sculptor would be able to reproduce in its imagined ideal proportions.

Messerschmidt's sculptures set him apart from the courtly spirit of absolutism, and he made use of the most personal and private motifs for his late art, although not without incorporating some elements of a more generalized ideal.

After his trip to Italy in 1731, Johann Christian Wenzinger (1710–97) spent the period between 1735 and 1737 at the Paris Académie des Beaux-Arts before setting up in business as an artist in the Breisgau area. Influenced partly by Italian terracotta work, he used the amorphous material of clay to achieve a more direct realization of his sculptural ideas. At the same time, this led him to pro-

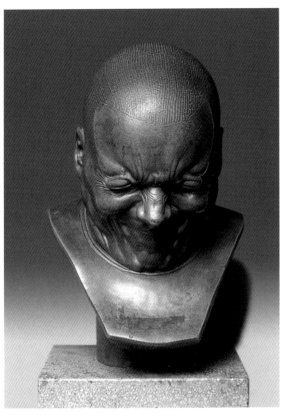

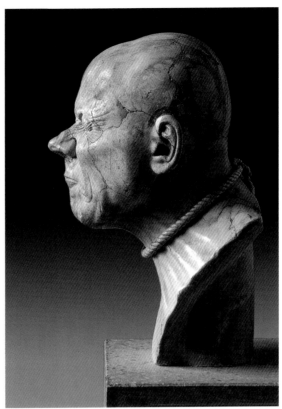

Franz Xaver Messerschmidt
Four character heads,
1770–83
Österreichische Galerie, Vienna

ABOVE LEFT:
Arch-villain
Lead, height 38.5 cm

ABOVE RIGHT:
Hanged Man
Alabaster, height 38 cm

BELOW LEFT:
Lascivious Fop
Marble, height 45 cm

BELOW RIGHT:
Second Beak-Head
Alabaster, height 43 cm

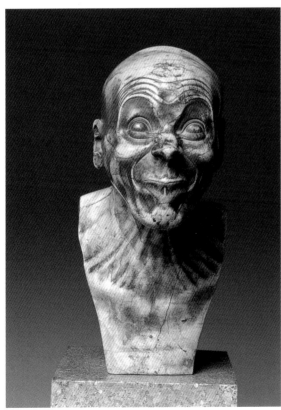

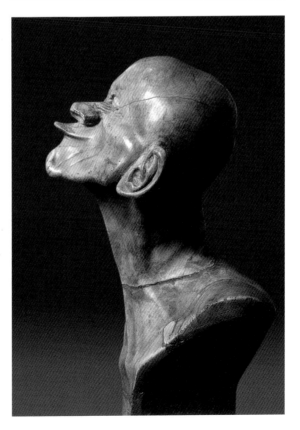

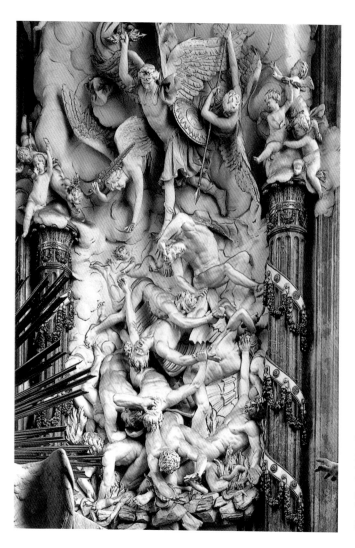

Karl Georg Merville
Fall of the Angels, 1781
Plasterwork on choir wall
St. Michael, Vienna

duce models or maquettes. The figures from the Mount of Olives (see below) which Wenzinger made in 1745 for the church at Staufen seem, as large-scale free-standing models, like preliminary versions of a composition, while at the same time displaying the sure touch of the virtuoso sculptor in the handling of the material. Not only are the inner emotions vividly represented in the figures, but the coloring creates an almost crude naturalism. Further, the conditions of contemporary life are suggested by the figure of the vagrant, in whom the consequences of the War of the Austrian Succession are personified only too graphically. Ragged and tattered, maimed and dull-witted, the discharged mercenary stumbles around like a marauder.

As court sculptor in Würzburg, Bamberg, and Trier, the Bohemian artist Adam Ferdinand Dietz (1708–77) was occupied mainly in producing garden figures of sandstone. At Seehof Palace near Bamberg, Dietz and his workshop had turned out four hundred statues by the time they finished work on the project.

The subject of these pieces was that of classical mythology, which outside the ecclesiastical realm enjoyed a considerable freedom of expression. Dietz' numerous figures of Mercury (see right), for example, illustrate the almost sunny lightness and sense of movement which typify his figures in the taste of the time. As the classical home of Apollo and the Muses, the *Parnassus* in the Great Lake of the prince-bishop's summer residence at Veitshöchheim is incorporated into the garden as nature enhanced by architecture (see right). The ensemble is divided into three areas intended to be read iconographically: the "shady forest" area symbolizes the state of nature,

RIGHT:
Johann Christian Wenzinger
Mourning Spirit, 1745
Staufen church, Mount of Olives
Terracotta, painted, height 82 cm
Liebighaus, Frankfurt

FAR RIGHT:
Johann Christian Wenzinger
Vagrant with Canteen, 1745
Staufen church, Mount of Olives
Terracotta, painted, height 54.5 cm
Liebighaus, Frankfurt

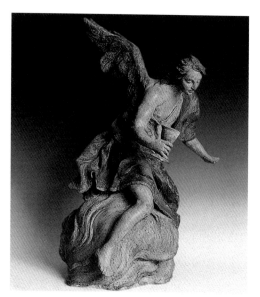

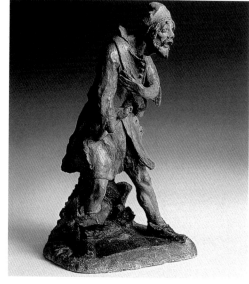

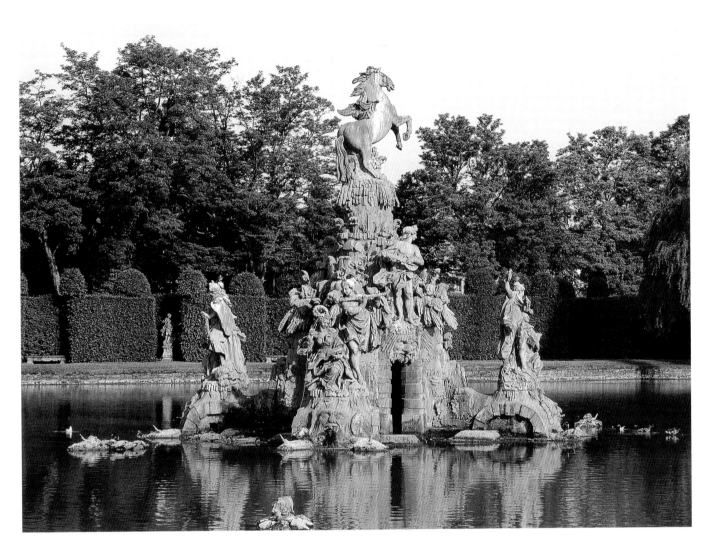

while the half-shady foliage area suggests the state of culture, and the lake area, totally open to the light, represents the state of absolute higher aspiration. The formerly gilt sandstone group at the lake embodies the force of inspiration in art as much as in princely rule. Both acquire a higher cosmological status in the statues of the gods of Olympus which surround the lake with the allegories of the seasons. There was also a musical device built into the body of the winged Pegasus that sounded in time with the water arts of Parnassus.

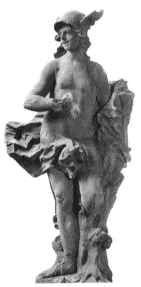

Adam Ferdinand Dietz
Parnassus, 1766
Sandstone, formerly gilded
Palace garden, Veitshöchheim, near Würzburg

Adam Ferdinand Dietz
Mercury, 1758
Sandstone, about lifesize
Gardens of former Electoral Palace, Trier

349

Franz Ignaz Günther
Pietà, 1758
Painted wood
Parish church of St. Rupert,
Kircheiselfing, near Wasserburg

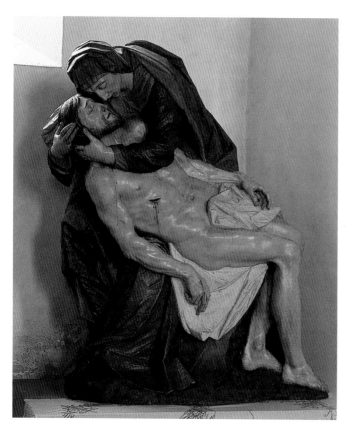

Ignaz Günther and the End of Rococo

The more difficulty there is in defining historical periods, the more questionable they seem to become. Three sculptures on a single theme by the hand of a single artist span the divide between the fading rococo style and the flourishing taste for neo-classicism. The sculptures in question are by Franz Ignaz Günther (1725–75) and represent the *Pietà*, the mother of God mourning her son's death on the cross. Taught by Straub in Munich and Egell in Mannheim, Günther is considered the outstanding master of southern German rococo.

The first of the three *Pietà* sculptures by Günther was made, according to the signature, in 1758 (see above). The dead Christ lies on a rocky plinth on which Mary also sits, clasping his torso to her bosom. Even in death the body appears strained, with the mouth closed and the right hand clenched. Mary bends right over him, reinforcing the sense of the intensity of her maternal pain. Although this sort of suffering and loving mother of God can be traced back to Byzantine models, and appears strangely old-fashioned in this respect, the sculpture would certainly have had an emotional impact on the contemporary viewer. Mourning and pain are here concentrated in an extremely confined space, and the believer is intended to share profoundly in the suffering of each figure.

Only a few years later (1764) the *Pietà* in Weyarn was created (see right). Here too Christ lies on a rock beside Mary, his upper body, apparently relaxed in death, resting on her lap. She supports his left arm, while the head and right hand fall slackly, as do the legs which slip from her lap. The sword in Mary's breast relates to local folk traditions. The anatomically naturalistic style of the naked male body is clearly contrasted with the more abstract treatment of the drapery, the geometrically carved ornamental folds, and the modeling of the drapery of Mary's lower left leg and of the loincloth, for example. As well as the contrasts illustrated within the sculpture, this piece contrasts emotionally with the earlier *Pietà*. Here the intensity of mourning is reduced. Mary sits upright, gazing at her dead son with inclined head, while his body presents itself in the direction of the onlooker rather than towards her. This sculpture is not designed to draw the believer directly into Mary's grief, which here seems to be remote from the actual figure of the corpse. In fact, this composition creates a perceptible distancing effect, allowing the viewer a less manipulated response to the subject.

The third of Günther's *Pietà* (see right) goes much further still. This piece was made for the cemetery chapel of the Virgin in Nenningen in 1774. Once again Christ rests on the rock beside Mary, his upper body resting in her lap. But here he appears to be neither alive nor quite dead. The right knee seems to rest on the rock as if supported by it. And his head, held up by Mary's right hand, is strangely wakeful for a dying man. While the half-closed eyes apparently watch the viewer, the mouth, half opened as if to speak, is taut with pain. Mary's head is likewise not inclined, and she is seated altogether upright. Her sorrowing gaze is no longer directed at her son, but slips over him into the distance.

The effect that must have deeply moved the beholder in earlier such images, the intense fusion of death on the cross and mourning, would have derived from the rhetorical force of baroque sculpture. In the Nenningen *Pietà*, this fusion is broken. The mourning is generalized, and ultimately releases the beholder from an empathetic response. The formal transformation is matched by the change in content. The unmistakable person of the sorrowing Virgin, one of the central figures of Christian iconography, is transformed on the threshold of a new age into an intimate and human grieving figure. The sorrowing mother of God takes on the image of any sorrowing female, whether mother, daughter, or sister. This generalization process at the same time incorporates an elevation of meaning, marking a fundamental change in the specific significance of Christ's sacrificial death and Christian mourning. When Ellen Spickernagel observes of the historical pictures of Jacques-Louis David (1748–1825) that they were intended "to awake an attitude of sacrifice through the aesthetic staging of the new bourgeois order of the sexes and anchor it in the

Franz Ignaz Günther
Pietà, 1764
Painted wood, height 113 cm
Former monastic church of Augustinian
canons, Weyarn

Franz Ignaz Günther
Pietà, 1774
Painted wood, height 163 cm
Cemetery chapel, Nenningen

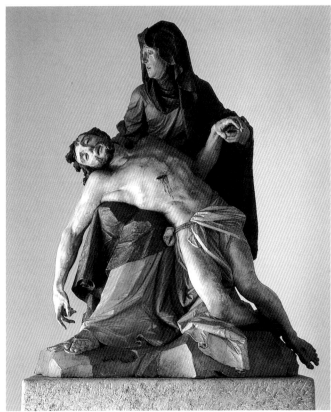

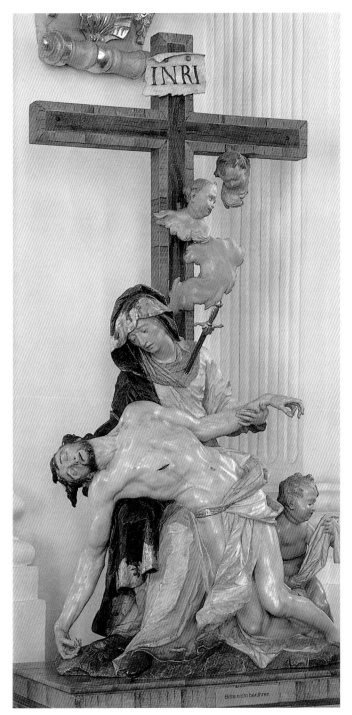

mentalities of the sexes," it is clear that this is a process that had already been introduced in the Nenningen *Pietà*. In the same way that Mary becomes a symbol of the almost heroically sorrowing woman, Günther's Christ seems to symbolize what is expected of men in their future roles. The noticeably large gaping wound in Christ's side, right in the center of the sculpture, sets him in the role of victim, which after the French Revolution will be defined as a hero's role in the warlike struggle for the ideals of the new bourgeois society. Günther's artistic greatness lies in his evident awareness of this change long before it was verbalized in manifestoes. It is not by chance that he graphically renders this concept precisely in a place where the encounter with death is everyday and individual, and has a rather private character, specifically in a cemetery chapel. The Nenningen *Pietà* is Günther's last work of importance. A year after it was completed he died, at the age of just fifty. With his work, German rococo comes to an end.

Small Sculptures and Collections

Small sculptures, because of their intimacy of scale, tended to appeal to ordinary people for use in the domestic interior. This was particularly true of religious subjects which could be used for private devotions. Countless crucifixes, statuettes of saints, and indeed entire miniature altars were in fact created expressly for this purpose. Not only was it easy to set them in particular positions in the house, but they were also very portable and could therefore be taken on journeys. The little altar by Leonhard Sattler (1744), for example, could be used exactly in this way (see below, left). Lavishly decorated in early eighteenth-century style, this piece can nonetheless be taken apart, which reinforces the idea that it was originally intended for travelers. This factor does not absolutely establish its actual use, however, since its portability would also have made it suitable for processional use as well as private devotion. However, this diminutive altar could only have been a model for a larger portable version.

Piecing together the history of small sculptures in this way is inevitably riddled with complications. This is because artists were no longer working just on specific commissions but were also supplying a collectors' market that had developed since the Renaissance. With small-scale copies of classical sculptures in bronze, known as "autonomous small bronzes," a virtually new category of art had emerged at the end of the fifteenth century. They were principally intended to supply the new collections of Italian princes of the Renaissance with collectable art objects. Thus a market arose which steadily expanded with the demand from new collectors. From the first half of the sixteenth century, increasingly well-to-do burghers had also started to build up private collections, if on a much smaller scale than those of the rich princely houses.

The papal nepotism of early seventeenth-century Rome encouraged the establishment of the great specialized private collections. The popes and their families, the Barberini, Borghese, and Pamphili, were the main figures with both the means and taste to provide the patronage that was the ideal basis for the development of Roman baroque art. Collectors were, of course, inspired by a variety of motives. In the first place there was a concern to demonstrate *buon gusto*, good taste, of the kind which a collector reveals in the choice of art works. In this respect, autonomous small bronzes began to lose their original value as collectibles, as they were increasingly reduced to the quality of mere scale reproductions of contemporary large-scale sculptures by artists such as Bernini or Algardi. Their function as an independent genre began to be superseded by small sculptures in other materials, with ivory becoming pre-eminent. Ivory is an exotic luxury medium with the possibility of being formed with the most sophisticated artistic and conceptual skill.

The Frankfurt-based sculptor Justus Glesker created a small statuette which Alfred Schädler numbers among the most outstanding ivory sculptures in the Palazzo Pitti's Museo degli Argenti [Silver Museum], in Florence. It shows St. Sebastian, his suffering represented with

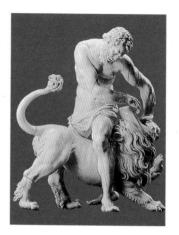

striking baroque pathos (see below). On closer inspection, the statuette proves to be a work of the highest aesthetic quality. As if hung up on the branches of a tree, the body is extraordinarily rich in anatomical detail, developing an ingenious rhythm as the flow of movement is interrupted several times. Vittoria's *St. Sebastian* in S. Salvatore in Venice (see p. 277) must have served as the model for Glesker's ivory statuette. However, the greatest skill in concept and execution was required in carving ivory sculptures from a single piece, as seen in Glesker's *St. Sebastian*. One almost expects to be able to trace the outline of the tusk in the contour of the statuette. But Glesker goes further: ivory figures are usually carved to follow the direction of the natural shape of the tusk and this is the case here, except that the bent knee of Sebastian acts like a barb in the flow of the material. This is a bold stroke that indicates an utterly sure touch in the sculptural handling of the ivory and at the same time an ability to translate an extraordinary artistic concept into material form. Unforunately, nothing is known of the provenance of this piece. All that is certain is that it must have been made

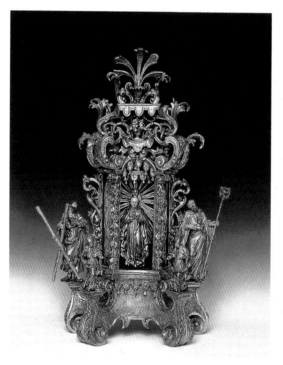

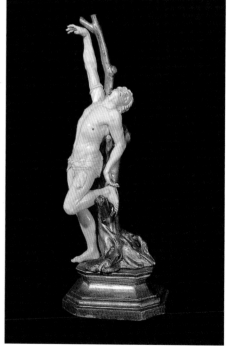

Andrea Brustolon
Jacob's Struggle with the Angel
1700–10
Boxwood, height 46.5 cm
Liebighaus, Frankfurt

Leonhard Kern
Imago pietatis, c. 1614
Alabaster, partially gilt
Height 36.5 cm, breadth 23.2 cm
Liebighaus, Frankfurt

BELOW:
Joseph Götsch
St. Elizabeth, 1762–63
Limewood maquette, height 17.5 cm
Liebighaus, Frankfurt

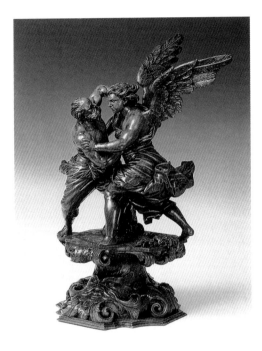

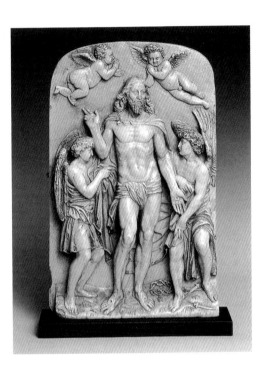

during Glesker's stay in Italy around 1645.

Probably the most innovative German sculptor of the early seventeenth century was Georg Petel, whose small sculptures are of such high quality that Joachim von Sandrart, the "German Vasari," commissioned a silver cast of one of his ivory crucifixes. Petel never fully abandoned the stylistic tricks of Italian mannerism, and many of his works contain unmistakable echoes of the last phases of the previous period. His *Hercules with the Nemean Lion* (see left), a typological substratum of a lost classical and not infrequently imitated scene, nonetheless displays many characteristic features of his personal personal style. Thes figures of the naked hero and the animal he is attempting to subdue are both softly modeled with anatomical accuracy but are imbued with a powerful physicality.

Almost every important collection of his time includes works by Leonhard Kern (1588–1662), one of the main designers of small sculpture in the early German baroque period. The richly diverse output of his workshop includes objects of soapstone, alabaster, wood, and ivory. Among them is the *Imago pietatis*, an alabaster relief (see above) now

in the Liebighaus in Frankfurt. The unusual iconography shows two flanking angels presenting the wounds of Christ, suggesting the influence of Protestant imagery which Kern was confronted with both in his birthplace of Forchtenberg in Württemberg and in the Protestant district of Schwäbisch-Hall. The balanced asymmetry of the figures, the athletic, physical presence of the Christ figure and the only slightly offset pose in which the upper body is parallel to the frame, convey a static feeling which can be related to the sculptural compositions of the late Italian Renaissance. In this sense, Kern's sculpture tends towards a fairly conservative style.

The figure scenes of the *Sacrifice of Abraham* and *Jacob's Struggle with the Angel* (see above) are attributed to the sculptor Andrea Brustolon (1662–1732), who came from Belluno and worked in Venice; they were conceived as a pair. The Jacob piece shows the scene from the Old Testament in which the future progenitor of Israel struggles with God, embodied in the figure of the angel. It is a masterpiece of sculptural drama. The idea of a physical struggle with God and the depiction of superhuman power is dramatically sharpened by the intersecting of contrasting axes of motion in the

encounter of the heads, which manifest extremes of tension.

The close attention paid by baroque collectors to the development of artistic theory also gave rise to a whole new genre of collectable objects, that of the artistic study or maquette, made of clay, wood, wax, or other materials, which collectors sought to acquire direct from the artist. As the earliest vehicle of the

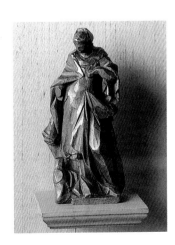

concept or artistic idea produced in material form, maquettes were not seen just as a basis for the negotiations of commissions, but came to represent tangible evidence of the artist's inspired genius. They were often therefore considered more significant than the finished sculpture itself, especially when the latter was carried out by pupils or workshop associates.

The small limewood maquette of St. Elizabeth (see below) is a study by Joseph Götsch (1728–93) for a life-size figure in the former Benedictine abbey of Rott am Inn. In solicitous familiarity, the saint turns towards a figure on her right who is only suggested. Her inner emotions are realized as an artistic idea in which features of the stylistic translation to the sculpture itself are already present. However, elements which appear compact on a small scale and richly detailed merely represent the distortions of scale that are corrected in the large-scale work, the effect of which is in fact cool and distancing.

By the end of the baroque period, a new material became popular with collectors. Whereas ivory had owed its exotic charm to biological and geographical strangeness, porcelain reflected a human talent for invention. Invention during this period was closely associated with the vainglorious ambition of alchemists to make gold, and porcelain was at first prized mainly for its status as a miraculous modern material rather than for its possibilities as an artistic medium.

353

José Ignacio Hernández Redondo

Baroque Sculpture in Spain

Over the last two centuries, art historians have demonstrated a certain degree of prejudice against Spanish baroque sculpture, generally rejecting the idea that it has any aesthetic merit whatsoever. Such views have only recently been modified, and it is now widely recognized that sculpture represents one of Spain's most brilliant and original contributions to European art. Curiously enough, the quality of Spanish sculpture during the seventeenth century can be attributed to some extent both to the economic decline and to the political and ideological isolation of the country during this period.

Sculptors were inevitably affected by these conditions. Important Spanish artists rarely seem to have travelled abroad during the seventeenth century—in contrast to the practice of the preceding century. The number and status of foreign artists in Spain during this period was in no way comparable to those who were active there during the sixteenth century, with the notable exceptions of the Flemish artist José de Arce and Manuel Pereira, an artist from Portugal.

The tendency to associate a new epoch in art with the beginning of a new century is a more or less conventional custom, but inevitably neither ever represents a complete break with the past. Nonetheless, a change does seem to have occurred in Spanish sculpture around 1600 and it continued to gather momentum. As will be seen, this change involved a transition from Roman mannerism to baroque naturalism, a process that can be seen as having been completed by around 1630.

The accession of the Bourbon dynasty in 1700 signaled the emergence of a new political and cultural milieu. In spite of this turning-point, the period from around 1600 up to 1770 will be treated here as different chapters of the same movement. It was only later that new academic theories brought about a profound alteration in the themes and materials of sculptural art, effecting a change which genuinely represented the beginning of a new era.

The Seventeenth Century

The Spanish church, which clung obstinately to its role as defender of the Catholicism of the Counter-Reformation, and stood in open opposition to Protestantism, found in the combined power of painting and the rhetoric of the pulpit the basic tools necessary to ensure the accessibility of its doctrines and thereby encourage popular devotion. The sheer quantity of devotional sculptures produced in Spain during this period far outnumbers that of secular sculptures. This was the expression of a deeply religious society, where the quest for the salvation of the soul was the abiding concern, and in which even secular festivals became appendages of sacred ceremonials.

Numerous examples reinforce this idea. The nobility dedicated most of their artistic initiatives to the construction of funerary monuments and chapels. Relics were collected and displayed or stored in a wide variety of decorative containers such as arm reliquaries, busts, and vessels in settings of wood or precious metals. Sometimes these reliquaries were shown in confined, overcrowded spaces, as in the church of S. Miguel, Valladolid (see right, above), which housed a veritable treasure trove of religious art. Cathedrals, parish churches, and monasteries endowed substantial sums for the creation of sculpture; in addition, town councils might donate funds for large altarpieces. The clearest expression of the role of sculpture in the religious life of the period is indicated by the considerable increase in the number of Holy Week processions, ceremonies which survive to this day. On such occasions, whole towns are transformed into huge sacred spaces in which floats with sculptural groups representing the Stations of the Cross draw vast crowds.

In this context, the demand for works of art was largely restricted to altar sculpture and three-dimensional devotional works. Other forms of religious art certainly did not disappear during the seventeenth century, but a distinct decline in their production can be perceived, especially in comparison to the levels of the sixteenth century.

Praying figures in Spanish funerary monuments of this period are characterized by an austerity of composition that is far removed from the allegorical complexity and decorative richness of similar subjects of the Renaissance. This austerity can also be seen in the choir-stalls of the first third of the century, which are modeled on the example of the Escorial; the lack of sculptural ornament reduces them to the level of joiner's work executed to the design of an architect. This tendency toward stylistic sobriety lasted only a short time, however; during the course of the century elaborate relief carving regained its predominance, as can be seen in the choir-stalls of Málaga cathedral, mostly decorated by craftsmen from the workshop of Pedro de Mena (see right below).

Many scholars of the baroque have accepted the central thesis of Emile Mâle's *L'Art Religieux après le Concile de Trente* [Religious Art after the Council of Trent] since its publication in 1932, which contends that the most significant feature of this Counter-Reformation art lies in the creation of a new iconography. If one examines the themes which appear most frequently in baroque art, it becomes apparent that it was used by the Catholic church as a defence against the attacks of the Reformation upon established doctrine. This accounts for the increasing popularity of the cult of the Virgin Mary whose role in the salvation of humanity was even compared to that of Christ, as suggested by the juxtaposition of the *Ecce Homo* and the *Mater Dolorosa*. Efforts to force the recognition of the Immaculate Conception as an essential tenet of church dogma became a passionate preoccupation of Spanish society; the iconographic model of the Virgin of the Immaculate Conception became an endlessly repeated theme in churches, monasteries, and even private chapels. To the same end, the authority of the papacy was reinforced with sculptures showing St. Peter as Prince of the Apostles, the value of the sacraments was emphasized by images of penitent saints, and the merit of good works was extolled through further

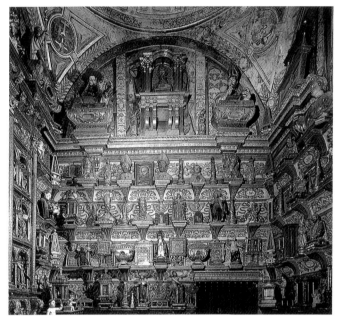

Valladolid, S. Miguel
Reliquary chapel, 17th century
Predominantly polychrome wood

Pedro de Mena
Málaga cathedral
Choir-stalls, detail, 1658–62
Cedarwood

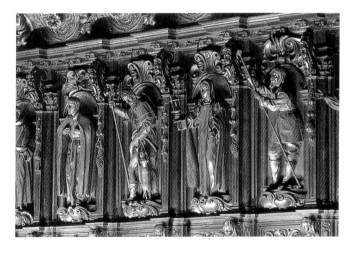

saintly examples. Particular attention was given to those saints who had been canonized relatively recently, such as St. Teresa of Ávila, St. Ignatius Loyola, and St. Francis Xavier.

Considering the major role that images were to play in promoting ecclesiastical doctrine, it made sense that sculptors began to

Francisco Rincón
Paso with *Raising of the Cross*, 1604
Polychrome wood, life-size
Valladolid, Museo Nacional de Escultura

move stylistically toward popular realism in their work. Wood, which could be painted in attractive colors, emerged as the ideal medium for emphasizing the life-like qualities of the sculpture. While the tradition of Spanish sculptural art was preserved, at the same time a range of technical innovations was introduced which allowed the desired degree of realism to be achieved. Among various efforts in this direction, perhaps the most bizarre is illustrated by the use of *postizos* or additions, a practice which would have seemed unthinkable in the sixteenth century. From about 1610 sculptures were often elaborated with wigs of real hair, crystal eyes or tears, ivory teeth, horn fingernails, and cork or leather representing wounds. Such accessories, combined with the realistic coloring of skin and fabrics, are characteristic of Spanish baroque sculpture (although some bishops forbade the use of additions of this kind). The somewhat curious nature of these sculptures probably accounts for their subsequent neglect by art historians. Nonetheless, these pieces reflect the same skill of handling that is evident in works by major sculptors of the period executed in more highly valued materials, such as stone or alabaster.

Scholarship in the field of seventeenth-century sculpture generally relies on an analysis of the characteristic traits of particular schools, an approach that will also be employed here. While acknowledging that works of the highest artistic quality were produced in Castile and Andalusia, the impact of the court in Madrid on contemporary artists must also be addressed, since it was the meeting point of several artistic trends. These remarks are not intended, however, to imply that the other regions of Spain were in any way artistically impoverished; on the contrary, the range of artistic production was evidently so widespread that every town of any size possessed active workshops. Although the pre-eminence of the schools named above can be clearly established, areas of artistic production like Catalonia and the east have sunk into relative obscurity, largely as a result of the disturbances created by the Civil War.

A survey of the main centers of Spanish baroque sculpture, Castile, and Andalusia, should avoid dealing in generalizations. Nonetheless, it is probably fair to say that Andalusian sculpture tempered the dramatic qualities of Castilian works with a stylistic language that tends towards elegance, emphasizes detail, and avoids the portrayal of cruelty, or at least softens its impact. As a result, in Andalusia a greater richness can be seen both in the draperies of the figures and in the use of decorative silver, as well as an emphasis on such pleasing or engaging themes as the childhood of Jesus and of Mary; by contrast there are very few representations of Corpus Christi (the body of the dead Christ), a theme characteristic of Castilian sculpture.

The following section will consider the specific contributions of major Spanish sculptors of the period.

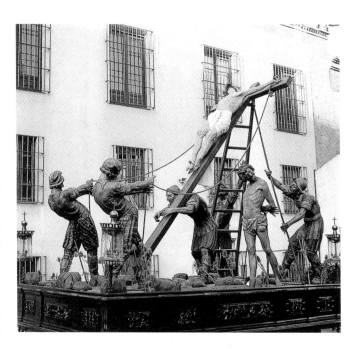

Castile

Valladolid is always regarded as the most important center of baroque sculpture in Castile, and this reputation had already begun to develop during the sixteenth century. By the end of the century, the sculptor Juan de Juni was still vividly remembered; his work had anticipated in many respects the baroque aesthetic. At the same time the sculptural work of Esteban Jordán served as a crystallization point for some of the elements of Roman mannerism. The residence of Philip II's court in Valladolid between 1601 and 1605 further enlivened the creative life of the town; this was mainly due to the presence of the king's sculptor, Pompeo Leoni, and his circle. Opportunities for work at the court attracted a large number of sculptors, the most prominent among whom was Gregório Fernández. The master's distinctive style (characterized by a remarkable naturalism) was disseminated after his death throughout Castile and the regions of northern Spain by a vast number of his imitators, pupils, and followers.

The sculptor Francisco de Rincón, born around 1567, played a fundamental role in the development of the new style. The sober manner of his early work had evolved within the context of Roman mannerism. However, his later work is very much in keeping with contemporary trends. Although it is constantly stressed that the young Gregório Fernández was active in Rincón's workshop, the innovations and creative powers of the older master, which extended to composition and iconography, should not be ignored. Rincón's early death at the age of forty certainly represented a great loss to Spanish art. His *Raising of the Cross*, now housed in the Museo Nacional de Escultura in Valladolid (see left), is testimony to his singular talent. Mentioned in documents of 1604, this piece is the earliest of a series of *paso* or life-size processional groups of polychromed wood. Previously only the figures of Christ and the Virgin had been executed in wood in such groups, while the other scenes were constructed with ephemeral figures made of cardboard which was, of course, much lighter. The composition of the *Raising of the Cross* must be seen as one of the finest examples of the baroque depiction of movement: the artist attempts to capture the moment when the men are straining to raise the cross and the head of Christ falls dramatically to one side in an abrupt turn.

The work of Gregório Fernández can be seen as representing the high point of Castilian baroque sculpture. He can in fact be considered as the founder of the Castilian school, since his work established the iconographic models which reflect the religious nature of the Spanish heartland and characterize the style of the area.

Born in 1576 in Sarria, Galicia, Fernández, like many other sculptors, adopted his father's profession and had certainly been used to the environment of the artist's workshop from his earliest childhood. On arrival in Valladolid at the beginning of the seventeenth century he had already completed his apprenticeship and began working for Rincón as a qualified assistant.

The presence of sculptors at court and the opportunities to study imported works of art created the aesthetic context for the emergence of his own early style, notable for its mannerist elegance, as typified by his *Gabriel* (see right), now in the diocesan museum in Valladolid, a piece almost certainly inspired by the work of Giambologna. The number of commissions for monumental altarpieces that he took on at the beginning of the 1620s suggests that his reputation was already well established at this stage; we can also assume that he was already employing a number of assistants in his workshop, which in due course came to produce the largest output of sculpture in Spain. Other smaller but still remarkable works were created around 1614, such as the delightful relief *The Adoration of the Shepherds* in the monastery of Las Huelgas at Valladolid (see p. 358, left) and the *Reclining Christ*, commissioned by Philip III and donated to the Capuchin convent of El Pardo in Madrid.

It has always been thought that the processional group of the vespers paintings with the two thieves (1616) (most of which is preserved in the Museo Nacional de Escultura in Valladolid) opened up a new naturalistic phase in Spanish sculpture which gradually began to supersede idealized forms. At the same time, a broken, angular style became apparent in the depiction of folds in clothing, with a stark contrast between light and shade. Two further devotional paintings (both owned by the brothers of atonement of Vera Cruz in Valladolid), designed for the Holy Week processions, demonstrate the mature style of the master. The *Flagellation of Christ* (see p. 358,

right) is a development of one of the iconographic peculiarities of Castilian baroque. In contrast to the earlier representations of the sixteenth century, this shows a low column which allows a graphic perspective on the tortures inflicted on the naked body. If the merit of a work of art can be measured by its long-term impact, then this figure is certainly successful: it continues to enjoy huge popularity in the streets of Valladolid even today.

One of the most extraordinary examples of processional art, however, is Fernández' monumental *Descent from the Cross* (1623) (see p. 359), an exceptional example of the expressive skills of the artist. The remarkable portrayal of two men standing on the ladder holding the corpse which appears to float freely in the air represents a sophisticated solution to the complex problem of balance, and of situating the figures in space.

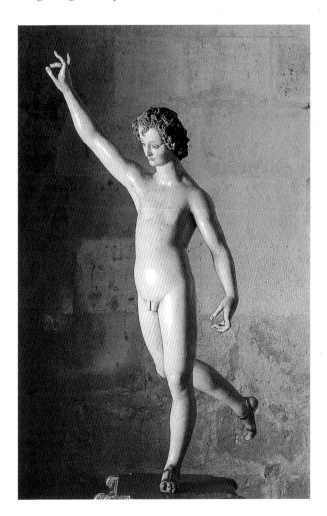

Gregório Fernández
Adoration of the Shepherds, 1614–16
Polychrome wood
Central panel 187 x 102 cm
Monasterio de las Huelgas (Valladolíd)

Gregório Fernández
Flagellation of Christ, c. 1619
Polychrome wood, 177 cm
Valladolíd, Vera Cruz

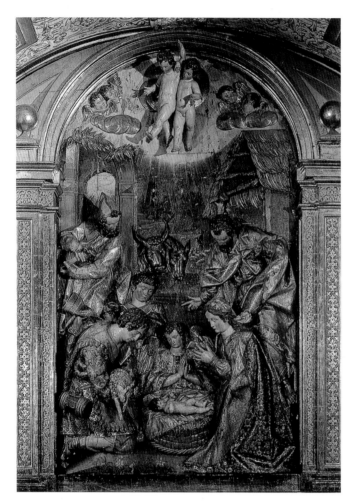

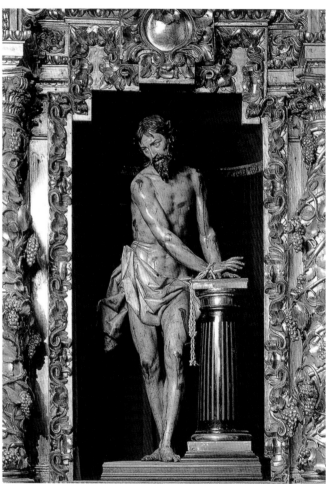

OPPOSITE:
Gregório Fernández
Paso with *Descent from the Cross*,
1623–25
Polychrome wood, over-life-size
Valladolíd, Vera Cruz

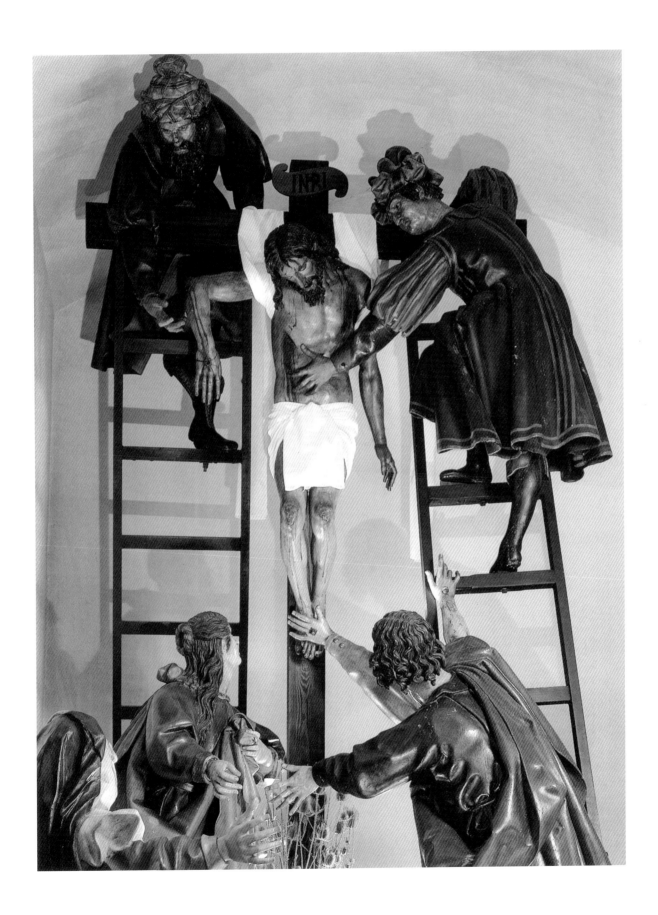

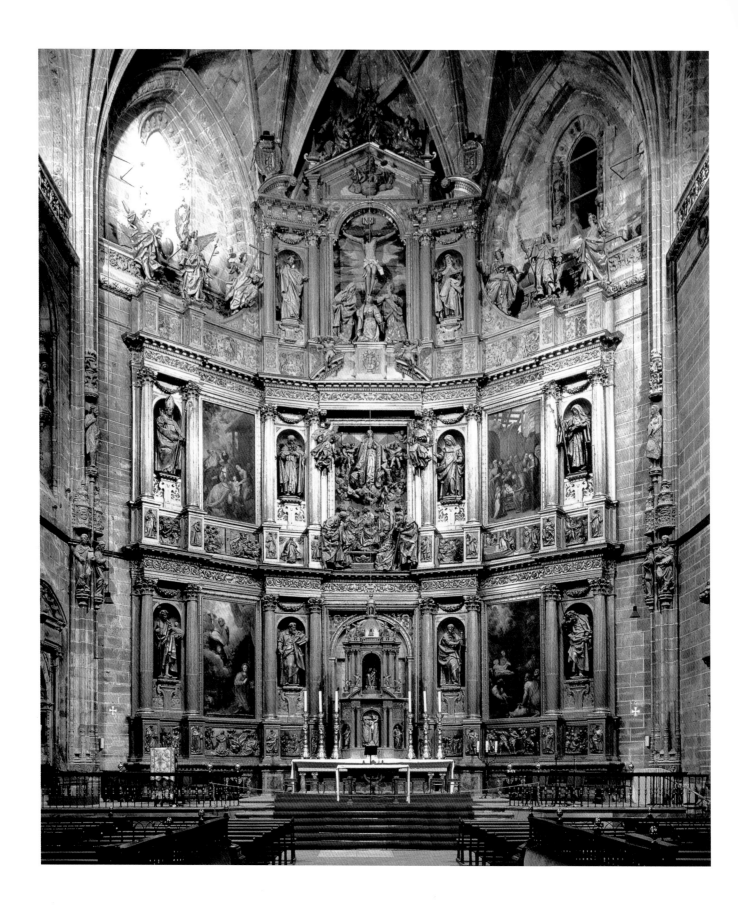

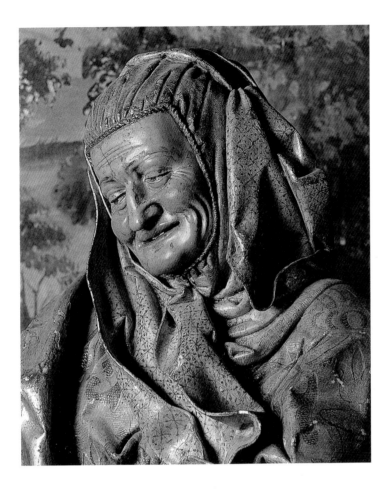

In 1626 the work of Gregório Fernández entered an intensely creative phase which was to last until his death. The workshop employed a great number of assistants, who were needed to work on large altarpieces. The altarpiece (see left) produced for Palencia cathedral (1625–32) is recognized as the sculptor's masterpiece. Although in poor health and overworked, the master retained his extraordinary skills during his last years, as demonstrated by the *Christ of the Light* in the collection of the Museo Nacional de Escultura in Valladolid (currently housed in the chapel of the Colegio Santa Cruz). The importance of Fernández' role in the development of Castilian sculpture can ultimately be measured by the fact that his works were faithfully copied for years after his death.

The seated figure of *St. Anne* in the church of Villaveliz near Valladolid (see above), a piece from a workshop at Toro (Zamora), should be briefly mentioned here. The figure, made as a collaborative effort by Sebastián Ducete and Esteban de Rueda, contemporaries of Fernández, marks the transition point in sculpture from the style of Juan de Juni to the baroque, a change which is reached here without the intermediate stage of courtly mannerism.

Andalusia

The second major school of seventeenth-century Spanish sculptors was in Andalusia where two important centers emerged: the western region, of which Seville was the capital, with minor centers in what are now the provinces of Huelva, Córdoba, and Cádiz, and the eastern region, centered on Granada as well as the provinces of Málaga, Jaén, and Almería. The style of sculpture in the two regions is particularly distinctive in spite of the vibrant and long-standing tradition of artistic exchange between them. With some exceptions, Sevillian sculptors tended toward large-scale works imbued with a certain mystical quality and elegance of manner, while the sculpture of Granada was more frequently typified by smaller-scale virtuoso work. Their smaller size naturally made these pieces more portable and they were thus disseminated as prototypes throughout Spain.

Seville

In Seville, which had been expanding since the discovery of America, groups of artists came together and gradually, from the last third of the sixteenth century, began to be defined as a distinct school. The consolidation of their style and the growing fame of these artists can be attributed to the important Seville master Martínez Montañés (1568-1649). His successful career, established from an early age, will be explored only briefly here; as a sculptor his works illustrate the

Juan Martínez Montañés
Christ of the Chalices, post-1605
Polychrome wood, height 190 cm
Seville cathedral, sacristy

Juan Martínez Montañés
St. Jerome, 1611
Polychrome wood, 160 cm
Santiponce, monastery of S. Isidoro
del Campo

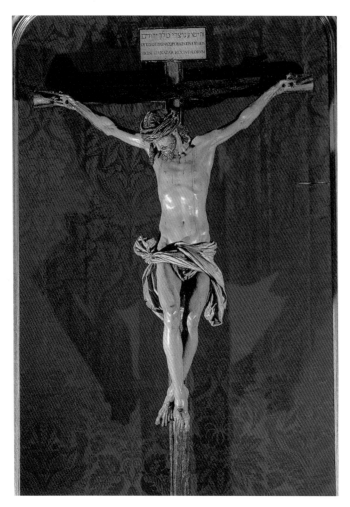

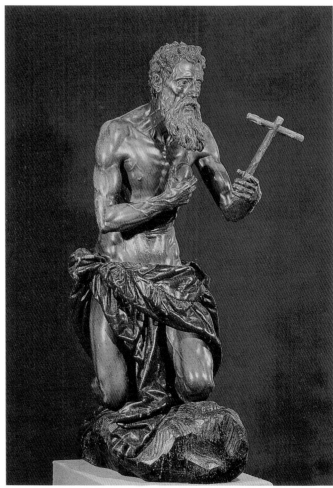

transition in sculpture from the late mannerist style to baroque. His work characteristically aspires to a balanced beauty, an ideal expressed in powerful gestures of great serenity, as suggested by one of his masterpieces, the *Crucifix of the Chalices* in Seville cathedral (see above left). The conditions of his contract for this piece are often referred to in the literature as they reveal a great deal about the original specifications given to Montañés by his patron for this sculpture. They state that "He [Christ] must still be alive, at the point of His last breath, His head bent towards His right arm, His gaze directed at some other person who is standing at His feet in prayer, as if He would speak to him and complain that His suffering is due to him..." Unlike the drama of Castilian sculpture, the delicate and naturalistic modelling of the body contrasts with the deeply

carved folds of the loincloth. Polychrome was applied to the wood by the painter Francisco Pacheco in mat tones in order to make it appear more life-like.

The period from 1605 to 1620 is generally regarded as the most important in Montañés' career; it was during this time that he produced, among other works, the *St. Jerome* for the central niche of the high altar of the convent of St. Isidoro del Campo at Santiponce in Seville (see above right), a work which would normally have been seen only from the front. However, the figure is carefully modelled in the round as it was intended to be removed for processions. The anatomical accuracy of the piece is again of unusually high quality: the tensed arm with its realistic musculature and the veins showing beneath the skin are scrupulously detailed.

Juan de Mesa
Christ the Almighty, 1620
Polychrome wood, height 181 cm
Seville, Iglesia de Jesús

Francisco Ruiz Gijón
Dying Christ (El Cachorro), 1682
Polychrome wood, height 184 cm
Seville, Iglesia del Patrocinio

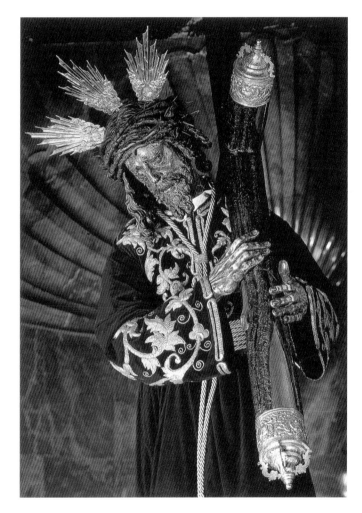

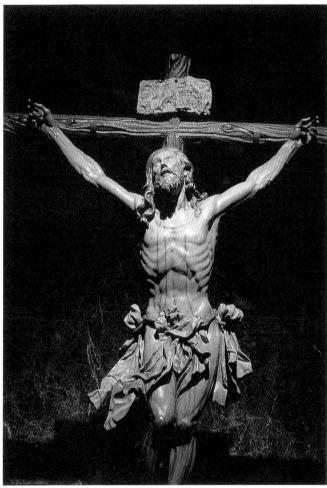

After recovering from a long illness in 1629, Montañés began to develop a later style in the high baroque manner. Well into old age he continued to produce masterpieces such as the *Virgin of the Immaculate Conception* for the chapel of the Alabastros in Seville cathedral. In 1635–36 he was summoned to the court of Philip IV to produce a bust in clay of the king, which may have been intended to serve as a model for the equestrian statue of the same subject by the Italian sculptor Pietro Tacca.

Like Gregório Fernández in Castile, Montañés was to exert a considerable influence on the sculpture of Seville both during and after his lifetime. The short-lived Juan de Mesa (1583–1627) of Córdoba became his pupil and most important assistant. In his works, predominantly processional sculpture, the authenticity of

anatomy and the emotional force anticipate the realism of the Seville school. This is exemplified by Mesa's most celebrated devotional image, that of *Christ the Almighty* (1620) in the Basilica del Gran Poder in Seville (see above left). This piece may have been inspired by Montañés' *Jesus of the Passion*; the observer is drawn into the humanity of the subject by such details as the crown of thorns piercing the forehead, the face aged by pain, and the corpse-like pallor of the skin.

Two artists figure prominently in the development of Sevillian sculpture during the second third of the century. One was Alonso Cano, to whom we will return in the context of Granada; the other was José de Arce, the Flemish sculptor who arrived in Seville in 1636, bringing with him the dynamic compositional style that effec-

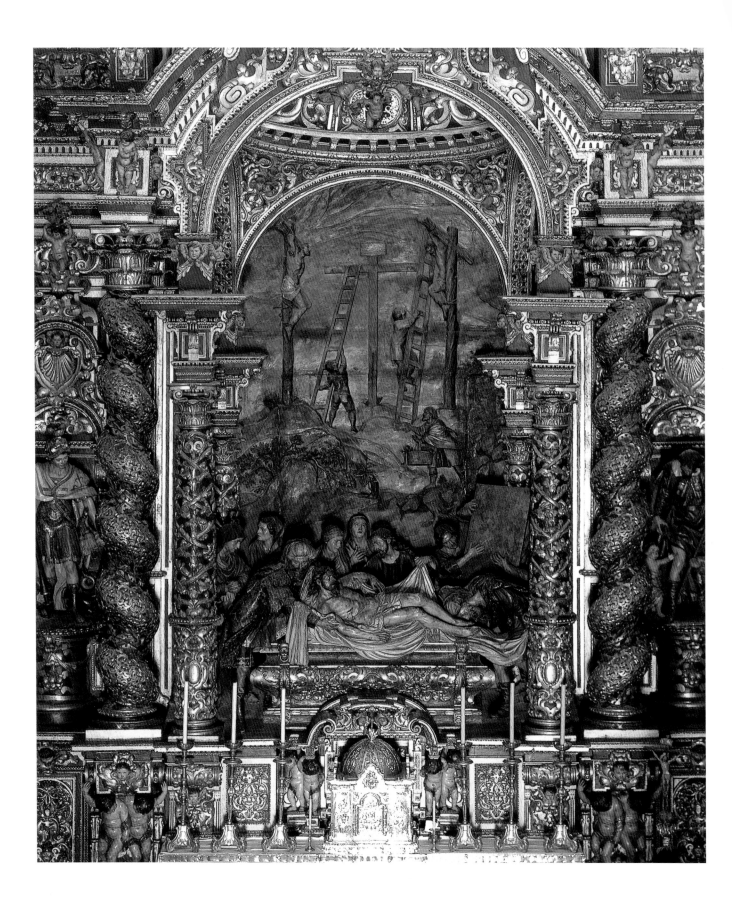

tively introduced European baroque into the city. Examples of his work can be found in the church of S. Miguel in Jerez de la Frontera, a commission which Montañés had passed onto him shortly before his death.

During the last third of the century the baroque style became fully established in Seville. The outstanding figure of this era is Pedro Roldán (1624–99). Although originally from Seville, he was trained in the workshop of Alonso de Mena in Granada between 1638 and 1646. After returning to his native city in 1647, he came under the influence of José de Arce and adopted elements from his compositions, with their distinctive hairstyles. The sense of dramatic pathos embodied in the sculpture of this period finds its strongest expression in monumental ensembles illustrating scenes of the Passion, the subject of numerous altarpieces. One of the most impressive examples of this is the retable in the church of the Hospital de la Caridad in Seville (see left), which features an over-life-size *Entombment* (1670–72) by Pedro Roldán.

Luisa Roldán (1650–1704), daughter of Pedro Roldán, was the most important female artist at the end of the century. The quality of her work was of a very high standard and she was, in fact, the only famous woman sculptor of seventeenth-century Spain. She achieved full royal recognition, obtaining the title of court sculptor. Her most distinctive works are small colored terracotta figure groups. Her contemporary, Francisco Ruiz Gijón, the last great master of the seventeenth century in Seville, created the *Dying Christ* popularly called *El Cachorro* (see p. 363, right). As in the *Crucifix of the Chalices* created by Montañés at the beginning of the century, Christ is shown still alive in this piece. But he turns his gaze beseechingly upwards, while his loincloth appears to move in the wind. A comparison of these two works underlines the changes that had occurred in the work of Sevillian sculptors in the course of the seventeenth century.

Granada

If one can argue that an artistic school exists wherever common elements consistently feature in the artistic output of a town or region, then it is a concept which can certainly be applied to Granada. The city was the source of small-scale wooden sculptures, intimate and exquisite pieces designed to delight the connoisseur. These objects enjoyed widespread popularity throughout the seventeenth century, as evidenced by the numerous examples which have survived in other regions of Spain.

While Alonso Cano (1601–67) is generally considered to have been the actual founder of the school of Granada, outstanding contributions were made at an early stage by Pablo de Rojas, the García brothers, and, most significantly, Alonso de Mena (1587–1646), a key figure of the early baroque. Mena's workshop produced a number of important artists, including his own son Pedro de Mena, and Pedro Roldán. When Alonso de Mena died in 1646, his son was

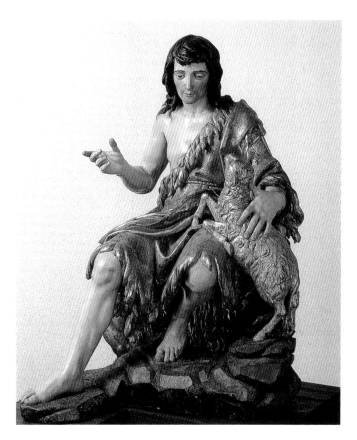

still very young and Roldán had moved to Seville. This change might well have led to an impoverishment of the artistic life of Granada if it had not been for the well-timed return of the versatile Alonso Cano to his native city, where he soon became active as an architect, painter, and sculptor. As a young man Cano had followed in the footsteps of his father, Miguel Cano, moving with him to Seville. He had obtained an excellent training in the workshop of Francisco Pacheco, where he also made friends with Velázquez; he remained in Seville until 1693, when the powerful count of Olivares, first minister of Philip IV, summoned him to Madrid. During his time in Seville Cano had mainly been influenced by the work of Montañés, as indicated by his *Virgin de la Oliva* and *St. John the Baptist*, now in the Museo Nacional de Escultura (see above), very much representative of the idealized naturalism that was to become an essential characteristic of his work.

During the subsequent period in Madrid, Cano devoted himself primarily to painting. In 1652 he decided to return to Granada to take up a position as a prebendary in the cathedral, a privilege which

Pedro de Mena
Málaga cathedral, 1658–62
Choir-stalls, detail
Cedarwood

Alonso Cano
Virgin of the Immaculate Conception,
1655
Polychrome decoration, 55 cm
Granada cathedral

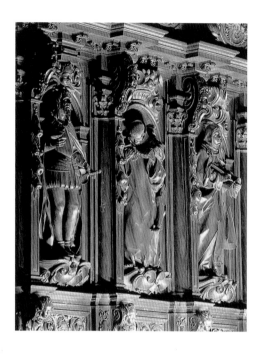

Pedro de Mena
Málaga cathedral, 1658–62
Choir-stalls, detail
Cedarwood

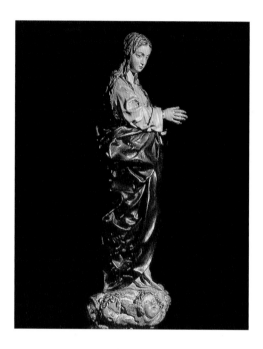

Alonso Cano
Virgin of the Immaculate Conception,
1655
Polychrome decoration, 55 cm
Granada cathedral

not only required him to be ordained as a priest within the year but also to take on the unfinished decoration of the church. He renewed his activity as a sculptor, achieving the high aesthetic standards evident in such finely executed small pieces as the famous polychrome cedarwood *Virgin of the Immaculate Conception* in the sacristy of the cathedral (see above right). The wooden sculpture, based on an oval form, has a harmonious and fluid quality which invites the observer to survey it by walking around the object. The composition is perfect complemented by the simple coloring in blue and greenish tones, set off by lavish gilding. Only an artist practiced in both media could achieve such a perfect symbiosis of sculpture and painting.

Cano's work was a decisive influence on his colleague Pedro de Mena (1628–88), the most outstanding personality of the school of Seville. Pedro de Mena was active in Granada but settled in Málaga in 1658 in order to create the choir-stalls of the cathedral (see above, left and p. 355, below). Carl Justi claimed that these are "the most original and perfect works of Spanish art, even of the whole of modern sculpture. They are probably the last and definitive word in Spanish sculptural art."

During a trip to Madrid and Toledo, Pedro developed a knowledge of Castilian sculpture, appropriating a series of iconographic models hitherto unknown in Andalusia. Above all, however, he was influenced by its profoundly emotional character, a feature which was to distinguish all his subsequent work. Rarely has the mysticism of Spanish baroque sculpture been more powerfully conveyed than in his *Penitent Magdalene* (1664; see right). This work was given on

long-term loan to the Museo Nacional de Escultura in Vallodolid in 1933 by the Prado; a few years ago it was brought back to Madrid for conservation and is currently on display there. It is to be hoped that this piece will in due course be returned to Vallodolid where it can be restored to its position as the centerpiece of Spain's most important collection of sculpture. In the meantime Pedro de Mena is well represented there by *St. Peter of Alcántara* (see far right). The structure of the head and hands of the saint displays an impressive, almost tangible realism. St. Teresa of Ávila observed of this sculpture that it seemed to be made out of roots, and that the patchy nature of the monk's habit, constructed from various pieces of wood, further emphasized the humility of the saint's demeanor.

Madrid

The final part of this general survey of the sculpture of the seventeenth century will concentrate on the court in Madrid, which became an important center for sculpture. Commissions from the royal court and from noble families led to the importation of foreign works of art and transformed Madrid into a meeting-point for the two great Spanish schools. What might be considered some of the greatest sculptures of the century were produced here. While the Castilian influence very much predominated during the first third of the century, the impact of the Andalusian style, and particularly that of Granada, is clearer later in the century. This was due to the visits to Madrid of Alonso Cano, Pedro de Mena, and José de Mora.

Pedro de Mena
Penitent Magdalene, 1664
Polychrome wood, 165 cm
Valladolid, Museo Nacional de Escultura
(currently in Prado)

Pedro de Mena
St. Peter of Alcántara, 1633
Polychrome wood, 78 cm
Valladolid, Museo Nacional de Escultura

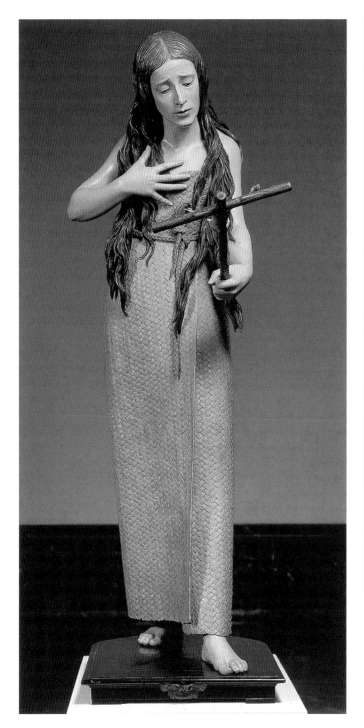

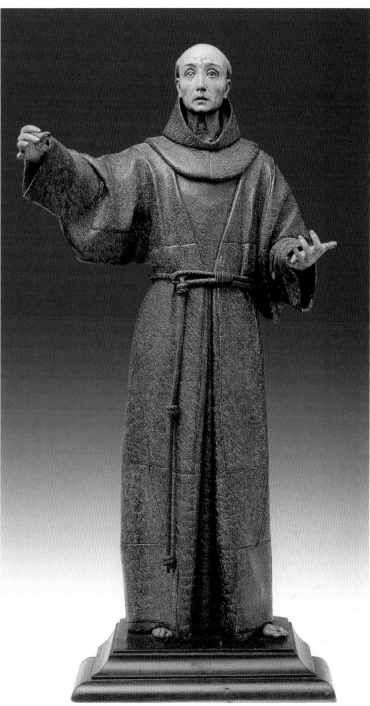

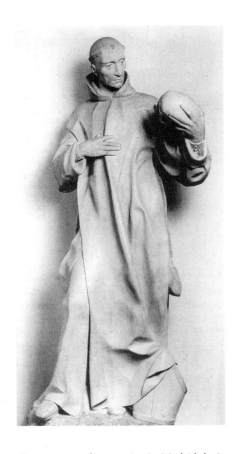

The most important sculptor active in Madrid during the seventeenth century was Manuel Pereira (1588–1683) of Portugal. His *St. Bruno* (1652), created for the portal of the hospice of the charterhouse of El Paular in Madrid (and now in the collections of the Royal Academy of Fine Arts of San Fernando, Madrid), is one of the most remarkable stone sculptures of its time (see above). This figure—a meditation on death—is unpainted, and its subject matter bears eloquent witness to the more ascetic side of Spanish art. According to Palomino, every time Philip IV drove past the statue, he ordered the state coach to stop so that he could gaze on it in peace.

Other sculptors such as Domingo de la Rioja and Juan Sánchez Barba maintained Pereria's high aesthetic standards in Madrid into the following century.

The Eighteenth Century

Spanish sculpture of the eighteenth century has been unfairly neglected by art historians. It was to some extent overshadowed by the work of the previous century and was also heavily criticized during the reign of neo-classicism. These rather biased views have only recently been revised. The period will be examined here briefly for two main reasons. First, there are a few great names which cannot reasonably be ignored in an account of Spanish baroque sculpture. Second, during the first third of the eighteenth century some late baroque works were produced which are of considerable significance for their role in the development of the style, representing the continuation and perfection of some of the artistic tendencies introduced in the last decades of the preceding century.

The structure of contemporary altarpieces illustrates this development particularly effectively. Churches were filled with arrangements of columns, entablatures, reliefs, and sculpture in an attempt to create a sense of the *Gesamtkunstwerk*, or total work of art. This concept, was, as we have seen, characteristically baroque. The large and richly decorated altarpiece of the Santiago church at Medina de Rioseco (see right) is an example of this tendency; it was the product of a collaboration between two of the best known artists of the day, having been designed by Joaquín de Churriguera (1674–1724) and constructed in the workshop of the sculptor Tomás de Sierra.

The Tomé family, another important group of artists, is closely associated with the *Transparente* in Toledo cathedral (see right and p. 103), one of the masterpieces of Spanish sculpture. This is a *trasaltar* or a sacramental chapel in the ambulatory behind the chancel and high altar, intended to display the sacrament in both directions, hence the link with "transparent." The use here of bronze and marble was not typical for Spain and suggests the influence of other European countries. Narciso Tomé (1690–1742) completed the piece after twelve years' work with the help of his brothers Diego and Andrés. It is an impressive architectural and technical statement, a monumental altarpiece lit by a window in the vault above and combining architecture, sculpture, and painting in the service of a eucharistic scheme which vibrantly asserts the mysticism of Catholicism.

During the course of the century, Madrid became a center of Spanish sculpture. The accession of the Bourbon dynasty brought an end to the isolation of Spanish art and architecture; many foreign sculptors, at first mostly French and later Italian, were put under contract to decorate the new royal palaces. By contrast, decorative pieces in the churches of Madrid, much in demand, were characterized by a reliance on traditional forms of representation, demonstrated, for example, by the famous *Head of St Paul* by Juan Alonso Villabrille y Ron (see p. 370), now in the Museo Nacional de Escultura in Valladolid. This is another explicit illustration of the cruelty of martyrdom: the head of the tortured saint with its staring eyes and furrowed brow set into a carved ground is depicted with exaggerated realism.

The next generation of sculptors, born in the eighteenth century, formulated the characteristic elements of the final stage of Spanish baroque sculpture. Traditionally crafted, and retaining some of the realistic tendencies of the past, what might be seen as a substantially

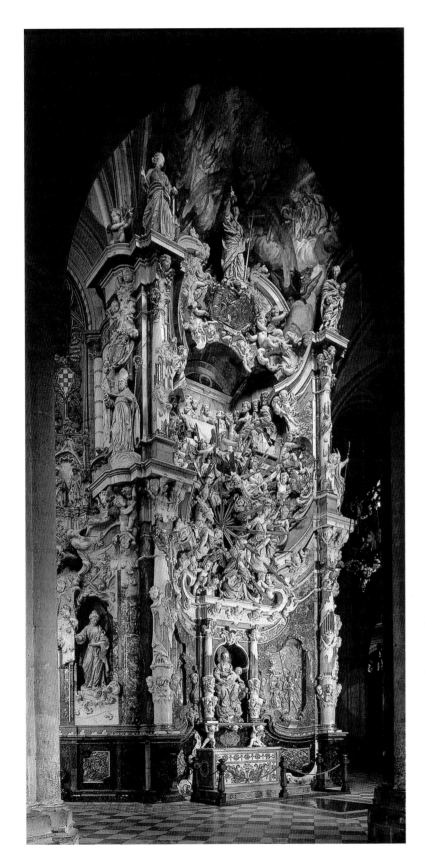
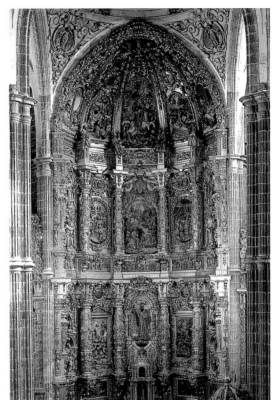
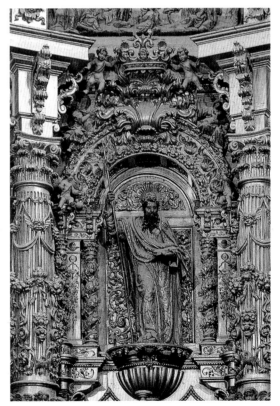

Juan Alonso Villabrille
Head of St. Paul, 1707
Polychrome wood, height 55 cm, width 61.5 cm
Valladolíd, Museo Nacional de Escultura

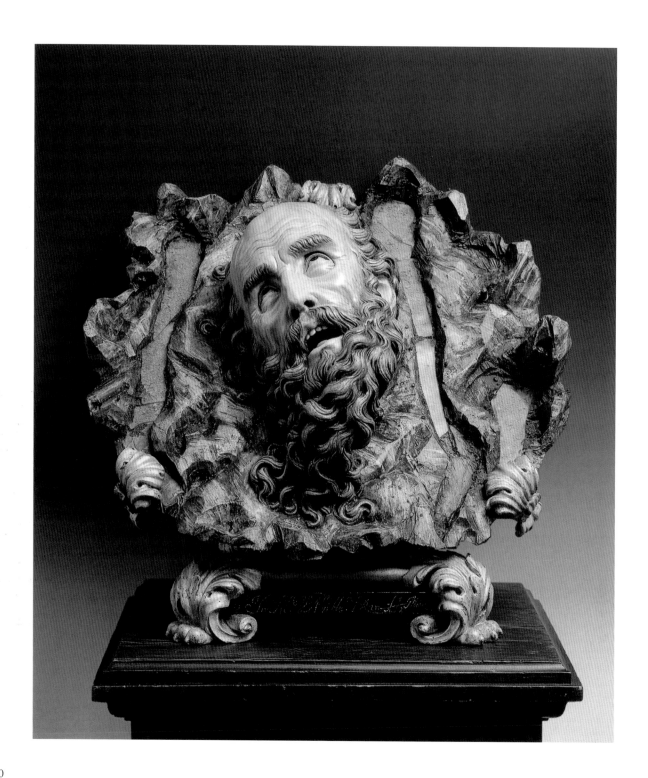

Luis Salvador Carmona
Holy Shepherdess, mid-eighteenth century
Polychrome wood and silver, 90 cm
Nava del Rey (Valladolid), Capuchin convent

Francisco Salzillo
Last Supper, 1760
Polychrome wood, life-size
Murcia, Museo Salzillo

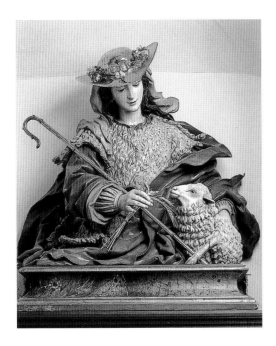

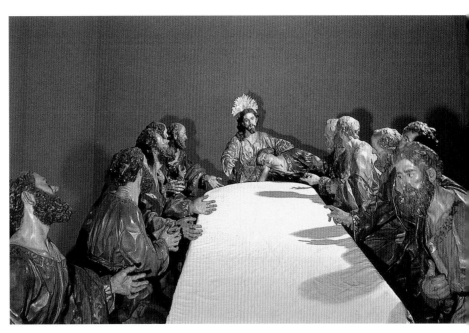

more "pleasing" art based on rococo was established from the second third of the century. Luis Salvador Carmona (1708–67) was the chief representative of the Madrid school whose influence gradually spread into other provinces. The *Holy Shepherdess*, a bust preserved in the convent of the Capuchin nuns of Nava del Rey, (Carmona's birthplace), conveys a new image of the Virgin as co-redeemer: the Virgin is a much gentler and more earthly figure than previously depicted, and this is suggested both by her facial expression and by the aristocratic silver accessories—hat, staff, earrings, and ring—with which she is adorned (see above left).

The work of Francisco Salzillo (1707–83) of Murcia exemplifies the impact of the rococo idiom on Spanish sculpture of the period. Economic and cultural exchange with other Mediterranean countries was a feature of this region, which attracted such artists as the Frenchman Antonio Dupar and the Neapolitan Nicolás Salzillo, Francisco's father; they prepared the way for a sculptural idiom that reflected a wider European influence. Francisco Salzillo perfected his style in processional groups like the *Last Supper* of 1762 (see above right). In this ambitious composition, the twelve apostles seated around the table are distinguished by a precisely rendered psychological characterization. It is worth noting that from its beginnings in Castile until its final flowering in Murcia the outstanding examples of Spanish baroque sculpture were represented in the same guise, namely that of processional art, although they often incorporated radically different compositional solutions.

An interest in neo-classicism was established during the reign of Charles III (1760-88). After his accession the king demanded a more severe and functional art, a requirement that was actually enforced by decree. The new regulations determined that the use of wood in sculpture should be avoided, since marble or other appropriate types of stone could be found in the vicinity of every town in the kingdom. To justify this ruling, reference was made to the danger of fire posed by wooden sculpture and to the high cost of producing colored versions.

The real reason, however, was quite different and appears to have been based solely on aesthetic considerations. This is suggested by the fact that wood was still used for religious sculpture on altarpieces; this was not only permitted but was also cheaper to produce; However, figures were often painted white in order to simulate marble. Plaster and ceramic sculpture also gained in popularity during this time. It was these drastic measures that effectively brought the production of baroque sculpture to an end; one of the most authentic expressions of Spanish art was thus brought to a close.

Karin Hellwig

Painting in Italy, Spain, and France in the Seventeenth Century

An interesting characterization of the different ways of life in Italy, Spain, and France during the seventeenth century comes from the mouth of a fool in Lope de Vega's novel *El peregrino en su patria*. The fool says that he would prefer to be born in France, live in Italy, and die in Spain; the first because of the straightforward honesty of the nobility and the king, the second because of the freedom and joy in life, and the third, finally, because of the purity and truth of the Catholic faith. The desire to live in Italy expressed by Lope's character is typical of many French and Spanish artists of the time. Not only Poussin and Claude Lorrain, but also Velázquez and Ribera—to name only four great masters—were all, despite their quite different roots, drawn to Italy and above all to Rome. Italian painters of this time frequently change the location of their activity, but mostly stay on their native soil. However, during the seventeenth century some in Spain and France voiced their concern at this state of affairs. Thus, for example, the Spanish art historian Antonio Palomino stresses that only mature artists were in serious demand in Rome; young painters wasted years there, became disoriented and dazed by "the astonishing labyrinth of wonders," and might die in poverty. Many artists, continues Palomino, learned to their disadvantage that it was better to frequent Hispanic schools than Roman inns.

Appreciation of those seventeenth-century masters who are now numbered among the most distinguished artists of their time has undergone considerable fluctuation in the course of the last two hundred years. Early criticism of baroque art in the eighteenth and nineteenth centuries, however, was at first directed less towards painting than towards architecture. In his study *Renaissance und Barock* (1888), Heinrich Wölfflin expressed criticism of the preference of that era for "massive effects, the colossal, the overpowering," and found fault with its apparent violation of renaissance concepts of harmony. Later, in his *Kunstgeschichtliche Grundbegriffe* [Basic Concepts in Art History] (1915), he appears to have discovered a relationship between the baroque and modern world of forms. Between these two works came Alois Riegl's *Die Entstehung der Barockkunst in Rom* [The Origins of Baroque Art in Rome] (1908), a positive appreciation of the architecture of the era. Comprehensive analyses of baroque painting began to appear after monographs on artists had been published. Among the major accounts were Hermann Voss's *Die Malerei des Barock in Rom* [Baroque Painting in Rome] (1925) and Nikolaus Pevsner's and Otto Grautoff's *Barockmalerei in den romanischen Ländern* [Baroque Painting in the Romance Countries] (1928).

The work of Italian baroque painters has received a variety of responses over the past two centuries. Caravaggio's œuvre, which had already divided his contemporaries into two camps, with his opponents taking exception to his apparent disregard for decorum and the lack of *historia*, was interpreted as a forerunner of modernism as early as the last century. Poussin was hailed by his contemporaries as *peintre philosophe* and highly regarded by David and

Ingres. The evaluation of Guido Reni reads as a story of brilliant fame, which was marred only by the commercial exploitation and trivialization of his paintings.

The work of the Spanish painters has had a mixed reception: masters such as Diego Velázquez, Francisco Zurbarán, and, above all, Jusepe Ribera strongly appeal to the modern observer, but Bartolomé Esteban Murillo has made less of an impact. Velázquez was discovered in the mid-nineteenth century by French painters such as Courbet and Manet, who had an unrestrained admiration for the *peintre des peintres*. Only later did art historians begin to take him more seriously: numerous monographs were produced, among which Carlo Justi's early *Diego Velázquez und sein Jahrhundert* [Diego Velázquez and his Century] (1888) has remained a worthwhile discussion of the subject. In the eighteenth century, Murillo's paintings were already so popular that their export was prohibited under Charles III in 1779. However, since the end of the nineteenth century Murillo's work has been dismissed in increasingly critical terms for what is seen as its saccharine sentimentality. Only in the last two decades of the twentieth century has there been a reassessment of this painter which has attempted to do justice to the status of his art. Zurbarán's work has also been reassessed only in recent years. Mainly preserved in the monasteries of Andalusia and Extremadura, these paintings were for a long time inaccessible to the public, and their spiritual figures and monastic asceticism make it difficult to classify them according to current perceptions of baroque style. An extraordinary public interest in the painters of the period is suggested by the appearance of many specialist publications as well as numerous exhibitions devoted to these masters during the last twenty years, including Caravaggio, Guercino, Gentileschi, Claude, Murillo, Poussin, Reni, Ribera, Valdés Leál, Velázquez, Vouet, and Zurbarán.

During the course of the seventeenth century, the arts were increasingly used to promote political purposes and either taken into the service of the Counter-Reformation by the Church or adopted by the absolutist courts for the programmatic glorification of the ruler. At the same time, panel painting became a particularly desirable collector's item for noblemen, courtiers, and kings as well as for the bourgeoisie, which was going through a process of emancipation. Even more markedly than during the Renaissance, artistic life was now concentrated in the large centers, either the seats of courts—Madrid and Paris as well as papal Rome—or places of particular economic importance such as the trading cities of Naples and Seville. Nonetheless, the centers of gravity shifted: Florence and Venice, the most important centers of art during the Renaissance, were hardly to play a role in artistic life between 1600 and 1700.

During this time a powerful change was occurring between the various centers of art. Influenced by political and economic factors, the painter's contractual situation changed in individual cities, and many were forced into frequent changes of residence. Caravaggio

left Lombardy and went to Rome; from there he traveled to Naples, then to Malta and back again to Naples. The Carracci and many of their pupils moved from Bologna to Rome, some of them returning to their native city. Artemisia Gentileschi was active not only in Rome but also in Florence, Naples, and England. Ribera left Valencia for Rome, and finally settled in Naples. Claude Lorrain, from Lorraine, and Poussin, from Paris, settled in Rome and were active there until the end of their lives. In addition, this period saw an increase in the quantity of exported art, resulting in a lively exchange of works of art between the centers: Poussin painted in Rome for French and Spanish clients, and Ribera in Naples created a number of works for the Spanish nobility and court.

The plentiful surviving information, in addition to the works of art, on the individual painters and their work and on the theory and practice of art as well as the aesthetic values of the seventeenth century, is mainly derived from archive material. There are also a number of documents which record contemporary views on art and artists. The painter and art historian Giorgio Vasari created a prototype in 1550 with the first edition of his work on the lives of Italian and particularly Florentine painters, *Le vite de' più eccellenti pittori, scultori, e architetti*, which was to be taken up in the course of the following century by a number of authors, some of them artists. Among the outstanding Italian art historians of the seventeenth century are Giovanni Baglione (*Le vite de' pittori, scultori, ed architetti, dal pontificato di Gregorio XIII del 1572 fino a' tempi di Papa Urbano VIII nel 1642*, Rome 1642), his successor Giovanni Battista Passeri (*Vite de' pittori, scultori ed architetti che ànno lavorato in Roma morti dal 1641 fino al 1673*, Rome 1642), and the learned librarian and antiquarian of Queen Christina of Sweden, Giovanni Pietro Bellori (*Le vite de' pittori, scultori, ed architetti moderni*), Rome 1672), as well as the Florentine abbot Filippo Baldinucci (*Notizie de' professori di disegno da Cimabue in qua*, Rome 1672), from whom we can discover much about the artists who were active in Rome, both indigenous and foreign masters. The painter and literary man Bernardo de Dominici (*Vite dei pittori, scultori, ed architetti napoletani*, Naples 1742-43) provides detailed information about artistic life in Naples.

The lives and works of Spanish painters are reported in detail by the Seville painter and art historian Francisco Pacheco (*El arte de la pintura*, Seville 1649), the historian and musician at the court of Philip IV, Lázaro Diaz del Valle (*Origen y illustracion del nobilissimo y real arte de la pintura y dibuxo*, 1656–59), and also the painter and art historian Antonio Palomino (*El parnaso español pintoresco laureado*, Madrid 1724). Finally, French painters are addressed in the writings of André Félibien (*Entretiens sur les vies et les ouvrages des plus excellents peintres anciens et modernes*, Paris 1666–85), and more can be gleaned on this subject from the art-lover and connoisseur Roger de Piles (*Abrégé de la vie des peintres*, Paris 1699).

Biographies of individual artists were still a rarity in the seventeenth century. Of the artists mentioned here, only one biography is known, a life of Velázquez produced by his pupil Juan de Alfaro (1640–80), long since out of print.

Rome

Rome was, of course, the most important center of painting in seventeenth-century Italy. In a nostalgic tone, the historian Giambattista Passeri reports in 1673: "When Urban VIII became pope it really seemed that the golden age of painting had returned; for he was a pope of friendly disposition and open-minded in nature, and had noble intentions." Indeed, the history of painting in Rome is primarily the history of the artistic patronage of the popes. This was not only because Italian baroque painting was almost exclusively produced in the service of the Church, but also because many artists were summoned to Rome on various commissions by the popes, their nephews and other relatives, and members of families with whom they were on friendly terms.

After the triumph of the Counter-Reformation, the new incumbents of the Holy See had abandoned their predecessors' dream of world supremacy for the papacy, and now transferred their bid for power to a spiritual realm, to whose wealth the capital city of Rome was to bear witness. They considered themselves the heirs of the Roman emperors and planned to revive the splendor of ancient Rome. The election of Paul V Borghese (1605–21) as pope signified a radical change in the cultural life of Rome. While the pontificates of Sixtus VII and Clement VIII were marked above all by the tendencies of the Counter-Reformation, under Paul V, and particularly with his nephew Scipione Borghese, a desire for ostentation and a love of luxury were also to play a significant part in papal schemes. His villa on the Pincio became a meeting place for the literary figures and artists of the city. Each new pontificate during the seventeenth century almost inevitably resulted in the building of a palace or a villa, the foundation of a family chapel in one of the most important churches in Rome, and the establishment of an art collection.

The papal metropolis was thus very attractive, for it promised not only well-paid commissions but also the possibility for an enhancement of social rank. A further attraction lay in its overwhelming wealth of superb classical and modern works of art. Rome became the adopted home of many ambitious artists. Every inhabitant of the chair of St. Peter, as soon as he took up his pontificate, began to commission works of art with feverish haste, in order to demonstrate as quickly as possible his wealth and power. With the death of a pope, his family as well as his friends usually fell into disfavor. The fortunes of the busy artists were often of similarly brief duration, since with every new pontificate new families determined the demands made upon them, often striving also to make use of artists from their own home town.

After Pope Julius II had initiated the rebuilding of St. Peter's and its transformation into the foremost church of the Catholic world, during the pontificates of Urban VIII and Alexander VII the completion and decoration of the church became the focus of attention, as did a number of town-planning measures of vast proportions. A high point in the artistic life of Rome was represented by the pontificates of Urban VIII Barberini (1623–44), Innocent X Pamphili (1644–55), and Alexander VII Chigi (1655–67). Urban VIII was only fifty-five years old and in the best of health when he was elected pope. During his reign he employed such artists as Bernini and Pietro da Cortona; the severity of the Counter-Reformation was mitigated by luxury, and a grandeur and extravagance hitherto unprecedented. Rome became the most important cultural center of Italy, and offered a rich sphere of activity for painters. There was great demand for paintings for the decoration of churches, private chapels, and art-lovers' collections, as well as for frescos to adorn the vaults of churches and the ceilings of the many newly built palaces. In about 1600, Annibale Carracci was commissioned to decorate the galleria of Palazzo Farnese. In the 1630s Pietro da Cortona created the frescos for the galleria of Palazzo Barberini and in the 1650s those for the galleria of Palazzo Pamphili. In addition to the popes, there were many clients offering commissions, among them the orders founded in connection with the Counter-Reformation like the Oratorians, Jesuits, and Theatines, which all required new and sumptuous houses of worship. The many new churches, including S. Maria della Pace, the Gesù, S. Ignazio, S. Andrea al Quirinale, and S. Carlo al Corso were supplied with splendid fresco cycles.

The relationship between painter and client was a complex one. In some cases an artist might be regularly employed by a particular client, living in his palace and receiving a monthly salary as well as the customary fees. Thus, we know that Andrea Sacchi lived in the palazzo of Cardinal Antonio Barberini between 1637 and 1640. However, it was more common for a painter to be independent and have his own workshop. If an artist received an important commission, a contract was usually drawn up which included a written record of the agreed extent and destination of the work, its subject, the date by which the work was to be completed, and the fee to be paid. In these cases, the subject was often formulated in very general terms. For example, Urban VIII commissioned an altarpiece for the church of S. Sebastiano showing the martyrdom of St. Sebastian with eight figures; the choice of the eight figures was left to the artist. The fee for the painting was often based on the number of principal figures in the composition, for which many artists had fixed prices. Further, the level of the artist's reputation played a part, so that with increasing fame an artist was able to raise his prices. Thus, Domenichino charged one hundred and thirty ducats per figure in his frescos for Naples cathedral, but Lanfranco is known to have charged only one hundred. Guercino adopted a businesslike attitude towards miserly clients. He wrote to Antonio Ruffo: "Since my usual fee per figure is one hundred and twenty five ducats and since Your Excellency has set an upper limit of eighty ducats, you will have a good view of only half of each figure." Apart from commissioned works, most painters kept a small stock of incomplete pictures which could be shown to visitors and quickly finished as required. Most painters, however, were not rich by any normal standard. Malvasia says of Reni that despite his position as court painter to the pope, he announced on his return to Bologna in 1612 that he was weary of trying to earn a living as a painter and could make money more easily as an art dealer.

The Roman School of Artists

It was from Rome under Annibale Carracci and Caravaggio that the decisive impulses emerged for the development of painting throughout Europe. Michelangelo Merisi, known as Caravaggio (1573–1610) after his home town of Caravaggio, came from Lombardy and had received his education in Milan; he arrived in Rome about 1590, spending most of his life and creating his most important works there. Caravaggio's innovations lay in his revolutionary handling of his subject matter. He brought secular elements into the representation of holy lives, practiced a flagrant realism, and was not afraid to portray human ugliness. His heroes are not idealized figures but are often old, sometimes even with dirty feet. His paintings are frequently characterized by a profound darkness from which figures and objects appear under a striking shaft of light. Soon after Caravaggio, a series of Bolognese painters arrived in Rome, where they came to dominate the art scene. Annibale Carracci (1560–1609), of the Carracci family of painters, was summoned to Rome by Cardinal Odoardo Farnese in 1595 to collaborate on the decoration of Palazzo Farnese. His most important work was the ceiling fresco of the Galleria Farnese, on which he collaborated with his brothers Agostino and Domenichino. The Carracci's aim was the revival of the art of Raphael, whose work had sunk into oblivion during the mannerist period. Gian Lorenzo Bernini's observation of 1665 confirms that Carracci had succeeded in this, for he "had combined everything that was good: the graceful line of Raphael, the precise anatomy of Michelangelo, the distinguished manner of Correggio, the coloring of Titian, and the imagination of Giulio Romano and Mantegna."

Domenico Zampieri, known as Domenichino (1581–1641), also came from Bologna. He worked with Annibale Carracci on the painting of the Galleria Farnese, creating not only a number of images of saints, but also the frescos of S. Andrea della Valle. Domenichino is regarded as the earliest representative of a consistent classicism in Rome. His clear simple compositions enhance the lucidity and accessibility of his style, which is marked by a gentle, serene intimacy. Guido Reni (1575–1642), another representative of the Bolognese school, introduced a slightly different dimension to his work. After studying under the Flemish painter Denys Calvaert he entered the Carracci's academy in 1594. His life in Bologna was interrupted by several stays in Rome between 1600 and 1603, 1607

and 1611, and 1612 and 1614. In Rome, Reni was employed by Scipione Borghese on a fixed salary. The emotional content of his artistic compositions and his achievements as a colorist decisively shaped the genres of monumental religious painting, private devotional pictures, and history painting. Giovanni Francesco Barbieri, called Guercino (1591–1666), born at Cento near Bologna, was mainly active there and, after Reni's death, in Bologna. In 1621 he was summoned to Rome by Gregory XV and stayed there only for the two-year duration of his pontificate. His most significant work here, apart from altarpieces, was the decoration of the Casino Ludovisi. Representing pronounced movement and foreshortening in his figures, Guercino filled his work with a dramatic quality which anticipated the high baroque manner of the work of Pietro da Cortona. His model was not classical antiquity; rather, he tended towards a picturesque style that emphasized color.

Pietro da Cortona (1596–1669) came to Rome in 1613, and was active there as a painter and architect. In addition to paintings, he created a number of frescos, including those decorating the gigantic vault of the ceremonial hall of Palazzo Barberini (1633–39) and the frescos in S. Maria in Vallicella (1633–39). Pietro's multi-figured compositions imbued with pathos established his reputation as the founder of Roman high baroque. A quite different position was taken up by Andrea Sacchi (1599–1661) who represented instead a strict classicism. He studied in Rome under Francesco Albani, went to Bologna in 1616, and from 1621 until his death in Rome worked chiefly for the Barberini. Sacchi produced several altar paintings as well as frescoes. His fresco *Divine Providence*, painted in 1630 in Palazzo Barberini, excited the greatest admiration. Sacchi avoided all exaggeration of action and gesture and instead preferred rigidity of form and the clear closed structure as expressions of ceremonial calm. His works lean towards classical Roman art and towards Raphael.

By the seventeenth century Rome was already considered a mecca for artists from all over Europe. Inevitably, therefore, many painters attempted to make their fortunes in the Eternal City. Among them, the *Bamboccianti* came from the Netherlands and Flanders; their founder was Pieter van Laer (1599–1642). They represent an artistic movement which effectively introduced a new genre into Roman painting, a naturalistic depiction of contemporary street and inn scenes which avoided any attempt at idealization. The name of the group derived from van Laer, whom his friends called *Bamboccio* (the word for a deformed puppet or simpleton) because of his peculiar physical appearance.

The *Bamboccianti* had good connections with the French painters in Rome, among whom Poussin and Claude were the most famous. Nicolas Poussin (1594–1664) came from a small village in Normandy and went to Paris, where he worked with Philippe de Champaigne. In 1624 he came to Rome where he was to spend most of his life. Here the master developed an enthusiasm for classical art which led to the creation of a number of small mythological paintings for private clients. After 1648 Poussin discovered landscape painting and produced a series of works in which he skillfully achieved the illusion of depth through the use of color, inserting figures only as accessories. Claude Gellée, known as Claude (1600–82), was also to settle in Rome. He is considered one of the first landscape painters in the modern sense. His sensitively composed subjects are evidence of the artist's confrontation with nature. Often real places are not represented in his works, but grandiose classical landscapes into which Roman or high renaissance buildings are harmoniously set and which become the scenes of meetings between gods and mortals. The German art historian Sandrart, however, observed a certain lack of skill in the painter's rendering of figures in such scenes. Claude prepared drawings after his paintings which were brought together in the *Liber Veritatis* in order to protect his copyright and guard against unauthorized copies.

Among the most important painters active in Rome in the second half of the century were Carlo Maratta and Fra Andrea Pozzo. Carlo Maratta (1625–1713) was a pupil of Sacchi in Rome and is considered the chief representative of the classicist element in Roman painting during this period. Maratta mainly produced altar paintings and religious-historical works, but also distinguished himself as a portrait painter. Fra Andrea Pozzo (1624–1709) from Como was active in Milan and in 1665 became a Jesuit lay brother. He specialized in architectural painting in perspective and in 1681, through the agency of Maratta, he was summoned to Rome, where he created his most important work in S. Ignazio.

In the Rome of the seventeenth century, then, no absolutely coherent artistic school can be identified; rather, a number of significant trends can be detected. Among these stylistic tendencies is the academicism of the Carracci and their followers, whose principal aim was to recapture the classical beauty and harmony of the Renaissance. On the other hand the realism of Caravaggio, whose critics accused him of a lack of *invenzione, disegno, decoro,* and *scienzia,* found many followers in Italy as well as in Spain and the Netherlands. The middle of the century witnessed both the exhilarating high baroque painting of Pietro da Cortona and the severe classicism of Sacchi. Bellori, in his *Idea del pittore, scultore, et architetto* published in 1664, established a programmatic theory based on the official tenets of classicism. One of his basic principles was that it was the artist's duty to select the most beautiful and perfect elements from nature and to create from these a perfect form which would actually surpass the imperfections of the natural world. Religious themes dominated the art of the century, for the Counter-Reformation insisted that the primary responsibility of art was to transmit the articles of faith in a convincing manner to every observer. Mythological representations were equally widespread, and it is notable here that, in contrast to France and Spain, no state allegories were created even among representatives of the leading families. The mythological cycles in the galleries of the palaces are restricted to Roman classical antiquity, and any suggestion of a direct link between this period and the current era was avoided.

The Academies

The second academy on Italian soil was founded in Rome in parallel to the various medieval guilds to which the artists belonged. In 1564 Vasari had founded the Accademia del Disegno in Florence, and in 1593, on the initiative of Federico Zuccari, the Accademia di San Luca was established in the papal metropolis. In its statutes the education of artists was described as its chief aim. This meant not only practical instruction and life drawing, but also lectures and discussions on art theory. The Academy was directed by the elected president, the *principe,* an artist member, who was advised by *consiglieri.* The Accademia also achieved great influence in the world of art politics, for all public commissions now came under its control. Its members included not only native but also foreign artists such as Velázquez, Poussin, and Claude. In the 1630s the Accademia was the scene of the famous controversy between Pietro da Cortona and Sacchi, who argued about the manner in which great paintings achieved their effects. Cortona stressed the advantage of lavish compositions with a number of figures in which the main theme was illustrated by subsidiary episodes in order to establish a richness of content and great splendor. He compared history painting with the epic poem in which the main theme was also extended by means of decorative sub-themes. By contrast, Sacchi's ideal painting was like a tragedy, the impact of which was enhanced by the smallest possible number of characters. He argued that a large number of figures and subsidiary groups achieved only a *confusione,* rather than a transmission of the emotions and feelings of the observer. Sacchi reproached Cortona with losing himself in magnificence, instead of occupying himself with more substantial matters. The dispute between these two men, who were both of the highest reputation, is in some respects representative of the different concepts of the high baroque displayed in Roman painting.

In addition to the Accademia di San Luca, Rome also had the Académie de France, founded in 1666 at the initiative of Colbert and intended as a branch of the Paris Academy. The aim of this academy was to enable gifted students at the Paris Académie, by means of a four-year grant, to pursue their education and enjoy life in Rome without financial worries. By way of recompense, it was expected that they should produce copies of the most valuable works of art there for the French court.

Caravaggio
Conversion of St. Paul, 1601
Oil on canvas, 230 x 175 cm
Rome, S. Maria del Popolo,
Cerasi chapel

Caravaggio
Crucifixion of St. Peter, 1601
Oil on canvas, 230 x 117 cm
Rome, S. Maria del Popolo,
Cerasi chapel

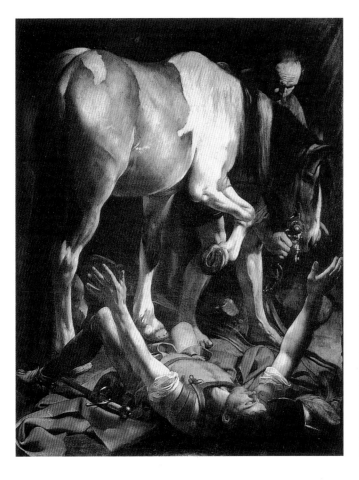

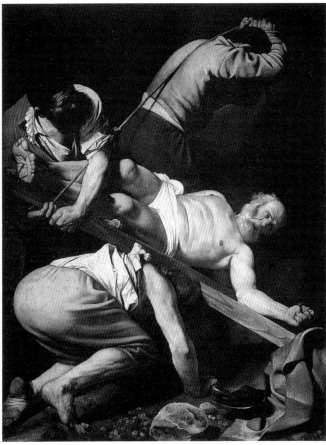

One of Caravaggio's most important commissions in Rome was the decoration of the Cerasi chapel in the church of S. Maria del Popolo. In 1600 he entered into a contract which committed him to complete two paintings for the family chapel of Tiberio Cerasi, Clement VII's treasurer, on the subjects of the conversion of St. Paul and the crucifixion of St. Peter, two themes already treated by Michelangelo in the Cappella Paolina in the Vatican. As in other cases, Caravaggio had to prepare a second version of both paintings on the insistence of the dissatisfied clients.

The painter has chosen the moment when Saul, who, as governor of Damascus, had led the persecution of the Christians, falls from his horse and is blinded, struck down by an overpowering apparition of Christ. Saul lies supine on the ground, his arms outstretched, his eyes closed; his body, severely foreshortened and projecting into the background of the painting, glows with heavenly light. Only Saul's horse and servant are witnesses to the event. In a very dark, unrecognizable setting, a harsh light picks out the figure of Saul, the body of the horse, and the face of the servant. The drama of the event is enhanced not only by the silhouette-like composition, in which the horse fills almost the entire picture, but also by the handling of the light. Caravaggio gives no indication of a miracle, excluding any representation of a divine manifestation which is often seen in other paintings with this theme. Divine power is replaced by the powerful shaft of light. Neither horse nor servant is aware of the significance of the event; the apparition of Christ takes place only within the chosen disciple.

The pendant illustrating the crucifixion of St. Peter shows Peter being fastened to the cross by three of Nero's henchmen. The three men employ tremendous force in fixing the apostle to the cross. While only one of the men's features can be clearly seen, both the face and body of the saint are in full view. Peter is represented with raised head, as a vigorous man who accepts his martyrdom in full consciousness. As in the *Conversion of St. Paul*, Caravaggio restricts the events to the four main figures and has no need of additional witnesses. He heightens the drama with a composition in which the shape of the cross, projecting across the image, is repeated in the four human figures which stand out from the surrounding darkness under a stark shaft of light. The observer is not drawn into the events represented in the painting; the figures are entirely preoccupied with their activity or with suffering, and not a glance or a gesture is directed outwards.

In these two paintings for the Cerasi chapel, Caravaggio emphasizes the discrepancy between the earthly and the spiritual and mystic spheres, showing the saint's unconscious state in the *Conversion of St. Paul*, or execution in the *Crucifixion of St. Peter*, without reinforcing our sense of the saint's own religious experience through the conventional depiction of a visible heavenly apparition.

377

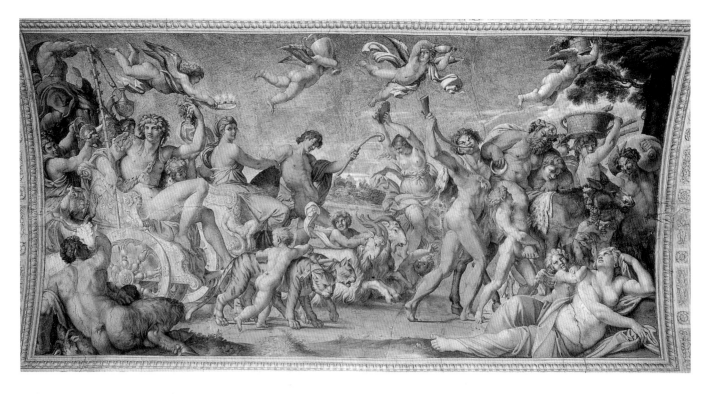

Annibale Carracci
Ceiling frescos of Galleria Farnese, Rome, Palazzo Farnese, c. 1600
General view (left), *Triumph of Bacchus and Ariadne*, detail (above)

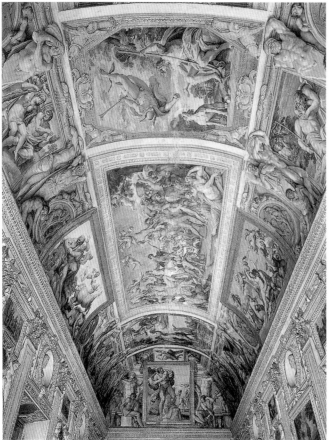

The ceiling fresco of the Galleria Farnese, commissioned by Cardinal Odoardo Farnese, is considered the masterpiece of the Bolognese artist Annibale Carracci; he executed it with the assistance of Agostino Carracci and Domenichino. The Galleria is a space twenty meters long and six meters wide and is surmounted by a semicircular barrel vault in which the Farnese sculpture collection was stored. The essential idea behind the scheme was the glorification of the house of Farnese through mythological association. The cardinal's father, Alessandro Farnese, commander to Philip II, and later governor of the Netherlands, had established a high reputation and fame for the house of Farnese.

Carracci divided the barrel vault lengthwise into three distinct areas. The lateral panels contain a number of smaller mythological scenes, while the four corners contain personifications of the virtues and the two large paintings on the front sides show scenes from the Perseus legend. The five monumental paintings in the central panels in the vertex of the ceiling are particularly important. In the center can be seen the triumphal procession of Bacchus and Ariadne and next to them are scenes showing Pan and Diana, and Paris and Mercury; finally in the last sections are representations of Ganymede and Hyacinthus. The triumphal procession shows the couple sitting in a chariot,

accompanied by joyful nymphs and satyrs. Bacchus, the god of wine and ecstasy, had rescued Ariadne after Theseus had abandoned her on Naxos.

The frescos impressively document Carracci's main artistic aim: to reclaim the naturalistic ideal of renaissance art. Figures of Atlas and herms painted as stone-gray statues support the central section. Real and painted architectural and sculptural elements, garlands, cartouches, and medallions stand beside *quadri riportati, tondi,* and unframed figurative scenes which take place behind the caryatids and nudes. In many areas of the design there is a deceptive element to the closure of spaces, for example at the corners, where the whole is open to the heavens. Often there is no clear dividing line between architecture and painting.

In spite of this complex system of ornament, the images on the ceiling remain easily "readable" due to the stepped axial symmetry of the scheme beginning at the center. The mythological scenes show either the loves of the gods or love between gods and chosen mortals. The central theme of the paintings is the elevation and transformation of the human soul through the power of divine love.

Domenichino and Reni were both Bolognese pupils of Annibale Carracci who came to work in Rome. However, their relationship to history painting was quite different. Their varying aims in the representation of a *historia* are exemplified by the frescos in the Oratorio di S. Andrea, which is part of the church of S. Gregorio Magno. Here, in a commission of 1609 from Cardinal Scipione Borghese, they created on opposite walls frescos of equal size showing scenes from the life of St. Andrew. Andrew was one of the twelve apostles of Jesus, who, according to legend, preached the gospel in Asia Minor and founded the church of Byzantium. He confronted Aegeas, governor of Patras, but could not convert him to Christianity in a disputation. Aegeas subsequently had him scourged and sentenced him to a slow death on an X-shaped cross. Hanging on the cross for two days before he died, Andrew preached to the people and died enveloped in heavenly light. The governor, as he mocked Andrew, was struck with madness and also died.

The two painters depict different stages in the saint's martyrdom. Domenichino's fresco shows the scene of the scourging of St. Andrew, while Reni's illustrates the saint on his way to his crucifixion at the moment when he catches sight of the cross and—remembering Christ—falls to his knees. Domenichino's painting is clearly structured. The action takes place in front of a Roman temple. On the right-hand side of the painting the saint is being scourged by four torturers, while on the left a group of women fearfully observe the proceedings; more observers are visible in the background and the governor is seen seated on his throne between the two groups. Domenichino sets the scene in the martyrium of Achaea and its architecture serves to frame the event. The observer of the painting is also kept at a distance by the rear view of the soldier who is restraining the women hurrying to the rescue.

Guido Reni, on the other hand, composes his scene with a number of figures in a turbulent landscape. In the center, Andrew, surrounded by three henchmen, falls to his knees and raises his hands in prayer in the direction of the cross which can be seen on a hill in the distance. The procession accompanying the saint—Roman soldiers, women with children and men as observers—is thus brought to a disorderly halt. Yet on closer examination it is possible to discern the way in which the various groups of people are set in relation to each other through looks and gestures. The artist draws the observer into the scene: the line of accompanying figures is so broken up in the center that it appears to allow participation in the main events.

The two paintings by Reni and Domenichino, positioned opposite each other in this manner, gave rise to heated discussion. Bellori speaks of a *duello* between the two artists, which can be summed up by the so-called *vecchiarella* [old woman] anecdote. According to this story, Annibale Carracci, asked which of the works of his two pupils he preferred, responded that he himself had understood the essential difference between the frescos because of the behavior and commentary of an old peasant woman or *vecchierella*. This woman—so Bellori relates—was visiting the Oratorio with her nephew, and first gazed at Reni's fresco attentively and presumably with approval, but then turned away from it without a word. But in front of Domeni-chino's *Scourging* she had shown a lively interest and had explained to the child all the details of the events shown. According to this account, preference was not to be given to Reni's work, in which there was nothing to "read." On the other hand, even a person unable to read, like the old woman, could "read" Domenichino's painting, so that the observation of the painting replaced the reading of a text.

Reni's work appeared to provide his opponents with evidence that the artist was not capable of the *maniera grande* [grand manner] essential to history painting. Despite these critical voices, however, Reni's work soon came to be valued by many as a masterpiece of baroque painting. The art of the following years was to demonstrate the extent of the influence of Reni's work in general. The critique of the two representations of St. Andrew and the *vecchiarella* anecdote graphically illustrate the two disparate artistic styles that were established during the seventeenth century—the *storia*, *invenzione*, and *istruire* as suggested by Reni's painting on the one hand, and the *grazia*, *delicatezza*, and *piacere* demonstrated by Domenichino's design on the other.

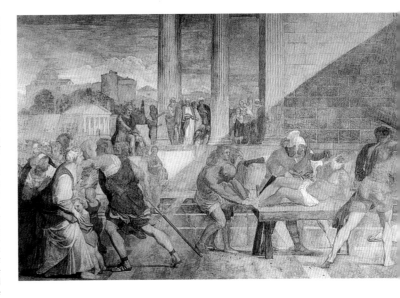

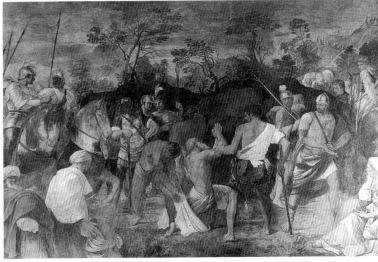

Guido Reni
St. Andrew on his Way to Crucifixion, 1609
Rome, S. Gregorio Magno,
Oratorio di S. Andrea, fresco

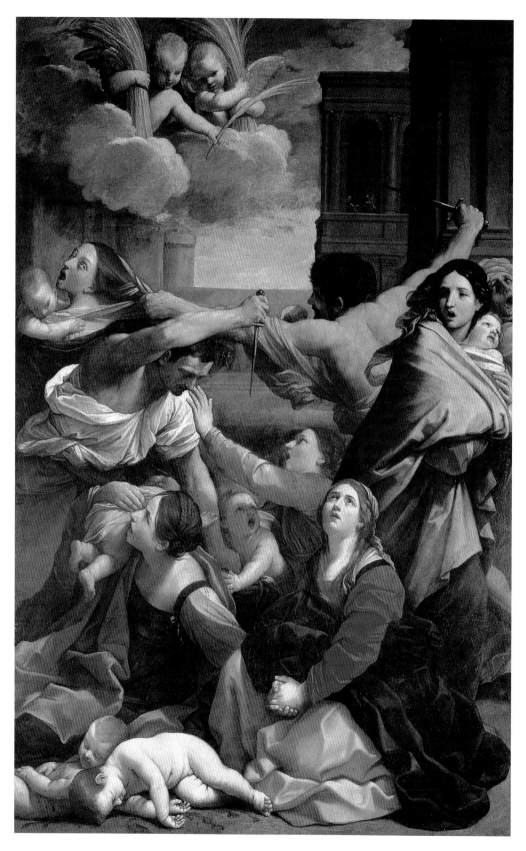

Guido Reni
Massacre of the Innocents at Bethlehem,
1611
Oil on canvas, 268 x 170 cm
Bologna, Pinacoteca Nazionale

The *Massacre of the Innocents at Bethlehem* is one of the works already hailed as a masterpiece by Reni's contemporaries; it was painted towards the end of his second stay in Rome, from 1607 to 1611, shortly before his return to Bologna. Reni created the painting for the Bolognese Beró family for a chapel in the church of S. Domenico in Bologna. The scene shows the episode in the gospel of St. Matthew (2, 1–19), which records that Herod, after he had learnt from the Magi of the East of the "newborn King of the Jews" in Bethlehem, and had failed to find the child, ordered that all children under the age of two in Bethlehem should be murdered.

Reni reduces the event to its essential elements and portrays it in an almost silhouetted style. The principle of the composition is an inverted triangle, the vertex of which is balanced on the lower edge of the painting. At the same time, the two halves are structured with strict symmetry. Each figure in the left-hand half of the painting corresponds to one on the right. In the upper zone, two figures on each side—two women and two soldiers, represented in pairs, in each case one facing forward, one turned away—are contrasted by their gestures. The somber architecture is effectively set-off by the light which floods the background. The focus of the scene is the anguish of the women. While only two soldiers are observed pursuing their brutal task, extensive space is devoted to the suffering of the six women with their pathetic desperate gestures, almost fainting as they try to protect their children from death.

Guercino
Aurora, 1621–23
Rome, Casino Ludovisi, ceiling fresco

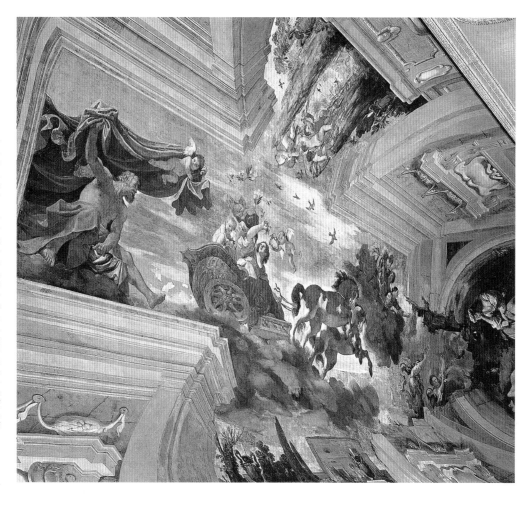

The only ceiling fresco created by Guercino is this *Aurora* with the personifications of Fama, Honor, and Virtus for the Casino of Cardinal Ludovico Ludovisi on the Pincio. The low vault of the Casino was illusionistically raised by the painter Agostino Tassi through painted "mock" architecture, with extremely foreshortened columns. Guercino takes this factor into account and foreshortens the figure of Aurora. In her golden chariot, the goddess, accompanied by putti with flowers and birds, sweeps through the firmament, allowing the dawn to break. Alongside this procession can be seen two landscapes: on one side a realistic view of the Casino, and on the other silvery-green poplars with romping flying putti above. Aurora, scattering flowers and driving away the night, passes the seated, bearded Tithonus. In front of her, emerging from the clouds, are the three Horae, the female guardians of heaven. In his dramatic representation of the scene, set before a sky which opens upwards out of the illusory architecture, the artist's work appears to anticipate the baroque style of Pietro da Cortona.

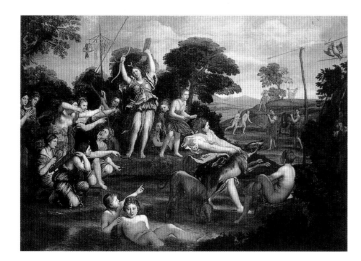

Domenichino
The Retinue of Diana Shooting Birds, 1617
Oil on canvas, 225 x 320 cm Rome, Galleria Borghese

Domenichino was commissioned to produce the painting *The Retinue of Diana Shooting Birds* by Cardinal Aldobrandini. However, the work later ended up in the collection of Scipione Borghese, who wanted at all costs to own it himself.

A shooting contest is in progress here, with Diana's nymphs shooting at a bird tethered to a perch. Three female archers, seen to the left in the picture, have each already completed their master shots; one arrow is stuck in the post, the second has loosened the binding, and the third has hit the bird as it flies away. Diana, acting as judge of the contest, holds in her right hand a golden circlet which is to be bestowed on the victorious archer, seen left, with the upper part of her body exposed.

Domenichino relies here on Virgil's description in book V of the *Aeneid* where he reports on the championships held by Aeneas, exiled to Sicily with the vanquished Trojans, in honor of his father Anchises. In the center of the painting stands the tall upright figure of the goddess Diana, around whom the remaining figures are arranged in an oval formation. The onlooker hidden in a bush to the right, holding his forefinger to his lips as an indication of silence, has recently been identified as Actaeon. This skillful hunter, according to Ovid, had watched the goddess of hunting while she was bathing, and as a punishment had been transformed into a stag, which was torn to pieces by the hounds. The identification is supported not only by the naked nymphs in the foreground but also by the two hounds, one of which is seen leaping in the direction of his owner, the hidden onlooker. The role of the observer of the painting is thus equated in a way with that of Actaeon, and becomes that of a voyeur and unwanted onlooker.

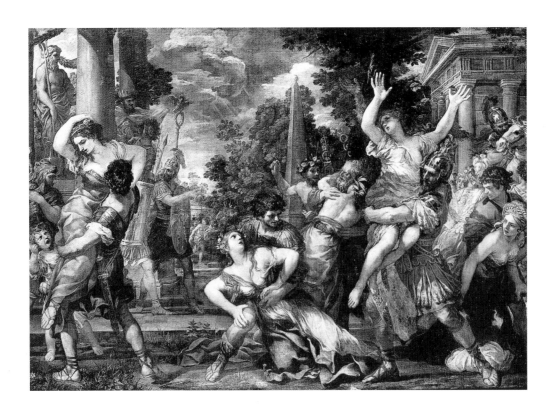

Pietro da Cortona
Rape of the Sabine Women, c. 1629
Oil on canvas, 280 x 426 cm
Rome, Pinacoteca Capitolina

Andrea Sacchi
Vision of St. Romuald, c. 1631
Oil on canvas, 310 x 175 cm
Rome, Pinacoteca Capitolina

The works of Pietro da Cortona and Andrea Sacchi also demonstrate the different ways in which great paintings achieve their effects. While Pietro favored the multi-figure history painting, with main and subsidiary action, Sacchi argued for fewer figures in order to achieve a more concentrated impact. Pietro's painting was executed on the commission of Cardinal Sacchetti, whose choice of theme was intended to portray his family as established, although it had in fact only recently settled in Rome. This painting was produced as a companion to Pietro's *Sacrifice of Polyxena*.

The theme of the rape of the Sabine women is based on the legend of Romulus, the founder of Rome; perceiving the great surplus of male citizens, he invited the Sabines to view the new city and take part in a great banquet. When the visitors least expected it, the Romans fell upon the wives and daughters of the Sabines and put the men to flight.

Pietro places the events in front of a temple of Neptune, where he distributes various scenes of *raptus*, seizure. In the foreground, three couples are shown in groups on a proscenium. For the physical poses of the group on the right Pietro takes as his model Bernini's *Pluto and Proserpine*. In its sculptural execution, the arrangement of the main groups, and the flat background which looks like a stage set Cortona's work is reminiscent of the relief compositions of the sixteenth century. Its artistic style and the use of impressive color effects, which was in fact criticized by contemporary observers

as a manifestation of decadence, stands in contrast to the classical aesthetic of Andrea Sacchi.

Sacchi's rather different approach becomes clear in the monumental painting the *Vision of St. Romuald* for the high altar of the church of S. Romualdo in Rome, since demolished. St. Romuald first lived as a Benedictine monk at Ravenna, then spent the rest of his life in France and Italy as a hermit, founding many eremitic settlements, including the most important, Camaldoli. In Sacchi's painting St. Romuald is shown in a white habit with a walking-stick, sitting in a landscape with three brothers of his order. With his left hand the saint points towards the upper left portion of the painting, where his vision is graphically portrayed. Like Jacob before him, Romuald sees a ladder, upon which his monks, dressed in white, ascend to heaven where the future monastery can be seen.

Sacchi emphasizes the supernatural event by contrasting the dark, almost threatening landscape, in which the trunk and branches of a tree frame two sides of the painting, casting a strong shadow on the gleaming white garments of the monks, with the vision, which is depicted in very light and delicate tones.

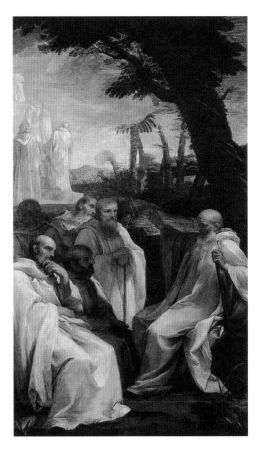

Pieter van Laer
Flagellants, c. 1635
Oil on canvas, 53.6 x 82.2 cm
Munich, Bayerische Staatsgemälde-
ammlungen, Alte Pinakothek

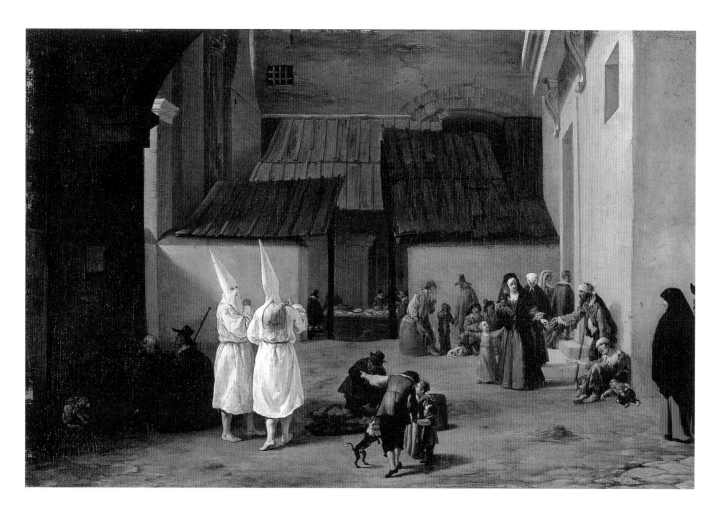

Among the few genre paintings produced in Rome during the seventeenth century were the works of the *Bamboccianti*. In *Flagellants* Pieter van Laer depicts a modest Roman square in front of a church with varied scenes of everyday life. Among the groups of different people such as churchgoers, passers-by, children playing, fruit-sellers, and kneeling pilgrims, two barefooted figures in white hooded mantles stand out. These are flagellants, Christians who scourged themselves with whips in penance for their sins.

Flagellation, which had already been condemned by the Church during the middle ages and had in fact almost disappeared by about 1400, experienced a revival in the seventeenth century among certain groups of *disciplinati*. The painting illustrates several forms of religious devotion which were propagated by brotherhoods and other religious associations. Piety is denoted by the praying pilgrims, self-chastisement by the flagellants, and charity by the alms-giving passers-by. In the background, in the interior of a

room fish are being sold, possibly an allusion to Christ. The numerous references to the austere, self-denying aspect of the Christian faith suggest that the painting should be interpreted as an allegory of the period of fasting.

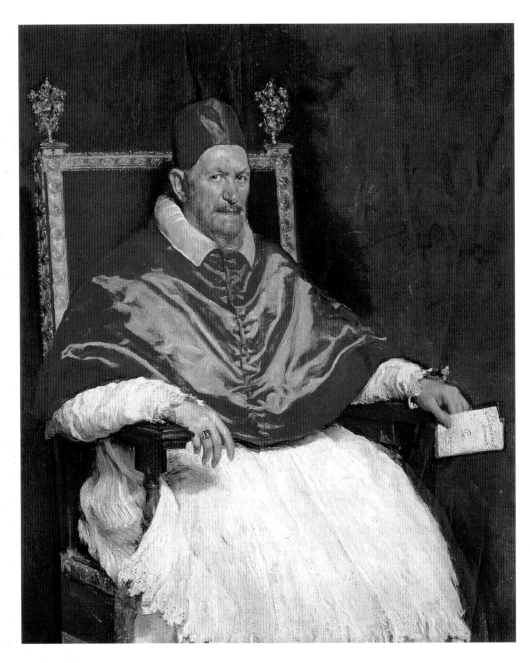

Diego Velázquez
Portrait of Innocent X, 1650
Oil on canvas, 140 x 120 cm
Rome, Galleria Doria Pamphili

Diego Velázquez stayed twice in Rome and these periods were of exceptional importance for the painter's artistic development. During the course of his second visit, from 1649 to 1651, he produced one of his masterpieces, the *Portrait of Pope Innocent X*. This is one of few painted portraits of the pope, although several sculptural portraits by Algardi and Bernini have been preserved.

Little is known about the exact circumstances of its creation. It may well have been a commissioned work, for Velázquez' fame as an outstanding portraitist had long since reached Rome. But the painter might also have offered to portray Innocent X, whom he already knew from his time as nuncio to the court of Philip IV. Velázquez had a very specific interest in obtaining the favor of the pope: he had been trying for years to achieve entry into the nobility through reception into the order of Santiago, and hoped to gain the goodwill of Innocent X by painting a successful portrait. The art historian Palomino reports that Veláz-quez, practicing the portrayal of a head from life, first created a portrait of his assistant Juan de Pareja, who had accompanied him. Only later did he start work on the papal likeness.

Velázquez here falls back on the tradition established by Raphael for the three-quarter portrait of a seated figure, which Titian also employed in his portrait of Pope Paul III. The distinctly unflattering rendering of the features of Innocent X, described by his contemporaries as unattractive and disagreeably delineated, is said to have induced the subject to exclaim: "Troppo vero!" [Too true!] In this portrait, Velázquez dis-penses with such elements as room settings and concentrates entirely on the psychological moment, treating the facial features and hands of the subject with particular care. The coloring is dominated by various shades of red. The loose brushwork, which requires the painting to be observed from a distance, is Velázquez' tribute to the Venetians and above all to Titian. The portrait met with strong approval and resulted in the admission of the painter to the Accademia di San Luca.

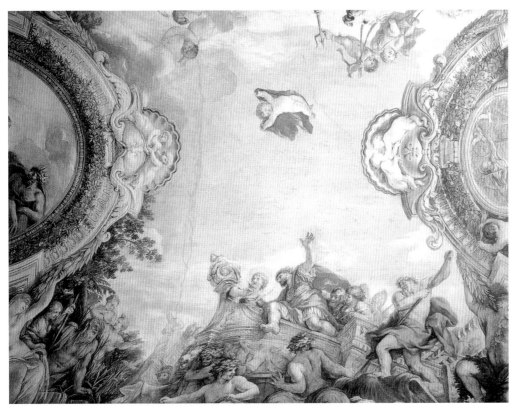

Pietro da Cortona
Landing of the Trojans at the Mouth of the Tiber, 1655
Detail of ceiling fresco, Galleria Pamphili
Rome, Palazzo Pamphili

BELOW:
Galleria Pamphili, general view
At about the time when Velázquez was painting his portrait, Innocent X ordered new decoration for his family palace on Piazza Navona and commissioned Pietro da Cortona to paint the frescos in the Galleria.

The theme of these images is the last phase of the wanderings of Aeneas, who, after the destruction of Troy, found himself in Italy with his companions, where he was to conquer Latium and become the ancestor of the *gens Julia*. All the scenes here, which are of different proportions according to significance and content, are connected with this historic event.

Pietro structures the ceiling into several adjoining areas, with boundaries that become slightly blurred; the scenes are partly distinguished as *quadri riportati*, images within an image. A narrative thread leads the observer from scene to scene, and the large square painting in the central field of the vault showing Jupiter reconciling the disputing goddesses Juno and Venus plays a central role. Juno had taken the side of the Greeks in the Trojan war, while Venus, Aeneas' mother, protectively accompanied the hero on his wanderings, finally leading him to Latium. Jupiter reconciled the goddesses so that the outcome of the battle against Turnus, king of the Rutulians, would be victorious for Aeneas. Above Jupiter, Fate is personified by a female figure holding the scales of Justice. Another painting shows the successful landing of Aeneas and his cheering companions at the mouth of the Tiber, where the river god welcomes them. The episodes which take place on earth are shown at the foot of the vault, and, in contrast to the heavenly scenes, are not framed. Thus open, silhouette-like compositions are created, achieving the illusion of a spatial continuum and breaking through the boundaries of the ceiling.

Pietro's frescos are based on a differentiated iconographical scheme: Aeneas' journey is seen as an *itinerarium mentis*, a journey of the soul or process of psychological development, which leads from the *vita voluptuosa* (Troy in flames) through the *vita activa* (Carthage) to the goal, the *vita contemplativa* (Rome). Interpreted in a mystical spirit, the *Aeneid*, according to the commentary of Cristoforo Landino, represents the triumph of the Church and the papacy, which saw itself as the legitimate successor to the *imperium Romanum*.

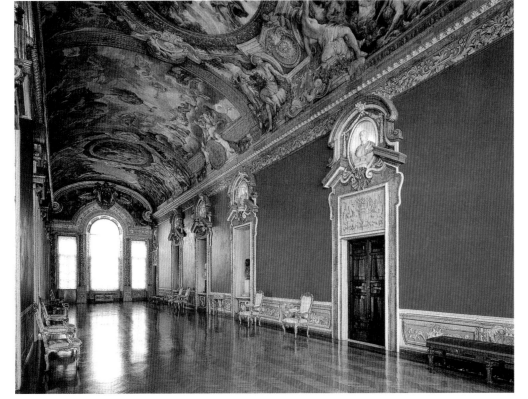

Nicolas Poussin
Kingdom of Flora, 1631
Oil on canvas, 131 x 181 cm
Dresden, Staatliche Kunstsammlungen,
Gemäldegalerie Alte Meister

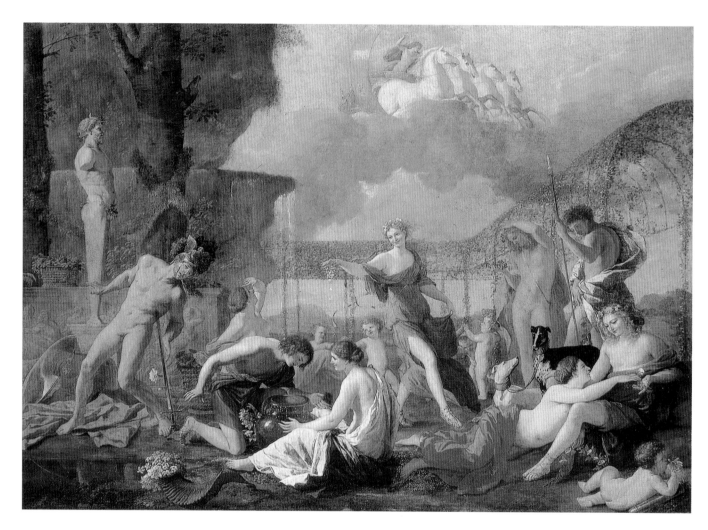

Another direction in painting is represented by the two French artists living in Rome, Poussin and Claude Lorrain. Poussin's *Kingdom of Flora* is among his early works; it was created in Rome, commissioned by the Sicilian nobleman Fabrizio Valguarnera.

The flower goddess Flora is shown dancing at the center of a charming landscape, surrounded by recumbent and standing figures. These are Greek heroes and demigods who met their deaths through various misfortunes and were turned into flowers. In front of a herm of the god of nature stands Ajax, the Greek; after the armor of Achilles was not given to him but to Odysseus, he fell in disap-

pointment on his sword. Hyacinths grew where his blood flowed on to the ground. To his right, kneeling, is Narcissus, who was so passionately in love with his reflection that he was turned into a narcissus. Opposite him sits the enamored nymph Echo; despised by Narcissus, she pined away to a shadow. Behind her is Clythia, the jealous lover of Apollo, who became a sunflower. At the front, to the right, recline Krokos and Smilax, a pair of lovers who changed into a saffron plant and a twining plant similar to the convolvulus. Behind them is Adonis, the lover of Venus who was killed by a wild boar, from whose bleeding wounds the Adonis rose grew. Beside him, to his left,

stands Hyacinthus, Apollo's lover, whom he accidentally killed with a discus, and from whose blood the hyacinth then bloomed. Both Adonis and Hyacinthus are pointing to their wounds. In a higher realm, Apollo, the sun god, drives his chariot below the roof of the vault of heaven.

The lively, delicate coloring, a uniform light which unites the whole scene, the harmonious dance-like movements of the figures, the well-balanced composition, and the ornamental enlivenment of the surface by means of rhythmically connected, clearly accentuated forms all provide evidence of Poussin's debt to classical antiquity. The arrangement of

the figures, which appear on a narrow area in the foreground, is intended to give a natural impression and at the same time to bring out the role of each individual figure. The only movement in the distance is denoted by the glance of Clythia, who is watching Apollo's progress in the firmament.

In choosing his theme, Poussin has relied both on Ovid's *Metamorphoses* and on a poem by Giambattista Marino. The painting illustrates the idea that life as a whole is eternal, but its forms are caught up in a process of constant change.

Nicolas Poussin
Stormy Landscape with Pyramus and Thisbe, 1651
Oil on canvas, 192.5 x 273.5 cm Frankfurt am Main,
Städelsches Kunstinstitut

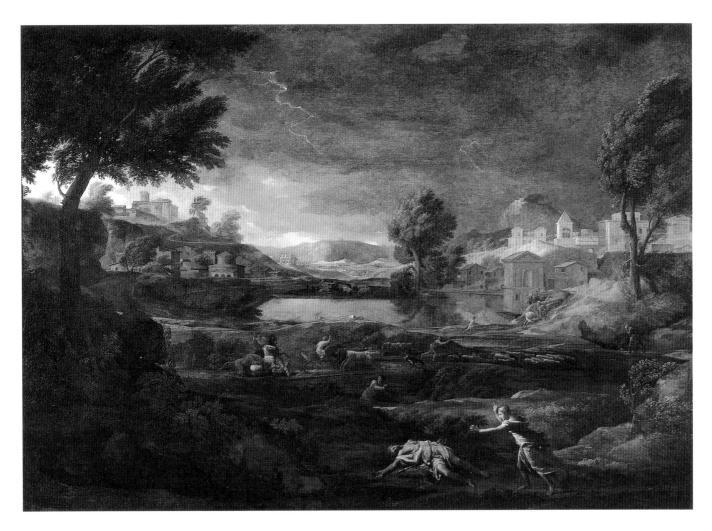

Quite different intentions lie behind the painting of *Pyramus and Thisbe* created by Poussin for his friend, the scholar and antiquarian Cassiano dal Pozzo. It was produced at a time when the artist was predominantly concerned with the problems of landscape painting. This is one of few large-format works by this artist. Poussin places the story of Pyramus and Thisbe in a broad impressive hilly and stormy landscape which extends widely into the background, with a lake in the center and a town on the right.

The story of the two unhappy Babylonian lovers is derived from Ovid's *Metamorphoses*. Pyramus had arranged to meet Thisbe by a spring in order to run away with her as their fathers had forbidden their relationship. Pyramus arrived late, when Thisbe, waiting at the spring, had already taken flight from a thirsty lioness. In fleeing she dropped her veil, which the lioness tore, her jaws still bloody from tearing the flesh of an ox. When Pyramus reached the scene, finding the tracks of a lion and the torn veil, he assumed that his beloved was dead, and in his guilt fell despairingly on his sword. Thisbe, finding her lover dying, also took her own life. Poussin portrays the moment of the greatest desperation of the two lovers: Thisbe is seen in the foreground, hurrying with frantic gestures towards Pyramus as he lies dying.

Nature participates in the dramatic events: a wild storm is raging, with a fierce gale and bolts of lightning, while the tempestuous sky breaks up in a narrow strip to the left. Dominating the tragic event, which takes place almost casually in the foreground, is the landscape, marked by the outbreak of elemental natural forces. By his own admission, Poussin was primarily concerned here with the mastery of the artistic problems associated with the depiction of a stormy landscape, and only secondarily with the tragic fate of the two lovers. The central idea of the painting is the helplessness of humanity against the capricious power of Fortuna.

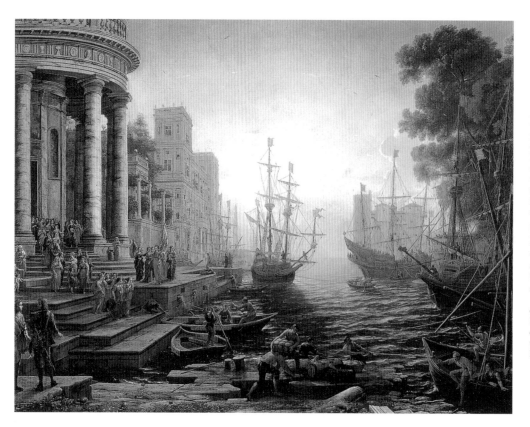

Claude Lorrain
Embarkation of St. Ursula, 1642
Oil on canvas, 113 x 149 cm
London, National Gallery

Claude produced the *Embarkation of St. Ursula* in Rome for Cardinal Poli. According to legend, Ursula, the daughter of the Christian king of Brittany, had promised her hand to Aetherius, the son of the king of England, on condition that he convert to the Christian faith within three years. In the meantime, she traveled from England to Rome with several thousand virgins, so that they could be baptized there. In Rome, Ursula learned that she was to go to Cologne as a martyr. After being received by Pope Cyriacus in Rome, the saint, with eleven thousand virgins, left for Cologne, where the group was attacked by Attila the Hun and most of them killed. As the only survivor, Ursula was finally killed by an arrow shot by Attila, whom she had rejected.

Here Claude shows the saint with her companions on their departure from the harbor of Rome. The banner with the red cross and the arrow on a red ground in the hands of St. Ursula are references to her impending martyrdom.

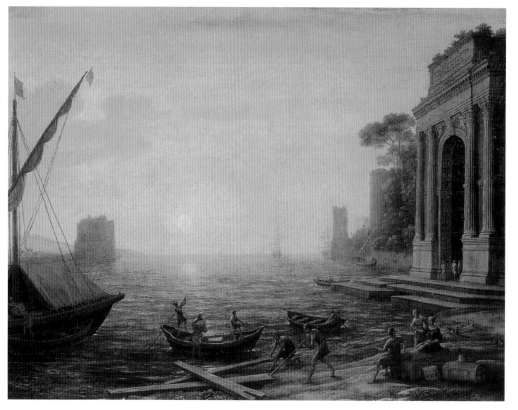

Claude Lorrain
Harbor at Sunrise, 1674
Oil on canvas, 72 x 96 cm
Munich, Bayerische Staatsgemäldesammlungen, Alte Pinakothek

Claude's *Harbor at Sunrise* in Munich is the last of three versions of this subject by the artist. An impressive sunrise by the sea is set off by a seaport with classical ruins; the portico on the right is reminiscent of the Arch of Titus in Rome. In the foreground, several laborers are engaged in transporting bales of goods from land to a barge, while others are struggling with heavy planks. A group of people on the shore is observing the activity, and another group is standing within the triumphal arch. Mythological figures are replaced here by realistic figures going about their business in an everyday scene. The busy activity of the seaport does not, however, detract from the atmosphere of calm.

Neither the time nor setting for the scene is identifiable, and there is thus something timeless about the whole piece. Clearly the painter is primarily concerned with the illustration of a natural phenomenon, the sunrise, which penetrates the veil of the early morning mist over the sea.

Claude Lorrain
Landscape with Noli Me Tangere, 1681
Oil on canvas, 84.5 x 141 cm
Frankfurt am Main, Städelsches Kunstinstitut

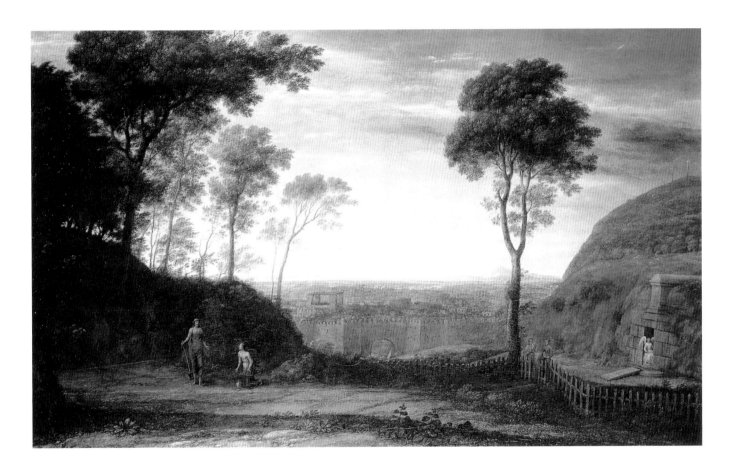

Landscape with Noli Me Tangere is among Claude's late works. It shows the meeting of St. Mary Magdalene with Christ, as described in the gospel of St. John. When Mary Magdalene went to the tomb of Christ to anoint his body, she found the tomb empty. Turning, she saw Christ with a spade, and believing him to be the gardener asked if he had taken away the body. Then Christ made himself known to her and said: "Do not touch me" (Noli me tangere).

The meeting is set in a wide landscape, opening out into the background. Claude designates the garden with Christ and the kneeling Magdalene, who has a jar of ointment, as a holy place by the wooden fence which separates it from the rest of the landscape. The mountain on the right is identified as Golgotha by the three crosses. The gentle morning light which appears behind the figure of Christ has been interpreted as a reference to the Resurrection. In the background, the view opens out to the city of Jerusalem, still veiled by early morning mist, and behind it the immediately adjoining coastline. The landscape, with its exceptionally fine nuances and richly atmospheric effects, and Claude's ability to transform observed natural phenomena into the most delicate values of light and color, suggest an intensive study of nature.

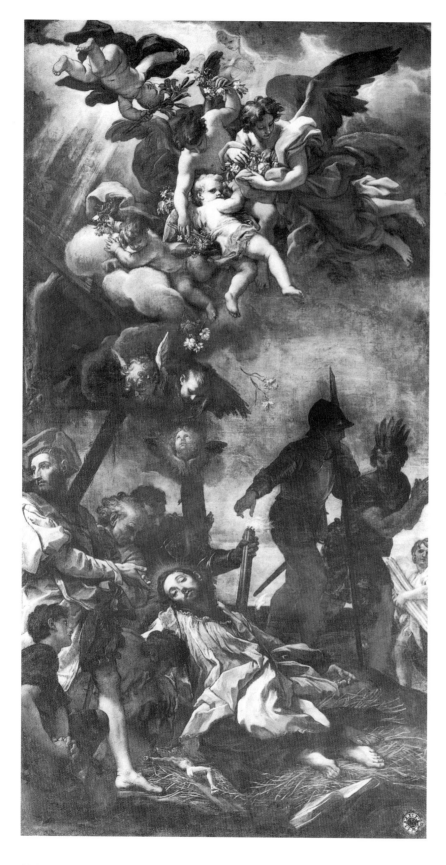

Carlo Maratta
Death of St. Francis Xavier, 1674–78
Oil on canvas, undated
Rome, the Gesù, altar of right-hand
transept

Carlo Maratta painted the *Death of St. Francis Xavier* for the altar of the right transept of the Gesù. St. Francis Xavier, one of the chief saints of the Jesuit order, joined Ignatius Loyola as early as 1533 and was active as a missionary in Asia, particularly in Goa, Japan, and China. In 1619 he was beatified and in 1662 canonized.

Maratta's painting, together with another by Gaulli for S. Andrea al Quirinale, is among the first images of the saint. Maratta shows the death of Francis Xavier, who according to legend died on the island of Shangchwan; he is totally abandoned, but comforted by angels.

The painting is divided into two areas. In the lower part Maratta shows the saint lying on the point of death surrounded by several people. In the upper part a number of angels attend the missionary's death, perhaps in expectation of his ascension to heaven. The presence of the figure of an Indian refers to Francis Xavier's missionary activity in general, and specifically to Goa; he is intended as an individual attribute of the saint, and here raises his hands in prayer at the sight of his death.

In Maratta's work (he was a pupil of Sacchi), the emphasis is on classical compositions with few figures and impressive gestures, and with particular value laid upon the three-dimensional quality of the bodies.

Fra Andrea Pozzo
Allegory of the Missionary Work of the Jesuits, 1691–94
Rome, S. Ignazio, ceiling fresco

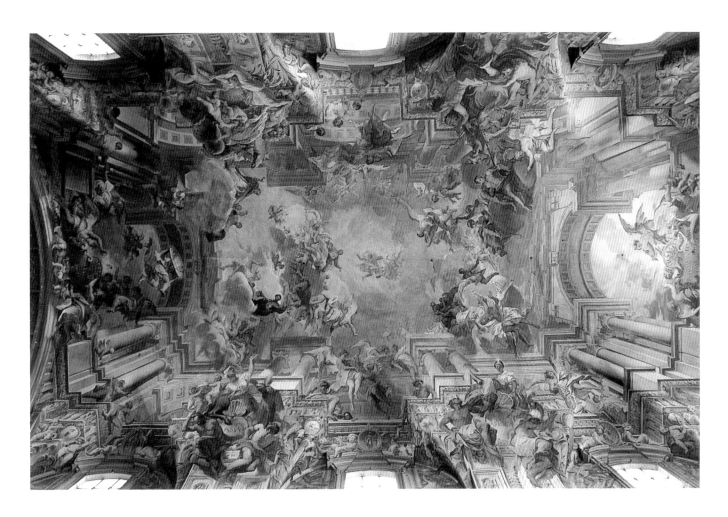

Fra Andrea Pozzo was summoned to Rome to create the ceiling paintings for S. Ignazio, the largest Jesuit church in the city after the Gesù. These are the frescos in the apse and a monumental fresco in the barrel vault above the nave, seventeen meters wide and thirty-six meters long. While the apse contains scenes from the life of St. Ignatius, the founder of the order of the Society of Jesus, the ceiling is dedicated to his apotheosis.

The content of the ceiling fresco, *Allegory of the Missionary Work of the Jesuits*, relates to one of Christ's sayings (Luke 12, 49). In the center of the picture hovers the Holy Trinity, from which a ray of light passes to St. Ignatius, who is borne on clouds by angels. The ray divides into four beams which fall on the four continents known at the time which are represented on the highest level of the *trompe-l'oeil* architecture. The divine fire is thus passed from Christ to Ignatius, who carries it to all parts of the world. Further Jesuit saints, placed closer to or further away from Ignatius according to rank, as well as a great number of praying devotees, populate the heavens. The personifications of the continents, transfigured, turn towards the saint, for the efforts of the Jesuit orders to convert heathens have freed them from heresy and idol-worship. Real architectural elements blend into painted architecture, while the barrel-vaulted ceiling is transformed by the fresco into a dome flooded with light.

The artist negates the boundaries between the actual space of the church and the painted heavens so ingeniously that it is almost impossible to see how he has achieved it. Pozzo himself indicated with a marble panel in the center of the nave the position to be taken up by the observer who wished to take in the central perspective of the construction of the painted *trompe-l'œil* architecture.

Naples

The kingdom of Naples and Sicily was ruled by viceroys under the Habsburg empire between 1516 and 1700. During the Renaissance, Naples had little importance as an art center and produced no painting of European standard. In the seventeenth century, however, things changed when the city became not only one of the leading cultural and commercial centers of Europe, but also the major Mediterranean port. It was the largest city of Europe apart from Paris at the beginning of the seventeenth century; with a population of 450,000 it was three times the size of Rome. The viceroy as well as a number of noblemen and well-to-do merchants led a luxurious existence. Several palaces were built for the court, and streets and squares were widened. In addition to this wealth, Naples was also a vibrant urban center. As a result of dense population, it was marked by social inequalities and further distinguished by great popular piety—towards the end of the century there were more than five hundred churches. It was described as a fascinating mixture of *paura e meraviglia* [fear and wonder].

The history of the city in the seventeenth century is marked by a number of catastrophic events. For a start, in 1624 Naples was hit by famine and in 1631 by an eruption of Vesuvius. Several years later, after the tax on fish and the price of bread had been raised by the viceroy, the Duke of Arcos, a rebellion broke out led by the fishseller Masaniello. At first the uprising was not directed against the Spanish rulers, but after Masaniello's murder, Naples declared itself an independent republic, a rebellion which was, however, immediately crushed by the Spaniards. A further disaster was the plague epidemic of 1656 which reduced the city's population by half.

The most important clients for artists, apart from the Church and the religious orders, were the viceroys, the Spanish and local nobility at the court, the major landowners such as the Colonna, Maddaloni, and Montleone, and also the merchant nobility. But despite the concentration of wealth and power in Naples, the sort of artistic patronage of the kind created by the popes in Rome was never really established here. The viceroys not only acquired paintings for their own collections but were also required by the Spanish king to buy works for him. Thus they obtained for Philip IV a great number of paintings by Claude Lorrain, Poussin, Lanfranco, and Ribera. The Count of Monterrey, viceroy from 1631 to 1637, owned a large art collection. On his return to Spain he took with him forty shiploads of paintings and classical sculptures. The Marquis of Carpio, viceroy from 1683 to 1687, had some thousand paintings. Another important patron of the arts was the Flemish merchant Gaspar Roomer, whose outstanding picture gallery included a number of works by Ribera. Nevertheless it was primarily the churches, monasteries, and brotherhoods which supplied the most important commissions to artists. A major contract for Caravaggio, the altarpiece *The Seven Works of Mercy*, came from the charitable association Pio Monte de la Misericordia, a confraternity which had been founded by noblemen and patricians with the principal aim of caring for the poor. The decoration of churches and monasteries involved further important commissions for the painters. Reni and Domenichino were called from Rome to Naples to paint the ceiling of the Cappella del Tesoro of the cathedral. Lanfranco also came from Rome in the mid-1630s to carry out the fresco decoration of the Certosa di San Martino. The Neapolitan painters Luca Giordano and Andrea Vaccaro collaborated on the decoration of the church of S. Maria del Pianto.

Trade connections with other European countries, as well as with Asia and the Spanish rulers, meant that Naples was particularly open to the widest variety of artistic influences. Hardly a single painter of the so-called "Neapolitan School" actually came from Naples. The city must have been very attractive to artists. New trends like "Caravaggismo" took hold quickly, and art developed in a number of directions. Some painters came to Naples because they had not achieved the success they had hoped for in the papal metropolis, or had left it because of the unfavorable nature of the contracts they had received. At the same time, however, painters traveled from Naples to Rome, Florence, or even Spain to work there. Some, although they were only passing through the city, made a powerful impact on it.

Caravaggio (1573–1610), for example, during his flight from Rome where he was wanted for manslaughter, spent the year 1607 in Naples, where the Spanish viceroy the Count of Benevento became his patron. After an interval of several months which he spent in Malta, he came to Naples for a further year shortly before his death in 1610. Despite the brevity of his stay, Caravaggio had a great influence on the Neapolitan art scene. It was here that the so-called "School of Caravaggio" originated. Artemisia Gentileschi (1597–1651), who came from Rome and had studied under her father, Orazio Gentileschi, first went to Florence and then came to Naples, where she spent the years 1630 to 1637. After a stay in England, she returned to Naples in about 1640, where she produced several altarpieces for churches as well as a number of paintings for the Spanish court and art-collectors. Jusepe Ribera (1591–1652), after studying with Francisco Ribalta in Valencia, left his native land and in 1609 went first to Parma and then to Rome. His time there was not particularly successful and he finally settled in Naples in 1616. He became known as "Lo Spagnoletto" [the Little Spaniard] and ran a large workshop with many pupils, gradually coming to dominate the art market. Ribera had originally worked much in the manner of Caravaggio, but then distanced himself from the *tenebroso* [shadowy] style and became famous above all for his light-filled color. Salvator Rosa (1615–73), born in Naples, was at first active there, then went to Rome and finally to Florence. Rosa achieved fame not only as a painter but also as a poet and musician. He became known primarily for his battle scenes and landscapes, but also for *vanitas* paintings. His romantic landscapes were praised for their poetic content and

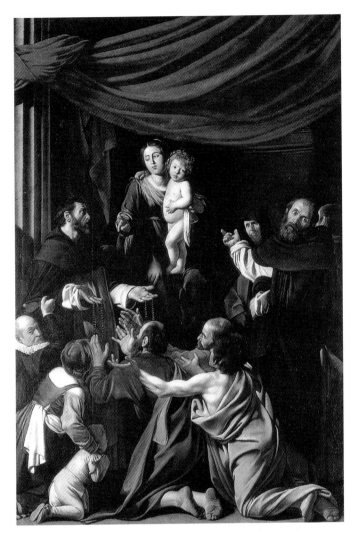

Caravaggio
Madonna of the Rosary, 1607
Oil on canvas, 364 x 249 cm
Vienna, Kunsthistorisches Museum

Naples was an important stage in the career of many important painters, but only a few of these spent their whole lives in the city.

Among the painters who were to have the most lasting effect on artistic life there was Caravaggio. His *Madonna of the Rosary* is first documented in 1607, when it came up for sale. It was probably intended for the Dominican church. Legend recounts that the Virgin Mary appeared to St. Dominic and gave him the rosary. She taught him how to use it for prayer and charged him with disseminating the use of the rosary among the people. The subject became popular during the Counter-Reformation after the victory at Lepanto in 1571, in which the Christian West held off the advance of the Turks, ascribed to the effect of the rosary prayer. Above all, however, the rosary was one of the new forms of piety propagated by the Church. These demanded self-discipline and individual initiative, but on the other hand also contributed to the structuring of everyday life through ritual, thus binding the faithful more closely to the Church.

In the center of the painting, fully facing the observer, slightly shifted to the left of the longitudinal axis, the Madonna is enthroned with the infant Jesus standing on her lap. To her left, St. Dominic, with an ecstatic expression, assisted by other monks to her right, is distributing rosaries to the people. At the left-hand edge of the painting the figure turning his gaze towards the observer is probably the donor. Another figure looking out of the picture is the counterpart of St. Dominic, St. Peter the Martyr. The shabbily clad people turn towards St. Dominic with strongly dramatic gestures.

Caravaggio dispenses with the strict division into a heavenly and earthly realm which was traditional in the depiction of this scene—the event takes place in a room and the figures are grouped closely together—but nevertheless he has taken care to preserve a strict hierarchy. The Virgin is not only placed at a higher level but is also the only figure completely visible to the observer. The powerful influx of light and the robust modeling of the bodies through the use of chiaroscuro which casts a strong light on some parts of the body are striking. Here Caravaggio deploys a characteristic early baroque color composition with intensely glowing pigments, each of which appears only once, and divides the painting into three sections, the upper and lower being strictly enclosed fields of color, while black and white predominate in the central section.

The *Madonna of the Rosary* is one of Caravaggio's most traditional works, yet it was to have an enormous impact, for in it the painter develops the archetype of the baroque altar panel. The painting alludes to the strict hierarchy of the Church, newly propagated during the Counter-Reformation, according to which the people have no direct access to the Virgin, but have need of the mediation of the saints.

pathos. Between 1620 and 1630 the first still lifes were created in Naples. The painters Giuseppe Recco (1634–95), Giovanni Battista Ruoppola, and Paolo Porpora were famous for their large-format still lifes of flowers, fruit, fish, and kitchen scenes. In the second half of the century, Luca Giordano (1632–1705), a pupil of Ribera, became one of the most successful painters. His extraordinary productivity—during his life he created no fewer than five thousand paintings—made him known as "Luca fa presto" [Speedy Luca]. Due to the considerable versatility with which he imitated the styles of various masters, he was also referred to as "proteo della pittura," a reference to Proteus, the god of transformation.

As in many other Italian centers of art, such as Venice, Genoa, and Bologna—with the exceptions of Rome and Florence—artistic life in Naples was still closely linked with medieval tradition. The guild of painters was reconstituted in 1665, with the support of the Jesuits, as the brotherhood of SS. Anna e Luca. Its main task, apart from teaching painting, was the support of impoverished painters and the upkeep of its chapel in the Jesuit church. It was not until 1755 that the Accademia del Disegno was founded. There was great competition among the artists for important commissions. De

Dominici, chronicler of the Neapolitan artists, reports that Ribera, Corenzio, and Caracciolo had offered fierce resistance when the renowned painters Reni, Domenichino, and Lanfranco were summoned from Rome to decorate the chapel of S. Gennaro in the cathedral.

There were a great number of artistic personalities in seventeenth-century Naples who cannot simply be classed together as a "Neapolitan School." Among the characteristics of Neapolitan painting of this period are the strongly naturalistic tendencies of the followers of Caravaggio, which rapidly became popular, and, by contrast, the representatives of the classicism of the Carracci, which asserted itself somewhat late in the day. The realism of ordinary lives and the tendency towards somber drama of Caravaggio or Ribera were better suited to Neapolitan religiosity and the city's stark social contrasts than the balanced approach of the Carracci or Reni.

Artemisia Gentileschi
Judith and Holofernes, c. 1630
Oil on canvas, 168 x 128 cm
Naples, Galleria Nazionale di Capodimonte

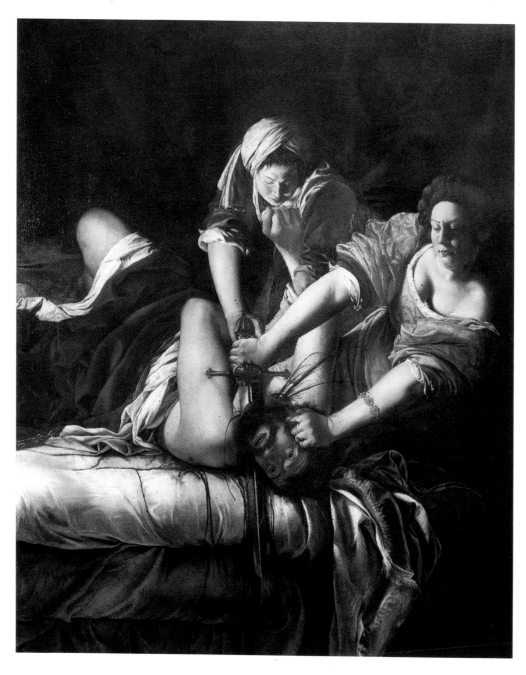

Artemisia Gentileschi created a whole series of large-format paintings with biblical and historical themes in which women play a central role. In numerous paintings such as *Susanna and the Elders* and *Judith and Holofernes* she deals with the problem of the sexual threat posed to women by men. She tackled the apocryphal story of Judith, who beheaded Holofernes, in several paintings; one version was produced in 1630, either in Naples or shortly before she moved to that city.

Judith was an exceptionally beautiful widow who lived in the Israelite town of Bethulia, which was under siege by the Assyrians under their king, Holofernes. After several days of water shortage the council of elders agreed to surrender the town to the enemy. Judith, known to be God-fearing, made a plan to save the town. She went to Holofernes, pretending a wish to help him to victory. Alone in the tent with the king, who was impressed with her beauty and gripped by greed, she cut off his head as he lay drunk and brought it to the town. There it was hung on the battlements of the city walls where it helped the Israelites to victory over the Assyrians, who took to flight in terror.

Gentileschi chooses to illustrate the high point of the story in her painting: Judith is on the point of beheading the king. Her young maid powerfully supports her by holding down the monarch who is trying to defend himself. Holofernes' features are contorted by fear. The facial expressions of Judith and her maid are not, as in other paintings on this theme, arrogant or triumphant, but determined and tense as they concentrate on their task. The center of the painting is formed by the head of Holofernes and the hands of the women overpowering the king. Some clues suggest a struggle has already taken place. In her portrayal Gentileschi restricts herself to the essentials, namely the beheading of Holofernes, and shows the event in a silhouette-like form, so that none of the figures is completely visible. She also dispenses with any characterization of the surrounding space.

The painter clearly owes her use of strong contrasts of light and dark to the influence of Caravaggio, as well as her glowing range of colors and her silhouette-like elements which concentrate the composition on a central statement. Primary colors predominate: the dark background contrasts with the glowing hues of the blue garment of Judith, the red one of the maid, and the white blood-spattered sheet. The drama of the brutal scene is heightened by the stark light that illuminates the upper part of Holofernes' body, the hands of the women, and Judith's head.

While Holofernes is shown by many painters as the victim of a cruel, cold-hearted woman, Gentileschi's version interprets the story somewhat differently. Her Judith is not a symbol of dangerously provocative, unpredictable womanhood, and neither, therefore, is the beheaded Holofernes shown as a victim of female castration mania. Artemisia Gentileschi's theme is the disempowerment and punishing of the male, but more emphasis is in fact laid on the strength of women when they act in collaboration.

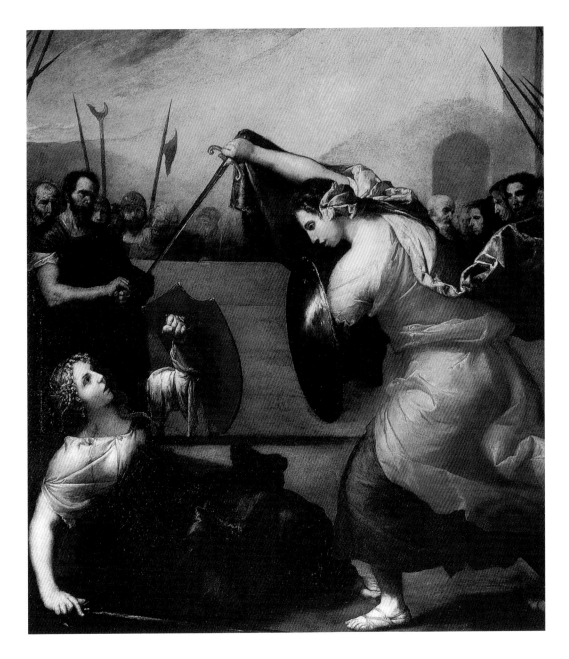

Jusepe Ribera
Battle of the Women, 1636
Oil on canvas, 235 x 212 cm
Madrid, Prado

Women and power are also the subject of
Jusepe Ribera's *Battle of the Women*. The
painting was formerly in the collection of
Philip IV; as early as 1666 it is mentioned
in the inventory of the Alcázar of
Madrid. Two women are shown fighting
with swords in an arena. Ribera chooses
a most dramatic moment for his scene:
while one woman has already sunk to the
ground, clearly in defeat, the other is
ready to pierce her with her sword. In the
background are a number of onlookers

who follow the event with the greatest
interest. It is presumed that here Ribera is
recording an incident which took place in
Naples in 1552. At that time, in the presence of the viceroy, the Marquis of Vasto,
two Neapolitan noblewomen, Isabella de
Carazi and Diambra de Petinella, fought
a duel over a young man named Fabio de
Zeresola.

The figures are presented in a manner
similar to that of late Roman reliefs on
the theme of Amazons: in the center of
the action are the life-size, three-
dimensionally represented figures of the
two women. The witnesses of the tense
battle, remaining in the background, are
of only secondary importance and are

therefore only sketched in. Ribera's
subtly graduated combinations and harmonies of color and, above all, the predominant golden tones reveal him as a
great colorist in the tradition of the
Venetian masters Titian and Veronese.

Apart from the portrayal of a histori-
cally documented event in Neapolitan
society, the battle between the two
women has also been interpreted as the
battle between virtue and vice.

Jusepe Ribera
Apollo Flaying Marsyas, 1637
Oil on canvas, 182 x 232 cm
Naples, Museo Nazionale di San Martino

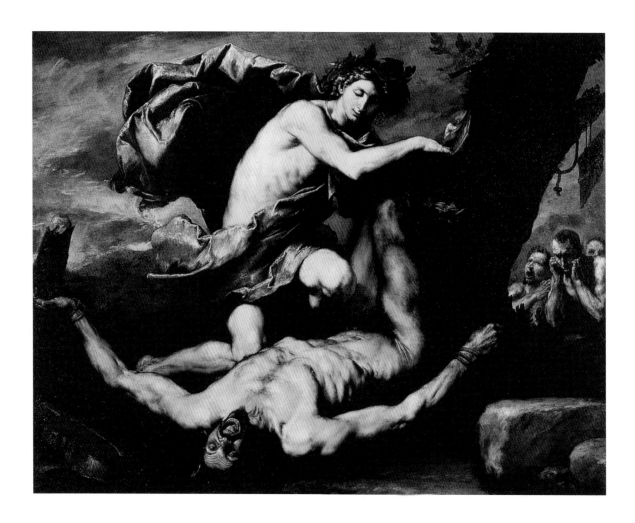

Jusepe Ribera is mainly known today for those paintings in which he describes in a crude, savage manner the martyrdoms of saints and mythological characters. He treated the theme of Apollo flaying Marsyas in a number of versions intended for private collections.

The Phrygian satyr Marsyas had achieved such mastery on the flute that he dared to challenge Apollo to a competition. The victor was to do what he wished with the loser. The two were at first on equal terms, until Apollo, who was playing the lyre, challenged Marsyas to play his instrument the wrong way around, which was not possible with the flute. Apollo thus became the victor and

punished Marsyas by hanging him from a pine tree and stripping off his skin.

In the Christian world this myth corresponded to the martyrdom of St. Bartholomew. Ribera chooses for his painting the scene of punishment: Marsyas, naked and manacled, lying on the ground, is seen being tortured by Apollo. Only the lyre in the left-hand corner of the painting refers to the competition which has just taken place. In the background, horror-struck observers are witnesses of the dreadful event.

Ribera succeeds in emphasizing the dramatic moment with a powerful diagonal composition which he achieves by allowing Marsyas' body to project, as it

were, out of the painting. The drama of the scene is further heightened by the contrast between the face of Marsyas, contorted in pain, the floating red garment of the god, and the turbulent sky on the one hand, and the calm features of Apollo, carrying out his cruel deed with a restrained gesture, on the other.

Salvator Rosa
Landscape with Apollo and the Cumae-
an Sibyl, c. 1661
Oil on canvas, 171 x 258 cm
London, Wallace Collection

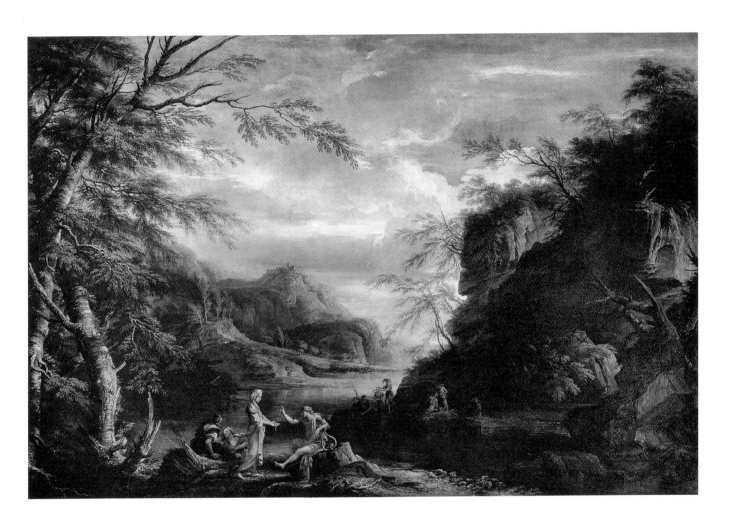

Salvator Rosa's late work includes atmospheric landscapes peopled by mythological figures, such as the *Landscape with Apollo and the Cumaean Sibyl*. As Ovid relates (*Metamorphoses*, XIV, 129–53), Apollo had offered to grant the Sibyl every wish if she would bestow her favors upon him. The Sibyl picked up a handful of dust and asked for as many years of life as there were grains of dust.

Her wish was granted, but as she continued to refuse Apollo's wooing, the god took his revenge. The Sibyl had forgotten to ask for eternal youth, and from then on continued to age. She lived in misery for more than seven hundred years and her only wish was to die.

Rosa portrays the scene of the meeting between the Cumaean Sibyl and her two companions with Apollo, who is seated on a tree-stump with his golden lyre. In the midst of a wild craggy landscape the cave where the Sibyl lives is shown on the right. On the hill in the background stands the Acropolis of Cumae where a temple to Apollo once stood. Here Rosa proves himself to be a master of the use of light. While the right-hand mountainside lies in shadow, the left-hand one is illuminated from behind, in the direction of the golden-brown evening sky. The scene with the figures stands out from the dark background because of its strong colors: Apollo's gar-

ments are salmon-pink, the Sibyl's are painted in lemon yellow and royal blue.

Rosa was clearly influenced by Claude in his choice of subject matter, but presents a different view of nature in his work. His landscapes are not marked by solemn calm, transparency, and clear harmonies like those of the French artist, but rather by passionate movement and tumultuous lighting, which lend his paintings a sinister, desolate, and lonely mood.

Luca Giordano
St. Gennaro Liberates Naples from the Plague, c. 1660
Oil on canvas, 400 x 315 cm
Naples, S. Maria del Pianto

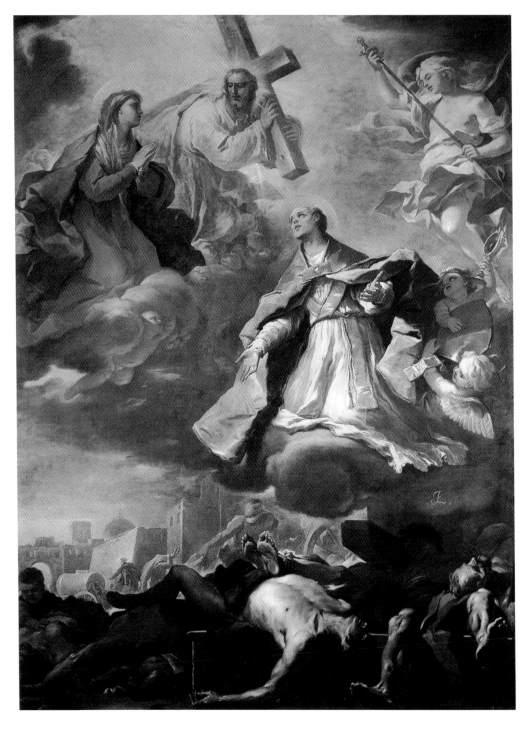

The figure of St. Gennaro, the patron saint of Naples, is set at the center of the painting which was produced by Luca Giordano in 1660 for the church of S. Maria del Pianto. *St. Gennaro Liberating Naples from the Plague* was commissioned, together with its pendant piece, *The Patron Saints of Naples Worshipping the Cross*, by the viceroy, the Count of Peñaranda. The church had been built after the dreadful plague epidemic of 1656 above the *grotte degli sportiglioni* in Poggioreale, where many had died. At the same time as Giordano's commission, Andrea Vaccaro was asked to produce his *Virgin Mary Praying for the Souls in Purgatory*. De Dominici reports that at first there was violent rivalry between Giordano and Vaccaro over which painting should be used for the high altar.

St. Gennaro (Januarius) of Benevento was one of the martyrs beheaded in AD 305 for refusing to sacrifice to idols. As patron saint of Naples, he protected the city above all against earthquakes. Today his blood is still preserved in two phials in the cathedral of S. Gennaro; according to popular belief it liquefies annually on his name-day, September 19, a sign of his concern for the people of Naples.

Giordano organizes his painting, which was in fact to adorn the high altar, into two sections. In the heavenly realm, St. Gennaro is shown kneeling on clouds and surrounded by angels gazing upwards towards Christ and the Virgin Mary as he pleads for mercy for the plague-stricken city. With his left hand the saint indicates the many corpses of plague victims lying on the ground. Giordano succeeds in representing the cruelty of the plague with great sensitivity: to the left, a weeping child tries to awaken its dead mother.

Giuseppe Recco
Still Life with Fruit and Flowers, c. 1670
Oil on canvas, 255 x 301cm
Naples, Galleria Nazionale di Capodimonte

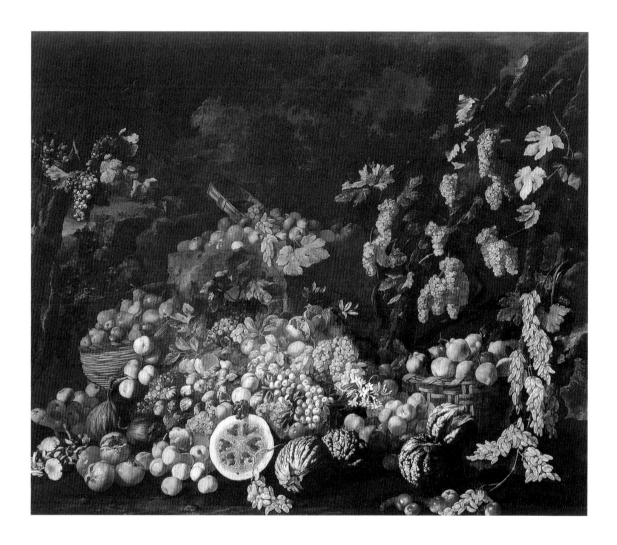

Giuseppe Recco's monumental painting *Still Life with Fruit and Flowers* is among the artist's late works. It shows a lavish arrangement of various kinds of fruit and flowers, with some spread out on the ground and some in baskets. The whole piece is set in a landscape with a rich foliage of blossoming shrubs and trees. There is a powerful contrast between the dark coloring of the natural scene and the bright hues of the individual fruits and flowers which appear to gleam out from it.

While Recco's painting appears at first glance similar to Dutch flower still lifes, on closer observation a number of differences become evident. The coloring is inspired by the work of Caravaggio and the composition is asymmetrical, with flowers and fruit arranged in less ornamental fashion; the Neapolitan's painting is further distinguished from Dutch works by its monumental size.

By placing the arrangement of flowers and fruit in a landscape, the artist puts the two main features of the painting on an equal level. The many still lifes of the period which show fruit have sometimes been interpreted as a reflection of the increasingly abundant supply of goods. They are also seen as representative of the growing interest in the scientific observation of nature which inspired the voyages of research during this period. In addition, the medicinal properties of plants, vegetables, and fruit were being explored. Thus scientific discovery and the spiritual assimilation of the everyday can be seen as the main impetus for this still life rather than higher levels of symbolic meaning. This particular genre was extremely popular in the merchant city of Naples, with its prolific Mediterranean vegetation.

Madrid

In the seventeenth century Madrid was among the youngest of the European cultural centers. It was not until 1561 that Philip II (1556–98) designated the city the country's capital. His decision in favor of Madrid was influenced by its advantageous position in the center of the country and its good climate. With the arrival of the court, Madrid, hitherto an insignificant town, achieved a certain importance as a center of economic and cultural exchange. Under Philip II, the city emerged as an impressive royal residence: the Moorish alcázar was extended, numerous churches built, streets and squares expanded, and summer residences created in the close vicinity of the capital including the Casa del Campo, Aranjuez, El Pardo, and El Escorial. For the decoration of El Escorial, the king summoned a series of Italian painters, among them Federico Zuccari, Bartolomé Carducho, and Patricio Cajés, some of whom never returned to their homeland. The painters Alonso Sánchez Coello and Juan Pantoja de la Cruz as well as Anthonis Mor, who had emigrated from the Netherlands, made their names as portraitists.

During the reign of Philip III (1598–1621) Madrid's position was undermined, for under the influence of his favorite, the Count of Lerma, the king moved the capital to Valladolid. As a result of violent protest from the nobility he reversed his decision five years later. Madrid, however, did not play a major role either as an industrial or commercial center during the seventeenth century. Alfonso Núñez de Castro's words of praise in 1658, "Sólo Madrid es corte" [There is no capital but Madrid], was reversed by mockers into "Madrid es sólo corte," arguing that Madrid was nothing beyond the court, a phrase which accurately summarizes the situation. The city acquired a more impressive character as the result of town-planning measures such as the extension of the Plaza Mayor. Philip III, whom history recorded as the *rey piadoso*, the pious king, was not, however, outstanding as a patron or collector of art.

It was only during the reign of Philip IV (1621–65) that several large artistic projects were undertaken. These included the decoration of the palace of Buen Retiro as well as the rebuilding and redecoration of rooms in the Alcázar (Salón de los Espejos, Salón Dorado, Salón Ochavado). During the 1630s the hunting seat Torre de la Parada was newly furnished by Rubens and members of his workshop with mythological paintings and by Velázquez with portraits of members of the royal family in hunting dress. Under Charles II (1665–1700), the last Spanish Habsburg, the chief artistic projects were the painting of the staircase of El Escorial, the Casón of Buen Retiro, and the decoration of several churches in Madrid such as Nuestra Señora de Atocha and San Antonio de los Alemanes with vast fresco cycles.

The most important clients for artists in Madrid were the court and the Church, for in Spain there was no self-confident bourgeoisie with a taste for art. The king was considered the chief patron and connoisseur. In 1700 the royal collection comprised 5,500 paintings, of which more than half had been acquired by Philip IV. There were also a number of collectors among the nobility: the Marquis of Leganés owned more than 1,100 paintings and the Marquis of Carpio more than 3,000 works. These collections revealed a similar emphasis: among the Italian masters, the Venetians were unequivocally preferred in Madrid because of their treatment of *colore*. Thus many works by Titian, Tintoretto, and Veronese adorned the walls of the royal Alcázar, El Pardo and the Buen Retiro. Similarly, early Flemish masters were collected, such as van Eyck, Rogier van der Weyden, and Hieronymus Bosch. Among contemporary painters, the French masters in Rome, Poussin and Claude Lorrain, as well as the Flemish Rubens and the Spaniard living in Naples, Jusepe Ribera, enjoyed great popularity. Paintings by foreign, particularly Italian and Dutch, artists formed the bulk of these collections, for collectors had little interest in the works of native painters. This contempt for Spanish masters, as we learn from the painter and writer Jusepe Martínez, is said to have persuaded Ribera to stay in Naples. While his works were very popular in Spain, if he should return— according to Ribera—he would be enthusiastically received during the first year, but would soon be forgotten. Spain, he said, was a beneficent mother to foreigners, but a cruel stepmother to her own sons.

Around the turn of the century, the successors of the Escorial painters summoned from Italy by Philip II achieved a certain importance. Among them should be mentioned the court painters of Philip IV, still under the strong influence of Italian mannerist painters, such as Vicente Carducho (1576–1638), the brother of Bartolomé from Florence, Eugenio Cajés (1574–1634), son of Patricio from Arezzo, and Angelo Nardi (1584–1665). The Flemish still-life painter Juan van der Hamen y León (1596–1631) and Juan Battista Maino (1581–1649), the son of Italian parents, and the drawing-master of Philip IV were also appreciated.

Many painters came from Seville to Madrid to make their names at court, above all Diego Velázquez (1599–1660), who replaced Philip IV's court portraitist, Rodrigo de Villandrando, after the latter's death. During his early career Velázquez was still strongly influenced by Caravaggio. In Madrid he encountered at first hand the many paintings by Titian in the royal collection and was decisively inspired by his meeting with Rubens, staying in Madrid for the second time between 1628 and 1629. Francisco Zurbarán (1598–1664), who was mainly active in Seville, also carried out a number of commissions for the court during the 1630s. Alonso Cano (1601–67), who came from Granada and settled in Seville, completed his education not only as a painter but also as a sculptor and architect; he came to Madrid where he worked both for the court and the Church. He seems to have been in greater demand as a painter and as a designer of ephemeral architecture than as a gifted sculptor. Antonio Pereda (1611–78) was particularly successful as a painter of *vanitas* works. Under Charles II several native masters

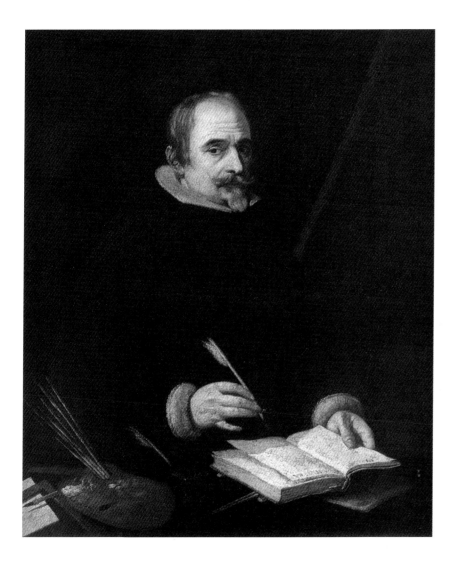

Vicente Carducho
Self-Portrait, c. 1633
Oil on canvas, 101 x 86 cm
Glasgow, Pollok House
Stirling Maxwell Collection

While portraits of painters and sculptors were common in Italy and the Netherlands, they were a rarity in Spain, where artists were not considered appropriate subjects because of their low social status. Vicente Carducho's self-portrait of 1633 is a successful example of this genre. The painter and art historian depicts himself seated at a table, turning slightly to the right, and fixing his concentrated gaze on the spectator. Wearing court costume, a pen in his hand, his treatise on painting in front of him, Carducho presents himself primarily as the author of the *Diálogos*. At the same time the attributes of ruler and T-square refer to the artist as a scientist. Easel, pencil, palette, and brushes on the other hand characterize him as a painter. Carducho evidently placed great value on portraying himself as a *pictor doctus*, a learned painter. He created the portrait in 1633, after a tax dispute between the painters of Madrid and the Real Consejo de Hacienda, the court tax authority, was finally decided in the artists' favor after eight years.

such as Francisco Herrera the Younger (1627–85) from Seville, José Antolínez (1635–75), Francisco Rizi (1614–85), Claudio Coello (1642–93), and Juan Carreño de Miranda (1614–85) achieved fame not only through their paintings but also because of their numerous ceiling frescos.

Apart from religious paintings, portraits and still lifes were the most sought-after works. Paintings of mythological subjects were, however, considered indecent and were not bought for fear of the Inquisition, since the Church regarded them with mistrust: the clergy saw them chiefly an excuse to represent nudity. In Spain painters did not generally specialize in specific themes, as was common in the Netherlands, but were active in several genres. However, most painters—Velázquez was a remarkable exception—succeeded in achieving a reputation for their mastery of a particular genre. For example, Antonio de Pereda had produced outstanding paintings on the *vanitas* theme, but showed little talent in the composition of his history paintings.

The educational standard of these painters was, except in a few cases, not particularly high. Some were even illiterate, as was reported of Antonio Pereda. From the inventories of several artists'

estates we know how many books a painter owned, and which ones. While the painter and art historian Vicente Carducho owned 306 books, Velázquez' estate included only 156. The majority of painters lived in impoverished conditions. They earned their daily bread with pictures of saints for private devotions, which they sold at the markets. However, some painters were also active as art dealers and owned their own shops. An important element of some painters' incomes was the painting of the polychrome sculptures which at that time predominated in the decoration of churches. A court artist such as Velázquez, with a fixed income and many extra payments for various official positions and special commissions, of course enjoyed a higher standard of living. He employed a servant, owned silk garments and a carriage, and led the life of a nobleman. However, neither the successful Velázquez nor Murillo left property to their descendants and both died in debt.

Juan van der Hamen y León
Still Life with Sweets, Vase of Flowers,
Clock, and Dog, 1625–30
Oil on canvas, 228 x 95 cm
Madrid, Prado

Juan van der Hamen y León
Still Life with Sweets, Vase of Flowers,
and Puppy, 1625–30
Oil on canvas, 228 x 85 cm
Madrid, Prado (pendant of adjacent
painting)

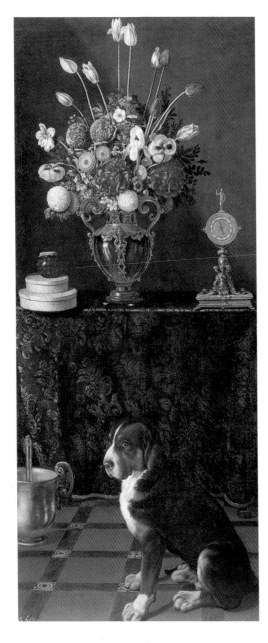

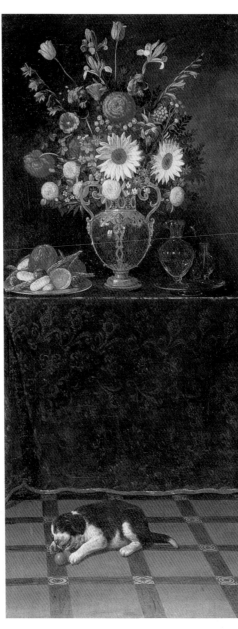

Still lifes, along with portraits, are among
the few paintings on secular subjects
which were produced in Spain. Several
still-life painters worked in the environs
of the court, and a number of still lifes
are mentioned in the contemporary
inventories of the royal collection.

One of the leading still-life painters
of Madrid was Juan van der Hamen y
León (1596–1631), whose Flemish parents had settled in the city. He belonged
to a group of intellectuals in the circle of
Lope de Vega. In his paintings he chiefly
shows subjects that refer to the daily life
of the court circles in which he was
active: there are choice pastries and con-
fectionery, the finest of tableware,
Venetian glass, and gilded goblets and
silver bowls, as well as Chinese porcelain,
all exquisitely presented.

The two paintings in vertical format
produced around 1625 flanked a door in
the house of the courtier Jean de Croy,
Count of Solre, in the Calle de Alcalá in
Madrid. They were designed to serve a
trompe-l'oeil function since they continued the pattern of the actual floor. After
the count's death the paintings ended up
in the royal collection and formed part of
the decoration of the room in which
Philip IV took his meals.

Diego Velázquez
Los Borrachos
(The Triumph of Bacchus), 1629
Oil on canvas, 165 x 227 cm
Madrid, Prado

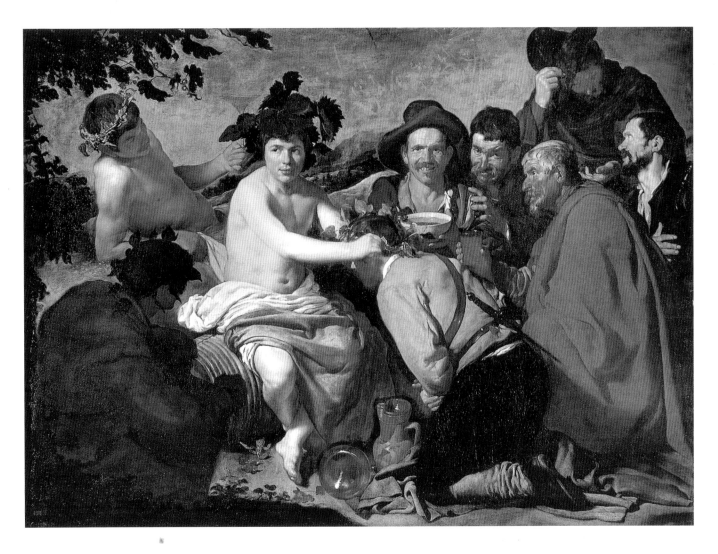

As suggested earlier, mythological painting was poorly represented in Spain. After Velázquez had been appointed as court portraitist to Philip IV, he made a number of portraits of the royal family as well as several mythological scenes.

The *Triumph of Bacchus* was painted shortly before his first stay in Rome (1629–31). Produced for the royal collection, the painting hung in the king's summer bedroom. It shows Bacchus surrounded by eight drinking peasants seated in a landscape and crowning one of his companions. The figure of Bacchus is closely based on Caravaggio's representation of the same subject, but suggests Velázquez' uncertainty in the handling of the human body at this stage: the figure appears doughy and not fully modelled, a technical difficulty that was to be overcome only during the course of the artist's stay in Italy (1629–31).

It has been demonstrated that Velázquez' painting relies on a sixteenth-century Flemish print. According to the inscription on the print, the peasants begged Bacchus to make them forget their troubles. The god of wine granted their request and allowed mere mortals to participate in his pleasures and forget their misery. More recent interpretations have seen the painting as referring to the reign of Philip IV: just as Bacchus washes away the cares of humanity with wine, the king was supposed to alleviate the sorrows of his subjects.

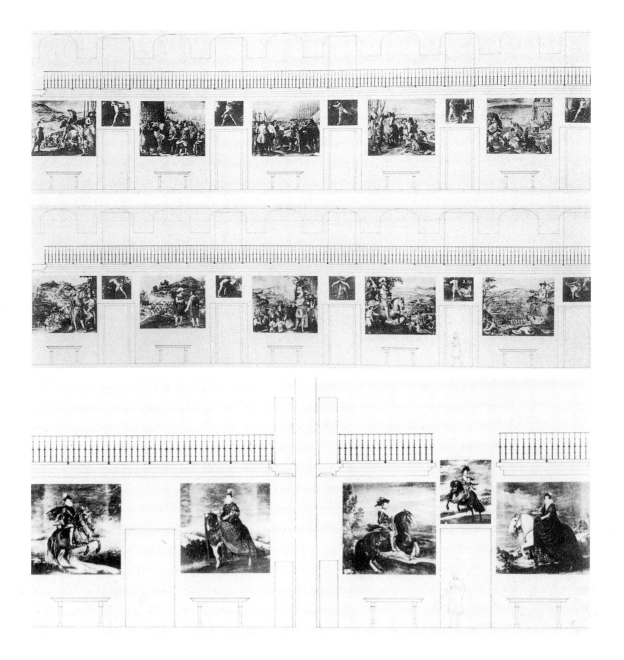

Reconstruction of the Salón de los Reinos in the Buen Retiro
From Jonathan Brown, *Velázquez, Painter and Courtier,*
New Haven/London, 1986

If the Escorial is regarded as the chief project of the reign of Philip II, the building and decoration of the palace of the Buen Retiro is considered among the great artistic tasks from Philip IV's reign. The building, constructed between 1632 and 1634, lay to the south of Madrid and was commissioned on the initiative of Count Olivares, the prime minister and favorite of Philip IV. The Buen Retiro

became a setting for the king's activity as an art collector and patron. The palace was particularly famous for its gardens and theater. The decoration of the Salón de los Reinos [Hall of Kingdoms], a showpiece in the tradition of princely halls of virtue, was carried out between 1633 and 1635.

The complicated iconographic scheme was designed for the glorification of the reigning house of Habsburg in Spain. The ceiling was adorned by frescos with floral motifs and grotesques, and on the pendentives between the windows were the coats of arms of the twenty-four kingdoms of the Spanish monarchy. On the shorter walls of the hall hung five eques-

trian portraits of the royal family by Velázquez and his assistants, portraying the immediate royal predecessors, the reigning royal couple, Philip III and Queen Margaret, and their child, the Infante Baltasar Carlos.

Twelve monumental battle scenes on the longer walls of the hall between the French windows celebrated the most recent victories of the Spanish army in various theaters of war. They were intended to glorify Philip IV's military successes, and at the same time to justify the high costs of waging war which had been the inevitable result of the expansionist policy of the king and Olivares. The commissions for the battle scenes

went to the most important painters in the court circle: Diego Velázquez, Vicente Carducho, Antonio de Pereda, Felix Castelo, Francisco Zurbarán, Eugenio Cajés, and Jusepe Leonardo. While most painted battle scenes follow a predictable formula, with the general posing in the foreground as a confident victor while the events of battle are played out in the background, Velázquez and Maino chose instead to emphasize the inhumanity and terrors of war; the clash of weapons can hardly be heard here.

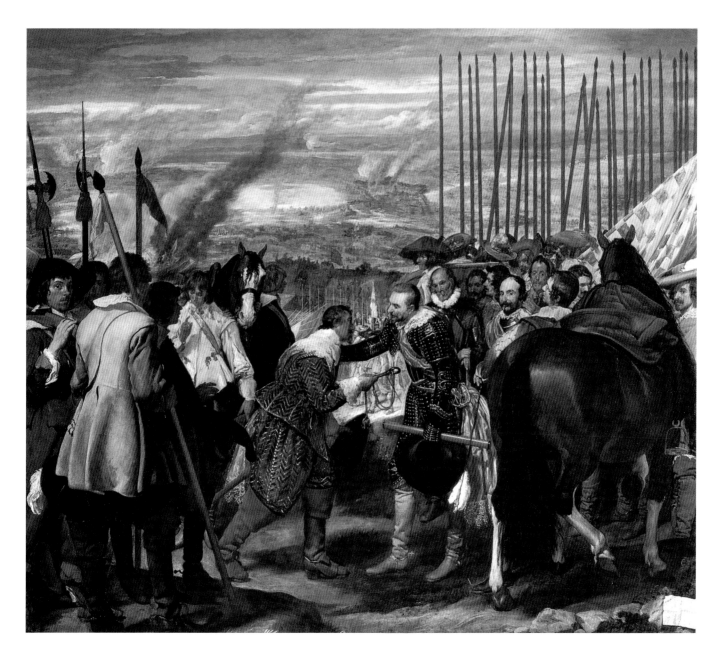

Diego Velázquez
The Surrender of Breda (Las Lanzas), 1635
Oil on canvas, 307 x 370 cm
Madrid, Prado

The most famous painting in the Salón de los Reinos is Velázquez' *Las Lanzas*. It recreates the moment after the capture of Breda by the Spanish army when the Dutch commander Justin of Nassau hands over the keys of the city to the Spanish general, Ambrogio Spinola. This scene takes place in a calm atmosphere and clearly demonstrates the victor's respect for the vanquished enemy. Velázquez shows it as a meeting in which the victor approaches the defeated commander with an almost friendly demeanour. His magnanimous behavior rests on his awareness that he owes his victory to fortune, which on this occasion happened to be on his side. We see neither a humble loser nor a triumphant victor, but a meeting of two commanders on equal terms.

Nevertheless some differences are subtly established: while the victorious army is presented as an orderly group with upright lances—which give the painting its Spanish title—the defeated troops stand around in a resigned, disorderly throng. Velázquez refrains from the allegories commonly ascribed to battle and victory scenes which are generally inserted for the glorification of the victor. He thus breaks the pattern of triumph and humiliation which dominates similar paintings, and at the same time introduces a new dimension, one of humanity and generosity in the spirit of the victor, and thus of the Spanish monarchy.

Velázquez used Flemish prints as the basis for the landscape in the background; in his composition he follows a model from the *Quadrins historiques de la Bible*, published in Lyons, in 1553, showing the meeting of Abraham and Melchisedek. The benevolent gesture of Spinola, who has dismounted from his horse to accept the keys and is turning towards his opponent Justin of Nassau, has literary parallels: Calderón de la Barca describes the scene in a similar way in his play of the same name, in which Spinola says to the governor: "Justinus, I accept them and acknowledge how brave you are, for the courage of the defeated creates the fame of the victor."

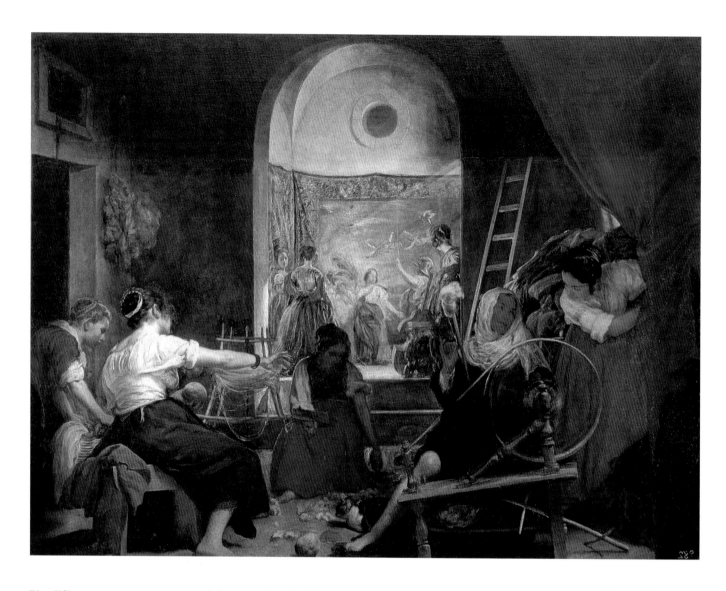

Diego Velázquez
Las Hilanderas (The Spinners), 1656
Oil on canvas, 117 x 190 cm
Madrid, Prado

Like the famous *Meninas,* the *Spinners* belongs to the late work of Velázquez; both paintings were produced in 1656. Both are based on complex themes which are not initially evident to the spectator. Each picture considers the status of the arts and the social position of the artist in Spanish society. In *Las Meninas* Velázquez portrays himself openly in the company of the royal family; in the *Spinners* this message is conveyed in a somewhat more obscure way.

In a manner similar to that of some early *bodegón* scenes (see p. 413), the action takes place on several planes: the manufacture of Gobelin tapestries is shown with several women spinning and

winding yarn in the foreground. Accordingly the picture is interpreted in the first instance as a workshop picture, a scene in the royal carpet factory of Santa Isabel. On a second plane, three women are viewed inspecting a tapestry through an opening which resembles a stage. The tapestry shows a scene from the legend of Arachne from Ovid's *Metamorphoses* (book 6) and is the key to the interpretation of the painting. The mortal Arachne had presumed to challenge the goddess Athene, the patron of weaving and spinning, to a contest in the art of weaving. When the judge declared the carpets produced by Arachne and Athene to be of equal merit, it effectively represented a victory for Arachne since it suggested that her weaving was of divine quality. At the same time, Arachne had insulted the goddess: she had depicted the rape of Europa by Jupiter, who had approached her in the form of a bull. Arachne was thus clearly mocking the gods. Athene

promptly turned Arachne into a spider. The tapestry in the painting shows the enraged goddess and to her right Arachne with her completed tapestry. Her punishment is indicated in the painting only by a musical instrument on the stage, for music was the traditional antidote to the bite of a spider.

As in the *Kitchen Scene with Christ in the House of Mary and Martha* (see p. 413), the scene in the foreground has been interpreted as a reference to the one in the background. The weaving women can in fact be associated with the legend of Arachne, since Ovid relates that the goddess disguised herself as an old woman when she sought out Arachne. In the theme of Arachne's tapestry, Velázquez recalls Titian's painting of the *Rape of Europa* in the royal collection. Arachne's tapestry therefore refers to Titian's artistic invention, and thus to the renaissance concepts of *disegno* and *idea*—to the creative genius of the artist which is found in every

work of art. The gifted painter Titian is compared to Arachne, who could weave divinely. In the sketchily rendered, light-filled, colorful scene in the background, we may see an allusion to painting as a divine art. In contrast, the figures in the dimly lit foreground are following a lowly occupation.

This late painting by Velázquez intentionally refers to the painter's masterly technique, for example in the skillfully suggested turning of the wheel. In this mythological painting Velázquez once again demonstrates his ability to work in this most difficult and also most highly valued of genres.

Alonso Cano
Miracle of the Well, c. 1646–48
Oil on canvas, 216 x 149 cm
Madrid, Prado

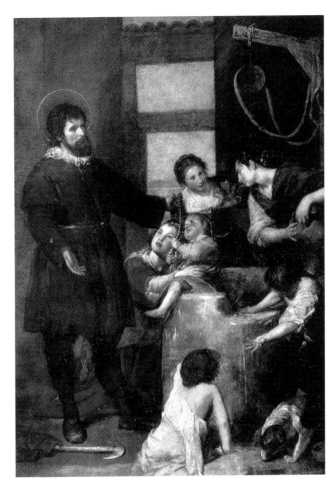

One of the most important paintings by Alonso Cano of Granada is the *Miracle of the Well* which he created for the high altar of the church of Santa Maria de la Almudena in Madrid. It depicts a scene from the life of St. Isidore of Seville, the patron of the city of Madrid. After the son of St. Isidore had fallen into a well, the water level rose in response to the saint's prayers and the child came to the surface unharmed. Several figures are closely grouped around the well: in the left-hand corner of the picture stands the full-length figure of the saint, a rosary in his hand. Partly concealed by him, the child's mother gazes at him in astonishment with the rescued child in her arms. In the background two more women turn towards each other, astonished by the miracle. The circle is closed by two children playing with the overflowing water and a dog.

The painting found great favor with the artist's contemporaries and was seen as a "true miracle" mainly because of its coloring—warm brown and green tones are delightfully complemented by orange and red. Here Cano turned to a manner of painting in which harsh contours are abandoned in favor of modeling loosened by light and shade, with many highlights and surface reflections.

In the painting, two moments from the legend are combined: the rescue of the child and the recognition of Isidore's saintliness by the women. In the composition the saint is isolated and conveys a certain grandeur as the only figure in the painting who is visible from head to foot and standing up. Nonetheless, Cano's painting hardly has the effect of an altarpiece, for the scene has a silhouette-like quality and the figures, as in the work of Murillo, are realistically portrayed in a manner which lends the character of an everyday event to a miraculous occasion.

Antonio Pereda
The Cavalier's Dream, c. 1650
Oil on canvas, 152 x 217 cm
Madrid, Museo de la Real Academia de San Fernando

In addition to scenes from the lives of the saints, *vanitas* paintings, which point to the transitory nature of earthly things through symbolism and allegory, play an important part in Spanish painting. In *The Cavalier's Dream* by Antonio Pereda a nobleman is shown asleep at a table. A number of objects are piled up in front of him: jewelry and coins, books, a mask, a burnt-out candle—a warning of the possibility of sudden death—as well as flowers, a skull, weapons, and armor, all emblems of power, wealth, and the transience of life. In the background an angel, with a banner with an inscription referring to unexpected death, turns towards the sleeping man. Pereda reminds the spectator that the path to salvation lies only in turning away from the temptations of earthly things and towards prayer, penance, and chastity.

407

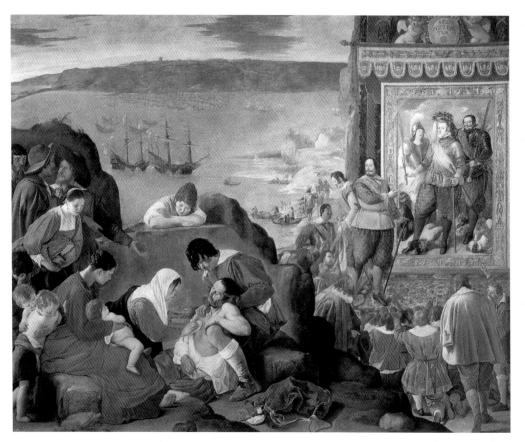

Juan Bautista Maino
Recapture of Bahía, 1635
Oil on canvas, 309 x 381 cm
Madrid, Prado

Juan Bautista Maino also produced a painting for the Salón de los Reinos. After the harbor of Bahía had been occupied by the Dutch, the Spaniards succeeded in recapturing it on May 1, 1625, the name-day of St. Philip. In Maino's painting the victorious army and the defeated enemy are presented with a wall-hanging which depicts Philip IV (who was not actually present on this occasion) being crowned with a laurel wreath by Victory, the personification of victory, and the minister Olivares. At the king's feet lie three figures personifying war, heresy, and anger. In the foreground, women are caring for the wounded, while children play nearby.

Maino's painting is characterized by sympathy for the wounded and tenderness towards the children. Thus the subject becomes not only the triumph of the victor but also the misery of the defeated. Like Velázquez' painting, the *Recapture of Bahía* is far from an unreflecting glorification of the misfortune and suffering brought by war.

Francisco Zurbarán
Death of Hercules, c.1635
Oil on canvas, 136 x 167 cm
Madrid, Prado

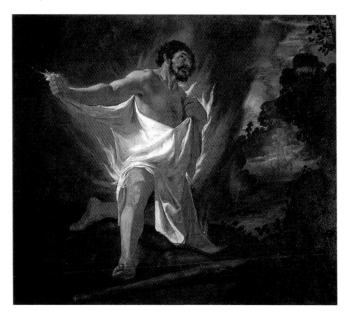

The decoration of the Salón de los Reinos included ten paintings of Hercules by Zurbarán which were hung above the French windows. The choice of Hercules was clearly not arbitrary, for he represented the embodiment of *virtus*, the virtue and strength of a just ruler, an allegory of the capable regent; he was also considered a forerunner of the Habsburgs, who traced their ancestry back to the legendary hero. The mythical hero as subject points to the fact that the Spanish kingdom was engaged in constant Herculean struggles with external threats, specifically unorthodoxy and heresy. Nine paintings depicted the Labors of Hercules, the tenth his last battle and the earthly death of the hero.

Hercules is shown here kneeling with his right arm outstretched, his features contorted in pain. His torture derives from the garment soaked in the blood of Nessus, which his jealous wife Deianira had sent him and which is now burning his flesh. In Zurbarán's painting, Hercules, obeying the command of the oracle of Delphi, subjects himself to burn on a funeral pyre; from its flames he will ascend to the heaven of the gods. The stark contrast of light and dark gives the hero's body a powerful three-dimensional quality. The coloring of the idyllic landscape, where the sketchily illustrated centaur Nessus lies wounded by Hercules' fatal arrow is modelled on Titian and contrasts with the dark foreground which is lit only by the flames.

The Hercules cycle alluded to the Spanish dynasty, since Hercules was considered to be its ancestor and founder, and to its physical and spiritual virtues; it was also intended to emphasize the almost superhuman ability and godlike quality of the regent, Philip IV.

Diego Velázquez
Philip IV at Fraga, 1644
Oil on canvas, 135 x 98 cm
New York, Frick Collection

As court painter, Velázquez' main task was to produce portraits of the royal family. Among the portraits of Philip IV painted on the occasion of a particular event is the so-called "Fraga portrait". After the Catalan revolt of 1640, the French army had occupied parts of Catalonia and Aragon. In 1644 the Spanish army set out to reconquer these areas and in the same year the king also traveled to the theater of war in Catalonia, accompanied by Velázquez.

The portrait was painted during their stay in Fraga, originally occupied by the French, after it had been liberated by the Spaniards. According to Palomino's report, Velázquez painted the portrait within three days in order to send it to the queen in Madrid. The king is portrayed three-quarter length in the costume of the supreme commander which he wore after the victory when he entered Lérida. With his right hand he braces his military staff against his thigh, holding his hat with the other hand. The king's dress, a red jacket richly decorated with white embroidery, a broad lace collar, and wide hanging sleeves, conveys an impression of wealth and splendor and stands out starkly from the gray-brown neutral background. While Velázquez' early portraits of Philip IV usually show him dressed in black in front of a dark background, conveying a certain austerity and sobriety, in the Fraga painting a change is evident: the king is here shown in a more relaxed and informal mood. The painter achieves this effect through a more free handling of color in the rendering of the costume and the use of vivid pigments. The absence of such attributes as insignia of power and allegories in glorification of the regent is typical of Spanish painting.

In Madrid, the portrait was set up under a canopy in the church of San Martín on the occasion of the Catalan victory celebration. As in Maino's *Bahía* painting, the work fulfilled the function of representing the absent king who could be present throughout his kingdom with the help of portraits.

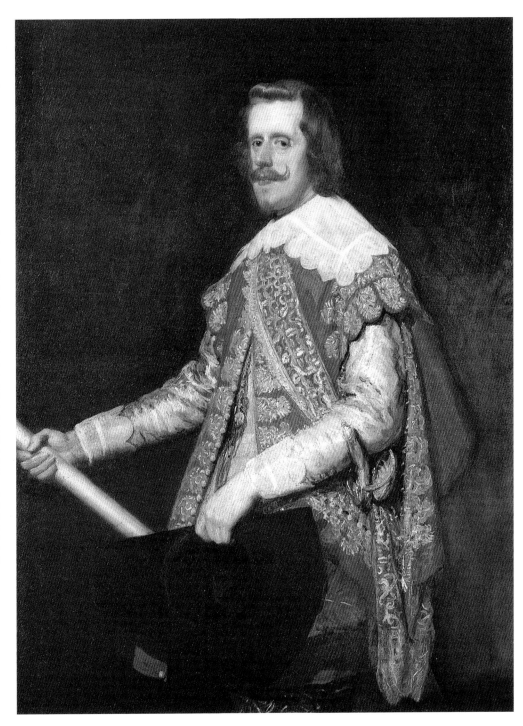

Francisco Herrera the Younger
Triumph of St. Hermengild, 1655
Oil on canvas, 328 x 229 cm
Madrid, Prado

José Antolínez
Workshop Scene, c. 1670
Oil on canvas, 201 x 125 cm
Munich, Alte Pinakothek

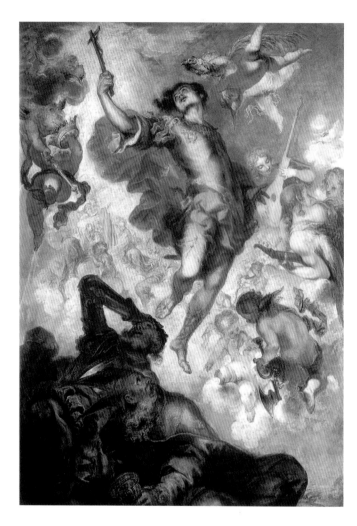

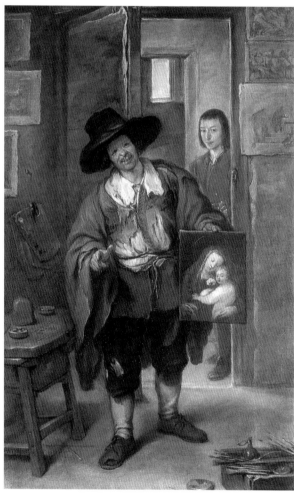

The Seville artist Francisco Herrera the Younger became court painter to Charles II in Madrid. One of his fourteen paintings for the main altar of the monastery of the Discalced Carmelites in Madrid, dating from 1655, is the *Triumph of St. Hermengild*. Palomino describes Herrera as a proud, even vain man: fully conscious of having produced a masterpiece, he demanded that his painting should be hung to the sound of drums and trumpets.

The work shows the apotheosis of St. Hermengild of Seville, the son of the Arian Visigoth King Leovigild; after steadfastly refusing to adopt the Arian heresy, he was imprisoned and executed by his heretic father. The saint, carrying the cross in one hand and conducted by angels, floats up to heaven in glory. The painting has a strongly theatrical character: the upper part shows the saint drifting upwards in glory while his body, accentuated by bright light and color, is extended in length and forms a bold curve as he floats. Below, at the feet of Hermengild, crowded closely together in the left-hand corner of the picture and colored in dark tones, lie his father Leovigild and an Arian bishop holding the chalice from which the saint had refused to drink.

Jose Antolínez' *Workshop Scene* effectively illustrates the everyday life of the artist in the capital. The room shown is characterized as an artist's workshop by the presence of artist's tools and paintings. An elderly man in ragged clothes, probably a picture dealer, presents a painting of the Virgin to an imaginary client, or to the spectator. A second man appears in the background, younger and well-dressed, also looking towards the spectator and pointing to the old man with his left hand. The young man is presumably Antolínez himself, receiving the picture dealer in his studio. The coins on the table also indicate a financial transaction.

The impoverished surroundings suggest that the painting includes a critical reference to the low status of the artist in Spain, where paintings were subject to tax at the same rate as ordinary goods and many painters lived at subsistence level.

Francisco Rizi's *Auto da Fé of 1680* has particular historical and documentary value in its depiction of contemporary events. An *auto da fé* was a ceremony organized by the Inquisition which was generally combined with some other solemn occasion such as the king's accession to the throne or the birth of a royal heir. The aim of these occasional rituals was to celebrate the triumph of the true faith, and also to arouse fear and horror in its enemies. People arrested for heresy, accompanied by the *familiares*, those close to the members of the Inquisition, therefore took part in a solemn procession, followed by monks as well as secular and spiritual dignitaries, right up to the bishop. This procession passed through the streets of the city to the festival square. An altar was erected in the center of the square, behind which sat the representatives of the Church; those under sentence were placed opposite them. The trial, during which the accused were sentenced either to death, to serve in the galleys, or to prison, was followed by many observers.

The *auto de fé* depicted by Rizi took place in 1680 in the reign of Charles II in the Plaza Mayor in Madrid. The spectator has a bird's-eye view of the proceedings. From the balcony of the Casa de Panadería, the king, his consort Marie-Louise of Orléans, and the queen mother, Marianna of Austria, observe the trial. The painter appears to have been concerned mainly with giving an accurate account of the events.

Claudio Coello's *La Sagrada Forma* also refers to a particular event during the reign of Charles II. Coello, with Rizi and Carreño, is considered one of the most important painters in Madrid of the second half of the century. In 1685 he received the commission to carry out the monumental altar painting for the sacristy of El Escorial. This painting, which is his major work, depicts the ceremony of the transfer of the miraculous host by Charles II into a specially constructed chapel which adjoined the sacristy of El Escorial. This was the host of Gorkum, presented to Philip II by Emperor Rudolf II, the *Sagrada forma*, a monstrance from which blood had flowed in 1572 when it was desecrated by Calvinists.

The scene of the event is the chapel in which the king hands over the host to the bishop in the presence of triumphant angels. A number of accurate likenesses, including that of Charles II, give the painting the character of a group portrait. The warm coloring, with dominating yellow and gold tones, enhances the triumphal character of the event. The representation of space in the painting seems to continue the architecture of the sacristy. Coello reveals here his mastery of illusionistic painting, which he further demonstrated in his frescos and ceiling paintings.

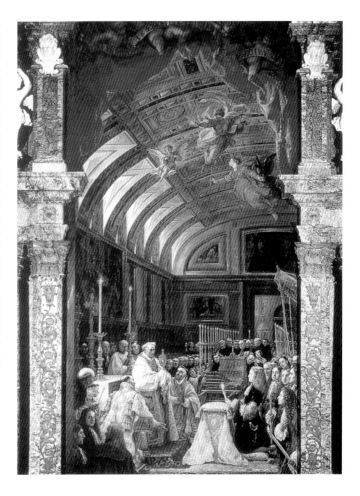

Claudio Coello
La Sagrada Forma, 1685–90
Oil on canvas, 500 x 300 cm
El Escorial, sacristy

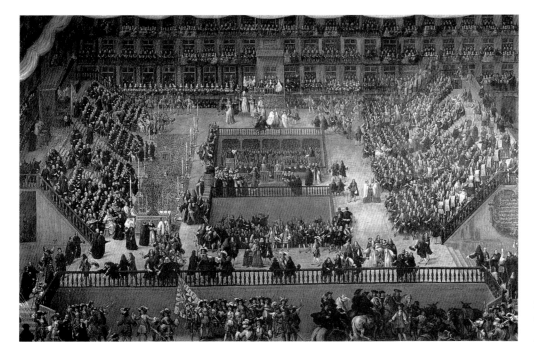

Francisco Rizi
Auto da Fé of 1680, 1683
Oil on canvas, 277 x 438 cm
Madrid, Prado

Seville

During the seventeenth century Seville, the capital of Andalusia, was the most important artistic center of the Spanish kingdom after Madrid. At the beginning of the century Seville was also still also its most important commercial center; after the colonization of America it was here that the flourishing trade with the *Indias*, the Spanish colonies overseas, developed. Along the river Guadalquivir the merchant ships brought wealth from the New World, especially gold and silver. The city emerged as the main shipping center for sea trade. However, during the political and economic crisis which gripped the whole of Spain during the first decades of the century, the city went into depression. Seville also faced a demographic crisis: the plague epidemic of 1649 and the famine that followed reduced its population by nearly half.

The arts, however, were only belatedly affected by this decline. As a result of the efforts of the Counter-Reformation which followed the Council of Trent (1545–63), in which Spain took the lead, the first half of the seventeenth century saw a boom in the foundation of monasteries in Seville: the thirty-seven monasteries and convents already in existence were augmented by fifteen new foundations, and a number of hospitals were also built. The decoration of these monasteries, their churches, sacristies, refectories, and cloisters, as well as the many hospitals with altarpieces and large cycles of paintings, opened up a rich field of employment to the painters and sculptors of Seville. An additional market of considerable importance was created by the American colonies, to which stacks of paintings with biblical themes and scenes from the lives of the saints were conveyed by the shipload. Portrait-painting represented a further source of income for painters. The nobility in the city and the dignitaries of the Church as well as the local representatives of the Dutch trading colonies had their portraits painted.

Yet Seville already enjoyed special esteem in Spain during the Renaissance, not only as an economic center, but also as an intellectual one. As a *nueva Roma* [new Rome] it attracted a number of important individuals. Around 1600 Francisco Pacheco, the painter and art historian known as Velázquez' teacher, had gathered a circle around himself consisting of humanists, writers, and theologians. They were to play an important part in the artistic life of the city. This circle of scholars, known as the "Pacheco Academy," produced several literary works as well as texts on art. Pacheco himself published one of the three great seventeenth-century Spanish treatises on art, *El arte de la pintura*, in which he deals exhaustively with theoretical and practical questions of painting and in the same thorough fashion considers questions of Christian iconography and the appropriate representation of religious art. His views reflected the concerns of the Inquisition which, with the help of specially nominated censors—of whom Pacheco was one—made certain that no heretical ideas crept into art and that in general the country was preserved from the "Lutheran heresy."

Around 1600 Pacheco was one of the most important representatives of the Seville school of painters, together with Juan de las Roelas and Francisco Herrera. However, the paintings of these masters are often heavily indebted to Dutch or Italian prints and copies after Italian masters, and are not particularly innovative in style. The works of the young Diego Velázquez, Francisco Zurbarán, Alonso Cano, Francisco Herrera the Younger, Bartolomé Esteban Murillo, and Juan de Valdés Leal were soon to transform Seville into one of the most important centers of art of the Spanish *Siglo de Oro* after the capital.

These painters obtained their education in the craft-oriented setting of the workshops. After seven years' apprenticeship in Pacheco's workshop, Diego Velázquez (1599–1660) obtained his master's diploma from the Seville painters' guild committee, and was thus entitled to open his own workshop. However, as early as 1622 he left his home town and in 1623, as discussed earlier, he settled in Madrid as court painter to Philip IV, at the start of a brilliantly successful career. Francisco Zurbarán (1598–1664), after studying for only three years with a little-known Seville church painter, Pedro Díaz de Villanueva, had completed his journeyman years and was at first active in his hometown, Llerena, and its environs, before settling in Seville in 1626. He obtained a number of commissions there, but he also took part in important projects for the court at Madrid in the 1630s, remaining there even during the plague epidemic of 1649 before finally moving to the capital in 1658. By contrast, Bartolomé Esteban Murillo (1617–82), who was born a generation later in Seville and had learned his craft in Juan de Castillo's workshop, stayed in his native town all his life, was hugely successful there, and in 1656 was mentioned as "the best painter in the city." He ran an extensive workshop enterprise where he employed several assistants and trained apprentices. Murillo is recorded as having visited the capital only once, in 1658. Juan de Valdés Leal (1622–90), who probably studied with Antonio del Castillo in Córdoba, also moved to Seville in 1656, where, apart from a short stay in Madrid in 1664, he remained for the rest of his life.

These artists were active not only as producers of oil paintings however. Often polychrome sculptures played a more significant role than panel paintings in the decoration of church and monastery altars. In the preparation of such splendid sculptural schemes the painters were closely involved as *doradores* [gilders] and *policromadores* [sculpture painters], activities which represented an important source of income for them. The Hermandad de S. Luca, the Seville painters' guild, regulated both training and the production of art by means of strict *ordenanzas* or decrees.

In 1660, on the instigation of such major painters as Murillo and Herrera the Younger, an Academy was founded; however, it was forced to close as early as 1674 because of financial problems. The Academy was a private initiative by the artists, who aimed to extend their inadequate training in drawing. Teaching in the workshops

Diego Velázquez
Kitchen Scene with Christ in the House of Mary and Martha, 1618
Oil on canvas, 60 x 103.5 cm
London, National Gallery

The *bodegónes* produced in Seville and Toledo are among the few secular forms of Spanish painting, uniting elements of still-life and genre scenes. Ordinary people are shown at their everyday occupations such as pouring water, cooking, or eating and drinking. In the representation of individuals and in the presentation of the objects and foodstuffs, there is a particular concentration on tactile values and a painstaking structuring of surfaces. In the early work of Velázquez *bodegónes* play an important role.

Among the most significant of these is the *Kitchen Scene with Christ in the House of Mary and Martha* from his Seville period. Two women are depicted in the foreground; the older one looks towards the spectator, pointing to the younger woman, who is preparing a meal. There are several vessels on the table with ingredients such as fish, eggs, and garlic. In the background to the right is a small image of Christ's visit to the house of Mary and Martha, which leaves open the question of whether this is a painting or a view of another room. Such

CONTINUED P. 414

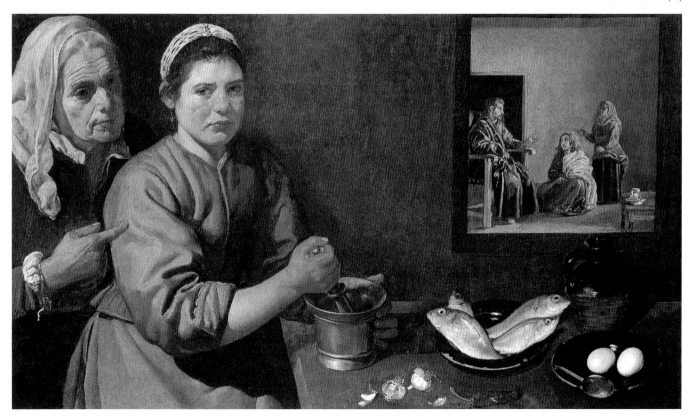

concentrated on the purely practical aspects of a painter's activities, while theory, which included drawing, was somewhat neglected. The Seville artists met every evening under the aegis of this Academy in the Casa de la Lonja, the stock exchange, where they practiced life drawing.

The artistic as well as material success of the important Seville artists was very variable. While at the beginning of the century the artists' sphere of activity was predominantly restricted to Seville, in the course of the century Madrid became more attractive as an artistic center. Several painters, including Velázquez, Zurbarán, and Herrera the Younger, attempted with varying success to establish themselves in the capital. While Velázquez succeeded in being promoted to chief court painter to Philip IV and Herrera the Younger became court painter to Charles II, Zurbarán, although he did carry out several commissions in the capital, spent his main creative period in his native city. Other painters, such as Murillo and Valdés Leal, were active in Seville almost all their lives and were committed to the Academy, but in spite of their fame were not offered commissions by the court in Madrid.

During the early decades of the century, the work of the young Velázquez and Zurbarán, as well as of Murillo, appeared to be heavily indebted to the influence of Caravaggio and his followers. In their paintings human bodies and objects are defined by precisely delineated contours and appear to possess a certain sculptural hardness created through a contrived deployment of light and shade, which is strictly divided and highly contrasted. The composition in general has a two-dimensional effect, and a coolness of tone is evident in the predominantly dark coloring; this style of painting in Murillo's work has been described as *estilo frío*. In the second half of the century the influence of Titian and other Venetians, as well as Rubens, van Dyck, and the Flemish painters, became dominant in Seville. The paintings of this period are characterized by loose outlines and a doughy modelling of the body, gentle illumination with a blurring of the boundaries between light and shade, light and misty backgrounds, warm coloring, and pronounced spatial composition.

images, structured on two levels, and in which two scenes belonging to different areas of space are united, can already be found in the second half of the sixteenth century in the work of Dutch masters such as Pieter Aertsen (see p. 469).

So far there has been no satisfactory explanation of the content of the paint-ing. One plausible interpretation, how-ever, is that the older woman is didacti-cally pointing out to the maid in the foreground the different ways of life, the *vita activa* and the *vita contemplativa* represented by Martha and Mary in the scene in the background. This interpreta-tion is placed in the context of the con-troversy as to which is better, strong faith and pious seriousness, or hard work and diligence. At the same time the painting might contain a reference to the remark of St. Teresa of Ávila that Christ was to be found among the kitchen pots and pans.

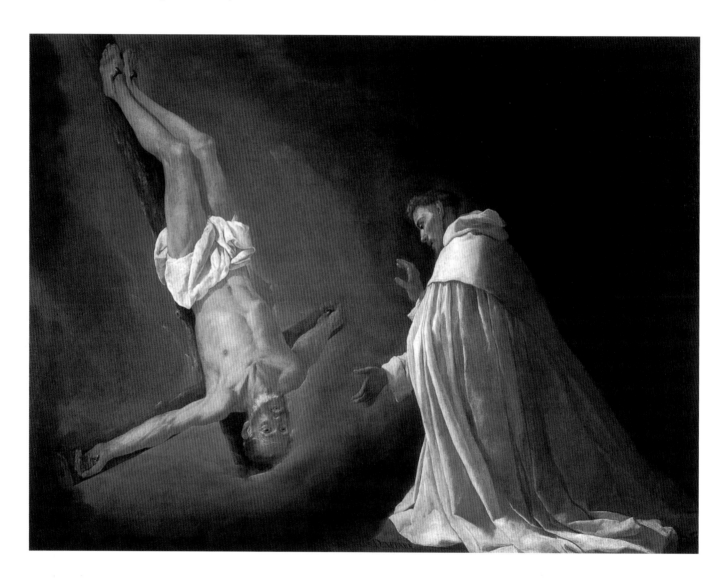

Francisco Zurbarán
Vision of St. Peter Nolasco with the Crucified Apostle Peter, 1629
Oil on canvas, 179 x 233 cm
Madrid, Prado

Cycles depicting the lives of saints were rich in images and proved to be an impor-tant source of work for artists. In the 1620s, Francisco Zurbarán painted three large series for churches and cloisters: two cycles for the Dominicans, depicting the lives of St. Dominic and St. Bonaventura, and one for the order of the Mercedarians, based on the life of St. Peter Nolasco, can-onized in 1628. Peter Nolasco, who died in Barcelona in 1249, was the founder of the Mercedarians. Zurbarán committed himself to the production of twenty-two large-scale paintings; it is unlikely that all of them were executed. The original aim of this order of knights was to ransom or liberate Christian captives from the Moorish regime.

One painting shows a vision of St. Peter Nolasco with the crucified apostle Peter. When the saint had persisted in praying for days for permission to under-take a pilgrimage to the tomb of the apostle Peter, Peter suddenly appeared to him and told him that there were other more urgent tasks for him as a Christian, in particular the liberation of the penin-sula from the Moors.

Zurbarán sets the visionary event in an undefined space in which Peter Nolasco kneels to the right, receiving the message of the crucified apostle with half-closed eyes and humbly outstretched arms, and bending slightly forwards. The apostle, enveloped in a cloud of light, is presented in such a way that fastened to his inverted crucifix he is almost in direct eye-contact with St. Peter Nolasco. Zurbarán lends a realistic quality to the event by avoiding any distinction between the heavenly and earthly spheres.

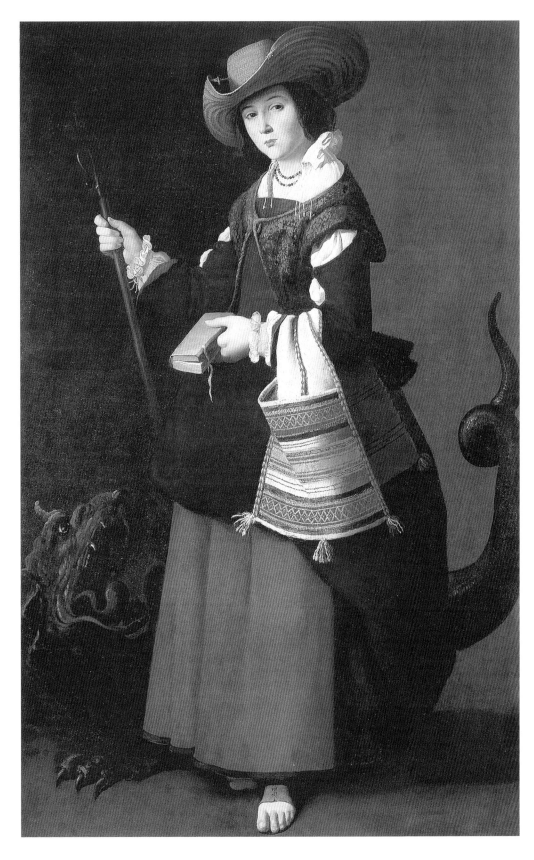

Francisco Zurbarán
St. Margaret, c. 1635
Oil on canvas, 194 x 112 cm
London, National Gallery

Among the representations of saints during this period, the portrait-style image occupies a special place. In pictures of saints who resemble ladies of the nobility, Zurbarán created a portrait type which has become known as *retrato a lo divino*. Zurbarán delivered twenty-four *Standing Virgins* to a convent in Lima, now lost but which perhaps were in the style of the painting of St. Margaret shown here, which was produced in 1635–40.

Zurbarán presents the saint to the spectator at full length in an appealing attitude wearing shepherdess's dress and with a Bible in her hand. The halo indicating her sainthood is not shown. St. Margaret, a virgin from Antioch, refused as a Christian to marry the prefect Olibrius and was therefore disowned by her father who had remained a pagan. During the persecution of Christians under Diocletian she suffered a cruel martyrdom and was finally beheaded. The shepherdess costume refers to her childhood in the country, and the dragon at her feet, which she attempts to drive away with the cross, to the dragon which devoured her but from which she emerged unscathed.

With its severe outlines and the sharp contrasts of light and shade in the manner of Caravaggio, this painting achieves a powerful sculptural effect.

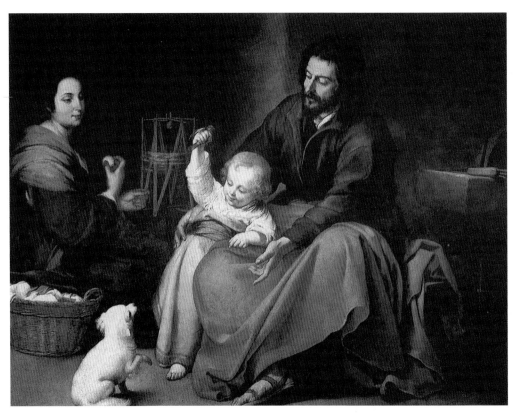

Bartolomé Esteban Murillo
Holy Family with a Little Bird,
c. 1650
Oil on canvas, 144 x 188 cm
Madrid, Prado

Murillo also dispenses to a considerable extent with the distance between the earthly and the heavenly realms in his many religious paintings. His saints are depicted as kindly and sympathetic human friends. His approach to religious themes is well exemplified by one of his early works, the *Holy Family with a Little Bird*. The Holy Family is shown in a dark, poorly furnished room. The Virgin Mary sits at the distaff, lovingly watching the Child who holds a bird in his right hand and is teasing a dog. A strong *chiaroscuro* which outlines the figures as in a relief is characteristic of the artist's early style. There is not a single indication of the holiness of the people represented. Clearly Murillo is chiefly interested in describing emotions like parental love, tenderness, and pride. It should be noted that the figure of Joseph is closer to the center of the picture than that of Mary. This indicates the re-evaluation of Joseph during the reforms of the Council of Trent.

Bartolomé Estebán Murillo
St. Thomas of Villanueva Heals a Lame Man, c. 1670
Oil on canvas, 220.8 x 148.7 cm
Munich, Bayerische
Staatsgemäldesammlung,
Alte Pinakothek

Murillo dedicated several paintings to the life of St. Thomas of Villanueva (1488–1555). With St. Teresa of Ávila and St. Ignatius Loyola he is among the most important Spanish saints of the Counter-Reformation. About 1670, Murillo produced this painting with its companion piece, *St. Thomas as a Child Distributes His Clothes*, for the altar of the chapel of St. Thomas in the church of the Augustinian monastery in Seville. The masterly composition and technical composition of *St. Thomas of Villanueva Heals a Lame Man* establishes it among his masterpieces.

The scene refers to *caritas*, the saint's love for his fellows, a theological virtue which characterized the saint from his childhood. Thomas was court preacher to Charles V and in 1544 was appointed archbishop of Seville. According to the reports of the *Acta Sanctorum* St. Thomas ordered that food should be given to the poor every day in the courtyard of the archiepiscopal palace in Valencia. When one day he saw a lame man walking with crutches, he called him over and asked him what he needed. The lame man answered that he was a tailor who mended clothes and it was his dearest wish to be able to practice his craft again, which he was unable to do because of his disability. The saint made the sign of the cross over the lame man and ordered him to go to work. The healed man dropped his crutches and ran in haste down the steps of the palace in order to take up his work again.

To illustrate the event, Murillo makes use of a practice widespread in the middle ages: he depicts two scenes simultaneously, thus rejecting the unity of place and time more common in the seventeenth century. The foreground shows the scene of the healing of the lame man. In the presence of two pupils, St. Thomas makes the sign of the cross over the man kneeling before him. In the distance, on a different level, the saint is shown feeding the poor in front of the archiepiscopal palace, with the lame man already happily healed, running down the steps without his crutches.

The contrast between the monumental, sinister scene, painted in dark, somber colors, with the supernaturally tall saint in his black habit in the foreground, and the cheerful scene in the background with a bright, glowing play of colors, is evidence of the painter's exceptional talent as a colorist.

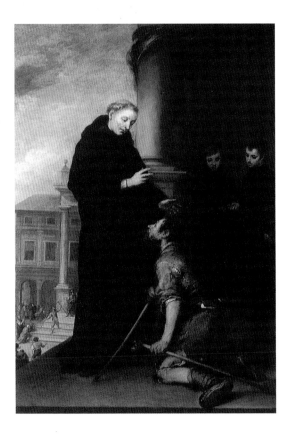

Juan de Valdés Leal
In ictu oculi (left) and *Finis gloriae mundi* (right), 1670–72
Oil on canvas, 220 x 216 cm
Seville, Hospital de la Caridad

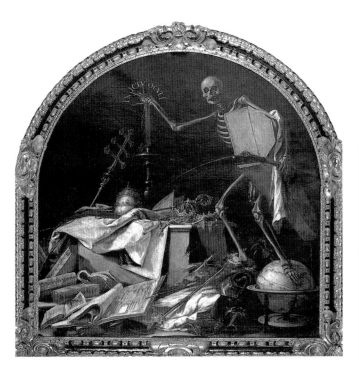

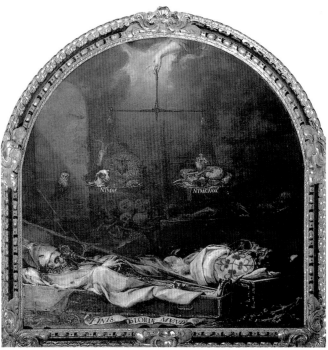

Murillo collaborated with Valdés Leal on several paintings for the church of the Hospital de la Caridad in Seville. The two companion pieces created by Valdés Leal for the church, the allegories *In ictu oculi* [In the Face of Death] and *Finis gloriae mundi* [The End of Worldly Glory], are based on the concept of *vanitas*, the illusory and transient nature of all earthly things.

The hospital was founded by the wealthy Seville merchant Miguel de Mañara, who entered the brotherhood of the Caridad in 1662 after the death of his wife, and committed himself to doing good deeds on behalf of the poor and sick.

Charitable work as the only chance of salvation from eternal damnation is the theme of Valdés Leal's paintings. In the first painting death is shown as the destroyer and annihilator of everything that human beings have amassed in the course of their lives—knowledge, office, dignity, and possessions. Death appears in the form of a skeleton, extinguishes the light of life, and brings time to a halt. Even power and scholarship are useless to mankind in the face of death.

The second painting is a view of the inside of a vault full of corpses in various stages of decay; in the foreground the

remains of a bishop and a knight of Calatrava are particularly noticeable. Above, the hand of Christ holds a set of scales. In one bowl are the symbols of the Seven Deadly Sins and in the other are the symbols of the Christian faith: charity, prayer, and penance. Both allegories remind the spectator that death seizes all equally and without discrimination and that their good and bad deeds will be judged at the Last Judgment.

Paris

Around 1600 a unified French state was formed, and the absolute monarchy which gradually established itself put an end to the feudal fragmentation of the country, the internal unrest, and the religious conflicts of the preceding century. These changes were to be of decisive significance for French painting of the seventeenth century. With the conversion of Henri IV (1589–1610) to Catholicism in 1593 and the Edict of Nantes in 1598 the Wars of Religion ended and freedom of religious thought was granted in France. At the same time a political and economic crisis, which had also inevitably affected the arts, was brought to an end.

By the end of the sixteenth century, Paris had already become the most important artistic center in the country. The systematic urban planning schemes of Henri IV transformed the city into a modern metropolis. The relatively progressive attitudes of the state were further reflected in the reorganization and beautification of the capital. Louis XIII (1610–43) and his chief minister, Cardinal Richelieu, had already placed art at the service of the state, but the conscious exploitation of art as propaganda which was so vigorously pursued under Louis XIV (1661–1715) was unprecedented. Jean-Baptiste Colbert, chief minister of the "Sun King," was not only responsible for finance but was also the ultimate arbiter in matters of art. He drew the most renowned artists in the land to the court in order to realize a vast project, the building and decoration of the palace of Versailles, on which work was to continue for many decades. Colbert, who bore the title of *surintendant et ordonnateur général des bâtiments, arts, et manufactures de France*, organized the arts and used them for political purposes. A number of artists were subordinate to him: Charles Perrault, Louis Le Vau as *premier architecte du roi*, Charles Le Brun as *premier peintre du roi,* and André Le Nôtre as *premier jardinier du roi*. The Académie Royale de Peinture was founded in 1648 in Paris with Colbert as political director and Le Brun as artistic director; it soon became a very effective instrument of royal artistic propaganda.

In addition to the court, which commissioned a number of works of art, the Church also had many projects to distribute among painters. Paris was an important center of the Counter-Reformation and there were even efforts on the part of the Catholic church to transform the city into a "New Rome." The great orders settled in the city; between 1600 and 1640, sixty new monasteries and twenty new churches were built.

It is not until the generation of the painters born around 1600, Le Nain, Vouet, and La Tour, however, that one can speak of a French school of painters. Simon Vouet (1590–1649) spent twenty years in Rome and achieved such a high reputation there that in 1624 he was elected president of the Accademia di San Luca. Returning to Paris in 1627 he entered the service of Louis XIII, but also worked for the Church and for private clients. Vouet ran a large workshop and had several pupils. He threw off the influence of Caravaggio as well as of

Guercino and Reni and introduced the vocabulary of the Roman baroque to Paris. Georges de La Tour (1593–1652) lived and worked mainly in the provinces. However, he also had contacts at the court of Louis XIII and in 1639 was granted the title of *peintre ordinaire du roy*. But his most important clients were found in the bourgeois circles of Lunéville and Nancy. La Tour became famous primarily for his night scenes, which reflect the influence of Caravaggio. Artificial lighting usually dominates his scenes, allowing the artist to achieve a strongly sculptural effect with strong lighting and sharp outlines. La Tour mainly created paintings of mystical and philosophical content, with themes such as becoming, passing away, and prediction, distinguished by the monumentality of their composition, a small number of figures, and a strong concentration on atmosphere. The Le Nain brothers, Matthieu (1607–77), Louis (1593–1648), and Antoine (1588–1648), also came from the provinces, from Laon, but then went to Paris where they were among the founder members of the Academy. They worked together and signed their works only with their family name, so their paintings are difficult to distinguish from each other. They were known for their genre scenes but also for portraits, mostly of ordinary people. While in the Netherlands the theme of everyday peasant life was generally treated in a satirical or coarse manner, the Le Nain brothers brought out the human dignity and seriousness of the people in their clearly composed paintings.

Philippe de Champaigne (1620–74) came from Brussels. He acquired his training with the landscape painter Jacques Fouquières and in 1621 came to Paris, where he immediately enjoyed great success. As chief painter to the queen mother, Marie de' Medici, he supervised the decoration of the Palais du Luxembourg. His fame was based chiefly on his court portraits. Philippe de Champaigne was a sympathizer of Jansenism, a strict movement within the bourgeoisie directed against Jesuits alleged laxity in matters of doctrine. This explains the severity and dignity of the figures he portrays. Nicolas Poussin (1594–1665) left France as early as 1624 and went to Rome, but he never quite lost contact with his native land. The many paintings he created for high French officials and friends and patrons in Paris and his prolific correspondence give evidence of his continuing relationship with France. At the urging of Louis XIII, Poussin returned to Paris for two years (1640–42) and participated in the decoration of the Louvre.

Charles Le Brun (1619–90), a pupil of Vouet, was also drawn to Rome where he spent a long period. Appointed *premier peintre du roi* in 1664, Le Brun carried out the decoration of a number of *hôtels* in Paris and created large cycles of paintings for the king. His most important works were produced at Versailles where he took over the decoration of the Gallery of Mirrors, the Halls of Peace and War, and the Ambassadors' Staircase. Le Brun's significance lies not only in his artistic achievement, but also in his influence on the various artistic projects undertaken by Louis XIV. As an important and extremely active figure in the artistic policy of Louis XIV, he enjoyed the favor of Colbert and became director of the Académie Royale de Peinture. The death of his patron Colbert in 1683 also meant the end of Le Brun's career, for Colbert's successor, Louvois, preferred Mignard, his rival.

Pierre Mignard (1612–95) first studied with Jean Boucher in Bourges and later with Vouet in Paris. In 1636 he went to Rome where he stayed for twenty years. He achieved great fame as a portraitist and after Le Brun's death in 1690 became director of the Academy; here he fought on the side of the followers of Rubens for the recognition of the importance of color in painting. Another pupil of Vouet was Eustache Le Sueur (1616–55), who painted a number of painting cycles for churches, palaces and *hôtels* as well as portraits. One of his major commissions was for twenty-two paintings on the life and work of St. Bruno for the Carthusians of Paris. The influence of Poussin is noticeable in the elegant neo-classicism and freely handled coloring of his work. Hyacinthe Rigaud (1659–1743) came from Perpignan and came to Paris at the age of about twenty, where in the course of his studies at the Académie Royale he obtained the second prize in historical painting in 1682. On the advice of Le Brun, however, Rigaud concentrated on portrait painting. He created several grand portraits but also images of friends, which are inevitably more private in character.

Since painting in France in the seventeenth century was placed in the service of the state to a much greater extent than elsewhere, fewer individual movements emerged in art. There are, however, two contrasting aesthetic currents evident at this time: one—substantially larger—group of painters aspired to a strict classicism, while the other leant more towards baroque. The exceptional dependence of the court painters was quite remarkable for its time, and was not found in the other art centers of Europe. The absolutist system was glorified in numberless allegorical and mythological paintings, while religious paintings by comparison declined in importance. At the same time, a new style of grand portrait develops which proclaims the virtue and glory of the ruler by means of a number of symbols and allegories.

In Paris at the beginning of the century, artists were also organized into guilds and companies. Despite the resistance of Henri IV, who opposed the guild system because it inhibited his plans for the improvement of Paris, in 1622 the privileges of the guilds were newly confirmed: according to the rules only guild members were allowed to carry on a trade. The guild masters caused further conflict between the two factions by demanding a reduction in the number of court painters. 1648 saw the inaugural meeting of the Paris Academy, where the formulation of the statutes was based on the academies of Rome and Florence. The emphasis lay on theoretical education and on life drawing for which two hours daily were reserved. However, the Academy was not yet financially supported by the state, and it came into conflict with the guilds. As a rival

establishment the painters' guild, under the direction of Vouet, opened its own academy, the Académie de Saint-Luc. After violent debates the two academies were finally amalgamated in 1651 as the Académie Royale, which was given new statutes in 1655. The new Academy moved into rooms in the Louvre and was supported by a subsidy from the king which gave it the status of a royal institution. With Colbert as vice-rector (1661) and protector (1672) the Academy was increasingly placed in the service of the state; in general, the absolutist regime had mastered the skill of acquiring control over all aspects of culture and in particular of subjugating painters and their work. Colbert had founded the Académie Française as early as 1635 in order to strengthen the French language and preserve it from "impurity" and to exercise influence over philosophy and literature.

The Académie Royale did not take over the full professional training of the artist, but only the theoretical part of it which included drawing from life and lectures. The lectures were intended above all for the instruction of students, whereas in Rome they represented a forum for artists, giving them the opportunity to clarify their ideas. The practical part of their training still took place largely in the master's workshop. Prizes were awarded at regular intervals to particularly gifted students and occasionally exhibitions of the work of Academy members were organized. The lectures represented an attempt to set up a system by which a work of art could be precisely evaluated. Thus, Fréart de Chambrai and Le Brun sought to analyze works of art according to the categories already defined by Italian writers on art—invention, proportion, color, expression, and composition. At the same time a strict hierarchy of painting genres was promulgated; according to these standards everything that was not *histoire* was considered of little significance. In establishing this order of precedence, reliance was placed upon norms and categories taken from philosophy and the practice of art. The contents of paintings were considered according to their respective values, and here the Aristotelian and Neoplatonic division of reality into form and substance played a role. The depiction of God and man as the expression of form was allocated the highest value. Nature followed in a subordinate position as substance, first living, animated things, then, in the lowest place, inanimate objects. In addition, attention was paid to the various artistic conditions that must be fulfilled by the painter. A history painting demanded mastery of drawing and composition. The historical painter must also give evidence of *ingenium* as well as theoretical knowledge. The portrait painter, on the other hand, was expected only to have practical experience and skill in handling color. According to this hierarchy, still lifes were placed on the lowest level, below landscapes, animal paintings, and the portrait, while the highest rank was, of course, allowed to history painting.

During the last thirty years of the seventeenth century a violent debate took place at the Académie Royale. Two movements had developed in contemporary painting, each championed and represented by prominent painters. The so-called Poussinists were in no doubt as to the supremacy of *dessin*, outline, over color. In opposition to this approach, the Rubenists saw color as the most important element of painting. The discussion between the Poussinists and the Rubenists was continued in the *Querelle des anciens et des modernes*. This controversy among the Academicians began in the years 1671–72 and was to persist until 1699. Charles Perrault's treatise of 1688, the *Parallèle des anciens et des modernes*, gives an account of the basic elements of this debate. Two fundamental approaches to painting were discussed, based on the relationship between classicism and modernism on the one hand and on the contrast between Poussin and Rubens on the other. The Poussinists and their spokesman Le Brun saw in classical antiquity an unsurpassable artistic model and considered its rules to be still binding. They regarded Poussin as the greatest painter of their time and gave absolute preference to form, the principle of drawing, and thus to classicism. For Poussin, as for many members of the Academy, classical antiquity remained the standard. Even nature was to be corrected where it did not conform to the Greek or Roman ideal of beauty.

The opposing party, the Rubenists, led by Mignard and with Roger de Piles as spokesman, prized the coloristic qualities of Rubens and gave preference to color over drawing. In his dialogue on color, Roger de Piles places the Venetians above Raphael and Rubens above Titian. The Rubenists mocked the Poussinists' trust in authority and believed that in the *siècle Louis le Grand* [the century of Louis the Great] a pinnacle of artistic perfection had been reached.

Thus the opposing forces in this polemical debate were Poussin and Rubens, old and new art, form and color, classicism and baroque. Not least, however, this was a quarrel between two generations of artists. That this quarrel also involved political elements is evident from the fact that Louvois, the successor to Colbert, supported the Rubenists and Mignard was therefore appointed head of the Academy. From an aesthetic point of view, this meant equality between *couleur* and *dessin*. At the same time a step was taken which would initiate new directions in eighteenth-century art: works of art were no longer judged solely according to a rigid catalogue of rules, but the emotions arising on contemplating them were also taken into account. A certain stylistic pluralism began to establish itself, and the works of Venetian and Flemish masters could now take their place beside Roman and French paintings.

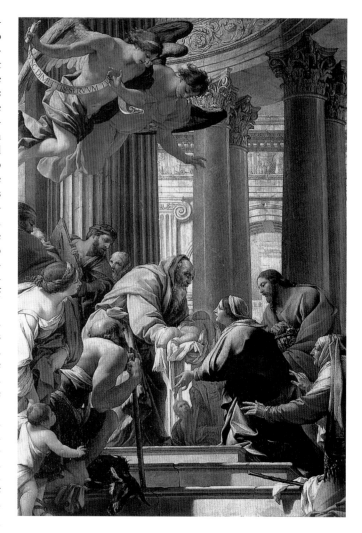

Simon Vouet
Presentation of Jesus in the Temple, 1641
Oil on canvas, 383 x 250 cm
Paris, Musée du Louvre

Among Simon Vouet's numerous religious paintings is the *Presentation of Jesus in the Temple*. The painting was commissioned by Richelieu in 1641 as part of the altarpiece for the Jesuit church of Saint-Louis. It contains the scene described by St. Luke in which the Virgin Mary hands the child over an altar to the high priest Simon.

Vouet places the event in the setting of a splendid temple architecture, showing it from an aerial perspective. The Virgin kneels on steps and presents the peacefully sleeping child to Simon. Next to her stands Joseph, gazing lovingly at the child. Other observers behind Simon also appear to be moved by the event. Several *repoussoir* figures on both sides separate the action from actual space. All the figures are strongly outlined with sculpturally draped garments. The painter does not particularly emphasize the supernatural or emotional content of the scene.

Here Vouet seems to have moved beyond the Caravaggism of his early work: the composition contains hardly any baroque elements and should be viewed rather as directly anticipating neo-classicism.

Georges de La Tour
St. Irene with the Wounded
St. Sebastian, c. 1640
Oil on canvas, 166 x 129 cm
Berlin, Gemäldegalerie Dahlem

One of La Tour's most important works is *St. Irene with the Wounded St. Sebastian*. La Tour does not, like most painters, choose as a representative scene from the legend of Sebastian the saint's martyrdom, but depicts Irene and her companions mourning the martyr's death. Sebastian, the commanding officer in the Emperor Diocletian's bodyguard, had converted to the Christian faith. He was betrayed and as punishment he was tied to a tree and shot with arrows by archers. Left for dead, he was found by Irene, the widow of the martyr Castulus, who nursed him back to health. The saint, who had thus miraculously survived his execution, confronted the astonished Diocletian, reproaching him for his senseless persecution of Christians. However, he was then beaten to death with clubs.

La Tour chooses to depict a night scene lit only by a torch held by a maiden. To her right stands Irene in an attitude of mourning, and behind her two other women, one praying, the other drying her tears with a cloth. The figures of the women express dignified, restrained sorrow. The saint is pierced by only one arrow and his perfect body already suggests neo-classical elements. The martyr's nakedness is reminiscent of depictions of dead heroes and Sebastian is thus represented as a hero of his faith. The light of the torch held by one of the women enigmatically illuminates the gentle, quiet grief of the women and emphasizes the supernatural quality of the scene. There is an unreal calm, with no sign of movement in the picture. La Tour's painting is characterized by simple, clear forms and masterly color composition. Ugliness, which could well have been introduced into the wounded body of the saint, and drama, as they are found in Caravaggio, evidently have no place here.

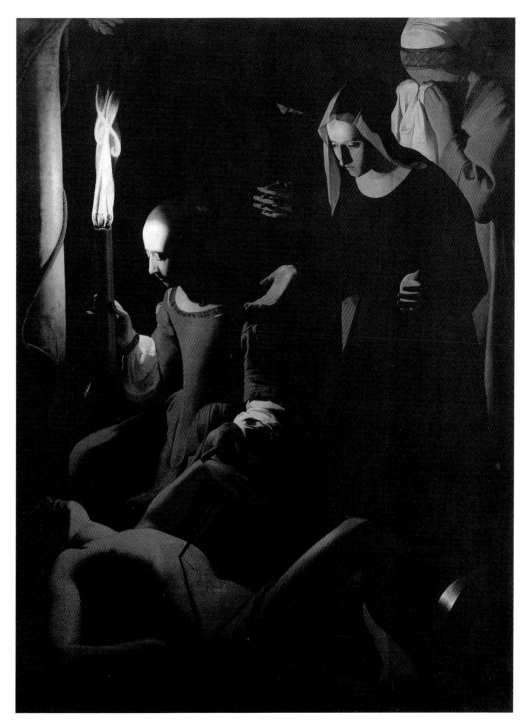

Matthieu and Louis Le Nain
Venus in Vulcan's Forge, 1641
Oil on canvas, 150 x 115 cm
Reims, Musée Saint-Denis

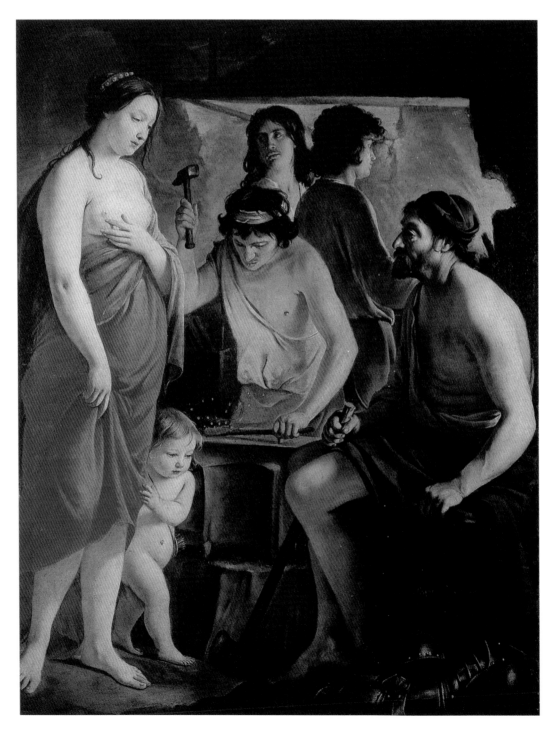

One of the favorite subjects for artists during the sixteenth and seventeenth centuries was the amorous adventures of Venus, the goddess of love. Venus had several times deceived her husband, Vulcan by consorting with Mars, the god of war. Most popular of all was the scene in which Vulcan surprises the adulterous couple, throws an invisible net over them, and exposes them to the mockery of the gods.

The Le Nain painting shows Venus, accompanied by Cupid, in Vulcan's forge. The god of metalworking and crafts is seated, oddly inactive; only his assistants, the Cyclopes, are occupied in making armor for the gods. It is not clear why Venus is visiting her husband at the forge, although the armor on the right at the feet of the seated god, towards which both Venus and Cupid are looking, could be the armor of Aeneas which Venus ordered from Vulcan in order to help the hero in his victory over the Latins. The heads of the two Cyclopes in the background are brightly illuminated by the furnace fire. The physical disability of Vulcan, who was born lame, is evident from his bent back and the legs crossed in an unnatural position.

No communication can be observed between the figures in the group. They are shown almost motionless and strangely rigid; only the Cyclops in the background gazes at Venus. The relationship of the two gods is established by posture but not through eye contact; their alienation is underlined.

Nicolas Poussin
Self-Portrait, 1650
Oil on canvas, 98 x 74 cm
Paris, Musée du Louvre

Philippe de Champaigne
Portrait of Cardinal Richelieu, 1635–40 Oil
on canvas, 222 x 165 cm
Paris, Musée du Louvre

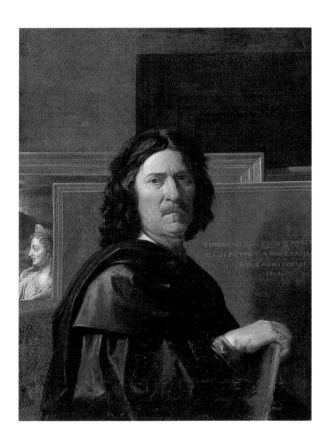

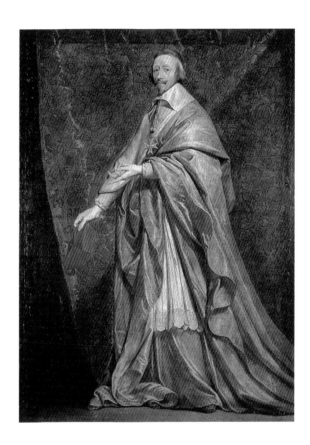

In Rome, Nicolas Poussin received a number of commissions from his friends. The self-portrait which he made in Rome was for Fréart de Chantelou, one of his Parisian patrons. Poussin painted it himself because the portraits a Roman artist had made of him did not come up to his expectations.

The painter presents himself, a portfolio in front of him, half-length in a dark green garment covered by a stole, gazing with a serious expression at an imaginary spectator. Three picture frames in the background characterize the location as a workshop.

On the basis of several details Poussin's self-portrait has been interpreted as "painted art theory" while several signs of respect for the recipient have been discovered. As we know, the artist occupied himself intensively with questions of theory and was working on a treatise on painting. The canvas at the front, which is empty but for an inscription which dates the painting

and describes its subject, is a reference to the *disegno interno*, that is, *idea* and *concetto*, which—before the practical execution of the painting—are the prerequisites for the creation of any picture.

With the particular emphasis on the significance of *disegno* in painting, the special creative activity of the artist was contrasted with the practical (*disegno estero*). As early as the fifteenth century a positive theory of *disegno* had already been developed in Italy, and it was on this basis that the intellectual claims of painting were based. Only a small part of the second canvas in the painting is shown, a woman's profile clasped by two hands. The woman, who wears a diadem with one eye, has been interpreted as an allegory of painting, which, as the noblest of the three arts (architecture, sculpture, and painting), is the only one to which a crown is attributed. The embrace may be an emblem of the friendship which bound Poussin to the recipient of the portrait.

A further reference to Poussin's friendship with Chantelou is to be found in the ring worn by the subject, which has a diamond cut in the shape of a four-sided pyramid. The pyramid is an emblem of Constantia, or constancy. The ring probably, therefore, referred to the durability of the artist's feelings of friendship, but might also allude to his adherence to the doctrine of strict classicism in art.

Philippe de Champaigne created several versions of his portrait of Cardinal Richelieu. Richelieu, Louis XIII's prime minister, came from the lower echelons of the nobility of officialdom; at the age of twenty-one he had already become bishop of Luçon, and shortly afterwards Marie de' Medici appointed him secretary of state. The full-length portrait, the impressive posture, the red of the cardinal's robes, the ceremonial folds in the garments, and the splendid carpet in the background are all intended to convey a sense of grandeur.

The composition is notable for its monumentality and severity. Richelieu appears as a distinguished and power-hungry politician rather than as a God-fearing and world-renouncing priest. His aged and pallid face, as well as the rhetorically moving hands, establish Richelieu as a representative of modern rationalism, absorbed in the ascetic work ethic.

423

Eustache Le Sueur
Three Muses, 1652–55
Oil on canvas, 130 x 130 cm
Paris, Musée du Louvre

From 1646 to 1647 Eustache Le Sueur produced a series of mythological scenes for the Cabinet de l'Amour of the Hôtel Lambert in Paris. Two of the paintings represented the Muses. The Muses were associated with their leader Apollo as daughters of Zeus and the Titaness Mnemosyne. Classical writers ascribed inspiration to them. Le Sueur depicts three muses as garlanded virgins clothed in pastel-colored garments within an Arcadian landscape. Clio, the muse of history, dominates the image from her slightly left-of-center position. With exposed breasts, cradling in her right arm a trumpet, the attribute of Fama (the personification of rumor), she leans on a leather-bound folio. To her right Eutherpe, the Muse of lyrical poetry accompanied by flute music, plays her instrument. Sitting with her back to the viewer, Thalia, the Muse of Comedy, gazes at a mask. The varied "responsibilities" of the Muses have been clarified by Le Sueur through his color scheme. Just as the three Muses encompass all the genres of poetry, their garments incorporate the whole spectrum of tones making up by the primary colors, yellow, red, and blue.

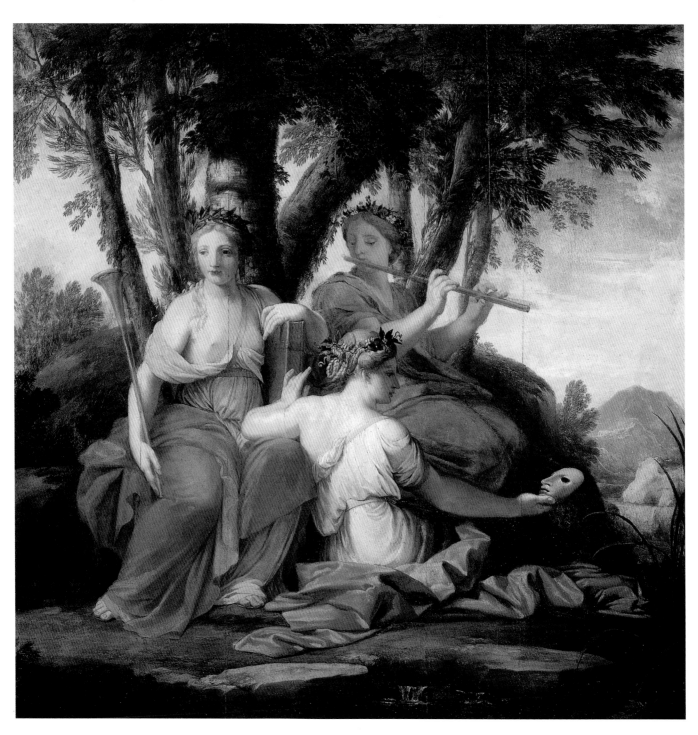

Charles Le Brun
Alexander's Entry into Babylon, c. 1664
Oil on canvas, 450 x 707 cm
Paris, Musée du Louvre

Charles Le Brun
Martyrdom of St. John at Porta Latina,
1641–42
Oil on canvas, 282 x 224 cm
Paris, Saint-Nicolas du Chardonnet

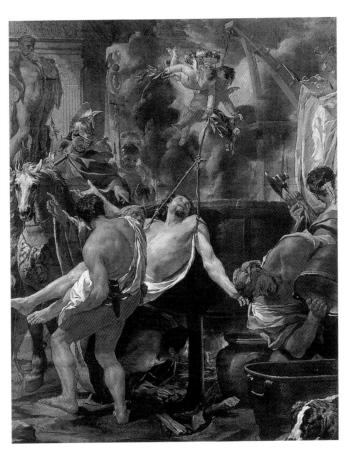

Alexander's Entry into Babylon is part of a cycle made by Le Brun for Louis XIV between 1662 and 1668. In 1661 he received a commission from the king to paint a scene from the life of Alexander the Great, and decided in favor of the *Family of Darius*. The extraordinary success of this work inspired Le Brun to create a monumental cycle of four paintings. These are the *Crossing of the Granicus*, *Battle of Arbela*, *Alexander's Entry into Babylon*, and *Poros before Alexander*, which depict triumphs and victories of the Macedonian king.

The entry into Babylon took place after Alexander's victory over the Persians in the battle of Gaugamela near Arbela (331 BC). Accompanied by his victorious army and captured enemies and seen in a gilded carriage drawn by elephants, Alexander, who has had himself proclaimed king of Asia, enters the subjugated Babylon. The center of the painting is occupied by the carriage with the triumphant Alexander. In the foreground, lively events are being played out: mothers with children and a lyre-player watch the procession with astonishment, and several slaves carry a bier. The artist's special interest in the representation of the human figure is indicated by the variety of features and reactions represented here: the stolid stare of one of the bier-carrying slaves, the admiring glance of the lyre-player, and the somber expression of a Babylonian who leans against the statue of Semiramis, the builder of Babylon.

Le Brun treats the event in the manner of a relief. In the background are seen the hanging gardens of Babylon. The magnificently laid out classical ensemble and its archeological details are contrasted with the realistic, anecdotal happenings in the foreground. The series was conceived as a homage to the king, who saw himself as a successor to Alexander, the greatest military commander of classical times and the conqueror of Asia. The Alexander cycle was created at the time of the overthrow of Flanders (1667), which marked the beginning of the period of Louis XIV's greatest military success. Le Brun's paintings were not only made into prints, but Gobelins tapestries were also designed after them. The painter himself regarded the cycle as his masterpiece.

The *Martyrdom of St. John at Porta Latina* is one of Le Brun's early works which he produced at the age of twenty-three for the church where it still hangs. It depicts the martyrdom of St. John the Evangelist who was tortured in Rome under Trajan. He survived the torture unharmed and later died a natural death.

Le Brun chooses the moment when the Evangelist is about to be lifted into a cauldron of boiling oil. Angels observe the proceedings with flowers and palm branches, the symbol of his "martyrdom." In the composition, which strongly emphasizes the spatial, and the violent movement which dominates the painting, Le Brun demonstrates that he is still clearly under the influence of Vouet. He is evidently concerned to represent the emotions expressed in the faces of the participants as well as defining the Roman military standard and the lictors' bundles with antiquarian precision.

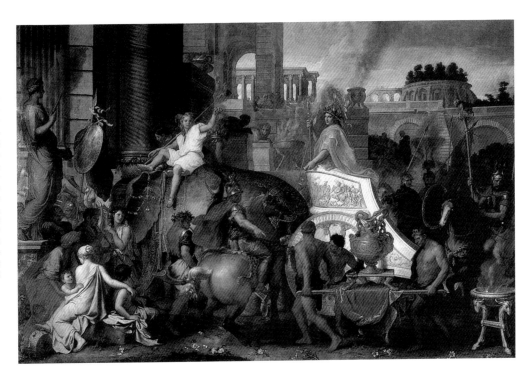

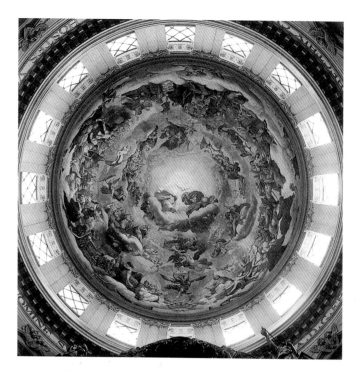

Pierre Mignard
Paradise, 1663
Paris, Val-de-Grâce, dome fresco

The church of Val-de-Grâce is among the most important baroque ensembles in Paris. It was founded by Anne of Austria, the wife of Louis XIII; after a long period of childless marriage she took a vow that if she bore a son she would have a splendid house of God built for the Benedictine monastery of Val-de-Grâce. The church was designed by François Mansart, who planned the church with a nave and with a central construction, the dimensions of which exceed the width of the central nave.

Mignard created the ceiling painting for the magnificent dome based on the model of St. Peter's. God is seen in celestial glory, surrounded by saints and martyrs, as well as important dignitaries of the church. This is a circular composition with a view of more than two hundred figures. Below, the founder of the church, led by St. Louis, presents the model of the building. The painting was enthusiastically received by contemporaries and was celebrated by Molière among others.

Pierre Mignard
Perseus and Andromeda, 1679
Oil on canvas, 150 x 198 cm
Paris, Musée du Louvre

Mignard painted *Perseus and Andromeda* for the Grand Condé (as Louis II, prince of Bourbon was known), and it hung in his collection at Chantilly. The painting is among Mignard's many mythological works.

The scene depicted is from the legend of Perseus which Ovid describes in his *Metamorphoses*. Perseus, the son of Zeus and Danaë, after beheading Medusa, reached the shores of Phoenicia riding the winged horse Pegasus. There he came upon Andromeda who was chained to a rock expecting to be devoured by a seamonster as punishment for the boast of her mother, Cassiopeia, that her daughter was more beautiful than the Nereids. Andromeda's father Cepheus promised her in marriage to Perseus and offered his kingdom as a dowry if he vanquished the seamonster and freed his daughter. Perseus killed the beast with one stroke of his sword—according to another version he held the head of Medusa up to it, whereupon it turned to stone—and took the king's daughter as his wife. Mignard depicts the moment when Perseus has freed Andromeda and the king and his wife are hastening gratefully towards him with a crowd of people behind them expressing astonishment at the event. The whole scene is spectacular and filled with movement. In the center of the painting stands Perseus with Pegasus, who sprang out of the blood of the slain Medusa, behind him. At the feet of the hero, who is

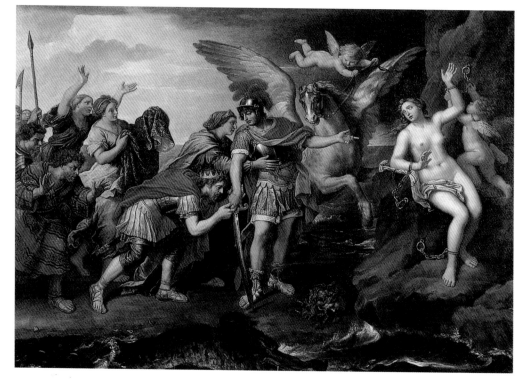

pointing towards Andromeda, lies the head of Medusa, while in the foreground lies the slain seamonster. Mignard demonstrates his talent as a superb colorist with the lavish hues of the natural forms and the splendid garments of the figures.

Hyacinthe Rigaud
Portrait of Louis XIV, 1701
Oil on canvas, 279 x 190 cm
Paris, Musée du Louvre

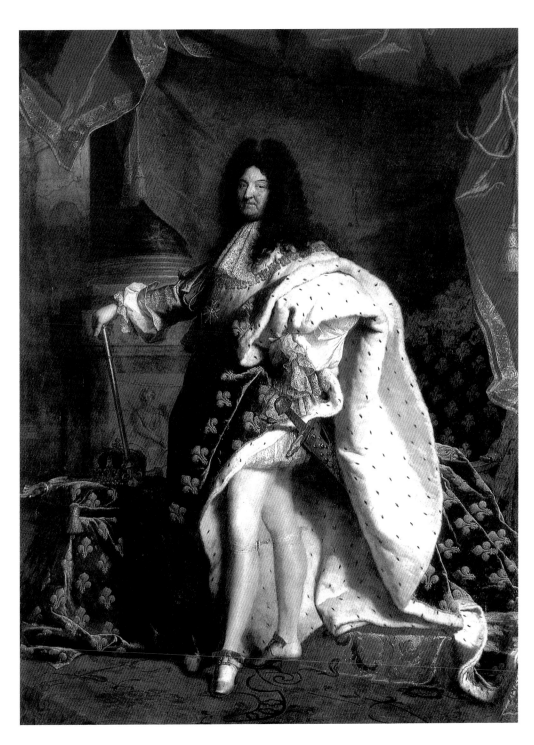

This painting, in which Rigaud portrays Louis XIV at the age of sixty-three, was originally intended as a present for the king's nephew, Philip V of Spain. Since he particularly liked the painting, the king had a copy made of it and kept the original himself.

In a slight *contrapposto*, Louis XIV leans with his right hand on his military scepter, while he braces his left arm on his hip. The king is shown in full state regalia. He wears a cloak of rich fabric with the Bourbon lily on a blue ground and with an ermine lining. The throne is seen behind him on a rostrum, surmounted by a baldacchino. The crown lies to the left on a cushion and behind it stands a column symbolizing dignity, power, and endurance. The exposed legs of the king correspond to the pose of a ruler from the classical era.

Louis XIV is portrayed by Rigaud as a shining example of royal power, but ultimately as the embodiment of the French monarchy. The features of the elderly king are realistically rendered by the artist. While in his *Portrait of Richelieu* (see p. 423) Champaigne was chiefly concerned to convey the character of the cardinal, Rigaud's main aim was to establish the status of his subject.

Emblems

Ehrenfried Kluckert

During the baroque age the emblem exerted a specific and pervasive influence on culture. It generated all sorts of references which touched on writing, rhetoric, painting, and festival ritual. The emblem is essentially an image which can be interpreted on a number of levels and is based on allusion, allegory, and symbol. Its curious language of signs can be traced back to the hieroglyphs popular in the Renaissance. It was during this period that supposed Egyptian hieroglyphs were rediscovered. Florentine humanists believed that behind the mysterious language of signs found in these ancient objects the original wisdom of humanity was concealed and encoded in order to preserve it from profane intrusion.

Horapollo's *Hieroglyphica*, a compendium of Alexandrine knowledge from the fifth century AD, was used as a source; a Greek version of it was brought to Italy in about 1500 and soon became widely known. The *Hypnerotomachia Poliphili* by Francesco Colonna, including images and signs consisting of Egyptian hieroglyphs, Pythagorean symbols, and cabalistic numerology, published in Venice in 1499, influenced both later books of emblems and, in particular, the subject matter of painting and writing, and even the planning of ornamental flower-beds in horticulture. The most famous book of emblems, which was soon widely dispersed throughout Europe, was the *Emblematum Liber* of Andrea Alciati, which was translated into German in 1531 in Augsburg, and later into other European languages. Other important books of emblems are the *Emblemata nova de secretis naturae chymica* published by Michael Maier in 1618, known as *Atlanta fugiens*, and the *Iconologia* by Cesare Ripa, published in 1758.

An emblem is composed of the *pictura*, the image, the *inscriptio*, the motto, and the *subscriptio*, a Latin epigram. The image, also called *imago* or *symbolon*, includes almost every conceivable motif, whether from everyday life or the animal or vegetable kingdoms. The motto, which is placed above the image, refers to the subject of the emblem. Finally, the *subscription* clarifies and interprets what is illustrated. Often a wise saying or a piece of moralistic advice is incorporated. The German baroque painter Georg Philipp Harsdörffer observed in his *Poetical Funnel*: "Poetry is called a speaking picture but painting a silent poetry." Here the spoken word is required to be graphically represented, for the "silent word" (the picture) explains what the "speaking picture" (the word) is unable to convey.

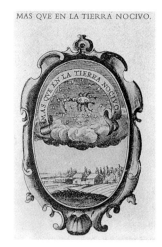

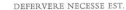

Emblem from *Idea de un principe politico christiano* by Diego de Saavedra, 1640

For Harsdörffer these so-called "picture-poems" are important elements of poetry and drama. Daniel Casper von Lohenstein's tragedy *Epicharis*, which appeared in 1665, is concerned with the fall of the Emperor Nero. Gaius Piso is to be declared ruler in his stead. However:

"What has Rome to expect from Piso? Does not every vice already come from him?
The poison may yet be healed/ wherewith the scorpion
On earth injures us; but when he injures/ He who is transferred to the high throne of stars/
His poisoned torch often infects whole lands."

This enigmatic aphorism is inspired by an emblem which is solved by the riddle. It comes from the book of emblems *Idea de un principe politico christiano* by Diego de Salver of 1640 (see above). The motto reads "More harmful than on earth" and refers to the scorpion which is seen in the heavens. Below is an earthly landscape. The motto is explained in the *subscriptio*: the scorpion, although distant in heaven, exerts a more terrible influence on mankind on earth than if he were still there. A king whose conduct is morally dubious, having once ascended the throne and thus ruling "from above," is capable of corrupting mankind and nations.

The use of visual metaphor was far more widespread during the baroque period than today. Emblem books were widely circulated and there was a broad general knowledge of the allusions made in them.

The decoding of seventeenth-century Dutch genre paintings is particularly fascinating, since almost all hidden allusions or symbols can be traced to emblem books or folk literature of the period. In Jan Steen's *Leaving the Tavern* (see right) of about 1660, a small boat with a party of revellers can be seen. Three men and four women are preparing to depart, while a further high-spirited drinker is shaking out the last drops from the barrel for a farewell drink. This young man, who stands in the center of the painting, appears repeatedly in Jan Steen's paintings. The artist links events which occur simultaneously: on the left are the lively people getting ready to leave and on the right are the tipplers crowding out of the tavern, while in the foreground are a group of figures who have evidently sunk into a blissful alcoholic stupor. A small splinter group at the right-hand corner of the painting are squatting behind a tree playing cards. The man's posture is schematic and suggests the deeper meaning of the picture, demonstrating the essential purpose of the collective conviviality: pouring out, drinking, and enjoying. Such motifs were widely distributed at the time but were not merely intended to describe the superficial jollity of a drinking party.

There is a cryptic message here, a mischievously conveyed moralizing which in the last instance was ignored. The painting incorporates the theme of the five senses, a subject frequently entertained in Dutch painting—drinking (taste),

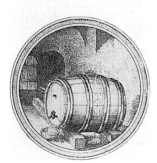

"It is necessary to restrain exuberance"

smoking (smell), embracing (touch), and singing (hearing), as well as the play of glances and facial expressions of the occupants of the boat (sight) can be clearly identified, but only by means of corresponding models in the literature of emblems. In "Vader Cats" popular collections of emblems, that is, Jacob Cats' *Mirror of the Times* of 1632 (*Spiegel van den Ouden ende Nieuwen Tijdt*, see below), the five senses turn up as a travelling group in a ship intended as an allegory of life. At the stern and bow stand a skeleton (Death) and a spirit (Life) pointing the way. The man with the barrel might symbolize the "overflowing desire of youth." In an emblem with the motto "Defervere necesse est" [It is necessary to restrain exuberance]; (see above right) we see a wine-barrel in a cellar dripping with wine. In the *subscriptio* the fermentation

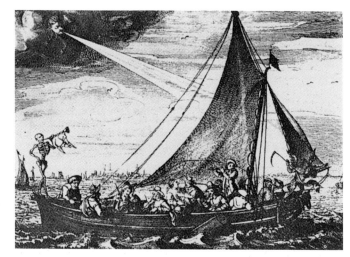

Depiction of the five senses from Jacob Cats' *Mirror of the Times*, 1632

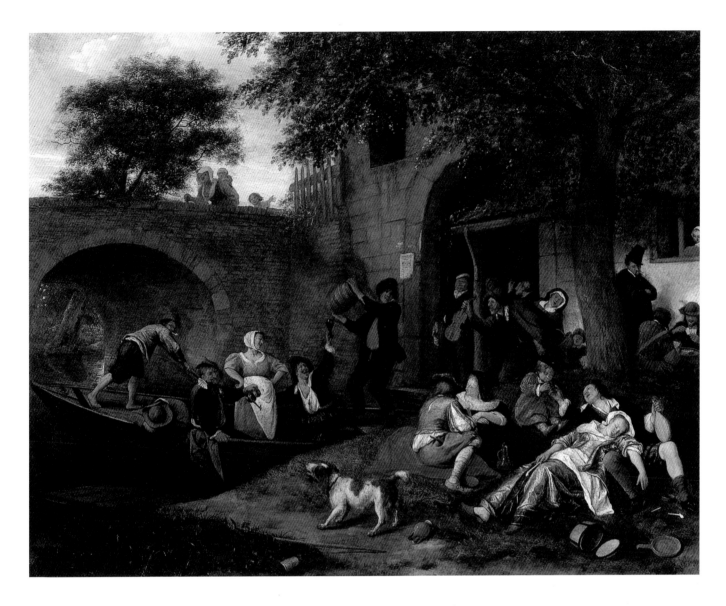

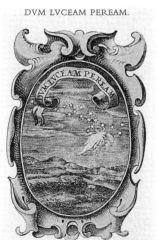

process of the young wine is compared with the awakening desire of youth. It is also possible that the typical Cythera theme familiar to us from Antoine Watteau is being touched on here and transformed into a decidedly bourgeois mode: the little group of people who have happily taken their places in the boat might be seen as traveling towards the paradise of their joyful emotions.

The emblem can be seen as an aid to the interpretation of the baroque culture of images. The transfer was simple, since the model image could be decoded without difficulty from the motto and the *subscriptio*. Thus the court culture of festivals made use of emblems in order to directly convey the message of, for example, a firework display on the occasion of a wedding or the visit of a dignitary. In addition to the craftsmen and technicians who prepared the celebration, the *inven-tor* was responsible for the settings and images. Often he would design well-known emblems and had frameworks, decorations, and illuminations made. The Elector Johann Georg II of Saxony was known for his extravagant celebrations in Dresden. In 1637 he ordered festivities in the course of which ten emblematic pictures were illuminated, centering on such themes as "War," "Triumph of Power," "Fear of God," and "Justice."

The use of the book of emblems in the cultural activity of the baroque era was thus reflected in a variety of media.

Jan Steen
Departure from the Inn
Oil on canvas, 84 x 109 cm
Stuttgart, Staatsgalerie

429

Kira van Lil

Painting in the Netherlands, Germany, and England in the Seventeenth Century

Introduction

The seventeenth century is always described as a golden age for the Netherlands. This concept can be traced back to the Dutch writer Arnold Houbraken: in 1721 he published his *Groote Schouburgh* in which he gathered together the lives of the Dutch artists of the preceding century. No other country or era has produced so many artists whose work is still considered to be significant today. The concept of "paradise on earth" refers above all to Holland in the northern part of the Netherlands, the dominant of the seven northern provinces. As a land of peasants and fishermen, the north had not distinguished itself culturally by the beginning of the seventeenth century and in this respect was quite unlike the southern provinces, particularly Flanders where the important commercial cities of Bruges and Ghent had a flourishing cultural life by the fifteenth century; painters such as Jan van Eyck, Hans Memling, and Rogier van der Weyden could confidently compare their work to that of the great Italian masters. In the sixteenth century, Antwerp and Brussels gained in industrial importance. Cultural life in these cities began to flourish again, reaching a high point in the paintings of Pieter Brueghel.

All the provinces of the Netherlands had been under Burgundian and then Habsburg rule for a time, until the Spanish king Philip II succeeded his father, Emperor Charles V. After the iconoclasm of 1566, Philip crushed the Protestant uprising and established a brutal regime with the assistance of the Inquisition. After the murder of Egmont in 1568 the War of Independence broke out; it was to last for eighty years. But only the northern provinces, under the strong influence of Calvinism, finally achieved their goal; the predominantly Catholic South remained dependent on Spain. In 1579 the northern provinces joined the Union of Utrecht and in 1609 they secured an armistice. This effectively marked the birth of an independent republic of the northern Netherlands.

The rise of Amsterdam as a new commercial center began when the Spaniards conquered Antwerp in 1585 and blockaded the river Schelde, which literally left the city isolated for commercial purposes. The Dutch had rapidly built up a strong fleet, which by 1588 had already defeated the Spanish fleet. By 1602 the East India Company had been founded, and Holland grew into a mighty commercial power which by the middle of the century was battling with England for supremacy at sea. A new nation was beginning to develop its own culture.

Art was at first closely connected with the tradition of Flanders, which had been introduced by the many emigrants into the cities of Holland. Soon, however, an individual character emerged, based on a new view of the world and marked by the citizens' national pride about the independence they had won for themselves and their unprecedented prosperity. The Calvinist religion reinforced this pride. After Calvin's teachings on predestination, economic success was considered a sign that the nation had been chosen by God. This explains the turning towards material reality, the "love of objects" which the Dutch historian Johan Huizinga considered were the distinguishing characteristics of the Dutch mentality during this period. Artists responded with a realism of an exceptional quality, which not even Caravaggio had been able to achieve quite so consistently. In the Netherlands, the skillful true-to-life rendering of objects became especially valued. However, the pictures are never simple copies of reality, they are always staged to make a particular pictorial statement. This aspect was often overlooked after Dutch realism was rediscovered in the mid-nineteenth century by the French realists and Impressionists. In contrast to the classical taste of the eighteenth century, nineteenth-century critics and observers had a sense of common interest with these artists, prizing the very devotion of the Dutch to a realism that was apparently without any idealized exaggeration. Until well into our own century, it was assumed that Dutch painters of this period had boldly renounced the introduction of any higher meaning into their work.

This would, however, have been unthinkable during the seventeenth century. "Nothing is without meaning in anything," wrote Roemer Visscher, one of the most famous Dutch writers of emblem books. In such books the meanings underlying objects were revealed and conveyed in mottoes and verses (see pp. 428–29). The sermon on the transience of all earthly things was hardly to be evaded in Calvinistic Holland. In the face of the eternal values of God they must be counted worthless and "vain." This concept of *vanitas* can in fact be seen as the leitmotif of the baroque age. But it appears to have been particularly volubly expressed in Holland, where the citizens continually assessed their earthly ambitions and admonished themselves to behave in a moral and virtuous manner.

These are also important themes in the art of the southern Netherlands. But while the Dutch developed new kinds of allegories with the subliminal meanings of everyday things, artists like Rubens and Van Dyck fell back on the figures of classical mythology; in spite of the often unequivocally sensual rendering of these subjects, they remain remote from real life. Flemish art emerged under quite different conditions. Here, as in other countries, there was a demand for large-format altar paintings. Here the artists followed the Italian tradition, even though a coarsely sensual element gives an individual character to the art of Rubens and Jordaens.

In the northern provinces, however, the Church virtually ceased to commission works of art while Calvinism strictly maintained the prohibition of images. Dutch churches were places of assembly rather than of devotion. Dogs were brought into churches as a matter of course, children were fed and allowed to play there, and conversations were conducted even during the sermon. The church was a sociable place, not an awe-inspiring one. In the whitewashed space of the church, in which no decoration was permitted except for coats of arms, memorial tablets, and tombs, the bright light

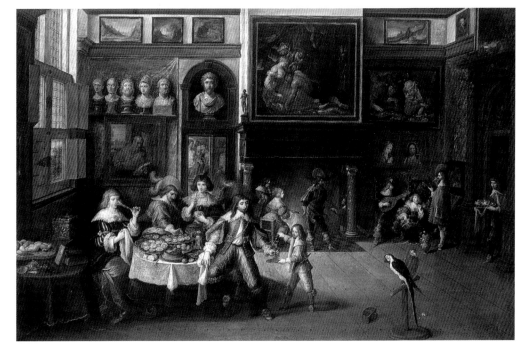

Frans Francken
Banquet at the House of Mayor Rockox,
c. 1630–35
Oil on wood, 62.3 x 96.5 cm
Munich, Bayerische
Staatsgemäldesammlungen,
Alte Pinakothek

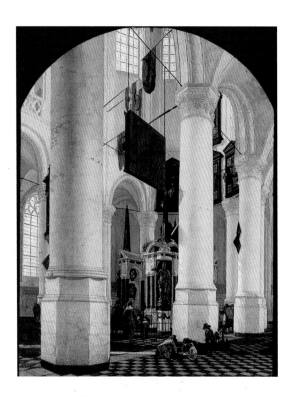

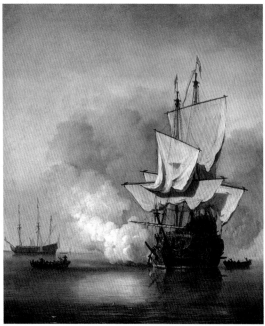

created a variety of effects. Next to the complicated perspectival construction of images, this was the particular charm of the church interior, a style which developed only in Holland.

Like the Church, the nobility were not prominent as patrons of art in Holland. A feudal court culture of the kind that was developing to a high point in the rest of Europe could hardly have evolved in the north. In Brussels, the *stadholders*, or governors, of Philip II conducted a court which encouraged the arts. In The Hague too there was a court headed by the *stadholder*, a status which was granted to the descendants of the national hero William of Orange-Nassau. The house of Orange, however, maintained an unpretentious lifestyle as it was dependent on the city patricians; the supreme power lay unequivocally with the States General. The citizens also replaced each other intermittently in the office of *stadholder*. Houkgeest's church interior (see left) must have been painted for a supporter of the court or for the court itself, for it focuses on the tomb of William of Orange, recalling the services of the house of Orange towards the liberty of the people. It was painted in 1650, the year when the *stadholder* was removed from office.

The dominating structures of city and bourgeoisie decisively characterized the arts, and the works of the painters conformed to the interests of the citizens. Under these conditions, completely new genres of painting were established: landscape and still life, until then merely tolerated as decorative concomitants of history painting, became emancipated and were adopted as independent themes. In addition, representations of everyday scenes, which had hitherto been considered genre works, became viable for the first time as large-scale paintings.

Since classical antiquity, art theorists had considered the ability of a painter to narrate stories as they were found in literature a particular challenge, although only one moment could actually be illustrated. The subject was presented in the foreground, and the manner in which it was depicted was considered to be of secondary importance. In the new categories, landscape, still life, and genre, on the other hand, it seemed to matter very much that the subject was well represented. For the Dutch, landscape paintings displayed the fruitfulness of the land while the precious objects in the still lifes and the domestic interiors mirrored prosperity and the abundance of goods available from exotic parts of the world. Dutch seafarers made this trade possible and marine painting therefore acquired particular significance (see left).

Most artists specialized in one of these categories and frequently even in a particular genre: the phenomenon of specialist painting was more marked in the Netherlands than anywhere else. Hendrik Avercamp, for example, mainly painted winter sports on the ice, Paulus Potter predominantly painted cows, Aert van der Neer specialized in moonlit landscapes, and still-life painters such as Willem Kalf and Pieter Claesz managed all their lives with only a few props. Gerard ter Borch demonstrated a particular skill in the painting of satin fabrics, while others were noted for their rendering of metal objects; some painted only flowers and others dead game. Rubens employed particular specialists: Jan Brueghel often painted the flowers, Frans Snyders the animals, and Jan Wildens and Frans Woutens the landscape backgrounds. Many landscape painters were not even able to paint small stock figures and required the assistance of specialist colleagues.

Subjects, objects, compositions, and the manner of execution were strongly influenced by the preferences of the city where an artist lived. This situation can be largely attributed to the guild system, which was more powerful in the Netherlands than anywhere else. An artist might sell his work only where he was a member of the guild, which strictly supervised the conditions of production. Painters mainly came from craft families: Rembrandt's father was a miller, Jan van Goyen's a shoemaker, and Ruisdael's a framemaker. In Holland, painting was considered to be a craft, although artists in Italy had claimed since the Renaissance to belong to the *artes liberales* and thus to be recognized as intellectual workers and not as craftsmen.

But even in Holland, some artists were highly paid, highly respected, and heaped with honors. Success and failure, as in absolutist states, depended on the favor of the mighty. But the wielders of power were more frequently subject to change than feudal rulers since offices were elected. Rembrandt's rise and fall is a startling example of this dependence (see pp. 441–43), while more diplomatic characters such as ter Borch and Gerard Dou were better able to handle the constant shifts of power.

Most painters, however, could not live by painting alone. Vermeer was an art dealer on the side, van Goyen speculated in real estate and tulip bulbs, Jan Steen was a licensed publican, and Philips Koninck operated a ferry between Amsterdam and Rotterdam. Some women painters also became well-known. Judith Leyster painted portraits and genre scenes in the style of Frans Hals, her painting master. Clara Peeters, about whose life little is known, influenced early still-life painting, and towards the end of the century Rachel Ruysch and Maria Oosterwijk achieved international fame with their flower still lifes.

Prices for paintings rose enormously with the popularity of the artist, and some works achieved sensational prices. For this reason works of art were also regarded as objects of speculative investment. The production of painting was no longer mainly based on fixed commissions, and what can be seen as a modern art market began to emerge. Gallery-owners obtained commissions for their artists, but bookshops and print shops as well as annual fairs also served as commercial centers for art. Even at the ordinary weekly markets paintings were sold among the fruit and vegetables. The Golden Age introduced a remarkable expansion in painting.

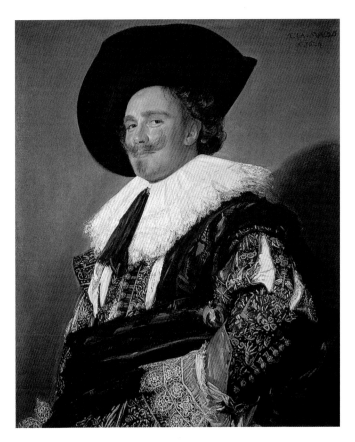

Portraits

The portrait served as a vehicle for the self-representation of the citizens. Anyone with any sense of their own significance had themselves painted. As with aristocratic portraits, Dutch artists understood the importance of conveying the status and dignity of the subject. But more than ever before, a new value was placed on a directness and faithfulness to life. As in landscape, genre studies, and still lifes, portrait artists also sought to achieve a realism which destroyed the imported formulas. The pioneering steps were taken at the beginning of the century by artists in the wealthy coastal city of Haarlem: Esaias van de Velde with landscape, Willem Buytewech with genre painting, and Frans Hals with the portrait. Rembrandt, of course, towers high above the many other portraitists of his time.

Frans Hals lived in Haarlem all his life. He painted portraits exclusively, some of which can also be classified as genre paintings. They show ordinary people, mountebanks, women selling fish, laughing children, or the mad *Malle Babbe* with her jug of drink. The vitality and freshness of these figures is also achieved in the

Frans Hals
Stephanus Geraerdts, 1650–52
Oil on canvas, 115 x 87 cm
Antwerp, Koninklijk Museum voor
Schone Kunsten

Frans Hals
Isabella Coymans, 1650–52
Oil on canvas, 116 x 86 cm
Private collection

Frans Hals
Man with Slouch Hat, 1660–66
Oil on canvas, 79.5 x 66.5 cm
Kassel, Staatliche Kunstsammlungen,
Gemäldegalerie Alte Meister, Schloss
Wilhelmshöhe

artist's most dignified grand portraits. His *Laughing Cavalier* (see p. 433) is shown, according to tradition, as a half-length figure; the classical pose of the subject, which is slightly foreshortened, with the hand resting on the hip unmistakably transmits his sense of self-confidence. However, Hals succeeds in freeing his subject from the static stiffness which usually accompanies such an attitude. This can be attributed quite simply to the sheer brilliance of the painting: the deep black pigment contrasts with the gleaming white areas and is enhanced by the sparkling colors of the richly embroidered jacket. Subtle compositional techniques are also introduced here: none of the decisive lines corresponds to the right angles prescribed by the picture edges. The play of shadows impels the man forward, out of the surface of the image, his right arm in particular straining out of the picture. His massive physical presence is certainly impressive. But it is ultimately the man's facial expression that makes him appear so real to us. In conventional portraits the subjects often gaze into the distance, look through the spectator, or pensively look past him. This man, however, appears to respond to the gaze of the spectator, almost to speak to him. His smile appears about to break at any moment into a hearty laugh which could topple his elegant pose. This sense of immediacy essentially constitutes the particular fascination of Hals' work.

Portraits were often commissioned for special occasions, for example as a memento of a wedding. This could be a double portrait, like the one by Rubens (see p. 438), but usually there were two separate panels. The picture of the woman was always intended as the right-hand piece since she traditionally sat to the man's left. Unfortunately the panels were sometimes separated, a fate that is particularly unfortunate in the case of Hals' companion pieces *Stephanus Geraerdts* and *Isabella Coymans* (see below, left and center). No other work in the history of portraiture radiates such a natural attraction between the partners. Isabella expresses the joyfulness of youth in her lively posture as she turns towards her husband, while he, seated, unlike his wife, embodies a stately dignity. The couple's gaze has met; she offers him a rose which he is about to take from her. Separated from each other, neither the gaze nor the gestures of the couple can be understood. Hals has here captured a moment from a sequence of events even more skillfully than in *The Laughing Cavalier*, and which is extended in the imagination. Again the static quality of the portrait has been subverted. In order to achieve this in his work, as early as the 1620s Hals developed a new type of portrait, establishing a style which is also represented in the *Man with Slouch Hat* (see below right), one of his last portraits. The subject turns towards the spectator as though the latter had spoken to him. Leaning his arm on the arm of the chair, he adopts an uncomfortable position which can only be temporary. He gives the impression that he is about to turn away again so that he can lean back in his chair. This understood movement is preserved in the enormous sweep of the big hat, but is conveyed above all by the extremely dynamic brushwork. This is typical of the artist's late style, one which Edouard Manet was to discover for himself in the nineteenth century. The brushwork of the portrait of *The Laughing Cavalier* at the beginning of his artistic career had already demonstrated a high level of confidence in his technique. But now the face consists of juxtaposed spots of color and is no longer carefully modeled. The hand is indicated by only a few brushstrokes, so that it is

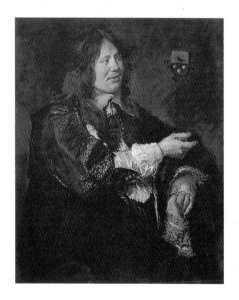

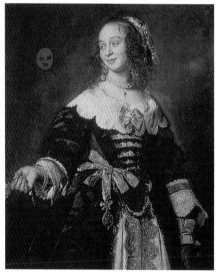

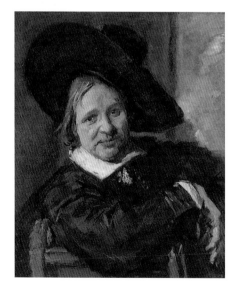

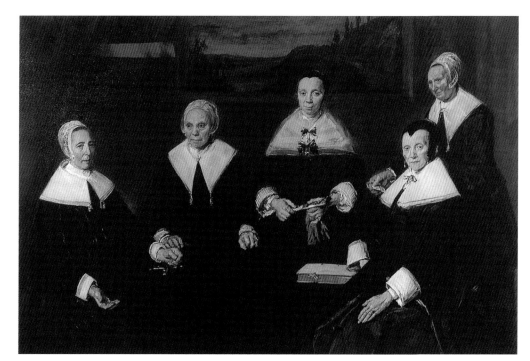

Frans Hals
*The Lady Regents of the Old Men's
Home*, Haarlem, 1664
Oil on canvas, 170.5 x 249.5 cm
Haarlem, Frans Hals Museum

In this portrait the female directors of an old people's home display their selfless and generous commitment to good social causes as well as their social status, for honorary positions such as these were given by the city authorities only to members of the upper classes. In a composition of studied simplicity Hals expresses the calm and discipline of the women, whose severe dignity resonates in the great dark surfaces of the painting. Only the applied color breathes life into these women; the light brushstrokes define the forms so fluidly that they appear almost to dissolve. In this bold work, the painting of the eighty-year-old Hals, who had became dependent himself on a pension from the city council, reaches its high point.

not clear whether the painting is to be seen as finished. But these bold slashes of the brush are deployed to establish liveliness of expression. This was a particular challenge in the case of a picture like this one which consists largely of black areas. The few white accents on the collar and sleeves or the highlighted areas of the face and hands would not suffice on their own. But in the black areas themselves, there is a certain fascination in the lively interaction between the different materials.

Rembrandt's work underwent a similar stylistic development. In the 1650s and 1660s he gave up the smooth style of painting and careful modeling which distinguish, for example, his self-portrait of 1640 and the portrait of his wife Saskia (see p. 441). In the *Portrait of Margaretha de Geer* (see p. 436, above), painted during the last decade of the painter's life, Rembrandt modeled the paint in certain areas to the level of relief, either using a palette knife or working directly with his fingers. In other places, the color is applied quite thinly and transparently, and a broad, liquid brushstroke remains visible. Thus an interesting tension is created in the surface of the painting, although Rembrandt almost completely renounced color contrasts and concentrated on nuances of brown tones. By variations in modeling he was able to emphasize certain elements: hands and faces are worked up with dense volumes of paint, while the background and cloak are applied thinly over broad surfaces. Nevertheless, the cape is recognizable as fur and the fine weave of the deep black garment is carefully suggested. The broad surface painting contrasts with the millstone ruff, worn in highly starched folds, which Rembrandt renders with delicate, careful brushstrokes. The handkerchief, however, is dashed on crudely, almost gracelessly with thick white paint. In these two light-colored passages of the painting two opposing sides of Margaretha de Geer's personality seem to be evident. She is alert and vital, but also disciplined and decorous, obviously well used to prosperity and luxury, but at the same time—observe the hands—rooted in the soil and accustomed to an active working life. In the portrait of this seventy-eight-year-old woman, who belonged to one of the most influential families of the country, Rembrandt uncovers a variety of qualities which characterize the founding generation of the republic.

The young modern generation as represented by Stephanus Geraerdts and Isabella Coymans behaved quite differently. Decent black did nothing for them and they are dressed in the latest fashions. The demure ruff is discarded and Isabella reveals a low neckline without embarrassment. Such exposure was just as much a political issue as Stephanus' long hair. In 1652 church councillors in Haarlem pilloried "wild hair" in men, and a heated dispute over the propriety of this fashion raged for several years. Finally a synod decided that persons who were inclined to such worldly vanities could be excluded from holy communion.

After the middle of the century, when this young generation was taking over power, the loose, dynamic style of Rembrandt and Hals became unfashionable and was dismissed as daubing. The young patricians, who were able to succeed to their inheritances without a care, cultivated a neo-classical taste in art which met their demands for explicit elegance and *grandezza*. The new model for portraiture was the aristocratic style of Anthony van Dyck and a fine application of color. This change in taste meant that the two great portraitists Hals and Rembrandt had difficulty in obtaining commissions towards the end of their lives. They had been the founding painters of the new generation.

For decent and devout Calvinists the requirement of moderation was central to their lives. Boastful behavior was outlawed, and respectable people were required to distance themselves from the splendidly dressed *landsknechte* [mercenary foot-soldiers] and dan-

Rembrandt
Margaretha de Geer, c. 1661
Oil on canvas, 130.5 x 97.5 cm
London, National Gallery

Rembrandt
The Anatomy Lesson of Dr. Tulp, 1632
Oil on canvas, 169.5 x 216.5 cm
The Hague, Mauritshuis

OPPOSITE:
Rembrandt
The Night Watch, 1642
Oil on canvas, 349 x 438 cm
Amsterdam, Rijksmuseum

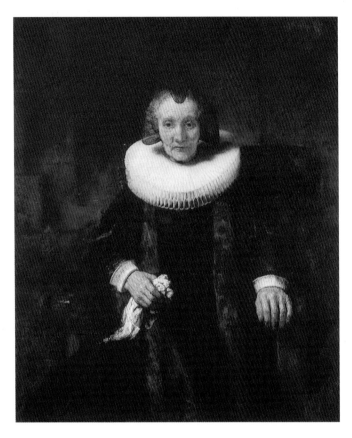

societies was an expression of high social status. This explains the exceptional importance of the group portrait in Holland.

For the painter, the challenge of the group portrait consisted of making a loosely organized, lively arrangement of the many individuals, rather than lining them up stiffly in a row. Rembrandt achieved this in his *Anatomy Lesson of Dr. Tulp* (see below) so convincingly that the painting hardly appears to be a group portrait at all. It seems more like a historical painting illustrating an anatomy lesson. This was in fact a significant event which took place over a period of three days, for the city council allowed a cadaver to be supplied only once a year; usually it was the body of an executed criminal. The lesson is being held by Nicolaes Tulp, the praelector of the guild of surgeons, surrounded by members of the guild. The situation appears as life-like as if Rembrandt had actually painted it during the anatomy class. Each of the figures represented responds individually to the lesson, and even the viewer participates in a sense, for a free space has been left for them in the circle. It is quite possible to imagine that Rembrandt attended an anatomy class for study purposes. His portrait is a sophisticated construction: the men are ranged behind each other in such a way that in reality there would have been nowhere for them to stand. It was the only way for him to show so many large figures in the painting. Each subject paid a certain amount to have himself immortalized in art. The portrait was hung in the assembly hall of the guild with other paintings.

The same purpose was served by what is probably Rembrandt's most famous work, the *Night Watch* (see right). This is a group portrait of some members of a company of the Amsterdam civic guards' guild. For such group portraits the most popular composition was an apparently informal banquet where the banners and other necessary

dies like those seen in a painting by Buytewech (see p. 460). The black fabrics that seemed so modest were in fact more costly than the most shimmering of garments; the ruffs were sewn from the finest batiste into artful constructions. Even with a modest appearance and decent behavior there was no way of denying that a portrait mainly served to represent the individual. Thus it was easy to lay oneself open to reproaches of vanity and surrender to sensual pleasures and worldly possessions. Correspondingly, the northern provinces produced no paintings like the one by the Antwerp artist Frans Francken of a mayor surrounded by his possessions (see p. 431).

One possible method of self-denial for the subject of a portrait was to have themselves depicted in a social or political function as the holder of an office. As such, a person was rarely portrayed as an individual but was seen in the company of other important postholders actively demonstrating their selfless commitment to the community. There were guilds in the medieval tradition, societies based on academic professions, or the citizens' militia, the so-called Schuttersgilden. The acquisition of official status in one of these

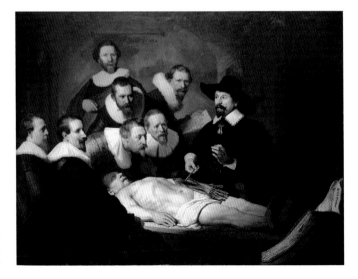

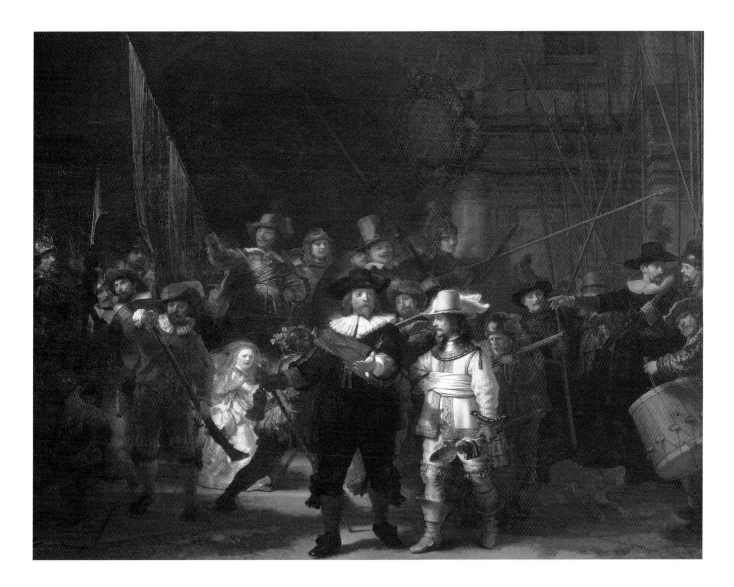

props usually nonetheless appeared very posed. Rembrandt, by contrast, shows a moment that could actually have taken place. The captain and lieutenant have moved out of the throng and are moving forward, others are slowly forming an ordered procession, some of the men are still cleaning or loading their guns, and the drummer is giving the signal for the company to set off. It is implied that a significant moment is being represented—a famous company just before a victorious battle during the War of Independence, or some similar event—or so the spectator is prompted to assume.

During the armistice, however, the citizens' militia had only a nominal function and even after it ended there were no battles on the northern terrain; mercenary forces were contending in the actual theaters of war in the south. It was ultimately a matter of honor to belong to one of the guilds of the civic guards. Rembrandt suggests a historic moment here only as a way of lending a noble aspect to his bourgeois clients, as the latter were well able to appreciate. It is a myth that they were not satisfied with the painting. But this artistic subterfuge was also an excuse for the painter to illustrate a lively situation.

Incidentally, this is not in fact a night scene; this error, which gave the picture its name, is probably due to the heavily darkened varnish which was later cleaned. Rembrandt set the event in shadow so as to allow the figures to emerge brightly and festively from the dark. A girl in a shimmering gold garment, perhaps a supplier to the camp, is the most brightly lit figure, reinforcing her central role in the scene. She carries, in a sense, the symbol of the company on her belt: the hen's claws derive from the same root as the *Kloveniers*, the armed militia. It is this motif that identifies the group in the first place.

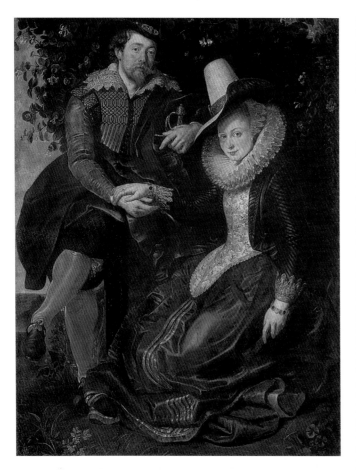

Peter Paul Rubens
Rubens and Isabella Brant in the Honey-suckle Bower, c. 1609–10
Oil on canvas, stretched on wood,
178 x 136.5 cm
Munich, Bayerische Staatsgemälde-sammlungen, Alte Pinakothek

Peter Paul Rubens
Portrait of Isabella Brant, the Painter's First Wife, 1622
Pen and ink on light brown paper,
38 x 29 cm
London, British Museum

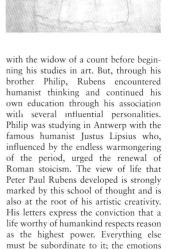

Rubens and Rembrandt

Among the many important Dutch painters of the seventeenth century, Rubens and Rembrandt stand out as the two giants whose status is comparable to that of Velázquez or Poussin. Both dedicated themselves primarily to the traditional genres of historical and portrait painting as well as producing important landscape works. In spite of several similarities between the two, there are striking differences which essentially determine the artistic relationship between the two painters, who never came to know each other personally. Background, training, milieu, and career, but above all their positively antithetical personalities marked the diverse character of their artistic achievements. Rembrandt began his career thirty years after Rubens. When he was still a pupil, Rubens was already a famous artist and in the 1630s, while Rembrandt was trying to find clients, Rubens was having difficulty in fending off commissions.

Peter Paul Rubens

Rubens had traveled extensively. Immediately after completing his studies he set off for Italy; commissions were hard to obtain in Antwerp which was suffering under Spanish rule. In Italy he came to the attention of the Duke of Mantua who instantly engaged him as court painter. Meanwhile, Rubens also spent time in other cities, and while studying the great masters of the Renaissance began to develop his own style. Through the Gonzaga he came into contact with other provincial princes early in his career: he was sent to the Spanish court on an official mission, for example, and worked for Rudolf II in Prague. In 1609 the *stadholders* of the Spanish king in Brussels appointed him their court painter; however, Rubens continued to live in Antwerp. The art–loving Infanta Isabella in particular gave him continued support. Through Isabella he was able to establish further contacts with the dynastic rulers of Europe.

Success

Rubens quickly became spoiled by success and his new social status was soon reinforced by his marriage to Isabella Brant, the daughter of a respected patrician and state secretary, barely a year after his return. In his marriage portrait, the *Honeysuckle Bower* (see above), Rubens demonstrates love and pride in equal measure. He evidently adored his wife throughout her life, and an intimate affection is undoubtedly clear in this painting. Such representations of emotional attachment were not commonly represented in formal portraits intended for display, since love between the couple was not generally established as the basis of marriage. As Rubens and Isabella turn almost imperceptibly towards each other, a harmonious interplay is staged, and the honeysuckle twining around the bridal couple, as if by chance, expresses their sense of unity on a symbolic level.

At the same time, however, this is decidedly a show portrait, despite the intimate, natural surroundings of the bower. An awareness of rank is indicated not only by the strikingly rich clothing but also by the confidence of the full-length type of portrait. The superior position of the man is firmly established; Isabella sits at his feet, a posture that cannot be disguised even by her tall hat. The dagger as part of the insignia of the aristocracy in the man's left hand is almost as important to Rubens as the woman to whom he offers his right hand. Rubens was showered with official honors: in 1624 the Spanish king elevated Rubens to the ranks of the nobility, in Cambridge he was awarded the degree of master of arts, and he was knighted at Whitehall.

Reason and Discipline

This sort of career had not been inevitable. The painter's father, Jan Rubens, as a Protestant lawyer and adviser to the Duchess had to flee Antwerp after the period of iconoclasm, and Peter Paul was born in Siegen in western Germany. His mother, who had remained a Catholic, returned from there to the Schelde after his father's death. As he was the younger son, there were only enough funds to pay for a short period at the Latin school, after which he went into service as a page with the widow of a count before beginning his studies in art. But, through his brother Philip, Rubens encountered humanist thinking and continued his own education through his association with several influential personalities. Philip was studying in Antwerp with the famous humanist Justus Lipsius who, influenced by the endless warmongering of the period, urged the renewal of Roman stoicism. The view of life that Peter Paul Rubens developed is strongly marked by this school of thought and is also at the root of his artistic creativity. His letters express the conviction that a life worthy of humankind respects reason as the highest power. Everything else must be subordinate to it; the emotions must be kept under control and discipline preserved.

In his painting of the *Drunken Silenus* (see right) Rubens graphically illustrates the animal-like qualities of man that are released through the exces-

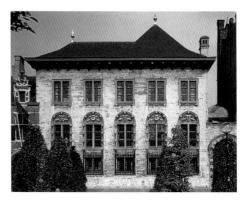

Antwerp
Rubens' House

Peter Paul Rubens
Drunken Silenus, 1618–26
Oil on wood, 205 x 211 cm
Munich, Bayerische Staatsgemälde-
sammlungen, Alte Pinakothek

Peter Paul Rubens
*Arrival of Marie de' Medici at
Marseilles*, 1625
Oil on canvas, 394 x 295 cm
Paris, Musée du Louvre

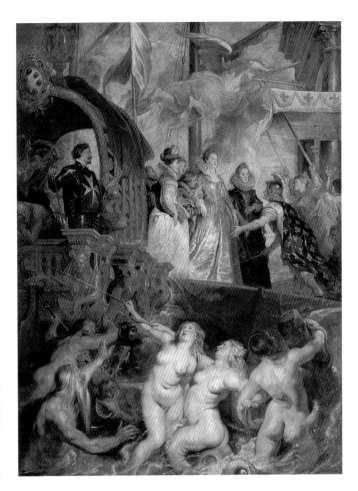

sive consumption of wine. The helpless state of the old man, who is part of the entourage of the wine god Bacchus, is explicitly portrayed. "Drunkenness disables the use of the limbs and the intellect," as the story of Silenus teaches us. "It wastes money, stimulates the blind passions of Venus and Mars, and brings about premature death," we are warned by a print after another depiction of Silenus by Rubens. But in both works the painter describes human weakness with a degree of amused sympathy which acknowledges that carnal impulses are part of the human personality and no one can entirely overcome them.

Reason and discipline were iron rules in the artist's own life and they made it possible for him to acquire wealth to a degree that was almost unheard of for a painter. With a keen head for business, he organized his workshop as though it were a factory. His status as court painter enabled him to exceed the limit of the number of pupils prescribed by the guilds. He approached the Spanish king with a plea for ennoblement, well aware of the guild-free and tax-free status that would be assured to him as a nobleman. Soon Rubens acquired extensive real estate property in his hometown, and as

early as the 1620s moved into a grand town house (see left below) which, in addition to his residence, housed his studio, sales premises, and important art collection. Rubens had the house furnished so that he could receive important visitors there.

Diplomacy

A further element in the artist's success, however, was his diplomatic talents. This ability was first demonstrated in the early 1620s, when Rubens received from Marie de' Medici, the widow of the French king, the commission to produce a twenty-one-part cycle of paintings about her life. This project, although apparently very promising from a financial angle, was soon revealed as a decidedly delicate undertaking. After her husband's murder, Marie had taken over the regency on behalf of her son, then a minor, who subsequently became Louis XIII. This difficult assignment could hardly be mastered by the artist's natural flair, since Cardinal Richelieu, with his increasing influence over Louis, was planning to remove Marie from power. When she ordered the cycle of paintings, Marie had already been obliged to surrender power. She was barely tolerated at

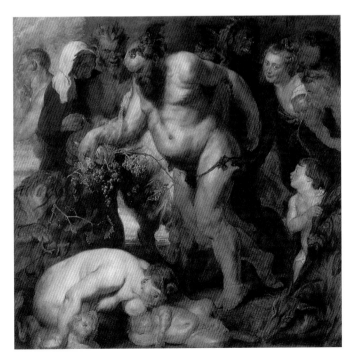

court and was later forced into exile. While struggling for the restoration of her position, she required Rubens' painting to represent nothing less than the justification of her actions as regent.

In a frenzy of splendid garments, and supported by armies of mythological characters, Rubens contrived to portray Marie's reign as a blessing for France. In one of the paintings, the magnificent ship of the Medici is moored at Marseilles, and Henri's future consort sets foot on French soil for the first time (see above). Humble, and yet with a spring in her step, she is greeted by two female figures representing France and the city of Marseilles. Her crossing from Italy had apparently been personally supervised by Neptune, with an entourage of tritons and naiads. In each of the paintings of the cycle, Marie's life is always seen under the protection of the gods. The young Marie, for example, is personally educated by Athena, the goddess of wisdom.

These had been the traditional means of glorifying a would-be divine ruler since the Renaissance and such iconography reached its high point during the absolutist seventeenth century. Admittedly Rubens did not actually put Marie on a level with the gods. Rather, she is posi-

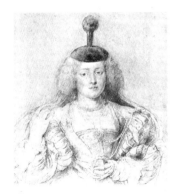

Peter Paul Rubens
Hélène Fourment, c. 1635
Chalk and ink drawing,
61.2 x 55 cm
London, Count Seilern Collection, Courtauld Institute Galleries

439

Peter Paul Rubens
"The Little Fur", c. 1635–40
Oil on wood, 176 x 83 cm
Vienna, Kunsthistorisches Museum

Peter Paul Rubens
Self-Portrait, c. 1638–40
Oil on canvas, 109.5 x 85 cm
Vienna, Kunsthistorisches Museum

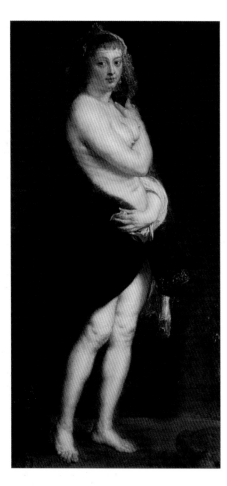

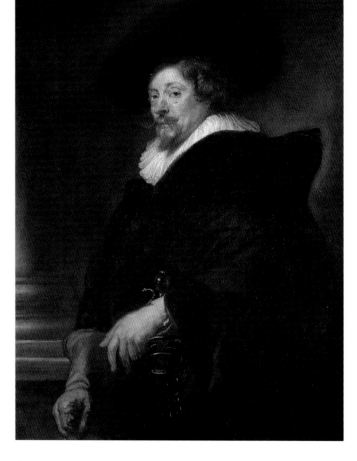

tively supervised, led, and conducted by them. In this way Rubens referred to higher powers and put the sovereignty of the regent into a relative context—a clever method of avoiding the danger of uncritical glorification. Maria, on her part, declared herself well satisfied and immediately gave Rubens a further commission for a cycle on the life of her murdered husband, Henri IV, which was never completed.

After the twelve-year armistice between the northern provinces of the Netherlands and Spain had ended in 1621, and England and France had entered the war, Rubens gave further evidence of his diplomatic skill, this time in peace negotiations in the service of the Spanish crown. Over a period of years this second career made great demands upon him. In 1627 he traveled to

Rotterdam, Delft, Amsterdam, and Utrecht on the pretext of meeting the painters of the northern provinces, while he was actually meeting English negotiators in order to prepare for direct dealings with the English king, with whom he finally worked out a peace agreement.

Withdrawal
Meanwhile his first wife had died, and in 1630, four years after her death, Rubens married Hélène Fourment. The aging painter was plagued by gout and longed for a private life far from the international stage and aristocratic circles. The sixteen-year-old Hélène gave the fifty-three-year-old painter new zest for life: "I have taken a young wife from a good though bourgeois house, although all the world tried to persuade me to set up a household in court circles. But I feared

the notorious weakness of the nobility, arrogance, particularly with the opposite sex, and therefore I preferred to take a wife who does not blush to see me take up the paintbrush. And to tell the truth, it would have seemed hard to me to exchange the precious treasure of freedom for the caresses of an old lady." Hélène was his model for several portraits, and even in the mythological and biblical scenes of these years her features are repeatedly represented. Rubens now painted most of his work himself, including carefree tributes to love such as the *Festival of Venus* (now in Vienna) and the *Garden of Love* (now in Madrid).

In 1635 the *stadholders* finally yielded to Rubens' plea to be liberated from the diplomatic service, and Rubens could, as he wrote, "cut through the golden knot of ambition." He had "no

further aim in this world but to live in peace." He carried out this intention in retirement at Het Steen, a property in the country (see p. 459), where he could reflect on his Flemish home and his life together with his young wife.

The complexity of Rubens' personality at the end of his active life can be grasped through an examination of three pictures from his final years. Two years before his death, in 1640, he painted probably his most risqué portrait of Hélène, the so-called *"Little Fur"*, a unique testimonial to his admiration of vitality and the joy of life. The *Self-Portrait* of 1636, however, expresses his official side: highly respected, well-heeled, supplied with all the honors that could be bestowed upon a painter. The three-quarter-length or so-called knee-length portrait was one which Rubens

Rembrandt
Saskia in Rich Costume, c. 1642
Oil on wood, 99.5 x 78.8 cm
Kassel, Staatliche Kunstsammlungen,
Gemäldegalerie Alte Meister, Schloss
Wilhelmshöhe

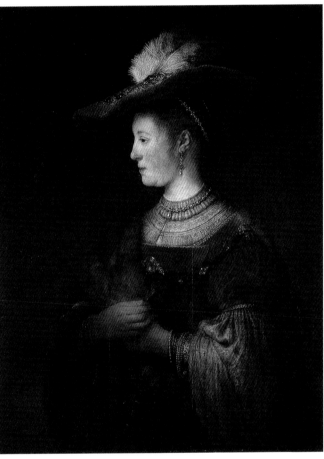

otherwise reserved for official state portraits. There are numerous motifs implying the dignity of the subject: the column is a standard component of the aristocratic portrait, just like the glove carelessly held in the hand, and the dagger draws attention to the subject's knighthood. Impressive volume is provided by the big hat and splendid robe. The dignity is not merely external, however: wisdom and experience speak from the alert but serene gaze. One eye flashes inquisitively, open to the world, the other is dark, serious, turned in on itself.

Rubens' tireless efforts for peace were finally disappointed—he was not to live to see the end of the war in Europe. In 1638 his disturbing painting *The Consequences of War* expressed his disillusionment (see p. 449). It must have seemed to him as though humanity would never again come to its senses.

Rembrandt van Rijn

If Rembrandt had anything in common with Rubens apart from outstanding artistic gifts, it was enormous ambition. The thirty-two-year-old Rubens had demonstrated an aristocratic self-confidence in his wedding portrait, and at thirty-four Rembrandt also displayed himself as someone who had arrived: in velvet and silk, furs and jewels, he depicts himself as a dignified, self-confident man. To an expert it would also be evident that he not only presented himself in the costume of the early sixteenth century, but he also took up a particular posture, with which he alluded to well-known portraits by Titian and Raphael representing Ariosto and Castiglione. Rembrandt thus surrounded

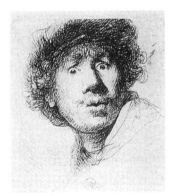

Rembrandt
Self-portrait with Eyes Wide Open, 1630
Etching, 5.1 x 4.6 cm
Amsterdam, Rijksmuseum

himself by an aura of exceptional culture and sophisticated manners as represented by these two renaissance figures. And like Titian, the prince of painters, from 1633 Rembrandt signed his works only with his Christian name, self-consciously placing himself in a great tradition.

Success

By about 1640 Rembrandt had indeed reached the peak of his career. Nine years earlier he had left his home town, Leyden, where he had completed his studies in art and run his first workshop, and moved to Amsterdam, where there were more commissions. In his first four years there he painted about fifty portraits, for each of which he received up to five hundred guilders, at a time when a laborer would have earned only about one hundred guilders a year. Rembrandt

even obtained a commission from the *stadholder* for a series on the Passion.

He came from a modest background, however; his father was a miller in Leyden. But, like Rubens, Rembrandt constantly strove to improve his education. He registered at Leyden University and learned Latin, a language that was indispensable for a prospective historical painter. In Amsterdam he associated with Jewish intellectuals and his house was in the Jewish quarter. He did not travel very much, however, for he was convinced that Amsterdam offered sufficient artistic stimulation.

Like Rubens, Rembrandt ran his workshop in great style: over the decades he took on some one hundred and fifty pupils and assistants. They produced copies of his own works which he then signed; original works by his pupils were

also sold under his name. This was permissible under the guild statutes, but no one took the custom quite to the extremes that Rembrandt did. For some years this workshop practice has been the subject of considerable debate. The master's enormous output, which during his lifetime established his fame, is now being evaluated in a manner that does justice to the work of his pupils.

Rembrandt's promising rise to fame, like that of Rubens, involved a suitable marriage. In 1634 he married Saskia van Uylenburgh who came from a Friesian patrician house and was furnished with a substantial dowry. Soon Rembrandt was able to consider himself a prospective patrician also; after all he was the favorite painter of the generation which set the new standards in art. Like Rubens, he moved into a large town house. His young wife often modeled for him.

In the year of their marriage he began one of the most ostentatious of his many portraits of her, demonstrating splendor and wealth (see left). But, unlike Rubens' wedding portrait, it was not their own wealth he was showing off, for Saskia is playing a historical role in a splendid *portrait historié*, a historical costume portrait very popular among their contemporaries. She is wearing renaissance dress, which matches the strict profile portrait that was quite rare in the seventeenth century. Rembrandt did not complete the portrait of his wife until after her early death in 1642; the feather on her cap alludes to the transience of life.

Decline

Saskia's death marked the point at which Rembrandt passed the height of his success, and a decline began which had become inexorable by the early 1650s at the latest. He had taken up with Geertje Dirckx, who had entered his household as nurse to his son Titus. But he soon tired of his liaison with this woman of nearly forty, and instead took the young Hendrickje Stoffels into his house as a maid. In 1649, however, Geertje sued Rembrandt over his verbal promise of marriage, and as a result he was forced to make regular maintenance payments to her. Hendrickje, on the other hand, was excluded from holy communion by the council of the Reformed Church in 1656 because she was living in an unlawful relationship with Rembrandt; the artist himself was not accused, since it seems that he did not belong to the Church.

About the same time Rembrandt painted a picture of Hendrickje paddling in a river, her simple garment carefully

Rembrandt
Woman Bathing in a Stream
(*Hendrickje*), 1655
Oil on wood, 61.6 x 47 cm
London, National Gallery

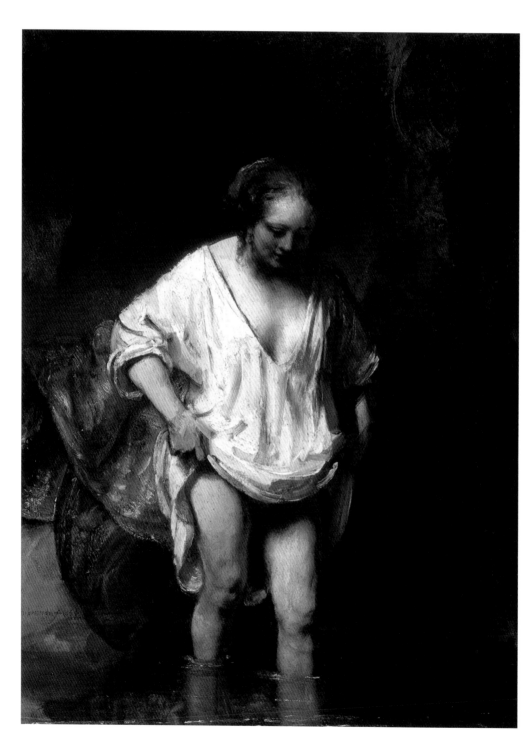

lifted (see left). The broad surface painting, with its fresh and dynamic sketchy technique, is representative of the master's late style. Tentative, but with a playful delight at the same time, Hendrickje has a very youthful look. One can imagine that the forty-eight-year-old Rembrandt prized the same qualities in the woman twenty years his junior as Rubens did in his Hélène. But Rembrandt did not want to marry Hendrickje since he would then have had to repay Saskia's fortune to her family. He was no longer in a position to do so. In 1656 he had to declare himself officially bankrupt and his possessions were impounded.

Rembrandt, quite unlike Rubens, was not good at handling money; he speculated unwisely, acquired a large art collection which was beyond his means, and carelessly spent whatever money he happened to have. In 1660 Hendrickje and Rembrandt's eighteen-year-old son Titus founded a company which took over the financial responsibility for the artist's affairs in order to protect him from his creditors. Hendrickje died in 1663, probably of the plague, followed by Titus in 1668, a year before his father. His unseemly affairs had put a strain on Rembrandt's reputation among respectable citizens.

Rembrandt did not have Rubens' ingratiating and diplomatic manner when dealing with potential clients. At the outset of his time in Amsterdam, Saskia's uncle, Gerrit van Uylenburgh, had obtained commissions for him. But in his personal contacts with his clients Rembrandt became increasingly temperamental and boorish. He was unable to sustain his promising relationship with the court in The Hague and received no further commissions. He also demonstrated little understanding of the constantly fluctuating balance of power among the Amsterdam upper classes and was unable to make allies of the right people. The biggest official commission offered by the city of Amsterdam, the decoration of the new city hall on the Dam, went to his former pupil Govaert Flinck, who enjoyed great popularity. It was only after the latter's early death that the commission was divided between several artists, and in 1661 Rembrandt was able to contribute a large painting of the conspiracy of Claudius Civilis. However, in the end the councillors did not accept it, and he was stuck with the gigantic work for which he was unable to find a buyer.

Rembrandt
Self-Portrait, 1640
Oil on canvas, 102 x 80 cm
London, National Gallery

Rembrandt
Self-Portrait, 1658
Oil on canvas, 133.7 x 103.8 cm
New York, Frick Collection

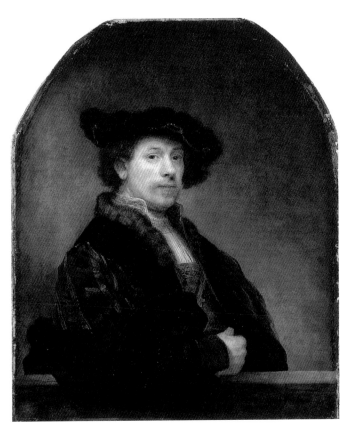

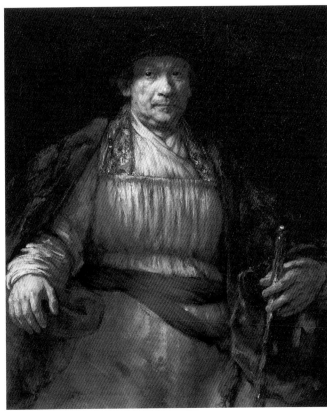

Self-Portraits

During the last twenty years of his life, during which he had to struggle against many hardships, Rembrandt again painted several self-portraits. Altogether he portrayed himself more than eighty times. This suggests a certain self-confidence and self-regard, but it was only partly narcissistic. Above all, Rembrandt used his own image as a model which was always available to him, and an object of study for the empirical psychology on which his creative work is based. It is difficult to determine how far he is revealing his character and psychological makeup in his portraits and the extent to which he is posing in order to be able to study variants of possible expressions.

He painted himself in all sorts of costumes: as a soldier, a beggar, an oriental, a representative of various levels of society—and with many different facial expressions. At the beginning of his career such self-portraits certainly served as promotional samples of his artistic abilities, but they soon became desirable as collectors' items in their own right. These portraits also open up to us the unstable, unsettled personality of the artist, who, unlike Rubens, found no support in the rigid regulation of life, but discovered the freedom of development in shifting situations. At the lowest point of his financial difficulties, far removed from prosperity and fame, Rembrandt paints himself in a powerful self-portrait (see above) like a king: he sits as though on a throne, clothed in garments that appear to be of gold. Benevolent and wise, he looks down on the spectator. This is equivalent to Rubens' late self-portrait. But while Rubens confidently wears the knightly dagger, Rembrandt is playing a part, posing as a king with his maulstick as a scepter.

Rembrandt rarely represented himself as a painter. In one of his last self-portraits he sits with his maulstick in front of a canvas on which he is painting the portrait of an old woman. But here too he is playing a part, that of the classical painter Zeuxis, who was supposed to have died from excessive laughter which caused him to choke while he was painting a comical wrinkled old woman from life. Perhaps this is a last, sarcastic comment on the many portraits which Rembrandt created from life with unsurpassed realism.

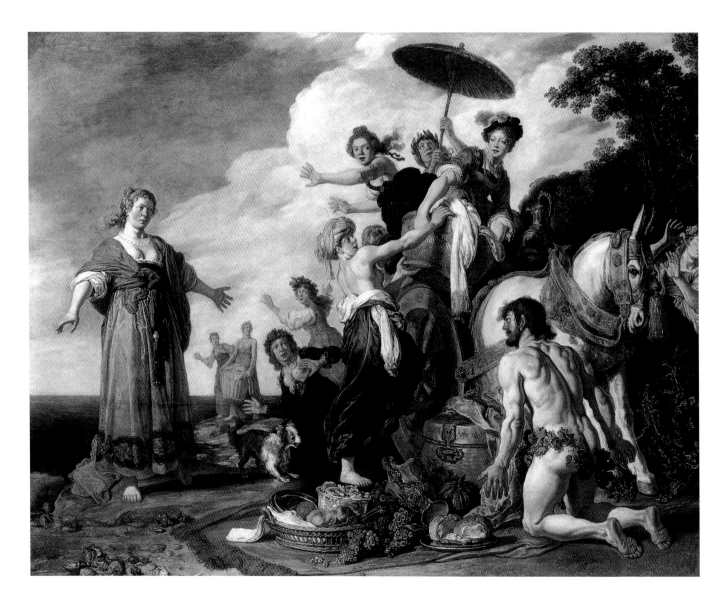

History Painting

"The most noble deeds and strivings of rationally thinking beings" were presented to the eyes by history painting, wrote Rembrandt's pupil Samuel van Hoogstraeten in 1678 in his *Inleyding tot de hooge schoole der schilderkonst*. It therefore deserved to be ranked most highly among all the categories of painting. Nonetheless, artists and collectors in Holland did not seem particularly to favor history painting, but unequivocally responded to landscapes, genre paintings, and still lifes. Many more paintings were produced in these categories than in the traditionally predominant field of history painting. However, higher themes, such as historic events, mythological stories, and biblical narratives remained the subjects of discussion in intellectually cultured circles.

One of the forerunners of Dutch history painting was the Amsterdam artist Pieter Lastman. From 1603 to 1607 he was in Italy, where he was influenced by Caravaggio and Adam Elsheimer, a German painter living in Rome. Lastman's lively narrative style

was based on his intense powers of observation and imagination. Unlike mannerist artists, he no longer considered the invention of cleverly devised compositions and complicated figural poses to be of prime importance; the theme of the picture should not merely be an excuse for a demonstration of artistic virtuosity. Lastman took the stories he wanted to tell seriously, and again concentrated on conveying their content clearly and memorably. He gave his attention in the first instance to human emotions, an interest which he passed on to Rembrandt, who as a young painter came to Amsterdam from Leyden for several months specifically to study with Lastman. In *Odysseus and Nausicaa* (see above) Lastman employs a theme from classical mythology. Odysseus, cast ashore, surprises the king's daughter and her entourage on an excursion and pleads for her help. While the other women express with distraught gestures their alarm at the sight of the "wild man," the naked Odysseus, and attempt to flee, the king's daughter retains her composure and confronts the unknown man. Lastman shows her outlined as a single figure against the sky and greatly foreshortened from the point of view of the kneeling Odysseus, a posture which gives her a monumental appearance. The scene is arranged diagonally to create a sense of depth, a novel means of composition which introduces a dynamic element into the picture and therefore can effectively be incorporated into the baroque narrative structure. The axis between Odysseus and Nausicaa accommodates the uncertainty of the moment, a field of tension between hope and fear, alarm and curiosity, rejection and attraction. We cannot yet foresee that Nausicaa will bring Odysseus to her father, who will make a ship available to him. After ten years of wandering Odysseus was thus finally able to return home.

Mythological themes traditionally corresponded to the tastes of the aristocracy and were therefore not produced in very great numbers in Holland. But scenes from the New Testament are also rare, since the Calvinist church adhered to the prohibition of images, and even pictures for private devotion were found in very few households. However, Utrecht, the only bishopric in the northern provinces during the middle ages, remained Catholic for the time being and produced painters who specialized in religious subjects. They also formed their own stylistic school within Dutch painting, the so-called "Utrecht Caravaggisti." The search for models and for inspiration had taken Dutch painters to Italy since the beginning of the sixteenth century. A century later, Utrecht artists in Rome such as Hendrick ter Brugghen, Gerrit van Honthorst, and Dirck van Baburen encountered the wholly innovative art of Caravaggio, whose methods they adopted and introduced to Holland: realism, non-idealized figures based on ordinary people, and the use of *chiaroscuro*, the creation of dramatic intensity through the contrast of light and shade. Without the work of the Utrecht Caravaggisti, Rembrandt's painted experiments with light are unthinkable for Rembrandt himself never actually visited Italy.

In his painting *Christ Before the High Priest*, Gerrit van Honthorst makes dramatic use of a single candle which illuminates the interrogation of Christ in the dark room. Christ's white robe reflects the light over a broad surface, as if it were emitted from his own person. The effect is unavoidably reminiscent of the words of Christ: "I am the light of the world. He that follows me shall not remain in darkness but shall have the light of life." Thus the figure of Christ is idealized, his inner calm standing in contrast to the seething anger of the high priest, who urges him to justify himself in the face of the accusations of the witnesses. Christ is about to confirm that he is the Son of God. "Thereupon they spat at him, covered his face, and beat him with fists." Honthorst did not, however, choose this particular scene, full of foreground drama, for his painting. Instead he illustrates the moment immediately preceding it: the words have not yet been spoken and the inner tension of the conversation is hanging in the air. Night scenes like this one were Honthorst's specialty—in Italy he was nicknamed Gherardo delle

Notti, Gerard of the Nights. In Rome, where he lived from 1610 to 1620, he had already achieved an excellent reputation. On his return to Utrecht, Honthorst rose to become one of the most famous painters in Holland, painting regularly for the *stadholder* in The Hague and for Christian IV of Denmark. He was finally summoned to England by Charles I.

In Flanders the demand for altar and devotional pieces remained fairly constant, and was even considerably heightened by the propaganda of the Counter-Reformation. The Church, as well as private individuals and associations, commissioned religious paintings, very much in the tradition of the middle ages when families or guilds maintained their own chapels in the churches. In Antwerp, for example, the guild of archers commissioned a descent from the cross

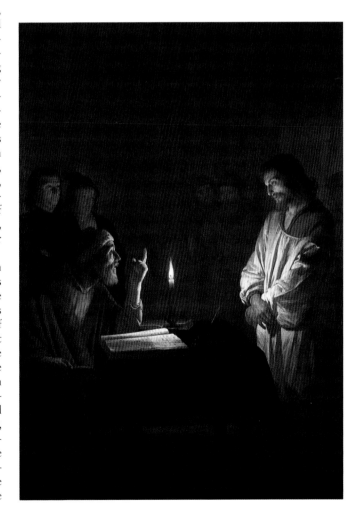

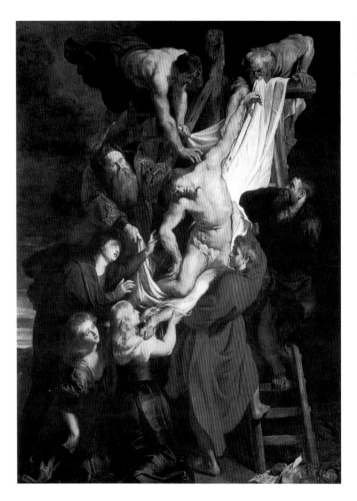

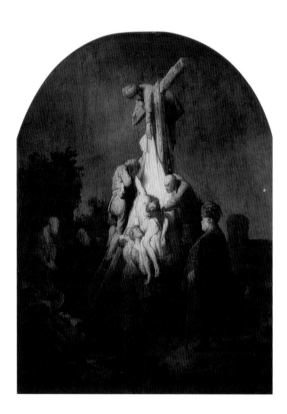

Peter Paul Rubens
Descent from the Cross, central panel
of triptych, 1612–14
Oil on wood, 462 x 341 cm
Antwerp cathedral

Rembrandt
Descent from the Cross, 1633
Oil on wood, 89.4 x 65.2 cm
Munich, Bayerische
Staatsgemäldesammlungen,
Alte Pinakothek

from Rubens for the cathedral instead of large group portraits of its members. Rubens' monumental *Descent from the Cross* of 1612–14 is one of the landmarks of baroque. The white shroud creates a diagonal line running from the upper right to the lower left of the image, linking all the figures in the composition. One movement leads to another, one hand grasps the next; the difficult task is carried out safely and without agitation, in devout concentration. Although Christ is given prominence as the central character, the theme here is the co-operation of those who are taking him down from the cross. This unusual emphasis is explained by the function of the painting as an altarpiece for the archers' guild. Rubens is showing the members of the civic militia, who have by their office devoted themselves to the common good, the importance of their commitment. In his preoccupation with humanistic thought, he had come to believe that dignity was bestowed upon humanity only when personal interest took second place to community spirit.

With this *Descent from the Cross*, Rubens became the pre-eminent Flemish artist of his time. He was the new major force against whom all others had to be measured. Rembrandt met the challenge by creating his own version of the famous *Descent from the Cross* (see above right). It was probably not a commissioned piece but resulted from the urge to meet the challenge of the master within his own style. Later Rembrandt's *Descent from the Cross* came into

the possession of the *stadholder* Frederik Hendrik, who then ordered from him further scenes of the Passion for a cycle. Rubens' altar painting is twenty times larger than Rembrandt's, which was intended as a picture for private devotion. Rembrandt never actually saw Rubens' painting himself; he worked from a print, and as a result the composition is reversed. In Rembrandt's version, the scene unfolds further back in the picture space, as if seen through a keyhole, while Rubens directly involves the spectator. Rembrandt's painting is distinguished by a muddy quality which makes the pale blue coloring of the assisting figure on the upper left the strongest tone in the picture; Rubens on the other hand dramatizes the event with powerful accents of color in front of a threatening sky, with the figures illuminated as if by cold flashes of lightning. In Rembrandt's image, the light seems to emanate from Christ himself. The crucified Christ is unquestionably the main figure here, while the other characters seem to form a frame around him. The figure dressed in blue is a self-portrait of Rembrandt himself. He involves himself in the biblical event and thus confronts himself with his own guilt as a sinner over the death of Christ—a concept which was constantly being invoked in contemporary chorales, for example.

In addition to portraits, Rembrandt dedicated himself mainly to history painting. The high point of his creative work in this field is the great painting *Jacob Blesses the Sons of Joseph* (see right). The

Rembrandt
Jacob Blesses the Sons of Joseph,
1656
Oil on canvas, 175 x 210 cm
Kassel, Staatliche
Kunstsammlungen,
Gemäldegalerie Alte Meister,
Schloss Wilhelmshöhe

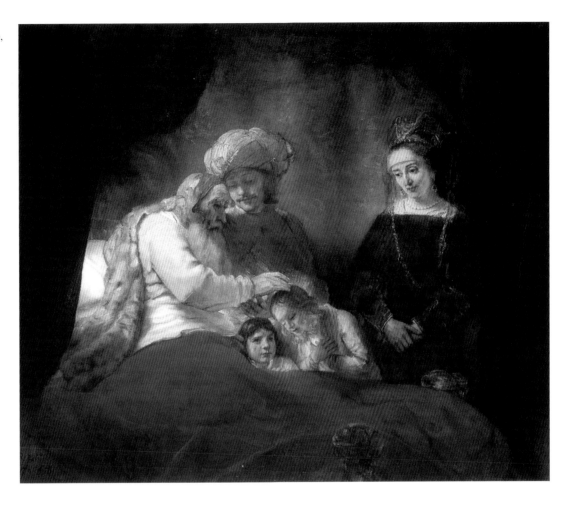

scene from the Old Testament shows the aged Jacob, who, sensing the approach of death, sits upright once more in order to bless his grandchildren. Since the middle ages this story had been frequently depicted as it is a key passage in the Christian religion. Ephraim and Manasseh, through the patriarch's blessing, are accepted among his sons, the progenitors of the twelve tribes of Israel. However, Jacob blessed the younger grandson instead of the firstborn, Manasseh, with his right hand, crossing his hands over in order to do so. Ephraim, the founder of Christianity, was thereby promised a greater future than had been given to Manasseh and Judaism: "His younger brother," said Jacob, "shall be greater than he, and his seed shall become a multitude of nations."

Rembrandt, however, does not seem to have concerned himself with this fateful decision. His version departs significantly from the biblical narrative and its traditional motif, particularly because Jacob does not cross his hands and blesses only one of the grandsons. This must be ascribed to some special interest on the part of the unknown client, about which only speculation has so far been possible. For the Calvinist and other Protestant interpretations of the scene the preference for one grandson over the other does not play a central part, and Jewish exegetes such as Rembrandt's friend Rabbi Menasseh ben Israel could certainly have interpreted it in a Judaic sense. It is also possible that Rembrandt created the picture without a specific com-

mission. The biblical painting offered him the opportunity to take his own understanding of painting as a subject. It is a story in which the sense of touch is particularly significant. In many of Rembrandt's works, the hands are emphasized and, unlike the sketchy treatment of limbs in the work of Frans Hals, are usually modeled very carefully with thickly applied paint. Jacob's hand, conferring the blessing, is shown by Rembrandt in a gesture of feeling the way. The old man cannot perceive with his eyes—he is blind and his face is in shadow—but he recognizes by touch. "Rembrandt presents the sense of touch as the symbol of the sense of sight," suggests Svetlana Alpers in her description of the apparently contradictory gesture. Only through touch, one might be intended to conclude, does one achieve sight, the "recognition" of seeing. The sense of touch plays an important role in Rembrandt's perception of the world, for painting is recognition through touch. But the particularly impressive aspect of *Jacob Blessing the Sons of Joseph*, profound interpretations aside, is the heavily charged tension of the scene and the high authority and certainty of the aged Jacob. Robed in white, he draws all the light to himself. All eyes are bent on the gesture of blessing, no details distract from it, and the room is scarcely suggested. This painting is the culmination of Rembrandt's late style. He increasingly dispensed with foreground drama and concentrated on internal processes which he allowed to unfold in an intense silence.

Rembrandt
The Deception of Samson, 1636
Oil on canvas, 205 x 272 cm
Frankfurt, Städelsches Kunstinstitut

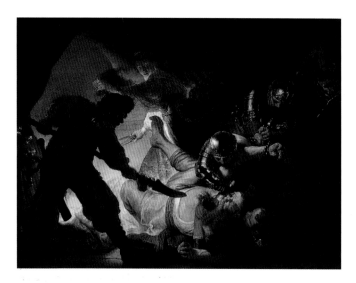

Rembrandt dedicated some thirty works to the Old Testament, creating images of subjects in which the Dutch were particularly interested. The Calvinist preachers counselled careful study of biblical stories, and there was of course a relationship with the Old Testament within the large Jewish community. The Jews who had emigrated to Holland, predominantly from Portugal, were not confined to a ghetto in Amsterdam, but lived in more or less close contact with their fellow citizens and had to a great extent the same rights as their Christian neighbors. From the end of the 1630s onward Rembrandt lived in the Jewish quarter and had close friends among cultured Jews.

It can be assumed that any client who commissioned Old Testament scenes wanted them to have some contemporary relevance in order that they could be projected as paradigms of his own existence in the present. The stories might, like parables, present models of morality: Susanna professed virtuous chastity, while Daniel was the embodiment of conscientiousness, since he saved Susanna from being sentenced. The name of Solomon became proverbial for wisdom, and Abraham, trusting entirely in God and prepared to sacrifice his son Isaac, represented unshakable obedience; his faith and hope were considered exemplary. On the other hand, the fund of narratives also offered the possibility of expressing warnings against weakness of character or an evil cast of mind. Delilah, for example, illustrates moral weakness—out of selfish greed she allows herself to be tempted into the worst betrayal of the common good.

The ominous consequences of such behavior were illustrated by Rembrandt in an expressive early work, *The Deception of Samson* (see above). Samson, of the Jews, has been furnished by God with

unconquerable powers. In order to undermine this threat, the Philistines bribe his wife Delilah to find out the secret of his powers so that he can be overcome. Exploiting his trust, at a favorable moment she cuts his hair and thus robs him of his strength. Rembrandt shows the moment immediately following when the Philistines burst out from their ambush and fall upon the defenseless Samson, while Delilah flees the scene of horror, the hair and scissors in her hand. The light falling through the opened curtains harshly reveals the cruel deception in a drama of emotions in which the spectator is inescapably involved. In contrast to his late works, here Rembrandt chooses a mood of extreme drama, selecting the moment of the story which permits the most dramatic treatment. But here too, the emotions accompanying the events are apparently his main concern: pain and aggression, tension and alertness are mirrored in the faces of the Philistines, while Delilah's expression wavers hesitantly between terror and triumph.

The theme can also be seen as an allusion to the political situation in the northern provinces, in particular to the War of Independence against Spain. Scenes from the Israelites' struggle for freedom could easily be interpreted in the Netherlands as referring to its own situation. After his hair had grown back, Samson did ultimately destroy the Philistines. The picture, which was painted in 1636, more than a decade before the Peace of Westphalia, could equally be understood as an expression of the wish finally to achieve independence. In addition to the story of Samson, the Dutch particularly liked David's heroic battle against Goliath, equating David with William of Orange. Another frequently painted subject was Esther, the Jewish woman married to the Persian king Ahasuerus. She risked her life in order to persuade the king to lift an edict against the Jews. The Dutch saw in the Jews persecuted in the Persian kingdom a parallel to their own situation as a community of faith not tolerated by Catholic Spain.

While the Dutch thematized the war with the assistance of Old Testament stories, painters like Rubens relied on mythological and allegorical figures. His allegory *War and Peace* (see right) suggests a unique combination of his diplomatic and artistic activities. Rubens had been sent to England in 1627 to negotiate a peace agreement with the king, a mission in which he actually succeeded. To seal this diplomatic success, while still in England he painted this picture for Charles I, intended to validate retrospectively the king's decision.

Peter Paul Rubens
War and Peace, 1629
Oil on canvas, 203.5 x 298 cm
London, National Gallery

BELOW:
Peter Paul Rubens
The Consequences of War, 1637–38
Oil on canvas, 206 x 345 cm
Florence, Palazzo Pitti

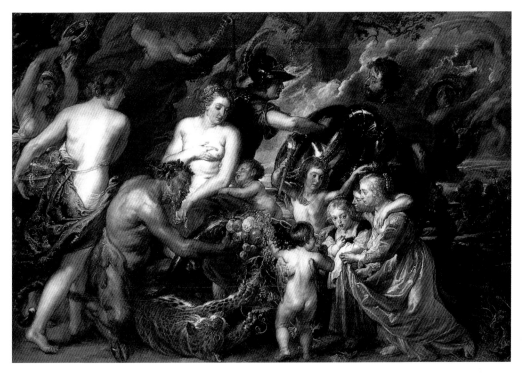

Here Rubens illustrates a Golden Age reflecting the effects of the new peace treaty. He chooses an allegorical image: in the center sits Venus, the goddess of love, feeding a boy with a stream of milk. A satyr is pouring fruit from a cornucopia, a woman brings precious armor and jewels; humanity is seen generally enjoying riches and abundance. Another woman dances to a tambourine, suggesting the enjoyment of the sensual pleasures of the world of Bacchus. In this idyll even the wild animals have been tamed. In the background, however, hate and war are being vigorously fended off. Minerva, the goddess of wisdom, protects freedom and prosperity by forcefully pushing aside the god of war, Mars, and the fury Alecto. The message is supported by the composition: the group around Venus is placed in a pyramidal scheme; but the warlike characters, in an extremely turbulent diagonal, are being literally driven out of the picture. Rubens has essentially represented a diplomatic dispute in a magnificent painting. He is appealing to the English king to use the wisdom of diplomacy to end the war and bring about peace.

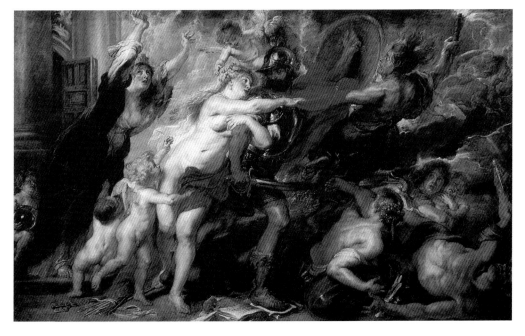

Only eight years later Rubens painted an allegory of war for the Duke of Tuscany which indicates how disappointed and disillusioned he was. He had retired from the diplomatic service in the meantime, having been forced to recognize that all his efforts and partial successes had in fact failed to lead to peace. The whole of Europe was afflicted by the Thirty Years War. As Rubens' new allegory demonstrates, Mars could no longer be held in check. However much Venus deploys all her charms, "attempting to hold him back with caresses and embraces," as Rubens wrote, she has to realize that this time the fury is stronger than she. The dreadful figures of Plague and Hunger hasten forward. With a bloodstained sword the god of war stamps out all the aspects of a civilized Europe: arts and sciences, family life, and fertility are personified in the figures writhing on the ground. Jakob Burckhardt wrote of this painting that it was "the eternal and unforgettable frontispiece to the Thirty Years War."

449

Esaias van de Velde
The Cattle Ferry, 1622
Oil on wood, 75.5 x 113 cm
Amsterdam, Rijksmuseum

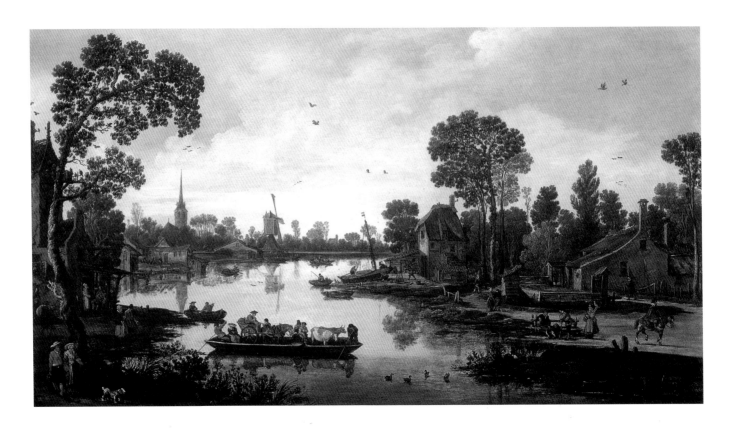

Landscape

A simple ferry with peasants, cows, and a horse-cart is the central feature of Esaias van de Velde's *The Cattle Ferry* (see above). On the river bank a small boatyard can be seen, ramblers and tipplers sit beneath the crooked porch of an inn, and in the background a church tower and windmill stand out above the trees. An everyday setting of this kind would be unusual in Italian or French painting of the same period; only historical subjects were considered worthy of depiction, and landscape paintings would be considered relevant only if they represented idealized scenes incorporating heroically impressive or idyllic themes, with shepherds and sheep, the bliss of Arcadia. There must be more to see in a landscape painting than the viewer would find on a walk in familiar, ordinary surroundings. Art was supposed to illustrate an ideal realm which transported the spectator beyond the everyday.

In Holland, by contrast, the approach to landscape was somewhat different. The independence of the young republic from the long-standing cultural traditions of these nations and a pride in the country expresses itself, for example, in the patriotic symbol of the *hollandse tuin*, the fruitful enclosed garden; such ideas encouraged

artists to represent their native landscape without idealization. Instead of astonishing views, they were more interested in scenes which might be regarded as typical. Similar subjects had already been represented in sixteenth-century Flanders, but only in drawings and prints. In the 1620s Esaias van de Velde was the first to apply the new concept of landscape to painting: seemingly trivial and modest views of the Dutch countryside such as one might encounter at any time in the course of a stroll.

The Dutch thereby set themselves apart from the wider European traditions of landscape, on the model of German renaissance painters such as Albrecht Altdorfer, which had been adopted in sixteenth-century Flanders. The aerial perspective allowed the spectator a broad view over scenery in a manner that would otherwise have been inconceivable. All the elements of landscape were assembled in one picture: high mountains and ranges of hills, forests and fields, rivers and oceans, city and country. And somewhere in all this a few very small figures representing the Temptation of Christ, St. George, or the Flight into Egypt.

Jan Brueghel, at the beginning of the seventeenth century, was still part of this tradition. The eldest son of the great "Peasant,"

Bruegel first became well-known as a flower painter, but he also produced a number of landscapes, mostly in small format, with lively scenes of daily life. His *Landscape with Windmills* (see right) is already imbued with the new spirit to the extent that it contents itself with an apparently accidental glance at a simple flat plain without particular motifs. In many respects, however, it remains trapped in the conventional Flemish pattern. The spectator's view is not from ground level but from a higher standpoint, which allows an exceptionally broad field of vision. In addition Brueghel has raised the horizon so that he is working against the correct perspective. This is cleverly disguised as he merges the horizon imperceptibly with the sky. In order to suggest depth, the picture is divided horizontally into three strips; the front section is defined by brown tones, the middle one by yellow and green, and the background by blue tones. Beyond the foreground, which lies in shadow, the gaze is attracted by the luminous middle ground, while the blue in the background seems to recede, reinforcing the sense of depth. This still corresponds to the pattern developed in the sixteenth century by Flemish painters such as Joachim Patinir, although Brueghel was skillful enough to transform it subtly.

As has been suggested, the Dutch painters were the first to free themselves from this pattern in the 1620s. The little *Dune Landscape with Trees and Wagon* by Pieter de Molijn in Braunschweig (see right) is considered an important milestone in this development. No distant view distracts from this modest motif. Molijn creates a uniform coloring in a reduced palette of green, yellow, and brown tones which are combined in the painting to create a light and airy effect.

A comparison with the painting by Esaias van de Velde reveals another unusual aspect of this work. In order to create a sense of depth in the landscape, Esaias fell back on the traditional formula in which elements of the picture appear to recede into the distance in a zigzag formation. Molijn's composition, by contrast, depends on a single diagonal, which is determined by the course of the brightly lit sandy path. This element, which was fundamental to later landscapes, probably goes back to Adam Elsheimer, the German painter active in Rome around 1600 (see p. 476), whose works were known in Holland through prints. Molijn achieves a powerful dynamic through the use of the diagonal: the path seems to pass only faintly through the picture and the cart rattling along will soon have disappeared from view. The spectator has the impression of being able to enter and exit the landscape along the path. Esaias' painting shows a static situation closed in on itself: the river looks like a lake, framed on all sides by the trees on the banks. On each side the protruding trees form the conventional *repoussoir* which closes off the view to the edges of the picture. The area of dark shadow in the foreground also serves to round off the image at the front. Molijn's dune landscape, on the other hand, does not offer a closed-off view, but shows an apparently incidentally chosen section from a greater whole

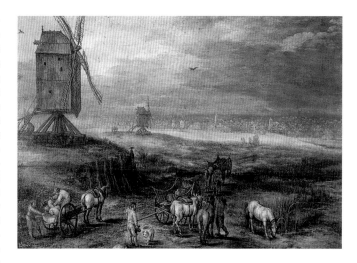

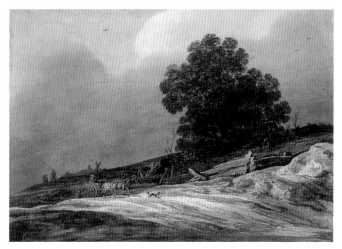

which might continue beyond the edges of the picture. This is characteristic of many works by Dutch landscape painters up to Philips Koninck. Inevitably, the sense of a scene almost chosen at random is somewhat undermined by the fact that the composition itself had to be carefully contrived in order to create a picture that would have the power to command the viewer's attention.

Molijn's innovations in composition and color were further developed by his Haarlem artist colleagues Salomon van Ruysdael and Jan van Goyen. Van Goyen's landscape with a view of his native town, Leyden (see p. 452), is also based on a diagonal composition, although it is not as clearly defined as in Molijn's work. Van Goyen's muddy, almost monochrome coloring is unsurpassed. On account of

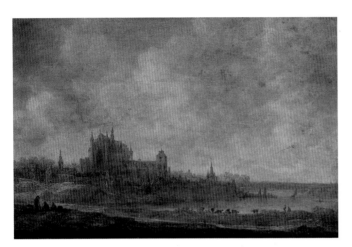

the thinly varnished application of color, the beige primer on the wood panel shows through the whole picture, contributing to its atmospheric effects: the outline of the church by the river appears almost to dissolve into damp mist and the veiled sunshine, while the shimmering light is suggested by the lively, ill-defined brushstrokes. The sober interpretation of the subject and poetic transfiguration enter into a tense liaison as nature and the work of man become blurred in the vibration of the damp air into an inseparable unity.

In spite of their patriotism, several Dutch artists were drawn to Italy from where they brought the southern light and the charming landscape of the Roman Campagna back to the North Sea coast. In about 1620, a colony of Dutch artists established a circle in Rome around the landscape painter Cornelis van Poelenburgh and Bartholomaeus Breenbergh; they became known as the "Schilderbent," the band of painters. It was a boisterous, hard-drinking club; each new member was accepted as a "Bentvueghel," a bird of the band, with a parody of ancient rituals, and supplied with a nickname. Rome's reputation soon spread as "the heart of Sodom," as the English moralist Joseph Hall wrote. Samuel von Hoogstraeten shuddered at the thought of his stay in Rome, and warned that three things above all should be avoided there: fellow-countrymen, wine, and women. But through their close contact with their fellow-countrymen, Dutch artists were also able to maintain a degree of independence from the strict guidelines of the Roman Academy. Between the 1630s and 1650s they were followed by a second generation of landscape painters, including Nicolaes Berchem, Jan Both, Jan Asselijn, and others. They took as their models the so-called "heroic landscapes" of the French artist living in Rome, Claude Lorrain, but preferred to give them an idyllic mood by adding small figures of shepherds or gypsies. The term *bambocciate* is associated with these lively landscape scenes after the nickname given to Pieter van Laer.

These genre scenes often incorporate a moralistic element. In Nicolaes Berchem's landscape (see right above), the woman seated on a horse holds an upturned bowl while the man catches the water in his hat. Drinking was seen as a vice of excess, and is here commented upon by the animal behavior of the urinating horse, while the woman, by contrast, virtuously demonstrates moderate restraint.

The great appeal of Italian landscapes, indicated by high prices for the paintings, induced even artists who had never themselves been in the south to adopt its warm light, sometimes even projecting it onto native subjects. The Dordrecht painter Aelbert Cuyp, for example, bathed his *River Landscape* (see right below) in a golden evening light. His painting, now in the Karlsruhe Kunsthalle, is dominated by the cows standing by the water which appear transfigured, almost glorified by the golden light. The field of vision recedes far into the distance, an effect which is reinforced by the sloping ground in the front of the image and seems almost to monumentalize the animals. In Holland the cow was not considered a mundane subject at all. It not only stood for earth, spring, fertility, and prosperity, but became, like the *hollandse tuin*, a symbol of Holland itself: the *hollandse kuh*, fat, fertile, and peaceable.

Aelbert Cuyp belongs to the second generation of Dutch landscape painters who came to artistic maturity around the middle of the century. These artists distanced themselves from the consistent realism of the founding fathers who wanted to capture the essential character of the northern landscape, and introduced instead heroic and sublime aspects into their landscapes. The most important landscape painter of this generation, if not of the whole century, is considered to be Jacob van Ruisdael, who developed a variety of new motifs and meanings. He integrated real life into a superior course of events more distinctly than any of his predecessors. The dramatic settings of his landscapes diverge from the calm serenity which distinguishes the works of van Goyen or Salomon van Ruysdael, an uncle of Ruisdael. In order to achieve a tension in the structure of his painting, Ruisdael often concentrates on a central element of the scene, which may appear somewhat surprising in a landscape painting. And yet a tree, a windmill, even a cornfield or a path among the dunes may, as in a historical painting, become the chief protagonist of an event. This is certainly the case with the dramatic *Waterfall with Mountain Castle* (see p. 455, below) now in Braunschweig.

A view like this can no longer be seen as a straightforward representation of a landscape, for the picture is made up of various set-pieces, each inspired by a different event in Ruisdael's life. The motif of the castle on the rock goes back to a journey to Germany which he undertook at the beginning of the 1650s with Nicolaes Berchem. This was the only time he ever left the Netherlands. Here Ruisdael discovered the castle of Bentheim, towering on a little rock above the plain, which later appeared, in a guise considerably glorified and exaggerated by dramatic imagination, in some of his paintings and

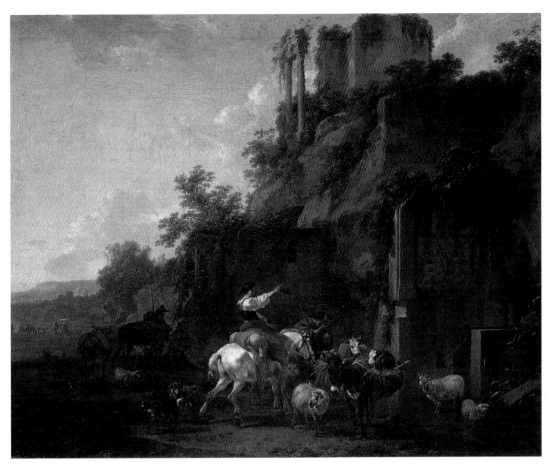

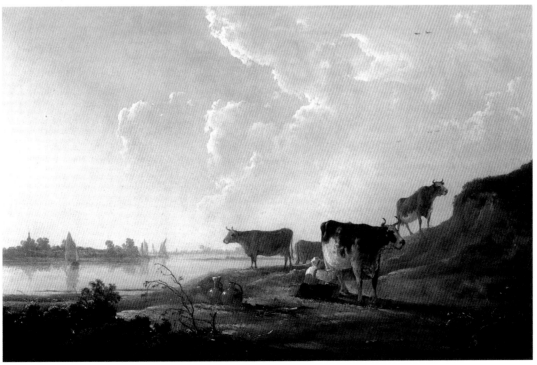

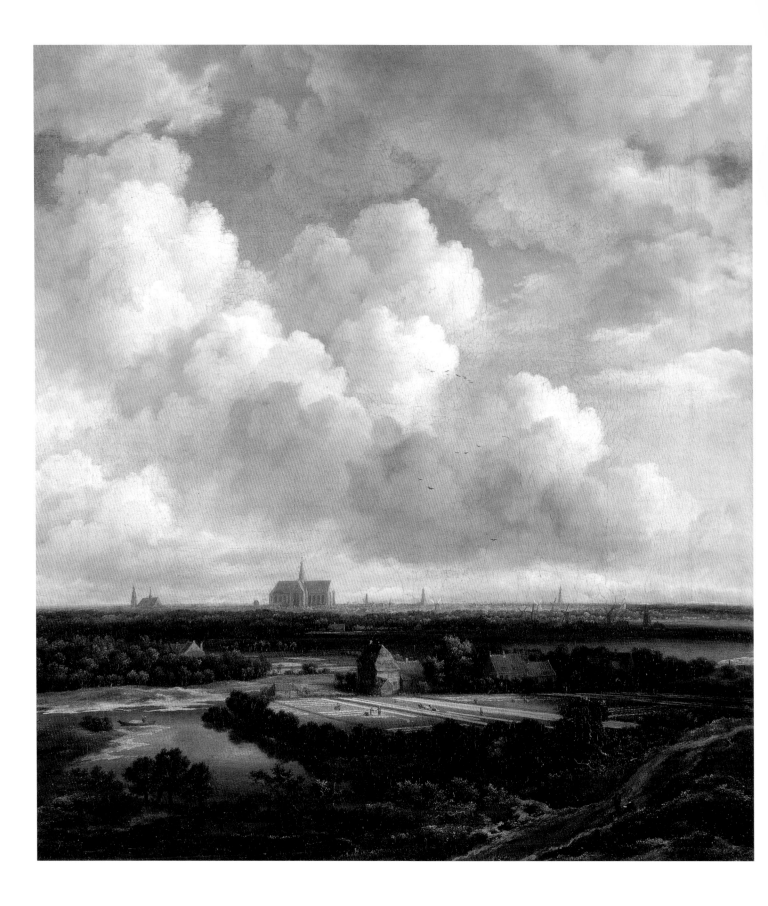

drawings, effectively transferred from the north German lowland plain to the Alpine regions. More than a decade later this image persisted in the Braunschweig painting. But the work of other artists also served as sources for motifs. The drama of this image expresses to some extent Ruisdael's tragic understanding of the world. It is not necessary to go back to contemporary emblem literature to understand the waterfall which carries everything along with it as a symbol of the transience of life. However, the castle gleaming in light high above on the rock seems to be conversing with heaven itself; the source here may be the biblical concept of the eternal city on Mount Zion.

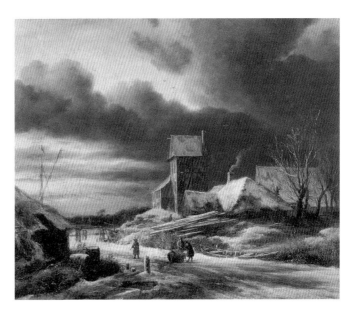

The awareness of the constant presence of death penetrates many of Ruisdael's landscapes. In his winter landscapes black and gray clouds convey a gloomy mood. The lively activity on the frozen lakes and rivers of the kind seen in the work of Hendrik Avercamp would be inconceivable in Ruisdael's melancholy winter scenes. In the *Winter Landscape* now in the Amsterdam Rijksmuseum all life seems to have come to a stop, and is positively frozen, like the boat on the shore and the ships' masts in the background. But smoke is rising from the houses, which are colored in warm tones, suggesting that life here is waiting for the spring, which seems to be heralded by the sunny blue of the opening heavens.

The symbolism in Ruisdael's work is unobtrusive, but it is offered somewhat more explicitly than in the pictures of van Goyen for example. In his *View of Leyden* sky and earth, the earthly and the heavenly spheres, seem to mingle into an inseparable unity. It suggests a different understanding of the world from that implied by Ruisdael. In Ruisdael's *Bleaching Fields near Haarlem* (see left) the separation of the two spheres is intensified. Only the town's churches, in particular the mighty Grote Kerk of St. Bavo, are able to push through the horizon and penetrate the regions of the heavens. The unusual choice of the vertical format allows Ruisdael to describe an expanse of sky which seems to promise freedom, while the human sphere of activity seems relatively very small. The two realms are linked, apart from the churches, only by the echo that the white clouds find in the gleaming areas of the outspread sheets in the bleaching fields in the foreground. In contemporary literature and in emblem books, white clean linen corresponds to the chaste souls of saints. Only those who leads virtuous and modest lives can gain entrance into heaven—such was the Christian rule of life that could be read into a simple town view.

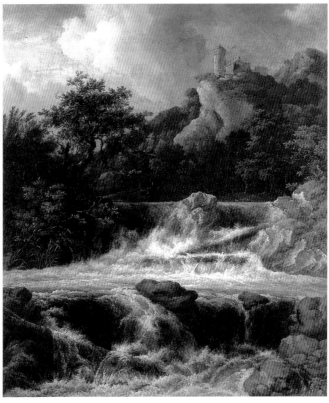

Rembrandt's landscapes express an even higher degree of moral content than is suggested by Ruisdael; they can actually be read as Christian historical paintings. Nature also served Rembrandt as a medium for certain themes. His aesthetic interest in nature itself only emerged later, particularly in drawings. The ten landscape paintings, however, were all created relatively early in his career, between 1636 and 1640. The *Landscape with Storm* (see p. 456) was painted by Rembrandt at about the same time as the *Deception*

Jacob van Ruisdael
Mill at Wijk near Duursteede,
c. 1670
Oil on canvas, 83 x 101 cm
Amsterdam, Rijksmuseum

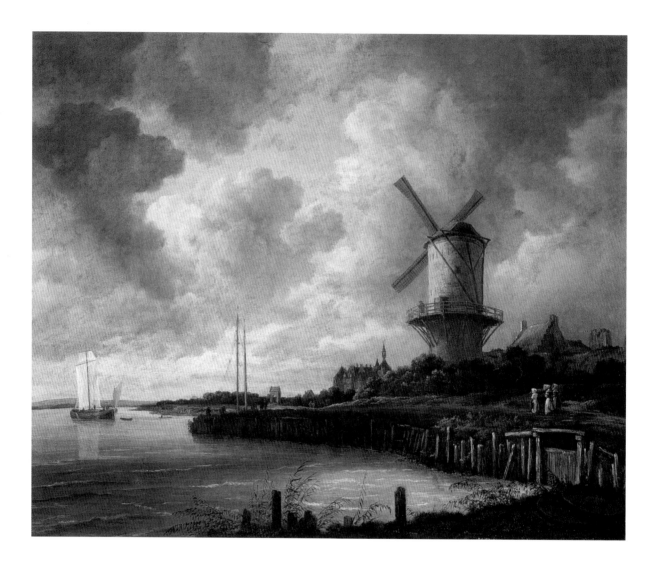

Ruisdael brings together the distinguishing elements of the Dutch landscape. At the point where land, water, and sky intersect stands the windmill; the work of mankind appears to be mercilessly exposed and unprotected from nature. This impression arises from the fact that the mill is seen from a lower point of view than the rest of the landscape; as a result it appears severely foreshortened and tipped slightly forwards. Just as the mill is exposed to nature, so mankind is subordinate to the power of God. At the moment depicted, the wind has dropped and the sailing boat lies motionless on the calm water, but the sky is turbulent, dark clouds are rising, and one last ray of sunshine falls upon the mill—soon there will be rain and thunder. This moment in time, the fixing of a particular instant, is a special quality of Dutch landscape painting, and Ruisdael brought this mood to its culminating point.

Meindert Hobbema
Avenue of Middelharnis, 1689
Oil on canvas, 103.5 x 141 cm
London, National Gallery

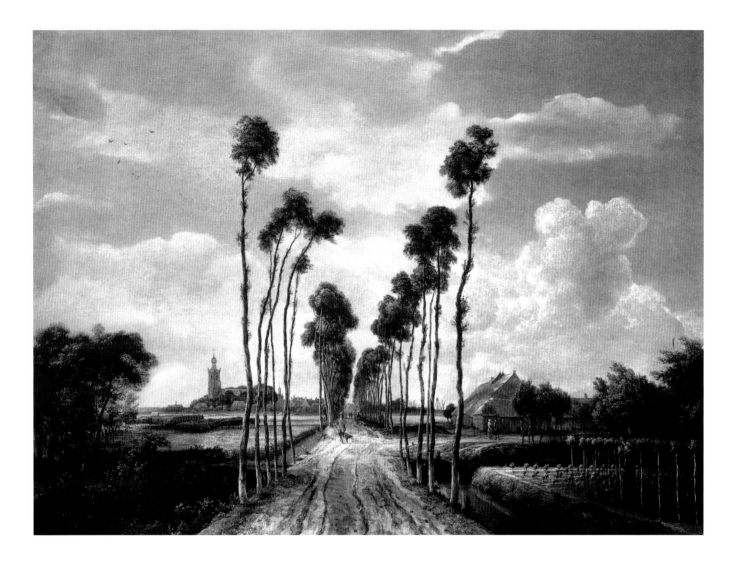

If Ruisdael's *Mill at Wijk near Duursteede* has become the representative image of the mill, then the famous *Avenue of Middelharnis* of his pupil Meindert Hobbema is the quintessential Dutch avenue. The windswept poplars assert themselves with difficulty in the broad plain, illustrating the way in which human beings have attempted to take possession of this land with rational systems. Hobbema here demonstratively abandons the diagonal model which had dominated Dutch landscape painting for years and resorts to the old central perspective. The avenue divides the picture into two parts with a striking consistency and runs in a dead straight line towards the town. The spectator is thus drawn directly into the image and has the impression of being on their way to the town, perhaps slightly elevated on the box of a coach; soon they will meet the hunter with his dog. This painting is distinguished not only by its bold composition but above all by the clean clarity of its light.

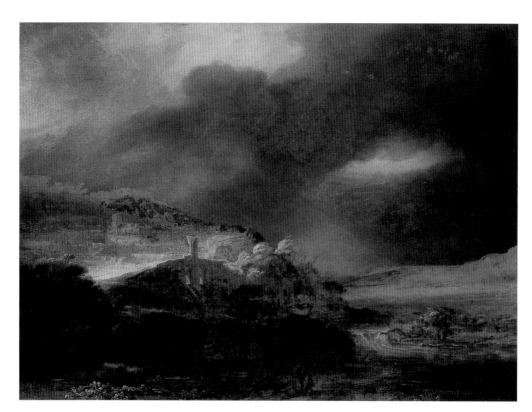

Rembrandt
Landscape with Approaching Storm,
c. 1638
Oil on wood, 52 x 72 cm
Braunschweig, Herzog Anton
Ulrich Museum

Philips Koninck
*Dutch Landscape with View from the
Dunes to the Plain,* 1664
Oil on canvas, 122 x 165 cm
Dresden, Staatliche Kunstsammlungen
Gemäldegalerie, Alte Meister

of Samson, one of his most dramatic pictures (see p. 448). The landscape illustrates such a vivid play of natural forces that the viewer might begin to see in it a manifestation of divine power. A knowledge of the use of metaphor in contemporary literature can positively transform the landscape into a religious image: a vehicle halfway to a high-lying town approaches a bridge where a waterfall rushes down the mountain. The carriage can be compared to the wandering soul searching for salvation, which shines out invitingly in the form of the brightly lit town at the top of the mountain. On its way there, the soul must leave behind the transient world, represented by the waterfall, in order to find salvation in the "heavenly Jerusalem" with Christ who is symbolized by the bridge.

However, landscape painting also offered history painters like Philips Koninck and Rubens an opportunity to dispense with moralizing content. Philips Koninck developed an unconventional form of panoramic landscape (see right). Every element seems to cowers under the sky as its clouds sweep over the land. In contrast to the Flemish landscape tradition, here the sky takes over more than half the height of the picture. Koninck boldly dispenses with any accent that might fix the image, whether in the center or at the edge of the picture. Only the reflection of the clouds in the river which runs through the scene provides any kind of focus. In spite of the path in the foreground which runs at an angle, the field of vision is no longer closed by a diagonal composition, but is built up from horizontals parallel to the picture plane, graduated in strips in the background. Here Koninck alludes to the Flemish formula, but without being tied to the color perspective. By subtle balancing of the light and dark zones he creates a wide plain which is open on all sides, but still creates a self-contained image.

Rubens, who produced a whole series of landscapes, was also indebted to the Flemish landscape model. In his *Autumn Landscape with View of Het Steen in Morning Light* (see right) the high standpoint extends the view into the distance; the town of Mechelen is seen on the horizon. Unlike Koninck, Rubens effects this aerial perspective through the use of brown, green, and blue pigments which are dissolved into delicate tones by the carefully considered treatment of light. A tall tree in the foreground to the right, which would have framed the view of the landscape in a conventional way, was evidently overpainted by the artist. Here Rubens celebrates the rich

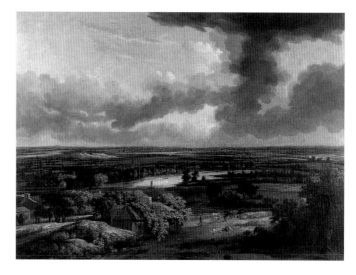

Peter Paul Rubens
*Autumn Landscape with View of Het
Steen in Morning Light*, c. 1636
Oil on wood, 131 x 229 cm
London, National Gallery

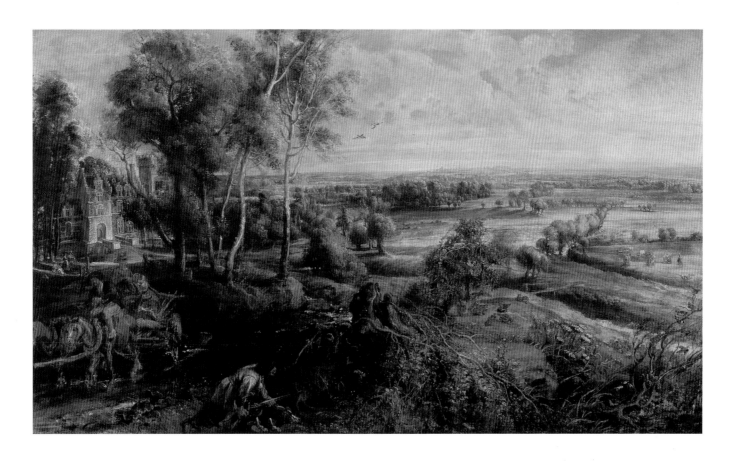

fertility of the delightful Flemish landscape on a sunny autumn morning, a scene enlivened by a wealth of narrative details. The artist had in fact just bought the country house seen on the left and he spent the last five years of his life here with his young wife and growing family. In this environment he again remembered the Flemish tradition and took pleasure in the simple life of the country, which he undoubtedly idealized, alluding in this work to the classical pastoral idiom. Life in the Flemish countryside is represented here as a lost Arcadia, a paradise on earth. The late landscapes were painted by Rubens for himself and this painting very probably hung at Het Steen. Here the painter expresses his personal feelings and his deep affection for this spot of earth; this above all differentiates his landscape from the sober Dutch approach that is exemplified by Koninck's panorama.

The English landscape painter John Constable clearly grasped this when he saw the *Autumn Landscape with Het Steen in Morning Light*, which had come into English possession at the beginning of the nineteenth century. He marvelled at the special qualities of

Rubens' landscapes—"the freshness and dewy light, the joyous and animated character which he has imparted to it, impressing on the level monotonous scenery of Flanders all the richness which belongs to its noblest features"—declaring that "in no other branch of the art is Rubens greater than in landscape."

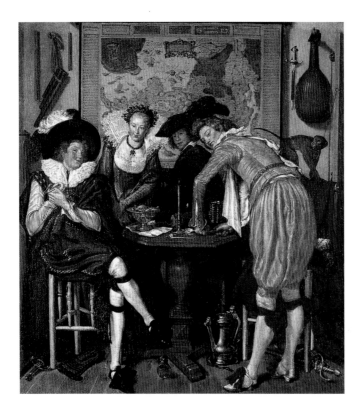

Willem Buytewech
Merry Company, c. 1620–22
Oil on canvas, 72.2 x 65.4 cm
Budapest, Museum of Fine Arts

Adriaen van Ostade
Peasant Interior with Men and Women,
c. 1635
Oil on wood, 29.1 x 36.3 cm
Munich, Bayerische
Staatsgemäldesammlungen,
Alte Pinakothek

of the picture with careful thought, and the apparently trivial scene was conceived with reference to a more profound meaning. This is an allegorical representation of the five senses, represented by everyday objects: the wine represents the sense of taste, the burning candle indicates sight, the cigar suggests smell, the musical instruments hearing, and the man's hand on the woman's arm and the bowl with the glowing ashes the sense of touch. Buytewech further describes what happens when one abandons oneself to the charms of the senses without the control of reason: the four young people are uninhibitedly indulging in the enjoyment of earthly pleasures. But this is also somewhat cryptically implied. The monkey stands for sin and sensuality, the musical instruments and the dagger in its sheath are potential erotic symbols, and the gesture of the man dressed in green is still perfectly comprehensible today. The woman with the striking lace collar is in the tradition of "Dame World"; she is the embodiment of all earthly wishes. Her traditional attribute, the globe, is replaced here by a map. The invitation from "Dame World" to give way to the worldly joys of the senses is one to which the three young men have surrendered entirely. References to such meanings which were given to everyday things are found in contemporary literature and emblem-books as well as contemporary prints from paintings, which were provided with appropriate commentaries. Next to the deceptively authentic representation of reality, the Dutch valued the game of revealing the veiled meanings of paintings—as if one were to find a big bunch of grapes under a pile of leaves, as the Dutch folk writer Jacob Cats wrote. No less was expected from such genre scenes than the highly cultured renaissance humanists anticipated from mythological representations. In

Genre

The English artist Sir Joshua Reynolds deplored the waste of the Dutch genre painter Jan Steen's talent on unworthy subjects. He could have become one of the great masters of art if instead of painting "vulgar figures," he had devoted himself to "the selection and imitation of what is great and elevated in nature." Scenes of daily life, without a historical, biblical, or mythological narrative, were regarded as essentially unworthy subjects. But genre scenes were very common in Dutch painting and very popular among the citizens. During Reynolds's time, in the eighteenth century, the more profound significance of these works was overlooked and these meanings have only been reconstructed during the last few decades. Like landscape paintings, they are sometimes explicitly, and sometimes only subliminally, thematized.

Haarlem artists initiated the first attempts to represent everyday scenes from their own time and environment. Willem Buytewech, only ten of whose paintings have survived, anticipated some of the elements of genre painting with his so-called "Merry Companies." His followers included such artists as Pieter Codde, Willem Duyster, and Dirck Hals, the brother of the great portrait painter Frans Hals. Convivial social activity had already been represented in painting in Flanders during the sixteenth century, but always as an illustration of biblical narratives such as the calling of Matthew or the story of the prodigal son. They generally showed appropriate historical dress and were thus removed from contemporary experience.

Buytewech's *Merry Company* (see above) appears as natural as if the painter had just come upon the group—the four young people seem to have been disturbed in their sociable circle by someone entering the room. In fact Buytewech has assembled all the elements

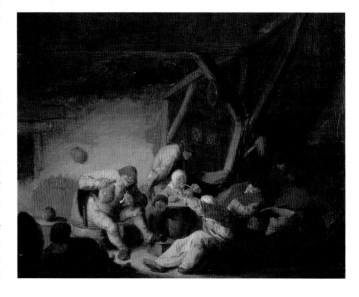

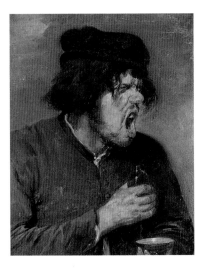

Adriaen Brouwer
The Bitter Drink, 1636–37
Oil on wood, 47.5 x 35.5 cm
Frankfurt, Städelsches
Kunstinstitut

Adriaen Brouwer
The Smokers, c. 1637
Oil on wood, 46 x 36.5 cm
New York, Metropolitan
Museum of Art

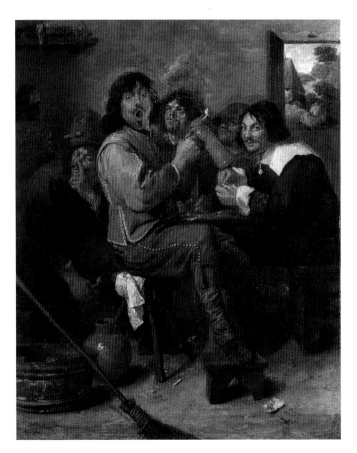

Dutch genre painting, however, only an alert mind rather than a special education was required to connect the images to everyday wisdom; the "reading of pictures" was a sport of ordinary people, not a cultured self-affirmation of the elite.

In addition to Arcadian figures and representatives of the rich upper classes, simple peasants in the inns also appeared in these works. This feature goes back to the Flemish artist Pieter Bruegel the Elder, who had depicted peasant feasts in the mid-sixteenth century. Adriaen Brouwer is considered to have successfully revived this tradition at the beginning of the seventeenth century. He influenced both the Flemish and the Dutch peasant genre and artists like Adriaen van Ostade in Haarlem and David Teniers in Antwerp. Coming from northern Flanders, he spent five of his mere fifteen creative years in Holland and then became active in Antwerp. His artistic faculties were and are highly regarded. Both Rubens and Rembrandt owned several of his works. The reception of his work is typical of the misunderstanding of Dutch genre painting. It seemed obvious that Brouwer himself should have moved in the circles depicted in his paintings. He may even have portrayed himself as a frequenter of inns—the central figure in the Metropolitan Museum painting has been seen as a self-portrait. Nevertheless his paintings are constructions, and the choice of milieu was above all dependent on artistic considerations. Brouwer painted his works in the studio, not in the public house. He may well have made studies there, but he also fell back on current types, such as those of Pieter Bruegel. The exceptional quality of his painting, the care taken with the settings, and the well-considered application of color speak against the concept of Brouwer as a good-for-nothing who was only concerned with drinking sprees.

The peasant genre often serves to belittle in moralistic fashion the fool who behaves like an animal. After all, it was not peasants who bought these paintings but well-mannered citizens who could thus observe how cultured they themselves were by contrast to these unwholesome characters. At the same time these images served as warnings against surrendering to sensual excess. Smoking or "drinking tobacco" was considered as much a sin as consuming alcohol, gambling, or sexual debauchery. Excessive consumption of tobacco was reputed to reduce male potency. Adriaen van Ostade shows how undignified a person's behavior can become if he gives way to alcohol and tobacco (see left, below).

Adriaen Brouwer, by contrast uses such scenes of excess in the first instance to illustrate human emotions. His *Smokers* (see above) could indeed be seen as an allegory of taste, but Brouwer seems mainly concerned with depicting the various reactions to unaccustomed pleasure. His characters display quite openly how they feel. They are also shown as individuals, not as types, as they are in Ostade's work. Each person brings his own story with him and his own character, which allows him to express his particular feelings. Brouwer's theme is human emotion, which he was able to represent with unique ability. His whole interest lies in the facial expression of sorrow, anger, enjoyment or disgust. In the Frankfurt painting *The Bitter Drink* (see above left) he represents a single human emotion: the deep revulsion in reaction to an evil-tasting drink. There are no accessories, no background, and no narrative suggested here—just this one emotion.

The simple milieu of the lower classes allowed Brouwer to portray human behavior in a natural manner. The citizens of the higher classes were bound by cultural constraints and could not give free rein to their emotions. This higher social group is the world of Gerard ter Borch from the obscure town of Deventer. He took genre painting into a new phase around the middle of the century, often showing well-to-do women surrounded by servants and dressed in elegant clothing. In his best paintings Gerard ter Borch never commits himself to a statement; the feelings and thoughts of his characters remain ambiguous. While Brouwer portrayed well-defined emotions, the thoughts of Gerard's *Woman Drinking Wine* are not

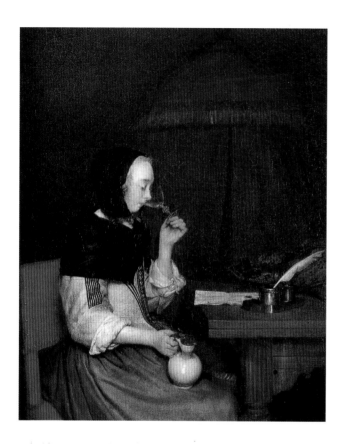

Gerard ter Borch
Woman Drinking Wine, 1656–57 Oil on canvas, 37.5 x 28 cm
Frankfurt, Städelsches Kunstinstitut

In the Netherlands there were definite ideas about the appropriate role of women. In well-to-do houses a woman took responsibility for the household and had to supervise the domestic staff. Most women understood this task as a challenge and a moral duty. A well-conducted house, after all, bore witness to the exemplary character of the lady of the house. Many paintings show that everything is turned upside down if she neglects her duties. In addition, the education of children above all was entrusted to her. Pieter de Hooch shows a young mother who has probably just finished feeding her child and is now lacing up her bodice (see right, below). It was not usual, however, for a well-off woman to nurse her own children. The folk writer Jacob Cats, whose widely read books gave advice about suitable behavior in all possible situations of middle-class life, recommended that: "One who bears children is a mother only in part, but she who nurses her children is a mother in every way." It was thought that moral and intellectual qualities were passed on with the mother's milk.

Pieter de Hooch developed a particular sense of depth in his paintings by allowing a view of the back room from the front room of a house, so that people really appeared to be moving within the interior and not in some uncertain corner of a room. The light comes not from an undefined source, but streams through the window as the bright light of day, unfolding in the house in a precisely observed treatment of light.

These initial efforts were followed by Jan Vermeer who brought Dutch genre painting to its highest level. The artist, who lived in Delft, left behind hardly more than thirty works which stand out like precious jewels from the enormous number of paintings produced during the seventeenth century. He worked very slowly and carefully, as his financial independence permitted him to do. Badly paid artists such as van Goyen, however, had to paint a great quantity of material, and therefore painted fast, in order to sell more pictures and earn a living. Vermeer had married a wealthy woman and inherited his parents' inn. Above all, however, he was regularly supported by a Delft collector and in the 1660s his paintings reached high prices. He began as a history painter, but soon turned to genre painting. Pieter de Hooch, three years older than Vermeer, encouraged the younger painter to paint spacious interiors in which the figures would have plenty of surrounding room and freedom of movement, while the theme of courtship goes back to Gerard ter Borch, whom Vermeer had met.

In the *Girl with Wineglass*, now in Braunschweig (see right, above), Vermeer opposes surrender to human urges with a call for moderation: the man in the background has succumbed to the numbing effect of tobacco, while the gentleman in the foreground is concentrating fully on the attractive young woman—surrender to wine is surrender to love. The woman in the stained glass of the window has suggested to some a depiction of temperance who shakes the reins as a metaphor for moderation. The ancestral por-

entirely obvious. Clearly she has received a letter and has now laid out her writing utensils in order to reply to it. The writing and receiving of letters is one of the great themes of Dutch genre painting. Usually it refers to amorous relationships. This is indicated in many paintings by playing-cards with hearts or—as here—the explicit depiction of a bed in the background, surrounded by a canopy. Prosperous citizens adopted from the aristocracy the game of *billets d'amour*, and advisers were consulted as to how allusions in love-letters should be properly formulated and how they should be responded to.

The drinking of wine, also a constantly recurring theme of genre painting, was considered quite simply unseemly for women of good breeding. If a woman was fond of wine, she could be easily seduced. A low neckline was a further unmistakable sign. The young woman here, however, is very modestly dressed. The spectator is moved by her evident conflict of conscience. Gerard portrays her sympathetically, well aware that everyone undergoes a similar conflict at some time between the temptations of the senses and the virtue of reason. The young woman's final decision is left open.

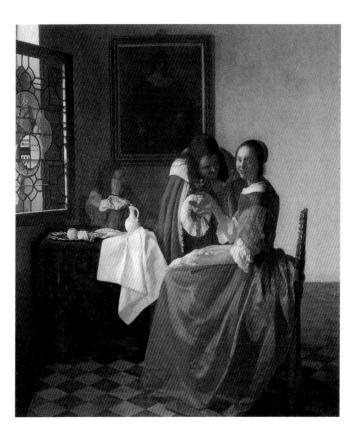

trait on the wall opposes exemplary discipline to the reprehensible behavior of the two men. It has frequently been assumed that the woman is being seduced. However, her low neckline, the provocative red dress, and ultimately her sublime indifference to her admirer and her the conspiratorial glance at the spectator show clearly that it is the woman who is in charge of the situation. She is not being seduced; it is she who is seducing the man.

From the end of the 1650s Vermeer painted indoor scenes almost exclusively, always with a window on the left-hand side through which bright light pours into the room. Obviously he chose this model because it offered the best opportunity to study and depict the effect of light on the observer's perception of space and objects. In order to examine more accurately the influence of light on objects, he occasionally used a *camera obscura* which is reflected in the characteristic luster of the highlights in his pictures. The French Impressionists were to rediscover Vermeer from a similar interest in the effects of light.

In his delicate manner of painting the Delft artist was influenced by Gerard Dou, the founder of the Leyden school of "fine painting," to which, in addition to his pupil Frans van Mieris, artists like Gabriel Metsu and Gottfried Schalcken also belonged. Dou was famous for his remarkably fine color technique which, as a contemporary remarked, often approached the smoothness of enamel. We know he used a magnifying glass for painting and hung a cloth as a canopy over his easel, so that not an atom of dust could settle in the layer of paint. Dou had studied with Rembrandt between 1628 and 1631 as one of his first apprentices. But while the master soon aban-

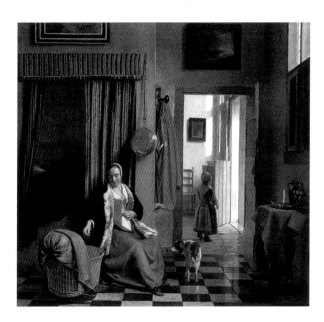

doned this smooth manner of painting, Dou developed it further into his own style of "fine painting."

Gerard Dou became one of the most successful and highly-paid artists in Holland. His reputation by far exceeded that of Rembrandt, and his art was approved by classicists. After the restoration of the Stuarts in 1660 the States General, in order to win the favor of King Charles II, presented to him with precious *objets d'art* and several paintings. These included Dou's *Young Mother* (see p. 466), reinforcing the idea that the artist was held in high esteem during this period. The painting shows the companionship between a young mother and her children in a simple setting; they are established as good role models through the luxurious effect of "fine painting." The virtuous character of the young woman is underlined by many features which have special emblematic significance.

The large academic element in the university city of Leyden cherished a particular interest in cryptic meanings or those which were complex in structure. Such cryptic meanings also marked the work of the Leyden artist Jan Steen, whose earthy peasant scenes effectively disguise the fact that they are essentially moral lectures in paint (see pp. 428-29). Steen, however, almost always included writ-

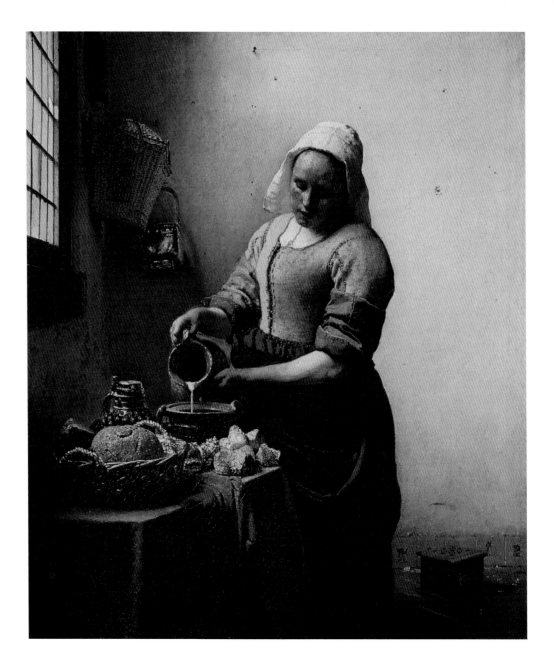

Johannes Vermeer
Kitchen Maid, c. 1660–61
Oil on canvas, 45.5 x 41 cm
Amsterdam, Rijksmuseum

This painting of a simple kitchen maid requires no anecdotal content or symbolic allusions. It grips the spectator through the physical presence of the maid, but also through her oblivious concentration on her actions. It is a mood, not a story, that is being conveyed here. The well-rounded but dignified vitality of the woman is stressed by the fact that she fills up a great part of the composition. With a full, dry brush Vermeer creates a painterly surface relief which gives her a sculptural quality. At the same time the painting is imbued with a sense of timelessness, as though the flow of milk would never end.

If Vermeer gives this earthy woman a physical heaviness, he allows the fine features of the *Woman with Scales* (see right) to appear positively Madonna-like and ethereal (she is believed to be Vermeer's wife, who bore him fourteen children). She is evidently of a higher social status, which is matched by the fine coloring of the piece. But both women, completely absorbed in their tasks, radiate an unshakable harmony— the kitchen maid in her oblivious manner, the elegant woman in her conscious effort. She holds the scales in such a precise manner that the weighing seems to take on a higher significance. This secular

activity is associated with the Last Judgment, which is depicted in the painting in the background.

Due to the numerous symbolic elements in the picture, this work has always been seen as an allegory, and gave rise to a number of inconsistent interpretations: pearls, for example, could stand for seduction by worldly luxury, but also for the purity of the Virgin. The woman in the picture, however, is weighing neither pearls nor gold, as has long been assumed; the scales are empty. Here a symbolic weighing of her own actions is intended which corresponds to the significance of the mirror on the wall at the left

464

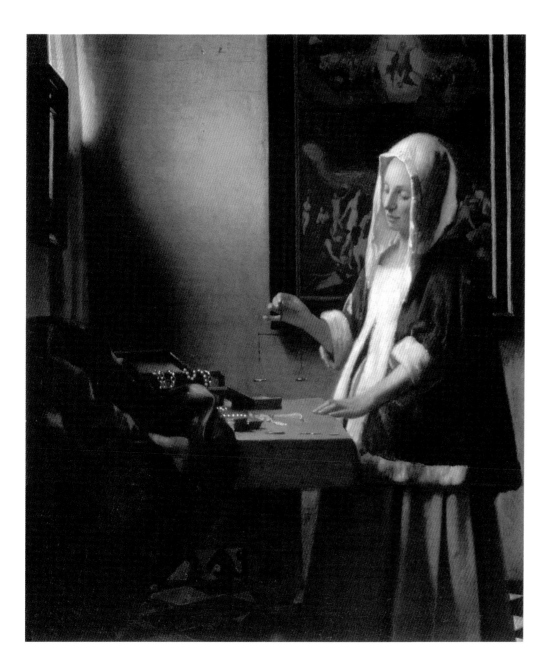

Johannes Vermeer
Woman with Scales, c. 1664
Oil on canvas, 42.5 x 38 cm
Washington, National Gallery

as a sign of self-knowledge. At the same time, however, it refers to narcissistic vanity—just like the precious objects on the table. It is essential, as the *Last Judgment* implies, to renounce vanity in the knowledge of the transience of human existence.

The woman's activity has also been related to Ignatius of Loyola. Vermeer, after his marriage converted to Catholicism, the faith of his wife, and maintained contacts with Jesuits. Ignatius had counseled weighing one's sins as though one were standing before one's judge on the day of judgment: "I shall be like the balanced scales, ready to

follow the way that leads to the fame and praise of God, Our Lord, and to the salvation of my soul." Balance, in fact, could be considered the theme of the painting: the alignment of the scales is only a symbol for this, while the composition in general, as well as the emotional state of the young woman, directly illustrate this desirable state.

Both paintings are quite remarkable in their varied handling of light: the first captivates us with the contrasting colors of yellow and blue, which were much prized by Vermeer; the other dispenses with color accents and relies for its effects on the tension between light and dark.

The face and hands of the young woman emerge from the diffused dark as if bathed in light, and framed in pure white. This positively dissolves the outlines and they seem to be wreathed in an aura. Similar effects of light can be observed on the kitchen maid, in particular on her hands and arms.

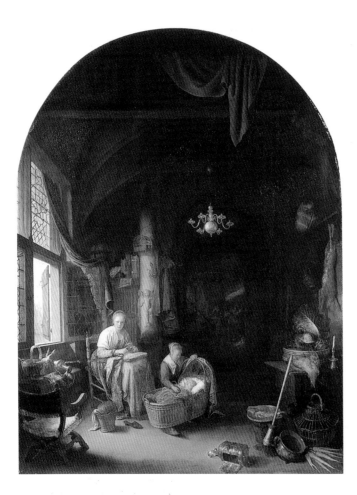

Gerard Dou
The Young Mother, 1658
Oil on wood, 73.5 x 55.5 cm
The Hague, Mauritshuis

the planks of the ceiling and blows soap bubbles which are traditionally a symbol of transience. A clock is also clearly in view on the back wall. Steen does not hold up the moralizing finger of a teacher, but concludes sympathetically that human beings are inescapably trapped by their urges as their lifespan is limited.

Sympathy for the earthy, compulsive side of human nature also marks the work of the Flemish painter Jacob Jordaens by whom Jan Steen was influenced. In 1649–50 Jordaens had furnished the summer residence of the *stadholder*, Huis ten Bosch near The Hague, with large cycles of paintings. This was possible after the Peace of Westphalia as he was a Protestant. The sumptuous furnishings of his scenes made him particularly prized in aristocratic circles. It is true, however, that the furnishings of his history paintings and the virtuosity of his technique often stand in stark contrast to the themes depicted.

In his painting *The King Drinks* (see right, below) the golden glow on the jewelery, festive dishes, and velvet robes gives the impression of a feast of noble companions. A closer look reveals that somewhat crude characters are celebrating here in a boisterous and uninhibited manner. It is the feast of the Bean King, which in Flanders was held on the feast of Epiphany. Jordaens' representation of this feast was so popular that his workshop produced a whole series of variations on this theme. The king was the guest who found the bean baked into a piece of bread. He then reigned over the table and led the entertainment. The moment is shown in which the king raises his glass and the company enthusiastically shouts "the king drinks." It was the king's task to allocate roles to the other participants in the banquet. The queen, the cupbearer, the minstrel, the doctor, and the fool had slips of paper with their new roles fastened to them, and were thus officially appointed—two of these "orders" lie on the floor in the foreground. Jordaens' model for his king, with his unmistakably striking head, was his old teacher Adam van Noort with whom the artist kept up a friendly relationship. Despite his evident sympathy for the subject, which is conveyed less by the explicit characterization of the individuals than by the fine painting and light brushwork, here Jordaens, as a cultured citizen, is essentially concerned with moderation. "Nil similius insano quam ebrius" is written in the cartouche above as a motto—nothing is more like a madman than a drunkard. Above this is the thunderously laughing face of a satyr framed by bunches of grapes and demonstrating Bacchus' mastery over the scene. It is the same theme that Rubens demonstrates in his *Drunken Silenus* (see p. 439). But while Rubens depicts a mythological figure, Jordaens illustrates the consequences of excess in a genre scene with people from his own circle, in which his contemporaries could recognize themselves.

ten sayings in his pictures in order to draw attention to the underlying message. He had to accept accusations that he was in the first instance a writer, which did not sit well with his painting. Unlike Dou, Steen was unable to live from the sale of his paintings. As an additional source of income, he therefore ran a brewery in Delft and in 1762 obtained a licence to manage an inn at his house in Leyden. As they did with Brouwer, and with as little justification, people have drawn conclusions from the paintings about the crude character of the artist. This unfavorable judgment hardly corresponds with his role as holder of several important offices and his activity in the professional association of rhetoricians. Steen painted in Leyden but also lived for a long time in Haarlem, Delft, and The Hague, where he met his future wife, the daughter of the landscape painter Jan van Goyen. In the 1660s he produced large, complex paintings which incorporate his views on humanity. In *The Life of Mankind* (see right, above) he literally pulls aside the (painted) curtain and grants the spectator a look at the stage of life. The people shown are following their impulses: some are gazing deeply into their glass, others indulging their passion for gaming, yet others flirting with each other. The inherent theme of the piece is evident from the many oysters which are being offered, eaten, and finally discarded everywhere. Oysters were considered an aphrodisiac and thus function as a sign of unfettered sexual urges. Unnoticed by the persons in the tavern room, a boy looks down at the goings-on through a gap in

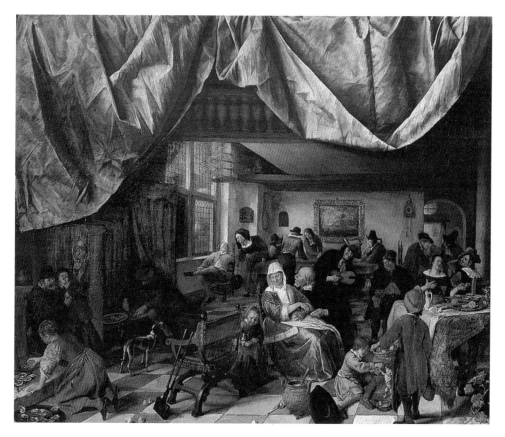

Jan Steen
The Life of Mankind, 1665
Oil on canvas, 68.2 x 82 cm

Genre painters portrayed human weakness with considerable sympathy. They shared their fellow-citizens' high-spirited love of life and enjoyment of pleasure, although in church they were constantly admonished towards restraint, reason, and discipline. Speaking the truth through laughter, as counselled by the Calvinist humanist and folk writer Jacob Cats, could be the motto of many genre paintings. To a certain extent genre painting served as social education. But while the moral sermon was painted in the most beautiful colors, the pictures themselves were a constant temptation to surrender to sensual pleasures. And the more seductive the sensuality of his paintings, the more highly prized was the painter in Holland. This deliberate ambiguity constituted the charm of genre painting.

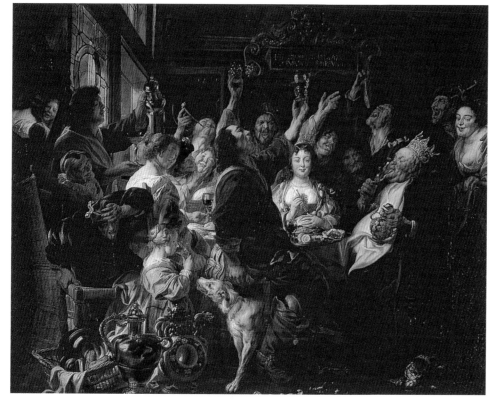

Jacob Jordaens
The King Drinks, pre-1656
Oil on canvas, 242 x 300 cm
Vienna, Kunsthistorisches Museum
The Hague, Mauritshuis

Jan Brueghel
Allegory of the Sense of Taste, 1618
Oil on wood, 64 x 108 cm
Madrid, Prado

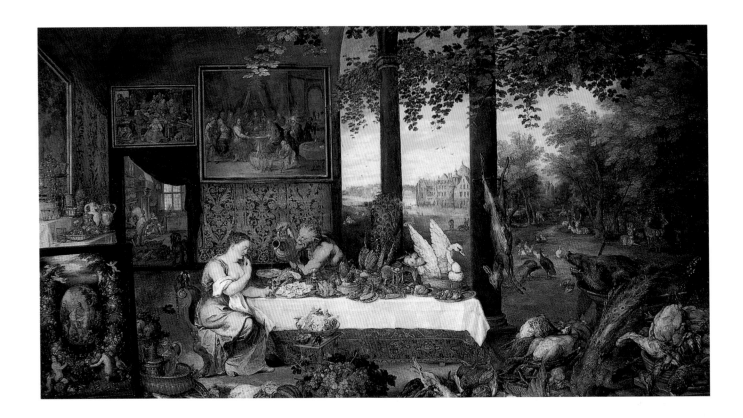

Still life

The ambiguity between seductive sensuality and moralizing content is characteristic not only of genre paintings, but also of the many still lifes which were created in the Netherlands. As a result of flourishing trade and the strength and variety of production in agriculture and business a new, rich assortment of wares became available which was to influence the lives of many people. This also inspired the depiction of consumer goods in still-life paintings. In Flanders this development had begun to emerge some time earlier, but pure still lifes were first created about 1600.

The depiction of secular objects, like landscapes and genre scenes, at first legitimized itself in the guise of history painting. A work by the Flemish painter Pieter Aertsen is dedicated to the story of Christ in the house of Martha and Mary (see right, below). The scene itself is played out only in the background, while a still life in the foreground is prominently displayed, showing a large haunch of meat, bread rolls, and flowers among other things. It is true that the story of the title serves here not only as an excuse to show a kitchen piece, but also for a confrontation between *vita activa* and *vita*

contemplativa, between Martha's leaning towards earthly things and Mary's devotion to the word of God. But the moralizing interpretation is hidden behind the presence of the secular objects which here literally take the foreground.

The new category of independent still lifes developed as kitchen pieces, market scenes, or tables laden with food took up ever more space in history paintings. Jan Brueghel unites these early forms of still-life in a sumptuous *Allegory of the Sense of Taste* (see above), part of a cycle of five paintings illustrating allegories of the senses. Here Brueghel gathers together everything that arouses the sense of taste, but is not yet ready to dispense with personification as a classic form of allegory: a female figure embodies the sense of taste. In the pure still life—as in genre painting—the objects themselves represent the various senses: musical instruments, for example, stand for hearing, flowers for smell, and foodstuffs for taste.

Around the turn of the century, Antwerp artists such as Osias Beert and Clara Peeters developed the early forms of the so-called "laid table," a sub-category of the still life, which was to be varied and further developed over the following decades. The display still

468

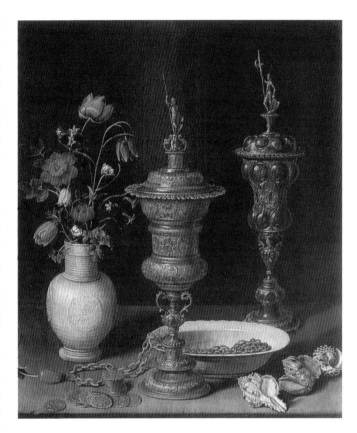

lifes are in this tradition. For special occasions display tables would be arranged in households with valuable possessions such as goblets, porcelain wares or gold and silver containers together with delicacies on a sideboard. A still life like the one by Clara Peeters (see right) is, however, not simply a copy of such a table, but was designed in conformity with the picture's own rules. This is signalled, for example, by the fact that each of the bosses on the lidded goblet reflects the image of the artist at her easel with her brush and palette. As in Flemish landscapes, a high viewpoint is adopted here and the upwardly raised horizon corresponds to the table surface, which is almost imperceptibly tipped forward. This ensures that each of the objects is easy to see. They have been arranged in such a way that wherever possible they do not overlap.

Clara Peeters was active in the second decade of the century in The Hague and Amsterdam, where she influenced still-life painting for a time; in Haarlem artists such as Floris van Schooten, Floris van Dyck, and Nicolaes Gillis also painted *ontbijtjes*, breakfast pieces, following a similar pattern. Here however, as early as the 1620s, the composition was altered in a manner which pointed the way for others. Willem Claesz Heda and Pieter Claesz abandoned the raised angle of vision and preferred to arrange the objects in an extended diagonal rising from left to right, enlivening the static structure of the composition. The pioneering invention of the diagonal in landscape painting, which can also be attributed to Haarlem, was adopted by the still-life painters. Willem Claesz Heda in his Dresden still life boldly leaves a large area of the picture's surface empty while still creating a coherent artistic scheme. In comparison to Clara Peeters' display table, the objects do not appear to have been consciously arranged. Rather there is the impression that someone has ended his meal in such a hasty manner that his wineglass has broken. In fact, here too everything has been chosen and arranged with considerable forethought.

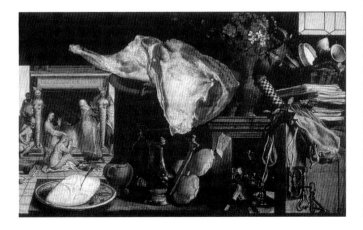

Characteristic of the Haarlem still life from the 1620s to the 1640s is almost monochrome coloration with subtle use of tones of brown, green and gray, a phenomenon which relates to the muddy landscapes of Jan van Goyen. These so-called monochrome *banketjes* present a special challenge to the artist in the reproduction of such diverse materials as those of a pie, pewter plate, silver bowl, and wineglass. Over several decades Heda used variations of the same objects in his paintings, which were nonetheless so carefully selected that they offered a view of a great variety of materials which he evidently considered an inexhaustible source of interest.

But the choice of the objects is also dependent on their higher meanings, which are again intended to transmit a moral message. As in the genre paintings and landscapes, this level of meaning is more or less explicit. The moralizing content in the so-called *vanitas* still lifes, is however, unmistakable, reminding the observer of the transience of all earthly existence. Pieter Claesz, for example, combined four *vanitas* elements at once—a pocket watch, a skull, an overturned glass, and a candleholder, with the wick of the candle just burning out (see p. 471, above). The striving after knowledge,

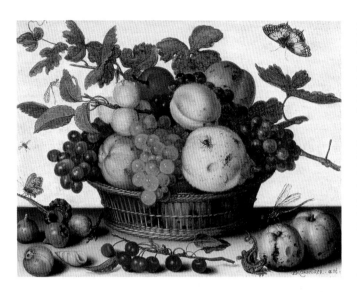

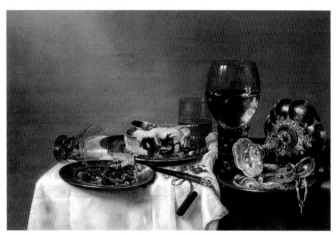

intellectual ambitions and exhorted themselves to exercise restraint. In many still lifes the Christological interpretation of earthly things which had already been associated with them in devotional pictures of the middle ages continues to have a lasting influence. There is hardly a Madonna, Annunciation, or Adoration in which flowers or fruits, animals or insects do not symbolically inform the event. In this tradition, the *Fruit Basket* of Balthasar van der Ast (see left) can be read as a confrontation between good and evil, death and resurrection. The bruises on the fruit where it has begun to rot are quite noticeable and flies, butterflies, and dragonflies flutter around them. Insects are frequently associated with the power of evil, and are seen as creatures of the devil. Opposed to these are symbols of the Resurrection: lizards, because they shed their skins, are believed to have many lives, the apple refers to Christ's taking upon himself mankind's original sin, and grapes are interpreted as the disciples of Christ since Christ referred to himself as *vitis vera*, the true vine.

Some still lifes effectively became devotional paintings: in a painting by Simon Luttichuys the few objects are arranged in a niche, which often housed pictures of saints or devotional images since the arch is considered an attribute of dignity. Wine and bread in the painting refer to the Last Supper. The stem of the wineglass consists of a skillfully formed serpent, a reminder of the original sin which was overcome by Christ.

Many special forms of still life developed, with books, fish, birds, game, kitchen equipment, or flowers, the preferences varying from place to place. Flower still lifes were produced in many areas, beginning with Ambrosius Bosschaert in Utrecht and Jan Brueghel in Antwerp and Brussels. Like the laid tables, Brueghel's painted bouquet of flowers (see p. 474, above) only appears to be as he might have found it. In fact the flowers are piled up to such a height that it would have been impossible for their stems to reach the vase. In order to show so many blooms, Brueghel would have had to spread them out on a surface but he nevertheless managed to convey the illusion of a round bouquet. It is such a finely constructed edifice, from very small flowers to large heavy blooms, that it gives the impression that the whole world of flowers has been assembled here. In fact these flowers would never in reality be seen all together in a vase, for they bloom at different times of the year: peonies and irises, tulips and roses, carnations and anemones, lilies and narcissi. Brueghel painted the flowers straight from the model, without preliminary sketching. It took a correspondingly long time for him to be able to produce a picture of this kind, for he could only paint the flowers when they were in bloom. "It is irksome," he complained, "to paint everything from nature, so I would rather make two more landscape paintings."

Many of the flowers depicted had just been introduced from distant lands and were still considered rarities in 1600. Their expensive cultivation was for a long time a privilege of the nobility. But the easily grown tulips soon became objects of speculative investment in

represented by a book, various papers, and a quill pen is set against the endless wisdom of God beside which human efforts appear vain and arrogant. In the university city of Leyden special book still lifes were created which illustrate the abundance of reading material (see right, below). Today it is astonishing to discover that as early as 1600 Barnaby Rich deplored the great number of books as one of "the great diseases of our time, which so fill the world that it is not able to digest the superfluity of worthless stuff which every day is hatched and brought into the world." Often the books in the still life themselves are clearly falling apart, and it is obvious that the paper will soon disintegrate. All knowledge is frail in view of the transience of life. Thus the scholars bore in mind the limits of their

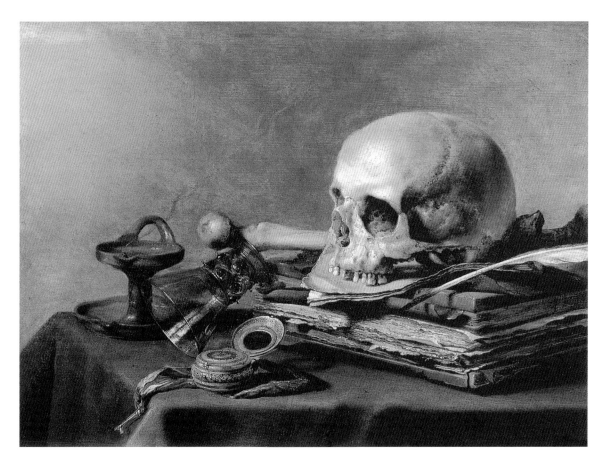

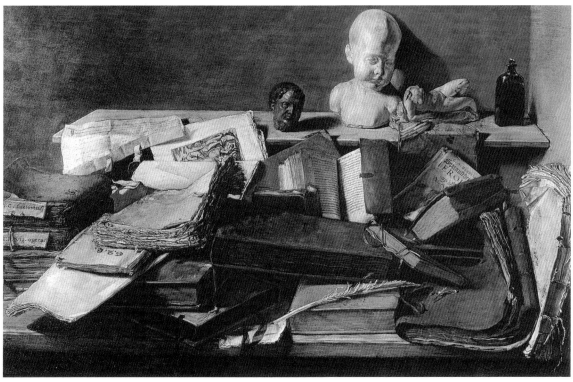

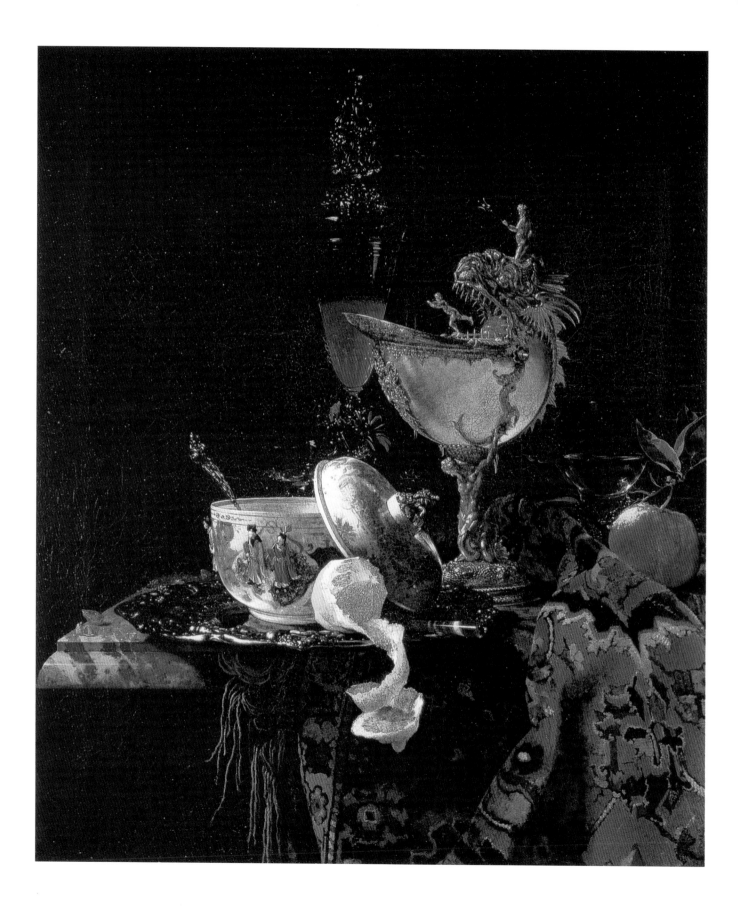

Jan Davidsz de Heem
Still Life with Fruit and Lobster, c. 1648–49
Oil on canvas, 95 x 120 cm
Berlin, Staatliche Museen,
Stiftung Preussischer Kulturbesitz, Alte Pinakothek

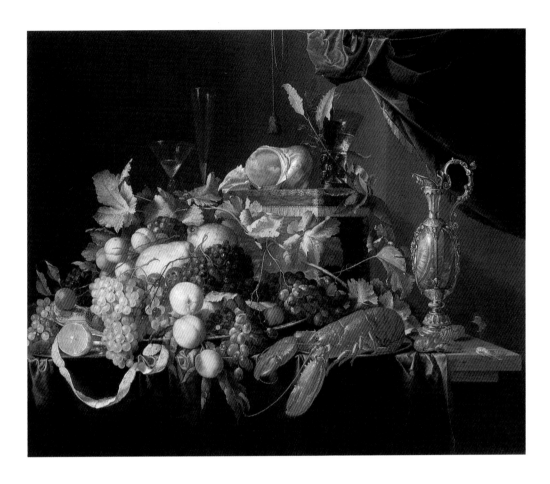

While in the second quarter of the century simple still lifes with few objects and a reduced palette predominated, the increasing wealth and self-confidence of citizens also enhanced their wish for self-representation. The new generation no longer had any reservations about displaying splendor and imitated the way of life of the aristocracy. The so-called display still lifes emerged at this time, often in very large formats and modeled on works created for the high nobility in the southern Netherlands. Jan Davidsz. de Heem at first painted in Utrecht and Leyden, but in 1636 went to Antwerp, where he found appropriate clients for his pictures. However, he remained in contact with the republic, where Abraham van Beyeren and others were following in his footsteps. De Heem's brilliant coloring and his ability in fine painting, acquired in Leyden, were unsurpassed in the field of still-life painting.

In contrast to de Heem, Willem Kalf restricted himself to a small number of objects, mainly of outstanding quality, which he used repeatedly with variations in his still lifes. The costliness of the objects corresponds to the costliness of his painting. It reaches new dimensions in the suggestion of the varied nature of the surfaces of the objects: one almost imagines oneself able to touch the rough surface of the lemon, as well as the cold smoothness of the Chinese bowl. The mother-of-pearl layer of the nautilus cup is translucent and the glass is so gossamer thin that one senses its fragility. Here too, aesthetic considerations were certainly not the definitive ones for the choice and arrangements of the objects. The lemon and wine, for example, which are shown in many still lifes, stand for the opposing characteristics of sweet and sour. Sometimes the lemon is actually placed in the glass of wine, the idea being to combine contrasting elements. This can be taken to refer to human qualities and thus illustrates a lesson for life.

Kalf allows the objects to shine out of the deep darkness with jewel-like brilliance, a characteristic which was much imitated by others. A bright ray of light seems to have found its way in, perhaps through a gap in the curtain, and illuminates the objects. In a moment, perhaps, they may subside into total obscurity.

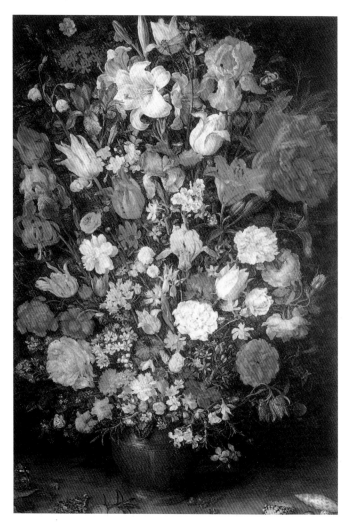

and plates were valuable as long as the majority of the population used wooden plates and cups. Thus the still lifes thematized the seduction of mankind by luxury goods and earthly charms. These are almost always opposed by an admonition about transience. Both are united in flowers. They were considered the epitome of beauty, but at the same time were short-lived and thus demonstrated the transience of earthly attractions. "Why do you gaze upon the flowers that stand so beautifully before you/ And yet through the might of the sun pass away all too fast?/ Take heed of God's word alone, that blossoms eternally./ What does the rest of the world become? Nothing" reads the inscription on a copper plate in another of Brueghel's still lifes.

The depiction of the beauty and preciousness of flowers placed high demands on the abilities of painters. "In this painting I have done the best that I am able to do," wrote Brueghel to his client, the Milanese Cardinal Borromeo. "I believe that never before have so many rare and diverse flowers been completed with such care.... Among the flowers I have painted a piece of jewelry with handmade medals and rarities of the ocean. I leave it to Your Honor to judge whether the flowers do not surpass the gold and jewelry." Jan Brueghel rendered the blossoms with great mastery as realistically as possible; they appear deceptively authentic, almost as if they could be touched and smelled.

Pleasure in illusionistic deception in imitation of nature is typical of all categories of painting in the Netherlands, but it produced positively excessive effects in the specialization of *trompe-l'œil* still lifes, known in Dutch as *bedrijghertje*. Dutch painters took up the chal-

Holland and many people tried to make their fortune from them. In the 1620s the tulip was quite simply the fashionable flower. Unusual varieties fetched astonishingly high prices. The *Semper Augustus* with red-streaked leaves and white stripes was at the top of the list; a single bulb could sell for one thousand guilders, and at the height of "tulip mania" it changed hands for four thousand guilders in cash and a coach with two dapple-grey horses worth two thousand guilders. In 1636–37 a point of extreme inflation was reached which drove many into ruin, among them the landscape painter Jan van Goyen. The Grand Council of Holland finally brought an end to this by declaring all post-1636 transactions to be invalid.

Flowers like those seen in the pictures were not affordable for everyone. The bag of game in Frans Snyders' extensive still life (see right) indicates aristocratic circles, for the hunt was a privilege of the nobility which then shared out the game to the people on their estates. Such a luxurious still life met the special requirements of the court or nobility, hanging either in dining halls, galleries, or hunting lodges. But most of the objects shown in Dutch still lifes were luxury goods anyway, above all delicacies such as lemons, pies, light-colored bread, meat, oysters, lobsters, and wine. Even pewter pots

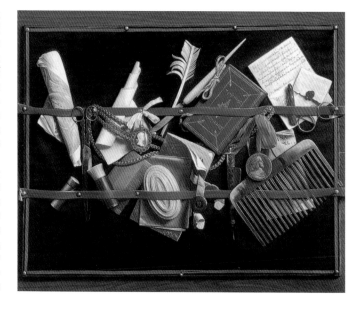

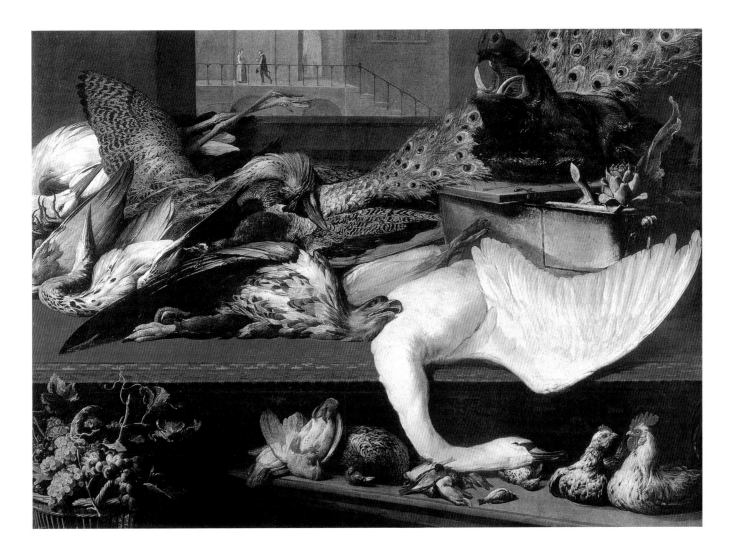

lenge of the two classical painters Zeuxis and Parrhasius, who, according to Pliny, attempted to surpass each other in their skill at illusionistic painting. Zeuxis painted grapes so convincingly that the birds tried to peck at them, but he had to recognize that Parrhasius excelled even this when he tried to pull aside a curtain in front of the latter's work which turned out to be painted. Such painted and partly drawn curtains are often found in Dutch still lifes: doors, windows, and cupboards are apparently open and nails protrude from the walls on which objects are hung.

Samuel van Hoogstraeten, a pupil of Rembrandt, also found enjoyment in *trompe l'oeil* and became a recognized master of this skill. However, he considered this type of picture only a game, while the true task of the artist lay in history painting for this required *inventio*, not merely *imitatio*. Admittedly one could achieve high esteem with the *Bedrijghertjes*. He himself had received a medal of honor from the Habsburg Emperor for a successful exercise in deception. His Karlsruhe *Pinboard* (see left, below), full of references to his life and his works, is a kind of representation of his extensive training as a painter—the spectacles symbolize the sense of sight—and as a writer—indicated by writing equipment and two of

his own plays, while the combs refer to the ordering of thoughts. With the gold chain of honor given by the Emperor and a poem of praise he openly boasts of his own talents: "You who doubt that Zeuxis' master hand/ deceived the birds with flat painted grapes, that a noble dispute could rob him of the mastery/ through the work of a more delicate brush and a white painter's garment,/ come and see Hoochstraet! The ruler of all the world/ falls into the same error through the art of his brush."

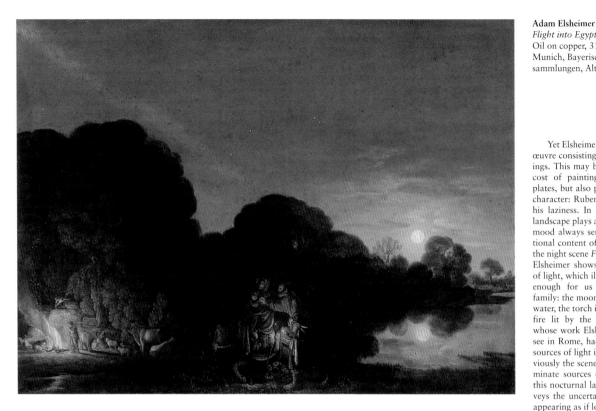

Adam Elsheimer
Flight into Egypt, 1609
Oil on copper, 31 x 41 cm
Munich, Bayerische Staatsgemälde-
sammlungen, Alte Pinakothek

Between the Netherlands and Italy: Germany in the Seventeenth Century

"Now we are wholly, indeed more than wholly, devastated!
The throngs of impudent folk, the raging trumpet,
The sword thick with blood, the thundering cannon royal,
Have consumed all our sweat and work and provision.
The towers stand in flames, the church is turned upside-down,
The council hall lies in horror,
The strong ones are mown down,
The maidens are dishonored,
And wherever we look is fire, plague, and death, which drives through heart and spirit."

Germany in the seventeenth century was dominated by the events of the Thirty Years War. Andreas Gryphius' poem *Tears of the Fatherland* of 1636 illustrates the extent of the destruction. After the Peace of Westphalia of 1648 it took the whole of the second half of the century to overcome the consequences of the devastation. Only slowly did art begin to flourish again and it was not until the late baroque and rococo periods that Germany was to experience a cultural blossoming. In southern Germany and Austria in particular, artists such as Johann Michael Rottmayr, Cosmas Damian Asam, Johann Baptist Zimmermann, and Franz Anton Maulpertsch developed their own solutions from the type of ceiling painting that had been invented in Rome.

But in the seventeenth century there were a number of active artists of German origin. The painter Joachim von Sandrart collected their biographies in his *German Academy of the Noble Arts of Architecture, Sculpture, and Painting* of 1675. In their native land they certainly had few opportunities. As a result of the war, there was a lack of teachers and collectors, and young aspiring artists found themselves obliged to go abroad. German artists were frequently regarded as members of the Dutch or Italian schools. The northern Germans Jürgen Ovens and Christopher Paudiss studied with Rembrandt and the genre painter Matthias Scheits from Hamburg with Philips Wouwerman in Haarlem. Later they were again able to work in Germany. Govaert Flinck's German origin has, however, been largely forgotten. He is considered one of the important history and portrait painters of Holland, who for a time was thought by his contemporaries superior to Rembrandt, whom he trained under. However, Flinck was actually born in Klev on the lower Rhine. Caspar Netscher from Heidelberg, a pupil of Gerard ter Borch, is numbered among the Dutch genre painters, and Ludolf Bakhuysen, born in Emden in East Fresia, is considered an Amsterdam marine painter. The circle of *Bamboccianti* (see p. 375) active in Rome included Johannes Lingelbach and Johann Heinrich Roos, the first from Frankfurt, the second from the Palatinate. Both had received their training in Holland, where Lingelbach had for a time painted stock figures for Jacob van Ruisdael. Jan Both, one of the most important Dutch Italianists, attracted German pupils in Rome such as Johann Franz Ermels and Wilhelm van Bemmel. Bemmel founded a family of landscape painters in Nuremberg which continued over several generations.

While many of the great Dutch masters hardly traveled and developed their style in confrontation with the tradition of their city, German artists seem to have responded to a variety of stimuli, even from several different countries. Their work is correspondingly difficult to categorize, and a specifically German version of baroque painting could not have developed in these circumstances. Some individual artistic personalities created their own style of art and exercised great influence on other artists.

Among these, Adam Elsheimer is by far the most important. This painter, who came from Frankfurt, went via Venice to Rome, where he worked for ten more creative years before he died at the age of thirty-two in 1610. In Rome he had contacts with Dutch artists and in particular with the landscape painter Paul Bril and with Rubens. Rubens was not the only artist to admire Elsheimer's work. His pictorial inventions, which were dispersed throughout Europe in the form of engravings, were the foundation of some of the essential elements of baroque composition.

Yet Elsheimer left behind only a small œuvre consisting of scarcely thirty paintings. This may be attributed to the high cost of painting on miniature copper plates, but also probably to the painter's character: Rubens, at any rate, deplored his laziness. In many of his works the landscape plays an important role, but its mood always serves to convey the emotional content of the story being told. In the night scene *Flight into Egypt* (see left) Elsheimer shows three different sources of light, which illuminate the picture just enough for us to recognize the holy family: the moon and its reflection in the water, the torch in Joseph's hand, and the fire lit by the shepherds. Caravaggio, whose work Elsheimer had been able to see in Rome, had been the first to show sources of light in the picture itself—previously the scene had been lit by indeterminate sources outside the painting. In this nocturnal landscape, Elsheimer conveys the uncertainty of the holy family, appearing as if lost under the wide starry sky, but also the confidence which will enable them to travel on and soon spend the night with the shepherds in a sheltered spot.

In addition to Elsheimer, Johann Liss, twenty years his junior, is considered one of the most important German painters of the seventeenth century; he too was active mainly in Italy. During his fifteen creative years Liss assimilated a great number of different artistic sources which he had observed during his years of journeyman travels: in Haarlem the genre painting of Buytewech, in Antwerp the art of Jordaens, but also of Jan Brueghel, in Paris the coloring of Valentin de Bourgogne, in Rome the monumental half-length figures of Caravaggio, Feti, and Strozzi with their dramatic effects of light and dark, but at the same time the careful fine painting of Elsheimer in his small formats. His work is not only stylistically confusingly rich, but also diverse in subject matter: genre scenes, religious and mythological scenes, miniature paintings, monumental half-length pictures, and large altarpieces. Sandrart, who stayed with Liss in Venice in 1629, could not decide which of the diverse pictures he should prize the most. In Venice, where Liss worked for the last years of his life, he produced paintings which were far ahead of their time. They were to have a considerable impact on rococo painting in the eighteenth century.

This is particularly true of a work like the *Inspiration of St. Jerome* (see right), which Liss painted for the church of S. Nicolò dei Tolentini in Venice where

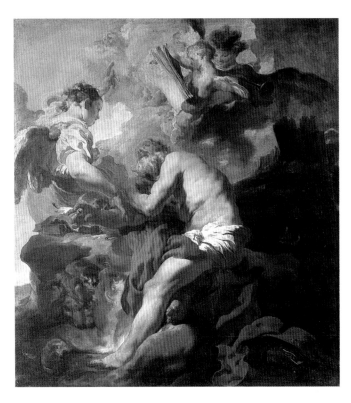

Johann Liss
Inspiration of St. Jerome, 1627
Oil on canvas, 225 x 175 cm
Venice, S. Nicolò dei Tolentini

it still hangs in the place for which it was painted. The Venetian travel guides of the seventeenth and eighteenth singled out the painting for special praise, and it was copied many times; Fragonard, for example, made an etching after it. The coloring is unusual for the early seventeenth century as it is dominated by pastel tones which did not become popular until the rococo, but the most innovative aspect of the composition lies in the fact that it is not built out of the figures, but is based completely on the ensemble of color surfaces. Thus a continuum of color is created in which the earthly and heavenly spheres mingle with each other. In this way Liss reflects the importance of the moment depicted, in which St. Jerome becomes aware of the divine power. Between light and shadow a rich spectrum of subtle color tones is opened out, enlivened by a vibrant brushwork which links Liss to the great Venetian painters of the late sixteenth century and which was conveyed to artists who were to introduce a second flowering of Venetian art: Piazzetta, Ricci, and Tiepolo.

A third German painter of European status is Johann Heinrich Schönfeld. He spent eighteen years in Italy, mainly in Naples. In his work Schönfeld skillfully combined such opposite qualities as elegance and drama, charm and theatricality. His formative years in Rome owed less to the powerful Roman baroque than to the fine classicism of Nicolas Poussin—but his scenes have a lighter and more free effect. Schönfeld's figures are elegantly elongated, appearing light-footed and slender. His colors are correspondingly delicate, carried by the gentle basic color of the hazy atmosphere of the background. The highly diverse gray-blue tones belong to Neapolitan painting, as does the muddy darkness, which is dramatically lit up by bright shafts of light and diagonal shafts of light. Magnificent processions such as those shown in Schönfeld's *Triumph of David* (see below) were very popular in the baroque era and were staged at every possible opportunity. Schönfeld was able to experience them in Naples at the court of the Spanish viceroy.

Next to the commercial city of Augsburg, where Schönfeld was active for another thirty years after his stay in Italy, Frankfurt, as one of the most important trade centers of Europe, was also a major artistic center. Here great auctions were held, for the rich citizens were also potential art buyers. Georg Flegel from Bohemia found his clientele here. He is considered the most important German still-life painter, with an outstanding talent for reproducing the surface quality of a wide range of materials, as in the *Cupboard Picture* (see p. 478,

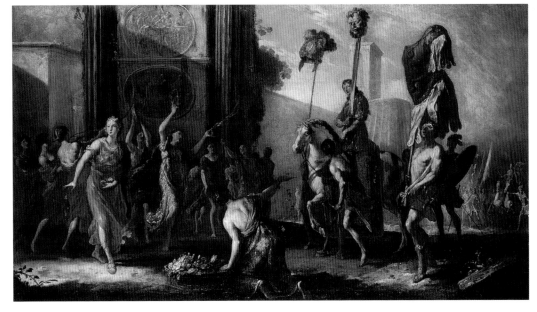

Johann Heinrich Schönfeld
Triumph of David, 1640–42
Oil on canvas, 115 x 207 cm
Karlsruhe, Staatliche Kunsthalle

477

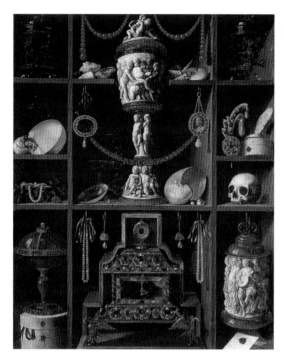

Georg Flegel
Cupboard Picture with Flowers, Fruit and Goblets, c. 1610
Oil on canvas, 92 x 62 cm Prague, National Gallery

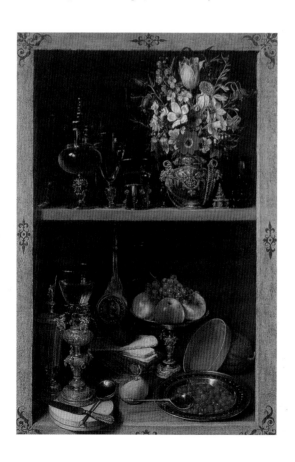

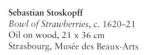

Georg Hinz
Kunstkammer Shelves, 1666
Oil on canvas, 114.5 x 93.3 cm
Hamburg, Kunsthalle

Sebastian Stoskopff
Bowl of Strawberries, c. 1620–21
Oil on wood, 21 x 36 cm
Strasbourg, Musée des Beaux-Arts

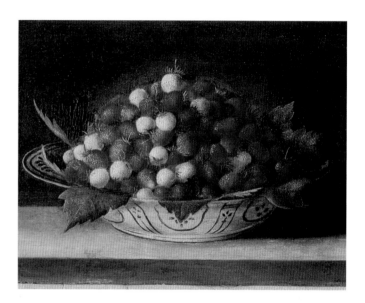

above right), which unites all the gifts with which a host would honor his guests. This tradition, inherited from classical times, may possibly have been known to this humanistically educated painter from Philostratus' *Imagines*.

Flegel developed his painting style in confrontation with the Flemish tradition which was present in Frankfurt and Hanau where a large community of Protestant refugees from Flanders had been taken in. In Hanau a new town had been founded in 1597 especially for immigrants; Daniel Soreau, a painter from Antwerp, had been involved in its planning. Here he founded a special school of still-life painting. In addition to his sons Isaak and Peter, his workshop included Peter Binoit as well as Sebastian Stoskopff who came from Strasbourg, and who took over the workshop on his teacher's death.

Stoskopff's individuality lies in the clear structure and strict composition of his paintings; he often limited himself to a few objects, such as a bowl of strawberries, for example (see above), in which he celebrates the sheer wonder of color. With this isolated illustration of a few objects in a painting, Stoskopff influenced French still-life painters such as Jacques Linard and Louise Moillon in Paris, where he lived for many years.

Hamburg offered similar economic conditions to those in Frankfurt, and here too artists found their clients. The still-life painter Georg Hinz developed

the individual category of *Kunstkammer Shelves* (see above left), unique in the whole of European still-life painting. It is a *trompe-l'œil* cabinet piece, a picture imitating a set of shelves. Various objects are tidily stored here, just like those that the princely and bourgeois collectors of the baroque liked to gather together in their cabinets of curiosities. Rare objects stand beside valuable and wonderful ones, artifacts are measured against naturalia. The *Kunstkammer Shelves* of Georg Hinz represented an attempt at an encyclopedic understanding of the world by means of representative objects. At the same time, however, the choice and combination is also at the service of the central theme of the era: an admonition about the transience of earthly splendor and the promise of resurrection after death.

Anthony Van Dyck
Sir Endymion Porter and Van Dyck,
c. 1635
Oil on canvas, 119 x 144 cm
Madrid, Prado

Anthony Van Dyck
Charles I on Horseback, c. 1635–40
Oil on canvas, 367 x 292.1 cm
London, National Gallery

Anthony Van Dyck in England

While German artists could look back on a tradition of great masters from Dürer to Holbein, painting was first developed as a significant medium in the British Isles only in the seventeenth century. Around 1680 an interest in the subject emerged that established the foundations for the subsequent golden age of English painting from Hogarth to Turner. But up to the eighteenth century foreign painters were dominant in England, and commissions were almost exclusively limited to portrait painting. The influence of Hans Holbein the Younger, who had been active at the English court during the 1530s, remained decisive for several generations. His followers included Nicholas Hilliard under Elizabeth I; his iconic, emphatically two-dimensional portrait type was finally replaced by the styles of Dutch painters such as Paul Somer, Cornelis Johnson, and Daniel Mytens. Their work introduced the more realistic Dutch portrait to the English court. In 1632, exactly one hundred years after Holbein, Anthony Van Dyck, a pupil of Rubens, arrived in London. His style was to define English portrait painting up to the death of Sir Thomas Lawrence in 1830.

Van Dyck was recruited by King Charles I, who can be described as the first great art patron among British rulers. His interest in art was inspired to some extent by Rubens' nine-month stay in London. The artist had come on a diplomatic mission but the king preferred to discuss art rather than politics with him and his wish to obtain the services of Rubens' pupil Anthony Van Dyck as court painter was reinforced by the visit. James I had already promised the young painter an annual income after a short stay in England in 1620, which meant that in practice he had already entered royal service. Nevertheless he soon set off for Italy to continue his education and then tried to establish himself in Antwerp. But as long as Rubens continued to exercise his enormous influence there, it was not possible for Van Dyck to develop an independent artistic personality. Thus Charles finally succeeded in bringing him to the court. Charles offered exceptional conditions, and Van Dyck was attracted by court life. Unlike Rubens, who deliberately avoided taking a noblewoman as his second wife, he married Lady Mary Ruthven, a member of the queen's closest circle.

In his self-portraits Van Dyck liked to portray himself as an aristocratic personality. He had a well-defined sense of the exquisite, of worldly sophistication and aristocratic refinement. His friendship portrait with Endymion Porter (see left) is the only one in which he depicted himself with another person. Porter, as adviser to the king in artistic matters, played a decisive role in finally binding Van Dyck to England. The portrait emphasizes Porter's gentle, friendly character and the warmth of his affection. The close connection between the painter and the king's confidant is symbolized by

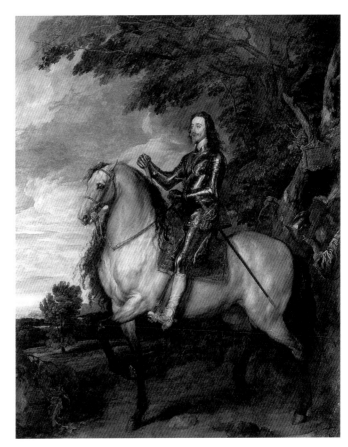

the hands of the two men, which rest closely together on a rock—an image of the indestructibility of their friendship. In the ten years which remained to Van Dyck before his early death, he painted forty portraits of Charles I alone, and thirty of his consort Henrietta Maria. Commissions from the aristocracy began to multiply.

His position at the court is comparable to that of Velázquez in Spain; both were highly esteemed and well-paid members of the court, and both were ennobled. Paradoxically Charles was interested in Van Dyck above all because he saw him as the true heir of Titian. He admired the Venetian prince of painters especially because of his impressive portrait of the great Emperor Charles V, whom he saw as a role model. Van Dyck justified the king's expectations: the equestrian portrait (see above), for exam-

ple, is clearly based on Titian's painting of Charles V on horseback. Charles is presented as Carolus Rex Britanniae, as is announced by the notice attached to the tree, ruler of all Britain. The armor and the horse shown in motion lend him an aura of energy and decisiveness, and his steady gaze conveys dignity and nobility. It is a conscious idealization of the king, who had very precise ideas about how a monarch ought to present himself without in fact possessing the abilities of a great ruler.

Van Dyck's portraits in England epitomized a certain aristocratic manner. His rich palette contributed to this, as did the loose brushwork which enlivened the portraits despite their static poses. He gave his subjects an obvious dignity; they radiate pride and elegance and, with a touch of melancholy, maintain the elective nature of their status. At the same

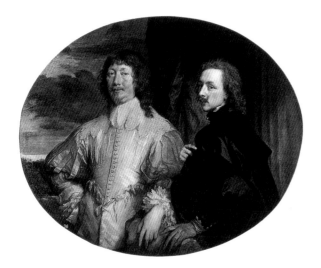

Anthony Van Dyck
Philip, Lord Wharton, 1632
Oil on canvas, 133 x 106 cm
Washington, National Gallery

Peter Lely
Louise de Kéroualle, c. 1671
Oil on canvas, 121.9 x 101.6 cm
Malibu, J. Paul Getty Museum

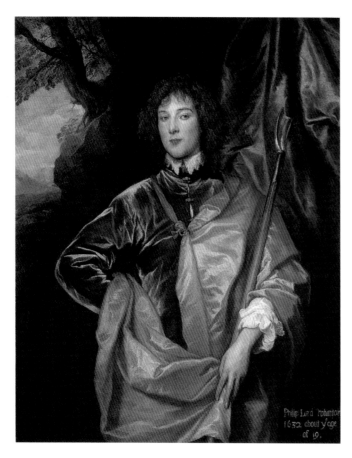

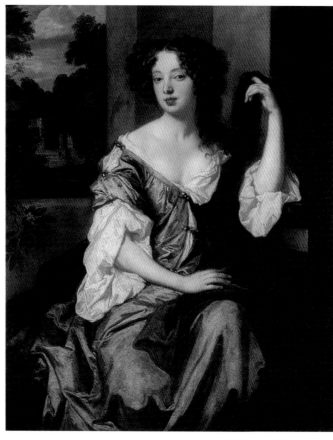

time Van Dyck did not rely on significant attributes, but was able to attain an appropriate aura by gaze and posture alone.

The nineteen-year-old Philip Lord Wharton was one of the first people to be portrayed by Van Dyck in England (see above). The gentle tones of the landscape lend particular delicacy to the noble features. The clear reference to Arcadia suggests Neoplatonic ideals of beauty and idyllic love; here Van Dyck was alluding to the occasion for the portrait, the marriage of the young lord.

The king's court painter was ultimately so constrained by time that he had to speed up his painting methods. The French writer Roger de Piles reports that Van Dyck arranged specific consultations; each client was allowed exactly an hour for a sitting, then the brushes were

rinsed out and another palette taken up for the next client. In this way Van Dyck was able to work on several portraits at the same time. But the idyll of a peaceful and prosperous existence which is expressed in many of his portraits was deceptive. The Civil War loomed—in 1649 Charles was to be beheaded. The influence of Van Dyck was already enormous in Genoa, Antwerp, and Amsterdam, but in England above all every portraitist was soon imitating his style.

Van Dyck's most important follower was Sir Peter Lely, the first court painter to the restored monarchy. He was also foreign by birth. Born in Soest, Westphalia, he had studied in Haarlem and came to London in the early 1640s. Van Dyck's work was a constant source of inspiration to him. His portrait of

Louise de Kéroualle, the mistress of Charles II, emphasizes Lely's brilliant technique. Like Van Dyck, however, he did standardize his portraits to some extent for the sake of high volume. Van Dyck, in spite of the enormous demands placed on him, had developed an individual pose for each of his clients in order to give them some element of individuality.

Appendix

Glossary

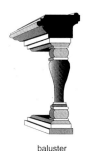

baluster

acanthus: a type of ornament based on the thick scalloped leaves of a Mediterranean plant; used in classical architecture to decorate the capital of Corinthian columns.

aedicule: the framing of a door, window, or niche with two columns or pilasters supporting an architectural device such as an entablature and pediment

aisle: in a church, parallel to the main span and divided from it by an arcade of piers or columns

alcázar (Arab./Sp.): a term used to describe a fortified palace, usually a closed construction consisting of four wings

allegory: the use of figures or elements in a work of art to symbolize a higher meaning, moral or religious

alternate support: alternation of columns and piers

amphitheater: circular or oval arena with rising tiers of seats

anagogic (Gr.): literally "leading upward"; interpretation of a text that finds in it a higher spiritual or mystical sense

anthropomorphic: the ascribing of human form or attributes to non-human things

apartment: suite of rooms in a grand house or residential building

apotheosis: deification, transfiguration of a person

apotropaic: intended to avert evil

appartement double (Fr.): double suite of rooms

apse: a semicircular or polygonal extension, usually to a chancel or chapel

arcade: a series of arches carried on piers and columns

arch: curved covering section over an opening in a wall which appears in a variety of shapes

arch forms: commonly used in baroque: round arch, basket arch, lancet arch, segmental arch, flying buttress

architrave: horizontal stone beam which supports the frieze and cornice in the classical entablature

archivolt: continuous architrave molding of the face of an arch

artes liberales (Lat.): the seven liberal arts: grammar, dialectic, and rhetoric (the trivium), music, astronomy, arithmetic, and geometry (the quadrivium)

ashlar: natural stone worked on all sides

Atlas (pl. Atlantes): support for an entablature in the form of a male full or half-length figure

atrium: in the Roman period an open inner courtyard; in early Christian and medieval architecture a colonnaded forecourt of a basilica

attic: a storey above the main entablature of a building in strict architectural relationship to it, the space within the sloping roof of a house

auricular: developed in the late sixteenth and early seventeenth centuries, with a smooth undulating surface resembling parts of the human ear

auto da fé: "act of faith"; the announcement and execution of a sentence passed by the Inquisition

azulejo (Sp./Port.): colorfully painted and glazed wall or floor tiles

baldacchino (It.): canopy or roof-like structure over a throne, altar, tomb, doorway, etc.

baluster: thick supporting post with profiled shaft, *see left*

Bamboccianti: an artistic movement of the seventeenth century dedicated to representing the everyday life of Rome in a naturalistic non-idealized manner; from the nickname "Bamboccio" [deformed puppet or buffoon] given to its founder, the Dutch painter Pieter van Laer

Bandelwerk (Ger.): scrollwork

Banketje (Dut.): painting showing a meal

baptistery: a free-standing building (generally central-plan) for performing baptismal rites, often separate from the main church

barocchetto (It.): term applied to the Italian variation on rococo art in the second and third quarters of the eighteenth century

barrel vault: see vault forms

base: profiled foot of a pillar or column, between the shaft and the plinth

basilica: originally Roman market-hall or meeting hall; in Christian architecture, a church divided into a nave and two or more aisles lit by the windows of a clerestory

bas-relief: low relief

bay: a vaulted section of a room

bedrijghertje (Dut.): illusionistic (see *trompe l'œil*)

binding-vault: supporting arch running diagonally to the longitudinal axis of a vault

bodegón (Sp.): still life

boiserie (Fr.): wooden paneling or wainscoting; the term is more specifically applied to seventeenth- and eighteenth-century paneling decorated with low-relief carvings

bosquet: pleasure grove, group of bushes and shrubs in an informal part of a garden

boss: an ornamental knob or projection covering the intersection of ribs in a vault or ceiling; often carved with foliage

bozzetto (It.): rough oil sketch; also plaster or wax model for sculpture

broderie (Fr.): literally embroidery; general term for decorative pattern; in a garden, a boxwood hedge

Calvinism: the theological system of the Franco-Swiss reformer Jean Calvin (1509–64) and his followers, marked by strong emphasis on the sovereignty of God, the sinfulness of mankind, and the doctrine of predestination

Camarín (Sp.): chapel-like room behind or above the high altar of Spanish churches

canonization: enrolment in the canon or list of saints

capela-mor (Port.): main chapel, usually choir chapel in Portuguese churches

capital: the head or crowning feature of a column; *see* diagram p. 484

capriccio (It.): in art, works characterized by a freedom of handling, a rejection of hierarchies of genre and form, and, above all, the supremacy of fantasy

cartouche (Fr.): scroll or escutcheon; a decorative motif which became popular during the Renaissance showing a framed panel with scrolled edges and a concave or convex central section

castle: originally for defense, later (as palaces) the residence of a ruler or noble, designed to impress with its grandeur, baroque types *see* diagram below right

castrum doloris (Lat.): funerary structure, usually richly decorated, for the lying in state of a high-ranking person

catafalque: temporary ornamental funerary sculpture

cathedral: bishop's church (*Dom* or *Münster* in German, *duomo* in Italian)

centralized structure: a building which is circular, polygonal, or in the form of a cross with arms of equal length

chapel: small room used for sacral purposes, free-standing or part of a larger church

chapter house: place of assembly for abbot or prior and members of a monastery for the discussion of business; usually situated in the eastern part of the cloister

chartreuse (Fr.): Carthusian monastery where the monk's cells are separate small rooms connected only by the cloister

cherub (pl. cherubim): in Christian iconography, belonging to the highest order of angels and representing divine wisdom

chiaroscuro (It.): literally, "light-dark"; in painting, the technique of modeling form by almost imperceptible gradations of light and dark

choir: the part of a church where divine service is sung, usually part of the chancel

choir, monks': a separate space in a monastery church reserved for the monks, furnished with choirstalls

church forms: *see* diagram below

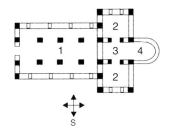

S

1 Nave and side aisles
2 Transept
3 Crossing
4 Choir

Churriguerismo (Sp.): florid late baroque architecture named after the Spanish Churriguera family of artists

Cinquecento (It.): sixteenth century

classicism: collective term for styles of art based on those of Greek and Roman antiquity

cloister: open rectangular courtyard of a monastery or convent, surrounded by roofed or vaulted passages and connecting the church with the domestic parts of the monastery

coffering: form of ceiling decoration for a vaulted or flat ceiling consisting of sunken square or polygonal ornamental panels

collage: a work of art assembled from a variety of materials

college: an institution of higher education; a building used for educational or religious purposes; a body of clergy supported by a foundation

colonnade: row of columns carrying an entablature or arches

colossal order: order of columns of pilasters rising through several storeys (also called giant order)

column: supporting member of circular section, consisting in classical architecture of base, shaft, and capital

communs (Fr.): outbuildings of a French noble residence for the accommodation of the domestic staff or for administration

composite order: late Roman combination of elements from the Ionic and Corinthian orders; see orders of architecture

conch: a semicircular niche surmounted by a half-dome

corbelling: a continuous projecting course of stones supporting beams or other horizontal members

cornice: projecting ornamentation along the top of a building, wall, arch, etc.; in classical architecture the top projecting section of an entablature

corps de logis (Fr.): the main building or residence as opposed to the wings or pavilions in grand houses

cross, stations of the: sculptural and architectural representations of Christ's journey to Mount Calvary, ending with the crucifixion

Dome resting on a tambour

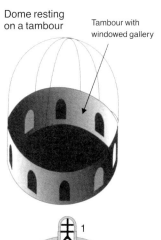

Tambour with windowed gallery

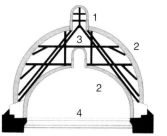

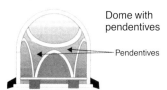

1 Lantern   2 Dome covering **a** interior **b** exterior
3 Suspension   4 Tambour

Dome with pendentives

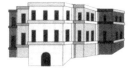

Pendentives

Palace types

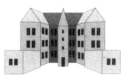

Italian

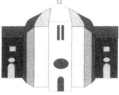

French hôtel

Austrian

Church forms:

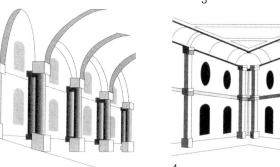

1 Gallery basilica
2 Hall church
3 Single-aisled church
4 Central-plan church

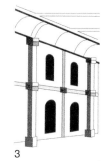

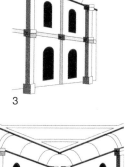

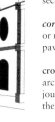

483

crossing: in church architecture, the space at the intersection of the nave, chancel, and transept

cross-vault: a vault produced by the intersection at right angles of two tunnel vaults of identical shape

crypt: in a church, a chamber or vault beneath the main floor, not necessarily underground, usually containing tombs and relics

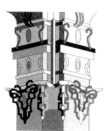  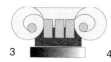

1 Decorative baroque capital
2 Rococo capital
3 Doric capital
4 Ionic capital
5 Corinthian capital
6 Tuscan capital

couleur (Fr.): color, application of color

cour d'honneur (Fr.): literally "court of honor"; principal part of the baroque palace, enclosed by the wings of the building

cupola: a small dome on a circular or polygonal base crowning a roof or turret

decorum, *decoro* (It.): literally decoration; in art theory, the notion of appropriateness in design

diamond cut: dressed stone the surface of which is cut like that of a diamond; used as facade decoration in the Renaissance and baroque

diaphanous: of such fineness and delicacy of texture that it is almost transparent

dilettante (Fr.): an admirer and amateur practitioner of the arts

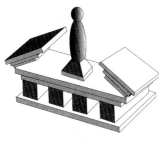

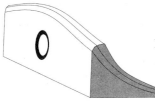

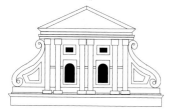

disegno (It.): term which describes the practice of draftsmanship but also embodies renaissance traditional art ideals of artistic invention and originality

dome forms: forms of the dome used in the baroque include the tambour and pendentive; *see* diagram p. 483

donjon, keep: central defensive tower of a castle occupied as a residence when under siege or permanently

Doric order: *see* orders of architecture

dormer: vertical window in a roof with a roof of its own

dormitory: sleeping quarters of a monastery

eclecticism: mixture of various historical styles

egg-and-dart: classical ornamental molding consisting of a pattern based on an alternation of egg forms and arrowheads

emblem: symbol consisting of three elements: 1. icon (an allegorical image); 2. *lemma* (inscription); 3. *subscriptio* (explanaltion); *see* pp. 428–29

Empore (Ger.): gallery-like construction in church interior; its function is to separate certain groups (courtiers, women) during the holy service

en face (Fr.): opposite

enfilade (Fr.): suites of rooms on one axis

entablature: upper part of an order consisting of architrave, frieze, and cornice

entre cour et jardin (Fr.): situated between courtyard and garden

entrée solonnelle (Fr.): ceremonial entry

epiphany (Gr.): appearance or manifestation, especially of a divine being or perception

estilo desornamentado (Sp.): term used for the "unornamented" Spanish architecture created under the influence of Juan de Herrera

estípite (Sp.): in Spanish architecture, a supporting member tapering downwards

exedra: in classical times a semicircular or rectangular recess with raised seats; also an apse opening onto a larger space

facade: the front face of a building

false facade: a facade attached for design purposes to the front of a building which does not correspond to its construction

fan vault: type of vault consisting of a number of ribs radiating out from the support or from a central point

figura serpentinata (It.): term for a twisted human figure, seen predominantly in mannerist art

filler: material in undressed stone and mortar used to fill spaces between walls

flagellant: member of a religious brotherhood whose purpose was self-flagellation

fluting: vertical grooves in the shaft of a pillar or column

flying buttress: a horizontal arch between the upper part of a wall and an outer support

frieze: middle division of an entablature below the cornice and above the architrave; also long narrow horizontal panel or band used for decorative purposes; *see* temple

gable: usually a decorative termination or a saddle roof, a window, or aedicule; triangular, stepped, or in arch form; the tympanum or area enclosed by the gable often supports sculptural decoration; *see* diagram left

gallery: originally a roofed passage open on one side; in palace architecture, an extended ceremonial hall; from the nineteenth century a roofed shopping arcade

genre (Fr.): literally type, kind; in art, a representation of everyday life

giant order: see colossal order

Gothic revival: neo-gothic movement predominant in Britain during the eighteenth and nineteenth centuries

Greek cross: a cross with arms of equal length

hall church (Hallenkirche, Ger.): a church with several naves of equal height

half-timbering: method of construction of walls built of interlocking wooden posts, beams, and props; the spaces between them are filled with non-structural walling such as lath and plaster, wattle and daub

helm roof: roof with four inclined faces joined at the top, with a gable at the foot of each

herm: bust on a pillar base

hermitage: small garden structure in imitation of a hermit's retreat

hipped roof: *see* roof forms

historie (Ger.), *histoire* (Fr.), *historia* (Sp.), *storia* (It.): literally story; in art history, term used for the narrative content of a work of art

history painting: representation of historical/mythical subjects

holy of holies: in ecclesiastical architecture a separate space for the altar or sacrament

horror vacui (Lat.): horror at the sense of a physical or spiritual vacuum

hôtel (Fr.): French term for a town house or mansion

iconography: study of images or symbols associated with a subject

idea (It.): design of the content of a work of art

imitatio (Lat.): imitation

Ornament

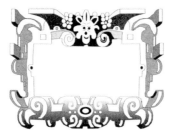

Scrollwork

Bandelwerk

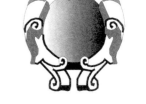

Cartouche

immaculata conceptio (Lat.): Immaculate Conception

impost: molding between the top of a pillar or pier and an arch, often in combination with a capital

impresa: image representing a concept in cryptic form; often combined with a motto; *see also* emblem

Inquisition: the Catholic church's inquiry into heresy and the preservation of religious belief

intercolumniation: space between columns, measured in diameters

inventio (Lat.), **invenzione** (It.): literally invention, the concept of the content of a painting

Ionic order: *see* orders of architecture

Isabelline: late Gothic style of architecture and decoration named after the Spanish Queen Isabella I (1451–1504)

Jansenism: after the Dutch theologian Cornelius Jansen the Younger (1583–1636), a religious and moral reform movement, mainly in the Netherlands

keep: central defensive tower of a castle occupied as a residence

keystone: stone in the apex of an arch or rib vault, sometimes carved

lambrequin: textile hanging with tassels or lace

lancet arch: *see* arch forms

landscape garden (English garden): the informal parkland schemes of early eighteenth-century English gardens, in contrast to the geometric formality of the baroque garden

lantern: window at the top of a dome to light the space below

Latin cross: cross with vertical and horizontal arms of different lengths

lintel: the beam which supports the wall above a window or door, sometimes decorative, often in gable form

loge: gallery opened to an interior space; box, as in the theater

loggia: arcade or open arched hall at ground level or on the upper floor of a building

lucarne: opening in an attic or a spine, often richly decorated

lunette: semicircular space above doors and windows

maison de plaisance (Fr.): country mansion for the court, a temporary summer pleasure house

mannerism: artistic style in Europe of the late sixteenth century, characterized by a "mannered" quality incorporating spatial incongruity and sometimes the elongation of the human figure

mansard roof: roof form named after the French architect Mansart with a double slope, the lower one longer and steeper than the upper one; *see* roof styles

mansion: also called town house, *see* palace diagram p. 483

Manueline: a style of decoration of the late Gothic to early Renaissance periods in early sixteenth-century Portugal; named after Manuel I (1469–1521)

martyrium: a church or other building erected over the tomb relating to a martyr

masonry bond: natural or artificial stone or brickwork laid according to a variety of traditional patterns

mausoleum: term deriving from the tomb of King Mausolus of Halicarnassos (completed 353 BC) used for monumental tomb structures

memento mori (Lat.): "remember thou must die"; saying taken from an Alemannic poem as a reminder of the transient nature of life, often interpreted as an image during the baroque period

metamorphosis (Gr.): transformation

monastery: residence of a community of monks since the early Christian period; the monastery complex includes the church, open courtyard (cloister), meeting-hall (chapter hall), dining hall (refectory), sleeping quarters (dormitory), and other functional buildings

monolith: column, pillar, or other architectural feature made from a single block of stone

monopterus: building with a single row of columns on all sides

narthex: vestibule leading into a Byzantine church; also transverse vestibule preceding nave and aisles

nave: central, middle section of the western limb of a church, flanked by aisles

neo-classicism: term used to denote recent versions of antique classicism, particularly during the period 1760–1830

nocturne: night piece; painting with the theme of night or moonlight; also the emphasized contrast between darkness and artificial lighting

nymphaeum: shrine to nymphs; usually a multi-storey structure of pillars with niches and water-basins

obelisk: a monolith erected on a square base which tapers upwards into a pyramidal form; form of monument arising from the architecture of ancient Egypt which remained popular up to the nineteenth century

octagon: eight-sided structure or design

oculus: circular window opening

ontbitje (Dut.): still life representing breakfast scene

orangery: a garden building for growing oranges with large windows on the south side, often arched

oratory: gallery in the choir of a sacral building; also a private chapel

orders of architecture: for baroque and classical forms; *see* diagram

ornament: geometric, figurative, or abstract decoration; *see* diagram

palace chapel: the sacral room within a palace reserved for the ruler and their family

Palladian motif: also known as a Venetian or Serlian window; a taller and broader central archway or window flanked by two narrower openings, surmounted by an arch

Palladianism: a style derived from the buildings and publications of Andrea Palladio; Inigo Jones introduced the style to England in the seventeenth century, but the great Palladian revival began there in the early eighteenth century under Campbell and Burlington

panneau (Fr.): framed field with painted, sculpted or ornamental decoration

paseo (Sp.): promenade, walk

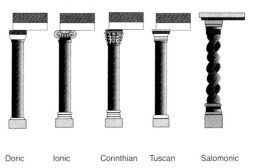

Doric   Ionic   Corinthian   Tuscan   Salomonic

paso (Sp.): procession; also a portable devotional painting carried in a procession

pavilion: a projecting subdivision of a larger building; also ornamental building often used as a pleasure-house

pedestal: plinth, base of statue

pendentive: a concave spandrel leading from the angle of two walls to the base of a circular dome; one of the means by which a circular dome is supported over a square or polygonal compartment

pendentive dome: dome erected above pendentives

pergola: stepped framework; also an open avenue

peripteros (Gr): temple arranged with a circle of columns

peristyle: hall of columns which surrounds a building or courtyard

Pfalz (Ger.): medieval palace of princes who had no fixed residence

piano nobile (It.), **belle étage** (Fr.): main storey of a house

pier: a solid masonry support without the entices (curvature) of the classical column, but which can also have a base and capital

pilaster: shallow pier projecting only slightly from the wall; in classical architecture conforms with one of the orders

pitched roof: *see* roof styles

place royale (Fr.): literally royal square, a monumental square built in one style, usually with the statue of the ruler; in seventeenth-century France it attained a particularly imposing significance in the planning of the town

plafond: flat ceiling

Plateresque: from the Spanish word *platero*, silversmith, term used to denote an ornate architectural style popular in Spain during the sixteenth century

plaza mayor (Sp.): a regular-shaped, imposing town square, usually surrounded by porticos; *see also* place royale

polychrome: multi-colored

polygonal: many-sided

portico: roofed space, open or partly enclosed, forming the entrance of the facade of a temple, house, or church, often with columns and a pediment; *see* diagram below.

presbytery: the part of the church which lies east of the choir where the high altar is placed; in the middle ages the often raised ceremonial room used by a priest

propylaea (Gr.): entrance to a temple area, term used since classical period

proscenium: raised front part of a stage

quadratura: illusionistic architectural painting of ceilings and walls

quadro riportato (It.): freestanding painting marked out by a frame within a wall or ceiling painting

querelle de anciens et des modernes (Fr.): debate conducted in the late seventeenth century at the Paris Académie Royale about the relationship between the classical and the modern as well as about the value of *dessin*, contour and color; linked to the contrast between the painting of Nicolas Poussin and that of Peter Paul Rubens.

raptus: group or painting depicting a robbery or abduction scene

redoute (Fr.): ballroom

reducción (Sp.): in Spain's American colonies, an Indian community set up under ecclesiastical or royal authority to facilitate the conversion of Indians to Christianity, to protect them, and to teach them better farming methods and simple crafts; best known are the Jesuit *reducciones* in Paraguay and Argentina

refectorium (Lat.): refectory, dining-hall of a monastery

repoussoir (Fr.): in painting, object or figure in the foreground which leads

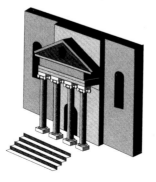

Church spires

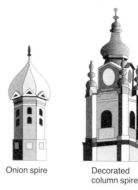

Onion spire   Decorated column spire

the observer into the picture and suggests spatial depth

respond: a half-pier banded into a wall and carrying one end of an arch

ressaut (Fr.): a particularly accentuated element of a building which projects from the outline of a wall, frequently in the center of a building

retable: a superstructure on the rear of an altar, often monumental in form and painted or carved

retrato a lo divino (Sp.): image of a saint with portrait-like features

reveal: the inside of a door-frame; also soffit, intrados

rib: element of a gothic vault; skeletal framework on which the non-load-bearing panels are built up; the rib became decoratively elaborated during the late gothic period

rocaille: (Fr.): literally shellwork; deriving from the rock and shell forms of grotto decorations; one of the most important decorative forms of rococo

rococo: a light frivolous style of decoration devised in France which spread throughout Europe during the early eighteenth century; characterized by asymmetrical or curvilinear forms including c-scrolls and s-scrolls, rock work, shellwork, and delicate scrollwork, sometimes incorporating exotic motifs

Romanism: trend in sixteenth-century Dutch art influenced by Roman painting

roof forms: *see* diagram

rose window: circular window designed in the form of a rose and subdivided by tracery

rotunda: building built on a circular plan, usually domed

rustication: stonework with massive blocks, smooth or rough-hewn, separated by deep joints; normally used to give a sense of solidity and bold texture to the lower part of a building

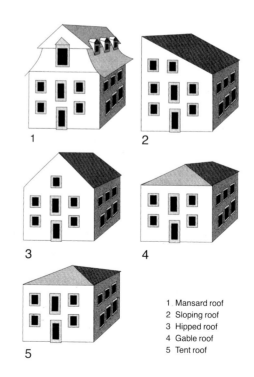

1. Mansard roof
2. Sloping roof
3. Hipped roof
4. Gable roof
5. Tent roof

486

sacristy: side-room of a church used for the priest to put on his vestments and for the storage of liturgical vessels

Salomonic: barley-sugar column found in baroque architecture; named after its use in the temple of Solomon in Jerusalem; *see* orders of architecture

saddle roof: *see* roof forms

sanctuary: holiest space in the church, generally the choir with the altar

Schilderbent: a community of Dutch painters in Rome founded in 1620 by Cornelis van Poelenburgh and Bartholomeus Breenbergh

segment: section of a circle

segment gable: *see* gable forms

Seicento (It.): seventeenth century

Settecento (It.): eighteenth century

skeleton, or frame construction: method of construction consisting of a framework and an outer covering which has no load-bearing function

spires: *see* diagram

still life: representation of inanimate or motionless objects; also called *nature morte* (Fr.), *natura morta* (It.)

Stoicism: the philosophy of the Stoics (c. 300 BC) which held that the wise man should be free from passion, unmoved by joy or grief, and submissive to natural law

summer palace: from the Renaissance a palace in an attractive rustic or garden setting, for use as a place of relaxation and entertainment

soprapporta (It.): a painting above the door of a room; usually framed in harmony with the doorcase

tabernacle: a canopied recess to contain an image or the host; a free-standing canopy

tambour: circular wall carrying a dome or cupola

tempietto (It.): literally little temple; often a small circular temple in a landscaped garden

temple: non-Christian devotional building, particularly in classical antiquity; the classical temple facade had a great influence on the design of baroque facades

tenebroso (It.): literally dark; painting with strong contrasts between light and dark, and stark highlights

thermae: Roman public baths with bathing rooms of different temperatures, steam baths, and recreation rooms

tholos: beehive-shaped chamber built of stone and roofed corbelling

three-winged style: basic form of the baroque palace with *corps de logis* and side wings enclosing the *cour d'honneur*

tondo: round painting or relief

tower facade: facade constructed with one or more towers; since medieval times a favored motif and majestic form in devotional architecture

transept: the transverse arms of a cross-shaped church

transubstantiation: according to Roman Catholic dogma, the transformation of bread and wine into the body and blood of Christ at their consecration

trefoil: three-lobed design; style of church architecture with three semicircular or polygonal apses arranged in the form of a clover leaf

Tridentine: of the Council of Trent (1543–63), focus of the Counter-Reformation

trionfo (It.): triumphal entry or departure of a ruler; also the artistic or literary representation of this event

triumphal arch: in classical times a monumental arch to honor an emperor or victorious general; in a Christian church, the arch between the nave of the choir and the crossing; sometimes applied as a secular decorative motif

trompe l'œil (Fr.): literally deception of the eye; a manner of representation intended to suggest that the observer is looking at a real object; in baroque, frequently used to demonstrate the virtuosity of the artist

Tuscan order: *see* orders of architecture

tympanum: area between the lintel of a doorway and the arch above it; also the triangular space enclosed by the moldings of a pediment

undressed stonework: wall- made of layered, irregular, unworked stone

urbanism: the study of town planning

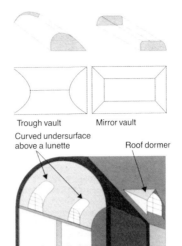

Trough vault   Mirror vault

Curved undersurface above a lunette   Roof dormer

Barrel vault with curved undersurface above a lunette and roof dormer

vanitas: work of art intended to remind the observer of the transience of life

vault: an arched roof or ceiling of stone or brick, sometimes imitated in wood or plaster

vault forms: trough vault, mirror vault, barrel vault; *see* diagram

veduta (It.): topographically correct city view or landscape painting

vestibule: anteroom

villa: originally a country residence, since the Renaissance designed as a palace

villa suburbana (Lat.): villa on the edge of town

volute: a spiral scroll on a Ionic capital

votive painting or structure: painting or structure dedicated to the fulfillment of a vow

voute (Fr.): ceiling molding

wall-pier church: single-nave church with inserted buttresses with chapels between them

window types: distinguished by the shape of the opening: rectangular, arch of circular; in French architecture windows are occasionally shaped like doors

Zwinger (Ger.): area between the front and main wall of a fortress; in Dresden interpreted as a baroque form of architecture

Bibliography

The bibliography is arranged according to the sequence of the main contributions to this volume. It combines references to the literature used by the respective authors with suggestions for further reading. This arrangement inevitably leads to occasional repetition of titles. Needless to say, in each case only a very limited selection has been possible.

**BARBARA BORNGÄSSER/
ROLF TOMAN**
Introduction

Alewyn, Richard: Das große Welttheater. Die Epoche der höfischen Feste, Munich 1989
Alpers, Svetlana: Kunst als Beschreibung. Holländische Malerei des 17. Jahrhunderts, Cologne 1985
Bauer, Hermann: Barock. Kunst einer Epoche, Berlin 1992
Burckhardt, Jacob: Der Cicerone (reprint of original edition), Stuttgart 1986
Burke, Peter: Ludwig XIV. Die Inszenierung des Sonnenkönigs, Frankfurt 1995
Busch, Harald (ed. Lohse Bernd): Baukunst des Barock in Europa (4th edn), Frankfurt am Main 1966
Croce, Benedetto: Der Begriff des Barock. Die Gegenreformation, Two essays, Zurich 1925
Dinzelbacher, Peter (ed.): Europäische Mentalitätsgeschichte, Stuttgart 1993
Elias, Norbert: Die höfische Gesellschaft, Neuwied, Berlin 1969
Haskell, Francis: Maler und Auftraggeber. Kunst und Gesellschaft im italienischen Barock, Cologne 1996
Hubala, Erich: Die Kunst des 17. Jahrhunderts (Propyläen-Kunstgeschichte, vol. 9), Berlin 1972
Huizinga, Johan: Holländische Kultur im 17. Jahrhundert, Frankfurt am Main 1977
Kaufmann, E.: Architecture of the Age of Reason, Harvard 1955
Keller, Harald: Die Kunst des 18. Jahrhunderts (Propyläen-Kunstgeschichte, vol. 10), Berlin 1971
Kultermann, Udo: Die Geschichte der Kunstgeschichte, Frankfurt 1966
Lavin, Irving: Bernini and the Unity of Visual Arts (2 vols), New York, London 1980
Möseneder, Karl: Zeremoniell und monumentale Poesie. Die "entrée solennelle" Ludwigs XIV in Paris, Berlin 1983
Norberg-Schulz, Christian: Barock (Weltgeschichte der Architektur), Stuttgart 1986
Norberg-Schulz, Christian: Spätbarock und Rokoko (Weltgeschichte der Architektur), Stuttgart 1985
Pevsner, Nikolaus: Europäische Architektur (7th edn), Stuttgart 1985
Riegl, Alois: Die Entstehung der Barockkunst in Rom, Vienna 1908
Tintelnot, Heinrich: Zur Gewinnung unserer Barockbegriffe, in: R. Stamm (ed.), Die Kunstformen des Barockzeitalters, Munich 1956. 13–91
Tintelnot, Heinrich: Barocktheater und barocke Kunst, Berlin 1939

Weisbach, Werner: Der Barock als Kunst der Gegenreformation, Berlin 1921
Wölfflin, Heinrich: Renaissance und Barock. Eine Untersuchung über Wesen und Entstehung des Barockstils in Italien, Basle 1888
Wölfflin, Heinrich: Kunstgeschichtliche Grundbegriffe. Das Problem der Stilentwicklung in der neueren Kunst, Munich 1915
Zapperi, Roberto: Der Neid und die Macht. Die Farnese und Aldobrandini im barocken Rom, Munich 1994

WOLFGANG JUNG
Architecture and the city in Italy from the early Baroque to early Neo-Classicism

An architectural progress in the Renaissance and Baroque. Sojourns in and out of Italy. Essays in architectural history, presented to Hellmut Hager on his sixty-sixth birthday; University Park, Philadelphia, 1992
Architettura e arte dei gesuiti, eds. R. Wittkower and I.B. Jaffe, Milan 1992
Argan, G.C.: Studi e note dal Bramante a Canova, Rome 1970
Argan, G.C.: Borromini, Milan 1978
Argan, G.C.: Immagine e persuasione. Saggi sul Barocco, Milan 1986
Il Barocco romano e l'Europa, eds. di M. Fagiolo and M.L. Madonna, Rome 1992
Bassi, E.: Architettura del Sei e Settecento a Venezia, Naples 1962
Von Bernini bis Piranesi. Römische Zeichnungen des Barock, revised by Elisabeth Kieven, Stuttgart 1993
Blunt, A.: Some Uses and Misuses of the Terms Baroque and Rococo as applied to Architecture, Lectures on Aspects of Art, Henriette Hertz trust of the British Academy, London 1975
Blunt, A.: Neapolitan Baroque and Rococo Architecture, London 1975
Blunt, A.: Roman Baroque Architecture: The Other Side of the Medal, in: Art History 3, 1980, 61–80
Borromini, F.: Opus architectonicum, ed. M. de Bendictis, Rome 1993
Brandi, C.: La prima architettura barocca. Pietro da Cortona, Borromini, Bernini, Bari 1970
Bruschi, A.: Borromini: manierismo spaziale oltre il Barocco, Bari 1978
Burckhardt, J.: Der Cicerone. Eine Anleitung zum Genuss der Kunstwerke Italiens (reprint of original edition), Stuttgart 1986, particularly Der Barockstil, 346–85
Connors, J., S. Ivo della Sapienza. The First Three Minutes, in: Journal of the Society of Architectural Historians, 55:1, March 1996, 38–57
Connors, J.: Borromini's S. Ivo della Sapienza: the Spiral, in: Burlington Magazine, vol. 138, Oct. 1996, 668–82
Essays in the History of Art, presented to Rudolf Wittkower, ed. by Douglas Fraser, Howard Hibbard, and Milton J.Levine, London 1967
Contardi, B.: La Retorica e l'Architettura del Barocco, Rome 1978
Gallacini, T.: Trattato di Teofilo

Gallacini sopra gli Errori degli Architetti, Venice 1767
Guarino Guarini e l'internazionalità del barocco. Atti del convegno internazionale, 2 vols. Turin 1970.
Hager, H. and Munshower, S. (eds): Architectural Fantasy and Reality, Drawings from the Accademia Nazionale di San Luca in Rome, Concorsi Clementini 1700–1750, University Park, Philadelphia, 1982
Hager, H. and Munshower, S. (eds): Projects and Monuments in the Period of the Roman Baroque, "Papers in Art History from the Pennsylvania State University" I, 1984
Hager, H. and Munshower, S.: Light on the Eternal City. Observations and discoveries in the art and architecture of Rome, "Papers in Art History from the Pennsylvania State University" II, 1987
Krautheimer, R.: The Rome of Alexander VII 1655–1667, Princeton 1985
Kruft, H.-W.: Geschichte der Architekturtheorie, Munich 1991, particularly Zwischen Gegenreformation, Akademismus, Barock und Klassizismus, 103–21
Lavin, I.: Bernini and the Crossing of St. Peter's, New York 1968
Lavin, I.: Bernini & L'Unità delle Arti Visive, Rome 1980
Lotz, W.: Die Spanische Treppe, in: Römisches Jahrbuch für Kunstgeschichte 12, 1969, 39–94
Macmillan Encyclopedia of Architects
Marder, T.: The Porto di Ripetta in Rome, in: Journal of the Society of Architectural Historians 39, 1980, 28–56
Marder, T.: Alexander VII, Bernini, and the urban setting of the Pantheon in the seventeenth century, in: Journal of the Society of Architectural Historians 50, 1991
Milizia, F.: Le vite dei più celebri architetti d'ogni nazione e d'ogni tempo, Rome 1768
Millon, H.A.: Filippo Juvarra and Architectural Education in Rome in the Early Eighteenth Century, in: Bulletin of the American Academy of Arts and Sciences, 7, 1982
Millon, H.A.: Filippo Juvarra Drawings from the Roman Period 1704–1714, Rome 1984
Millon, H.A. and Nochlin, L., eds.: Art and architecture in the service of politics, Cambridge (Mass.) 1978
Noehles, K.: La chiesa di SS. Luca e Martina nell'opera di Pietro da Cortona, Rome 1970
Oechslin, W.: Bildungsgut und Antikenrezeption des frühen Settecento in Rom. Studien zum römischen Aufenthalt Bernardo Antonio Vittones, Zurich 1972
Ost, H.: Studien zu Pietro da Cortonas Umbau von S. Maria della Pace, in: Römisches Jahrbuch für Kunstgeschichte 13, 1971, 231–85
Pastor, L. von: Geschichte der Päpste, Freiburg im Breisgau 1901
Pevsner, N.: Academies of Art, Past and Present, Cambridge 1940
Pinto, J.: Filippo Juvarra's Drawings Depicting the Capitoline Hill, in: Art

Bulletin, 62, 1980
Pinto, J.: The Trevi Fountain, London-Newhaven, 1986
Portoghesi, P.: Roma Barocca, revised and newly edited, Rome-Bari 1995
Steinberg, L.: Borromini's San Carlo alle Quattro Fontane: A Study in Multiple Form and Architectural Symbolism, New York and London 1977
Thelen, H.: Zur Entstehungsgeschichte der Hochaltar-Architektur von St. Peter in Rom, Berlin 1967
In Urbe Architectus: Modelli Misure. La Professione dell'Architetto. Rome 1680–1750, catalogo della mostra, a cura di B. Contardi e G. Curcio, Rome 1991
Vagnetti, L.: L'architetto della storia di occidente, Florence 1974
Bernardo Vittone e la disputa fra classicismo e barocco nel Settecento. Atti del Convegno internazionale promosso dall'Accademia delle scienze di Torino nella ricorrenza del secondo centenario della morte di B. Vittone, 21–24 settembre 1970, Turin 1970
Wilton-Ely, J.: Piranesi as Architect, in: Piranesi Architetto; American Academy in Rome, Rome 1992, 15–45
Wittkower, R. and Brauer, H.: Die Zeichnungen des Gianlorenzo Bernini, 2 vols, Berlin 1931
Wittkower, R., Art and Architecture in Italy 1600–1750, Harmondsworth 1990
Wittkower, R., Studies in the Italian Baroque, London 1975, particularly Piranesi's Architectural Creed, 235–58
Wölfflin, H.: Kunstgeschichtliche Grundbegriffe, Munich 1915

BARBARA BÖRNGASSER
Baroque Architecture in Spain and Portugal

Bottineau, Yves: Baroque Ibérique, Espagne-Portugal-Amérique Latine, Fribourg 1969
França, José-Augusto et al.: Arte portugues (Summa artis, 30), Madrid 1986
França, José-Augusto: Lisboa Pombalina e o Iluminismo, Viseu 1987
Haupt, Albrecht: Geschichte der Renaissance in Spanien und Portugal, Stuttgart 1927
Kubler, George and Soria, M.: Art and Architecture in Spain and Portugal and their American Dominions 1500–1800, Harmondsworth 1959
Kubler, George: Portuguese Plain Style between spices and diamonds, 1521–1706, Middletown 1972
Levenson, Jay A. (ed.): The Age of the Baroque in Portugal, Washington 1993
Pereira, José Fernandes: Arquitectura barroca em Portugal, Lisbon 1986
Pereira, José Fernandes (ed.): Dicionário da arte barroca em Portugal, Lisbon 1989
Triomphe du Baroque. exhibition catalogue, Brussels 1991

Baroque Architecture in Ibero-America

Bernales Ballesteros, Jorge: Historia del arte Hispano-Americano, vol. 2, siglos XVI a XVIII, Madrid 1987
Bonet Correa, Antonio and Villegas, Victor Manuel: El barroco en España y en Mexico, Mexico 1967
Bury, John: Arquitetura e Arte no Brasil Colonial (with English summary), São Paulo 1991
Bonet Correa, Antonio: El Urbanismo en España y en Hispanoamérica, Madrid 1991
Bottineau, Yves: Baroque Ibérique, Espagne-Portugal-Amérique Latine, Fribourg 1969
Gasparini, Graziano: América, barroco y arquitectura, Caracas 1972
Gutiérrez, Ramón: Arquitectura y urbanismo en Iberoamérica, Madrid 1992
Hubala, Erich: Die Kunst des 17. Jahrhunderts (Propyläen-Kunstgeschichte vol. 9), Berlin 1972
Kubler, George and Soria, M.: Art and Architecture in Spain and Portugal and Their American Dominions 1500–1800, Harmondsworth 1959
Sebastián López, Santiago et al.: Arte iberoamericana desde la colonización a la Independencia (Summa artis 28, 29), Madrid 1985
Zanini, Walter: História Geral da Arte no Brasil, 2 vols. San Paulo, 1963

Baroque Architecture in France

Blunt, Anthony: Art and Architecture in France 1500 to 1700 (Pelican History of Art), Harmondsworth 1953
Blunt, Anthony: François Mansart and the origins of French classical architecture, London 1941
Chastel, André: L'Art français. Ancien Régime, Paris 1995
Eriksen, S.: Early Neoclassicism in France, 1974
Evans, J.: Monastic Architecture in France from the Renaissance to Revolution, Cambridge 1964
Feray, J.: Architecture intérieure et décoration en France. Des origines à 1875, 1988
Hautecoeur, Louis: Histoire de l'architecture classique en France, vol. I, 3 – IV, Paris 1948–67
Hubala, Erich: Die Kunst des 17. Jahrhunderts (Propyläen-Kunstgeschichte vol. 9), Berlin 1972
Kauffmann, E.: Architecture in the Age of Reasons. Baroque and post-Baroque in England, Italy and France, Cambridge, Mass. 1955
Keller, Harald: Die Kunst des 18. Jahrhunderts (Propyläen-Kunstgeschichte vol. 10), Berlin 1971
Kimball, F.: Le style Louis XV, Paris 1949
Lavedan, Pierre: French Architecture, Harmondsworth 1956
Middleton, Robin and Watkin, David: Klassizismus und Historismus, 2 vols (Weltgeschichte der Architektur), Stuttgart 1986
Norberg-Schultz, Christian: Barock (Weltgeschichte der Architektur), Stuttgart 1986

Norberg-Schultz, Christian: Spätbarock und Rokoko (Weltgeschichte der Architektur), Stuttgart 1985
Pérouse de Montclos, Jean-Marie: Histoire de l'architecture française de la Renaissance à la Révolution, Paris 1995
Pillement, G.: Les hôtels de Paris, 2 vols, Paris 1941–45
Szambien, Werner: Symétrie, goût, caractère. Théorie et terminologie de l'architecture à l'âge classique, 1986
Tapié, Victor-Louis: Baroque et classicisme, 1957

Baroque Architecture in England

Colvin, M.: A biographical dictionary of English architects, 1660–1840, London 1954
Crook, J.M.: The Greek Revival. Neoclassical Attitudes in British Architecture 1760–1870, London 1972
Downes, K.: Hawksmoor, London 1959
Fleming, J.: Robert Adam and His Circle, London 1962.
Fürst, V.: Wren, London 1956
Hubala, Erich: Die Kunst des 17. Jahrhunderts (Propyläen-Kunstgeschichte vol. 9), Berlin 1972
Kauffmann, E.: Architecture in the Age of Reason. Baroque and Post-Baroque in England, Italy and France, Cambridge, Mass. 1955
Keller, Harald: Die Kunst des 18. Jahrhunderts (Propyläen-Kunstgeschichte vol. 10), Berlin 1971
Kidson, P. et al.: A History of English architecture, Harmondsworth 1965
Middleton, Robin and Watkin, David: Klassizismus und Historismus, 2 vols (Weltgeschichte der Architektur), Stuttgart 1986
Norberg-Schultz, Christian: Barock (Weltgeschichte der Architektur), Stuttgart 1986
Norberg-Schultz, Christian: Spätbarock und Rokoko (Weltgeschichte der Architektur), Stuttgart 1985
Pevsner, Nikolaus: The Buildings of England, 47 vols, Harmondsworth 1951–74
Pevsner, Nikolaus: Christopher Wren 1632–1723, Milan 1959
Saxl, Fritz and Wittkower, Rudolf: British art and the Mediterranean, Oxford 1969
Stutchbury, H.E.: The Architecture of Colen Campbell, Manchester 1967
Summerson, John: Architecture in Britain, 1530–1830, Yale 1993
Summerson, John: Inigo Jones, Harmondsworth 1966
Waterhouse, E.K.: Three decades of British art. 1740–70, Philadelphia, Pa. 1965
Whistler, L.: The Imagination of Sir John Vanbrugh, London 1953
Whistler, L.: Sir John Vanbrugh, Architect and dramatist, London 1938

Baroque Architecture in the Netherlands

Braun, Joseph: Die belgischen Jesuitenkirchen, Freiburg i.Br. 1907
Gelder, H.E. van et al.:

Kunstgeschiedenis der Nederlanden, 12 vols. Antwerp 1963–65
Gerson, H. and Ter Kuile, E.H.: Art and architecture in Belgium 1600 to 1800 (Pelican History of Art), Harmondsworth 1960
Hubala, Erich: Die Kunst des 17. Jahrhunderts (Propyläen-Kunstgeschichte vol. 9), Berlin 1972
Kauffmann, E.: Architecture in the Age of Reason, Baroque and post-Baroque in England, Italy and France, Cambridge, Mass. 1955
Keller, Harald: Die Kunst des 18. Jahrhunderts (Propyläen-Kunstgeschichte vol. 10), Berlin 1971
Kleijn, Koen et al.: Nederlands bouwkunst. Een geschiedenis van tien eeuwen architectuur, Alphen aan den Rijn 1995
Kuyper, W.: Dutch Classicist Architecture, Delft 1980
Leurs, C.: De geschiedenis der bouwkunst in Vlaanderen, Antwerp 1946
Mazières, Th. de: L'architecture religieuse à l'époque de Rubens, Brussels 1943
Middleton, Robin and Watkin, David: Klassizismus und Historismus, 2 vols (Weltgeschichte der Architektur), Stuttgart 1986
Norberg-Schultz, Christian: Barock (Weltgeschichte der Architektur), Stuttgart 1986
Norberg-Schultz, Christian: Spätbarock und Rokoko (Weltgeschichte der Architektur), Stuttgart 1985
Ozinga, M.D.: De protestantse kerkenbouw in Nederland, Amsterdam 1929
Parent, P.: L'architecture des Pays-Bas méridionaux aux XVI–XVIII siècles, Paris, Brussels 1926
Rosenberg, J. et al: Dutch Art and Architecture 1600 to 1800 (Pelican History of Art), Harmondsworth 1966
Taverne, E. and Visser, I. (eds.): Stedebouw. De geschiedenis van de stad in de Nederlanden van 1500 tot heden, Nijmegen 1993
Vermeulen, F.A.J.: Handboek tot de geschiedenis der Nederlandsche Bouwkunst, The Hague 1928–41
Vermeulen, F.A.J.: Bouwmeesters der klassicistische Barok in Nederland, The Hague 1938
Vriend, J.J.: De bouwkunst van ons land, 3 vols. Amsterdam 1942–50

Baroque Architecture in Scandinavia

Cornell, H. Den svenska konstens historia, vol. 2, Stockholm 1966
Fett, H.: Norges kirker i 16 og 17 aarhundrede, Kristiania 1911
Hubala, Erich: Die Kunst des 17. Jahrhunderts (Propyläen-Kunstgeschichte vol. 9), Berlin 1972
Josephson, R.: Tessin, 2 vols, Stockholm 1930–31
Keller, Harald: Die Kunst des 18. Jahrhunderts (Propyläen-Kunstgeschichte vol. 10), Berlin 1971
Lund, H. and Millech, K.: Danmarks Bygningskunst, Copenhagen 1963
Middleton, Robin and Watkin, David: Klassizismus und Historismus, 2 vols

(Weltgeschichte der Architektur), Stuttgart 1986
Norberg-Schultz, Christian: Barock (Weltgeschichte der Architektur), Stuttgart 1986
Norberg-Schultz, Christian: Spätbarock und Rokoko (Weltgeschichte der Architektur), Stuttgart 1985
Paulsson, Th.: Scandinavian architecture, London 1958

EHRENFRIED KLUCKERT
Baroque Architecture in Germany, Switzerland, Austria and Eastern Europe

Alewyn, R. and Sälzle, K.: Das grosse Welttheater. Die Epoche der höfischen Feste, Munich 1989
Alpers, S. and Baxandall, M.: Tiepolo und die Intelligenz der Malerei, Berlin 1996
Aurenhammer, H.: J.B. Fischer von Erlach, London 1973
Bauer, H.: Barock. Kunst einer Epoche, Berlin 1992.
Bottienau, Y.: Die Kunst des Barock, Freiburg 1986
Brucher, G.: Barockarchitektur in Österreich, Cologne 1983
Brucher, G.: Die Kunst des Barock in Österreich, Salzburg und Wien, 1994
Bußmann, Matzner, Schulze (eds.): Johann Conrad Schlaun. Architektur des Spätbarock in Europa. Westfälisches Landesmuseum für Kunst und Kulturgeschichte, Münster 1995.
Elias, N.: Die höfische Gesellschaft, Frankfurt am Main 1983
Förderkreis Alte Kirchen (eds.): Fachwerkkirchen in Hessen, Königstein/Taunus 1987
Freeden, M.H. von: Balthasar Neumann, Leben und Werk, Munich 1981
Giersberg, H.-J.: Friedrich als Bauherr. Studien zur Architektur des 18. Jh. in Berlin und Potsdam, Berlin 1986
Grimschitz, B.: Johann Lucas von Hildebrandt, Vienna 1959
Haas, D.: Der Turm. Hamburgs Michel. Gestalt und Geschichte, Hamburg 1986
Häring, F. and Klein, H.-J.: Hessen. Vom Edersee zur Bergstrasse, Cologne 1987
Hansmann, W.: Balthasar Neumann, Leben und Werk, Cologne 1986
Hansmann, W.: Der Terrassengarten von der Zisterzienserabtei Kamp im 18. Jh. In: Der Terrassengarten von Kloster Kamp, publ. by Landschaftsverband Rheinland, Arbeitsheft 34, Cologne 1993
Hansmann, W.: Im Glanz des Barock. Ein Begleiter zu Bauwerken Augusts des Starken und Friedrichs des Grossen, Cologne 1992
Hansmann, W.: Schloß Augustusburg und Schloss Falkenlust in Brühl. In: Das Weltkulturerbe. Deutschsprachiger Raum. Publ. by Hoffmann, Keller and Thomas, Cologne 1994, pp. 291–301
Hantsch, H.: Jakob Prandtauer, Vienna 1926
Hempel, E.: Baroque Art and Architecture in Central Europe, Bungay 1965
Himmelein and Merten et al.: Barock in Baden-Württemberg, Stuttgart 1981

Kalinowski, K.: Barock in Schlesien. Geschichte, Eigenart und heutige Erscheinung, Munich 1990
Kamphausen, A.: Schleswig-Holstein als Kunstlandschaft, Neumünster 1973
Kluckert, E.: Vom Heiligen zur Postmoderne. Eine Kunstgeschichte Baden-Württembergs, Stuttgart 1996
Kolb, Chr. Graf von: Potsdam als Darstellung Preussens. In: Das Weltkulturerbe. Deutschsprachiger Raum. Publ. by Hoffmann, Keller and Thomas, Cologne 1994, pp. 302–6
Ladendorf, H.: Der Bildhauer und Baumeister Andreas Schlüter, Berlin 1935
Lieb, N.: Barockkirchen zwischen Donau und Alpen, Hirmer (6th edn), Munich 1992
Lieb, N.: Die Vorarlberger Barockbaumeister, Munich/Zurich 1976
Löffler, F.: Der Zwinger in Dresden, Leipzig 1976
Lohmeyer, K.: Die Briefe Balthasar Neumanns von seiner Pariser Studienreise 1723, Düsseldorf 1911
Lorenz, H.: Johann Bernhard Fischer von Erlach, Zurich 1992
Schlosser, J. von: Die Kunst- und Wunderkammern der Spätrenaissance, Braunschweig 1978
Sedlmayr, H.: Die Schauseite der Karlskirche in Wien, in: Kunstgeschichtliche Studien für Hans Kauffmann, Berlin 1956, pp. 262–71
Sedlmayr, H.: Johann Bernhard Fischer von Erlach, Munich 1956
Sedlmayr, H.: Österreichische Barockarchitektur, Vienna 1930
Sobotka, B.J. (ed.): Burgen, Schlösser, Gutshäuser in Mecklenburg-Vorpommern, Stuttgart 1993
Streidt and Frahm: Potsdam. Die Schlösser und Gärten der Hohenzollern, Cologne 1996
Theiselmann, Chr.: Potsdam und Umgebung. Von Preussens Arkadien zur brandenburgischen Landeshauptstadt, Cologne 1993
Wiesinger, L.: Das Berliner Schloss. Von der kurfürstlichen Residenz zum Königsschloß, Darmstadt 1989
Wurlitzer, B.: Mecklenburg-Vorpommern, Cologne 1992

Urban Planning in the Baroque (pp. 76–7)
Garden Planning in the Baroque (pp. 152–61)
Emblems (pp. 428–9)

Braunfels, W. Abendländische Stadtbaukunst, Cologne 1977
Clifford, C.: Gartenkunst, Munich 1981
Criegern, A. von: Abfahrt von einem Wirtshaus. Ikonographische Studien zu einem Thema von Jan Steen. In: Oud-Holland, LXXXVI, 1971, pp. 9–32
Hansmann, W.: Gartenkunst der Renaissance und des Barock, Cologne 1983
Henkel and Schöne (eds.): Handbuch zur Sinnbildkunst des XVI und XVII Jahrhunderts, Stuttgart 1967]
Kruft, H.-W.: Städte in Utopia. Die Idealstadt vom 15. bis zum 18. Jahrhundert

Lablaude, P.-A.: Die Gärten von Versailles, Worms 1995
Mosser, Teyssot: The History of Garden Design, London 1991
Mumford, L.: Die Stadt. Geschichte und Ausblick, Munich 1979
Penkert, S.: Emblem und Emblematikrezeption, Darmstadt 1978
Schöne, A.: Emblematik und Drama im Zeitalter des Barock, Munich 1968

UWE GEESE
Baroque Sculpture in Italy and Central Europe

General:

Beck, Herbert, and Schulze, Sabine (eds.): Antikenrezeption im Hochbarock, Frankfurt am Main 1989 [Schriften des Liebieghauses, Museum alter Plastik, Frankfurt am Main]
Beck, Herbert, Bol, Peter C. and Maek-Gérard, Eva (eds.): Ideal und Wirklichkeit der bildenden Kunst im späten 18. Jahrhundert. [Frankfurter Forschungen zur Kunst, vol. 11]
Bialostocki, Jan: "Barock": Stil, Epoche, Haltung: in: id., Stil und Ikonographie, Cologne 1981
A.E. Brinckmann: Barockskulptur. Entwicklungsgeschichte der Skulptur in den romanischen und germanischen Ländern seit Michelangelo bis zum 18. Jahrhundert. 2 parts. Berlin-Neubabelsberg, undated (1919/20)
Busch, Harald and Lohse, Bernd (eds.): Barock-Plastik in Europa. Introduction by Werner Hager. Commentaries to illustrations by Eva-Maria Wagner, Frankfurt am Main 1964 [Monumente des Abendlandes – 9]
Exhib. cat. Frankfurt am Main 1986–1987: Die Bronzen der Fürstlichen Sammlung Liechtenstein. Ed. by Herbert Beck and Peter C. Bol, Frankfurt am Main, 1986
Geese, Uwe: Liebieghaus – Museum alter Plastik, Frankfurt am Main. Scientific catalogues. Nachantike große plastische Bildwerke vol. IV. Italien, Niederlande, Deutschland, Österreich, Schweiz, Frankreich 1540/50–1780. Melsungen, 1984 (with extensive literature)
Hager, Werner: Barock. Skulptur und Malerei. Kunst der Welt. Ihre geschichtlichen, soziologischen und religiösen Grundlagen, Baden-Baden 1969, 2nd edn, 1980
Hubala, Erich: Die Kunst des 17. Jahrhunderts. Propyläen-Kunstgeschichte vol. 9, Frankfurt am Main, Berlin 1990
Kauffmann, Georg: Die Kunst des 16. Jahrhunderts. Propyläen Kunstgeschichte vol. 8, Frankfurt am Main, Berlin 1990
Keller, Harald: Die Kunst des 18. Jahrhunderts (Propyläen-Kunstgeschichte vol. 10), Frankfurt am Main, Berlin 1990
Merk, Anton: Altarkunst des Barock. Ed. by Herbert Beck and Peter C. Bol, Liebighaus, Museum alter Plastik, Frankfurt am Main, undated.

Italy

Die Legenda aurea des Jacobus de Voragine, tr. from the Latin by Richard Benz. Heidelberg, 8th edition 1975
Exhib. cat. Berlin 1995: "von allen Seiten schön". Bronzen der Renaissance und des Barock. Ed. by Volker Krhan, Berlin 1995
Huse, Norbert: Zur "S. Susanna" des Duquesnoy; in: Argo. Festschrift Kurt Badt, Cologne 1970
Kauffmann, Hans: Giovanni Lorenzo Bernini. Die figürlichen Kompositionen, Berlin 1970
Kroß, Mathias: G.L. Bernini: Die Verzückung der Hl. Theresa, in: Tumult. Zeitschrift für Verkehrswissenschaft. Ed. by Frank Böckelmann, Dietmar Kamper and Walter Seitter. No. 6: Engel, Wetzlar 1983
Ranke, Winfried: Berninis "Heilige Theresa". Discussion report, in Martin Wahnke (ed.): Das Kunstwerk zwischen Wissenschaft und Weltanschauung. Gütersloh 1970
Pope-Hennessy, John: Italian High Renaissance and Baroque Sculpture, New York 1985
Schlegel, Ursula: Die italienischen Bildwerke des 17. und 18. Jahrhunderts in Stein, Holz, Ton, Wachs und Bronze mit Ausnahme der Plaketten und Medaillen. Berlin 1978 [Staatliche Museen Preussischer Kulturbesitz. Works in the Sculpture Gallery, Berlin, vol. Ia]
Scribner, Charles: Gianlorenzo Bernini, New York 1991
Valentiner, W.R.: Alessandro Vittoria and Michelangelo; in: id., Studies of Renaissance Sculpture, Oxford, New York 1950
Winckelmann, Johann Joachim: Ausgewählte Schriften und Briefe. Ed. by Walter Rehm, Wiesbaden 1948

France

Blunt, Anthony: Art and Architecture in France 1500–1700, Harmondsworth 1953
Chastel, André: L'Art Français, Ancien Régime 1620–1775, Paris 1995

Germany

Beck, Herbert: Das Opfer der Sinnlichkeit. Ein Rückblick auf den "Kunstverderber" Bernini; in Beck, Herbert and Sabine Schulze (eds.), Antikenrezeption im Hochbarock. Frankfurt am Main 1989 [Schriften des Liebieghauses, Museum alter Plastik, Frankfurt am Main]
Brucher, Gunter (ed.): Die Kunst des Barock in Österreich, Salzburg-Vienna 1994
Exhib. cat. Augsburg 1980: Welt im Umbruch. Augsburg zwischen Renaissance und Barock. Vol. I: Zeughaus; Vol. II: Rathaus. Augsburg 1980
Exhib. cat. Frankfurt am Main 1981: Dürers Verwandlungen in der Skulptur zwischen Renaissance und Barock.

Herbert Beck and Bernhard Decker, Frankfurt am Main 1981

Exhib. cat. Schwäbisch-Hall 1988: Leonard Kern (1588–1662). Meisterwerke der Bildhauerei für die Kunstkammern Europas, ed. by Harald Siebenmorgen, Schwäbisch-Hall 1988

Exhib. cat. Vienna 1993: Georg Raphael Donner 1693–1741, pub. by Österreichische Galerie, Belvedere, Vienna, 1993

Feuchtmayr, Karl (collected essays), Alfred Schädler (critical catalogue), Georg Petel 1601/2–1634. With contributions by Norbert Lieb and Theodor Müller, Berlin 1973

Geese, Uwe: Justus Glesker. Ein Frankfurter Bildhauer des 17. Jahrhunderts. Typescript, Marburg 1992 [Liebieghaus, Museum alter Plastik, Frankfurt am Main]

Germanisches Nationalmuseum Nürnberg: Führer durch die Sammlungen, Munich 1977. 2nd edn 1980.

Götz-Mohr, Brita von: Liebieghaus, Museum alter Plastik, Frankfurt am Main. Wissenschaftliche Kataloge. Nachantike kleinplastische Bildwerke Vol. III. Die deutschsprachigen Länder 1500–1800, Melsungen 1989

Goldner and Johannes, Bahnmüller, Wilfried, Die Familie Schwanthaler. Freilassing 1984

Hansmann, Wilfried, Gartenkunst der Renaissance und des Barock. Cologne 1983

id.: Die Familie Zürn. Freilassing 1979

id.: Die grossen Ritterheiligen von Martin Zürn. Studienhefte der Skulpturenabteilung 2, Staatliche Museen Preussischer Kulturbesitz, Berlin, undated.

Lankheit, Klaus: Egell-Studien; in: Münchner Jahrbuch für Bildende Kunst, issue 3, vol. VI, 1955

Lindemann, Bernd Wolfgang: Ferdinand Tietz 1708–1777. Studien zu Werk, Stil und Ikonographie, Weissenhorn 1989

Müller, Theodor: Deutsche Plastik der Renaissance bis zum Dreißigjährigen Krieg. Königstein i. Ts. 1963

Philippovich, Eugen von: Elfenbein. Ein Handbuch für Sammler und Liebhaber, Munich, 2nd edn 1982

Pühringer-Zwanowetz, Leonore: Triumphdenkmal und Immaculata. Zwei Projekte Matthias Steinls für Kaiser Leopold I; in: Städel Jahrbuch NF 6, 1977

Schädler, Alfred: Georg Petel (1601/02–1634), Barockbildhauer zu Augsburg. Munich, Zurich 1985

Schönberger, Arno: Deutsche Plastik des Barock. Königstein i. Ts. 1963

Spickernagel, Ellen: "Laß Witwen und Bräute die Toten klagen... Rollenteilung und Tod in der Kunst um 1800; in: Das Opfer des Lebens. Bildliche Erinnerungen an Märtyrer. Loccumer Protokolle 12/95. Dokumentation einer Tagung der Evangelischen Akademie Loccum vom 17. bis 19. März 1995, ed. by Detlef Hoffmann, Loccum 1996

Steinitz, Wolfgang: Ignaz Günther. Freilassing 1970, 4th edn 1979

Volk, Peter: Rokokoplastik in Altbayern, Bayerisch-Schwaben und im Allgäu. Munich 1981

Woeckel, Gerhard P.: Ignaz Günther. Die Handzeichnungen des kurfürstlich bayerischen Hofbildhauers Franz Ignaz Günther (1725–1775). Weissenhorn 1975

Zoege von Manteuffel, Claus: Die Bildhauerfamilie Zürn 1606 bis 1666. 2 vols, Weissenhorn 1969

Netherlands

Geese, Susanne: Kirchenmöbel und Naturdarstellung – Kanzeln in Flandern und Brabant. Dissertation. Hamburg 1993. Ammersbek 1997

Rosenberg, Jakob, Slive, Seymour, and Ter Kuile, E.H.: Dutch Art and Architecture 1600 to 1800. Pelican History of Art, Harmondsworth, London, 1966, Yale University Press, 1993

England

Whinney, Margaret: Sculpture in Britain 1530 to 1830. Pelican History of Art, Harmondsworth, London 1964. 2nd edn 1988

JOSÉ IGNACIO HERNÁNDEZ REDONDO
Baroque Sculpture in Spain

Alonso Cano en Sevilla, Colección Arte Hispalense, Diputación Provincial de Sevilla, 1982

Bernales Ballesteros, J. and García de la Concha Delgado, F.: Imagineros Andaluces de los Siglos de Oro. Biblioteca de la Cultura Andaluza, Sevilla, 1986

Bernales Ballesteros, J.: Pedro Roldán (1624–1699). Colección Arte Hispalense, Diputación Provincial de Seville, 1973

El arte del Barroco. Escultura, Pintura y Artes Decorativas. Historia del Arte en Andalucía, vol. VII, Ediciones Gever, Sevilla, 1991

Gómez Piñol, E.: El imaginero Francisco Salzillo. Exhibition catalogue. Murcia, 1973

Gómez-Moreno, M. E.: Escultura del siglo XV. Ars Hispaniae series vol. XVI. Plus Ultra, Madrid, 1958.

Hernández Díaz, J., Martín Gónzález, J. J., and Pita Andrade, J. M.: La Escultura y la Arquitectura Españolas del siglo XVII. Summa artis series, vol. XXVI, Espasa Calpe, Madrid, 1982

Hernández Redondo, J. I.: Spanische Skulptur des 17. Jahrhunderts. Ein Überblick. In: Spanische Kunstgeschichte, vol. 2, Reimer Berlin, 1992

Martín González, J. J.: El Escultor Gregório Fernández. Ministerio de Cultura, Madrid, 1980

Martín González, J. J.: Escultura Barroca Castellana. Fundación Lázaro Galdiano, vol. 1, Madrid, 1958 and vol. 11, Valladolid, 1971

Martín González, J. J.: Escultura barroca en España. Manuales de Arte Catédra, Madrid, 1983

Martín González, J. J.: Luis Salvador Carmona. Escultor y Académico. Editorial Alpuerto, Madrid 1990

Sánchez-Mesa, D.: Técnica de la Scultura Policromada Granadina. Universidad de Granada, 1971

Tovar, V. and Martín González, J. J.: El arte del Barroco I, Arquitectura y Escultura. Colección Conceptos Fundamentales en la Historia del Arte Español. Editorial Taurus, Madrid 1990

Urrea, J.: Anotaciones a Gregorio Fernández y su entorno artístico. In Boletín del Seminario de Arte y Arqueología. Universidad de Valladolid, 1980, p. 375

Urrea, J.: El Escultor Francisco Rincón. In Boletín del Seminario de Arte y Arqueología. Universidad de Valladolid, 1973, p. 245

Urrea, J.: Introducción a la Escultura Barroca Madrileña. Manuel Pereira. In Boletín del Seminario de Arte y Arqueología. Universidad de Valladolid, 1977, p. 253.

Valdivieso, E., Otero, R. and Urrea, J.: El Barroco y el Rococó. Historia del Arte Hispánico, vol. IV, Editorial Alhambra, Madrid 1980

Various authors: La Escultura en Andalucía, siglos XV a XVIII. Exhibition catalogue, Museo Nacional de Escultura, Valladolid 1984

Various authors: Pedro de Mena. III Centenario de su muerte. Conserjería de Cultura. Junta de Andalucía, Málaga 1985

Wethey, H.E.: Alonso Cano. Painter, Sculptor, Architect. Princeton 1955

KARIN HELLWIG
Painting in Italy, Spain, and France in the Seventeenth century

General:

Hager, Werner: Barock. Skulptur und Malerei, Baden-Baden 1969 (Kunst der Welt 22)

Held, Jutta and Schneider, Norbert: Sozialgeschichte der Malerei vom Spätmittelalter bis ins 20. Jahrhundert, Cologne 1993

Hubala, Erich: Die Kunst des 17. Jahrhunderts, Berlin and others, 1972 (Propyläen Kunstgeschichte 9)

Pevsner, Nikolaus: Die Geschichte der Kunstakademien, Munich 1986

Pevsner, Nikolaus and Grauthoff, Otto: Barockmalerei in den romanischen Ländern, Wildpark-Potsdam 1928 (Handbuch der Kunstwissenschaft)

Schlosser, Julius von: Die Kunstliteratur, Vienna 1924

Schneider, Norbert: Porträtmalerei. Hauptwerke europäischer Bildniskunst 1420–1670, Cologne 1994

Walther, Ingo F. (ed.): Malerei der Welt, 2 vols, Cologne 1995

Warnke, Martin: Hofkünstler. Zur Vorgeschichte des modernen Künstlers, Cologne 1985

Rome and Naples:

Barolsky, Paul: Domenichino's Diana and the Art of Seeing, in: Source Notes in the History of Art, 14, 1994, pp. 18–20

Bätschmann, Oskar: Nicolas Poussins Landschaft mit Pyramus und Thisbe. Das Liebesunglück und die Grenzen der Malerei, Frankfurt am Main 1987

Chastel, André: Die Kunst Italiens, vol. 2, Munich 1961

Claude Lorrain 1600–1682. Exhibition catalogue. Washington 1982

Guido Reni und Europa: Ruhm und Nachruhm, exhibition catalogue. Frankfurt am Main 1988/89

Haskell, Francis: Patrons and Painters, New Haven and London, 1980

Held, Jutta: Caravaggio. Politik und Martyrium der Körper, Berlin 1996

I Bamboccianti. Niederländische Malerrebellen im Rom des Barock. Exhibition catalogue. Cologne 1991

Il Guercino 1591–1666. Exhibition catalogue. Frankfurt am Main 1991/92

Locher, Hubert: Das Staunen des Betrachters. Pietro da Cortonas Deckenfresko im Palazzo Barberini, in: Werners Kunstgeschichte 1990, pp. 1–46

Nicolas Poussin 1594–1665. Exhibition catalogue. London 1995

Nicolas Poussin. Claude Lorrain. Zu den Bildern im Städel. Exhibition catalogue. Frankfurt am Main 1988

Painting in Naples. From Caravaggio to Giordano. Exhibition catalogue. London 1982

Preimesberger, Rudolf: Pontifex Romanus per Aeneam praesignatus. Die Galleria Pamphilj und ihre Fresken, in: Römisches Jahrbuch für Kunstgeschichte 16, 1976, pp. 223–87

Ribera 1591–1652. Exhibition catalogue. Naples/Madrid 1992

Stolzenwald, Susanna: Artemisia Gentileschi, Stuttgart/Zurich 1991

The Age of Caravaggio. Exhibition catalogue. New York 1985

Winner, Matthias: Poussins Selbstbildnis im Louvre als kunsttheoretische Allegorie, in: Römisches Jahrbuch für Kunstgeschichte 20, 1983, pp. 419–49

Wittkower, Rudolf and Margot: Künstler – Aussenseiter der Gesellschaft, Stuttgart 1989

Wittkower, Rudolf: Art and Architecture in Italy 1600–1750, Harmondsworth 1980 (The Pelican History of Art)

Madrid and Seville

Brown, Jonathan: Velázquez. Painter and Courtier, New Haven, London 1986

Brown, Jonathan, and Elliott, John: A Palace for the King. The Buen Retiro and the Court of Philip IV, New Haven, London 1980

Brown, Jonathan: The Golden Age of Painting in Spain, New Haven, London 1991

Carreño, Rizi: Herrera y la pintura madrileña de su tiempo [1650–1700]. Exhibition catalogue. Madrid 1986

Defourneaux, Marcelin: Spanien im Goldenen Zeitalter, Stuttgart 1986
Harris, Enriqueta: Velázquez, Ithaca 1982
Held, Jutta: Malerei des 17. Jahrhunderts II, in: S. Hänsel, H. Karge (eds.), Spanische Kunstgeschichte. Eine Einführung, vol. 2, Von der Renaissance bis Heute, Berlin 1992, pp. 47–62
Hellwig, Karin: Die spanische Kunstliteratur im 17. Jahrhundert, Frankfurt am Main 1996 (Ars Iberica 3)
Justi, Carl: Diego Velázquez und sein Jahrhundert, 2 vols, Bonn 1888
Karge, Henrik (ed.): Vision oder Wirklichkeit. Die spanische Malerei der Neuzeit, Munich 1991
Kubler, George and Soria, Martin: Art and Architecture in Spain and Portugal and their American Dominions 1500 to 1800, Harmondsworth 1959 (The Pelican History of Art)
Murillo. Exhibition catalogue, London, Madrid 1982/83
Pérez Sánchez, Alonso Emilio: Spanish Still Life from Velázquez to Goya. Exhibition catalogue. London 1995
Scholz-Hänsel, Michael: Malerei des 17. Jahrhunderts I., in: S. Hänsel, H. Karge (eds.), Spanische Kunstgeschichte. Eine Einführung, vol. 2, Von der Renaissance bis Heute, Berlin 1992, pp. 31–45
Velázquez. Exhibition catalogue. Madrid 1990
Waldmann, Susann: Das spanische Künstlerporträt im 17. Jahrhundert, Frankfurt am Main 1995 (Ars Iberica 1)
Zurbarán: Exhibition catalogue. Paris/New York 1987/88

KIRA VAN LIL
Painting in the Netherlands, Germany and England in the 17th century

Sources:

Gaehtgens, Thomas W. and Fleckner, Uwe (eds.): Historienmalerei, vol. 1, Berlin
König, Eberhard and Schön, Christiane (eds.): Stilleben (vol. 5), Berlin 1996
Hofstede de Groot, Cornelis: Beschreibendes und kritisches Verzeichnis der Werke der hervorragendsten holländischen Maler des XVII. Jahrhunderts. Nach dem Muster von John Smith's Catalogue Raisonné zusammengestellt, 10 vols, Esslingen am Neckar, 1907–1928
Hoogstraeten, Samuel van: Inleyding tot de Hooge Schoole des Schilderkonst: anders de Zichtbaere Werelt ..., Rotterdam, Utrecht 1969 (Rotterdam 1678)
Sandrart, Joachim von: L'Academia Tedesca della Architectura, Scultura e Pictura: Oder Teutsche Academie der Edlen Bau- Bild und Malerey-Künste ..., Nuremberg 1675–79
Wurzbach, Alfred (ed.): Arnold Houbraken's Grosse Schouburgh der Niederländischen Maler und Malerinnen, vol. 1 (1718–1721),

Quellenschriften für Kunstgeschichte und Kunsttechnik des Mittelalters und der Renaissance, Vienna 1880

Overviews

General:

Fuchs, Rudi: Dutch Painting, London 1984 (1978!)
Huizinga, Johan: Holländische Kultur des siebzehnten Jahrhunderts – Ihre sozialen Grundlagen und nationale Eigenart, Jena 1933
Haak, Bob: Das Goldene Zeitalter der holländischen Malerei, Cologne 1996 (New York 1984!)
Olbrich, Harald and Möbius, Helga: Holländische Malerei des 17. Jahrhunderts, Leipzig 1990
Zumthor, Das Alltagsleben in Holland zur Zeit Rembrandts, Leipzig 1992 (Paris 1959!)

Portraits

Schneider, Norbert: Porträtmalerei. Hauptwerke europäischer Bildniskunst 1420–1670, Cologne 1992
Tümpel, Christian (ed.): Im Lichte Rembrandts. Das Alte Testament im Goldenen Zeitalter der niederländischen Kunst, exhibition catalogue, Westfälisches Landesmuseum Münster 1994

Landscape

Bol, L.J.: Die holländische Marine-malerei des 17. Jahrhunderts, Braunschweig 1973
Leppien, Helmut R. and Müller, Levine, David A. and Mai, Ekkehard: I Bamboccianti – Niederländische Malerrebellen im Rom des Barock, exhibition catalogue Wallraf-Richartz Museum, Cologne, and Centraal Museum, Utrecht, Milan 1991
Karsten: Holländische Kirchenbilder, Hamburger Kunsthalle 1996
Stechow, Wolfgang: Dutch Landscape Painting of the Seventeenth Century, National Gallery of Art: Kress Foundation, Studies in the History of European Art, Oxford 1981 (1966!)
Sutton, Peter C.: Masters of Seventeenth Century Dutch Landscape Painting, exhibition catalogue, Rijksmuseum, Amsterdam, Museum of Fine Arts, Boston, Philadelphia Museum of Art, 1987/1988
Vignau-Wilber, Thea: Das Land am Meer, Holländische Landschaft im 17. Jahrhundert, exhibition catalogue, Staatliche Graphische Sammlung, Munich, Munich 1993

Genre

Renger, Konrad: Lockere Gesellschaft. Zur Ikonographie des Verlorenen Sohnes und von Wirtshausszenen in der niederländischen Malerei, Berlin 1970
Schulze, Sabine (ed.): Leselust – Nieder-

ländische Malerei von Rembrandt bis Vermeer, exhibition catalogue Schirn Kunsthalle Frankfurt, Stuttgart 1993
Sutton, Peter C.: Von Frans Hals bis Vermeer, Meisterwerke holländischer Genremalerei, exhibition catalogue Staatliche Museum Preußischer Kulturbesitz Berlin, Berlin 1984

Still Life

Alpers, Svetlana: Kunst als Beschreibung. Holländische Malerei des 17. Jahrhunderts, Cologne 1985 (London 1983!)
Gemar-Koeltsch, Erika: Holländische Stilleben-Maler im 17. Jahrhundert, Lingen 1995
Grimm, Claus: Stilleben. Die niederländischen und deutschen Meister, Stuttgart and Zurich 1988
Schneider, Norbert: Stilleben – Realität und Symbolik der Dinge, Die Stillebenmalerei der frühen Neuzeit, Cologne 1989
Segal, Sam: A Prosperous Past. The Sumptuous Still Life in the Netherlands 1600-1700, The Hague 1988

Artists

Adriani, Götz: Deutsche Malerei im 17. Jahrhundert, Cologne 1977
Alpers, Svetlana: Rembrandt als Unternehmer: sein Atelier und sein Markt, Cologne 1989 (Chicago 1988!)
Andrews, Keith: Adam Elsheimer - Werkverzeichnis der Gemälde, Munich 1985
Blankert, Albert and Montias, John Michael: Vermeer, New York 1988 (Paris 1986!)
Brown, Christopher and Kelch, Jan: Rembrandt – der Meister und seine Werkstatt, exhibition catalogue, Gemäldegalerie SMPK, Altes Museum, Berlin, Munich/Paris/London 1991
Brown, Christopher: Anthony van Dyck, Oxford 1982
Bushart, Bruno: Johann Liss, exhibition catalogue, Augsburg 1975
Büttner, Nils and Unverfehrt, Gert: Jacob van Ruisdael in Bentheim – Ein niederländischer Maler und die Burg Bentheim im 17. Jahrhundert, publ. by Landeskreis Grafschaft Bentheim and Museumsverein für die Grafschaft Bentheim, Bielefeld 1993
Buytewech, Willem: exhibition catalogue Museum Boymans-van Beuningen, Rotterdam 1974, and Institut Néerlandais, Paris 1975
Grisebach, Lucius: Willem Kalf, Berlin 1974
Hahn-Woernle, Birgit: Sebastian Stoskopff, with a Critical Catalogue of the paintings, Stuttgart 1996
Heinrich, Christoph: Georg Hinz – Das Kunstkammerregal, Hamburger Kunsthalle 1996
Imdahl, Max: Jacob van Ruisdael: Die Mühle von Wijk bei Duurstede, Stuttgart 1968 (Reclams Werkmonographien 131)
Jan Davidsz. de Heem und sein Kreis, Centraal Museum in Utrecht and

Herzog Anton Ulrich Museum, Braunschweig 1991
Jan Steen: Painter and Storyteller, exhibition catalogue, National Gallery of Art, Washington, D.C., and Rijksmuseum, Amsterdam 1996
Judith Leyster – A Dutch Master and her World, exhibition catalogue, Frans Hals Museum, Haarlem 1993
Millar, Oliver: Sir Peter Lely, 1618–80, exhibition catalogue, National Gallery, London, London 1978
Reiss, S.: Aelbert Cuyp, London/Boston 1975
Renger, Konrad: Adriaen Brouwer und das niederländische Bauerngenre, exhibition catalogue Bayerische Staatsgemäldesammlungen Munich, Alte Pinakothek, Munich 1986
Schwartz, Gary: Rembrandt, Erlangen 1991
Sello, Gottfried: Adam Elsheimer, Munich 1988
Slive, Seymour: Frans Hals, exhibition catalogue, Frans Hals Museum, Haarlem 1990
Slive, Seymour: Jacob Ruisdael, exhibition catalogue, Mauritshuis, The Hague 1982
Sutton, Peter C.: Pieter de Hooch, New York/Oxford 1979/80
Ter Borch, Gerard: exhibition catalogue, Landesmuseum Münster 1974
Vermeer, Johannes: exhibition catalogue, National Gallery of Art, Washington, D.C., and Mauritshuis, The Hague 1995
Warncke, Martin: Pieter Paul Rubens. Leben und Werk, Cologne 1977
Wettengel, Kurt (ed.): Georg Flegel – Stilleben, exhibition catalogue, Historisches Museum Frankfurt in cooperation with Schirn Kunsthalle Frankfurt, Stuttgart 1993
Wheelock, Arthur K. Jr. (ed.): Van Dyck – Paintings, exhibition catalogue, National Gallery of Art, Washington D.C. 1990
Wiegand, Wolfgang: Ruisdael-Studien. Ein Versuch zur Ikonologie der Landschaftsmalerei, Hamburg 1971

England:

Dynasties: Painting in Tudor and Jacobean England 1530–1630, exhibition catalogue, Tate Gallery, London 1995
Gaunt, William: A concise history of English painting, London 1962
Millar, Oliver: The Age of Charles I, Painting in England 1620–1649, Tate Gallery, London 1972
Pears, Iain: The Discovery of Painting – The Growth of Interest in the Arts in England, 1680–1768, New Haven/London 1988

Index of Personal Names

Page-numbers in italics refer to illustrations.

Index of Placenames

Page-numbers in italics refer to illustrations.

Photo credits

The majority of illustrations (approximately 450) that are not individually listed here are new photographs by the Cologne architectural photographer Achim Bednorz. In photographing for this book, he traveled through Italy, Spain, Portugal, France, Belgium, Netherlands, Germany, Austria, Switzerland and the Czech Republic. The publishing house and the publisher wish to thank the museums, archives, and photographers for making further photographs available and for allowing them to be reproduced. As well as the institutions already named in the picture captions, the following are listed here individually:

AKG photo, Berlin: 267 bottom right (Stefan Drechsler), 446 left, 458 bottom
Alinari: 15, 44 bottom left, 53 bottom, 63 top, 64 left, right, 294 right, 296
Anders, Jörg P. (BPK, Berlin): 331 top, bottom, 421, 463 bottom, 470 top, 473
Anderson: 295 left, 299 right, 382 top, 390
Artothek: 383 (Blauel/Gnamm), 387 (Ursula Edelmann), 388 bottom (J. Blauel), 410, 416 (Bayer & Mitko), 427, 431 (Blauel/Gnamm), 438 left (J. Blauel), 439 bottom left (Blauel/ Gnamm), 446 right (Blauel/Gnamm), 448 (J. Blauel), 453 top (Bayer & Mitko), 460 bottom (J. Blauel), 461 left (Ursula Edelmann), 471 bottom (J. Blauel), 474 bottom, 476 (Blauel/ Gnamm)
Bildarchiv Preußischer Kulturbesitz: 197 top left, top right, bottom
Blasi, Enrico: 385 top, bottom
Brunzel (Staatliche Museen Kassel): 434 right

Carafelli, Richard (National Gallery of Art, Washington): 465
Conway Library, Courtauld Institute of Art, London: 320 top, bottom left, bottom right.
By permission of the president and Council of the Royal College of Surgeons of England. Photo: Photographic Survey, Courtauld Institute of Art, London: 321 bottom
de la Riestra, Pablo: 121 left, right top, right bottom, 182 top, bottom left, bottom right, 183 top right
Edelmann, Ursula: 21 top, 389
Frahm, Klaus: 199, 200, 201
Frank (Staatliche Kunsthalle Karlsruhe): 453 bottom, 477 bottom
Giraudon (Bridgeman): 127
Grove, Bob (National Gallery of Art, Washington): 480 left
Józsa, Dénes (National Gallery of Art, Washington): 460 top
Jürgens (Ost u. Europa) Photo: 271 top
Keiser, B.P. (Herzog Anton Ulrich Museum, Braunschweig): 451 bottom, 455 bottom, 458 top, 462
Kersting, A.F.: 164, 165 top, bottom, 167, 168 top, bottom, 169 top, bottom left, bottom right, 170, 171 top, bottom, 172, 173 top, bottom, 174, 175 top, bottom, 176 top, bottom, 177 top left, top right, bottom, 178 top, bottom, 179 top, bottom
Klut (Staatliche Kunstsammlungen Dresden): 207 left bottom
Moser, Jean-Marc (Photothèque des Musées de la ville de Paris): 425 top
Orloff, Alexandre: 272 top, bottom, 273
Oronoz: 362 left, right, 363 left, 366 right, 371 right

Orsi Battaglini, Nicolò: 58 bottom, 352 bottom right
Orti, Dagli: 126, 136, 137, 146 left top
Pedicini, Luciano: 398, 399
Posselt, Milan (Nationalgalerie Prag): 478 bottom left
R.M.N.: 77 top (M. Bellot), 133 bottom (M. Bellot), 139 center (Gerárd Blot), 153 bottom, 154 top (Gerárd Blot), 302 top, 304 left (R.G. Ojeda), 304 right (C. Jean), 305 right (H. Lewandowski), 313 bottom, (R.G. Ojeda), 420 (Arnaudet), 423 left, right (G. Blot/C. Jean), 424, 425 bottom, 426 bottom (C. Jean), 439 top right (C. Jean/H. Lewan.)
Sächsische Landesbibliothek, Staats- und Universitätsbibliothek Dresden, Deutsche Fotothek: 202, 207 top left, right, 270
© Photo Scala, Florence: 18 top, 20, 39, 51 right, 52 bottom, 55 left, right, 65 top, bottom, 279 left, right, 280 left, right, 281, 284 right, 285 left, 377 left, right, 378 top, bottom, 380, 381 top, bottom, 382 bottom, 384, 394, 396, 449 bottom, 477 top
The Metropolitan Museum of Art, © Photograph: 461 right
von der Mülbe, Christian: 212
Walford, Elke (Bridgeman): 432 top, 478 top left
Westfälisches Amt für Denkmalpflege: 193 bottom